African Archaeology

BLACKWELL STUDIES IN GLOBAL ARCHAEOLOGY

Series Editors: Lynn Meskell and Rosemary A. Joyce

Blackwell Studies in Global Archaeology is a series of contemporary texts, each carefully designed to meet the needs of archaeology instructors and students seeking volumes that treat key regional and thematic areas of archaeological study. Each volume in the series, compiled by its own editor, includes 12–15 newly commissioned articles by top scholars within the volume's thematic, regional, or temporal area of focus.

What sets the *Blackwell Studies in Global Archaeology* apart from other available texts is that their approach is accessible, yet does not sacrifice theoretical sophistication. The series editors are committed to the idea that usable teaching texts need not lack ambition. To the contrary, the *Blackwell Studies in Global Archaeology* aim to immerse readers in fundamental archaeological ideas and concepts, but also to illuminate more advanced concepts, thereby exposing readers to some of the most exciting contemporary developments in the field. Inasmuch, these volumes are designed not only as classic texts, but as guides to the vital and exciting nature of archaeology as a discipline.

1. Mesoamerican Archaeology: Theory and Practice
   Edited by Julia A. Hendon and Rosemary A. Joyce

2. Andean Archaeology
   Edited by Helaine Silverman

3. African Archaeology: A Critical Introduction
   Edited by Ann Brower Stahl

4. North American Archaeology
   Edited by Timothy R. Pauketat and Diana DiPaolo Loren

5. Archaeologies of the Middle East: Rocking the Cradle
   Edited by Susan Pollock and Reinhard Bernbeck

6. The Archaeology of Mediterranean Prehistory
   Edited by Emma Blake and A. Bernard Knapp

Forthcoming:

Classical Archaeology
   Edited by Susan E. Alcock and Robin G. Osborne

Archaeology of Oceania: Australia and the Pacific Islands
   Edited by Ian Lilley

Historical Archaeology
   Edited by Martin Hall and Stephen Silliman

An Archaeology of Asia
   Edited by Miriam Stark

African Archaeology
A Critical Introduction

Edited by
Ann Brower Stahl

 **Blackwell**
Publishing

BLACKWELL PUBLISHING
350 Main Street, Malden, MA 02148-5020, USA
108 Cowley Road, Oxford OX4 1JF, UK
550 Swanston Street, Carlton, Victoria 3053, Australia

First published 2005 by Blackwell Publishing Ltd

Library of Congress Cataloging-in-Publication Data

African archaeology : a critical introduction / edited by Ann Brower Stahl.
     p.   cm. — (Blackwell studies in global archaeology)
   Includes bibliographical references and index.
   ISBN 1-4051-0155-5 (alk. paper) — ISBN 1-4051-0156-3 (alk. paper)
   1. Africa—Antiquities. 2. Antiquities, Prehistoric—Africa. 3. Archaeology—Africa. I. Stahl,
Ann Brower, 1954– II. Series.

   DT13.A354 2004
   960′.1′072—dc22
                                                                              2004003052
A catalogue record for this title is available from the British Library.

Set in 10 on 12.5 pt Plantin
by SNP Best-set Typesetter Ltd., Hong Kong
Printed and bound in the United Kingdom
by MPG Books Ltd, Bodmin, Cornwall

The publisher's policy is to use permanent paper from mills that operate a sustainable forestry policy,
and which has been manufactured from pulp processed using acid-free and elementary chlorine-free
practices. Furthermore, the publisher ensures that the text paper and cover board used have met
acceptable environmental accreditation standards.

For further information on
Blackwell Publishing, visit our website:
www.blackwellpublishing.com

Contents

 # Series Editors' Preface

This series was conceived as a collection of books designed to cover central areas of undergraduate archaeological teaching. Each volume in the series, edited by experts in the area, includes newly commissioned articles written by archaeologists actively engaged in research. By commissioning new articles, the series combines one of the best features of readers, the presentation of multiple approaches to archaeology, with the virtues of a text conceived from the beginning as intended for a specific audience. While the model reader for the series is conceived of as an upper-division undergraduate, the inclusion in the volumes of researchers actively engaged in work today will also make these volumes valuable for more advanced researchers who want a rapid introduction to contemporary issues in specific sub-fields of global archaeology.

Each volume in the series will include an extensive introduction by the volume editor that will set the scene in terms of thematic or geographic focus. Individual volumes, and the series as a whole, exemplify a wide range of approaches in contemporary archaeology. The volumes uniformly engage with issues of contemporary interest, interweaving social, political, and ethical themes. We contend that it is no longer tenable to teach the archaeology of vast swaths of the globe without acknowledging the political implications of working in foreign countries and the responsibilities archaeologists incur by writing and presenting other people's pasts. The volumes in this series will not sacrifice theoretical sophistication for accessibility. We are committed to the idea that usable teaching texts need not lack ambition.

Blackwell Studies in Global Archaeology aims to immerse readers in fundamental archaeological ideas and concepts, but also to illuminate more advanced concepts, exposing readers to some of the most exciting contemporary developments in the field.

Lynn Meskell and Rosemary A. Joyce

Figures

Tables

Notes on Contributors

Zelalem Assefa (Ph.D., SUNY Stony Brook, 2002) is currently a postdoctoral fellow at the Smithsonian Institution. His professional interests include the Middle Stone Age of East Africa, zooarchaeology, osteology, and geographic information systems.

Joanna Casey (Ph.D., University of Toronto, 1993) is Associate Professor of Anthropology at the University of South Carolina. Her research interests are the Later Stone Age and the dynamics of early settlements, ethnoarchaeology, and gendered economies in West Africa.

S. Terry Childs (Ph.D., Boston University, 1986) is an archaeologist in the Archeology and Ethnography Program of the National Park Service in Washington, DC. Her primary research interest is the Iron Age of sub-Saharan Africa, particularly involving the anthropology of technology, and she has worked in Tanzania, the Democratic Republic of the Congo, Zimbabwe, and Uganda. At the NPS, Dr. Childs works on archaeological collections management of objects, records, and reports (e.g., gray literature) and she has published extensively on related topics.

H. J. Deacon has taught courses on African prehistory over a number of years and is a co-author of a standard text, *Human Beginnings in South Africa*. He has investigated a number of significant archaeological sites, notably Boomplaas Cave and Klasies River, that have added significantly to our knowledge of the emergence of modern humans.

Manfred K. H. Eggert (Dr. phil., Johannes Gutenberg-Universität Mainz, 1973) is Professor of Pre- and Protohistory at the Institut für Ur- und Frühgeschichte und Archäologie des Mittelalters, Eberhard-Karls-Universität Tübingen, Germany. Besides intensive work on the methodology of prehistoric archaeology, his main research interests are divided between the early Iron Age of Central Europe and the settling of the Central African rainforest. From 1977 to 1987 he was engaged in archaeological, ethnohistorical, and ethnoarchaeological fieldwork in Zaire (now the Democratic Republic of Congo) and the People's Republic of Congo (now Congo-Brazzaville). Since 1997 he has been pursuing his rainforest research in southern Cameroon.

Jeffrey Fleisher (Ph.D., University of Virginia, 2003) is Adjunct Professor of Anthropology and African Studies at Lehigh University, Bethlehem, Pennsylvania. His research on the Swahili coast focuses on the growth of urban polities through the lens of economic and political interactions between rural and urban settlements, with particular attention to rural-urban population dynamics, the social uses of goods, and the establishment and maintenance of social inequality.

Diane Gifford-Gonzalez (Ph.D., University of California at Berkeley, 1977) is a zooarchaeologist and author of publications on zooarchaeology, the origins of pastoralism in Africa, archaeological theory, ethnoarchaeology, taphonomy, pinniped paleoecology, and visual anthropology. She recently edited a monograph on Adrar Bous, Niger, which yielded domestic cattle dating to 5500–4000 b.p. Ongoing research includes the origins of pastoralism, Holocene human ecology around Monterey Bay, California, and indigenous responses to Spanish colonization in New Mexico.

Eugenia W. Herbert (Ph.D., Yale, 1957) is the author of *Red Gold of Africa: Copper in Precolonial History and Culture* (1984), *Iron Gender, and Power: Rituals of Transformation in African Societies* (1993), and *Twilight on the Zambezi* (2002), as well as numerous articles and several films on African metalworking. She is E. Nevius Rodman Professor of History Emeritus at Mount Holyoke College.

Augustin F. C. Holl (Ph.D., Sorbonne, 1983) is Professor of Anthropology and Afro-American and African Studies and Curator of West African Archaeology at the University of Michigan. His research revolves around issues of social evolution, the advent of food-producing economies, and the emergence and growth of complex social systems in West Africa and the Levant. He has conducted fieldwork in the Saharan desert in Mauritania, the Negev desert in Israel, the Chadian plain in northern Cameroon, northwestern Burkina Faso, and Senegal. He has published six books, and has also co-authored one, and co-edited one.

Chapurukha M. Kusimba (Ph.D., Bryn Mawr College, 1993) is Associate Curator of Anthropology at the Field Museum of Natural History, Chicago, and Adjunct Associate Professor of Anthropology at the University of Illinois at Chicago and Northwestern University, Evanston, Illinois. His research interests are in precolonial trade, economy, and technology. His has published one book and two edited volumes, and is also the author of a number of papers and chapters in edited volumes on African history, archaeology, and ethnology.

Sibel B. Kusimba (Ph.D., University of Illinois, 1997) is Assistant Professor of Anthropology at Northern Illinois University. She has conducted archaeological research in Kenya, and is the author of *African Foragers: Environment, Technology, Interactions* and has edited, together with Chapurukha Kusimba, *East African Archaeology: Foragers, Potters, Smiths, and Traders*.

Paul J. Lane (Ph.D., Cambridge, 1986) has research interests in African historical archaeology, ethnoarchaeology, and maritime seascapes. His doctoral research comprised an ethnoarchaeological study of the use of space and time among the Dogon of Mali. Thereafter, he taught archaeology and museum studies at the University of Dar es Salaam, Tanzania, and at the University of Botswana until the late 1990s, helping to establish archaeology degree programs in both places. He is currently Director of the British Institute in Eastern Africa, based in Nairobi.

Adria LaViolette (Ph.D., Washington University-St. Louis, 1987) is Associate Professor of Anthropology, University of Virginia, Charlottesville, Virginia. Her Ph.D. research resulted in a monograph entitled *Ethno-Archaeology in Jenné, Mali: Craft and Status among Smiths, Potters, and Masons*. Her more recent area of research specialization is Swahili archaeology in the context of the eastern African Iron Age, with particular emphasis on households, craft production, urbanism, and regional systems.

Scott MacEachern (Ph.D., Calgary, 1991) is an Associate Professor of Anthropology at Bowdoin College in Brunswick, Maine. He has worked on and directed archaeological research projects in Kenya, Ghana, Nigeria, Cameroon, Chad, Canada, and the United States. Most of his research since the mid-1980s has taken place in and around the Mandara Mountains of northern Cameroon and Nigeria. His main research interests are in state-formation processes, ethnoarchaeology, and the archaeological study of ethnicity.

Curtis W. Marean (Ph.D., University of California at Berkeley, 1990) is Professor of Anthropology at Arizona State University and a member of the Institute of Human Origins. He has research interests in the origins of modern humans, the prehistory of Africa, and the study of animal bones from archaeological sites. He has a special interest in human occupation of grassland and coastal ecosystems. He has conducted research in Ethiopia, Kenya, Tanzania, and Somalia, and since 1991 has been conducting field research on the Middle Stone Age in South Africa.

Pierre de Maret is Professor of Archaeology and Anthropology, and Rector of the Université Libre de Bruxelles. He is also President of the Scientific Advisory Board of the Royal Central Africa Museum in Tervuren, Belgium. Since 1970 he has done extensive fieldwork in Africa. His teaching and research interests have focused on the archaeology of Central Africa, ethno-archaeology, and economic, medical, and applied anthropology, as well as museology and cultural heritage management. He has led global projects on AIDS prevention and rainforest conservation, and has been advisor to the European Union, the UN, the World Bank, and several governments.

Peter Mitchell (D.Phil., Oxford, 1987) is Lecturer in African Prehistory at the University of Oxford and Tutor and Fellow in Archaeology at St Hugh's College, Oxford. He has been researching the archaeology of Late Pleistocene and Holocene hunter-gatherers in southern Africa since 1983, and has conducted extensive fieldwork in Lesotho. He is author of *The Archaeology of Southern Africa* and *African Connections: An Archaeological Perspective on Africa's Links with the Rest of the World*.

Katharina Neumann (Dr.Phil. nat., Botany, 1988; *Habilitation*, Botany, J. W. Goethe Universität, Frankfurt am Main, 2001) is an archaeobotanist at the University of Frankfurt, Germany. Her research is focused on prehistoric plant use and the Holocene vegetation history of West Africa, with special emphasis on woody plants and the domestication history of African crops.

Thomas Plummer (Ph.D., Yale, 1991) is Associate Professor of Anthropology at Queens College, City University of New York. His research interests include Pliocene and Pleistocene hominin behavior and ecology, hominin paleontology, human osteology, paleolithic archaeology, and vertebrate paleontology. His current field project on the Homa Peninsula, Kenya, is investigating fossil- and artifact-bearing deposits ranging in age from the Holocene to the Late Pliocene, and includes the investigation of a ca. 2 million-year-old Oldowan occurrence at Kanjera South.

Gilbert Pwiti (M.Phil., Cambridge, Ph.D. Uppsala) is Dean of the Faculty of Arts and Professor of Archaeology at the University of Zimbabwe. His main research interests and publications over the last 18 years have focused on southern African archaeology, spatial archaeology, the development of complex societies, and archaeological heritage management.

Andrew Reid (Ph.D., Cambridge, 1991) is Senior Lecturer in Eastern African Archaeology at University College London. He previously lectured at the University of Dar es Salaam and the University of Botswana, and has conducted research on various aspects of states and cattle in eastern and southern Africa. His recent publications include *Ancient Egypt in Africa* (co-edited with David O'Connor) and *African Historical Archaeologies* (co-edited with Paul Lane).

Ann Brower Stahl (Ph.D., University of California at Berkeley, 1985) is Professor of Anthropology at the State University of New York, Binghamton (Binghamton University). Her early research focused on sedentism and subsistence in ceramic Late Stone Age contexts in Ghana (Kintampo complex), while her more recent research has centered on the effects of global entanglements along the savanna-woodland/forest margins in Ghana. She is the author of *Making History in Banda: Anthropological Visions of Africa's Past.*

Sarah Wurz (D.Phil., University of Stellenbosch, 2000) is a research associate in the Department of Geography and Environmental Studies at the University of Stellenbosch. She has taught courses in prehistory and human evolution and studied the stone artifact sequence at Klasies River. Her research interests include the evolution of music and language from a multidisciplinary perspective, and the methodology of stone artifact analysis.

To our archaeological predecessors

on whose work we respectfully build

1

Introduction: Changing Perspectives on Africa's Pasts

Ann Brower Stahl

When I teach the archaeology of sub-Saharan Africa at an American university, I begin by asking students to name African archaeological sites of which they know something. The resulting list is predictable in composition and length: Olduvai Gorge invariably tops the list, Great Zimbabwe is typically second, while students who enjoy archaeological documentaries may come up with Jenné-jeno or Gorée Island. Those who have taken an introductory course on human evolution may recall the classic quartet of Sterkfontein, Swartkrans, Makapansgat, and Kromdraai. At this point, the room grows quiet. "Any other sites? No?" As we move to talk about the images they hold of Africa, safaris and wildlife come easily to mind, as do images of exotic "otherness" invariably combined with those of violence and warfare (see Achebe 1978; also Comaroff and Comaroff 1992:3–48; Ebron 2002:163–216; Lane 2001). Two points emerge from these discussions: (1) students know little at the beginning of the course about African archaeology (which is neither a debility for them nor for the reader of this volume); and (2) their perceptions of Africa draw on imagery sustained by the media and a broader popular imagination. Some are motivated by this negative imagery to take courses on Africa. They seek knowledge that will enable them to counter ethnocentric presumptions and sustain more positive views of Africa. In this, the students are little different from a long tradition of scholars whose research has been motivated by a desire to create respect for the cultural achievements of African peoples past and present (e.g., Bates et al., eds., 1993; Ebron 2002:viii–xi).

As in the course I teach, the goal of this volume is twofold. First, and most conventionally, it is intended to familiarize readers with *some* of what we know of Africa's past through archaeological sources. In no sense is it an encyclopedic compendium. The volume samples the temporal, topical, and geographical spectrum encompassed by sub-Saharan African archaeology. Though an effort has been made to be temporally and spatially inclusive, major gaps remain. Temporally, the volume is ambitious, "covering" 2.6 million years from the earliest archaeological traces to sites occupied in the last century; yet coverage is uneven, favoring some regions while slighting or omitting others. Notable geographic omissions south of the Sahara include the Horn of Africa (see Munro-Hay 1989; Phillipson 1995, 1997, 2001), Mediterranean Africa, and the Nile Valley. Regrettably, by focusing on sub-Saharan Africa, the volume reinforces an artificial division between North Africa and Africa south of the Sahara (see O'Connor and Reid, eds., 2003 for an effort to surmount this division); however, publisher's page restrictions force selectivity. Within those restrictions, however, the conventional goal of the volume is to impart knowledge of Africa's past.

The second, less conventional goal of the volume is to encourage critical evaluation of archaeological knowledge; what questions are posed by archaeologists working in Africa and why? What presumptions (implicit and explicit) have shaped knowledge of African pasts? For whom is knowledge of Africa's pasts relevant? And how might that knowledge affect the present and future of African peoples? These questions are intended to bring into view the contexts in which knowledge about African pasts is produced (see also Hall 1990a:2–4, 1990b). This goal is motivated by the view that knowledge is always "interested" and has effects in the world. The concept of "interested" knowledge stands in juxtaposition to the ideal of "distinterested" knowledge that is sustained by simplistic perspectives on objectivity. Recent, often rancorous, debates over the nature of scientific inquiry have hinged on the issue of objectivity. From the time of Descartes' effort to free "mind" from the constraints of "body" (Descartes 1979), science became linked with objectivity. Objectivity was equated with removing oneself from the fray and letting evidence or scientific facts "speak for themselves." Objectivity was viewed as a prerequisite of rigorous scientific knowledge and linked to Enlightenment goals of producing generalizable knowledge. However, the last two decades have seen vigorous critiques of objectivity which some dismiss as nihilistic perspectives rooted in post-structural/post-modern perspectives of the last two decades (Wilson 1998). Yet the sources of these critiques are diverse (e.g., Alcoff and Potter, eds., 1993; Foucault 1972; Nielson, ed., 1990; White 1973) and cannot be equated with a denial of a "real world" or, for the purposes of this volume, denial of a "lived past." From Kuhn (1962) on, scholars have discussed the effects of "paradigms" (accepted ideas about the way the world works) on scientific thought. As Kuhn argued, paradigms structure what is "knowable." Change in what is "known" often proceeds less from an accumulation of new facts than from paradigm shifts that cast existing facts in a new light. But this does not negate the importance of empirical evidence which can, when data are allowed to "just say no" (Gould 1981:68–69, 74), lead to the rejection of entrenched ways of thinking (see Chapters 10, 13).

Though schisms remain between those who embrace a model of science as objective knowledge and those who embrace radically relativist views of knowledge (questioning the notion of reliable knowledge grounded in a knowable reality), there is a broadening awareness that knowledge is shaped by the social, political, and economic contexts in which it is produced (e.g., Schmidt and Patterson, eds., 1995; Shepherd 2002). This is not so much a condemnation of scientific inquiry as a recognition that science is a human product. As such, the goal of a critically aware science is *not* to strip away or disembed knowledge from its human context (arguably an impossible goal). Rather it acknowledges the contexts and concerns that shape scientific inquiry, and works to understand how that context affects the resulting knowledge (e.g., Wylie et al. 1989). In the case of archaeology, the questions that archaeologists ask of the past are shaped by the presumptions and concerns of the present (Trigger 1990:309). In this sense, new knowledge about the past often emerges as much from asking new questions as it does from newly discovered evidence.

Thus the last two decades have witnessed the emergence of critical perspectives that emphasize the "interested" character of knowledge. These perspectives are theoretically diverse. There is no single perspective within history or archaeology on what motivates change or how change occurs. Despite their diversity, however, they share a concern to explore the contexts that shape what we know of Africa's pasts and how we know it.

This second goal distinguishes this volume from the handful of published syntheses of African prehistory (although see Hall 1990a, 1996). Texts often present what is known within the context of a narrative, typically one of technological progress (below). This volume does not offer an overarching narrative of African prehistory because such narratives "paper over" significant interpretive debates and obscure how archaeologists generate and revise knowledge about the past. By introducing readers to the paradigms, points of debate, and implications of key case studies/topics, the volume is intended to provide a platform from which to enter the primary literature on African archaeology. Each chapter thus provides an extensive bibliography that allows readers to follow debates into the primary literature, and to expand geographical coverage of particular time periods and issues.

Given the second goal of the volume – to foster critical awareness of the contexts that have shaped archaeological knowledge of Africa's pasts – remaining sections of this chapter and Chapter 2 explore underlying assumptions and preoccupations that have shaped the questions archaeologists ask about Africa's pasts and the methods they have employed in answering those questions. Thus, these first two chapters explore the history and practice of African archaeology. This exploration is partial, and readers wanting to know more of the contextual history of African archaeology are referred to Robertshaw's (Robertshaw, ed., 1990) edited volume, which remains a standard. Remaining chapters of this book are temporally and topically organized, beginning with the earliest archaeological traces (Chapter 3) and the archaeology of Pleistocene Africa (Chapters 4–6). Chapters 6 through 10 explore Holocene contexts and pay particular attention to various forms of "intensification" that characterized later Holocene lifestyles. Chapters 11–13 are topically focused contributions that explore debates surrounding metallurgy, urbanism, and historical linguistic modeling of Bantu languages. These chapters lay the groundwork for an exploration of the last several millennia in Chapters 14–18. Here authors explore the mosaic of technological, social, and political-economic strategies that characterized different geographical regions over the last 2,000–3,000 years. This temporal organization mirrors to some extent the standard organization of synthetic volumes on African archaeology (e.g., Phillipson 1985, 1993). Yet a key difference is that this temporal organization is not overlaid with a narrative based on stages of technological progress. This will become most evident in final chapters devoted to the last several millennia, which explore complex interactions among groups that would previously have been considered as belonging to different "Ages" (i.e., stone tool-using hunter-gatherers interacting with metal-using agriculturalists).

Valuation, Significance, and Archaeological Knowledge

The sites listed by students in the opening sessions of my African archaeology class are strikingly similar to the roster of World Heritage sites approved by the United Nations Educational, Scientific and Cultural Organization (UNESCO). UNESCO World Heritage sites are chosen on the basis of their "outstanding universal value" to a human heritage in which we all share (World Heritage 2003). National parks meant to conserve African wildlife top the list of World Heritage sites in sub-Saharan Africa with more than 30 sites, underscoring a view of Africa as a place of natural rather than cultural heritage (compare this with other world areas where cultural sites outnumber natural sites 4 to 1; World Heritage 2003). Ancient cities and towns are a distant second (ten sites), and sites that have yielded ancestral fossil hominids are third (five sites). Royal palaces, royal burial grounds, and European sites are tied with four sites each, while the remaining seven sub-Saharan African sites include rock art (two sites), stelae (two sites), unique cultures (two sites), and a church (one site). The parallels between these lists raise the issue of *valuation* or *significance*. How do archaeologists choose sites for investigation? Why are some sites known to the general public or nominated to heritage lists, while others remain obscure?

The question of valuation or significance raises the issue of audience – *by whom* is a site valued? For many archaeologists, the importance of a site is determined by its significance to "the human story" – a story of physical and cultural change spanning our transition from terrestrial primate scavengers to proficient stone tool-using hunter-gatherers, to metal-using food producers living in urban settlements with complex political organizations. Local inhabitants, however, value sites for different reasons (Thiaw 2004). Contemporary groups may be very concerned with the interpretation of sites linked to their own past, but uninterested in those deemed to represent the past of others. Colonial processes often contributed to a people's sense of disconnection from, and therefore indifference toward, their cultural heritage (Pwiti and Ndoro 1999). Some archaeologists see this sort of disconnection as linked to the "plundering of the past" (Schmidt and McIntosh, eds., 1996), as for example in Islamic areas of West Africa where terracotta figurines valued by Western collectors may be seen as vestiges of a "pagan" past disconnected from the present. Archaeologists have struggled with how to foster a sense of local connection to cultural heritage as a means to combat illegal excavation and export of antiquities (Bedaux and Rowlands 2001; McIntosh 1996; Posnansky 1996; Sidibé 1995:32–33; and see Sowunmi 1998 on the need to foster more than simply pride in the past).

The question of valuation also helps us see how our knowledge of Africa's past is entangled with a broader political economy. Generating knowledge of the past through systematic survey and excavation requires access to financial and infra-structural resources (Abungu and Abungu 1998; Karenga-Munene 1996; Kibunjia 1997; Kusimba 1996; Lane 2001; Mabulla 2000; MacEachern 2001; Posnansky 1996; Pwiti 1997). Investment in relevant training, facilities and fieldwork is, under-standably, a low priority for African nations facing pressing social and economic problems and straining under burdensome debt loads (Ellison et al. 1996; Pos-nansky 1996). Consequently, archaeological research in Africa has been funded pri-marily through external sources, which therefore have the power to shape research priorities – determining the kinds of sites that are excavated, and thus the archae-ological knowledge that is generated (Andah et al. 1994; Shepherd 2002:192). So, for example, World Heritage designation, driven by the criterion of "outstanding universal value," opens coffers for research and preservation of select ancient cities, colonial forts and castles, and royal palaces. Research on sites deemed important to the project of "World Prehistory" may be funded by international agencies and non-African governments. And sites likely to yield ancient objects that suit the tastes of Western collectors become the focus of illegal excavations fueled by the illicit art market (Brent 1994, 1996; Shaw 1997; Sidibé 1995, 1996). So the possibilities and partialities of our knowledge of Africa's past are shaped by a complex mix of what "we" wish to know or possess and why we wish know or possess it. Since the rele-vance of that knowledge is often framed in terms of our human heritage, I turn now the "Project of World Prehistory."

Images of Africa and the Project of World Prehistory

Standard narratives of world prehistory frame the "human story" as one of pro-gressive development in which simple forms of technology and organization gave way to progressively more complex ones. These narratives have deep cultural roots in Western thought. Medieval notions of a "Great Chain of Being" (a single, hier-archical ordering of all creatures from creation; Lovejoy 1936) were incorporated first into Enlightenment conjectural histories that posited a universal sequence of development through stages of "savagery," "barbarism," and "civilization," and later into 19th-century social evolutionary formulations (Stocking 1987; Trigger 1989). The technologies and organizational forms highlighted by this narrative were not confined to a single world area; however, their appearance in some world areas was accorded greater significance in "the human story" compared to others, a signifi-cance based largely on time. Time has been a crucial standard for significance or valuation because world prehistory was cast as a race in which it mattered who "got there first" (Neale 1985, 1986). By extension, a preoccupation with origins was shaped by the esteem in which invention/innovation are held; once a technology, or a social or political form, was invented, later manifestations of that technology or form were though to be derivative unless a case for independent origins could be made (see Sinclair et al. 1993:9–13).

The project of "world prehistory" that emerged in the 19th century was shaped by the dual legacies of industrialization and colonization, and simultaneously grounded in the universalism of Enlightenment science. As the Crystal Palace exhibition (1851) made clear, England's increased industrial capacity was seen as an outgrowth of progressive technological innovation (Stocking 1987:1–6). Industrial modification of European landscapes fostered the growth of paleolithic studies, which reinforced this view of progressive technological development. Mining and construction disturbed the earth's surface at an unprecedented scale and led to the exposure of ancient remains that were only slowly accepted as proof of the deep antiquity of human occupation in Europe (Heizer, ed., 1962; Stocking 1987:69–74; Trigger 1989:87–94). Fossil remains of extinct animals in association with stone tools contributed to the rejection of Ussher's short chronology (a mere 6,000 years based on the Bible) in favor of "deep time" that could be known through two sources: (1) the material evidence of archaeology (traces from the past); and (2) the customs of non-European people who were perceived as living in the manner of the past (traces of the past in the present). The methods of 19th-century prehistory were aptly captured in the titles of prominent works such as Sir John Lubbock's (later Lord Avebury) *Prehistoric Times as Illustrated by Ancient Remains and the Manners and Customs of Modern Savages* (Lubbock 1865; see also Sollas 1915). The oxymoronic phrase "modern savages" betrayed the dual temporality embedded in the project of world prehistory. To be "modern" was to be living in the same time, coeval with, Europeans; but coevalness was simultaneously denied to "modern savages" who were perceived as remnant societies, survivals from earlier times and evolutionary phases (the past persisting into the present). This temporal "sleight of hand" framed European knowledge of colonized peoples well into the 20th century (Fabian 1983).

The knowledge of "modern savages" that flowed from colonization enabled fuller imaginings of pre-modern life in Europe (Orme 1973, 1974; examples in Heizer, ed., 1962), and laid the contours of a universal scheme of technological and social development in which savage societies stood in for early stages of development, while Europe manifested the pinnacle or end point of this trajectory. But as Laclau (1996) argued, the universal emerges *NOT* from widely documented shared features, as we might at first imagine, but rather from the elevation of a *specific instance* or example to *stand for* the universal. The particular instance (e.g., European society) thus became the exemplar of the universal. Other particularities (i.e., non-European societies) represented "stops along the way," steps in the direction of the purported universal. Thus in 19th-century Europe, the *present* of so-called savage societies became a key source of insight into a *European past*, while Europe, in its present, stood for the future of all (see Chapter 2 for fuller consideration of analogy).

Implied in the structure of the preceding paragraph is a distinction between "us" (Europeans) and "them" ("Others"; the "savages" and "barbarians" of 19th-century thought), a distinction that betrays the universal pretense of Enlightenment-inspired world prehistory (e.g., the singular "human story"; also Mehta 1997). True to its Enlightenment legacy, world prehistory espoused a universalist program in which

all societies passed through the same (or a broadly similar) sequence of technological and social development. Simple technological and social forms were superseded
by more complex ones. This trajectory was captured in the early terminology of the
Three Age System – Stone, Bronze, Iron (Rodden 1981). This system was later
elaborated into a ladder-like scheme of successive Paleolithic stages (Lower, Middle
and Upper) characterized by various chipped stone technologies, followed by a
Neolithic (or "new" stone age) marked by the advent of polished stone technologies, which gave way to successive ages of metal, first a Bronze and later an Iron
Age (Trigger 1989:73–79, 94–102, 155–160; on Africa, see Sinclair et al. 1993:3–9).
Initially defined on the basis of European archaeological materials, this age/stage
terminology was thought to manifest a universal sequence of human technological
or, in later formulations (Childe 1936), socio-economic development, and thus the
structure of world prehistory. As archaeological research began in other world areas,
this sequence acted as the universal standard against which the particularities of
"regional prehistories" were compared and often found wanting (Trigger 1989:
110–147).

Although some early colonial officers and amateur archaeologists in Anglophone
Africa employed European terminology in pioneering archaeological investigations
in Africa, a separate terminological framework was developed to emphasize the distinctive qualities of the African archaeological record (Bishop and Clark, eds., 1967;
Deacon 1990; Gowlett 1990:18–19; Hall 1990a:8–12; Robertshaw 1990a; Sinclair
et al. 1993:3–9). Goodwin, a student of European prehistorian Miles Burkitt, is
credited with introducing the framework of an Early, Middle and Later Stone Age
that has structured discussions of Africa's past in ensuing decades (Goodwin and
van Riet Lowe 1929). Though African researchers stressed the distinctive, local features of these "ages," they obviously paralleled in a general sense the threefold
Lower, Middle, and Upper Paleolithic of Europe. Other European terms appeared
even more problematic. The applicability of the Anglophone concept of "neolithic"
to Africa was a source of considerable debate (Shaw 1967; Sinclair et al. 1993:4–8;
Chapters 7–10), and it was recognized early on that, by contrast to Europe and the
Middle East, no discernible Bronze Age preceded the Iron Age in Africa. In Africa
there was apparently a "direct transition" from the Late Stone Age or "Neolithic"
to the Iron Age (Chapter 11). Africa's past (*their* past) was thus distinctive, a departure from the universal standard embodied by European prehistory (*our* past)
glossed as the *human* past writ large.

Yet despite the early recognition of diversity in prehistoric sequences around the
world, the terminological framing of world prehistory (Lower, Middle, and Upper
Paleolithic, followed by a Neolithic, then Bronze and Iron Age) hangs on a Euro-
pean/Near Eastern scaffolding. The perception of this *particular* sequence as the
embodiment of a universal one had implications for the narrative staging of world
prehistory (also Connah 1998). Picture the world as a stage on which the "human
story" is played out. As narration of the story proceeds, a spotlight trains our attention on different geographical areas. The area "illuminated" at any point in the story
is determined by temporal priority; in other words, the geographical area with the
"first instance" of a particular development occupies the spotlight as the "human

story" is told. In standard narratives, the spotlight is trained on Africa – home of our hominid ancestors – as the story begins. Thus the staging of world prehistory is, in theory, broadly encompassing in the earliest reaches of time (periods when "we" trace "our" common ancestry to Africa), but becomes less encompassing as the story of "our" ancestry shifts to the narrower geographic stage of the Near East, and narrower still as the "center" of civilization shifts to Europe. This entails an ever-narrowing "circle of we" that excludes major portions of the globe from a central role. Micaela di Leonardo (1998:123, 138, 140) explored the significance of a "circle of we" for patterns of inclusion and exclusion. "We," she argued, is a dynamic category with shifting boundaries that strategically include and exclude in relation to particular goals and contexts. Building on di Leonardo, it becomes important to ask who is included and who is excluded from the "circle of we" in world prehistory.

In standard narratives of world prehistory, the "circle of we" is inclusive in early human history. The Plio-Pleistocene hominids (Chapter 3) who forged new adaptations in the open woodlands of East Africa are portrayed as common human ancestors (see Dennell 1990 on geographical centers of human origins). Thus, early hominids do not belong to the particularity of "African prehistory" but are broadly relevant to "our" universal prehistory. This is captured in comments by Gowlett, who suggests that

> Archaeological studies of human origins differ from other areas of African archaeology, in that in principle, and perhaps for some researchers, the prime importance lies in the subject – human evolution – rather than the place . . . There is a theoretical contrast with any other field of African prehistory, since . . . those who choose to work in Africa have done so primarily because of their own interest in Africa. To many researchers in human evolution the continent has been important in its own right, but for others it has been merely the backdrop to a science which was the main interest. (Gowlett 1990:13)

Thirty years ago, when regional models of modern human origins prevailed (Chapter 4), the "circle of we" rapidly telescoped following the migration of Acheulean peoples out of Africa and into the Near East and Europe. The Middle Stone Age (MSA) of Africa (thought to be temporally and technologically comparable to the Middle Paleolithic of Europe and the Near East) was viewed as a parochial topic pursued by a few dogged individuals (part of Glynn Isaac's [1975] "muddle in the middle"). As explored in detail in Chapters 4 and 5, the last 15 years witnessed important changes in the perceived significance of the African MSA. Based on fossil evidence as well as more controversial mitochondrial DNA evidence, many students of human evolution now favor a more recent African ancestry for modern humans (Chapters 4, 5). In this view, all contemporary humans share a common African ancestry as recently as ca. 100,000 to 200,000 years ago. In light of these claims, African MSA studies have achieved new prominence and focus of research that will, no doubt, be claimed as integral to "our" human story. But the geographical telescoping of the story remains intact for periods after this;

the Later Stone Age of Africa is framed as a distinctive/*particular* Late Pleistocene response, while the Upper Paleolithic of Europe, with its rock art and finely worked stone and bone tools, embodies the prehistory of "us" (see Connah 1998:1). In standard narratives, the Near East remains in the "circle of we" through the neolithic and urban "revolutions" because of the temporal priority of these developments in the Near East compared to Europe (Chapters 10, 13). However, the "story of human development" narrows in focus to Europe as historians and archaeologists track the growth of "civilization" in its linguistically unmarked form.

Linguists distinguish marked and unmarked forms of words. The effect of marking is to modify – often to specify – the meaning of a word. Unmarked forms are taken to be general, while marked forms are specific. Yet Laclau's observations about the relationship between the particular and the universal are relevant here (i.e., that the universal is simply a particular form elevated to *stand for* the universal). Consider the broadly encompassing term "American." As Williams (1989) argued, the supposedly inclusive term carries with it exclusions based on race and ethnicity.[1] In practice the taken-for-granted referent of "American" is "white American," which accounts for the proliferation of linguistically marked forms of Americans (African American, Asian American and so on). So too with history. Unmarked "history" is taken as broadly encompassing (Schlesinger 1991); yet it simultaneously obscures exclusions embedded in the practice of history (e.g., Bernal 1987 on the exclusion of Africa from the history of Western civilization). From the 1950s to the 1970s, calls to make history more inclusive resulted in specialities like "women's history," "black history," and "African history." These linguistically marked forms of history were intended to broaden the scope of history, to reveal and correct exclusions in unmarked "history," yet their persistence as marked forms attests the persistence of exclusions they were intended to correct.

These issues of inclusion and exclusion through linguistic marking have implications for the narrative of world prehistory. The geographical telescoping of the narrative is obscured by representing world prehistory as "our story," begging the question of who was included in and excluded from the "circle of we." Yet exclusions from the main narrative are evident in the ancillary stories of "alternative developments" in "other world areas" to which final chapters of world prehistory texts are often devoted. Here is where we learn of the development of New World and African civilizations. New World prehistory is often considered distinct because of its geographical isolation. Yet African prehistory from the Middle, or more recently Later, Stone Age has long been treated as "ancillary" for at least two reasons: (1) Africa was explicitly perceived as a "late-comer" to technological and social developments highlighted by the narrative of world prehistory (e.g., agriculture, metallurgy, urban settlement, political complexity, and so on); and (2) there was an implicit perception that African prehistory was relevant to "them," not "us," underscoring the exclusion of Africa from the "circle of we."

The first perception, that Africa was at best a "runner up" in the race of progressive development, drew on deeply rooted Western imagery of Africa as a barbarous continent that stood outside the progressive human impulse. From Hegel to Trevor-Roper, Africa was portrayed as the most unprogressive of continents, an inversion of the civilized qualities of Europe (see Ebron 2002; Hammond and Jablow 1970; Holl 1995; Mudimbe 1994). This deeply rooted view, shaped and refined through the long history of the slave trade, was further reinforced by an early 20th-century pessimism about the ubiquity of innovation. Whereas 19th-century social evolutionists allowed that technological, social, and political innovations could develop independently, albeit at different rates, early 20th-century scholars were more pessimistic about the innovative qualities of humans. They believed that innovation was rare, that most inventions were singular, and that these subsequently spread through processes of diffusion and migration (see Trigger 1989:150–155, 161–167). The long-term exclusion of Africans from the "circle of we" (intimately linked to the dehumanization of the slave trade) was thus combined with a general pessimism about the innovative nature of humans, with important consequences for the development of African archaeology.

Thematics in African Archaeology

Though there was isolated attention to a handful of prominent sites in the late 19th century (e.g., Great Zimbabwe; Hall 1995; Kuklick 1991), systematic archaeological investigations in sub-Saharan Africa developed in the context of 20th-century colonial occupation and were further stimulated by nationalism and the end of colonial occupation (Robertshaw 1990b:4–5; Trigger 1990; see contributions in Robertshaw [ed., 1990] for the development of archaeological investigations in different parts of the continent). Early attention focused on Africa's Stone Age past (e.g., Chapter 17) which was seen as dynamic in relation to the perceived stagnation of Africa in more recent periods (Robertshaw 1990b:4). The so-called Iron Age was viewed as recent and inherently uninteresting, for it graded into the "ethnographic present" (see Clark 1990:189). Innovation was assumed to be a product of outside influence, and therefore diffusion or migration was invoked to account for apparent changes. Because archaeological investigations were in their infancy, there was often little direct evidence to sustain views of late, derivative development. This is clearly seen in the ambitious synthesis of African culture history offered by George Peter Murdock in 1959. His *Africa: Its Peoples and their Culture History* (Murdock 1959) is exemplary of the received view of African history on the eve of independence. First and foremost, the history was organized by tribal/linguistic units. The tribal mapping of African societies had profound effects on the structure of archaeological knowledge as archaeologists sought to trace the ancestors of contemporary "tribal" entities (Hall 1984, 1990a:13–16; Chapters 16, 17). This project came to be questioned from the 1970s as anthropologists and historians began to explore the extent to which so-called "tribal entities" emerged through colonial interventions and were therefore problematic units of historical analysis (e.g., Cohen and Odhiambo 1989; Goody 1990, 1998; Lentz 1994, 1995; Ranger 1993). Second, Murdock's history assumed the priority of diffusion over independent invention; much of the volume was devoted to tracking the spread of diverse traits and practices across the continent (e.g., Chapter 12). Unlike some of his contemporaries, Murdock did not assume that all cultural innovation was introduced to Africa. Based on the insights of botanists, Murdock postulated an independent development of agriculture in Africa (Chapter 10); however, "handicrafts," trade towns, complex political organizations, and other potent signs of progress were, in Murdock's (1959:72) view, introduced to the continent from the north.

Colonial insistence on the unprogressive quality of African societies and the external origins of all/most innovations led to a backlash in the period leading up to and in the wake of African independence. The growth of nationalism and the promise of independence coincided with growing interest in Iron Age archaeology. Newly forged nations required independent histories that overcame the biases inherent in the limited documentary sources relied upon by traditional historians (Temu and Swai 1981:18–22). The late 1950s and early 1960s witnessed the emergence of a vital tradition of African historical studies that emphasized the importance of "non-traditional" sources, including oral history and archaeology (Vansina 1961; Vansina et al., eds., 1964; on the limits of early interdisciplinary cooperation, see Stahl 2001:15). "Iron Age" archaeological studies (see Hall 1990a:8–10, 1990b:64 on the introduction of this term) were viewed as providing important evidence regarding the precolonial history of African societies. The precolonial past took on new significance as archaeologists embraced two new projects: (1) helping to forge national histories, which meant a greater focus on Iron Age sites; and (2) countering images of Africa as an unprogressive backwater (Andah 1995; Sinclair et al. 1993:16–31; Stahl 2001:13). These negative images had gained new force through the broadcasts and writings of Oxford historian Hugh Trevor-Roper, who excluded Africa from his program on world history on the grounds that "there is only the unrewarding gyrations of barbarous tribes in picturesque but irrelevant corners of the globe" (Trevor-Roper 1965:9). Trevor-Roper's words, uttered in the context of African independence, became a rallying cry for historians and archaeologists determined to prove that Africa had a progressive history much like Europe's (see Fuglestad [1992] and Neale [1985, 1986] for an extended discussion).

These new goals affected the kinds of sites that archaeologists targeted for investigation. New emphasis was placed on sites that promised to afford insight into the antiquity of agriculture, metallurgy, cities, and social complexity, all taken as hallmarks of cultural progress (Stahl 1999). The goal was to demonstrate that Africa too had a proud history of innovation and social complexity, one that rivaled other world areas in age and could therefore provide a platform for generating respect for African cultural history – in other words, that Africa was active in the story of human development (Rowlands 1989a, 1989b; Shepherd 2002:196–197). But in common with African history, these efforts to counter negative images of Africa through the production of new histories questioned the *details* of the narrative but *not its underlying presumptions* (Neale 1985, 1986; also Mudimbe 1994:xv). A focus on origins, kingdoms, and states was intended to stake a claim to the "right to universality, and thus the acknowledgment of African contributions to the make-up of humanity" (Jewsiewicki and Mudimbe 1993:1), in other words, to demonstrate that Africa's past was continuous with the standard of world prehistory. But by failing to question the presumptions of this narrative (i.e., the teleology of pro-gressive developmentalist models, the valuation of "complexity," and that the European/Middle Eastern sequence stood for the "universal"), archaeologists, like historians, fell into what Fuglestad (1992) termed the "Trevor-Roper trap." The epistemological framework and narrative conventions of earlier approaches remained intact (Jewsiewicki 1989:36), and in the case of archaeology, were rein-vigorated in the 1960s through American New Archeology, which reinfused evolu-tionary ideas into archaeology and reinforced the study of origins as a key issue (Trigger 1989:289–328; also Robertshaw 1990b:5). Nor did archaeologists ques-tion the standard of world prehistory which, as we have seen, was created through the elevation of a particularity to the status of the universal.

A renewed interest in origins flowed from the efforts to demonstrate Africa's place in the story of human progress, and led to archaeological investigations into the origins of agriculture (e.g., Harlan et al., eds., 1976; Stahl 1984; Chapter 10); metallurgy (Schmidt and Avery 1978; Tylecote 1975; van der Merwe 1980; van der Merwe and Avery 1982; see Killick 1996; Chapter 11); and urbanism (McIntosh and McIntosh 1984; see McIntosh 1999; Sinclair et al. 1993; Chapter 13). Radio-carbon dating promised new insight into the antiquity of these "key" developments, but proved disappointing after results suggested that some of these developments occurred later in Africa than in adjacent regions of the Old World. Arguments intended to generate respect for Africa now hinged on issues of *plentitude* or *diver-sity*. Sutton (1974), for example, argued that food production occurred late in Africa because of the natural endowment of Africa in the early to middle Holocene (Chapter 7). His proposal for an encompassing "aqualithic culture" stressed a *dis-tinctive* African pathway shaped by natural endowment; only later, under pressure from environmental deterioration, were African peoples forced to make the transi-tion to food production (see Chapters 9 and 10 for assessments of these arguments). In the case of metallurgy, a consensus emerged through the 1980s that, although smelting techniques may have been introduced to Africa, there was considerable innovation in the techniques of smelting within Africa, with others postulating a *distinctive* "African pathway" to the production of steel (Schmidt and Avery 1978; van der Merwe and Avery 1982; Chapter 11). Difference, diversity, and distinc-tiveness have thus been lauded as reasons to respect Africa's cultural history (e.g., McIntosh 1998). Yet we need to heed Ebron's (2002:30) observation that "even well-intended efforts to turn around the valences of 'Africa' and 'the West' . . . still tend to repeat the framework." Difference and distinctness are assessed in relation to a "standard," and the unquestioned standard that continues to lurk behind the *distinctive* qualities of Africa's past are the supposedly *universal* qualities of Europe's past. *Plus ça change, plus c'est la même chose!*

To this point I have argued that the thematics or "big questions" that drove early archaeological investigations into Africa's pasts were framed by the project of world prehistory – first in negative fashion (denying Africa a place), and then in "posi-tive" fashion (insisting on Africa's place) – but without questioning the broader framing of world prehistory. This is, however, a generalization that does not account for the questions that occupied archaeologists working in specific areas. When we examine regional trends, a second characteristic feature of African archaeological research becomes apparent, a feature shaped by the relationship between African archaeology and other disciplines. For a variety of reasons, which I develop below, the archaeology of Africa, particularly the archaeology of the last few millennia, was shaped by insights from linguistics, ethnography, and oral history. Historical reconstructions based on these sources were often in place before archaeologists put "spade to ground," and these reconstructions, often speculative, provided a ready-made scheme into which archaeological data were slotted as they became available (Chapter 12).

The unusual relationship between archaeology and other disciplines that characterized African studies relates to the fact that, unlike other world areas subject to European colonization (the western hemisphere, Australia, etc.), African cultures remained vital through the rather brief formal colonial period (in many areas, the period from ca. 1890 to the 1960s). Formal colonization of most of the continent followed the 1884 Berlin conference, at which European powers divided the continent among themselves based on existing coastal interests. The ensuing "scramble for Africa" forcibly imposed colonial rule and shaped the later configuration of African nation-states. Make no mistake. These 20th-century developments led to considerable change; however, "African Africa remained a going concern" (Moore 1994:12). Change was perceived as a thin, recent veneer over long-standing traditional practices. Because these practices were thought to be enduring, knowledge of present practices, forms of organization, and so on was thought to inform directly and unambiguously on the past (Stahl 2004; Chapter 2). At the same time, a growing interest in the "culture history" of larger cultural units led to ambitious reconstructions of regional and interregional history based on contemporary sources (e.g., Murdock 1959). In order to evaluate these reconstructions and their effects on archaeology, we need to consider the sources we use to gain insight into the past.

Learning about the Past: The Value of Archaeological Sources

Knowledge of the past can be derived from a variety of sources, including written documents, the material traces of archaeological sites, and oral histories. These sources stand in different temporal relationships to the past, relationships that we might conceive of as "direct" and "indirect." Documents and material residues are what we might consider "direct" sources, in that they were produced in the past. Though we might distinguish residues created by "actors" from those of "witnesses" (a distinction drawn by Hall [2000:9] in exploring differences between the archaeological and documentary records), both relate to events or circumstances of the time. We can consider other sources as "indirect" in the sense that they come from a time *after* the contexts about which we wish to know. Oral histories are an example. Oral histories are contemporary sources based on remembrances of a past from which they are temporally removed. This contemporary quality of oral histories sparked a controversy over their veracity as historical sources; because they can be edited, amplified, and so on, some argued that oral histories were inadequate as historical sources (e.g., Henige 1982; see Ebron [2002:81–113] on oral sources and state archives). Others developed techniques of source evaluation that would allow their use as credible historical sources (Vansina 1961, 1985). This was a particularly important development in African historical studies given the paucity of "standard" historical sources (i.e., written documents), and a fluorescence of oral historical research in the early independence period (after 1957) generated a wealth of new insights into African societies of the last millennium.

Linguistics is another indirect source of evidence that has significantly influenced historical reconstruction in Africa. Spoken languages are contemporary, but carry "traces of the past" in their vocabulary and structure that historical linguists study in order to discern historical relationships among languages. In the case of written languages, documents can yield important insights into the changing character of language over time. Historical linguists who study non-written languages must, however, glean historical insights solely from contemporary language. By comparatively analyzing the vocabulary and structure of related languages, historical linguists reconstruct the relationships among contemporary languages based on patterns of similarity and difference. Languages that differ to a greater degree than others are assumed to have diverged or split off from one another earlier in time than those that are more similar. Though geographical "homelands" of languages have been traced by a variety of methods, all draw on the contemporary distribution of languages to posit places of origin and paths of dispersal (see Chapter 12). The key point for our purposes is that historical linguists derive historical insights from sources *in the present*. An analogous use of indirect evidence in the study of domestic crops is described by Neumann in Chapter 10. Based on the *current* distribution of the wild plants thought to be progenitors or precursors of their domesticated relatives, botanists have tried to pinpoint the general location where domestication occurred in the past. The logic is that plants must have been domesticated in an area where wild progenitors occurred (and see Chapter 2 on ethnographic sources).

What is the significance of the distinction between "direct" and "indirect" sources for the relationship between archaeology and other disciplines interested in the history of African peoples? First, there are few *direct* sources of insight into Africa's past; the material evidence of archaeology is often the primary direct source given the paucity of documentary sources prior to the last century. Yet historical reconstruction has often, as readers will discover in later chapters, been driven by or based upon *indirect* sources (e.g., linguistics, contemporary distribution of ethnographic traits). The course of African archaeology has been plagued by a wealth of speculative reconstructions typically, though not exclusively, based on indirect sources and a dearth of empirical archaeological work. Murdock's *Africa* (1959) is a primary example. Based on comparative analysis of ethnographic traits and historical linguistic analysis, Murdock offered wide-ranging historical reconstructions of agriculture and crafts, population movement, and more. As Eggert (Chapter 12) explores in detail, the widespread distribution of Bantu languages became a source of historical controversy which shaped the agenda of Iron Age archaeology in the central, eastern, and southern subcontinent for decades. In another example, Neumann details (Chapter 10) how the study of plant domestication and agricultural origins has been shaped by early speculative scenarios based on the distribution of contemporary plant species and the ethnocentric assumptions of Western scholars.

Archaeological sources, as contributors to this volume demonstrate, provide valuable independent evidence against which to assess models of the past. A recurrent theme in the chapters that follow is how expanded, empirically based archaeological research has, on reflection, led us to revise earlier understandings of the past based on comparative ethnographic, linguistic, and other sources. Where earlier researchers tended to "fit" archaeological evidence to reconstructions drawn from ethnographic, linguistic, or oral historical sources, research over the last several decades has more often treated archaeological evidence as an independent source of insight that often modifies or extends our understanding of the past derived from other sources (e.g., Schmidt 1990; Stahl 2001).

A Final Word on the Goals of the Volume

As readers will discover, this volume is unified neither by a particular theoretical stance nor a limited sense of shared goals for African archaeology. What the contributions share instead is a commitment to *assessment* of or critical engagement with the state of archaeological knowledge (hence the subtitle of the volume, "A Critical Introduction"). Contributors go beyond a simple review of knowledge to critically assess the direction and substance of research in their areas. "Critique" is not, however, synonymous with "criticism." The goal is not simply to criticize past research upon which all present knowledge builds; rather, it is to explore the preoccupations and assumptions that framed that research; to assess the quality and veracity of evidence used to sustain understandings of Africa's past; and to chart emerging research directions and questions that can help us surmount limitations and build on strengths of earlier work. As readers will discover, knowledge of Africa's pasts has changed over the last several decades, but only partly as a result of new evidence. As important as new evidence are new questions and perspectives that reframe our understanding of old evidence (Ellison et al. 1996). More sophisticated understanding of site formation and taphonomic processes has led to reinterpretations of the material signatures of Plio-Pleistocene sites (Chapters 3–5). Simplistic views of hunting and gathering peoples as survivals of ancient lifestyles have given way to a recognition to the diversity of hunting-gathering lifestyles and the dynamic relationships among peoples pursuing diverse economic strategies (Chapters 6–10, 14). Similarly, the assumption that "farmers" and "herders" rely primarily on domesticated resources led us to ignore the archaeological evidence of mosaic subsistence strategies that rely on a complex mix of wild, cultivated, and domesticated resources (Chapters 8–10, 16). We are increasingly aware of the complex history of technologies (Chapter 11), language groups (Chapter 12, 16), and of how entanglements in global networks over long time periods have shaped and reshaped the contours of daily life (Chapters 13–18). And we are coming to recognize that historically and ethnographically documented social and political formations only go so far in helping us to imagine the variability of arrangements in the past (David and Sterner 1999; Guyer and Belinga 1995; Chapters 13, 16, 17, 18).

There is then much that is new in African archaeology (Lane 2001), but that which is new builds on previous work. The foundations of earlier work may be dissembled and reassembled, but it remains an important component of contemporary knowledge. What is new today will no doubt be subject to revision and reinterpretation in future as research continues. As readers will discover, there is often a lack of consensus on our understanding of Africa's pasts, and a central theme of this volume is that knowledge of the past is dynamic and open-ended rather than fixed and finished, forged as it is through differences of opinion, revision based on new evidence, and the posing of new questions and new interpretations. Our knowledge of Africa's pasts is thus a series of successive approximations, shaped by contemporary concerns and issues, but nonetheless anchored in the study of material residues that attest the dynamic and varied lifestyles of African peoples. It is an archaeology shaped by categories inherited from the past, but categories that we need to "write into as well against" in an effort to understand how "facts" about the past come to be (Ebron 2002:51; see e.g., Pikirayi 1999 on ceramic typologies).

This is an exciting time to be involved African archaeology. We hope the volume will motivate archaeologists-in-training to learn more about Africa's pasts, and practicing archaeologists to use emerging knowledge of Africa's pasts in reformulating the project of world prehistory. Conventional narratives of world prehistory continually reinscribe a temporalizing view of Africa as a place apart (Stahl 2004). And whether we care to acknowledge it or not, archaeological knowledge extends "beyond academics" (Sowunmi 1998), simultaneously informing and replicating media images and popular imaginings of Africa. We need, therefore, to concern ourselves with the kinds of questions we ask, the answers we seek, and the effects of our successive approximations of Africa's pasts on her present and future. Africa's pasts speak to *us* – conceived as an encompassing "circle of we" – not for what they tell us about teleologically conceived universal progress, or quintessential difference and diversity conceived as a departure from an ever-present phantom standard of "us-ness." Rather they offer insight into our humanness; to the struggles of humans as social actors to feed and care for family, to express commonalities and differences, to impose or resist power and hegemony, in short, to make our way in a world of entangled and changing natural and cultural circumstances.

NOTE ON THE EXPRESSION OF DATES IN THIS VOLUME

Dates derived from radiocarbon age estimations are expressed in this volume in several ways. "Raw" dates are expressed as "b.p." (before present) with "present" taken to be A.D. 1950, the date after which atomic testing led to elevated levels of radioactive carbon isotopes in the earth's atmosphere. Dates expressed as b.c./a.d. are uncalibrated dates that have been derived by subtracting the raw date from A.D. 1950. These dates do not take into account variations in radioactive carbon isotope concentrations in the earth's atmosphere. Dendrochronological evidence shows that radiocarbon levels have been relatively enriched or depleted during some periods in the past, and these variations must be taken into account in order to translate radiocarbon dates into calendric equivalents. Dates expressed as b.c./a.d. should not, therefore, be taken as equivalents of calendric dates. Dates expressed as B.C./A.D. have been calibrated (or adjusted) to account for these variations and may be understood as equivalent to calendric dates. On calibration see Bronk Ramsey (1995), Stuiver et al. (1998) and Taylor et al. (1996).

NOTES

1   "Consider, for example, the following two sentences: 1. Americans are still prejudiced against blacks. 2. Americans still earn less money than do whites. There is absolutely no difficulty understanding the first sentence; the second sentence is confusing. This is because in the first sentence 'American' is used as a metonym for 'whites'; in the second sentence 'American' was used as a metonym again, but this time for 'blacks' . . . most readers will understand the use of 'American' as a metonym for whites" (Stanley Lieberson, 1985, quoted in Williams 1989:430).

REFERENCES

Abungu, George, and Lorna Abungu, 1998 Saving the Past in Kenya: Urban and Monument Conservation. African Archaeological Review 15:221–224.

Achebe, Chinua, 1978 An Image of Africa. Research in African Literatures 9:1–15.

Alcoff, Linda, and Elizabeth Potter, eds., 1993 Feminist Epistemologies. New York: Routledge.

Andah, Bassey W., 1995 Studying African Societies in Cultural Context. In Making Alternative Histories. The Practice of Archaeology and History in Non-Western Settings. Peter R. Schmidt and Thomas Patterson, eds. pp. 149–181. Sante Fe: School of American Research Press.

Andah, Bassey W., A. Adande, C. A. Folorunso, and O. Bagodo, 1994 African Archaeology in the 21st Century; or, Africa, Cultural Puppet on a String? West African Journal of Archaeology 24:152–159.

Bates, Robert H, V. Y. Mudimbe, and Jean O'Barr, eds., 1993 Africa and the Disciplines. Chicago: University of Chicago Press.

Bedaux, R. M. A., and Michael Rowlands, 2001 The Future of Mali's Past. Antiquity 75:872–876.

Bernal, Martin, 1987 Black Athena: The Afroasiatic Roots of Classical Civilization. London: Free Association Books.

Bishop, W. W., and J. Desmond Clark, eds., 1967 Background to Evolution in Africa. Chicago: University of Chicago Press.

Brent, M. 1994 The Rape of Mali. Archaeology 47(3):26–35.

——1996 A View Inside the Illicit Trade in African Antiquities. In Plundering Africa's Past. Peter R. Schmidt and Roderick J. McIntosh, eds. pp. 63–78. Bloomington: Indiana University Press.

Bronk Ramsey, C., 1995 Radiocarbon Calibration and Analysis of Stratigraphy: The OxCal Program. Radiocarbon 37:425–430.

Childe, V. Gordon, 1936 Man Makes Himself. London: Watts.

Clark, J. Desmond, 1990 A Personal Memoir. In A History of African Archaeology. Peter Robertshaw, ed. pp. 189–204. London: James Currey.

Cohen, David William, and E. S. Atieno Odhiambo, 1989 Siaya: The Historical Anthropology of an African Landscape. London: James Currey.

Comaroff, John, and Jean Comaroff, 1992 Ethnography and the Historical Imagination. Boulder, CO: Westview Press.

Connah, Graham, 1998 Static Image: Dynamic Reality. In Transformations in Africa. Essays in Africa's Later Past. Graham Connah, ed. pp. 1–13. London: Leicester University Press.

David, Nicholas, and Judy Sterner, 1999 Wonderful Society: The Burgess Shale Creatures, Mandara Polities and the Nature of Prehistory. In Beyond Chiefdoms: Pathways to Complexity in Africa. Susan Keech McIntosh, ed. pp. 97–109. Cambridge: Cambridge University Press.

Deacon, Janette, 1990 Weaving the Fabric of Stone Age Research in Southern Africa. In A History of African Archaeology. Peter Robertshaw, ed. pp. 39–58. London: James Currey.

Dennell, Robin, 1990 Progressive Gradualism, Imperialism and Academic Fashion: Lower Palaeolithic Archaeology in the 20th Century. Antiquity 64:549–558.

Descartes, René, 1979[1641] Meditations on First Philosophy in which the Existence of God and the Distinction of the Soul from the Body are Demonstrated. Donald A. Cress, trans. Indianapolis: Hackett Publishing.

di Leonardo, Micaela, 1998 Exotics at Home. Anthropologies, Others and American Modernity. Chicago: University of Chicago Press.

Ebron, Paulla A., 2002 Performing Africa. Princeton: Princeton University Press.

Ellison, James, Peter Robertshaw, Diane Gifford-Gonzalez, Roderick J. McIntosh, Ann B. Stahl, Christopher R. DeCorse, Larry H. Robbins, Susan Kent, Adoum Ngaba-Waye, Mohamed Sahnouni, and A. K. Segobye, 1996 The Future of African Archaeology. African Archaeological Review 13:5–34.

Fabian, Johannes, 1983 Time and the Other. How Anthropology Makes its Object. New York: Columbia University Press.

Foucault, Michel, 1972 The Archaeology of Knowledge and the Discourse on Language. A. M. Sheridan, trans. New York: Pantheon Books.

Fuglestad, Finn, 1992 The Trevor-Roper Trap or the Imperialism of History. An Essay. History in Africa 19:309–326.

Goodwin, A. J. H., and C. van Riet Lowe, 1929 The Stone Age Cultures of South Africa. Annals of the South African Museum 27:1–289.

Goody, J. R., 1990 The Political Systems of the Tallensi and their Neighbours 1888–1915. Cambridge Anthropology 14(2):1–25.

——1998 Establishing Control: Violence along the Black Volta at the Beginning of Colonial Rule. Cahiers d'Études Africaines 150–152:38(2–4):227–244.

Gould, Stephen J., 1981 The Mismeasure of Man. New York: W. W. Norton.

Gowlett, J. A. J., 1990 Archaeological Studies of Human Origins and Early Prehistory in Africa. *In* A History of African Archaeology. Peter Robertshaw, ed. pp. 13–38. London: James Currey.

Guyer, Jane, and Samuel M. Eno Belinga, 1995 Wealth in People as Wealth in Knowledge: Accumulation and Composition in Equatorial Africa. Journal of African History 36:91–120.

Hall, Martin, 1984 The Burden of Tribalism: The Social Context of Southern African Iron Age Studies. American Antiquity 49:455–467.

——1990a Farmers, Kings and Traders. The People of Southern Africa 200–1860. Chicago: University of Chicago Press.

——1990b "Hidden History": Iron Age Archaeology in Southern Africa. *In* A History of African Archaeology. Peter Robertshaw, ed. pp. 59–77. London: James Currey.

——1995 Great Zimbabwe and the Lost City. The Cultural Colonization of the South African Past. *In* Theory in Archaeology. A World Perspective. P. J. Ucko, ed. pp. 28–45. London: Routledge.

——1996 Archaeology Africa. London: James Currey.

——2000 Archaeology and the Modern World. Colonial Transcripts in South Africa and the Chesapeake. London: Routledge.

Hammond, Dorothy, and Alta Jablow, 1970 The Africa that Never Was. Four Centuries of British Writing about Africa. Prospect Heights, IL: Waveland.

Harlan, Jack R., Jan M. J. De Wet, and Ann B. L. Stemler, eds., 1976 Origins of African Plant Domestication. The Hague: Mouton.

Heizer, Robert F., ed., 1962 Man's Discovery of his Past: Literary Landmarks in Archaeology. Englewood Cliffs, NJ: Prentice-Hall.

Henige, David P., 1982 Oral Historiography. London: Longman.

Holl, Augustin, 1995 African History: Past, Present and Future. *In* Making Alternative Histories. The Practice of Archaeology and History in Non-Western Settings. Peter R. Schmidt and Thomas C. Patterson, eds. pp. 183–211. Sante Fe: School of American Research Press.

Isaac, Glynn Ll., 1975 Sorting Out the Muddle in the Middle: An Anthropologists' Post-Conference Appraisal. *In* After the Australopithecines. Karl W. Butzer and Glynn Ll. Isaac, eds. pp. 875–887. The Hague: Mouton.

Jewsiewicki, Bogumil, 1989 African Historical Studies. Academic Knowledge as "Usable Past" and Radical Scholarship. African Studies Review 32(3):47–76.

Jewsiewicki, Bogumil, and V. Y. Mudimbe, 1993 Africans' Memories and Contemporary History of Africa. *In* History Making in Africa. V. Y. Mudimbe and Bogumil Jewsiewicki, eds. pp. 1–11. History and Theory. Studies in the Philosophy of History 32. Wesleyan University.

Karenga-Munene, 1996 The Future of Archaeology in Kenya. African Archaeological Review 13:87–90.

Kibunjia, Mzalendo, 1997 The Management of Archaeological Collections and Resources in Africa. African Archaeological Review 14:137–141.

Killick, David, 1996 On Claims for "Advanced" Ironworking Technology in Precolonial Africa. *In* The Culture and Technology of African Iron Production. Peter R. Schmidt, ed. pp. 247–266. Gainesville: University Press of Florida.

Kuhn, Thomas, 1962 The Structure of Scientific Revolutions. Chicago: University of Chicago Press.

Kuklick, Henrika, 1991 Contested Monuments. The Politics of Archeology in Southern Africa. *In* Colonial Situations. Essays on the Contextualization of Ethnographic Knowledge. George W. Stocking, Jr., ed. pp. 135–169. Madison: University of Wisconsin Press.

Kusimba, Chapurukha M., 1996 Archaeology in African Museums. African Archaeological Review 13:165–170.

Laclau, Ernesto, 1996 Universalism, Particularism, and the Question of Identity. *In* The Politics of Difference. Ethnic Premises in a World of Power. Edwin N. Wilmsen and Patrick McAllister, eds. pp. 45–58. Chicago: University of Chicago Press.

Lane, Paul, 2001 African Archaeology Today. Antiquity 75:793–796.

Lentz, Carola, 1994 "They Must be Dagaba First and Any Other Thing Second . . .": The Colonial and Post-Colonial Creation of Ethnic Identities in North-Western Ghana. African Studies 53(2):57–91.

——1995 "Tribalism" and Ethnicity in Africa: A Review of Four Decades of Anglophone Research. Cahiers de Sciences Humaines 31(2):303–328.

Lovejoy, Arthur O., 1936 The Great Chain of Being. Cambridge, MA: Harvard University Press.

Lubbock, J., 1865 Prehistoric Times as Illustrated by Ancient Remains and the Manners and Customs of Modern Savages. London: Williams & Norgate.

Mabulla, Audax Z. P., 2000 Strategy for Cultural Heritage Management (CHM) in Africa. A Case Study. African Archaeological Review 17:211–233.

MacEachern, Scott, 2001 Cultural Resource Management and Africanist Archaeology. Antiquity 75:866–871.

McIntosh, Roderick J., 1996 Just Say Shame. Excising the Rot of Cultural Genocide. *In* Plundering Africa's Past. Peter R. Schmidt and Roderick J. McIntosh, eds. pp. 45–62. Bloomington: Indiana University Press.

——1998 The Peoples of the Middle Niger. The Island of Gold. Oxford: Blackwell.

McIntosh, Susan Keech, 1999 Pathways to Complexity: An African Perspective. *In* Beyond Chiefdoms. Pathways to Complexity in Africa. Susan Keech McIntosh, ed. pp. 1–30. Cambridge: Cambridge University Press.

McIntosh, Susan Keech, and Roderick J. McIntosh, 1984 The Early City in West Africa: Towards an Understanding. The African Archaeological Review 2:72–98.

Mehta, Uday S., 1997 Liberal Strategies of Exclusion. *In* Tensions of Empire. Colonial Cultures in a Bourgeois World. Frederick Cooper and Ann L. Stoler, eds. pp. 59–86. Berkeley: University of California Press.

Moore, Sally Falk, 1994 Anthropology and Africa. Changing Perspectives on a Changing Scene. Charlottesville: University of Virginia Press.

Mudimbe, Victor Y., 1994 The Idea of Africa. Bloomington: Indiana University Press.

Munro-Hay, Stuart C., 1989 Excavations at Aksum: An Account of Research at the Ancient Ethiopian Capital Directed in 1972–4 by the Late Dr. Neville Chittick. London: British Institute in Eastern Africa.

Murdock, George Peter, 1959 Africa: Its Peoples and their Culture History. New York: McGraw Hill.

Neale, Caroline, 1985 Writing "Independent" History: African Historiography, 1960–1980. Westport, CT: Greenwood Press.

——1986 The Idea of Progress in the Revision of African History, 1960–1970. *In* African Historiographies: What History for Which Africa? Bogumil Jewsiewicki and David Newbury, eds. pp. 112–122. Beverly Hills: Sage.

Nielson, Joyce McCarl, ed., 1990 Feminist Research Methods: Exemplary Readings in the Social Sciences. Boulder, CO: Westview Press.

O'Connor, David, and Andrew Reid, eds., 2003 Ancient Egypt in Africa. Philadelphia: University of Pennsylvania Press.

Orme, B., 1973 Archaeology and Ethnography. *In* The Explanation of Culture Change: Models in Prehistory. Colin Renfrew, ed. pp. 481–492. London: Duckworth.

—— 1974 Twentieth Century Prehistorians and the Idea of Ethnographic Parallels. Man 9:199–212.

Phillipson, David, 1985 African Archaeology. Cambridge: Cambridge University Press.

—— 1993 African Archaeology. 2nd edition. Cambridge: Cambridge University Press.

—— 1995 Ancient Ethiopia. Aksum: Its Antecedents and Successors. London: British Museum Press.

—— 1997 The Monuments of Aksum. An Illustrated Account. Addis Ababa: Addis Ababa University Press.

—— 2001 Archaeology at Aksum, Ethiopia 1993–7. London: British Institute in Eastern Africa.

Pikirayi, Innocent, 1999 Taking Southern African Ceramic Studies into the Twenty-First Century: A Zimbabwean Perspective. African Archaeological Review 16:185–189.

Posnansky, Merrick, 1996 Coping with Collapse in the 1990s: West African Museums, Universities and National Patrimonies. *In* Plundering Africa's Past. Peter R. Schmidt and Roderick J. McIntosh, eds. pp. 143–163. Bloomington: University of Indiana Press.

Pwiti, Gilbert, 1997 Taking African Cultural Heritage Management into the Twenty-First Century: Zimbabwe's Masterplan for Cultural Heritage Management. African Archaeological Review 14:81–83.

Pwiti, Gilbert, and Webber Ndoro, 1999 The Legacy of Colonialism: Perceptions of the Cultural Heritage in Southern Africa, with Special Reference to Zimbabwe. African Archaeological Review 16:143–153.

Ranger, Terence, 1993 The Invention of Tradition Revisited: The Case of Colonial Africa. *In* Legitimacy and the State in Twentieth-Century Africa: Essays in Honour of A. H. M. Kirk-Greene. Terence Ranger and Olufemi Vaughan, eds. pp. 62–111. London: Macmillan.

Robertshaw, Peter, 1990a The Development of Archaeology in East Africa. *In* A History of African Archaeology. Peter Robertshaw, ed. pp. 78–94. London: James Currey.

—— 1990b A History of African Archaeology: An Introduction. *In* A History of African Archaeology. Peter Robertshaw, ed. pp. 3–12. London: James Currey.

Robertshaw, Peter, ed., 1990 A History of African Archaeology. London: James Currey.

Rodden, Judith, 1981 The Development of the Three Age System: Archaeology's First Paradigm. *In* Towards a History of Archaeology. Glynn Daniel, ed. pp. 51–68. London: Thames & Hudson.

Rowlands, Michael, 1989a The Archaeology of Colonialism and Constituting the African Peasantry. *In* Domination and Resistance. Daniel Miller, Michael Rowlands, and Christopher Tilley, eds. pp. 261–283. London: Unwin Hyman.

—— 1989b A Question of Complexity. *In* Domination and Resistance. Daniel Miller, Michael Rowlands, and Christopher Tilley, eds. pp. 29–40. London: Unwin Hyman.

Scheslinger, Arthur M., Jr., 1991 The Disuniting of America. Knoxville, TN: Whittle Direct Books.

Schmidt, Peter R., 1990 Oral Traditions, Archaeology and History: A Short Reflective History. *In* A History of African Archaeology. Peter Robertshaw, ed. pp. 252–70. London: James Currey.

Schmidt, Peter R., and Donald H. Avery, 1978 Complex Iron Smelting and Prehistoric Culture in Tanzania. Science 201:1085–1089.

Schmidt, Peter R., and Roderick J. McIntosh, eds., 1996 Plundering Africa's Past. Bloomington: Indiana University Press.

Schmidt, Peter R., and Thomas C. Patterson, eds., 1995 Making Alternative Histories: The Practice of Archaeology and History in Non-Western Settings. Sante Fe: School of American Research Press.

Shaw, Thurstan, 1967 Resolutions on Terminology. West African Archaeological Newsletter 7:33–37.

——1997 The Contemporary Plundering of Africa's Past. African Archaeological Review 14:1–7.

Shepherd, Nick, 2002 The Politics of Archaeology in Africa. Annual Review of Anthropology 31:189–209.

Sidibé, Samuel, 1995 Fighting Pillage: National Efforts and International Cooperation. *In* Illicit Traffic in Cultural Property. Harrie Leyten, ed. pp. 25–33. Amsterdam: Royal Tropical Institute.

——1996 The Fight Against the Plundering of Malian Cultural Heritage and Illicit Exportation. National Efforts and International Cooperation. *In* Plundering Africa's Past. Peter R. Schmidt and Roderick J. McIntosh, eds. pp. 79–86. Bloomington: University of Indiana Press.

Sinclair, Paul J. J., Thurstan Shaw, and Bassey Andah, 1993 Introduction. *In* The Archaeology of Africa. Food, Metals and Towns, Thurstan Shaw, Paul Sinclair, Bassey Andah and Alex Okpoko, eds. pp. 1–31. London: Routledge.

Sollas, W. J., 1915 Ancient Hunters and their Modern Representatives. 2nd edition. London: Macmillan.

Sowunmi, M. Adebisi, 1998 Beyond Academic Archaeology in Africa: The Human Dimension. African Archaeological Review 15:163–172.

Stahl, Ann B., 1984 A History and Critique of the Investigations into Early African Agriculture. *In* From Hunters to Farmers: Causes and Consequences of Food Production in Africa. J. Desmond Clark and Steven Brandt, eds. pp. 9–21. Berkeley: University of California Press.

——1999 Perceiving Variability in Time and Space: Evolutionary Mapping of African Societies. *In* Beyond Chiefdoms: Pathways to Complexity in Africa. Susan K. McIntosh, ed. pp. 39–55. Cambridge: Cambridge University Press.

——2001 Making History in Banda. Anthropological Visions of Africa's Past. Cambridge: Cambridge University Press.

——2004 Comparative Insights into the Ancient Political Economies of West Africa. *In* Archaeological Perspectives on Political Economies. Gary Feinman and Linda Nicholas, eds. pp. 253–270. Salt Lake City: University of Utah Press.

Stocking, George W., Jr., 1987 Victorian Anthropology. New York: Free Press.

Stuiver, Minze, Paula J. Reimer, and Thomas F. Braziunas, 1998 High-Precision Radiocarbon Age Calibration for Terrestrial and Marine Samples. Radiocarbon 40:1127–1151.

Sutton, John E. G., 1974 The Aquatic Civilization of Middle Africa. Journal of African History 15:527–546.

Taylor, R. E., Minze Stuiver, and Paula J. Reimer, 1996 Development and Extension of the Calibration of the Radiocarbon Time Scale: Archaeological Applications. *In* Quaternary Geochronology. pp. 655–668. New York: Elsevier Science.

Temu, Arnold, and Bonaventure Swai, 1981 Historians and Africanist History: A Critique. Post-Colonial Historiography Examined. London: ZED Press.

Thiaw, Ibrahima, 2004 Archaeology and the Public in Senegal: Reflections on Doing Fieldwork at Home. Journal of African Archaeology 1:215–225.

Trevor-Roper, Hugh, 1965 The Rise of Christian Europe. London: Thames & Hudson.

Trigger, Bruce G., 1989 A History of Archaeological Thought. Cambridge: Cambridge University Press.

—— 1990 The History of African Archaeology in World Perspective. *In* A History of African Archaeology. Peter Robertshaw, ed. pp. 309–319. London: James Currey.

Tylecote, R. F., 1975 The Origin of Iron Smelting in Africa. West African Journal of Archaeology 5:1–9.

van der Merwe, Nikolaas J., 1980 The Advent of Iron in Africa. *In* The Coming of the Age of Iron. T. A. Wertime and J. D. Muhly, eds. pp. 463–506. New Haven: Yale University Press.

van der Merwe, Nikolaas J., and Donald H. Avery, 1982 Pathways to Steel. American Scientist 70(2):146–155.

Vansina, Jan, 1961 De la tradition orale: Essai de méthode historique. Annales, Sciences Humaines, no. 36. Tervuren: Musée Royal de l'Afrique Centrale.

—— 1985 Oral Tradition as History. Madison: University of Wisconsin Press.

Vansina, Jan, R. Mauny, and L. V. Thomas, eds., 1964 The Historian in Tropical Africa. London: Oxford University Press.

White, Hayden, 1973 Metahistory: The Historical Imagination in Nineteenth-Century Europe. Baltimore: Johns Hopkins University Press.

Williams, Brackette, 1989 "A CLASS ACT:" Anthropology and the Race to Nation across Ethnic Terrain. Annual Review of Anthropology 18:401–444.

Wilson, Edward O., 1998 Consilience: The Unity of Knowledge. New York: Knopf.

World Heritage, 2003 World Heritage Information Kit. Electronic document. <http://whc.unesco.org/nwhc/pages/sites/main.htm>, accessed April 14.

Wylie, Alison, Kathleen Okruhlik, Leslie Thielen-Wilson, and Sandra Morton, 1989 Feminist Critiques of Science: The Epistemological and Methodological Literature. Women's Studies International Forum 12:379–388.

2

Barbarous Tribes and Unrewarding Gyrations? The Changing Role of Ethnographic Imagination in African Archaeology

Paul J. Lane

every man calls barbarous anything he is not accustomed to.

(Montaigne 1580:231)

Archaeologists frequently make recourse to ethnographic, ethnohistoric, and anthropological data in their efforts to interpret the material remains of past societies. These data may be collected by scholars in other fields or, increasingly, by archaeologists themselves. These practices of analogical modeling have been integral to archaeological inquiry from the moment the subject became a formal discipline, and it remains an important element of archaeological interpretation today; however, the ways in which archaeologists have used ethnographic data to interpret the material traces of earlier human societies and behavior have changed enormously.

This essay traces some of the most important developments in the use of African ethnographic material and explores its effects on the archaeology of the continent. This analysis requires that we examine how Africa and Africans have been portrayed in Western thought through time. Even in its most sophisticated form, the use of ethnographic data to facilitate archaeological interpretation entails a search for the exotic, and it is to this aspect that the first part of my title – "barbarous tribes" – refers (e.g., Trevor-Roper 1963:871; Chapter 1). This search for the exotic (or, at the very least, "difference") is an inescapable, and some would even argue desirable, fact of archaeological endeavor. Without it, all archaeological interpretations would end up casting the past entirely in terms of the present. We also need to ask whether the countless ethnoarchaeological studies made in Africa have been useful, or if they have amounted to little more than a series of "unrewarding [academic] gyrations."

In Search of the Exotic

Although ethnographic analogies are an inescapable element of archaeology, they introduce a fundamental paradox. Archaeologists often claim to be concerned with revealing human cultural and behavioral universals; however, by drawing on ethnographic data to interpret archaeological remains, they necessarily transform "the past" into something "other" than their own world, from which all archaeologists, "Western" or not, are temporally *and* spatially removed. In this way, to invoke L. P. Hartley's famous phrase, the past becomes "a foreign country [where] they do things differently" (1953:1; see Lowenthal 1985). This notion that "the past" is somewhere from which we have escaped is further reinforced by the widespread tendency to categorize past societies in terms of an evolutionary framework (Chapter 1).

[margin note: the prevalent archeological practise is to reframe the past as sth foreign]

The evolutionary concepts in common currency today differ markedly from 19th-century unilinear systems which graded all societies on a scale of progress from savagery, through barbarism, to civilization (Morgan 1877; Tylor 1865). Nonetheless, evolutionary concepts imply a process of "othering" in which non-European peoples are perceived as more or less distant from a European present (Chapter 1). Evolutionary categorizations long governed the use of analogy by guiding the selection of ethnographic analogs "appropriate" to the stage under consideration. Thus, archaeologists excavating Paleolithic sites in Europe often turned to ethnographic literature on African hunter-gatherers, especially the Kalahari San, for "parallels" regarding issues such as the division of labor, principles of social organization, and even ritual practices. That a group of contemporary people living on open sites in a hot, semi-arid nation-state with a capitalist economy should be thought of as a suitable parallel for the way early humans lived during an ancient Ice Age seems puzzling. But this form of analogical modeling is rooted in the deep-seated Western belief that hunter-gatherers like the San represent the timeless and essential qualities of humans as *biological beings* (Chapter 14). As such, they are thought to live lives closely resembling those of ancient humans.

[margin note: 19th C. unilinear system; savagery > civilization]

This use of analogs as a vehicle for imagining a distant past dates from the Age of European Discovery commencing in the late 15th century. Soon after the first written descriptions and visual images of Native Americans were published, antiquarians began to envision the clothing and artifact styles of Celts and Ancient Britons in terms of those observed among contemporary peoples in the non-Western world (Daniel 1950; Orme 1973, 1974, 1981; Piggott 1976). For the first time Europeans began to imagine that, at some time in the past, they too had lived in ways similar to contemporary non-Western peoples. This prompted recognition of stone tools and earthworks as human creations dating from periods before written history began.

Images of Africans contributed to new imaginings of Europe's past; however, European images of Africans were neither uniform nor stable. Early representations of Africans focused on *cultural* as opposed to physical differences between black Africans and Europeans (see Iselin 1994); however, these representations rapidly became less favorable. For instance, depictions of Khoikhoi inhabitants of southern Africa emphasized their "savagery" and predilection towards cannibalism (Smith 1993:10–11; Chapter 14). With few exceptions, Africans were depicted as essentialized representatives of "the primitive savage" well into the 19th century.

By the mid-19th century scholars influenced by evolutionary thinking (e.g., Edward Tylor, Lewis Henry Morgan) drew more explicit links between contemporary non-Western societies and the lifeways of ancient European societies. This "comparative approach" laid the basis for all subsequent uses of analogy within archaeology. One of the earliest proponents was Sir John Lubbock, who early on observed that:

> [d]eprived . . . of any assistance from history . . . the archaeologist is free to follow the methods which have been so successfully pursued in geology . . . [such that] if we wish to understand the antiquities of Europe, *we must compare them* with the rude implements and weapons still or until lately used by the savage races in other parts of the world. (Lubbock 1912:407–408, emphasis added)

Living modern "savages" and "barbarians" were believed to be "living fossils" who provided direct analogs for the way of life of peoples in the past with comparable technologies and subsistence practices. Subsequent approaches to the use of ethnographic analogy in archaeology have refined and amended this concept, but the discipline has yet to fully rid itself of the latent assumption that "the Other" represents not just different places but also different *times*.

Archaeology, Ethnography and Analogical Reasoning

Analogy is a form of inductive reasoning. In its simplest form, the method relies on the principle that if two objects or situations share some observable similarities, they likely share other, less observable similarities as well. The greater the number of observable similarities between items compared, the greater the likelihood that they have other factors in common, and hence the stronger the analogy. However, this is not necessarily the case, for the simple reason that observed similarities may not be relevant to the presence or absence of the other, inferred commonalities (Salmon 1982; Wylie 1985). As archaeology matured, simple formal analogies, often also referred to as "ethnographic parallels," became more commonplace and were based on the principle that "*similar cultural conditions may produce similar cultural phenomena*" (Curwen 1938:261, emphasis added).

African societies became an increasingly popular source for analogies in European archaeology, especially because the consolidation of "prehistoric" archaeology in Europe coincided with the era of "Colonial Anthropology" (1920–1950) aimed at documenting the societies that were now under colonial rule (see Kuper 1973). African ethnography was of less interest in North America, where archaeologists drew instead on the accumulating ethnographic information concerning Native Americans. Most often, archaeologists consulted available ethnographies for suitable parallels; however, others, derived their analogies from direct observation, as for instance O. G. S. Crawford following his visit to Anglo-Egyptian Sudan in 1950. An astute field archaeologist and pioneer of the use of aerial photography in British archaeology, Crawford's (1953) book is replete with ethnographic analogies drawn from African contexts. While they are relatively modest observations (e.g., the potential effects of tree falls on the alignment of trackways, the difficulties of archaeologically identifying nomadic pastoralists, or the archaeological traces of burned mud and wattle huts (Crawford 1953:76, plate 2a [facing p. 81], 148, 227–228, 147, plates 9a, 9b [facing p. 168]), they presage many of the concerns of the earliest ethnoarchaeological studies.

African archeology by way of analogy

In Africa, archaeologists drew analogies between archaeological sites and the material culture and practices of the local inhabitants in their research area. Known as the "Direct Historical Approach" (see Trigger 1989:124–125), this strategy sought to restrict the selection of analogies to specific geographical localities where continuities between past and present populations were assumed to exist. In early applications, *spatial* correspondences in the distribution of past and present populations were taken as sufficient justification for inferring *temporal* continuities. Thus, in her report on excavations in Zimbabwe, Caton-Thompson drew direct functional analogies between features she observed in Shona houses and formally similar features encountered during her excavations (e.g., Caton-Thompson 1931, plate XLII [facing p. 173]). These similarities provided further proof "of the unbroken continuity of a purely native African design and method exemplified from Zimbabwe to the present day," also evident at Great Zimbabwe (1931:173–4).

main disadvantage of analogical technique

With the rise of more explicitly scientific approaches associated with the "New Archeology" of the 1960s and 1970s, rather more critical perspectives developed. Initially, there was a reaction against the use of analogical reasoning, principally on the grounds that it projected the present into the past. This made it unlikely that archaeologists would ever discover evidence for the existence of types of behavior, types of artifacts, or social forms that had *no* direct parallel in the present (Wobst 1978). For some this suggested the need for greater caution in the application of ethnographic analogies. Others argued that archaeologists should abandon analogy altogether (e.g., Freeman 1968; Gould 1980). Freeman insisted on the need to *demonstrate* that patterns of behavior observable in the present were evident in the past, rather than simply assuming that this was the case. Gould argued that ethnographic analogies, by virtue of being culturally and historically specific, are "self-limiting" (1980:29), and archaeologists must rely instead on more general, universal propositions about human behavior, especially those drawn from ecology. Yet as Wylie showed (1982, 1985), despite his claims to the contrary, Gould's approach also relied on analogy, although his analogies were drawn from human ecology rather than ethnography.

From the mid-1980s on, concerns about the use of analogical reasoning within the discipline shifted from outright skepticism to growing acceptance and recognition of different types of analogy and awareness of the criteria that help distinguish "weak" from "strong" analogies. For example, Wylie distinguished between "formal" and "relational" analogies which lie at opposite ends of a continuum

(1985; see also Gifford-Gonzalez 1991; Salmon 1982; Stahl 1993). Formal analogies are based on the premise that, because two objects or contexts share a similar appearance or shape, they are likely to share other properties as well, typically that of function. An example is Mary Leakey's comparison of the circular arrangement of lava blocks at site DK in Olduvai Gorge Bed I (Tanzania), with the way modern Okombambi people of Namibia place stones to create a foundation when building temporary grass and brushwood shelters. The formal similarities between the two sets of circular stone arrangements encouraged Leakey to interpret the DK remains as evidence of a temporary hut or windbreak (Leakey 1971:24 and plate 2), an interpretation that is still cited in discussions about proto-human inhabitants of Olduvai (e.g., Gallay 1999:52, 57, figs. 34, 38; Michael and Fagan 2000).

Subsequent assessments of this kind of formal analogy have shown that similarly shaped objects or structural remains often have different functions or may have been created by different processes. For example, this has led to a rethinking of Mary Leakey's original interpretation of so-called "living floors" (i.e., the "Zinjanthropus" level at site FLK) and "butchering or kill sites" in Beds I and II at Olduvai Gorge (Chapter 3). The excavated portion of the "Zinj floor" ($290\,m^2$)had a high density of stone tools, waste flakes, and a variety of animal bones with limited vertical distribution (ca. 10–20 cm). Preservation was particularly good; even the bones of small rodents, insects, and insect-casts were recovered (Leakey 1971:40–60). The apparent clustering of material (Leakey 1971:260–261) led Leakey to interpret this as an "occupation floor." Though Leakey did not draw explicit ethnographic parallels, she, like most archaeologists at that time, had in mind a general model based on formal similarities between FLK and recently abandoned hunter-gatherer camps. She suggested that research among the Kalahari San might well clarify various issues, since in her view they "are undoubtedly one of the nearest modern parallels to the early hunter-gatherers of Africa" (1971:259).

Leakey's interpretations were widely accepted, and contributed to an image of early hominids as reasonably accomplished hunter-gatherers living in small bands of closely knit kin groups, each with its own home base and surrounding territory. By the mid-1970s, however, archaeologists were beginning to question whether the concentration of bones with artifacts necessarily represented hominid food refuse (Binford 1983; Isaac 1984). As a consequence, a wide range of ethnoarchaeological and taphonomic studies on natural and human site-formation processes were initiated which led to a rethinking of these images (Gallay 1999; Chapter 3). This trend was shaped by growing skepticism linked to the New Archeology, and a corresponding concern to demonstrate the relevance of observed similarities between past and present to particular contexts (Ascher 1961).

A concern with relevance is also at the heart of Wylie's (1985) "relational" analogies. For instance, ax-shaped, ground-stone objects are found on both "Pastoral Neolithic" and "Iron Age" sites across East Africa (see Chapters 8 and 16 for details on periodizations). Examples illustrated in Figure 2.1 are ethnographic specimens made and used by Pokot herdsmen of western Kenya for "horn-shaping" to modify the way livestock horns grow from the skull (see Brown 1990). These objects exhibit considerable formal variability, and could equally be used for other tasks, for

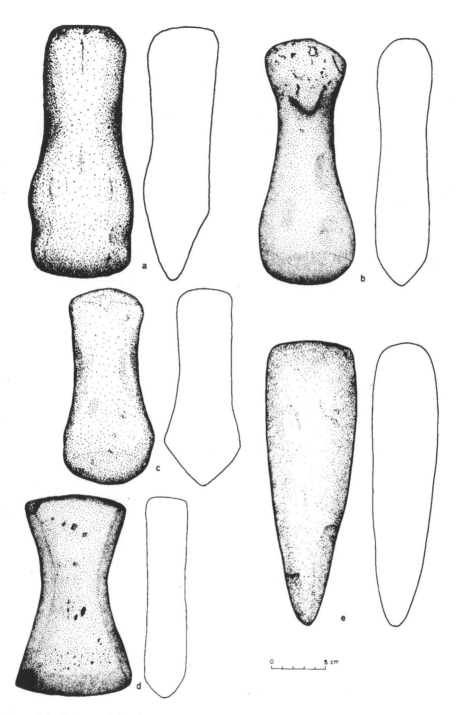

Figure 2.1. Pokot ox-horn shapers
Source: Brown 1990:58, fig. 1; © British Institute in Eastern Africa, reproduced with permission.

instance as a hammerstone (Figure 2.1b, 2.1c), the weighted end of a digging stick (Figure 2.1e), an axe/adze (Figure 2.1d) and as a blade for a simple plough (Figure 2.1a). For archaeologists to correctly interpret similar archaeological examples as "horn-shapers" rather than any of these other artifact classes, they would have to demonstrate why horn-shaping was the most probable function of such tools. This might involve showing from other evidence that: pastoralism provided the mainstay of the associated economy (ruling out other agricultural uses); the wear patterns on the objects were consistent with their use as horn-shapers and not other functions; cattle and goat skulls showed healed lesions in the appropriate place; and, perhaps, the practice of horn-shaping was an appropriate one within the society whose archaeological remains are being studied. Each of these points would strengthen the analogy, since they all help show why this specific comparison is more relevant than numerous others that could be made. Unfortunately, this kind of detailed argumentation is rare in archaeological interpretation, whether in Africa or elsewhere.

Wylie (1985) also stressed that, although relevance can be approached from either the "source" (i.e., ethnographic) or "subject" (i.e., archaeological) sides of an analogy, ideally both sides should be scrutinized. Strategies for doing this are commonly used in archaeological interpretation, and include the demonstration of shared operational, ecological, or technological constraints; the application of cross-cultural uniformities or structural parallels; and evidence of historical and/or cultural continuities between the archaeological and ethnographic sides of the analogy. This can also be illustrated with reference to the horn-shaping example above. For example Brown noted that horn-shaping appears to be restricted today to "the Turkana cluster of Eastern Nilotes and to some of the Kalenjin group of Southern Nilotes" (1990:64). One might expect, therefore, that archaeological examples, at least from relatively recent sites, would broadly conform to the spatial extent of these Nilotic language speakers. For earlier periods, the distribution could well be different (as indeed seems to have been the case, judging from the evidence presented by Brown), in which case, reasons for why their distribution changed should be proposed and tested against various sources of evidence.

Brown's use of ethnographic and historical sources exemplifies the "direct historical approach" which is quite common in African archaeology. Whereas such comparisons are an inevitable component of any attempt to produce a culture history for a given area, if used uncritically without due regard for the evidence for change, the "direct historical approach" is especially prone to reinforcing, albeit unwittingly, stereotypical views of African societies as conservative and unchanging.

The Direct Historical Approach

The strengths and weaknesses of the direct historical approach as commonly applied (cf. Stahl 2001:19–40) can be illustrated by the use of normative ethnographic models in southern African archaeology, known respectively as the Central Cattle Pattern and Zimbabwe Pattern, to infer aspects of social organization,

ethnography - n - the scientific description of races and
and cultures of humankind
albeit - conj - though

ideology, and worldview of the prehistoric inhabitants of the region. Both models are closely associated with the work of Thomas Huffman (1982, 1986), but they have been taken up by other archaeologists working on the "Iron Age" and later archaeology of southern Africa. Both models take as their starting point that in many societies, residential settlements are laid out according to principles that govern the organization of society into different social groups and mirror the ideological significance of these divisions. Thus the spatial organization of an archaeological settlement should reflect the core principles of social organization and ideological structure among its inhabitants. Since the majority of southern Africa's population to the east and south of the Kalahari are speakers of Eastern Bantu languages, proponents of the direct historical approach argue that these peoples should be the main source of any ethnographic or ethnohistorical analogy because their ancestors occupied the majority of archaeological settlements in the region over the last two thousand years (see Chapters 12, 15). Comparative analysis of ethnographic accounts and documentary sources concerning Sotho-Tswana, Nguni and other Eastern Bantu language groups indicates a very strong, consistent, and trans-ethnic tradition of settlement organization for at least the last 150 years. This spatial layout appears to have been correlated with a particular way of organizing society and a set of ideological beliefs centered around the economic, socio-political, and symbolic significance of cattle (Huffman 1986; Kuper 1980). Ethnographically, cattle byres were placed at the center of the settlement with houses and other structures (e.g., grain-bins) arranged around them in a circular or semi-circular fashion. Placement of houses was governed by the relative seniority of their occupants (Figure 2.2a). This spatial pattern generated a series of structural oppositions which contrasted: center with periphery; men with women; cattle with grain; seniors with juniors; front with back; and up with down. These structuring principles gave order and meaning to the social worlds of the Eastern Bantu language speakers and also influenced the positioning of other material elements of settlements, such as burials and courts.

This spatial layout is referred to by archaeologists as the Central Cattle Pattern (CCP), and elements of it have been noted on a wide range of archaeological sites of different time periods across southern Africa. These include 18th- and 19th-century Tswana settlements (e.g., Evers 1984), 15th- to 17th-century stone-walled sites associated with proto-Sotho-Tswana and proto-Nguni groups (e.g., Pistorius 1992), and various first millennium groups for which no direct historical association is available (e.g., Denbow 1986; van Waarden 1989). The latter include occupants of the fourth- to seventh-century site of Broederstroom (Huffman 1993) and the seventh- to 10th-century site of KwaGandaganda (Whitelaw 1994), which constitute some of the very first sites in southern Africa to be occupied by metal-using farming communities (Chapter 11). If these interpretations are correct, it implies that a worldview and ideology similar to that documented among southern Africa's Eastern Bantu language speakers during the early 20th century has existed in the region for over 1,500 years.

In marked contrast to the CCP, the Zimbabwe Pattern (ZP) has no modern or historic analog, all of the known examples being archaeological. The main sources

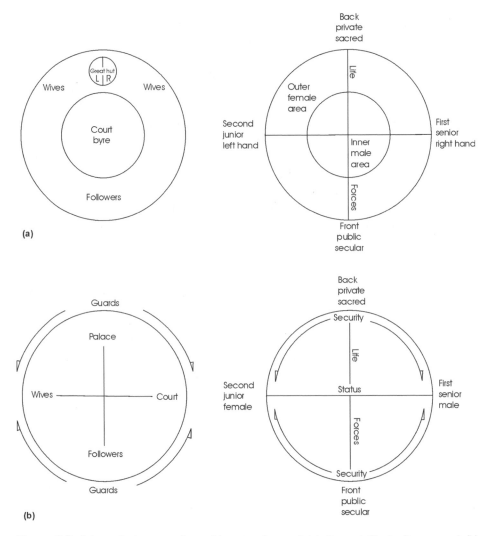

Figure 2.2. Schematic layout and cognitive correlates of (a) Central Cattle Pattern and (b) Zimbabwe Pattern settlements. Based on Huffman 2000:15–16 [figs. 1 and 2]

of analogy thus come from 16th-century Portuguese documents which provide descriptions of the elite settlements associated with the early phases of the Mutapa and Rozvi states (see Pikirayi 2001), and elements of recent Shona and Venda ethnography (Huffman 1996). The Shona are believed to be the direct descendants of the Zimbabwe Culture, while the Venda are historically related to the Shona but currently reside in what is now South Africa (Loubser 1991). Compared with CCP settlements, ZP examples have a more restricted spatial and temporal distribution, being limited to the known area of the first three phases of the Zimbabwe Culture tradition, with the earliest instance of the ZP appearing at Mapungubwe around

A.D. 1220–1300 (Huffman 2000:21; Chapter 15). Unlike the CCP, which appears to have been associated with both elite and commoner elements of precolonial societies, the ZP was restricted to elite settlements or parts thereof (Huffman 1986, 1996), while commoners retained a basic CCP settlement layout. A core feature which distinguishes ZP from CCP settlement structures is the removal of cattle enclosures from the elite areas of settlements, and its replacement with a court-cum-assembly area, said to reflect an increased emphasis on political decision-making. Other elements of elite areas not found on CCP settlements were a palace, an area for royal wives, a place for palace guards, and a place for followers (Figure 2.2b). In addition, the ZP is said to incorporate a topographic separation of elite and commoners, with the residential areas of the former on hilltops overlooking commoner sectors. Although the cognitive system continued to be expressed through a series of concentric and diametric spatial oppositions, these placed greater emphasis on the differences between commoners and the elite, whose power emanated from ritual kingship.

These interpretive models have profoundly affected archaeological research in southern Africa by directing research away from narrow concerns with artifact typology and economy to broader considerations of the symbolic, cognitive, and socio-political aspects of these societies (see also Chapter 13). However, both models have been critiqued from both subject-side (archaeological) and source-side (ethnographic/historical) perspectives. On the subject side, common criticisms have been that, while archaeological sites in the region may share aspects of the CCP layout, there are often variations around this norm on the more recent examples, while on earlier examples (before A.D. 1400) the evidence concerning spatial layout is often far more ambiguous than is claimed by proponents of the model (see e.g., Calabrese 2000; Lane 1994/95; Maggs 1992, 1994/95). On the source side, criticisms have focused on a failure to consider the historical context of the ethnography from which the models are derived, since this is in part responsible for the emphasis given by both informants and ethnographers to certain cultural traditions and the omission or limited discussion of others (e.g., Beach 1998). For example, the CCP model does not account for how gender relations were transformed with the penetration of waged economies under colonial rule (Lane 1994/95, 1998a; see Kent, ed., 1998). Also, Huffman's application of the direct historical approach does not accommodate evidence for divergence from norms or the possibility of social change arising from internal social dynamics rather than external forces. As a result, it has tended to reproduce a timeless image of southern African societies bound by an adherence to tradition and an innate predilection towards tribalism (Hall 1984).

Huffman has responded vigorously to many of these criticisms, arguing most recently that the current concern in archaeology with understanding "difference" is symptomatic of a broader Western conceit that all societies must change and must want to change. This, he argues, is nothing less than "a cultural appropriation that denies Africa the opportunity to speak for itself" (Huffman 2001:32). Clearly, the rise and subsequent collapse of the ZP is evidence for systemic change, so in this sense the models are not entirely unable to accommodate change. However, other aspects of Huffman's response misrepresent the nature of the criticisms leveled at the way these models have been used. First, it is the responsibility of archaeologists to acknowledge the possibility for change *and* continuity between past and present, and, as critically, to offer adequate explanation of both changes and continuities. Second, and as important, to talk of "difference" is not the same as insisting that change has occurred. Instead, it is an acknowledgment of the diverse ways in which the material world, beliefs, practices, traditions, and histories can be and often are understood – something which the last quarter-century of ethnoarchaeological research on the African continent has demonstrated.

"The Present Past" – or, On the Rise of Ethnoarchaeology

In response to the reaction against analogy in the 1960s and 1970s, many archaeologists believed that developing robust analogies required archaeologists to conduct their own ethnographic fieldwork designed to address research questions pertinent to archaeological concerns. Initially termed "action archaeology" (Kleindienst and Watson 1956) or "living archaeology" (Gould 1980), these field studies and research strategies subsequently came to be known as "ethnoarchaeology."

In its current form ethnoarchaeology entails research among contemporary communities for specifically *archaeological*, as opposed to ethnographic or anthropological, purposes. The precise aims and research goals of projects vary, as do definitions of the disciplinary sub-field (for a synopsis see David and Kramer 2001:12, table 1.1). However, the ultimate objectives of most ethnoarchaeological research fall into two categories. One concerns the study and documentation of the processes that affect the transition of material objects from their contexts of production and use in a living society to an archaeological context. "Formation processes," as they are generically known (see Schiffer 1976, 1987), can only be observed in the present. Their study is as central to understanding the physical traces of past societies, as is the study of the relationship between the material and non-material aspects of cultural behavior.

The second group of ethnoarchaeological approaches is concerned with relationships between the material and non-material elements of human cultures and societies. In a discipline that relies on the physical traces left by past human activities, the need for such research would seem self-evident. Without an understanding of how artifacts, buildings, and other physical entities relate to how societies are organized along socio-economic, political, and religious lines, or how items of material culture convey and are given meanings, we can not make useful statements about specific past societies, or more general processes of human behavior. Instead, all that archaeologists could hope to offer would be tedious descriptive accounts of the material remains they recover.

In summary, then, ethnoarchaeology "is neither a theory or method, but a research strategy" which embodies "a range of approaches to understanding the relationships of material culture to culture as a whole, both in the living context and as it enters the archaeological record, and to exploiting such understandings in order to inform archaeological concepts and to improve interpretation" (David and Kramer 2001:2). Over the last 30 to 40 years, the African continent has become a major setting for ethnoarchaeological research of both categories and has made significant contributions to working through the complexity of the issues involved. As a result, the procedures of archaeological inference and interpretation have been strengthened considerably. The following sections use select case studies to map out major developments within the two broad categories of ethnoarchaeological research (for additional material, see Atherton 1983; MacEachern 1996; Schmidt 1983a).

Formation of Archaeological Sites and Assemblages

Many early ethnoarchaeological studies in Africa were concerned with site-formation processes and these continue to be popular. These varied in scope, temporal focus, and substantive detail (Table 2.1). Topics included processes of site abandonment, house collapse and decay, discard patterns, site structure, butchery practices, and activity area analysis. In addition, taphonomic studies of natural formation processes have also been conducted (Chapter 3), sometimes in parallel with more strictly ethnoarchaeological work. Significantly, many of these have been inspired by concern to elucidate the causes and nature of patterning in Early and Middle Stone Age sites. There are various ways of categorizing this type of research. Some, such as Robbins' (1973) study of the abandonment of a Turkana pastoralist settlement in northern Kenya, and David's (1971) investigation of the re-use and recycling of houses and other structures among sedentary Fulani in northern Cameroon, fall into the category of "spoilers" (Yellen 1977a:8). They caution archaeologists against making simplistic or culture-specific assumptions about the real world. Other studies have been more concerned with identifying the diagnostic material or bio-chemical "signatures" of different processes and categories of human behavior. These are sometimes referred to as Middle Range Theory (see Binford 1983).

Collectively, site-formation studies have refined our understanding of how archaeological deposits and assemblages can be created and transformed through a variety of cultural and natural processes. This awareness has radically altered interpretation of spatial patterning within archaeological sites and structures. Most early interpretations were based on two rather simple assumptions. First, that the spatial patterning of objects recovered from archaeological contexts reflected the range of activities conducted at a site or within a structure during its occupancy. Second, that variations in artifact density and assemblage diversity were a straightforward indicator of differences in site function, on-site activities, and/or the wealth and status of its occupants. As awareness of the potential effects of site-formation processes on assemblage composition and patterning has grown, few archaeologists would now expect such one-to-one relationships to hold (see David and Kramer 2001:91–115; Hodder 1982a:47–67; Schiffer 1976, 1987).

A second category of site-formation studies relies on uniformitarian assumptions pertaining to the natural world. To some extent these cross-cut more strictly

Table 2.1. Selected examples of ethnoarchaeological studies of formation process and artifact manufacture in Africa

Main research theme	Foragers	Fishing communities	Pastoralists	Agro-pastoralists	Craft specialists and urban dwellers
Processes of house-site construction, abandonment, decay, and collapse	Kent 1993a	Gifford and Behrensmeyer 1977; Robbins 1980	Robbins 1973; Stiles 1979, 1980	Agorsah 1985; David 1971; Friede and Steel 1980; McIntosh 1974, 1977; Walicka Zeh 2000	Tobert 1988
The patterning of refuse disposal, activity areas, and site-structure	Bartram et al. 1991; Fisher and Strickland 1989; Hitchcock 1987; Kent 1991; O'Connell et al. 1991; Yellen 1977a, 1977b	Gifford 1978; Pétrequin and Pétrequin 1984; Stewart and Gifford-Gonzalez 1994	Mbae 1990; Parkington and Mills 1991	Foloronso and Ogundele 1993; Moore 1982; Posnansky 1984; Walicka Zeh 2000	
Hunting/fishing strategies, butchery practices, food-sharing, bone-processing and discard	Bartram 1993; Bunn et al. 1988; Fisher 1993; Kent 1993b; Lupo 1995; Marshall 1993, 1994; O'Connell et al. 1988, 1990, 1991; Yellen 1977b, 1993a, 1993b		Brain 1967, 1969; Mbae 1990		
Settlement systems	Brooks 1984; Hitchcock and Bartram 1998; Yellen 1976, 1977a		Hivernel 1980; Smith 1980	Hivernel 1980; Hol 1993; Stone 1991, 1993	
Plant/shellfish-gathering, crop-processing and agricultural practices	Vincent 1985			Butler et al. 1999; D'Andrea et al. 1999; Foloronso and Ogundele 1993; Stone 1994	Msemwa 1994
Artifact curation, recycling, and uselife				Bedaux 1986a, 1986b; Bedaux and van der Waals 1987	
Craft production and organization				Balfet 1965; Brandt 1996; Brown 1995; David and Hennig 1972; Gallay 1981	Clark and Kurashina 1981; Gallagher 1977; LaViolette 2000; Tobert 1988

taphonomic studies, although the boundaries between the two fields are sometimes hard to draw (see Gifford 1981). A classic example is McIntosh's (1974, 1977) attempt to identify the physical signatures of house floors and walls in archaeological sites around Begho, Ghana. Other studies have been concerned to develop cross-cultural generalizations about human behavior and adaptation, for example regarding processes of sedentism among pastoralist and forager communities in the Kalahari (Hitchcock 1987; Kent 1991; Kent and Vierich 1989), or studies of butchery practices and site structure in hunter-gatherer camps (e.g., Bartram et al. 1991; O'Connell et al. 1988, 1991; Yellen 1977a, 1977b, 1993a, 1993b; see Lane 1998b).

Unlike particularistic "cautionary tales," this category of ethnoarchaeological research relies on a belief in universal causal connections between certain classes of human behavior and the patterning of physical remains in the archaeological record. There is no doubt that patterned human behavior shapes the archaeological record. However, after over 30 years of research, the isolation of non-trivial causal connections between human behavior and the patterning of human residues has proved to be extremely difficult. Several of the post-1980 studies among hunter-gatherers have been influenced by Binford's arguments on site structure and how sitting positions around hearths constrain discard patterns (see Binford 1983, 1987 and references therein). While Binford's observations are clearly pertinent, it is evident that as soon as issues of intentionality and the meaning of discard are considered alongside the constraints imposed by the human body, the regularities proposed by Binford are less clear-cut. Recognition of this is growing, as is the realization that cross-cultural principles of human behavior are unlikely to be as invariable as the operation of the natural laws of physics and chemistry.

[margin note: Binford's arguments]

[margin note: variability of cross-cultural principles]

A final category of ethnoarchaeological investigation concerns artifact technology and manufacture. Many studies have focused on the technical aspects of artifact manufacture and raw material composition. Such studies (Table 2.1) provide a useful resource for cross-cultural comparison, yet they seldom provide details on the social context of production, the anthropology of techniques, or the chemical, physical, and/or mechanical properties of the processes, raw materials, and finished products. Most critically, such studies are founded on a premise that these manufacturing processes are "traditional" and therefore associated practices are of considerable antiquity.

Only rarely have ethnoarchaeologists sought to demonstrate that this is indeed the case. Typically, this has been accomplished within the context of broader investigations of technological processes involving a combination of archaeometric studies, direct observation of manufacturing processes, excavation and subsequent analysis and comparison of archaeological and ethnographic specimens. This "ethno-archaeometry" has been dominated by studies of iron-smelting (based on the recreation of lapsed technological processes), and pottery manufacture (Table 2.1). Probably the most comprehensive investigation has been that of Haya iron-smelting in northwestern Tanzania, initiated and coordinated by Peter Schmidt. This encompassed detailed documentation of the smelting process, the refractory properties of the furnace wall, chemical characteristics of slags, fluxes, and iron, experimental reconstructions, and comparison of the physical remains of the furnace pit with archaeological examples from the same area (Childs 1996; Schmidt 1997a). In addition, the relations of production and symbolic significance of Haya iron-smelting (Schmidt 1997a), oral traditions and myths (Schmidt 1983b), archaeological traces of iron-smelting (Schmidt and Childs 1985) and the long-term environmental impact of iron-smelting practices (Schmidt 1997b), have been investigated. Although similar elements have been investigated elsewhere in Africa (see Childs and Killick 1993; David and Kramer 2001:328–349), no other study has been so wide-ranging, or as controversial (for critiques see Killick 1996; Rehder 1986). A critical point with respect to these types of studies is that, precisely because the technical aspects of artifact manufacture are governed by natural laws, it is frequently possible to derive robust analogies with which to interpret similar categories of archaeological remains. As the following section illustrates, it is far harder to isolate similarly strong analogies concerning the cultural aspects of artifact manufacture and design.

Material Culture Theory

"Material culture" typically refers to objects and perhaps buildings and other types of physical structures. Recently, scholars from a variety of disciplines have adopted more encompassing definitions: the term now may refer to any kind of human "artifact," ranging in scale from isolated objects to landscapes (e.g., Tilley in press) and even the human body. Such an all-encompassing definition offers an epistemological challenge to binary classifications of the world (i.e., between "nature" and "culture," or "mind" and "matter") which have dominated Western thought for centuries. They also offer archaeology, concerned as it is with the study of the "histories of things," a far more central explanatory role within the humanities and social sciences than is currently the case.

Although archaeologists have long had an interest in the broader social and ideological significance of material things, explicit efforts to understand how meanings are ascribed to things and places and their role in shaping social values began in the 1980s. Ian Hodder (e.g., 1982a, 1982b, 1987) and his students, several of whom, like Hodder, conducted their fieldwork in Africa (e.g., Braithwaite 1982; Donley 1982, 1987; Lane 1987; Mawson 1989; Moore 1982, 1987; Welbourn 1984) pioneered these studies. Many drew on work by Lévi-Strauss (e.g., 1968, 1970) and other structuralist and semiotic analyses of material objects and the organization of space (e.g., Barthes 1973; Glassie 1975; Hugh-Jones 1979; Leach 1976; Tambiah 1969), and viewed things as communicating meaning in much the same way as language. In other words, any material thing from a pot to a T-shirt can operate as a sign with the potential to bear meaning, but the relationship between an object (signifier) and its meaning/s (signified) is arbitrary and independent from the formal and material constituents of the object (see Stahl 2002 on the implications for analogical modeling).

A related concern of many of these ethnoarchaeological studies was with the symbolic meanings of things and places, and how this contributed to the construction of age, gender, class, and ethnic identities. Hodder's work on such issues among the Tugen, Pokot, and Ilchamus (Njemps) around Lake Baringo, Kenya (1982b) was particularly influential and controversial. Hodder was concerned to examine the degree of correspondence between ethnic and material culture patterning, and establish the conditions under which isomorphic correspondences occur. When Hodder initiated his study, it was widely assumed within archaeology that similarity in material culture styles at the regional level directly reflected the degree of social interaction between groups (e.g., Plog 1976). In the Lake Baringo area, however, Hodder found the converse to be the case; despite frequent interaction between the three groups, their material culture exhibited a number of stylistic differences (1982b:13–57). Rather than attributing such patterning in a tautological fashion to "cultural" norms, Hodder argued that material culture styles were used strategically to maintain notions of difference between groups, and that material culture could be said to play an *active* role in the creation and recreation of identities (for substantive critiques, see Dietler and Herbich 1998; Graves 1982).

material culture as an active player in (re)creation of identities

The notion that material culture is actively involved in social processes rather than passively reflecting human behavior was subsequently elaborated upon by Hodder and others (for a review, see Shanks and Tilley 1987:79–117), and has had a profound influence on archaeological interpretation over the past few decades. This perspective drew on the "practice" or "action" theories of Bourdieu (1977) and Giddens (1979, 1981). These emphasize the contingent nature of social structures and norms, which, far from existing as a set of independent external rules, only emerge through the strategic action of individuals and thus are always in a state of "becoming." It is the routine and unreflective nature of much of this action that gives rise to what goes under the term "custom" – habitual, taken-for-granted ways of behaving and "being-in-the-world." Viewed in these terms, daily practice can be regarded as a central site for structural reproduction and the generation and regeneration of meaning in any society. However, since all actions are interpretive acts, there is always an inherent ambiguity to any action and a corresponding latent possibility that things will be "done differently." In other words, the potential for change is ever present, as is the potential for continuity, with the two coexisting in a permanent state of tension.

change and continuity

Other ethnoarchaeological studies of the symbolic, stylistic, and cultural aspects of contemporary objects, technologies, spaces, and landscapes have been conducted in various parts of Africa (Table 2.2). While some share similar theoretical perspectives as Hodder and his former students, others are inspired by different disciplinary debates. It is increasingly recognized, however, that material culture not only conveys multiple meanings, but that a correlation between stylistic and social boundaries occurs only under certain, highly specific circumstances. As Wiessner (1983, 1984) observed in a study of formal variations in San projectile points, different artifact attributes can convey different types of meanings within a group, and the significance and meaning content of a particular attribute can vary between groups. Similar conclusions regarding the complexity of factors affecting artifact styles were reached by Larrick (1985, 1986, 1991) in analyses of spear forms and their social correlates among the Lokop section of the Samburu of northern Kenya.

Table 2.2. Selected examples of ethnoarchaeological studies of the symbolic, ideological, and social significance of artifacts and technologies in Africa

Main research theme	Foragers	Fishing communities	Pastoralists	Agro-pastoralists	Craft specialists and urban dwellers
Artifact style and group and personal identities	Wiessner 1983, 1984		Hodder 1977, 1979, 1982b; Larrick 1986, 1991	Dietler and Herbich 1989, 1998; MacEachern 1992; Sterner 1989	LaViolette 2000
Residential spatial symbolism and power			Hodder 1987	Donley 1982, 1987; Lane 1987; Lyons 1996; Moore 1982, 1986; Smith and David 1995	
Symbolism and rituals of craft production					Barndon 1996; Rowlands and Warnier 1993; Schmidt 1997a
Mortuary practices				David 1992	
Artifact symbolism, meaning, and ideology			Hodder 1982b; Welbourn 1984	Braithwaite 1982; David et el. 1988; Donley-Reid 1990	Childs and Dewey 1996; Ray 1987
Material culture as a marker of social change				Moore 1987; Sargent and Friedel 1986	
Temporal structuring of material culture			Hodder 1991; Larrick 1985	Dietler and Herbich 1993; Herbich and Dietler 1993; Lane 1994	
Technology, style and chaînes opératoires				Gosselain 1992, 1998; Herbich 1987	Barndon 1996; Childs 1991

These studies have obvious ramifications for the way in which archaeologists seek ⌐
to define social boundaries from the spatial patterning of artifact styles. ⌐

Important studies on stylistic expression and social identity were conducted
under the auspices of the Mandara Archaeological Project in Cameroon and
Nigeria. The studies range from consideration of particular artifact types, decorative motifs, and burial forms associated with individual identities (David 1992;
David et al. 1988; Sterner 1989), through patterning at the intra-settlement level
(Lyons 1996; Smith and David 1995; Sterner 1989) to inter-ethnic variations in
potting techniques and styles (David et al. 1991; MacEachern 1998) and iron-
smelting furnaces (David et al. 1989). These researchers treat ethnicity as a situational construct, the particulars of which are historically determined, an approach
consistent with the project's concern with the historical trajectory of the region,
which is recognized to have played an important formative role in the patterning
of current group relationships and their corresponding material expressions. Considerable shifting in the historical composition of Mandara communities and ethnic
groups has resulted in enormous stylistic differentiation. Nevertheless, there exists
a series of broad-scale similarities in the conceptual frames of the different groups.
These are sufficiently ubiquitous to suggest that a common "symbolic reservoir"
cross-cuts contemporary ethnic and linguistic divisions (David et al. 1991; see
MacEachern 1994 for a critique).

This latter observation parallels recent work on "technological styles," such as
those related to iron-smelting and potting (e.g., Childs 1991; Childs and Killick
1993; Gosselain 1992, 1998, 1999). Various scholars have noted that objects which
serve similar functions can take a variety of forms. This suggests that, while artifact
form is partly constrained by functional considerations, the range of suitable forms
is open-ended, and that selection of one form out of many possibilities is a cultural
choice. Careful examination of the manufacturing process can reveal something of
the logic to the sequence of these cultural decisions taken at each stage. This type
of logic is sometimes referred to as a *chaîne opératoire* (Lemmonier 1986), and it
has been suggested that cross-cultural comparisons of the different logics employed
in a particular technique have the potential to reveal longer-term cultural and historical linkages between even geographically distant populations (Chapter 11). With
the exception of iron-smelting and potting, these have yet to be attempted on a very
large scale. However, one of the interesting issues to emerge from these is the apparent widespread existence among Bantu language speakers (Chapter 12) across sub-
Saharan Africa of a general "thermodynamic philosophy," which may account for
why these technical practices are the focus of routine symbolic elaboration. Critically, these studies illustrate the inadequacy of conventional distinctions between
artifact "style" and "function," "technology" and "magic," "nature" and "culture."

Conclusion

The use of observations drawn from the ethnographic present to understand materials from the archaeological past has been a feature of archaeological interpreta-

tion since the origins of the discipline. Africa and its peoples have been major sources of these analogies. However, over time interpretive strategies have changed. Initially, African societies were regarded as living fossils of earlier stages of human evolution. Subsequently, greater emphasis was placed on the formal similarities between past and present in terms of specific artifactual and architectural traditions, encouraging the formulation of piecemeal parallels. These were used rather indiscriminately to interpret archaeological remains both from Africa and elsewhere, especially western Europe. With the rise of ethnoarchaeology in the 1960s, more emphasis has been placed on developing analogies based on sound uniformitarian principles. These can take different forms. Many studies focused on issues governed by the natural laws of physics, biology, and/or chemistry. These include the material science of artifact manufacture and a wide range of processes that can influence the depositional and post-depositional history of archaeological sites and materials. The "direct historical approach" offers an alternative interpretive strategy. Here ethnographic data is restricted to the interpretation of archaeological remains believed to be directly ancestral to the living communities that provide the sources of the analogies. Cultural continuities between past and present justify the use of the specific analogies. Far too often, however, such continuities have been assumed rather than independently demonstrated (for an important exception, see Stahl 2001).

Another increasingly common approach has been the development of relational analogies concerning the role of material culture in the construction of symbolic meanings. On the one hand, these emphasize the historically and contextually specific nature of symbolic meanings. On the other, such studies are also concerned to illustrate the universal aspects of such processes as the use of metaphor and metonymy. Other emerging themes in the same vein are the role of memory and the embodied nature of routine practice. Ethnoarchaeological research has produced a vast body of knowledge concerning recent material traditions and practices across the continent. However, it is evident from Tables 2.1 and 2.2 that, regardless of interpretive strategy, the pattern of research has been uneven. For instance, few studies of site-formation processes have been conducted among contemporary urban dwellers, and there has been a disproportionate amount of research on bone-processing and discard among foraging communities compared to agriculturalists. By the same token, there is a dearth of ethnoarchaeological research on the symbolic ordering of residential space among hunter-gatherers, or on the symbolism and rituals of craft production among foragers, pastoralists, or fishing communities. Research on any of the obvious gaps suggested by these tables would be beneficial, and in the case of some themes, such as mortuary practices, material culture as icons of social change, and artifact curation among foraging, fishing, and pastoral communities, is particularly pressing.

A topic which has yet to receive sustained ethnoarchaeological study (cf. Lane 1987, 1994, 1996; Chapter 16), but which is currently of interest to historians and anthropologists of Africa (e.g., Greene 2002; Roberts and Roberts, eds., 1996; Weiss 1997; Werbner, ed., 1998) concerns the uses of material culture and the built environment in the construction of social and individual memory. More comparative work needs to be undertaken on the significance of material culture and architectural forms in the construction of memory and the production of historical knowledge in different African societies (e.g. Robertshaw and Kamuhangire 1996; van Dyke and Alcock, eds., 2003). In much the same way that biologists, agriculturalists, and others now study aspects of indigenous knowledge systems under the guise of terms such as "ethnobotany" and "ethnopharmacology," so the study of these non-Western historical epistemologies could quite legitimately be referred to as "ethnoarchaeology" (Lane 1996). As yet, we know virtually nothing about these "indigenous" African archaeologies. Establishing how they differ and what commonalities they share with the discipline of archaeology should become a research priority on the continent. The need for such research is partly driven by the urgency to develop cultural resource management (CRM) policies that are sensitive to local, non-Western understandings of the past (MacEachern 2001). Moreover, the way people in the past used material remains to construct their own historical narratives would have determined, to a certain extent, the type of material traces they left for us to study and produce our own historical narratives about the past (e.g., Bradley 2002). Consequently, if we want to understand the nature of the "mentions" and "silences" in Africa's archaeological records (Stahl 2001:1–41, 215–224), we first need to examine how such processes and concerns influence the archaeological record of the present.

Whereas older perceptions of African societies as living fossils of evolutionary stages have all but disappeared, and archaeologists working on the continent no longer seem to be in search of "barbarians" or overly concerned with their "unrewarding gyrations," the ghosts of these ideas continue to haunt many of their interpretations. Thus, for instance, there is still widespread, latent belief among "Iron Age" specialists that archaeological assemblages reflect the existence of discrete, bounded cultures, linguistic communities, and/or ethnic identities in the past, and that the "movement" of these peoples can be traced through studies of stylistic variation alone (Chapters 12, 17). Conversely, to judge from their routine interpretations, many "Stone Age" specialists seem to believe that these communities lived in worlds entirely devoid of socially constructed meanings (with perhaps the exception of those associated with their rock art), concerned only with the practicalities of extracting a living from the surrounding environment, and living largely outside history. Certainly this is the impression given by the continued use of San analogs to interpret "Stone Age" sites of varying age (cf. Chapters 6, 14). In these respects, then, it would seem that rather more, not less, ethnographic *imagination* is called for in African archaeology.

REFERENCES

Agorsah, E. Kofi, 1985 Archaeological Implications of Traditional House Construction among the Nchumuru of Northern Ghana. Current Anthropology 26:103–115.

Ascher, R., 1961 Analogy in Archaeological Interpretation. Southwestern Journal of Anthropology 17:317–325.

Atherton, John H., 1983 Ethnoarchaeology in Africa. The African Archaeological Review 1:75–104.

Balfet, Henri, 1965 Ethnographical Observations in North Africa and Archaeological Interpretation. *In* Ceramics and Man. F. R. Matson, ed. pp. 161–177. Viking Fund Publications in Anthropology 41. New York: Wenner-Gren Foundation for Anthropological Research.

Barndon, Randi, 1996 Fipa Ironworking and its Technological Style. *In* The Culture and Technology of African Iron Production. Peter R. Schmidt, ed. pp. 58–73. Gainesville: University of Florida Press.

Barthes, Roland, 1973 Mythologies. London: Paladin.

Bartram, Laurence E., 1993 Perspectives on Skeletal Part Profiles and Utility Curves from Eastern Kalahari Ethnoarchaeology. *In* From Bones to Behavior: Ethnoarchaeological and Experimental Contributions to the Interpretation of Faunal Remains. J. Hudson, ed. pp. 115–137. Occasional Paper 21. Carbondale: Center for Archaeological Investigations, Southern Illinois University.

Bartram, Laurence E., Ellen M. Kroll, and Henry T. Bunn, 1991 Variability in Camp Structure and Bone Refuse Patterning at Kua San Hunter-Gatherer Camps. *In* The Interpretation of Archaeological Spatial Patterning. Ellen M. Kroll and T. Douglas Price, eds. pp. 77–148. New York: Plenum Press.

Beach, David N., 1998 Cognitive Archaeology and Imaginary History at Great Zimbabwe. Current Anthropology 39:47–72.

Bedaux, Rogier M. A., 1986a Pottery Variation in Present-Day Dogon Compounds (Mali): Preliminary Results. *In* Variation, Culture and Evolution in African Population. R. Singer and J. K. Lundy. eds. pp. 241–248. Johannesburg: Witwatersrand University Press.

——1986b Recherches ethno-archéologiques sur la poterie Dogon (Mali). *In* Op Zoek Narr Mens en Materiële Cultuur. H. Fokkens, P. Banga, and M. Bierma, eds. pp. 117–145. Groningen: Universiteitsdrukkerji RUG.

Bedaux, Rogier M. A., and J. Diderik van der Waals, 1987 Aspects of Life-Span of Dogon Pottery. Newsletter – Department of Pottery Technology, University of Leiden (A Knapsack Full of Pottery) 5:137–153.

Binford, Lewis R., 1983 In Pursuit of the Past: Decoding the Archaeological Record. New York: Academic Press.

——1987 Researching Ambiguity: Frames of Reference and Site Structure. *In* Method and Theory for Activity Area Research: An Ethnoarchaeological Approach. Susan Kent, ed. pp. 449–512. New York: Columbia University Press.

Bourdieu, Pierre, 1977 Outline of a Theory of Practice. Cambridge: Cambridge University Press.

Bradley, Richard, 2002 The Past in Prehistoric Societies. London: Routledge.

Brain, C. K., 1967 Hottentot Food Remains and their Bearing on the Interpretation of Fossil Bone Assemblages. Scientific Papers of the Namib Desert Research Station 32:1–11.

——1969 The Contribution of Namib Desert Hottentots to an Understanding of Australopithecine Bone Accumulations. Scientific Papers of the Namib Desert Research Station 39:13–22.

Braithwaite, Mary, 1982 Decoration as Ritual Symbol: A Theoretical Proposal and an Ethnographic Study in Southern Sudan. *In* Symbolic and Structural Archaeology. Ian Hodder, ed. pp. 80–88. Cambridge: Cambridge University Press.

Brandt, Steve, 1996 The Ethnoarchaeology of Flaked Stone Tool Use in Southern Ethiopia. *In* Aspects of African Archaeology. Papers from the 10th Congress of the Pan-African Association for Prehistory and Related Studies. Gilbert Pwiti and Robert Soper, eds. pp. 733–738. Harare: University of Zimbabwe Publications.

Brooks, Alison S., 1984 San Land-Use Patterns, Past and Present: Implications for Southern African Prehistory. *In* Frontiers: Southern African Archaeology Today. Martin Hall, Graham Avery, D. M. Avery, M. L. Wilson, and A. J. B. Humphreys, eds. pp. 40–52. BAR International Series, 207. Oxford: British Archaeological Reports.

Brown, Jean, 1990 Horn-Shaping Ground-Stone Axe-Hammers. Azania 25:57–67.

——1995 Traditional Metalworking in Kenya. Monograph 44. Oxford: Oxbow Books.

Bunn, Henry, Laurence Bartram and Ellen Kroll, 1988 Variability in Bone Assemblage Formation from Hadza Hunting, Scavenging, and Carcass Processing. Journal of Anthropological Archaeology 7:412–457.

Butler, A., Z. Tesfay, A. C. D'Andrea, and D. E. Lyons, 1999 The Ethnobotany of *Lathyrus sativus* L. in the Highlands of Ethiopia. *In* The Exploitation of Plant Resources in Ancient Africa. M. van der Veen, ed. pp. 123–136. New York: Kluwer Academic/Plenum Publishers.

Calabrese, John A., 2000 Metals, Ideology and Power: The Manufacture and Control of Materialised Ideology in the Area of the Limpopo-Shashe Confluence, c. AD 900 to 1300. *In* African Naissance: The Limpopo Valley 1000 Years Ago. Mary Leslie and Tim Maggs, eds. pp. 100–111. Goodwin Series 8. Cape Town: South African Archaeological Society.

Caton-Thompson, Gertrude, 1931 The Zimbabwe Culture: Ruins and Reactions. Oxford: Clarendon Press.

Childs, S. Terry, 1991 Style, Technology and Iron-Smelting Furnaces in Bantu-Speaking Africa. Journal of Anthropological Archaeology 10:332–359.

——1996 Technological History and Culture in Western Tanzania. *In* The Culture and Technology of African Iron Production. Peter R. Schmidt, ed. pp. 277–320. Gainesville: University of Florida Press.

Childs, S. Terry, and William J. Dewey, 1996 Forging Symbolic Meaning in Zaire and Zimbabwe. *In* The Culture and Technology of African Iron Production. Peter R. Schmidt, ed. pp. 145–171. Gainesville: University of Florida Press.

Childs, S. Terry, and David Killick, 1993 Indigenous African Metallurgy: Nature and Culture. Annual Review of Anthropology 22:317–337.

Clark, J. Desmond, and H. Kurashina, 1981 A Study of the Work of a Modern Tanner in Ethiopia and its Relevance for Archaeological Interpretation. *In* Modern Material Culture: The Archaeology of Us. Richard A. Gould and Michael B. Schiffer, eds. pp. 303–321. New York: Academic Press.

Crawford, O. G. S., 1953 Archaeology in the Field. London: Phoenix House.

Curwen, E. C., 1938 The Hebrides: A Cultural Backwater. Antiquity 12:261–289.

D'Andrea, A. C., D. E. Lyons, M. Haile, and A. Butler, 1999 Ethnoarchaeological Approaches to the Study of Prehistoric Agriculture in the Highlands of Ethiopia. *In* The Exploitation of Plant Resources in Ancient Africa. Marijke van der Veen, ed. pp. 101–122. New York: Kluwer Academic/Plenum Press.

Daniel, Glyn E., 1950 A Hundred Years of Archaeology. London: Duckworth.

David, Nicholas, 1971 The Fulani Compound and the Archaeologist. World Archaeology 3:111–131.

——1992 The Archaeology of Ideology: Mortuary Practices in the Central Mandara Highlands, Northern Cameroon. *In* An African Commitment: Papers in Honour of Peter Lewis Shinnie. Judy A. Sterner and Nicholas David, eds. pp. 181–210. Calgary: University of Calgary Press.

David, Nicholas, and H. Hennig, 1972 The Ethnography of Pottery: A Fulani Case Study

Seen in Archaeological Perspective. McCaleb Module in Anthropology 21. Cambridge, MA: Addison-Wesley.

David, Nicholas, and Carol Kramer, 2001 Ethnoarchaeology in Action. Cambridge: Cambridge University Press.

David, Nicholas, Judy A. Sterner, and K. B. Gavua, 1988 Why Pots are Decorated. Current Anthropology 29:365–389.

David, Nicholas, K. B. Gavua, A. Scott MacEachern and Judy A. Sterner, 1991 Ethnicity and Material Culture in North Cameroon. Canadian Journal of Archaeology 15:171–177.

David, Nicholas, Robert R. Heimann, David J. Killick, and Michael Wayman, 1989 Between Bloomery and Blast Furnace: Mafa Iron-Smelting Technology in North Cameroon. The African Archaeological Review 7:183–208.

Denbow, James R., 1986 A New Look at the Later Prehistory of the Kalahari. Journal of African History 27:3–29.

Dietler, Michael, and Ingrid Herbich, 1989 Tich Matek: The Technology of Luo Pottery Production and the Definition of Ceramic Style. World Archaeology 21:148–164.

————1993 Living on Luo Time: Reckoning Sequence, Duration, History, and Biography in a Rural African Society. World Archaeology 25:248–260.

————1998 Habitus, Techniques, Style: An Integrated Approach to the Social Understanding of Material Culture and Boundaries. In The Archaeology of Social Boundaries. Miriam T. Stark, ed. pp. 232–269. Washington, DC: Smithsonian Institution Press.

Donley, Linda W., 1982 House Power: Swahili Space and Symbolic Markers. In Symbolic and Structural Archaeology. Ian Hodder, ed. pp. 63–73. Cambridge: Cambridge University Press.

——1987 Life in the Swahili Town House Reveals the Symbolic Meaning of Spaces and Artefact Assemblages. The African Archaeological Review 5:181–192.

Donley-Reid, Linda W., 1990 The Power of Swahili Porcelain, Beads and Pottery. In Powers of Observation: Alternative Views in Archaeology. S. M. Nelson and A. B. Kehoe, eds. pp. 47–59. Archaeological Papers of the American Anthropological Association, 2. Washington, DC: American Anthropological Association.

Evers, Tim, 1984 Sotho-Tswana and Moloko Settlement Patterns and the Bantu Cattle Pattern. In Frontiers: Southern African Archaeology Today. Martin Hall, Graham Avery, D. M. Avery, M. L. Wilson, and A. J. B. Humphreys, eds. pp. 236–247. BAR International Series, 207. Oxford: British Archaeological Reports.

Fisher, Jack, 1993 Foragers and Farmers: Material Expressions of Interaction at Elephant Processing Sites in the Ituri Forest, Zaire. In From Bones to Behaviour: Ethnoarchaeological and Experimental Contributions to the Interpretation of Faunal Remains. J. Hudson, ed. pp. 247–262. Occasional Paper 21. Carbondale: Center for Archaeological Investigations, Southern Illinois University.

Fisher, J., and H. Strickland, 1989 Ethnoarchaeology among the Efe Pygmies, Zaire: Spatial Organization of Campsites. American Journal of Physical Anthropology 78:473–484.

Foloronso, C., and S. Ogundele, 1993 Agriculture and Settlement among the Tiv of Nigeria: Some Ethnographic Observations. In The Archaeology of Africa: Food, Metals and Towns. Thurstan Shaw, Paul Sinclair, Bassey W. Andah, and Alex Okpoko, eds. pp. 274–288. London: Routledge.

Freeman, L., 1968 A Theoretical Framework for Interpreting Archaeological Materials. In Man the Hunter. Richard B. Lee and Irven DeVore, eds. pp. 262–267. Aldine: Chicago.

Friede, H., and R. Steel, 1980 Experimental Burning of Traditional Nguni Huts. African Studies 39:175–181.

Gallagher, John, 1977 Contemporary Stone Tools in Ethiopia: Implications for Archaeology. Journal of Field Archaeology 4:407–414.

Gallay, Alain, 1981 Le Sarnyéré Dogon, archéologie d'un isolat (Mali). Mémoire 4. Paris: Éditions Recherche sur les Civilisations.

——1999 A la recherche du comportement des premiers hominidés. In Comment L'Homme? A la découverte des premiers hominidés d'Afrique de l'Est. Alain Gallay, ed. pp. 9–94. Paris and Geneva: Éditions Errance/Géo-Découverte.

Giddens, Anthony, 1979 Central Problems in Social Theory. London: Macmillan.

——1981 A Contemporary Critique of Historical Materialism. London: Macmillan.

Gifford, Diane P., 1978 Ethnoarchaeological Observations of Natural Processes Affecting Cultural Materials. In Explorations in Ethnoarchaeology. Richard A. Gould, ed. pp. 77–101. Albuquerque: University of New Mexico Press.

——1981 Taphonomy and Palaeoecology: A Critical Review of Archaeology's Sister Disciplines. Advances in Archaeological Method and Theory 4:365–438.

Gifford, Diane, and Anna Behrensmeyer, 1977 Observed Formation and Burial of a Recent Human Occupation Site in Kenya. Quaternary Research 8:245–266.

Gifford-Gonzalez, Diane, 1991 Bones Are Not Enough: Analogues, Knowledge, and Interpretive Strategies in Zooarchaeology. Journal of Anthropological Archaeology 10:215–254.

Glassie, Henry, 1975 Folk Housing in Middle Virginia. Knoxville: University of Tennessee Press.

Gosselain, Olivier P., 1992 Technology and Style: Potters and Pottery among Bafia of Cameroon Man (N.S.) 27:559–586.

——1998 Social and Technical Identity in a Clay Crystal Ball. In The Archaeology of Social Boundaries. Miriam T. Stark, ed. pp. 78–106. Washington, DC: Smithsonian Institution Press.

——1999 In Pots We Trust: The Processing of Clay and Symbols in Sub-Saharan Africa. Journal of Material Culture 4:205–230.

Gould, Richard A., 1980 Living Archaeology. Cambridge: Cambridge University Press.

Graves, Michael W., 1982 Breaking Down Ceramic Variation: Testing Models of White Mountain Redware Design Style Development. Journal of Anthropological Archaeology 1:304–345.

Greene, Sandra E., 2002 Sacred Sites and the Colonial Encounter: A History of Meaning and Memory in Ghana. Indiana: Indiana University Press.

Hall, Martin, 1984 The Burden of Tribalism: The Social Context of Southern African Iron Age Studies. American Antiquity 49:455–467.

Hartley, L. P., 1953 The Go-Between. Harmondsworth: Penguin.

Herbich, Ingrid, 1987 Learning Patterns, Potter Interaction and Ceramic Style among the Luo of Kenya. The African Archaeological Review 5:193–204.

Herbich, Ingrid, and Michael Dietler, 1993 Space, Time and Symbolic Structure in the Luo Homestead: An Ethnoarchaeological Study of "Settlement Biography" in Africa. In Actes du XIIe Congrès International des Sciences Préhistoriques et Protohistoriques, Bratislava, Czechoslovakia, September 1–7. J. Pavúk, ed. pp. 26–32. Nitra: Archaeological Institute of the Slovak Academy of Sciences.

Hitchcock, Robert K., 1987 Sedentism and Site Structure: Organization Changes in Kalahari Basarwa Residential Locations. In Method and Theory for Activity Area Research: An Ethnoarchaeological Approach. Susan Kent, ed. pp. 374–423. New York: Columbia University Press.

Hitchcock, Robert K., and Laurence E. Bartram, 1998 Social Boundaries, Technical Systems and the Use of Space and Technology in the Kalahari. In The Archaeology of Social

Boundaries. Miriam T. Stark, ed. pp. 12–49. Washington, DC: Smithsonian Institution Press.

Hivernel, Françoise, 1980 An Ethnoarchaeological Model for the Study of Environmental Use. *In* Proceedings of the 8th Pan-African Congress of Prehistory and Quaternary Studies, Nairobi, September 1977. R. Leakey and B. Ogot, eds. pp. 27–28. Nairobi: International Louis Leakey Memorial Institute.

Hodder, Ian, 1977 The Distribution of Material Culture Items in Baringo District, W. Kenya. Man (N.S.) 12:239–269.

—— 1979 Economic and Social Stress and Material Culture Patterning. American Antiquity 44:446–454.

—— 1982a The Present Past. London: Batsford.

—— 1982b Symbols in Action. Cambridge: Cambridge University Press.

—— 1987 The Meaning of Discard: Ash and Domestic Space in Baringo, Kenya. *In* Method and Theory for Activity Area Research: An Ethnoarchaeological Approach. Susan Kent, ed. pp. 424–448. New York: Columbia University Press.

—— 1991 The Decoration of Containers: An Ethnographic and Historical Study. *In* Ceramic Ethnoarchaeology. William A. Longacre, ed. pp. 71–94. Tucson: University of Arizona Press.

Holl, Augustin, 1993 Community Interaction and Settlement Patterning in Northern Cameroon. *In* Spatial Boundaries and Social Dynamics: Case Studies from Food-Producing Societies. Augustin Holl and Thomas E. Levy, eds. pp. 39–61. Ethnoarchaeological Series 2. International Monographs in Prehistory. Ann Arbor: University of Michigan.

Huffman, Thomas N., 1982 Archaeology and Ethnohistory of the African Iron Age. Annual Review of Anthropology 11:133–150.

—— 1986 Archaeological Evidence and Conventional Explanations of Southern Bantu Settlement Patterns. Africa 56:280–298.

—— 1993 Broederstroom and the Central Cattle Pattern. South African Journal of Science 89:220–226.

—— 1996 Snakes and Crocodiles: Power and Symbolism in Ancient Zimbabwe. Johannesburg: Witwatersrand University Press.

—— 2000 Mapungubwe and the Origins of the Zimbabwe Culture. *In* African Naissance: The Limpopo Valley 1000 Years Ago. Mary Leslie and Tim Maggs, eds. pp. 14–29. Goodwin Series 8. Cape Town: South African Archaeological Society.

—— 2001 The Central Cattle Pattern and Interpreting the Past. Southern African Humanities 13:19–35.

Hugh-Jones, Christine, 1979 From the Milk River. Cambridge: Cambridge University Press.

Isaac, Glynn, 1984 The Archaeology of Human Origins: Studies of the Lower Pleistocene in East Africa 1971–1981. *In* Advances in World Archaeology, vol. 3. Fred Wendorf and Angela Close, eds. pp. 1–87. New York: Academic Press.

Iselin, Regula, 1994 Reading Pictures: On the Value of the Copperplates in the *Beschryvinghe* of Pieter de Marees (1602) as Source Material for Ethnohistorical Research. History in Africa 21:147–170.

Kent, Susan, 1991 The Relationship between Mobility Strategies and Site Structure. *In* The Interpretation of Archaeological Spatial Patterning. Ellen M. Kroll and T. Douglas Price, eds. pp. 33–59. New York: Plenum Press.

—— 1993a Models of Abandonment and Material Culture Frequencies. *In* Abandonment of Settlements and Regions: Ethnoarchaeological and Archaeological Approaches. Catherine M. Cameron and Steve A. Tomka, eds. pp. 54–73. Cambridge: Cambridge University Press.

—— 1993b Variability in Faunal Assemblages: The Influence of Hunting Skill, Sharing, Dogs and Mode of Cooking on Faunal Remains at a Sedentary Kalahari Community. Journal of Anthropological Archaeology 12:323–385.

Kent, Susan, ed., 1998 Gender in African Prehistory. Walnut Creek, CA: AltaMira Press.

Kent, Susan, and H. Vierich, 1989 The Myth of Ecological Determinism: Anticipated Mobility and Site Organisation of Space. *In* Farmers as Hunters: The Implications of Sedentism. Susan Kent, ed. pp. 97–103. Cambridge: Cambridge University Press.

Killick, David, 1996 On Claims for "Advanced" Ironworking Technology in Precolonial Africa. *In* The Culture and Technology of African Iron Production. Peter R. Schmidt, ed. pp. 247–266. Gainesville: University of Florida Press.

Kleindienst, Maxine R., and Patty Jo Watson, 1956 "Action Archaeology": The Archaeological Inventory of a Living Community. Anthropology Tomorrow 5:75–78.

Kuper, Adam, 1973 Anthropologists and Anthropology. London: Allen Lane.

—— 1980 Symbolic Dimensions of the Southern Bantu Homestead. Africa 50:8–23.

Lane, Paul J., 1987 Reordering Residues of the Past. *In* Archaeology as Long-Term History. Ian Hodder, ed. pp. 54–62. Cambridge: Cambridge University Press.

—— 1994 The Temporal Structuring of Settlement among the Dogon: An Ethnoarchaeological Study. *In* Architecture and Order: Approaches to Social Space. Michael Parker Pearson and C. Richards, eds. pp. 196–216. London: Routledge.

—— 1994/95 The Use and Abuse of Ethnography in the Study of the Southern African Iron Age. Azania 29–30:51–64.

—— 1996 Rethinking Ethnoarchaeology. *In* Aspects of African Archaeology. Papers from the 10th Congress of the Pan-African Association for Prehistory and Related Studies. Gilbert Pwiti and Robert Soper, eds. pp. 727–732. Harare: University of Zimbabwe Publications.

—— 1998a Engendered Spaces and Bodily Practices in the Iron Age of Southern Africa. *In* Gender in African Prehistory. Susan Kent, ed. pp. 179–203. Walnut Creek, CA: AltaMira Press.

—— 1998b Ethnoarchaeological Research – Past, Present and Future Directions. *In* Ditswa Mmung: The Archaeology of Botswana. Paul Lane, Andrew Reid, and Alinah Segobye, eds. pp. 177–205. Gaborone: Pula Press.

Larrick, Roy, 1985 Spears, Style and Time among Maa-Speaking Pastoralists. Journal of Anthropological Archaeology 4:206–220.

—— 1986 Age Grading and Ethnicity in the Style of Loikop (Samburu) Spears. World Archaeology 18:268–283.

—— 1991 Warriors and Blacksmiths: Mediating Ethnicity in East African Spears. Journal of Anthropological Archaeology 10:299–331.

LaViolette, Adria, 2000 Ethno-Archaeology in Jenné, Mali: Craft and Status among Smiths, Potters and Masons. BAR International Series, 838. Oxford: British Archaeological Reports.

Leach, Edmund, 1976 Culture and Communication. Cambridge: Cambridge University Press.

Leakey, Mary, 1971 Olduvai Gorge, vol. 3: Excavations in Beds I and II, 1960–63. Cambridge: Cambridge University Press.

Lemmonier, Pierre, 1986 The Study of Material Culture Today: Towards an Anthropology of Technical Systems. Journal of Anthropological Archaeology 5:147–186.

Lévi-Strauss, Claude, 1968 Structural Anthropology. London: Allen Lane.

—— 1970 The Raw and the Cooked. London: Cape.

Loubser, Jaanie, 1991 The Ethnoarchaeology of Venda-Speakers in Southern Africa. Navorsinge van die Nasionale Museum Bloemfontein 7:154–464.

Lowenthal, D., 1985 The Past is a Foreign Country. Cambridge: Cambridge University Press.

Lubbock, John (Lord Avebury), 1912 Prehistoric Times as Illustrated by Ancient Remains and the Manners and Customs of Modern Savages. 6th edition. London: Williams & Norgate.

Lupo, K. D., 1995 Hadza Bone Assemblages and Hyena Attrition: An Ethnographic Example of the Influence of Cooking and Mode of Discard on the Intensity of Scavenger Ravaging. Journal of Anthropological Archaeology 14:288–314.

Lyons, Diane, 1996 The Politics of House Shape: Round versus Rectilinear Domestic Structures in Déla Compounds, Northern Cameroon. Antiquity 70:351–367.

MacEachern, A. Scott, 1992 Ethnicity and Stylistic Variation Round Mayo Plata, Northern Cameroon. In An African Commitment: Papers in Honour of Peter Lewis Shinnie. Judy A. Sterner and Nicholas David, eds. pp. 211–230. Calgary: University of Calgary Press.

——1994 "Symbolic Reservoirs" and Inter-Group Relations: West African Examples. The African Archaeological Review 12:205–24.

——1996 Foreign Countries: The Development of Ethnoarchaeology in Sub-Saharan Africa. Journal of World Prehistory 10:243–304.

——1998 Scale, Style and Cultural Variation: Technological Traditions in the Northern Mandara Mountains. In The Archaeology of Social Boundaries. Miriam T. Stark, ed. pp. 107–131. Washington, DC: Smithsonian Institution Press.

——2001 Cultural Resource Management and Africanist Archaeology. Antiquity 75: 866–871.

McIntosh, Roderick J., 1974 Archaeology and Mud Wall Decay in a West African Village. World Archaeology 6:154–171.

——1977 The Excavation of Mud Structures: An Experiment from West Africa. World Archaeology 9:185–199.

Maggs, Tim, M. O'C., 1992 "My Father's Hammer Never Ceased its Song Day and Night": The Zulu Ferrous Metalworking Industry. Natal Museum Journal of Humanities 4:65–87.

——1994/95 The Early Iron Age in the Extreme South: Some Patterns and Problems. Azania 29/30:171–178.

Marshall, Fiona, 1993 Food Sharing and the Faunal Record. In From Bones to Behaviour: Ethnoarchaeological and Experimental Contributions to the Interpretation of Faunal Remains. J. Hudson, ed. pp. 228–246. Occasional Paper 21. Center for Archaeological Investigations. Carbondale: Southern Illinois University.

——1994 Food Sharing and Body Part Representation in Okiek Faunal Assemblages. Journal of Archaeological Science 21:65–77.

Mawson, Andrew N. M., 1989 The Triumph of Life: Political Dispute and Religious Ceremonial among the Agar Dinka of Southern Sudan. Unpublished Ph.D. dissertation, University of Cambridge.

Mbae, Bernard, 1990 The Ethnoarchaeology of Maasai Settlements and Refuse Disposal Patterns in the Lemek Area. In Early Pastoralists of South-Western Kenya. Peter Robertshaw, ed. pp. 279–292. Memoir 11. Nairobi: British Institute in Eastern Africa.

Michael, George H., and Brian M. Fagan 2000 Anthropology 3 Courseware: Exercise 4–5, The Archaeology of Olduvai Gorge. Electronic document, <http://www.archserve.id. ucsb.edu/Anth3/Courseware/OlduvaiArch/Sites/DK/PlanMap.html>, accessed June 2003.

Montaigne, Michel de, 1991[1580] Of the Cannibals. In Michel de Montaigne, The Complete Essays. M. A. Screech, trans. and ed. pp. 228–241. Harmondsworth: Penguin.

Moore, Henrietta L., 1982 The Interpretation of Spatial Patterning in Settlement Residues. In Symbolic and Structural Archaeology. Ian Hodder, ed. pp. 74–79. Cambridge: Cambridge University Press.

——1986 Space, Text and Gender. Cambridge: Cambridge University Press.

——1987 Problems in the Analysis of Social Change: An Example from the Marakwet. *In* Archaeology as Long-Term History. Ian Hodder, ed. pp. 85–104. Cambridge: Cambridge University Press.

Morgan, Lewis Henry, 1877 Ancient Society, or Researches in the Lines of Human Progress from Savagery through Barbarism to Civilization. New York: Henry Holt.

Msemwa, Paul, 1994 An Ethnoarchaeological Study on Shellfish Collecting in a Complex Urban Setting. Unpublished Ph.D. dissertation, Brown University.

O'Connell, James F., Kristin Hawkes, and N. Blurton-Jones, 1988 Hadza Hunting, Butchering, and Bone Transport and their Archaeological Implications. Journal of Anthropological Research 44:113–162.

——————1990 Reanalysis of Large Mammal Body Part Transport among the Hadza. Journal of Archaeological Science 17:301–316.

——————1991 Distribution of Refuse-Producing Activities at Hadza Base Camps: Implications for Analyses of Archaeological Site Structure. *In* The Interpretation of Archaeological Spatial Patterning. Ellen M. Kroll and T. Douglas Price, eds. pp. 61–76. New York: Plenum Press.

Orme, Bryony J., 1973 Archaeology and Ethnography. *In* The Explanation of Culture Change: Models in Prehistory. Colin Renfrew, ed. pp. 481–492. London: Duckworth.

——1974 Twentieth Century Prehistorians and the Idea of Ethnographic Parallels. Man (N.S.) 9:199–212.

——1981 Anthropology for Archaeologists. London: Duckworth.

Parkington, John, and G. Mills, 1991 From Space to Place: The Architecture and Social Organization of Southern African Mobile Communities. *In* Ethnoarchaeological Approaches to Mobile Campsites. C. Gamble and W. Boismier, eds. pp. 355–370. Ethnoarchaeological Series 1. International Monographs in Prehistory. Ann Arbor: University of Michigan.

Pétrequin, Anne-Marie, and Pierre Pétrequin, 1984 Habitat Lacustre du Bénin: Une approche ethnoarchéologique. Mémoire 39. Paris: Éditions Recherches sur les Civilisations.

Piggott, Stuart, 1976 Ruins in the Landscape. Edinburgh: Edinburgh University Press.

Pikirayi, Innocent, 2001 The Zimbabwe Culture: Origins and Decline of Southern Zambezian States. Walnut Creek, CA: AltaMira Press.

Pistorius, Julius, C. C. 1992 Molokwane: An Iron Age Bakwena Village. Johannesburg: Preskor.

Plog, Stephen, 1976 Measurement of Prehistoric Interaction between Communities. *In* The Early Mesoamerican Village. Kent V. Flannery, ed. pp. 255–272. New York: Academic Press.

Posnansky, M., 1984 Ethnoarchaeology of Farm Shelters at Hani, Ghana. AnthroQuest 30:11–12.

Ray, Keith, 1987 Material Metaphor, Social Interaction and Historical Reconstructions: Exploring Patterns of Association and Symbolism in the Igbo-Ukwu Corpus. *In* The Archaeology of Contextual Meanings. Ian Hodder, ed. pp. 66–77. Cambridge: Cambridge University Press.

Rehder, J. E., 1986 Use of Preheated Air in Primitive Furnaces: Comment on the Views of Avery and Schmidt. Journal of Field Archaeology 13:351–353.

Robbins, Lawrence H., 1973 Turkana Material Culture Viewed from an Archaeological Perspective. World Archaeology 5:209–214.

——1980 Appendix 3: Ethnoarchaeological Study of a Fisherman's Camp. *In* Lopoy: A Late

Stone-Age Fishing and Pastoralist Settlement in the Lake Turkana Basin, Kenya. Lawrence H. Robbins, ed. pp. 130–135. Anthropological Series 3/1. East Lansing: Michigan State University Museum.

Roberts, Mary Nooter, and Alan F. Roberts, eds., 1996 Memory: Luba Art and the Making of History. New York and Munich: The Museum of Modern Art/Prestel.

Robertshaw, Peter, and Ephraim Kamuhangire, 1996 The Present in the Past: Archaeological Sites, Oral Traditions, Shrines and Politics in Uganda. In Aspects of African Archaeology. Papers from the 10th Congress of the Pan-African Association for Prehistory and Related Studies. Gilbert Pwiti and Robert Soper, eds. pp. 739–743. Harare: University of Zimbabwe Publications.

Rowlands, Michael, and J.-P. Warnier, 1993 The Magical Production of Iron in the Cameroon Grassfields. In The Archaeology of Africa: Food, Metals and Towns. Thurstan Shaw, Paul Sinclair, Bassey W. Andah, and Alex Okpoko, eds. pp. 512–550. London: Routledge.

Salmon, Merilee H., 1982 Philosophy and Archaeology. New York: Academic Press.

Sargent, C. F., and D. A. Friedel, 1986 From Clay to Metal: Culture Change and Container Usage among the Bariba of Northern Benin, West Africa. The African Archaeological Review 4:177–196.

Schiffer, Michael B., 1976 Behavioral Archaeology. New York: Academic Press.

——1987 Formation Processes of the Archaeological Record. Albuquerque: University of New Mexico Press.

Schmidt, Peter R., 1983a An Alternative to a Strictly Materialist Perspective: A Review of Historical Archaeology, Ethnoarchaeology and Symbolic Approaches in African Archaeology. American Antiquity 48:62–79.

——1983b Cultural Meaning and History in African Myth. International Journal of Oral History 4:167–183.

——1997a Iron Technology in East Africa: Symbolism, Science and Archaeology. Bloomington: Indiana University Press.

——1997b Archaeological Views on a History of Landscape Change in East Africa. Journal of African History 38:393–421.

Schmidt, Peter R., and S. Terry Childs, 1985 Innovation and Industry during the Early Iron Age in East Africa: KM2 and KM3 Sites in Northwestern Tanzania. The African Archaeological Review 3:53–94.

Shanks, Michael, and Christopher Tilley, 1987 Social Theory and Archaeology. Cambridge: Polity.

Smith, Andrew B., 1993 Different Facets of the Crystal: Early European Images of the Khoikhoi at the Cape, South Africa. In Historical Archaeology in the Western Cape. Martin Hall and A. Markell, eds. pp. 8–20. Goodwin Series 7. Cape Town: The South African Archaeological Society.

Smith, A., and Nicholas David, 1995 The Production of Space and the House of Xidi Sukur. Current Anthropology 36:441–471.

Smith, Susan, 1980 The Environmental Adaptation of Nomads in the West Africa Sahel: Key to Understanding Prehistoric Pastoralists. In The Sahara and the Nile: Quaternary Environments and Prehistoric Occupation in Northern Africa. Martin Williams and H. Faure, eds. pp. 467–487. Rotterdam: A. A. Balkema.

Stahl, Ann B., 1993 Concepts of Time and Approaches to Analogical Reasoning in Historical Perspective. American Antiquity 58:235–260.

——2001 Making History in Banda: Anthropological Visions of Africa's Past. Cambridge: Cambridge University Press.

——2002 Colonial Entanglements and the Practices of Taste: An Alternative to Logocentric Approaches. American Anthropologist 104:827–845.

Sterner, Judy, 1989 Who is Signalling Whom? Ceramic Style, Ethnicity and Taphonomy among the Sirak Bulahay. Antiquity 63:451–459.

Stewart, K. M., and Diane P. Gifford-Gonzalez, 1994 Ethnoarchaeological Contribution to Identifying Hominid Fish Processing Sites. Journal of Archaeological Science 21:237–248.

Stiles, Daniel, 1979 An Ethnoarchaeological Study with the Boni, Eastern Kenya. Nyame Akuma 15:29–33.

——1980 Archaeological and Ethnographic Studies of Pastoral Groups of Northern Kenya. Nyame Akuma 17:20–24.

Stone, Glen D., 1991 Settlement Ethnoarchaeology: Changing Patterns among the Kofyar of Nigeria. Expedition 33:16–23.

——1993 Agricultural Abandonment: A Comparative Study in Historical Ecology. In Abandonment of Settlements and Regions: Ethnoarchaeological and Archaeological Approaches. Catherine M. Cameron and Steve A. Tomka, eds. pp. 75–81. Cambridge: Cambridge University Press.

——1994 Agricultural Intensification and Perimetrics: Ethnoarchaeological Evidence from Nigeria. Current Anthropology 35:317–324.

Tambiah, S. J., 1969 "Animals are good to think and good to prohibit". Ethnology 8:423–459.

Tilley, Christopher, In press Ethnography and Material Culture: A Review. History, Culture and Archaeology – The Interdisciplinary Crossroad 1.

Tobert, Natalie, 1988 The Ethnoarchaeology of the Zaghawa of Darfur (Sudan): Settlement and Transience. BAR International Series, 445. Oxford: British Archaeological Reports.

Trevor-Roper, Hugh, 1963 The Rise of Christian Europe: The Great Recovery. The Listener 70(1809):871–875.

Trigger, Bruce G., 1989 A History of Archaeological Thought. Cambridge: Cambridge University Press.

Tylor, Edmund, 1865 Researches into the Early History of Mankind. London: John Murray.

van Dyke, Ruth M., and Susan E. Alcock, eds., 2003 Archaeologies of Memory. Oxford: Blackwell.

van Waarden, Catrien, 1989 The Granaries of Vumba: Structural Interpretation of a Khami Period Commoner Site. Journal of Anthropological Archaeology 8:131–157.

Vincent, Anne, 1985 Plant Foods in Savanna Environments: A Preliminary Report of Tubers Eaten by the Hadza of Northern Tanzania. World Archaeology 17:131–148.

Walicka Zeh, Renata A., 2000 Building Practice and Cultural Space amongst the Bambara, Senufo and Bozo of Mali: An Ethnoarchaeological Study. Unpublished Ph.D. dissertation, University of London.

Weiss, Brad, 1997 Forgetting Your Dead: Alienable and Inalienable Objects in Northwest Tanzania. Anthropological Quarterly 70:164–172.

Welbourn, Alice, 1984 Endo Ceramics and Power Strategies. In Ideology, Power and Prehistory. Daniel Miller and Christopher Tilley, eds. pp. 17–24. Cambridge: Cambridge University Press.

Werbner, Richard, ed., 1998 Memory and the Postcolony: African Anthropology and the Critique of Power. London: Zed Books.

Whitelaw, Gavin, 1994 KwaGandaganda: Settlement Patterns in the Natal Early Iron Age. Natal Museum Journal of Humanities 6:1–64.

Wiessner, Polly, 1983 Style and Social Information in Kalahari San Projectile Points. American Antiquity 48:253–276.

—— 1984 Reconsidering the Behavioural Basis for Style: A Case Study among the Kalahari San. Journal of Anthropological Archaeology 3:190–234.

Wobst, Martin, 1978 The Archaeo-Ethnography of Hunter-Gatherers or the Tyranny of the Ethnographic Record in Archaeology. American Antiquity 43:303–309.

Wylie, Alison, 1982 An Analogy By Any Other Name Is Just as Analogical: A Commentary on the Gould-Watson Dialogue. Journal of Anthropological Archaeology 1:382–401.

—— 1985 The Reaction against Analogy. *In* Advances in Archaeological Method and Theory 8:63–111.

Yellen, John E., 1976 Settlement Patterns of the !Kung: An Archaeological Perspective. *In* Kalahari Hunter-Gatherers: Studies of the !Kung San and their Neighbors. Richard B. Lee and Irven DeVore, eds. pp. 47–72. Cambridge, MA: Harvard University Press.

—— 1977a Archaeological Approaches to the Present: Models for Reconstructing the Past. London: Academic Press.

—— 1977b Cultural Patterning in Faunal Remains: Evidence from the Kung Bushmen. *In* Experimental Archaeology. D. T. Ingersoll, John E. Yellen, and W. MacDonald, eds. pp. 271–331. New York: Columbia University Press.

—— 1993a Small Mammals: !Kung San Utilization and the Production of Faunal Assemblages. Journal of Anthropological Archaeology 9:1–26.

—— 1993b Small Mammals: Post-Discard Patterning of !Kung San Faunal Remains. Journal of Anthropological Archaeology 9:152–192.

3

Discord after Discard: Reconstructing Aspects of Oldowan Hominin Behavior

Thomas Plummer

The oldest known technology consists of modified stones found at sites in eastern, southern, and northern Africa from approximately 1.6–2.6 million years (my) ago (Figure 3.1). Cores were struck to produce sharp-edged flakes. One demonstrable use of these artifacts was animal butchery, but they may have been used to work wood and process plant foods as well. Artifacts older than 1.6 my in Africa are now commonly referred to the Oldowan Industry within the Oldowan Industrial Complex (type site Olduvai Gorge; Isaac 1984; Leakey 1971). The term Oldowan is applied to this ancient technology, to the artifacts produced by these technological practices, and to the sites where these artifacts are found.

Site assemblages attributable to the Oldowan Industrial Complex and artifact-assisted processing of fauna now extends to approximately 2.6 my (de Heinzelin et al. 1999; Semaw 2000; Semaw et al. 2003) (Table 3.1). The oldest well-dated occurrences are found in East Africa, but by ca. 1.7 my the Oldowan is known from Algeria to South Africa and as far west as the Democratic Republic of the Congo. Yet most inferences about Oldowan hominin behavior are based on assemblages from sites slightly younger than 2.0 my at Olduvai Gorge, Tanzania (Blumenschine 1995; Bunn and Kroll 1986; Capaldo 1997; Leakey 1971; Oliver 1994; Potts 1988; Selvaggio 1998) and Koobi Fora, Kenya (e.g., Bunn et al. 1980; Isaac, ed., 1997; Isaac and Harris 1978; Kroll 1994; Schick 1987; Toth 1987).

There is general agreement on some aspects of Oldowan hominin behavior (Table 3.2). It is clear that Oldowan hominins transported stone and some classes of food items (notably animal tissue, defined here as vertebrate muscle, viscera, and within-bone nutrients such as marrow and the brain). Artifact transport exceeded that seen in chimpanzees (*Pan troglodytes*) in which transport rarely exceeds 100 m and is frequently 20 m or less (Boesch and Boesch-Achermann 2000). However, tethering to raw material sources may have been higher during the Oldowan than in later stone tool industries (Potts 1994; Rogers et al. 1994). Refuse was repeatedly deposited at certain locales, leading to extensive horizontal and sometimes ver-

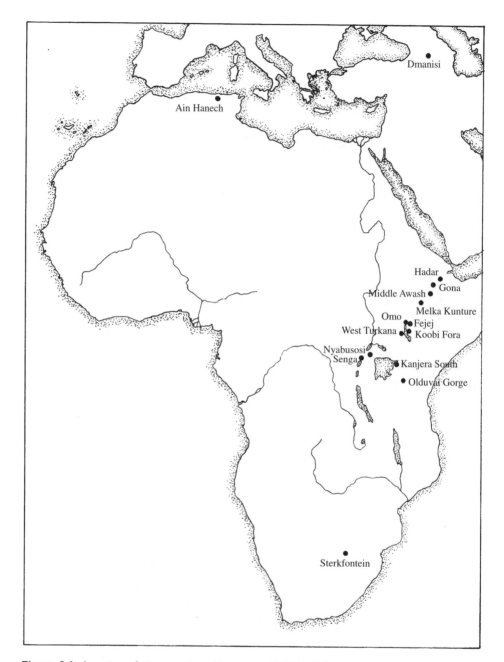

Figure 3.1. Location of sites mentioned in text and in Table 3.1

tical accumulations of archaeological material (Isaac, ed., 1997; Kroll 1994; Leakey 1971; Potts 1988). Transport of carcass parts provides the first hint of delayed food consumption in the fossil record, a distinctively human trait among living primates (Isaac 1978; Chapter 4). The size and taxonomic diversity of the butchered taxa as

Table 3.1. Major Oldowan occurrences

Locality	Excavation	Age (my)	Excavation size (m²)	Number of excavated artifacts	Raw material	Excavated terrestrial vertebrate fossils	Geomorphological and paleoenvironmental settings	References
Gona, Ethiopia	Kada Gona 2-3-4	2.58–2.63	NR	21	B, T	0	Streambank or adjacent floodplain	Roche 1996; Roche and Tiercelin 1980
	West Gona 1	2.4	10	19	B, T	5	Streambank or adjacent floodplain with seasonal flooding	Harris 1983; Harris and Capaldo 1993
	EG10	2.5–2.6	13	667	T > 70%	0	Floodplains close to stream channel margins	Semaw et al. 1997; Semaw, 2000
	EG12	2.5–2.6	9	444	T > 70%	0	Floodplains close to stream channel margins	Semaw et al. 1997; Semaw 2000
	OGS-6	ca. 2.6	NR	NR	NR	Surface fossil w/cut marks	Bank of ancestral Awash	Semaw et al. 2003
	OGS-7	ca. 2.6	2.6	265	La, T, R, C	34	Bank of ancestral Awash	Semaw et al. 2003
Hadar Ethiopia	AL 666	2.33	2.5	14	B, C	3	Predominantly open, with wetlands and bushed or wooded grasslands and with trees close to a water source	Hovers et al. 2002; Kimbel et al. 1996

Table 3.1. *Continued*

Locality	Excavation	Age (my)	Excavation size (m²)	Number of excavated artifacts	Raw material	Excavated terrestrial vertebrate fossils	Geomorphological and paleoenvironmental settings	References
Middle Awash, Ethiopia	Hata Mbr, Bouri Fm	2.5	NR	0	Not applicable	Several fossils w/stone tool damage	Broad, grassy, featureless margin of a shallow freshwater lake	de Heinzelin et al. 1999
West Turkana, Kenya	Lokalalei 1 (GaJh5)	2.34	67	417	Predominantly lava	>3415	Near intersection of ephemeral basin-margin streams and meandering, axial, ancestral Omo river.	Kibunjia 1994
	Lokalalei 2C (LA2C)	2.2	17	2067	Predominantly B, P (10 types)	239	Near intersection of ephemeral basin-margin streams and meandering, axial, ancestral Omo river. Open environment on alluvial plain, with patches of bushes or forest along ephemeral river	Brown and Gathogo 2002; Roche et al. 1999

Site/Formation	Locality	Age		Count	Lithology	Presence	Depositional environment	References
Omo Shungura Fm, Mbr E, Ethiopia	Omo 84 (stratigraphic position unclear)	2.4–2.5 Ma?	NR	200	Q (B, C)	Present, found below artifacts	Distal edge of fluviatile levees, behind gallery forests bordering open savanna	Howell et al. 1987
Omo Shungura Fm, Mbr F, Ethiopia	Ftji 1	2.3–2.4 Ma	18	367	Q (C, L)	Present, derived context	Deposited in braided stream system	Howell et al. 1987; Merrick and Merrick 1976
	Ftji 2	2.3–2.4 Ma	22	224	Q	0	Meandering stream system, distal edge of fluviatile levee, open floodplain between riparian forest and open savanna	Howell et al. 1987; Merrick and Merrick 1976
	Ftji 5	2.3–2.4 Ma	8	24	Q	Present, derived context	Deposited in braided stream system	Howell et al. 1987; Merrick and Merrick 1976
	Omo 57	2.3–2.4 Ma	NR	30	Q (C, Qt)	Present	Deposited in braided stream system	Chavaillon 1976; Howell et al. 1987
	Omo 123	2.3–2.4 Ma	NR	ca. 900	Q (C, Qt)	0	Meandering stream system, distal edge of fluviatile levée, open floodplain between riparian forest and open savanna	Chavaillon 1976; Howell et al. 1987

Table 3.1. *Continued*

Locality	Excavation	Age (my)	Excavation size (m²)	Number of excavated artifacts	Raw material	Excavated terrestrial vertebrate fossils	Geomorphological and paleoenvironmental settings	References
Upper Semliki Valley, Democratic Republic of the Congo	Senga 5A	2.0–2.3	Not applicable, sediments disturbed and redeposited	723	Q (Qt)	4400, but no definite behavioral association with artifacts	Not applicable, artifacts derived from Lusso Beds and subsequently redeposited	Harris et al. 1987; Harris et al. 1990
Kanjera Fm (S), Kenya	Excavation 1	ca. 2.0 Ma	175	>4000 (under analysis)	Under analysis, but includes A, B, C, E, J, M, N, P, Q, Qt, R, S	>3000 (under analysis)	Sites in wooded grassland at basin margin with braided, intermittently flowing streams	Plummer et al. 1999
Koobi Fora Fm, KBS Member	FxJj 10	1.9	13	294	L (I)	5–6	Artifact discard along the bank of a watercourse within a fluviodeltaic floodplain setting	Harris and Capaldo 1993; Isaac, ed., 1997
	FxJj 3	1.9	44.5	120	L (I, Q OV)	237	Side of a slight depression (pool) along the course of a silted up deltaic channel	Isaac, ed., 1997
	FxJj 1	1.9	65	136	L (I, OV)	689	Shallow swale in tuff-choked channel	Isaac, ed., 1997

Location	Site	Age					Environment	References
Olduvai Gorge, Tanzania	FLK N 1-2	1.75	106	1205	L, Qt	2274	Lake margin surrounded by relatively flat swampy floodplain. Pollen suggests open grassland and reed swamps with some gallery bush and trees	Bunn 1986; Harris and Capaldo 1993; Leakey 1971; Potts 1988; Rose and Marshall 1996
	FLK N 3	1.75	105	171	L, Qt		Lake margin	
	FLK N 4	1.75	82	67	L, Qt		Lake margin	
	FLK N 5	1.75	115	151	L, Qt		Lake margin	
	FLK N 6	1.75	36	130	Qt, B/ta, N (L, C)	>2258	Lake margin	
	FLK I 22 (Zinj)	1.76	290	2647	Qt, VB, L (B/Ta, N, G, F)	ca. 40172	Lake margin	
	FLK NN 3	1.76	209	72	B/Ta, N, L, Qt	>2261	Lake margin	
	DK 2 and 3	1.86	233	1163	B/Ta, VB, N, L, Qt (C, G, F)	>7855	Lake margin	
Nyabusosi (Toro-Uganda)	NY 18	ca. 1.5	16	536	Q, C	None mentioned	From a sequence of "fluvio-lacustrine" deposits	Texier 1995

Table 3.1. Continued

Locality	Excavation	Age (my)	Excavation size (m²)	Number of excavated artifacts	Raw material	Excavated terrestrial vertebrate fossils	Geomorphological and paleoenvironmental settings	References
Fejej, Ethiopia	FJ1 locality	1.88	Surface	>150 from surface	Q (B)	Present on surface	Not stated	Asfaw et al. 1991
Melka-Kunture, Ethiopia	Gombore I B	ca. 1.7	200	ca. 8000	B (O?)	Yes, amount not specified	Occupation of the banks of the Paleo-Awash River, riverine gallery forest	Chavaillon et al. 1979
Sterkfontein, South Africa	Member 5 Oldowan Infill	1.7–2.0	Not applicable – cave infill	3245	Q, Qt, C	Present, but perhaps not archaeological	Landscape near cave entrance wooded grassland to open grassland locally moist catchement in immediate vicinity of cave	Bishop et al. 1999; Kuman 1998; Kuman and Clarke 2000
Ain Hanech and El Kherba sites, Algeria	Unnamed	ca. 1.8	54 m² at Ain Hanech, NR at El-Kherba	1232 at Ain Hanech, 270 at El-Kherba	E, F (S, Qt)	Present but not tallied	Alluvial floodplain cut by meandering river	Sahnouni and de Heinzelin 1998; Sahnouni et al. 2002

Artifact lithology abbreviations

A = andesite, B = basalt, B/Ta = basalt/trachyandesite, C = chert/chalcedony/flint, E = limestone, G = gneiss, I = ignimbrite, J = ijolite, L = lava indet., La = latite, M = microgranite, N = nephelinite, P = phonolite, Q = quartz, Qt = quartzite, R = rhyolite, S = sandstone, T = trachyte, Ta = trachyandesite, VB = vesicular basalt. Rare lithologies (<3%) are placed in parantheses. NR = not reported

Source: after Potts (1991:156–157).

Table 3.2. Points of consensus regarding Oldowan hominin behavior

- Artifact transport in excess of that seen in *Pan*, with maximum transport distances of ca. 10 km
- Movement of carcass parts across landscape (delayed consumption)
- Items repeatedly deposited at certain locales, forming archaeologically visible "sites"
- Faunal utilization in excess of that seen in non-human primates
- Broad faunal search image with butchery of animals ranging in size from hedgehogs to elephants
- Medium and large mammals (weight >114 kg) probably scavenged
- Hominin tethering to raw material sources strong relative to the Acheulean, MSA or LSA
- Lithic technology represents a least effort method of dispensing flakes from cores, generally through hard hammer or bipolar techniques
- Selective use of lithic raw materials with preference given to lithologies with good edge and fracture characteristics

well as the sheer magnitude of some Oldowan accumulations suggests that hominins were consuming much greater quantities of animal tissue than observed in chimpanzees and baboons (Bunn and Kroll 1986; Leakey 1971; Plummer and Stanford 2000; Rose 1997; Strum 1981). In further contrast to nonhuman primates, wildebeest and larger-sized carcasses were probably scavenged (Blumenschine 1987; Bunn and Ezzo 1993). Technologically, Oldowan tool production represents a least effort method of dispensing flakes, generally through hard hammer or bipolar techniques (Toth 1985). Raw material for artifact manufacture was selected based on availability and fracture characteristics (Schick and Toth 1993). In sum, by 1.9 my and perhaps even at its inception, this simple core and flake technology allowed Plio-Pleistocene hominins to access animal products on a scale without precedent in primate evolutionary history.

However, contention remains within Oldowan hominin studies (Table 3.3). Researchers debate whether a uniformly high technological competency is demonstrated in all Oldowan artifact assemblages (Kibunjia 1994; Semaw 2000) and disagree on their behavioral significance. A number of behavioral models for archaeological site formation and hominin land use have been proposed, including variants of central place foraging (Isaac 1983a, 1983b; Rose and Marshall 1996); stone caching (Potts 1988); routed foraging (Binford 1988); refuging (Blumenschine 1991; Isaac 1983a); and the recurrent use of favored places (Schick 1987; Schick and Toth 1993). The range of models reflects differences in opinion over: the degree of spatial focus of hominin activity; the duration of site formation; the degree of group cohesion; the scale of carcass returns and likelihood of extensive food sharing; and the intensity of on-site competition with carnivores. Considerable debate exists over the environmental context and scale of hominin carnivory, including whether carnivory was most frequently practiced in particular habitats or seasons; whether hominins were capable of effectively competing with large felids and hyenids; whether hunting of small mammals was likely; the fre-

Table 3.3. Points of contention within studies of Oldowan hominin behavior, with exemplary references

---

Technology
- High versus low degree of variability in technological competency[1]

Socioeconomic function of archaeological sites and underlying taphonomic, geologic, and behavioral assumptions
- Models of archaeological site formation (e.g., stone cache, central place, routed foraging)[2]
- Degree of spatial focus of hominin activities (well versus poorly defined)[3]
- Duration of site formation of thin (<10cm) archaeological horizons (short accumulation with final burial over several years versus accumulation alone in 5–10 years)[4]
- Degree of group cohesion (high versus uncertain, possibly weak)[5]
- Likelihood of extensive food-sharing (very likely versus unlikely)[6]
- Intensity of on-site competition with carnivores (highly competitive versus low competition)[7]

Foraging ecology
- Degree to which Oldowan foraging was tool-dependent[8]
- Degree of hominin tethering to a specific habitat (strong woodland preference versus generalized habitat usage)[9]
- Seasonality of faunal utilization (predominantly late dry season versus year-round)[10]
- Place of hominins within Plio-Pleistocene carnivore competitive hierarchy (high versus low)[11]
- Likelihood of small mammal (<114kg) hunting (likely hunted versus very possibly scavenged)[12]
- Mode of scavenging (passive versus active) and scale of carcass returns (moderate versus high)[13]
- Faunal transport distance (short versus long)[14]
- Carcass resources exploited (meat[15] and within bone[16] or predominantly within bone?)[17]
- Relative importance of meat versus "high-quality" plant foods (i.e., underground storage organs, nuts, baobab fruit)[18]

---

1 Contrast Kibunjia (1994) with Semaw et al. (1997)
2 Contrast Binford (1981), Isaac (1978, 1984), Potts (1984)
3 Contrast Blumenschine and Masao (1991) with Leakey (1971)
4 Contrast Bunn and Kroll (1986) with Potts (1988)
5 Contrast Potts (1988) with Rose and Marshall (1996)
6 Contrast Binford (1984) with Oliver (1994)
7 Contrast Capaldo (1997) with Potts (1988)
8 Contrast Binford (1981) with Isaac (1978)
9 Contrast Plummer and Bishop (1994), Plummer et al.(1999), with Sikes (1994)
10 Contrast Bunn (1986) with Foley (1987)
11 Contrast Blumenschine (1987) with Bunn and Ezzo (1993)
12 Contrast Bunn and Ezzo (1993) with Cavallo and Blumenschine (1989)
13 Contrast Binford (1981) with Oliver (1994)
14 Contrast O'Connell et al. (2002) with Rose and Marshall (1996)
15 "Meat" here refers to organ and muscle tissue
16 "Within bone" here refers to brains and marrow
17 Contrast Dominguez-Rodrigo (1997) with Selvaggio (1998)
18 Contrast O'Connell et al. (1999) with Milton (1999)

quency and mode of scavenging of medium- and larger-sized mammals; the degree to which carcass parts were transported; the carcass resources most frequently exploited; and the relative significance of meat versus high-quality plant foods.

This chapter presents divergent views of Oldowan hominin behavioral ecology and assesses the commonalities and contrasts expressed by different researchers. Attention is focused on Oldowan technological studies, the socio-economic function of Oldowan sites, the degree of faunal transport, and the scale of carcass exploitation.

Background to the Oldowan

Timing and distribution

The best-documented Oldowan occurrences are from East Africa, largely from sites within the Eastern Rift (Table 3.1; Figure 3.1). Additional occurrences have been documented in the Chiwondo Formation, Malawi; between the major rift axes at Kanjera, Kenya; in the western rift at Senga 5A in the Democratic Republic of the Congo; in North Africa at Ain Hanech, Algeria; and in South Africa at Sterkfontein. Oldowan sites range in age from approximately 1.6 my to between 2.5 and 2.6 my. Until recently, the Oldowan was considered an exclusively African phenomenon. But the recovery of a comparable technology at Dmanisi, Georgia (in western Asia) at approximately 1.7 my suggests that the earliest travelers out of Africa brought the Oldowan tool kit with them (Gabunia et al. 2001).

The Oldowan is succeeded by the Developed Oldowan Industries A, B, and C, the Karari Industry and the Acheulean Industry (Harris and Isaac 1976; Isaac 1984; Leakey 1971) and is grouped with these industries into the Early Stone Age (ESA). The Developed Oldowan contains broadly the same range of artifacts as the Oldowan *sensu stricto*, but with greater emphasis on large, battered pieces (e.g., spheroids), scrapers, and proto-bifaces. The Karari and Acheulean Industries contain new artifact classes made on large flake blanks (Karari scrapers in the Karari Industry; handaxes and cleavers in the Acheulean; Harris and Isaac 1976; Isaac and Harris 1997). Developed Oldowan sites overlap the Acheulean in time and space within Africa, and may represent activity variants of this industry (Clark 1970). These industries clearly developed from the Oldowan, but are distinguished from it technologically and temporally and so are beyond the scope of this review. Here the term Oldowan only refers to the technology from 1.6 to 2.6 my, exclusive of the Developed Oldowan.

History of research

Research in the first half of the 20th century focused on constructing regional cultural-historical sequences (Clark 1970; Toth and Schick 1986). Crude "pebble tools" were documented in North Africa, East Africa, and South Africa (Biberson

1967; Clark 1970; Leakey 1935; Toth and Schick 1986); however, the term "Oldowan" was first applied to artifacts from the oldest layers at Olduvai Gorge, Tanzania and from Kanjera and Kanam West on the Homa Peninsula, Kenya (Leakey 1935). The practice of exposing large, horizontal surfaces to investigate spatial patterning of archaeological materials and relate these to prehistoric behavior was introduced to Africa by the Leakeys in their Acheulean excavations at Olorgesailie, Kenya in the 1940s (Isaac 1977) and became the standard in subsequent stone age research (e.g., Clark 1969; Isaac 1977; Leakey 1971). From the later 1960s research orientation shifted toward generating and testing hypotheses, and researchers began to consider Oldowan behavior in broader environmental and adaptive contexts (Binford 1981; Isaac 1984; Potts 1988). "Actualistic" studies, including artifact replication and use feasibility studies, studies of resource availability in different modern ecosystems, and applications of ethnoarchaeological data to the past (Chapter 2) emerged as important sources for generating data to interpret the paleoanthropological record (Blumenschine 1986; Bunn et al. 1988; Capaldo 1998; O'Connell et al. 1990; Selvaggio 1998; Sept 1994, 2001; Stahl 1984; Tappen 1995, 2001). Investigation of Plio-Pleistocene archaeological sites through excavation of relatively dense artifact distributions (sometimes called "maxi-sites") continued, but new research strategies emerged, including: (1) excavation of "mini-sites" believed to represent a single or few episodes of hominin activity; (2) "scatter between the patches" surface surveys which sought to investigate hominin activities from a landscape perspective, documenting areas of high hominin activity as well as the lower density scatters between them; and (3) dispersed, generally small-scale excavations of "landscape distributions" of archaeological material, also attempting to investigate hominin discard behavior beyond the bounds of single sites (Blumenschine and Masao 1991; Bunn et al. 1980; Isaac, ed., 1997; Isaac and Harris 1978; Isaac et al. 1981; Kroll 1994; Leakey 1971; Potts 1994; Potts et al. 1999; Stern 1993, 1994). The paleo-landscape approach may help to assess the degree of spatial focus of hominin discard behavior and investigate the relationship between discard and resource distribution (Blumenschine and Peters 1998; Potts 1994; Potts et al. 1999).

Oldowan Technological Characteristics

Artifact types and classification

Mary Leakey published the first formal description of Oldowan tools from Bed I and lower Bed II Olduvai Gorge, Tanzania (Leakey 1966, 1971), creating a typology that is still referenced. Flakes were produced by using one stone (a hammerstone) to knock flakes off of another (a core) in a technique termed hard hammer percussion. Cores were sometimes set on an anvil and struck from above, driving flakes off both ends in a procedure termed bipolar percussion. Stones may also have been thrown against a hard substrate, as has been argued for quartzite cores from Sterkfontein, South Africa (Kuman 1998). In Leakey's typology, hominin-modified lithics fall into three groups: tools; utilized material; and debitage. The tool category is further subdivided into heavy-duty (e.g., choppers, scrapers) and light-duty (e.g. retouched flakes) tools based on whether their mean diameter exceeds or is less than 50 mm (Leakey 1971; Schick and Toth 1993; Toth 1985; Figure 3.2). Artifacts shaped or damaged through use – hammerstones, anvils, or flakes with incidental edge damage – were termed utilized pieces. Unmodified flakes, flake fragments, and other knapping debris were termed debitage (debris). Manuports were natural stones transported and discarded without modification. Leakey believed that Oldowan hominins shaped their tools with a clear idea of the desired end product, and that different tool forms were used for different tasks. More recently, it has been argued that the Oldowan was a simple but effective method of producing sharp flakes from stones, and that flakes, not cores, were often the desired end product (Keeley and Toth 1981; Potts 1991; Toth 1985, 1987). Rather than following a mental template, Oldowan hominins relied on simple spatial concepts

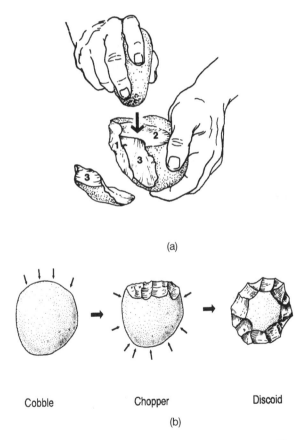

(a)

Cobble   Chopper   Discoid

(b)

Figure 3.2. (a) The production of flakes through hard hammer percussion. The resultant core form is a chopper in Mary Leakey's (1971) typology. After Schick and Toth (1993:121). (b) Much of the variation in Oldowan core forms is continuous. Here sequential removal of flakes around the perimeter of a cobble transforms it from a chopper to a discoid. After Potts (1993:61)

to coordinate flake production (Wynn 1981; Wynn and McGrew 1989). Core form was strongly influenced by the size and shape of raw material, its flaking characteristics and flaking extent (Potts 1991; Toth 1985). While Leakey's (1971) terms are still used in discussing ESA artifact assemblages, Isaac's terminology (e.g., Isaac 1984; Isaac et al. 1981) avoids assumptions about artifact usage. In his scheme, stones from which flakes have been removed are termed "flaked pieces" (FPs), while flakes and other forms of flaking debris are termed "detached pieces" (DPs).

Issac's typology/ artifact naming convention

Stone tool function

Assessing the function of Oldowan artifacts is an indirect exercise. The co-occurrence of artifacts and fossils at localities such as DK, FLK NN, FLK, and FLK N at Bed I Olduvai Gorge have long been thought to reflect hominin processing of animal tissue (Leakey 1971). However, a direct relationship between artifacts and bones was only established with detailed, taphonomically oriented studies of Oldowan fauna (e.g., Bunn 2001; Bunn and Kroll 1986; Potts 1988) Though disagreement remains over methodology (Bunn and Kroll 1986; Potts 1987), there is consensus that cut marks on bone reflect butchery and meat removal (Bunn 1981; Potts and Shipman 1981). Combined with percussion damage reflecting marrow extraction (Blumenschine 1995; Oliver 1994) they demonstrate hominin processing of animal carcasses with stone artifacts. Processing of faunal materials remains the single clear example of Oldowan artifact function. Otherwise, replicated artifacts have been used to assess the feasibility of carrying out tasks observed among living hunter-gatherers, such as woodworking, hide-slitting and scraping, butchery, and nut- and bone-cracking (Jones 1981; Schick and Toth 1993; Toth 1997). Many butchery and woodworking tasks were best conducted with simple flakes, highlighting the importance of DPs within the Oldowan. Some FPs were well suited for heavy-duty activities, such as wood-chopping and bone-breaking. Though the processing of an array of plant and animal tissues was possible, there is little direct evidence linking Oldowan artifacts to specific tasks other than butchery and bone-breaking. Microwear analysis of a small sample of 1.5 my Karari artifacts from Koobi Fora has shown that hominins (presumably *H. erectus*) were cutting meat, processing soft, siliceous plant materials (grasses or reeds), and working wood (Keeley and Toth 1981). Phytoliths recovered from the edges of handaxes from the roughly coeval site of Peninj, Tanzania also suggest woodworking (Dominguez-Rodrigo et al. 2001). This implies that hominins were making tools with other tools, a behavior rarely if ever observed among great apes (McGrew 1992). It also highlights that some (perhaps a substantial proportion of) ESA material culture was made of wood and other perishable materials.

Early Stone Age tool industry may be composed of wood?

Degree of technological variability

Research at localities other than Olduvai Gorge has underscored the variability in Oldowan technology (Roche et al. 1999; Semaw et al. 1997) in terms of reduction sequences, proportions of different tool "types," raw material utilization, and perceived degree of technological "competency" (e.g., Chavaillon 1976; Kibunjia 1994; Kibunjia et al. 1992; Roche 1989; Roche et al. 1999). This has led some to posit a *pre-Oldowan* "pre-Oldowan" phase in the archaeological record from 2.0 to 2.5 my, char- [*pre-Oldowan phase*] acterized by a less sophisticated approach to artifact production. For example, Kibunjia (1994) has argued that assemblages older than 2.0 my should be placed in the Omo Industrial Complex to highlight differences in flake production and technical competency before and after 2.0 my. Recently, Roche (Roche et al. 1999) emphasized the high degree of variability in technological competency in assemblages older than 2.0 my, arguing that later assemblages show more uniform evidence of a sophisticated grasp of flake production combined with refined motor precision and coordination. Others argue that archaeological sites from 1.6 to 2.6 my evince the same understanding of stone fracture mechanics and competency in flake production (Ludwig and Harris 1998; Semaw 2000; Semaw et al. 1997). These researchers have noted that hominins from ca. 2.6 my sites at Gona, Ethiopia had an understanding of stone fracture mechanics as sophisticated as that seen at ca. 1.8 my sites at Bed I Olduvai, Tanzania. Because assessment of assemblage "sophistication" is subjective, and differences due to blank shape, raw material type, and duration of flaking are important determinants of assemblage variation, there does not yet seem to be a compelling reason to erect different facies or industries for the first million years of the archaeological record.

Raw material selectivity

Oldowan hominins used a variety of lithic raw materials (Table 3.1). Quartz dominates the Fejej, Omo Shungura Fm, Nyabusosi, and Sterkfontein artifact samples. At Bed I Olduvai quartzite and several types of igneous rock (e.g., basalt, trachyandesite, nephelinite) were used. At Ain Hanech and El-Kherba, artifacts were predominantly made of limestone and flint (Sahnouni et al. 2002). At most other Oldowan sites the dominant raw material(s) tend to be locally available igneous rocks. Chert is a common, though low-frequency, element in the Oldowan raw material repertoire. At the assemblage level, raw material variation is limited by local availability of appropriately sized raw materials with suitable fracture properties. It is clear that Oldowan hominins preferred hard, fine-grained raw materials that fractured well when impacted (Isaac and Harris 1997; Leakey 1971; Toth 1985). Sites were often located at or near raw material sources, frequently stream channel conglomerates (Table 3.1), and hominins sometimes selected raw materials in the frequency they occurred in these conglomerates (Isaac, ed., 1997; Schick and Toth 1993). Several sites hint at preferential use of specific raw materials. At the East Gona sites EG10 and EG12 in Ethiopia hominins appear to have selected one raw material (trachyte) over others (Semaw 2000; Semaw et al. 1997). The small (n = 258) artifact sample from the nearby site of OGS-7 includes 12 percent chert debitage (Semaw et al. 2003). Chert is a rare element in the local conglomerates and so may have been selectively utilized and transported by hominins. At the Bed I Olduvai sites, Leakey (1971) found that heavy-duty tools (FPs) were commonly made of lava, while quartzite frequently dominated the light-duty tool, utilized flake,

Material character by preferred Oldowan hominin site location

and debitage (DP) categories. The Bed I manuport sample is dominated by lava stones (Kimura 2002; Potts 1988). This may suggest that quartzite was used somewhat differently than lava; transported pieces were flaked relatively rapidly, with percussion leading to the disintegration of cores and the production of many flakes and core fragments. These sharp shards may have been preferred for light-duty cutting tasks. The lack of the appropriate amount of lava debitage to account for the cores at many sites may indicate that lava cores were flaked elsewhere before being deposited on site and that lava core forms may have been preferred for certain heavy-duty tasks (Leakey 1971).

Raw material transport

While hominins throughout the Stone Age relied on local raw materials for tool manufacture, there is an increase in the maximum transport distance in industries following the Oldowan (Isaac 1977; Potts 1994; Rogers et al. 1994; Schick and Toth 1993). Transport distance provides information on hominin ranging behavior. While it is clear that Oldowan hominins regularly transported stone, the sourcing of raw materials has rarely been accomplished. Transport distances of several kilometers have been suggested for the Omo Shungura Fm archaeological sites (Merrick and Merrick 1976), but shorter distances are also a possibility (Rogers et al. 1994). The three published KBS Member sites sampled at Koobi Fora are thought to have been several kilometers from the nearest source of raw material (Isaac 1976; Isaac and Harris 1978; Toth 1997). However, this estimate is based on negative evidence: no appropriately sized stream gravels have thus far been found in the paleochannel deposits around the sites. Use of raw materials not found in local drainages at OGS-7 and Kanjera South are indicative of transport, though distance estimates have not yet been determined (Braun, pers. comm. May 2003; Semaw et al. 2003).

The most secure transport distances for the Oldowan are currently from Olduvai Gorge, Tanzania (Hay 1976; Leakey 1971). Lava was mainly used in the form of rounded cobbles, derived from conglomerates in alluvial fan deposits south of the gorge. The nephelinite, derived from the volcano Sadiman, was probably available within a few kilometers of the Oldowan sites. Naibor Soit, an inselberg of tabular quartzite widely used in Bed I and lower Bed II times, lies within 2–3 km of most of the archaeological occurrences (Hay 1976). This provides one of the few truly secure transport distances for the entire Oldowan. Kelogi gneiss is a rare element in several of the larger artifact samples (e.g., DK I and FLK Zinj) and was transported 8–10 km from its source near the Side Gorge (Hay 1976). Results from Bed I Olduvai thus demonstrate that hominins used a variety of raw materials from highly localized outcrops (Naibor Soit quartzite), relatively more widespread conglomerates (e.g., Sadiman nephelinite) and rare lithologies drawn from farther afield (Kelogi gneiss). Most artifacts were probably derived from sources within 2–3 km of a site.

Further evidence of transport comes from technological analysis of stone assemblages from Koobi Fora and Olduvai. By analyzing the range and characteristics of cores and flakes, Toth (1985, 1987, 1997) has demonstrated that some materials were flaked before they were introduced to the site, some were flaked on the site, and some materials were removed from the site after flaking. Analysis of flake types recovered from KBS and Okote Member excavations shows that flakes from later stages of core reduction are best represented archaeologically. This indicates that hominins were importing and flaking cores on site that had been previously worked elsewhere. In Bed I Olduvai there are discrepancies between the number of FPs and DPs of different raw material types, and detailed study has shown that there are no corresponding cores for flakes of particular raw materials, or that the number of flakes is too low to account for the number of flake scars on cores (Kimura 2002; Potts 1988).

Habitual transport may extend back to the first appearance of artifacts at 2.6 my. The Hata Member of the Bouri Formation in the Middle Awash, Ethiopia provides evidence for lithic transport at 2.5 my (de Heinzelin et al. 1999). The ancient lake margin zone lacked stream channel conglomerates and volcanic outcrops. Surface or *in situ* artifacts are rare, and low-density scatters of *in situ* fossils with cut marks and percussion damage occur without associated artifacts, suggesting that artifacts were transported away from the points of faunal utilization.

By at least 2.0 my hominins moved lithic materials over the landscape. Artifacts derived from multiple raw material sources, were worked at multiple points on the landscape, and were sometimes deposited in quantity at relatively restricted areas that we now designate as "sites." This suggests that the Oldowan was not simply an expedient technology; the repeated carrying of artifacts for use at different points on the landscape may reflect pressure to curate or economize based on current or projected need for stone (Bamforth 1986; Binford 1979; Odell 1996; but see Brantingham 2003).

Who Made the Oldowan Tools?

Historically Oldowan tool usage has been linked to the genus *Homo* (Leakey 1971; Leakey et al. 1964; Stanley 1992). *H. erectus* (*H. ergaster* to some) was a stone tool-maker, and some of the Oldowan sites between 1.6 and 1.9 my were probably produced by this taxon. *H. habilis sensu lato* or one of the constituent species therein (Wood 1992) was likely ancestral to *H. erectus* and thus also a stone tool-maker. The oldest secure date for any early *Homo* specimen is 2.33 my, but fragmentary material possibly attributable to *Homo* is known as far back as 2.5 my (e.g., KNM-BC1; Hill et al. 1992; Wood 1992). Whether the oldest Oldowan occurrences can be attributed to a late australopithecine (*A. garhi*; Asfaw et al. 1999) or an early member of the genus *Homo* is as yet uncertain.

Oldowan Site Formation

Oldowan sites consist of artifact concentrations of varying density, sometimes with associated faunal material (Table 3.1). Bone weathering and object refitting studies suggest that hominins visited certain favored locales intermittently but repeatedly, and materials in discrete (several inch thick) layers may have taken a decade to accumulate and be buried (Bunn and Kroll 1986; Kroll 1994; Potts 1988). Sites where archaeological materials are dispersed through a foot or more of sediment, or where archaeological layers are stratigraphically stacked (e.g., DKI, FLK NN I, FLK I, and FLK N I at Bed I Olduvai) are indicative of locales that remained attractive to hominins over tens or hundreds of years (Kroll 1994; Leakey 1971; Potts 1988). The density of archaeological material can vary dramatically (Harris and Capaldo 1993; Potts 1991; Rogers et al. 1994), suggesting variation in hominin discard behavior that presumably reflects resource distribution and landscape use (Schick 1987). Excavations tend to be small (Table 3.1) and the bounds of the archaeological concentration have typically not been reached (Kroll 1994). A variety of behavioral interpretations for these accumulations have been put forth, the most influential of which are summarized here.

Home base hypothesis

Based on excavations in Bed I and lower Bed II Olduvai Gorge, Leakey (1971) recognized four categories of sites: *living floors* (dense artifact and fossil accumulations with a vertical distribution of only a few inches); *butchery or kill sites* (artifacts associated with a large mammal skeleton or the skeletons of several smaller mammals); *sites with diffused material* (i.e., a substantial vertical dispersion of archaeological material); and *stream channel sites* (cultural debris in fluvial deposits). The living floors were interpreted as the campsites of early hunter-gatherers, and her interpretation of activities at these sites was strongly influenced by the work on the Kalahari San by DeVore, Lee, and others (Lee and DeVore, eds., 1976; see Chapters 2, 14). She envisioned small groups with enough adult males to hunt, scavenge from carnivore kills, and protect dependents from other hominin groups and carnivores. Plant food provided the bulk of the calories, with small mammals, reptiles, fish, snails, grubs, and insects supplementing the diet. Sites varied in the density of cultural material, with the large accumulation of artifacts and fauna on the FLK Zinj living floor being quite exceptional. Several sites were believed to provide evidence of structures (see Chapter 2). Evidence of Oldowan hominin hunting proficiency included driving large mammals into swamps (based on the skeletons of a deinothere and an elephant associated with artifacts) and dispatching antelope with blows to the head (based on several antelope crania from FLK N I with depressed fractures).

Isaac concurred that the dense scatters of artifacts and fossils represented Plio-Pleistocene base camps, and subsequently used the expression "type C" or "home base" to refer to them (Isaac 1976, 1978, 1983a; Isaac and Harris 1978). His home base hypothesis incorporated elements that distinguish hunter-gatherer and ape adaptations: use of a central place from which hominins dispersed and returned on a daily basis; a sexual division of labor whereby males hunted or scavenged for animal tissue and females gathered plant food resources; delayed consumption and transport of food to the base where food-sharing and social activities took place. Food-sharing was central to this behavioral complex and provided the selective milieu for enhanced cognition, language development, and cultural rules such as marriage systems. After articulating this hypothesis, Isaac and colleagues set out to test its underlying assumptions with continued fieldwork at Koobi Fora (Bunn et al. 1980; Isaac 1981, 1984; Isaac and Harris 1997; Kroll 1994; Schick 1997; Stern 1993, 1994), comparative study with material from Olduvai Gorge (Bunn 1986; Bunn and Kroll 1986), and actualistic research investigating foraging opportunities for plant foods (Sept 1986, 2001; Vincent 1985) and scavengable carcasses (Blumenschine 1986, 1987). Taphonomic analysis of the Bed I Olduvai collections by Potts and Shipman (Potts 1984, 1988, 1991; Potts and Shipman 1981; Shipman 1983, 1986) and an analysis of ethnographic butchery data, carnivore kill and den site data and the preliminary faunal information presented in Leakey (1971) by Binford (1981, 1985, 1988) provided additional critiques of the home base hypothesis.

The shift in research strategies toward testing the integrity of archaeological accumulations and proving rather than assuming a behavioral relationship between fauna and artifacts at Oldowan sites (e.g., Bunn 1981, 1983, 1986; Oliver 1994; Petraglia and Potts 1994; Potts 1983, 1988; Potts and Shipman 1981; Schick 1997) was a critical step in Oldowan studies. This work demonstrated that hominins and carnivores both damaged bones, but that the majority of the bones at sites like FLK Zinj were transported and deposited by hominins. Though Isaac (1981, 1983a, 1983b, 1984) reformulated the home base hypothesis, using the less emotive term "central place foraging," he and his colleagues viewed the archaeological record at Olduvai and Koobi Fora as consistent with the elements of the home base hypothesis: tool use, food transport, meat consumption on a scale allowing sharing (e.g., Bunn 2001; Bunn and Ezzo 1993; Bunn and Kroll 1986), possibly a sexual division of labor associated with pair bonding, and the existence of sites where hominins would come together and food debris and discarded artifacts would accumulate (Isaac 1981). The home base hypothesis still has proponents (e.g., Bunn 2001; Clark 1996) and it inspired a recent variant described below (the resource defense hypothesis). Several alternatives to the home base hypothesis have been developed and are also discussed here.

Carnivore kill sites and routed foraging

Binford (1981, 1984, 1985, 1988) was an early and vociferous critic of the home base hypothesis. He argued that it was a post-hoc interpretation lacking critical examination of its fundamental assumptions, such as the causal link between fossils and artifacts at Oldowan sites. Binford argued that the Oldowan artifacts and fossils needed to be "linked" through middle range theory to modern processes relevant to the formation of the archaeological record and the traces that these processes produce. In this view, actualistic experiments and naturalistic and ethnographic observations of the modern world provide the connection between specific processes and resultant traces that can be used to interpret archaeological residues. Rather than home bases, Binford (1981) argued that many sites were carnivore kills that had been picked over by hominins, providing such meager returns (some marrow or scraps of flesh) that sharing was unlikely. There was no transport of faunal material and hominins were unable to compete with contemporary large carnivores. He modified his view on transport somewhat in the "routed foraging model," in which hominins were recurrently drawn to fixed resources (stone outcrops, stands of trees acting as midday resting sites) where, with relatively minor transport, carcass parts would have accumulated over time (Binford 1984).

[handwritten marginalia:] Binford's suggestion based on most theoretical/ett based archaeology

Stone cache hypothesis

Based on his study of Olduvai Bed I fauna and artifacts Potts (1983, 1984, 1988, 1991, 1994) argued that stone in the form of both artifacts and manuports was deposited at various points in the foraging range of hominins. These "caches" became secondary sources of raw material, whether established consciously or as an unconscious by-product of hominin discard behavior (e.g., stones dropped at a carcass, underneath a recurrently visited shade tree). As debris accumulated at particular drop points, it drew hominins foraging nearby as need for stone dictated. Carcasses obtained by either hunting or scavenging would be disarticulated and transported away from the death site to the nearest cache for processing. Computer simulation indicated that the production and use of multiple caches across a given range was more energetically efficient (considering stone and carcass transport costs) than using a single home base. Potts' analysis of Oldowan site formation suggested that: sites were used intermittently over years; carnivore competition on site was intense; and hominin processing of fauna was hasty and incomplete. Sites were viewed as processing areas and lithic raw material stores rather than home bases. Social activities and sleeping would likely have taken place "off site" and in Potts' view no specific statements about food-sharing could be made. For Potts (1991, 1993) the key adaptation of the Oldowan was the establishment of novel transport behaviors, whereby food and stone from disparate sources were brought together.

Favored place hypothesis

Schick (1987; Schick and Toth 1993) also proposed that large archeological accumulations could act as secondary sources of stone raw material, but her model of site formation emphasized passive processes to a greater extent than the stone cache model. The anticipated need for stone tools led to the habitual transport of lithic material. Over time, occasional discard of lithics at "favored places" (frequently visited rich foraging areas where hominins would consume foods, rest, carry out social activities, sleep) would lead to the passive accumulation of a local store of raw material. This would depress the need for lithic transport while foraging in the immediate area and, over time, stone and debris from multiple butchery events would form dense archaeological concentrations. This model accounts for variations in site size (depending on visitation frequency and relative lithic import-export imbalance), for the occurrence of faunal remains with artifactual damage but without associated artifacts (Bunn 1994; de Heinzelin et al. 1999; e.g., lithics exported due to a lack of local raw material) and for the presence of stockpiles of stone greatly exceeding need as a store of material (e.g., lithic assemblage at FLK Zinj was likely in a rich, recurrently visited foraging area).

guild – n – an association of persons sharing the same interests

Resource defense model

Rose and Marshall (1996) considered Oldowan hominin carnivory from the perspective of nonhuman primate behavior and the likely characteristics of the Plio-Pleistocene predator guild. They noted that primates respond to predator pressure through increased sociality, cooperative protection against predation, and cooperative defense of resources. In their view meat from hunted and scavenged carcasses was transported to focal sites, places with fixed, defendable resources (trees, water, plant foods, sleeping sites). Group defense allowed focal sites to be used regularly for multiple diurnal and nocturnal activities, leading to the gradual accumulation of archaeological debris. The model resembles Isaac's home base model in many ways (delayed consumption, food transport to a central place, and potentially extensive food-sharing) without the emphasis on a sexual division of labor.

hominid response to primate aggression

Riparian woodlands model/refuging

Based on actualistic research at the Serengeti and Ngorongoro Crater, Tanzania, Blumenschine (1986, 1987) and colleagues (Blumenschine et al. 1994; Cavallo and Blumenschine 1989; Marean 1989) postulated that Oldowan hominins filled a "scavenging niche" based on consuming marrow, brains, and scraps of flesh from kills abandoned by large felids during the late dry season in riparian woodlands. Hominin theft of small antelopes cached by leopards in trees, as well as the potentially substantial residues of sabertooth felid predation of megafauna, might have provided additional woodlands-based scavenging opportunities. When yields were low and predation risk high hominins would have transported carcass parts a short distance to stands of trees where food could be consumed in safety ("refuging;" Blumenschine 1991; Isaac 1983a). Active sharing would not be expected, but tolerated scrounging might have occurred. If carcass yield and processing equipment needs were high, carcass parts might have been transported to a previously visited refuge site with remaining usable stone. Food-sharing would be more likely in the latter scenario, but would not have been the goal of the foraging strategy (as assumed by the home base hypothesis). Recurrent visits to such a site could have led to the accumulation of artifacts and bones. Transport distances were not expected to be great in the refuge model.

Near-kill accumulations

O'Connell (1997; O'Connell et al. 2002) has pointed out that the fossil assemblage and setting of some Oldowan sites (e.g., FLK Zinj) share characteristics with faunal accumulations formed near hunting blinds used by Hadza hunter-gatherers in Tanzania. The Hadza near-kill accumulations form in shaded areas near perennial water sources contain the remains of many individual animals, include taxa from diverse habitats, and are dominated by head and limb bones. O'Connell believes that Oldowan sites represent near-kill points on the landscape where hunting and scavenging opportunities were concentrated enough to allow the formation of large, taxonomically diverse assemblages over time.

These models provide a range of scenarios for how Oldowan site formation may have occurred. Binford's (1981) "carnivore kill site" model has largely been discarded. It was based on flawed skeletal part data (Bunn and Kroll 1986), and carcasses ravaged to the degree described by Binford occur today in highly competitive, dangerous contexts where utilizable residues are rare (Blumenschine 1987; Blumenschine et al. 1994). Researchers agree that lithic transport occurred, and the remaining models all postulate recurrent visitation of favored points or habitats on the landscape with some faunal transport. Several models (favored place, resource defense model) recall the home base hypothesis, without assuming a sexual division of labor or pair-bonding between males and females. Transport distance was short for the routed foraging, refuge, and near-kill accumulation models and unstated but potentially longer in the others. Several other critical variables for assessing the socio-economic function of Oldowan sites remain in dispute: the scale of returns from faunal acquisition (small returns imply little or no sharing, while large returns and active sharing are a must for the home base and resource defense models) and the degree of predator risk to hominins, particularly on site (high according to the stone cache model, low according to the others). These points are addressed below, with particular reference to the well-studied Oldowan assemblage at FLK Zinj.

Interpreting the Oldowan Assemblage at the FLK Zinj Site

Faunal transport distance

The largest and best-studied Oldowan faunal assemblage is from FLK Zinj, including approximately 46,000 bones (excluding microfauna), representing approximately 40 individual animals from at least 16 taxa (Bunn and Kroll 1986; Potts 1988). Isaac (1978) and others (Rose and Marshall 1996) argued that the size, taxonomic diversity, and habitat preferences of the animals suggest that hominins were transporting carcasses from multiple habitats to a central location. Though not specified, the implication is that transport distances frequently reached a kilometer or more. In the routed foraging, refuge, and near-kill models of site formation the assumption is that faunal transport was limited to several hundred meters (O'Connell 1997). Carcass encounter rates and transport decisions vary with prey body size (Bunn et al. 1988; O'Connell et al. 1990). Of relevance here is the expected transport distance for medium (wildebeest-sized) mammals. Medium-sized mammals are the most common in the Zinj assemblage and may frequently have been scavenged (Blumenschine 1995; Bunn and Ezzo 1993; Potts 1988). O'Connell et al. (2002) noted that Hadza hunter-gatherers armed with bows and hunting from blinds can form large, taxonomically diverse bone assemblages without long-distance transport. However, this may not be an appropriate analog for the frequency and spatial focus of scavenging opportunities provided by large carnivores, which is likely what Oldowan hominin medium-sized carcass acquisition depended on. Carnivores would have to have killed approximately 30 medium-sized mammals within a few hundred meters of the FLK Zinj locale over a period of perhaps 5–10 years (Potts 1988) for the Zinj assemblage to have formed through short-distance transport. This degree of kill concentration is generally inconsistent with large carnivore and landscape taphonomic studies in modern savannas (Behrensmeyer et al. 1979; Behrensmeyer and Dechant Boaz 1980; Blumenschine 1986; Foley 1987; Hill 1975; Kruuk 1972; Potts 1988; Schaller 1972; Tappen 1995, 2001). In the rare occurrences where catastrophic mortality concentrates carcasses in one place or carnivores make a mass kill, prey taxonomic diversity is low (Capaldo and Peters 1995; Kruuk 1972; Schaller 1972). So the size and taxonomic diversity of the FLK Zinj assemblage is suggestive of at least some transport events greater than a few hundred meters.

On-site competition

Potts (1984, 1988, 1996) has used several lines of evidence to argue that carnivores limited hominin on-site activities at Bed I Olduvai. Carnivore tooth marks occur on bones from each archaeological level analyzed by Potts, and some bones exhibit damage attributable to a large, bone-crunching carnivore like the spotted hyena (*Crocuta crocuta*). Small, immature carnivore remains are more common than expected in the environment in general, potentially reflecting individuals killed in on-site competition for animal tissue. Complete long bones lacking tool marks are not uncommon, and may indicate hasty hominin faunal processing and the abandonment by hominins of resources attractive to carnivores.

Researchers generally agree that the Bed I zooarchaeological assemblages show extensive carnivore damage. But measures of the intensity of bone damage at FLK Zinj suggest that carnivore ravaging was *extensive* but not *intensive* (Blumenschine 1995; Blumenschine and Marean 1993; Capaldo 1997; Oliver 1994). A wide range of skeletal parts show cut marks, and hammerstone processing was pervasive and thorough. Very little long bone fragmentation is attributable to carnivore activity (Oliver 1994). The representation of axial elements and long bone epiphyses is high relative to controlled spotted hyena feeding experiments (see below), suggesting that on-site competition for these elements was not intense (Blumenschine and Marean 1993; Capaldo 1997; Marean and Spencer 1991; Marean et al. 1992). Finally, long bones may have been abandoned by hominins satiated with flesh, and their survival on site may be further indication of low competition with carnivores (Capaldo 1997; Dominguez-Rodrigo 2002). Similarly at Kanjera South, the frequency of skeletal parts unlikely to survive intensive carnivore ravaging is consistent with faunal processing without a great deal of on-site competition (Plummer et al. 1999).

Carcass completeness and faunal acquisition strategies

Because resource availability depends on the timing of access, some researchers have relied on the relative frequency of body part representation (skeletal part profiles) to assess whether hominins had access to complete animal carcasses (Blumenschine 1995; Bunn 2001; Bunn and Kroll 1986; Capaldo 1997; Dominguez-Rodrigo 1997, 2002; Lupo and O'Connell 2002; O'Connell et al. 2002; Oliver 1994; Potts 1988; Selvaggio 1998). Early access, either through confrontational scavenging (driving carnivores off a nearly complete or complete kill) or hunting, provides most or all of a carcass. Late access through passive scavenging provides a smaller selection of carcass parts, often limited to within-bone nutrients (marrow and/or brains; Binford 1981; Blumenschine 1986). Oldowan faunal assemblages from Olduvai Gorge are frequently dominated by meat-bearing limb bones and skull fragments. This finding has been used to argue that hominins had early access to relatively complete carcasses and were disarticulating limbs and skulls for transport from death sites, thereby reducing transport costs and maximizing the utility of the transported remains (Bunn and Kroll 1986; Bunn et al. 1988). Following this line of reasoning, the scavenging of incomplete carcasses would yield a profile with fewer "high utility" skeletal parts than seen in the Olduvai assemblages. However, it is now clear that the action of large carnivores, particularly spotted hyenas, can lead to a "limb and head"-dominated skeletal assemblage even if axial bones were initially present. In experiments in natural and captive settings, spotted hyenas presented with a range of skeletal elements preferentially consumed grease-rich vertebrae and ribs, with innominates, scapulae, and foot bones also being differentially consumed in some experiments (Capaldo 1997, 1998; Marean et al. 1992). This suggests that carnivore ravaging of hominin-transported faunal elements could produce a "limb and head"-dominated skeletal assemblage, even if axial elements had originally been present. The carcass transport decisions made by modern hunter-gatherers also do not neatly fit a "limb and head" transport model (Monahan 1998; O'Connell et al. 1990; Oliver 1993; Yellen 1977), though hunter-gatherer cooking practices (particularly boiling bones in pots to extract grease and adhering meat scraps) provide a transport influence that would not have existed in the remote past. Some researchers have continued to rely on skeletal part frequencies to assess the timing of hominin access to carcasses (e.g., Brantingham 1998a, 1998b), but the issue of equifinality (multiple pathways to the same end result) argues that skeletal part data alone should not be used for this task.

The timing and agents involved in carcass utilization can also be studied through bone surface damage (Binford et al. 1988; Blumenschine 1988, 1995; Blumenschine and Marean 1993; Bunn 2001; Capaldo 1997, 1998; Dominguez-Rodrigo 1997, 1999, 2001, 2002; Lupo and O'Connell 2002; Marean and Spencer 1991; Marean et al. 1992; Oliver 1994; Selvaggio 1994, 1998). Carnivores and tool-wielding hominins process carcasses in different ways. Carnivores strip meat off of bones (leaving tooth marks), gnaw on bone ends (epiphyses) to access blood and grease, and, if the epiphyses are destroyed, attack shaft cylinders from the ends to access the fatty marrow (Brain 1981). Large cats such as lions (*Panthera leo*) can crack bones from impala-sized and smaller prey, but are limited to viscera and flesh of wildebeest and larger taxa (Blumenschine 1987). Spotted hyenas have specialized jaw and tooth morphology and are exceptional among living carnivores in their ability to completely consume the edible tissue of medium (wildebeest)-sized prey, including breaking long bone shafts to access marrow (Brain 1981; Lewis 1997).

Oldowan hominins lacked the meat-shearing and bone-crunching abilities of carnivores, but could carry out the same functions with their simple stone tool kit (Schick and Toth 1993). Sharp stone flakes were used to slice off meat and disarticulate carcass parts, sometimes leaving cut marks. Within-bone nutrients were accessed by placing bones on an anvil and striking them with a hammerstone. Resultant percussion marks include microstriations or pits and grooves containing microstriations (Blumenschine and Selvaggio 1988; Selvaggio 1994). Thus, bone surface damage can inform on the agents involved in bone modification and perhaps the timing of carnivore and hominin access if a dominant sequence of access held throughout the formation of an assemblage. Blumenschine and colleagues (Blumenschine 1988, 1995; Capaldo 1997, 1998; Selvaggio 1994, 1998) used experimental simulations in several modern Serengeti and Ngorongoro habitats to determine criteria sensitive to the timing of hominin and carnivore access to a set of bones. Several different actors were presented the same sets of bones, in an attempt to mimic the "dual patterning" of hominin and carnivore damage to Oldowan archaeological bone. Bones from small and medium-sized mammals were exposed first to carnivores (frequently spotted hyenas) in some experiments and to "hominins" (the researchers processing defleshed carcasses for marrow) in others. In Capaldo's (1997, 1998) whole-bone to carnivore models, bones were defleshed with tools but presented whole to carnivores (spotted hyenas) for consumption. Selvaggio (1998) presented a three-stage simulation, in which carnivore access to the assemblage preceded and followed hominin marrow-processing of bones. This body of work (supported by captive spotted hyena feeding experiments, Blumenschine and Marean 1993; Marean and Spencer 1991; Marean et al. 1992) suggests signatures of access to carcass parts. There were extensive tooth marks on long bones (including 82.6 percent of midshafts) when large carnivores (spotted hyenas and lions) had first access to a fleshed carcass. Midshaft tooth mark frequencies were depressed with hominin first access (10.5 percent in Blumenschine's models, 15.4 percent in Capaldo's), because meat and marrow removal made bone shafts less attractive. In the whole bone to carnivore models, 57.4 percent of midshaft fragments were tooth-marked, reflecting spotted hyena interest in grease and marrow. Spotted hyenas frequently consumed long bone epiphyses and axial elements when scavenging hammer stone-processed bones. When applied to the large FLK Zinj assemblage, three researchers (Blumenschine 1995; Capaldo 1997; Selvaggio 1998) suggested that the high midshaft tooth mark frequencies (57.9 percent), percentage of percussion marks, and deletion of long bone epiphyses were consistent with a three-stage access sequence of large felids defleshing carcasses, hominins removing remnant flesh and marrow-processing bones, and hyena scavenging of epiphyses.

Cut mark data have been interpreted in several ways. Bunn (1986, 2001) suggested that cut mark distribution on limbs from FLK Zinj was similar to that produced by the Hadza, clustering around areas of strong muscle attachments. This suggests that large muscle masses were stripped and consumed by Oldowan hominins. Oliver (1994) produced similar cut mark frequency estimates, and noted that, at least for small mammals and the forelimbs of medium- to large-sized mammals, cut marks were preferentially placed on upper (meat-bearing) elements. But the lack of an experimental framework relating cut mark distribution to flesh yield has led some to suggest that the cut marks at FLK Zinj reflect hominin removal of meat scraps surviving carnivore consumption, i.e. that the cut mark data could still be accommodated within a passive scavenging framework (Binford 1981; Blumenschine 1991, 1995; Capaldo 1997; Selvaggio 1998).

Dominguez-Rodrigo (1997, 2002) has analyzed cut mark data from experimental studies of carcasses with varying amounts of flesh (hominin first access versus hominin scavenging of carcasses partially or completely stripped of meat by lions) to establish a referential model for interpreting hominin meat-processing. He argued that there is a strong relationship between the amount of meat present and cut mark representation, with upper limb elements (humeri and femora) exhibiting the highest cut mark frequencies from defleshing. Carcasses consumed by lions in woodland settings were completely defleshed, leaving few scraps of meat for a scavenging hominin. Applying this referential framework to FLK Zinj, he argued that hominins were stripping substantial amounts of meat from carcasses in addition to marrow-processing, rather than only accessing within-bone nutrients from defleshed felid kills.

In addition to analyzing bone surface damage Oliver (1994) assessed load points and associated fracture surfaces to determine the roles carnivores and hominins played in fracturing long bones at FLK Zinj. Though carnivore tooth marking was common, breakage attributable to carnivore activity was not. This suggested to him that a large, bone-crunching carnivore like the spotted hyena was not a primary modifier of the FLK Zinj assemblage. Cut marks were focused on meat-bearing bones, and hammer stone-induced fracturing of bones was common, thorough, and likely destroyed some epiphyses. Carnivore tooth marking was evenly distributed across meat-bearing and non-meat-bearing bones. Oliver interpreted this overall pattern as reflecting early carcass access with subsequent defleshing and marrow-processing by hominins. Small carnivores scavenged flesh scraps but were unable to crack bones from the hominin residues.

In summary, all researchers agree that bones at FLK Zinj were transported there by hominins and that damage implicates both carnivores and hominins in nutrient extraction. Extensive hominin marrow-processing of limb bones is also generally accepted as is scavenging of hominin refuse by carnivores. The major point of contention is whether hominins accessed fleshy or largely defleshed carcasses, i.e. whether a hominin to carnivore two-stage model or a three-stage (carnivore to hominin to carnivore) model most accurately reflects the predominant mode of faunal use at FLK Zinj. This distinction is significant, because it provides a measure of whether hominins were handling faunal packages able to feed multiple individuals or marrow-processing bones likely to satiate a single individual (Blumenschine 1991; Isaac 1978; Rose and Marshall 1996). Blumenschine and colleagues clearly favor the three-stage model, while other authors generally favor the two-stage model. Several lines of evidence provide tentative support for the two-stage model, at least for FLK Zinj.

The first line of evidence is that bones with high economic value *when fleshed* (vertebrae, ribs, innominates, scapulae) are well represented in the FLK Zinj assemblage (38 percent MNE from Bunn and Kroll 1986; see also Capaldo 1997; Dominguez-Rodrigo 2002; Lupo and O'Connell 2002; Potts 1988). This probably underestimates the number of axial and girdle parts transported to the site because their fragile nature (low structural density) makes them susceptible to compaction (Lyman 1994) and they are often consumed by scavenging carnivores (Capaldo 1997, 1998; Marean et al. 1992). Their frequency likely signals the acquisition of fleshy carcasses by hominins (without a cooking/grease-rendering technology they are of low economic utility defleshed; Lyman 1994; O'Connell et al. 2002). The recovery of bones from every region of the ungulate skeleton in reasonably high proportions at FLK Zinj and other Oldowan sites supports the view that meaty carcass packages were transported to these sites (Bunn and Kroll 1986; Oliver 1994; Plummer et al. 1999; Potts 1988).

Complete long bones occur in many of the Bed I archaeological assemblages (Potts 1988) and may be another indirect indication of hominin access to fleshed carcasses. Carnivores abandon complete bones when satiated from flesh, particularly if group size is small and the prey is not fat-depleted (Bunn and Ezzo 1993; Dominguez-Rodrigo 2002; Potts 1988). The high frequency of complete bones, particularly metapodials (which contain the least marrow of the limb bones) may reflect hominin neglect of some within-bone nutrients due to satiation from flesh (Dominguez-Rodrigo 2002).

The experimental modeling done up to this point by Blumenschine and colleagues has been meticulous and well thought out, but almost certainly does not represent the full range of possible scenarios under which long bone midshafts can be tooth marked, an important pillar of the three-stage model of prey utilization (see also Dominguez-Rodrigo 2002; Lupo and O'Connell 2002). Given the possible range of actors who could have tooth marked the Oldowan faunal assemblages, including felids, hyenids, canids, and the hominins themselves, the confidant application of models using lions and hyenas as the sole tooth-marking agents seems premature. This is particularly true because the quantification of isolated "inconspicuous" tooth marks is an essential element of their methodology (Blumenschine and Marean 1993; Capaldo 1997), yet these marks can be produced by an extremely broad array of taxa (Dominguez-Rodrigo and Piqueras 2003). There are no criteria for attributing tooth marks to taxon, and a framework for inferring carnivore size from tooth marks is only now being developed (Dominguez-Rodrigo and Piqueras 2003; Monahan 1999; Selvaggio 1994; Selvaggio and Wilder 2001). Further, if hominins did not completely consume the carcasses they processed, either because of on-site competition with carnivores (Potts 1988) or satiation (Dominguez-Rodrigo 2002), or if in the course of defleshing carcasses with stone tools they left scraps of flesh on bone midshafts (Dominguez-Rodrigo 1997, 1999), the possibility of midshaft tooth marking occurring *after* hominin processing would exist. This in fact occurred at FLK Zinj. Hammerstone damage preceded tooth marking in 63 of 65 long bone (mostly midshaft) fragments where the order of damage agent could be determined (Oliver 1994).

Finally, while there is some ambiguity with interpreting flesh yield from cut mark frequencies (Lupo and O'Connell 2002), the distribution and frequencies of cut marks documented by Bunn and Kroll (1986) and Oliver (1994) are more consistent with the defleshing of substantial amounts of muscle tissue (Bunn 2001; Dominguez-Rodrigo 1997, 2002; Lupo and O'Connell 2002) than with removal of tissue scraps from passively scavenged felid kills (Dominguez-Rodrigo 1999). The balance of available evidence (reasonably high frequencies of axial and girdle bones and complete long bones, cut mark distribution, and evidence that at least some tooth marking occurred on midshaft fragments *following* hominin processing) suggests that FLK hominins had access to carcasses with substantial amounts of flesh. Bunn and Kroll's (1986) argument that they acquired carcasses through small mammal hunting combined with active scavenging of larger prey is consistent with this conclusion, as is the scavenging of carcasses cached by leopards (Cavallo and Blumenschine 1989) or from catastrophic death assemblages (Capaldo and Peters 1995). However, with the exception of Potts (1988) and Bunn (1986), the above series of studies has sought to explain the formation of an assemblage from a single level of a single site at a single locality – FLK Zinj. Recent research suggests that by approximately 2 my there was considerable variability in the environments used by Oldowan hominins (Plummer and Bishop 1994; Plummer et al. 1999; Sikes 1994). We should expect variation in hominin–faunal interaction, reflecting differences in habitat structure and resource distribution, predator taxonomic composition, and predator to prey ratio among other things. The obvious implication is that assemblages in addition to FLK Zinj need to be carefully scrutinized in order to fully document the breadth and extent of Oldowan carnivory.

Conclusion

Research over the last several decades has provided a wealth of data and often contradictory interpretation regarding Oldowan hominin behavior and the adaptive significance of the first lithic technology. A least effort method to dispense flakes from cores, the Oldowan provided a simple but powerful means to cut, pound, or scrape a wide array of materials in the environment. Technological studies suggest that tool transport was habitual, certainly by 1.9 my but perhaps as far back as 2.6 my. Butchery and consumption of meat and marrow appears to be characteristic of even the oldest Oldowan occurrences (de Heinzelin et al. 1999). Whether the Oldowan represented tool-assisted or tool-dependent foraging at its inception remains unclear, but by ca. 1.9 my the repeated carrying of artifacts for use at different points on the landscape may reflect pressure to curate or economize based on current or projected need for stone. Oldowan sites are distributed across much of Africa by 1.7 my and perhaps into Georgia as well.

The largest, most meaningful assemblages of Oldowan debris are still derived from Mary and Louis Leakey's pioneering work at Olduvai Gorge well over 30 years ago. There is a critical need to expand the sample of Oldowan site assemblages, particularly those preserving archaeological fauna as well as artifacts (Table 3.1). Though sometimes contradictory models of site formation have been proposed, there is a growing consensus on a number of points. Sites were part of complex transport and discard systems, with large assemblages forming where fossil and artifact discard was relatively high. High discard rates may have been more likely in rich, frequently visited foraging areas where the pressure to transport stone was relaxed (Schick 1987). Once established, stone assemblages served as secondary sources of lithic raw material (Potts 1984, 1988; Schick 1987). Transport distances for lithic raw materials were sometimes on the order of several kilometers, but this may represent cumulative movement over several separate transport events. Faunal transport distances almost certainly varied, but for FLK Zinj it seems likely that some transport events were greater than a few hundred meters. In other words, faunal transport may have been more goal-directed than simply seeking the nearest patch of shade. Carnivore modification was extensive but not intensive at FLK Zinj, reflecting a low degree of carnivore competition on site. Hominins appear to have had time to extensively process carcasses, and may have sometimes had food in excess of need (Dominguez-Rodrigo 2002). Thus, while the frequency of Oldowan hominin carnivory is difficult to assess (O'Connell et al. 2002), when carcasses were available at FLK Zinj they may have been in packages of tissue substantial enough to feed multiple individuals. Given the enormous geographic distribution of Oldowan sites (Figure 3.1) and the possibility that more than one taxon produced stone tools, it is reasonable to expect that Oldowan hominin lithic transport, curation strategies, and foraging behaviors varied across time and space, influenced by local ecology and stone tool raw material distribution. The adaptive significance of the first lithic technology has been incompletely explored, particularly at sites older than 2 my. Further detailed research is necessary to more clearly document whether hominins were accessing meaty carcasses over the geographic extent and temporal span of the Oldowan. Such research may provide clues to the frequency of carcass access, the likelihood of substantial sharing of meat, and the evolutionary significance of Oldowan carnivory.

REFERENCES

Asfaw, Berhane, Y. Beyene, S. Semaw, Gen Suwa, T. White, and G. WoldeGabriel, 1991 Fejej: A New Paleoanthropological Research Area in Ethiopia. Journal of Human Evolution 21:137–143.

Asfaw, Berhane, Tim White, Owen Lovejoy, Bruce Latimer, Scott Simpson, and Gen Suwa, 1999 *Australopithecus garhi*: A New Species of Early Hominid from Ethiopia. Science 284:629–635.

Bamforth, Douglas B., 1986 Technological Efficiency and Tool Curation. American Antiquity 51:38–50.

Behrensmeyer, Anna K., and Dorothy E. Dechant Boaz, 1980 The Recent Bones of Amboseli Park, Kenya, in Relation to East African Paleoecology. *In* Fossils in the Making. Anna K. Behrensmeyer and Andrew P. Hill, eds. pp. 72–92. Chicago: University of Chicago Press.

Behrensmeyer, Anna K., David Western and Dorothy E. Dechant Boaz, 1979 New Perspectives in Vertebrate Paleoecology from a Recent Bone Assemblage. Paleobiology 5(1):12–21.

Biberson, P. J., 1967 Some Aspects of the Lower Palaeolithic of Northwest Africa. *In* Background to Evolution in Africa. W. W. Bishop and J. Desmond Clark, eds. pp. 447–475. Chicago: University of Chicago Press.

Binford, Lewis R., 1979 Organization and Formation Processes: Looking at Curated Technologies. Journal of Archaeological Research 35:255–273.

——1981 Bones: Ancient Men and Modern Myths. New York: Academic Press.

——1984 Faunal Remains from Klasies River Mouth. New York: Academic Press.

——1985 Human Ancestors: Changing Views of their Behavior. Journal of Anthropological Archaeology 4:292–327.

——1988 Fact and Fiction about the Zinjanthropus Floor: Data, Arguments and Interpretation. Current Anthropology 29:123–135.

Binford, Lewis R., M. G. L. Mills, and Nancy M. Stone, 1988 Hyena Scavenging Behavior and its Implications for the Interpretation of Faunal Assemblages from FLK 22 (the Zinj Floor) at Olduvai Gorge. Journal of Anthropological Archaeology 7:99–135.

Bishop, L. C., T. Pickering, T. Plummer, and F. Thackeray, 1999 Paleoenvironmental Setting for the Oldowan Industry at Sterkfontein. Paper presented at the XV International Congress of the International Union for Quaternary Research, Durban, South Africa, 1999.

Blumenschine, Robert J. 1986 Early Hominid Scavenging Opportunities: Implications of Carcass Availability in the Serengeti and Ngorongoro Ecosystems. BAR International Series, 283. Oxford: British Archaeological Reports.

——1987 Characteristics of an Early Hominid Scavenging Niche. Current Anthropology 28:383–407.

——1988 An Experimental Model of the Timing of Hominid and Carnivore Influence on Archaeological Bone Assemblages. Journal of Archaeological Science 15:483–502.

——1991 Hominid Carnivory and Foraging Strategies, and the Socio-Economic Function of Early Archaeological Sites. Philosophical Transactions of the Royal Society of London B 334:211–221.

——1995 Percussion Marks, Tooth Marks, and Experimental Determinations of the Timing of Hominid and Carnivore Access to Long Bones at FLK Zinjanthropus, Olduvai Gorge, Tanzania. Journal of Human Evolution 29:21–51.

Blumenschine, Robert J., and Curtis W. Marean, 1993 A Carnivore's View of Archaeological Bone Assemblages. *In* From Bones to Behavior. J. Hudson, ed. pp. 273–300. Occasional Paper 21. Carbondale: Southern Illinois University.

Blumenschine, Robert J., and Fidelis T. Masao, 1991 Living Sites at Olduvai Gorge, Tanzania? Preliminary Landscape Archaeology Results in the Basal Bed II Lake Margin Zone. Journal of Human Evolution 21:451–462.

Blumenschine, Robert J., and Charles R. Peters, 1998 Archaeological Predictions for Hominid Land Use in the Paleo-Olduvai Basin, Tanzania, during Lowermost Bed II times. Journal of Human Evolution 34:565–607.

Blumenschine, Robert J., and Marie M. Selvaggio, 1988 Percussion Marks on Bone Surfaces as a New Diagnostic of Hominid Behavior. Nature 333(6175):763–765.

Blumenschine, Robert J., J. A. Cavallo and S. D. Capaldo, 1994 Competition for Carcasses and Early Hominid Behavioral Ecology: A Case Study and Conceptual Framework. Journal of Human Evolution 27:197–213.

Boesch, Christophe, and Hedwige Boesch-Achermann, 2000 The Chimpanzees of the Tai Forest. Oxford: Oxford University Press.

Brain, C. K., 1981 The Hunters or the Hunted: An Introduction to African Cave Taphonomy. Chicago: University of Chicago Press.

Brantingham, P. Jeffrey, 1998a Hominid–Carnivore Coevolution and Invasion of the Predatory Guild. Journal of Anthropological Archaeology 17:327–353.

——1998b Mobility, Competition, and Plio-Pleistocene Hominid Foraging Groups. Journal of Archaeological Method and Theory 5:57–98.

——2003 A Neutral Model of Stone Raw Material Procurement. American Antiquity 68:487–509.

Brown, F. H., and Patrick N. Gathogo, 2002 Stratigraphic Relation between Lokalalei A and Lokalalei 2C, Pliocene Archaeological Sites in West Turkana, Kenya. Journal of Archaeological Science 29:699–702.

Bunn, Henry T., 1981 Archaeological Evidence for Meat-Eating by Plio-Pleistocene Hominids from Koobi Fora and Olduvai Gorge. Nature 291:574–577.

——1983 Evidence on the Diet and Subsistence Patterns of Plio-Pleistocene Hominids at Koobi Fora, Kenya, and at Olduvai Gorge, Tanzania. *In* Animals and Archaeology, vol. 1: Hunters and their Prey. Juliet Clutton-Brock and Caroline Grigson, eds. pp. 143–148. BAR International Series, 163. Oxford: British Archaeological Reports.

——1986 Patterns of Skeletal Representation and Hominid Subsistence Activities at Olduvai Gorge, Tanzania, and Koobi Fora, Kenya. Journal of Human Evolution 15: 673–690.

——1994 Early Pleistocene Hominid Foraging Strategies along the Ancestral Omo River at Koobi Fora, Kenya. Journal of Human Evolution 27:247–266.

——2001 Hunting, Power Scavenging, and Butchering by Hadza Foragers and by Plio-Pleistocene Homo. *In* Meat-Eating and Human Evolution. Craig B. Stanford and Henry T. Bunn, eds. pp. 199–218. Oxford: Oxford University Press.

Bunn, Henry T., and Joseph A. Ezzo, 1993 Hunting and Scavenging by Plio-Pleistocene Hominids: Nutritional Constraints, Archaeological Patterns, and Behavioural Implications. Journal of Archaeological Science 20:365–398.

Bunn, Henry T., and Ellen M. Kroll, 1986 Systematic Butchery by Plio/Pleistocene Hominids at Olduvai Gorge, Tanzania. Current Anthropology 27:431–452.

Bunn, Henry T., Laurence E. Bartram and Ellen M. Kroll, 1988 Variability in Bone Assemblage Formation from Hadza Hunting, Scavenging, and Carcass Processing. Journal of Anthropological Archaeology 7:412–457.

Bunn, Henry, John W. K. Harris, Glynn Isaac, Zefe Kaufulu, Ellen Kroll, Kathy Schick,

Nicholas Toth, and Anna K. Behrensmeyer, 1980 FxJj50: An Early Pleistocene Site in Northern Kenya. World Archaeology 12(2):109–136.

Capaldo, Salvatore D., 1997 Experimental Determinations of Carcass Processing by Plio-Pleistocene Hominids and Carnivores at FLK 22 (Zinjanthropus), Olduvai Gorge, Tanzania. Journal of Human Evolution 33:555–597.

——1998 Simulating the Formation of Dual-Patterned Archaeofaunal Assemblages with Experimental Control Samples. Journal of Archaeological Science 25:311–330.

Capaldo, Salvatore D., and Charles R. Peters, 1995 Skeletal Inventories from Wildebeest Drownings at Lakes Masek and Ndutu in the Serengeti Ecosystem of Tanzania. Journal of Archaeological Science 22:385–408.

Cavallo, John A., and Robert J. Blumenschine, 1989 Tree-Stored Leopard Kills: Expanding the Hominid Niche. Journal of Human Evolution 18:393–399.

Chavaillon, J., 1976 Evidence for the Technical Practices of Early Pleistocene Hominids, Shungura Formation, Lower Omo Valley, Ethiopia. In Earliest Man and Environments in the Lake Rudolf Basin. Y. Coppens, F. Clark Howell, Glynn Ll. Isaac, and Richard E. F. Leakey, eds. pp. 565–573. Chicago: University of Chicago Press.

Chavaillon, J., N. Chavaillon, F. Hours, and M. Piperno, 1979 From the Oldowan to the Middle Stone Age at Melka-Kunture (Ethiopia). Understanding Cultural Changes. Quaternaria 21:87–114.

Clark, J. Desmond, 1969 Kalambo Falls Prehistoric Site, vol. 1. Cambridge: Cambridge University Press.

——1970 The Prehistory of Africa. New York: Praeger.

——1996 Comment on Rose and Marshall. Current Anthropology 37:323.

de Heinzelin, Jean, J. Desmond Clark, Tim White, William Hart, Paul Renne, Giday Wolde-Gabriel, Yonas Beyene, and Elizabeth Vrba, 1999 Environment and Behavior of 2.5-Million-Year-Old Bouri Hominids. Science 284:625–629.

Dominguez-Rodrigo, Manuel, 1997 Meat-Eating by Early Hominids at the FLK 22 (Tanzania): An Experimental Approach Using Cut-Mark Data. Journal of Human Evolution 33:669–690.

——1999 Flesh Availability and Bone Modification in Carcasses Consumed by Lions. Palaeogeography, Palaeoclimatology and Palaeoecology 149:373–388.

——2001 A Study of Carnivore Competition in Riparian and Open Habitats of Modern Savannas and its Implications for Hominid Behavioral Modelling. Journal of Human Evolution 40:77–98.

——2002 Hunting and Scavenging by Early Humans: The State of the Debate. Journal of World Prehistory 16:1–54.

Dominguez-Rodrigo, Manuel and Ana Piqueras, 2003 The Use of Tooth Pits to Identify Carnivore Taxa in Tooth-Marked Archaeofaunas and their Relevance to Reconstruct Hominid Carcass Processing Behaviours. Journal of Archaeological Science 30:1385–1391.

Dominguez-Rodrigo, M., J. Serrallonga, J. Juan-Tresserras, L. Alcala, and L. Luque, 2001 Woodworking Activities by Early Humans: A Plant Residue Analysis on Acheulian Stone Tools from Peninj (Tanzania). Journal of Human Evolution 40:289–299.

Foley, Robert, 1987 Another Unique Species: Patterns in Human Evolutionary Ecology. New York: John Wiley & Sons.

Gabunia, Leo, Susan C. Anton, David Lordkipanidze, Abesalom Vekua, Antje Justus, and Carl C. Swisher III, 2001 Dmanisi and Dispersal. Evolutionary Anthropology 10:158–170.

Harris, John W. K., 1983 Cultural Beginnings: Plio-Pleistocene Archaeological Occurrences from the Afar Rift, Ethiopia. The African Archeological Review 1:3–31.

Harris, John W. K., and S. Capaldo, 1993 The Earliest Stone Tools: Their Implications for an Understanding of the Activities and Behaviour of Late Pliocene Hominids. *In* The Use of Tools by Human and Non-Human Primates. A. Berthelet and J. Chavaillon, eds. pp. 196–224. Oxford: Clarendon Press.

Harris, John W. K., and Glynn Isaac, 1976 The Karari Industry: Early Pleistocene Archaeological Evidence from the Terrain East of Lake Turkana, Kenya. Nature 262:102–107.

Harris, John W. K., P. G. Williamson, J. Verniers, M. J. Tappen, K. Stewart, D. Helgren, J. de Heinzelin, N. T. Boaz, and R. V. Bellomo, 1987 Late Pliocene Hominid Occupation in Central Africa: The Setting, Context, and Character of the Senga 5A Site, Zaire. Journal of Human Evolution 16:701–728.

Harris, J. W. K., P. G. Williamson, P. J. Morris, J. de Heinzelin, J. Verniers, D. Helgren, R. Bellomo, G. Laden, T. W. Spang, K. Stewart, and M. J. Tappen, 1990 Archaeology of the Lusso Beds. Virginia Museum of Natural History Memoir 1:237–272.

Hay, Richard L., 1976 Geology of the Olduvai Gorge. Berkeley: University of California Press.

Hill, Andrew, 1975 Taphonomy of Contemporary and Late Cenozoic East African Vertebrates. Ph.D. dissertation, University of London.

Hill, Andrew, S. Ward, A. Deino, G. Curtis, and R. Drake, 1992 Earliest Homo. Nature 355:719–722.

Hovers, E., K. Schollmeyer, T. Goldman, G. Eck, K. Reed, D. Johanson and W. Kimbel, 2002 Late Pliocene Archaeological Sites in Hadar, Ethiopia. Journal of Human Evolution 42:A17.

Howell, F. Clark, P. Haesaerts, and J. de Heinzelin, 1987 Depositional Environments, Archeological Occurrences and Hominids from Members E and F of the Shungura Formation (Omo Basin, Ethiopia). Journal of Human Evolution 16:665–700.

Isaac, Glynn Ll., 1976 Plio-Pleistocene Artifact Assemblages from East Rudolf, Kenya. *In* Earliest Man and Environments in the Lake Rudolf Basin. Y. Coppens, F. Clark Howell, Glynn Ll. Isaac, and Richard E. F. Leakey, eds. pp. 552–564. Chicago: University of Chicago Press.

——1977 Olorgesailie: Archaeological Studies of a Middle Pleistocene Lake Basin in Kenya. Chicago: University of Chicago Press.

——1978 The Food-Sharing Behavior of Protohuman Hominids. Scientific American 238(4):90–108.

——1981 Archaeological Tests of Alternative Models of Early Hominid Behaviour: Excavations and Experiments. Philosophical Transactions of the Royal Society of London B 292:177–188.

——1983a Bones in Contention: Competing Explanations for the Juxtaposition of Early Pleistocene Artefacts and Faunal Remains. *In* Animals and Archaeology, vol. 1: Hunters and their Prey. Juliet Clutton-Brock and Caroline Grigson, eds. pp. 3–19. BAR International Series, 163. Oxford: British Archaeological Reports.

——1983b Aspects of Human Evolution. *In* Evolution from Molecules to Men. D. S. Bendall, ed. pp. 509–543. Cambridge: Cambridge University Press.

——1984 The Archaeology of Human Origins: Studies of the Lower Pleistocene in East Africa 1971–1981. *In* Advances in World Archaeology, vol. 3. Fred Wendorf and Angela Close, eds. pp. 1–87. New York: Academic Press.

Isaac, Glynn Ll., ed., 1997 Koobi Fora Research Project, vol. 5: Plio-Pleistocene Archaeology. Oxford: Clarendon Press.

Isaac, Glynn Ll., and John W. K. Harris, 1978 Archaeology. *In* Koobi Fora Research Project, vol. 1: The Fossil Hominids and an Introduction to their Context, 1968–1974. Meave G. Leaky and Richard E. Leakey, eds. pp. 64–85. Oxford: Clarendon Press.

————1997 The Stone Artefact Assemblages: A Comparative Study. *In* Koobi Fora Research Project, vol. 5: Plio-Pleistocene Archaeology. G. L. Isaac, ed. pp. 262–362. Oxford: Clarendon Press.

Isaac, Glynn Ll., John W. K. Harris, and Fiona Marshall, 1981 Small is Informative: The Application of the Study of Mini-Sites and Least Effort Criteria in the Interpretation of the Early Pleistocene Archaeological Record at Koobi Fora, Kenya. *In* Las industrias mas Antiguas. J. Desmond Clark and Glynn Ll. Isaac, eds. pp. 101–119. Mexico: X Congresso Union International de Ciencias Prehistóricas.

Jones, Peter, 1981 Experimental Implement Manufacture and Use: A Case Study from Olduvai Gorge. Philosophical Transactions of the Royal Society of London B 292: 189–195.

Keeley, Lawrence H., and Nicholas Toth, 1981 Microwear Polishes on Early Stone Tools from Koobi Fora, Kenya. Nature 293:464–465.

Kibunjia, Mzalendo, 1994 Pliocene Archaeological Occurrences in the Lake Turkana Basin. Journal of Human Evolution 27:159–171.

Kibunjia, Mzalendo, Helene Roche, Frank H. Brown, and Richard E. Leakey, 1992 Pliocene and Pleistocene Archaeological Sites of Lake Turkana, Kenya. Journal of Human Evolution 23:432–438.

Kimbel, W. H., R. C. Walter, D. D. Johanson, K. E. Reed, J. L. Aronson, Z. Assefa, C. W. Marean, G. G. Eck, R. Bobe, E. Hovers, Y. Rak, C. Vondra, T. Yemane, D. York, Y. Chen, N. M. Evensen, and P. E. Smith, 1996 Late Pliocene Homo and Oldowan tools from the Hadar Formation (Kada Hadar Member), Ethiopia. Journal of Human Evolution 31:549–561.

Kimura, Yuki, 2002 Examining Time Trends in the Oldowan Technology at Beds I and II, Olduvai Gorge. Journal of Human Evolution 43:291–321.

Kroll, Ellen M., 1994 Behavioral Implications of Plio-Pleistocene Archaeological Site Structure. Journal of Human Evolution 27:107–138.

Kruuk, H., 1972 The Spotted Hyena. Chicago: University of Chicago Press.

Kuman, Kathleen, 1998 The Earliest South African Industries. *In* Early Human Behavior in Global Context. Michael D. Petraglia and Ravi Korisettar, eds. pp. 151–186. New York: Routledge.

Kuman, Kathleen, and R. J. Clarke, 2000 Stratigraphy, Artifact Industries and Hominid Associations for Sterkfontein, Member 5. Journal of Human Evolution 38:827–847.

Leakey, Louis S. B., 1935 The Stone Age Races of Kenya. London: Oxford University Press.

Leakey, L. S. B., P. V. Tobias, and J. R. Napier, 1964 A New Species of the Genus Homo from Olduvai Gorge. Nature 202:7–9.

Leakey, Mary D., 1966 A Review of the Oldowan Culture from Olduvai Gorge, Tanzania. Nature 212:579–581.

————1971 Olduvai Gorge, vol. 3: Excavations in Beds I and II, 1960–1963. Cambridge: Cambridge University Press.

Lee, Richard B., and Irven DeVore, eds., 1976 Kalahari Hunter-Gatherers. Cambridge, MA: Harvard University Press.

Lewis, Margaret E., 1997 Carnivoran Paleoguilds of Africa: Implications for Hominid Food Procurement Strategies. Journal of Human Evolution 32:257–288.

Ludwig, Brian V., and John W. K. Harris, 1998 Towards a Technological Reassessment of East African Plio-Pleistocene Lithic Assemblages. *In* Early Human Behaviour in Global Context. Michael D. Petraglia and Ravi Korisettar, eds. pp. 84–107. New York: Routledge.

Lupo, Karen D., and James F. O'Connell, 2002 Cut and Tooth Mark Distributions on Large Animal Bones: Ethnoarchaeological Data from the Hadza and their Implications for

Current Ideas about Early Human Carnivory. Journal of Archaeological Science 29:85–109.

Lyman, R. Lee, 1994 Vertebrate Taphonomy. Cambridge: Cambridge University Press.

McGrew, William, 1992 Chimpanzee Material Culture. Cambridge: Cambridge University Press.

Marean, Curtis W., 1989 Sabertooth Cats and their Relevance for Early Hominid Diet and Evolution. Journal of Human Evolution 18:559–582.

Marean, Curtis W., and L. M. Spencer, 1991 Impact of Carnivore Ravaging on Zooarchaeological Measures of Element Abundance. American Antiquity 56:645–658.

Marean, Curtis W., L. M. Spencer, R. J. Blumenschine, and S. D. Capaldo, 1992 Captive Hyena Bone Choice and Destruction, the Schlepp Effect, and Olduvai Archaeofaunas. Journal of Archaeological Research 19:101–121.

Merrick, H. V., and J. P. S. Merrick, 1976 Archaeological Occurrences of Earlier Pleistocene Age from the Shungura Formation. In Earliest Man and Environments in the Lake Rudolf Basin. Y. Coppens, F. Clark Howell, Glynn Ll. Isaac, and Richard E. F. Leakey, eds. pp. 574–584. Chicago: University of Chicago Press.

Milton, Katharine, 1999 A Hypothesis to Explain the Role of Meat-Eating in Human Evolution. Evolutionary Anthropology 8:11–21.

Monahan, Christopher M., 1998 The Hadza Carcass Transport Debate Revisited and its Archaeological Implications. Journal of Archaeological Science 25:405–424.

——1999 Quantifying Bone Modification by African Wild Dogs and Spotted Hyenas: Implications of Models Estimating the Timing of Hominid and Carnivore Access to Animal Carcasses. Journal of Human Evolution 36:A14.

O'Connell, James F., 1997 On Plio/Pleistocene Archaeological Sites and Central Places. Current Anthropology 38:86–88.

O'Connell, James, F., Kirsten Hawkes, and Nicholas Blurton Jones, 1990 Reanalysis of Large Mammal Body Part Transport among the Hadza. Journal of Archaeological Science 17:301–316.

————1999 Grandmothering and the Evolution of Homo erectus. Journal of Human Evolution 36:461–485.

O'Connell, J. F., K. Hawkes, K. D. Lupo, and N. G. Blurton Jones, 2002 Male Strategies and Plio-Pleistocene Archaeology. Journal of Human Evolution 43:831–872.

Odell, George H., 1996 Economizing Behavior and the Concept of "Curation." In Stone Tools: Theoretical Insights into Human Prehistory. G. H. Odell, ed. pp. 51–80. New York: Plenum Press.

Oliver, James S., 1993 Carcass Processing by the Hadza: Bone Breakage from Butchery to Consumption. In From Bones to Behavior. J. Hudson, ed. pp. 200–227. Occasional Paper 21. Carbondale: Southern Illinois University.

——1994 Estimates of Hominid and Carnivore Involvement in the FLK Zinjanthropus Fossil Assemblage: Some Socioecological Implications. Journal of Human Evolution 27:267–294.

Petraglia, Michael D., and R. Potts, 1994 Water Flow and the Formation of Early Pleistocene Artifact Sites in Olduvai Gorge, Tanzania. Journal of Anthropological Archaeology 13:228–254.

Plummer, Thomas W., and L. C. Bishop, 1994 Hominid Paleoecology at Olduvai Gorge, Tanzania, as Indicated by Antelope Remains. Journal of Human Evolution 27:47–75.

Plummer, Thomas W., and Craig B. Stanford, 2000 Analysis of a Bone Assemblage Made by Chimpanzees at Gombe National Park, Tanzania. Journal of Human Evolution 39:345–365.

Plummer, Thomas, Laura C. Bishop, Peter Ditchfield, and Jason Hicks, 1999 Research on Late Pliocene Oldowan Sites at Kanjera South, Kenya. Journal of Human Evolution 36:151–170.

Potts, Richard, 1983 Foraging for Faunal Resources by Early Hominids at Olduvai Gorge, Tanzania. In Animals and Archaeology, vol. 1: Hunters and their Prey. Juliet Clutton-Brock and Caroline Grigson, eds. pp. 51–62. BAR International Series, 163. Oxford: British Archaeological Reports.

—— 1984 Home Bases and Early Hominids. American Scientist 72:338–347.

—— 1987 On Butchery by Olduvai Hominids. Current Anthropology 28:95–98.

—— 1988 Early Hominid Activities at Olduvai. New York: Aldine de Gruyter.

—— 1991 Why the Oldowan? Plio-Pleistocene Toolmaking and the Transport of Resources. Journal of Anthropological Research 47(2):153–176.

—— 1993 Archeological Interpretations of Early Hominid Behavior and Ecology. In The Origin and Evolution of Humans and Humanness. D. T. Rasmussen, ed. pp. 49–74. Boston: Jones & Bartlett.

—— 1994 Variables Versus Models of Early Pleistocene Hominid Land Use. Journal of Human Evolution 27:7–24.

—— 1996 Comment on Rose and Marshall. Current Anthropology 37:325–327.

Potts, Richard, and Pat Shipman, 1981 Cutmarks Made by Stone Tools on Bones from Olduvai Gorge, Tanzania. Nature 291:577–580.

Potts, Richard, Anna K. Behrensmeyer, and P. Ditchfield, 1999 Paleolandscape Variation and Early Pleistocene Hominid Activities: Members 1 and 7, Olorgesailie Formation, Kenya. Journal of Human Evolution 37:747–788.

Roche, Helene, 1989 Technological Evolution in Early Hominids. OSSA 14:97–98.

—— 1996 Remarques sur les plus anciennes industries en Afrique et en Europe. In The First Humans and their Cultural Manifestations, vol. 4. F. Facchini, ed. pp. 55–68. Forli: ABACO.

Roche, H., and J. J. Tiercelin, 1980 Industries lithiques de la formation Plio-Pleistocene d'Hadar: Campagne 1976. In Proceedings of the 8th Pan-African Congress of Prehistory and Quaternary Studies, Nairobi, September 1977. Richard Leakey and B. Ogot, eds. pp. 194–199. Nairobi: International Louis Leakey Memorial Institute.

Roche, H., A. Delagnes, J. P. Brugal, C. Feibel, M. Kibunjia, V. Mourre, and P.-J. Texier, 1999 Early Hominid Stone Tool Production and Technical Skill 2.34 Myr Ago in West Turkana, Kenya. Nature 399:57–60.

Rogers, Michael J., John W. K. Harris, and Craig S. Feibel, 1994 Changing Patterns of Land Use by Plio-Pleistocene Hominids in the Lake Turkana Basin. Journal of Human Evolution 27:139–158.

Rose, Lisa M., 1997 Vertebrate Predation and Food-Sharing in Cebus and Pan. International Journal of Primatology 18(5):727–765.

Rose, Lisa, and Fiona Marshall, 1996 Meat Eating, Hominid Sociality, and Home Bases Revisited. Current Anthropology 37:307–338.

Sahnouni, M., and J. de Heinzelin, 1998 The Site of Ain Hanech Revisited: New Investigations at this Lower Pleistocene Site in Northern Algeria. Journal of Archaeological Science 25:1083–1101.

Sahnouni, Mohamed, Djillali Hadjouis, Jan van der Made, Abd-el-Kader Derradji, Antoni Canals, Mohamed Medig, Hocine Belahrech, Zoheir Harichane, and Rabhi Merouane, 2002 Further Research at the Oldowan Site of Ain Hanech, North-Eastern Algeria. Journal of Human Evolution 43:925–937.

Schaller, G. B., 1972 The Serengeti Lion. Chicago: University of Chicago Press.

Schick, Kathy D., 1987 Modeling the Formation of Early Stone Age Artifact Concentrations. Journal of Human Evolution 16:789–808.

—— 1997 Experimental Studies of Site-Formation Processes. *In* Koobi Fora Research Project, vol. 5: Plio-Pleistocene Archaeology. Glynn Ll. Isaac, ed. pp. 244–256. Oxford: Clarendon Press.

Schick, Kathy D., and Nicholas Toth, 1993 Making Silent Stones Speak. New York: Simon & Schuster.

Selvaggio, Marie M., 1994 Carnivore Tooth Marks and Stone Tool Butchery Marks on Scavenged Bones: Archaeological Implications. Journal of Human Evolution 27:215–228.

—— 1998 Evidence for a Three-Stage Sequence of Hominid and Carnivore Involvement with Long Bones at FLK Zinjanthropus, Olduvai Gorge, Tanzania. Journal of Archaeological Science 25:191–202.

Selvaggio, Marie M. and Joseph Wilder, 2001 Identifying the Involvement of Multiple Carnivore Taxa with Archaeological Bone Assemblages. Journal of Archaeological Science 28:465–470.

Semaw, Sileshi, 2000 The World's Oldest Stone Age Artefacts from Gona, Ethiopia: Their Implications for Understanding Stone Technology and Patterns of Human Evolution between 2.6–1.5 Million Years Ago. Journal of Archaeological Science 27:1197–1214.

Semaw, S., P. Renne, J. W. K. Harris, C. S. Feibel, R. L. Bernor, N. Fesseha, and K. Mowbray, 1997 2.5-Million-Year-Old Stone Tools from Gona, Ethiopia. Nature 385:333–336.

Semaw, S., M. J. Rogers, J. Quade, P. R. Renne, R. F. Butler, M. Dominguez-Rodrigo, D. Stout, W. S. Hart, T. Pickering, and S. W. Simpson, 2003 2.6-Million-Year-Old Stone Tools and Associated Bones from OGS-6 and OGS-7, Gona, Afar, Ethiopia. Journal of Human Evolution 45:169–177.

Sept, Jeanne M., 1986 Plant Foods and Early Hominids at Site FxJj 50, Koobi Fora, Kenya. Journal of Human Evolution 15:751–770.

—— 1994 Beyond Bones: Archaeological Sites, Early Hominid Subsistence, and the Costs and Benefits of Exploiting Wild Plant Foods in East African Riverine Landscapes. Journal of Human Evolution 27:295–320.

—— 2001 Modelling the Edible Landscape. *In* Meat-Eating and Human Evolution. Craig B. Stanford and Henry T. Bunn, eds. pp. 73–98. Oxford: Oxford University Press.

Shipman, Pat, 1983 Early Hominid Lifestyle: Hunting and Gathering or Foraging and Scavenging? *In* Animals and Archaeology, vol. 1: Hunters and their Prey. Juliet Clutton-Brock and Caroline Grigson, eds. pp. 31–49. BAR International Series, 163. Oxford: British Archaeological Reports.

—— 1986 Scavenging or Hunting in Early Hominids: Theoretical Framework and Tests. American Anthropologist 88:27–43.

Sikes, N. E. 1994 Early Hominid Habitat Preferences in East Africa: Paleosol Carbon Isotopic Evidence. Journal of Human Evolution 27:25–45.

Stahl, Ann B., 1984 Hominid Dietary Selection before Fire. Current Anthropology 25:151–168.

Stanley, S. M., 1992 An Ecological Theory for the Origin of Homo. Paleobiology 18:237–257.

Stern, Nicola, 1993 The Structure of the Lower Pleistocene Archaeological Record: A Case Study from the Koobi Fora Formation. Current Anthropology 34:201–225.

—— 1994 The Implications of Time-Averaging for Reconstructing the Land-Use Patterns of Early Tool-Using Hominids. Journal of Human Evolution 27:89–105.

Strum, Shirley C., 1981 Processes and Products of Change: Baboon Predatory Behavior at

Gilgil, Kenya. *In* Omnivorous Primates. Robert S. O. Harding and Geza Teleki, eds. pp. 255–302. New York: Columbia University Press.

Tappen, Martha, 1995 Savanna Ecology and Natural Bone Deposition: Implications for Early Hominid Site Formation, Hunting, and Scavenging. Current Anthropology 36:223–260.

——2001 Deconstructing the Serengeti. *In* Meat-Eating and Human Evolution. Craig B. Stanford and Henry T. Bunn, eds. pp. 13–32. Oxford: Oxford University Press.

Texier, P.-J., 1995 The Oldowan Assemblage from NY 18 Site at Nyabusosi (Toro-Uganda). Comptes Rendus de l'Académie des Sciences Paris. Série II, vol. 320:647–653.

Toth, Nicholas, 1985 The Oldowan Reassessed: A Close Look at Early Stone Age Artifacts. Journal of Archaeological Science 12:101–120.

——1987 Behavioral Inferences from Early Stone Age Archaeological Assemblages: An Experimental Model. Journal of Human Evolution 16:763–787.

——1997 The Artefact Assemblages in the Light of Experimental Studies. *In* Koobi Fora Research Project, vol. 5: Plio-Pleistocene Archaeology. Glynn Ll. Isaac, ed. pp. 363–401. Oxford: Clarendon Press.

Toth, Nicholas, and Kathy Schick, 1986 The First Million Years: The Archaeology of Protohuman Culture. *In* Advances in Archaeological Method and Theory, vol. 9. M. B. Schiffer, ed. pp. 1–96. New York: Academic Press.

Vincent, Anne, 1985 Plant Foods in Savanna Environments: A Preliminary Report of Tubers Eaten by the Hadza of Northern Tanzania. World Archaeology 17:1–14.

Wood, Bernard, 1992 Origin and Evolution of the Genus *Homo*. Nature 355:783–790.

Wynn, Thomas, 1981 The Intelligence of Oldowan Hominids. Journal of Human Evolution 10:519–541.

Wynn, Thomas, and William C. McGrew, 1989 An Ape's View of the Oldowan. Man 24: 383–398.

Yellen, John E., 1977 Cultural Patterning in Faunal Remains: Evidence from the !Kung Bushmen. *In* Experimental Archeology. D. Ingersoll, J. E. Yellen, and W. Macdonald, eds. pp. 271–331. New York: Columbia University Press.

x Modern humans survive through technology
animals do so by their anatomy and behaviour

4

The Middle and Upper Pleistocene African Record for the Biological and Behavioral Origins of Modern Humans

Curtis W. Marean and Zelalem Assefa

There is currently one species of human on the planet (*Homo sapiens*), but this is a rare condition in human evolution. As recently as 35,000 (ky) years ago, modern humans shared the western Eurasian landscape with Neanderthals (*Homo neanderthalensis*). Shortly thereafter, modern humans became the sole human inhabitants of our planet, and variation within our species began to develop into what we see today. Research into this final major event in human biological evolution has become one of the most dynamic areas in paleoanthropology and is widely known as the problem of *modern human origins*.

When we think of human evolution, we generally think about changes in biological traits, and more specifically anatomy. However, modern humans are a cultural species, and this, combined with our large brains, is what separates us from other animals. The modern human adaptation is primarily a technological one, whereas other species adapt to their environments through anatomy (such as thick hair for cold environments) and behavior. This technological adaptation combined with our extraordinary ability to symbol, of which language is a complex form, is the root of our definition of "humanness." It is likely that this special "humanness" developed during the origins of modern humans, and thus this research problem targets an issue of great significance to all humans. The primary evidentiary record for the origins of modern human behavior is archaeology.

In the last 20–30 years there have been a number of discoveries that have led most paleoanthropologists to believe that Africa is the cradle of modern humans. This should not surprise, because time and again we find Africa to be a precocious place for human evolution. The first upright-walking hominins appeared in Africa between 5 and 6 million years ago (my). The first major increases in human brain size occurred in Africa between 3 and 2 my. Africa is where hominins first used stone tools, roughly 2.5 my ago. It should be no surprise that the capstone of human

[handwritten: & What is the Pleistocene]

evolution, the appearance of modern people, also occurred in Africa. The African continent consistently acted as a potent engine for human evolution, and our goal is to discover why. This chapter will examine the debates and evidence for that crescendo of human evolution.

The Temporal and Paleoenvironmental Background

The time range of interest here spans the Middle and Upper Pleistocene, roughly 787 to 40 ky. Building a reliable chronological framework for this time range is a major challenge. The well-established radiocarbon technique is not reliable beyond 45 ky, while argon/argon ($^{40}AR/^{39}AR$) is limited to assemblages found in association with volcanic deposits. For this reason dating of Middle and Upper Pleistocene sediments relies on fairly new chronometric techniques, such as uranium series, luminescence, electron spin resonance, and amino acid racemization. While progress is being made, it is still safe to say that most sites in this time range are coarsely dated.

For this reason we sometimes use chronologic systems to order sites, and the oxygen isotope stratigraphic record provides such a system as well as a global measure of temperature change. It is based on chemical principles of the oxygen isotopes ^{18}O and ^{16}O (Imbrie and Imbrie 1979): ^{18}O is heavier and tends to be less susceptible to evaporation. With declining moisture and formation of ice sheets during glacial periods, oceans were enriched with ^{18}O compared to ^{16}O. During their lifetime marine microorganisms, such as foraminifera, absorb both oxygen isotopes in ratios preserved in their skeletons. The $^{18}O/^{16}O$ ratio from deep-sea cores therefore provides an oxygen isotope stratigraphy that reflects worldwide temperature shifts, and we recognize oxygen isotope stages (OIS) defined by periods of relative stasis separated by more dramatic reversals in temperature (Figure 4.1a). These alternating cold and warm stages have been dated by a variety of methods and their boundaries are now reasonably secure.

The different stages of global climatic shifts are identified by a sequence of Arabic numerals (Figure 4.1a) starting from the current interglacial (the Holocene) with odd and even numbers referring to interglacial and glacial periods, respectively. Customarily, the lowest isotopic value or climatic minima in the last interglacial-glacial cycle, marked at 18 ky is referred to as Last Glacial Maximum (LGM), while Last Glaciation is used in reference to the preceding climatically milder period which includes OIS 4 to 2. OIS 5, an interglacial stage with several sub-stages, is commonly referred to as Last Interglacial.

Broadly speaking, most of Africa was subjected to greater aridity during cold stages and greater precipitation during warmer stages. This, combined with more localized paleoenvironmental data and computer modeling, has been used to develop basic vegetation maps for the past. Figure 4.1b shows one such reconstruction (Adams and Faure, eds., 1997) for the LGM and the early Holocene (a warm wet period) which represents a useful approximation of African paleovegetation during cold and warm stages.

[handwritten left margin: x Africa in general was arid during cold phases x rainfall was greater during warmer stages]

[handwritten bottom: paleo]

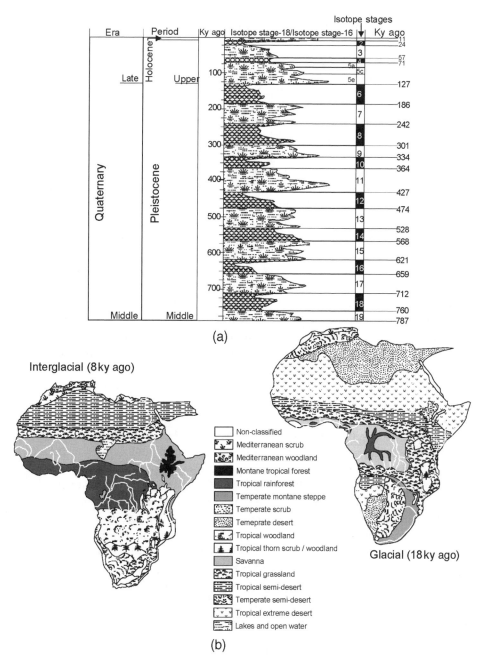

Figure 4.1. The geological and paleoenvironmental framework: (a) global climatic shifts through time as indicated by oxygen isotope data; (b) reconstructed vegetation distributions under interglacial (8 ky) and glacial (18 ky) conditions

X The Origins of Modern Humans

Models in science are simplifications of reality (Clarke 1978). These constellations of related hypotheses communicate complex sets of empirical observations and associated interpretations. Below we present four basic competing models for the origins of our species (Aiello 1993) that can be used to develop specific hypotheses for testing with evidence.

The *Multiregional Continuity* model (MRC), also known as the Multiregional Evolution model, argues that modern humans evolved simultaneously throughout the Old World from indigenous populations of more archaic humans linked by regular genic exchange (Thorne and Wolpoff 1992; Wolpoff 1989). Some implications are that modern human ("racial") variation has a deep time depth, and we might be able to recognize racially distinct traits in ancient fossil populations. This model does not anticipate a break in the fossil record linked to sudden replacement by outside populations since it denies that any one region played a primary role. Proponents argue that the transition to modern humans occurred 40 to 50 ky ago, and gene flow between populations kept humans from speciating. This model was very popular until recently. The *Assimilation* model accepts an African origin for modern humans, but rejects a massive immigration of Africans. It emphasizes gene flow from Africa, admixture between populations, and changing selection pressures that resulted in the shift to modern humans (Smith et al. 1989). The *African Hybridization and Replacement* model (AHR) argues that Africa is the sole source for modern humans (Bräuer 1984, 1989). Modern humans arose sometime before 100 ky, radiated throughout Africa, but traveled no further than the Levant. Sometime around 40 ky, Africans left Africa and spread throughout the Old World, hybridizing with but genetically swamping resident populations, and thus minimizing their genetic contribution to our genome. The *African Replacement* (Stringer 1990; Stringer and Andrews 1988) model (AR) argues that modern humans arose first in Africa and replaced resident archaic populations outside Africa, with little to no hybridization. A particularly strong variant of AR is the Eve Model, which argues that this new modern human species could not interbreed with archaics outside Africa (Stringer and Bräuer 1994). Geneticists have often used the term Garden of Eden (GOE) model (Harpending et al. 1993), with weak and strong forms, to cover the Assimilation, AHR, and AR models. Furthermore, the weak Garden of Eden model suggests that racial differences may predate the expansion of modern humans (Harpending and Rogers 2000).

Where do we stand today? While we cannot exhaustively review the evidence, it is useful to look at some of the test implications for each model. For example, the AHR and AR models argue that Africans migrated into Eurasia, and that anatomically modern humans were present in Africa prior to their appearance in Eurasia. Both implications appear to be true. The earliest modern humans in Europe had skeletons with tropical morphologies that eventually evolved into a colder environment form (Pearson 2000). As discussed below, there are fossil hominins in Africa that are contemporary with Neanderthals who resemble modern humans.

Recent advances in genetics have allowed us to use the genetic record of living people to look at past populations and their evolutionary and demographic history. The test implications for the models are clear. The MRC model anticipates genetic continuity between very early humans, as far back as *Homo erectus*, and modern people. GOE models argue that modern humans come from a restricted area (Africa) and that archaic populations living outside Africa contributed little or nothing to the modern gene pool. Thus, the GOE anticipates a bottleneck, or period of very low genetic diversity in the past (Relethford 1999). Overall, the most recent results suggest that our species went through a bottleneck in the late Middle Pleistocene or early Upper Pleistocene, and then there was an expansion of modern humans out of Africa. Thus, both the fossil and genetic records target Africa as central to the origins of modern humans (Harpending and Rogers 2000). A consistent result of these studies is that African people of Khoi and Pygmy ancestry represent some of the most ancient populations on this planet (Ingman et al. 2000).

How does archaeology fit in?

If anatomically modern humans arose in Africa, when did humans first attain their modern mental abilities? Archaeology uses material remains to understand human behavior, and much research effort to date has focused on where and when modern human behavior first arose. Accomplishing this hinges on our definition of "humanness," often based on differences between us and living great apes. Modern humans developed sophisticated technologies, often with multiple components. These technologies allowed modern humans using Stone Age technology to live in virtually any environment on this planet. Modern humans regularly collect food in bulk and store it for the future, showing the ability to plan and organize. Modern humans symbol in complex ways and express this behavior as art and body decoration. Perhaps most importantly, this ability to symbol is the foundation for language, which is a very complex form of symbol and analogy that is hardwired into our brains (Pinker 1997).

While distinctions between humans and other living apes seem clear, they are less so in regards to our closest past relatives, the Neanderthals. We do not know if Neanderthals had language. How then do we define ourselves relative to Neanderthals and other closely related species of humans? In this archaeologists have been guided more by tradition than theoretical rigor (Henshilwood and Marean 2003). Over time a trait-list of modern human behaviors developed (Gamble 1994; Klein 1998, 2000) that was rooted in a paper (Mellars 1973) on the differences between Middle Paleolithic (Neanderthal) and Upper Paleolithic (modern human) sites in southwestern France. This small region has a rich Paleolithic record for several reasons: researchers have been working there a long time; there is a dense distribution of sites; and many of these are in limestone caves that preserve fossil bone extremely well. The record in southwestern France easily surpasses in size and quality the entire known African record.

This list of traits morphed over time into a litmus test for behavioral modernity based on the idea that Neanderthals reflected non-modern behavior. Use of this approach led to a model that Henshilwood and Marean (2003) called the Later Upper Pleistocene model for the origins of behavioral modernity. This once favored model argued that traits sensitive to modern human behavior did not appear until after 40 ky. This accorded well with evidence from Eurasia, but the record in Africa was virtually unknown. The Eurasian record, defined by the southwestern French pattern, was by default assumed to be a broad evolutionary pattern and was extended to Africa. The projection of this pattern to Africa without an adequate African sample was a clear Eurocentric misstep.

The African record is now filling out, and it shows that Africa differed dramatically from Europe during this critical time (McBrearty and Brooks 2000). Understanding this record requires an appreciation of the environmental and biological context. To that end, we summarize the nature of the African fossil record before describing the archaeological evidence for behavior.

The Fossil Evidence for Modern Human Evolution in Africa

Despite all the debate surrounding the origins of modern humans, most researchers agree that by 30 ky anatomically modern *Homo sapiens* became the sole occupant of all regions of the Old World. However, the first appearances of modern humans in different regions followed disparate evolutionary trajectories. Africa shows a continuous anatomical evolution across this boundary. In contrast, the fossil evidence from Europe and eastern Asia prior to 40 ky lacks any trace of anatomically modern humans, while both modern humans and Neanderthals occurred at the gates to Africa in Southwest Asia (Bar-Yosef and Vandermeersch 1993). Beyond these basic facts, the relationships of the hominin specimens from the late Acheulean and Middle Stone Age (MSA) of Africa are still unresolved. However, several authors have provided broadly compatible summaries (Bräuer 1992; McBrearty and Brooks 2000) which we draw on for a general picture of the hominin record from the terminal Acheulean through the MSA.

There are two broad approaches to nomenclature for the hominin remains from this time. One system refers to all specimens that postdate the *Homo ergaster/erectus* group as *H. sapiens*, emphasizing the morphological distinctions from a more rugged and heavily built ancestral group. This approach extends the root of *H. sapiens* in Africa to 600 ky (the Bodo cranium; Clark et al. 1994) with a grade-based taxonomy of early archaic, late archaic, and anatomically modern *H. sapiens* (Bräuer 1992), or groups 1 through 3 (McBrearty and Brooks 2000). Other researchers employ a more taxonomically rigid system: early archaic fossils are assigned to *Homo heidelbergensis* or *Homo rhodesiensis*; the late archaic to *Homo helmei*; and the last to *H. sapiens*. *Homo heidelbergensis* is also found in Europe, and is considered to be a likely candidate for the last common ancestor of modern humans and Neanderthals (Rightmire 1996; Stringer and Gamble 1993).

The term "archaic *H. sapiens*" is often used in reference to Middle Pleistocene specimens, which are further classified into "early" and "late" archaic *H. sapiens*. Some of the best representatives of the early archaic group (Group I) include the Bodo (Ethiopia) cranium, the skeletal remains from Kapthurin (Kenya), and the Eyasi (Tanzania) cranial fragments (Figure 4.2). These specimens have a broad brow ridge, massively built and prognathic faces, thick cranial bones, large brains, long low crania, and large teeth. Postcrania, when present, are often robust and the long bones thick, suggesting a heavily muscled body. Whenever found associated with stone tools, early archaic *H. sapiens* are found with Acheulean tools and their

Figure 4.2. Map of Late Acheulean and MSA sites mentioned in the text

terminal appearance roughly correlates with the earliest occurrence of the MSA.

Late archaic *H. sapiens* includes specimens that are morphologically "intermediate" between anatomically modern humans and early archaic *H. sapiens*. Some of the best specimens of this group are Jebel Irhoud (Morocco), Omo II (Ethiopia), and Florisbad (South Africa). The late archaic group exhibits a trend toward a more modern and gracile cranium with a higher forehead (frontal), thus decreasing the length of the cranium, and a less pronounced brow ridge. These anatomical features are not, however, advanced enough to allow inclusion in anatomically modern humans, although there is temporal overlap between the two groups. The fossils in this group are found exclusively with MSA assemblages.

Members of anatomically modern *H. sapiens* in Africa associated with MSA technologies have many features in common with living humans and distinct from their contemporaries the Neanderthals. For example, the Klasies River (South Africa) specimens have chins while Neanderthals do not, and the mandibles of these specimens lack a retromolar space (such as at Haua Fteah in Libya), which Neanderthals have. They are more gracile than the preceding late archaic group, but are typically somewhat more robust with larger teeth than Later Stone Age (LSA) and living humans. Good examples of these include Omo I, Klasies River (Chapter 5), and Border Cave (South Africa). All of these specimens date to the Upper Pleistocene and are associated with MSA assemblages.

The Late Acheulean to Middle Stone Age: The Development of a Modern Technological and Cultural Adaptation

The long-lasting Acheulean Industrial Complex (about 1.6 my to 300 ky) is defined by the appearance of bifaces. Though once believed to be monotonous and unchanging, we now know that the Acheulean varied significantly through time and space. Unfortunately, the Acheulean in Africa remains poorly sampled and incompletely understood. We know that Acheulean hominins used caves and rockshelters, but these are so old that few survived, so we lack the dense lithic and faunal repositories that aid our investigation of the MSA and later periods. This is unfortunate because we expect that Acheulean hominins made significant behavioral advances that set them on the path to behavioral modernity. Here we focus on later Acheulean developments that set the stage for both the MSA and transition to modern humans.

Bifaces were fairly crude early in the Acheulean (Figure 4.3a), made by removing a minimum number of flakes from two sides. Two biface varieties were characteristic. Hand-axes (Figures 4.3a and 4.3b) come to a point, and cleavers (Figure 4.3c) have a long and flat edge similar to an ax. Retouched flakes were also an important component of Acheulean technology, though unretouched flakes typically dominate assemblages. Bifaces have historically been used as an indicator fossil for the Acheulean, but as we discuss below, this is problematic, particularly for the latest Acheulean. Over time bifaces became more standardized in shape, thinner, and often had a straight cutting edge (Figure 4.3b). The frequency of raw materials extracted

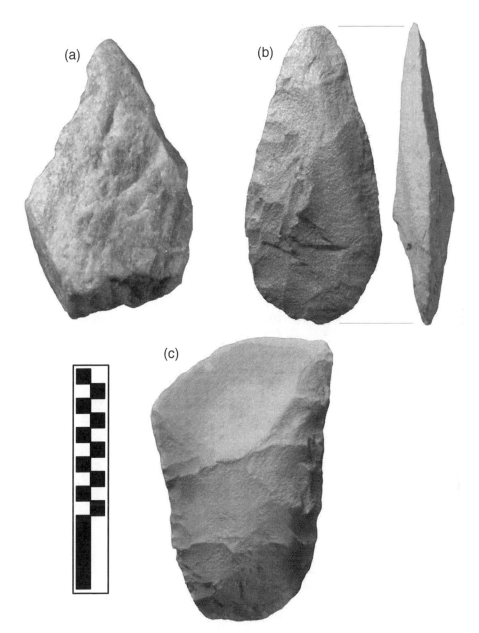

Figure 4.3. A selection of Acheulean stone tools: (a) Acheulean handax from Olduvai Gorge; (b) Acheulean handax from Kalambo Falls in plan (left) and profile (right); (c) Acheulean cleaver from Kalambo Falls. Scale is in cm.

from distant resources increased, and prepared core techniques of flake production (see Andrefsky 1998) appeared. These subtle and poorly dated shifts define stages within the Acheulean (Early, Middle, and Late). Our focus here is on the Late Acheulean and its transition to the MSA.

Acheulean traces are found throughout Africa and are widely distributed in Eurasia, though classic handaxes are absent from eastern Asia. For this reason the Acheulean is regarded as the technological adaptation of the first hominins to leave the African tropics and become *widely and permanently* established in temperate climatic zones. Since temperate zones have prolonged seasons during which plant foods are rare to absent (fall through early spring), it is likely that effective hunting strategies were developed during the Acheulean. Given the often cold conditions, we anticipate that controlled use of fire was also developed. Unfortunately, while there are probably hundreds of documented Acheulean sites in Africa, most have provided little information on hominin behavior because of poor preservation.

The Late Acheulean Record

Africa's densest concentration of excavated Acheulean sites is in the Rift Valley from Ethiopia to northern Tanzania. Olorgesailie in southern Kenya is a well-known locality. Olorgesailie once bordered a lake and most of the well-known sites are on a low rocky promontory that jutted into the lake or on sand beaches of small streams that drained into the lake (Isaac 1977). The sites are well dated by a series of volcanic ashes ranging in age from 999 ky to 49 ky (Deino and Potts 1990). Faunal remains are preserved in some areas, but never well. Olorgesailie is one of several Acheulean sites to display a puzzling pattern: hundreds, even thousands, of handaxes occur concentrated in one area. This pattern is also present at Kariandusi (Kenya), Isimila (Tanzania), and Amanzi Springs (South Africa). At Isimila the handaxes vary widely in size, from very large and unwieldy to just a few inches long.

Perhaps the most famous Acheulean locality in Africa is Kalambo Falls, Zambia (Clark 2001). Its fame arises from the very long sequence (Acheulean to Iron Age), and the preservation of organic material in Acheulean deposits. Sites are concentrated near where the Kalambo River plunges over a 200 m waterfall. Upstream the river is dammed at regular intervals by structural changes in the bedrock that formed small lakes, and these were places of dense prehistoric occupation. The waterlogged conditions preserved plant material, but destroyed fossil bone. Some pieces of wood show signs of being worked and in some cases burned. An arc of stone enclosing an area of about 2 m may represent the remains of a windbreak.

Acheulean sites are abundant in South Africa, and two of Africa's rare Acheulean cave sites are here: the Cave of Hearths (Mason 1988) and Montague Cave (Keller 1973). MSA is stratified above Acheulean at both sites, but the Acheulean and MSA are separated by an unconformity, and there is no technological transition between the two. At Elandsfontein Acheulean materials erode out of dune sands covering ancient land surfaces. Elandsfontein, thought to date between 700 and 400 ky (Klein and Cruz-Uribe 1991), has yielded fossil mammal skeletons that apparently rest where they died. At a site called Cutting 10, handaxes were associated with about 15 mammalian species, including elephants, rhino, and large and small bovids, and may represent a combination of butchering and natural deaths of animals near a waterhole (Klein 1978).

Transitions and turnovers at the end of the Acheulean

Until recently we had little firm data on the timing and nature of the transition between the Acheulean and MSA. At Baringo in the Kapthurin Formation, where sediments with volcanic ashes are present, several Acheulean and MSA occurrences overlap in time with no clear transition. Acheulean occurrences lacking classic handaxes occur at roughly the same time as early MSA sites that date before 285 ky (Tryon and McBrearty 2002). Tryon and McBrearty conclude that the Acheulean to MSA transition was gradual and characterized by simultaneous use of Acheulean, Sangoan (see below), and MSA technologies. New dates from Southwest Asia date the replacement of the Acheulean by the Middle Paleolithic to 247 ky at the earliest (Porat et al. 2002), suggesting that MSA technology in Africa may predate its occurrence in Eurasia.

The Sangoan is probably the only well-described industry that consistently occurs interstratified at the boundary of the Acheulean and MSA. It differs from the classic Acheulean in several ways: there are no handaxes or cleavers, small scrapers predominate, and there are robust tools called picks and core-axes. First recognized in 1923 (Wayland 1924), these assemblages have been found throughout equatorial Africa, typically in wooded or forested areas. Most have come from surface finds and are selected samples. The Sangoan is followed by an industry called the Lupemban, which is widely considered MSA. The Sangoan and Lupemban share several technological characteristics that often blend together, but the Lupemban has numerous distinctive lanceolate bifaces, fewer heavy-duty elements, and an MSA technology. The two together are often referred to as the Sangoan-Lupemban Industrial Complex.

Evidence to date suggests that the Acheulean-MSA transition occurred sometime between 300 and 250 ky, squarely within glacial OIS 8. The dramatic rotations between cold-dry and warm-wet climates during the late Middle and Upper Pleistocene posed a recurrent and amplifying cycle of vegetation change and habitability of the African continent. During cold-dry stages current desert and grassland habitats were probably very arid, forested areas in equatorial Africa more open, and coastal platforms more extensive as depressed sea levels exposed previously submerged land mass. Vast areas of northern and southern Africa were likely inhospitable except near coastlines and permanent rivers. We believe that at these times populations were found in two forms: clusters within equatorial Africa in what were then grasslands and wooded grasslands, and small, fragmented populations along the continental margins and other isolated refugia. It is possible that the Sangoan-Lupemban is the technological trace of the equatorial population. The tendency to find unconformities between Late Acheulean and fully developed MSA occupations in northern and southern Africa may represent periods of sparse occupation or abandonment.

During times of population fragmentation and stress biological and behavioral evolution is typically stimulated. Evolutionary shifts often take two forms: turnovers and transitions. By transition we mean a gradual change from one state to another. Turnovers are when one form replaces another, often by decreasing frequencies of old forms and increasing frequencies of new ones. We think it likely that a true transition from Acheulean to MSA occurred in just one region and spread outward, resulting in a widespread patchwork pattern of technological turnovers and eventual replacement of Acheulean by MSA technology. During OIS 8 some populations likely retained the traditional Acheulean technology, while others experimented with new technologies such as Sangoan-Lupemban. As populations contracted, expanded, and moved, this mix of old and new technologies was deposited on the landscape in a patchwork pattern, with the Acheulean gone for the most part by the end of OIS 8.

We would expect several patterns if this were true. First, areas uninhabitable during cold conditions (i.e., areas that are currently arid) should see a complete replacement of Acheulean by MSA with an unconformity or hiatus between. Second, habitable areas (areas that today are more wooded) should see several con-temporaneous technologies. Third, areas of true transition should be hard to find. The record bears this out. Northern and southern Africa (more arid parts of the continent) are characterized by patterns 1 and 2, while central and eastern Africa show pattern 3.

The MSA Record

MSA people refined and diversified late Acheulean technologies. Prepared core flake manufacture came to dominate MSA assemblages, and flakes and flake tools and pointed forms became common (Figure 4.4). Blade technology was common in the African MSA. When present, bifaces were small, falling within the size range and shape of projectile weapons. Clark (1988) argued that the MSA introduced a pattern of regional identity. Different regions showed different tool forms and assemblage composition, and Clark thought this signaled a significant step forward in behavioral modernity. Advances in dating techniques now allow us to expand Clark's idea: the MSA represents a stage of *both regional and temporal patterning.* Regionally unique and temporally restricted artifact types and technologies appear and disappear. Examples of these include the Aterian and pre-Aurignacian in north-ern Africa; the Lupemban in equatorial Africa; and the Howiesons Poort and Still-bay in South Africa (Chapter 5). All are regionally distinct, while some (perhaps all) are temporally distinct. It is unclear at this time exactly what this means. These could be very specific technological adaptations to particular conditions, or region-ally based stylistic entities.

The bibliographic sources for the empirical record on the MSA of Africa are vast. Clark's (1982) overview of the entire continent still stands as the definitive source. Other sources focus on the northern, eastern, or southern regions. The student of Africa faces a highly variable record in these regions resulting from: regional variation in scientific traditions derived from different colonial pasts; spurts of research that occurred at different times and with different methods of excava-tion and recovery; and varying geological conditions resulting in widely differing quality of preservation.

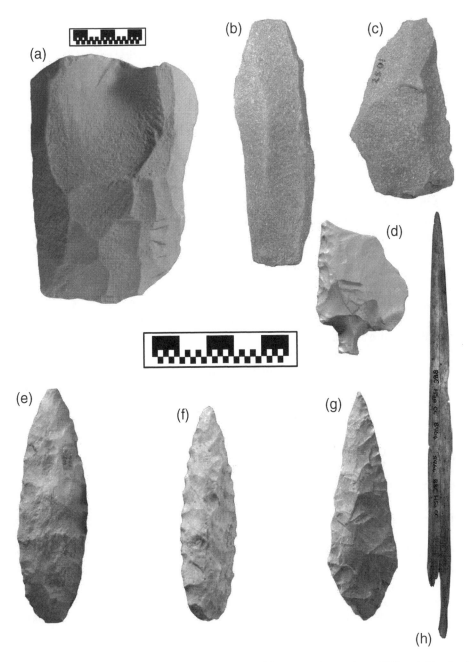

Figure 4.4. A selection of MSA tools from Africa: (a) prepared core from El Beyed, Mauritania; (b) blade and (c) point from Mossel Bay, South Africa; (d) Aterian tanged side-scraper from El Beyed; (e) Lupemban lanceolate from Lukala, Democratic Republic of the Congo; (f) Aterian lanceolate from El Beyed; (g) Stillbay lanceolate from Blombos Cave, South Africa; (h) bone point from Blombos Cave. Tools (b) through (h) all at central scale (large block = cm), and (a) on scale above. Photos (g) and (h) courtesy of Christopher Henshilwood

Under French influence, the MSA in northern Africa has been called Middle Paleolithic (Balout 1955; Ferring 1975; McBurney 1960; Wendorf and Schild 1992). The intensity of Stone Age research in northern Africa was greatest in the colonial period, particularly before 1960 (Sheppard 1990). Excellent preservation characterized the coastal zone of northern Africa where alkaline limestone formations that produce caves were natural attractors for human settlement. However, since many of these sites were excavated before the 1960s, many were subject to collection bias. It was common not to sieve the remains, and standard practice to only keep diagnostic lithics (retouched pieces) and fossils (cranial parts and the articular ends of bones).

Stone Age research in northern Africa has been shaped by the typological approach of the French tradition. Artifacts are placed into types defined by recurrent morphology and the frequency of types compared between samples (see Bordes 1972). This extends to the classification of technology where technological classes, such as levallois flakes, form the basis of comparisons. While this approach may have its weaknesses (Dibble 1995), its strength lies in its standardization, allowing wide-ranging (even intercontinental) comparisons.

Though eastern Africa has seen more research than northern Africa in the last 20 years, the record is still sparse and patchy. Limestone formations are rare in eastern Africa and the majority of the MSA sites have very poor, or non-existent, faunal preservation. Stone Age archaeology in eastern Africa was conducted under an Anglophone tradition. Unlike northern Africa, researchers working in eastern Africa have not developed a standard approach to lithic classification, and many sites are reported in widely varying ways. Clark's (1988) review of the MSA in eastern Africa covers most of the known sites. Since then there have been several advances in the application of dating techniques, faunal analysis, and some new fieldwork. Central Africa has seen sporadic research by British, Belgian, and American scholars working with a variety of approaches (de Maret 1990). Mortelmans (1957), Clark (1982), and Barham (2001) offer good summaries of this region.

The rich MSA record of southern Africa grew from a long tradition of research that was always of high quality for its time. Somewhat uniquely, much of the work on the MSA in southern Africa was developed by local, albeit European in derivation, scholars. Though influenced by an Anglophone approach, many developed a distinctly "South African style" that has its roots in the now classic monograph by Goodwin and van Riet Lowe (1929). While this approach has strengths, the approach to lithics is idiosyncratic. For example, researchers in South Africa seldom tabulate levallois technology, though this technology certainly exists there. As a result it is impossible to measure the geographic extent of this technology and its changing frequency, and develop an overall understanding of the pattern in Africa.

While Zimbabwe saw regular Stone Age research during the colonial period, work has slowed in the last 30 years. South Africa has an outstanding record, but like northern Africa, many of the best-known sites were excavated more than 20 years ago with imperfect techniques. For example, the Singer and Wymer (1982) excavations at Klasies River were relatively coarse, and much of the material selectively retained. This site and those excavations have had an enormous impact on our view of the South African MSA, and there may be much in need of revision. More recent research is being conducted with the highest standards, resulting in records of varying character that are difficult to compare to the older excavations. The record in South Africa is both dense and, sometimes, spectacularly preserved, often in the large coastal caves. This rich record has seen a sequence of excellent summaries (Clark 1959; Deacon and Deacon 1999; Sampson 1971; Volman 1984).

Western Africa has the sparsest excavated MSA record, and for the most part we leave it out of our discussion (see Chapters 7 and 9). We diverge from most other presentations in that we will refer to all these archaeological occurrences in Africa as MSA. We do so for several reasons. First, it is just simpler to do so. Second, we want to emphasize commonalities among all African assemblages that, we believe, separate them from Eurasia beyond the Levant. And finally, drawing a vast terminological line across the continent at the southern boundary of the Sahara seems unreasonable unless empirically justified, which it is not.

Northern Africa

Northern Africa is an arid region dominated by the Sahara desert where there are few areas with sufficient water to support a hunter-gatherer adaptation lacking wells and water storage technology. This was not always the case. The paleoenvironmental record shows that during inter-glacial periods much of northern Africa was wetter, with grassland and wooded grassland ecosystems and permanent sources of water extending throughout the Sahara. Recent results suggest that northern Africa went through several arid and humid phases that correlate with the worldwide oxygen isotope record (Macklin et al. 2002; Szabo et al. 1995). The natural aridity and climatic shifts produced a punctuated record where Stone Age remains appear during climatically favorable periods, and then disappear with the onset of aridity.

All MSA sites in the Sahara occur in association with evidence for standing water. Faunal remains suggest a grassland or wooded grassland ecosystem similar to that found in sub-Saharan Africa. Moreover, many sites have fauna suggesting permanent water (crocodiles, Nile perch). The Maghreb and Cyrenaica are exceptions and show more continuous occupation in a wider variety of contexts, perhaps due to more favorable rainfall regimes that did not expire during glacial periods. These areas were refugia for people during glacial periods when most of northern Africa was uninhabitable.

No site in northern Africa documents a smooth transition from Acheulean to MSA, there being an unconformity between the two when present together. In contrast, there is often a smooth transition between the two main MSA entities of northern Africa (Aterian and Mousterian), the former stratified above the latter. Some of the earliest Mousterian sites are Jebel Irhoud in Morocco (Grün and Stringer 1991) and Bir Terfawi in Egypt (Wendorf et al. 1993), and overall the evidence suggests that the MSA was in place by 230 ky. This suggests that the time of turnover from Acheulean to MSA may have dated a few thousand years earlier during the terminal periods of OIS 8, a cold period when much of northern Africa would have been desert and most of the region abandoned.

The Mousterian generally is dominated by levallois (Figure 4.4a) and/or disc technology, and includes high frequencies of side scrapers, denticulates, notches, and lower frequencies of points (sometimes Mousterian points). It typically lacks bifacial points. The distribution of Mousterian sites forms a northeasterly arc on the edge of the Sahara. These hunter-gatherers practiced a wide range of economies. In the Maghreb arid grassland species predominate (Thomas 1981), suggesting regular exploitation of open environments, while Barbary sheep dominate the occupations at Haua Fteah (Klein and Scott 1986), suggesting exploitation of steep mountainous areas. In the Nile Valley in the northern Sudan, several sites document shifting exploitation of terrestrial and aquatic resources, sometimes focused on wild cattle, other times on large deep-water species of fish (Shiner 1968).

Aterian assemblages typically have bifacial foliate points (Figure 4.4f), and the presence of these with pedunculates (tanged pieces, Figure 4.4d) is often used to define it relative to the Mousterian. The Aterian shares with the Mousterian the common occurrence of levallois technology, side scrapers, denticulates, and more rarely Mousterian points. In contrast with the Mousterian it often has Upper Paleolithic (UP) forms such as end scrapers and burins. It is generally recognized that the Aterian changes over time, with the earlier phases looking more Mousterian, and the later converging on the UP. The Aterian is far more abundant than the Mousterian in the central and western Sahara and Maghreb, but it does not occur east of the Nile. At Adrar Bous (Clark et al. 1973), Aterian sites are near a lake or swamp, and may have been positioned to ambush large mammals coming to drink. A fine vitrified tuff exploited for lithic production was procured from about 240 km away. Despite the lack of plant remains in both Mousterian and Aterian sites, we anticipate that plants were a significant component of the diet.

Several other lithic expressions are both temporally and regionally specific. Haua Fteah on the coast of Cyrenaica (Libya) has one of the longest uninterrupted sequences in Africa (McBurney 1967). The lowest occupation is assigned to a lithic industry called the pre-Aurignacian, a blade-dominated technology with many UP-like forms, followed by a more conventional Mousterian. The presence of seashells provides some of the earliest evidence for the use of shellfish as food. In general, the assemblages from Cyrenaica resemble those from the Levant, suggesting a pathway of connection between Asia and Africa. The Khormusan in the Nile is another northern African lithic entity with UP characteristics (Marks 1968).

The stratigraphic record, combined with new radiometric dates and the regional pattern of landscape use, presents an interesting picture for northern Africa. Dates in eastern Africa and Bir Terfawi suggest that the MSA dates back to OIS 7 and 8, so it seems likely that the Acheulean/MSA boundary is in OIS 8. This manifests itself as a period of dune migration, deflation, and lower water tables in northern Africa, lower sea level on the Maghreb coast, and general site abandonment. The earliest MSA technology in northern Africa likely dates to late OIS 8. Initial radiocarbon dates on the Aterian were interpreted to suggest an age between 40 to 20 ky (Camps et al. 1973), but more recent radiometric dates suggest an older time range, perhaps in isotope stage 5 (Cremaschi et al. 1998).

The Aterian is one of the most widely distributed MSA or MP industries yet documented. The core region for this technology was the Sahara, which during its heyday was a rich grassland ecosystem with abundant plant foods, large mammal migration ecosystems, and permanent water sources. It may have been one of the largest continuous stretches of grassland ever to exist on our planet. The Aterian was the dominant MSA technology west of the Nile during OIS 5 and likely represents a highly mobile grassland adaptation. On the fringes of this grassland ecosystem were other technological systems specially adapted to local conditions (such as the Khormusan). As the Sahara desiccated during OIS 4, the region was abandoned. Much of northern Africa shows little to no occupation until around 20 ky when there is a reoccupation of the Maghreb and Nile Valley by complex hunter-gatherers. The exception is Cyrenaica, which was continuously occupied right up to the origins of food production.

The MSA settlement of northern Africa documents shifting human settlement and technology in reaction to severe climatic perturbations acting on an already harsh environment. We often envision the Sahara as a vast wasteland, a sea of sand of only marginal interest to our current lives and economies. However, due to its size and likely productivity, the Sahara during the Aterian was home to a vast hunter-gatherer population equipped with a refined technology. As the Sahara opened to human settlement at the beginning of OIS 5, populations likely entered it from central Africa, the Maghreb, and the Nile Valley. These populations brought newly developed technologies that fused to form the Aterian technology which these hunter-gatherers used to exploit the rich grasslands. Aterian technology, with its combination of levallois production and emphasis upon hafted bifaces, may be a fusion of Mousterian and Lupemban elements.

The MSA in eastern and central Africa

South of the Sahara we enter a more environmentally heterogeneous area. Our knowledge of the MSA is concentrated in the Rift Valley that spans a variety of habitats, from arid near-desert conditions, through rich grassland ecosystems, dense woodlands, lowland rainforests, and montane forests. Eastern Africa has produced the oldest MSA dates, and likely documents the oldest MSA or MP in the world. While it might be tempting to argue that the MSA evolved here, these early dates reflect the presence of volcanic ashes that allow us to date the MSA. One of the first applications of potassium-argon dating to Africa yielded a date of 240 ky for the site of Malewa Gorge in the Kenyan Central Rift (Evernden and Curtis 1965). More recent applications have yielded dates consistent with this (Gademotta at 235 ky; Wendorf et al. 1994) and even older (Baringo at 280 ky; Tryon and McBrearty 2002).

Eastern Africa does not show the punctuated record of settlement so clear in northern Africa, and this might be due to several factors. First, eastern Africa falls at the confluence of two rainfall systems that may have had an ameliorating effect on glacial aridification. Second, variation in elevation provides a diversity of habitats, some of which could have remained productive through cool and arid conditions. There are several localities where occupation during glacial periods is probable, including Lukenya Hill GvJm46 (Marean 1992), Porc-Epic (Clark et al. 1984), and the long sequences at Nasera and Mumba Rockshelter (Mehlman 1989).

Nor does eastern Africa show the distinct shift in lithic technology that is so evident in northern Africa. Rather, the majority of MSA assemblages draw on a series of basic technological characteristics with much of the variation related to raw materials. The technological similarities include: an emphasis on prepared core technology, including levallois and disc forms; assemblages dominated by unretouched flakes; regular occurrence of blades; rare formal tools; and even rarer bifacial points. Bifacial points are found in a variety of shapes throughout the region, and when found in the past these have often been called "Stillbay" after the South African site. Backed blades resembling crescents have been discovered at Mumba Rockshelter, and some have noted these may provide a connection to the Howiesons Poort of South Africa (Chapter 5). However, they do not display the same regularity of manufacture, and there is no clear pattern of distribution yet described. The lithic raw materials vary from relatively poor quality quartzite and quartz, to high-quality volcanic glass obsidian. The obsidian was clearly highly valued, as geochemical analyses have documented its presence over 300 km from its point of extraction (Mehlman 1989; Merrick and Brown 1984).

Eastern African MSA sites document exploitation of a variety of ecozones. At Porc-Epic Cave, hunters used a cave far up an escarpment to hunt a variety of wooded grassland and woodland species (Assefa 2002). Lukenya Hill hunters lived in arid grassland and may have intercepted migrating herds through a tactical hunting strategy (Marean 1997). At Nasera Rockshelter and Loiyangalani hunters exploited the fauna of a rich grassland ecosystem. We anticipate that these economies focused primarily on plant foods through most of the year, supplemented by hunting.

The Lake Victoria basin marks a change in environment from these more easterly areas. It is just east of classic equatorial Africa, a mostly low-lying area dominated by wetter climates and forested conditions where the Sangoan-Lupemban Industrial complex occurs. The Lupemban is distinctive in that it has two rather unique tool forms: a bifacial lanceolate (Figure 4.4e) and a core axe. The Lupemban, like the Sangoan, is especially concentrated in areas that are forested today, and this pattern led Clark (1964) to suggest it was a forest adaptation. Unfortunately most Lupemban sites lack faunal remains. Recent results from western Kenya suggest that the association with forested conditions may be modern only (McBrearty 1991), though Barham (2001) has recently elaborated on the forest-adaptation argument. We believe that these dense rainforest locations were unproductive for foragers (Bailey et al. 1989), and that the Lupemban may have been a grassland adaptation dated to glacial OIS 6 (see below).

A somewhat unique series of sites has recently been reported from the Semliki Valley, just north of Lake Rutazinge in the Democratic Republic of the Congo. All occur at a locality called Katanda, which is a series of terraces that run parallel to the Semliki River (Brooks et al. 1995; Yellen et al. 1995). The MSA occurrences are a reasonably crude MSA technology that the researchers date to 90 ky. There are several important finds, including fish remains and finely made uniserial (one set of barbs) bone points (Chapter 7).

The MSA in southern Africa

Southern Africa shares with eastern Africa a heterogeneous environment with high-altitude zones, grasslands, and deserts. Yet there are notable differences. Southern Africa is less tropical, and as one moves into South Africa, somewhat temperate in climate. As a result it lacks the lowland and highland rain forests typical of the more tropical regions and has greater seasonality. It also has vast stretches of desert and arid lands on the borderline of habitability. Oceans off the coast are some of the richest in the world, providing abundant near-shore resources in the form of fish, shellfish, marine mammals, and sea birds, all of which were exploited from the MSA onward. This rich near-shore ecology far surpasses that found elsewhere in Africa, and likely explains the abundance of shell-middens relative to the north. Finally, the Rift Valley does not penetrate deeply into this region, so younger volcanic rocks and ashes are absent. This translates into different types of woodlands and grass-lands, and less secure dating.

The lithic assemblages in southern Africa have similarities to and differences from those to the north. The vast majority of unretouched flakes and blades were struck from prepared cores (Figure 4.4a). Blades are abundant (Figure 4.4b), more so than in eastern Africa, as are pointed forms (Figure 4.4c). Many of the cores are levallois, disc, or variants of these approaches specifically designed for blade removal. Retouched pieces are rare, and when present are often rather simple denticulates or scrapers. The assemblages often have relatively large flakes and blades, and this is partially explainable by the predominant raw material, quartzite, which is usually available in large blocks and cobbles. Classification systems have been diverse. Volman's (1984) MSA 1 through 3 sequence recognizes a temporal shift in size and shape of flakes and blades.

The relatively rare retouched pieces sometimes take on special forms. One such form is that of a backed blade, often forming a crescent, similar in shape but larger than LSA types and considered the hallmark of the Howiesons Poort (Chapter 5). Another is a bifacial point (Figure 4.4g) that varies from teardrop to foliate in shape. The latter is the defining feature of the Stillbay. There is now evidence to suggest that both the Howiesons Poort and the Stillbay are temporally discrete and region-ally restricted entities. That being the case, southern Africa shares with northern Africa the occurrence of a variable MSA technology based on prepared cores and unretouched flakes and blades, with entities that have unique and more specialized retouched forms.

One of the hallmarks of the southern African record is the presence of cave/rockshelter sites, often large and deeply stratified with long sequences of MSA material, and sometimes preserved fauna. Many were excavated prior to the 1960s and produced data that, because of less advanced excavation techniques, we now know is questionable. However, both old and new sites are the focus of renewed field research.

There are some basic distinctions between the archaeological record in the northern versus southern parts of southern Africa, and the record in Zambia and Zimbabwe seems to represent a transition from an equatorial character to the more classic South African record encompassed by Volman's system. Some of these more northern sites preserve Sangoan-Lupemban assemblages, or assemblages resembling these (Clark and Brown 2001; Clark et al. 1947). New uranium-series dates suggest that these Lupemban occupations may be as old as 266 ky, and worked pieces of pigment are present (Barham 2002). The influence of the Sangoan-Lupemban extends into Zimbabwe, as at the Matopos Hills sites. Several have assemblages that suggest a mixture of late Sangoan with early MSA (Cooke 1966). Stratified above these sites are more conventional MSA assemblages, similar to those to the south, which include unifacial and bifacial points, end and side scrapers, backed flakes, and even grinding stones. More than 100 sites with this type of assemblage are known from the Matopos Hills and to the west.

In South Africa there is a diversity of sites. Some, such as Montague Cave and Nelson Bay Cave, do not preserve fauna due to the acidic conditions in these quartzite formations. Others, such as Klasies River (Chapter 5) and Die Kelders Cave 1 have fauna preserved due to associated calcretes or limestones. Several sites preserve sequences that span the MSA and LSA transition. The long sequence at Border Cave dates this transition to around 40 ky (Butzer et al. 1978; Grün and Beaumont 2001), while at Rose Cottage it is more gradual and later (A. Clark 1999; Wadley 1996).

Klasies River has long been the benchmark sequence (Deacon and Geleijnse 1988; Singer and Wymer 1982). This was the first site found with substantial amounts of anatomically modern human fossil material, some with stone tool cut marks, now well dated to OIS 5. The Klasies River sequence also was the first to document that the Howiesons Poort lies between more conventional MSA layers, where it was once thought to be a transitional MSA/LSA industry (Chapter 5). Fauna and organic materials document a pattern of shifting faunal and floral exploitation in reaction to changing environmental conditions and sea levels. Antelopes were hunted throughout the sequence (Klein 1976), and during warmer periods shellfish and seals were exploited regularly, while cooler periods show a drop in sea use and a focus on terrestrial-based plant foods. The Klasies River faunal list is extremely diverse. Recent taphonomic work at Die Kelders Cave 1 shows that the small bovids were likely accumulated by large raptorial birds, suggesting that hunters at the site focused on eland, the largest antelope on the landscape (Marean et al. 2000).

Blombos Cave (Henshilwood et al. 2001a, 2001b, 2002) differs from the large and open caves so far discussed. It is a small cave set high up a steep cliff. Blombos Cave has a rich and well-preserved MSA sequence of three layers stratified below dune sand that blew into the cave during OIS 4, securely dated to 77 ky. There are two remarkable results from this site, including a bone tool industry and a rich ochre assemblage, much of which is worked, and perhaps most spectacularly two pieces are engraved with abstract designs. The faunal assemblage is rich in shellfish and terrestrial mammals, and fish are common as well.

The African Evidence for the Origins of Modern Human Behavior

We have outlined several models for the origins of modern humans, and noted that the weight of evidence favors a replacement scenario with Africa as the source of anatomically modern humans. The ultimate mechanism for this replacement is likely a behavioral difference between non-modern and modern populations. The nature of this behavioral difference is a key source of debate in the archaeological literature. There is no agreement among scholars as to what constitutes modern behavior. Some researchers have examined the antiquity and distribution of the material residues of behavioral traits thought to be modern or non-modern (Lindly and Clark 1990; McBrearty and Brooks 2000; Mellars 1995). This "litmus-test" approach assumes that if enough traits are absent, modern behavior is not present. For example, some argue that the ability to systematically manufacture formal tools from raw materials other than stone, and the ability to symbol in complex ways, are hallmarks of modern humans (Gamble 1994; Klein 2000). Thus, the presence of bone tools or art is taken as support for behavioral modernity, and their absence reflects non-modern behavior (for summaries of traits see Gamble 1994; Klein 1995; McBrearty and Brooks 2000).

How effective are these traits at measuring behavioral modernity? A recent analysis suggests that some may be more effective than others (Henshilwood and Marean 2003). It is instructive to reflect on how these traits came to be emphasized. A paper by Paul Mellars (1973) on the differences between the rich MP and UP records of southwestern France is the source. Mellars identified several material traits, thought to reflect important aspects of human adaptation that were absent in the MP and present in the UP, and established a Rubicon that eventually was projected across the Old World. The overlap between Mellars' list of traits and those found in Gamble (1994) and Klein (2000) is considerable.

Debate over the presence and antiquity of these traits has congealed into opposing models summarized by Henshilwood and Marean (2003): the Later Upper Pleistocene model (LUP); Earlier Upper Pleistocene model (EUP); a Later Middle Pleistocene model (LMP); and a Gradualist model. Simply put, LUP argues that modern human behavior did not appear until after 60 ky, and the support for this model is largely the extension of the "Mellars Rubicon" throughout the Old World. McBrearty and Brooks (2000) contested this, arguing that many of these traits appear in Africa well before 60 ky. The other models place the origins well before this time, for example at the Acheulean–MSA boundary (LMP) or the beginning of OIS 5 (EUP), or gradually through the late Middle and Upper Pleistocene (Gradual).

LUP was the favored model until recently. As McBrearty and Brooks (2000) have pointed out, the African empirical record is thin relative to the Eurasian record, and further archaeological research is needed to develop an adequate empirical test of the competing models. In light of this, Henshilwood and Marean (2003) argue that the projection of the Mellars Rubicon throughout Africa resulted from Eurocentric presumptions about the Stone Age past.

In the last 10 years there has been a burst of research on the MSA of Africa, and while the record is nowhere near as complete as that in France, progress is being made. We are finding exciting, but hotly contested, results that have steadily eroded the Mellars Rubicon in Africa, which holds somewhat firmer in Eurasia. We distill from our broader empirical review the new finds to suggest that the MSA in Africa is distinct from the MP in Eurasia, and explore new data from faunal exploitation that suggests some important similarities. More speculatively, these new results could suggest that cultural aspects of behavioral modernity in Africa extend far earlier than 50 ky.

Exchange networks and the integration of societies

Stone, the primary raw material for Stone Age technology, varies in quality and typically outcrops in a patchy manner. Archaeologists have discovered that more complexly organized societies develop trade and exchange systems that move materials greater distances on the landscape. Studying the transport of ancient raw materials allows us to examine, by proxy, the formation and character of past exchange systems. This potentially informs on the origins of modern human behavior since one characteristic of modern people is the ability to form complex social relations that rely on our brain's ability to plan and monitor social and economic contracts.

Prior to the UP lithic raw materials in Eurasia were generally procured within 40 km of the site of discard (Mellars 1996). This has been interpreted as indicating simple social networks that precluded long-distance flow of goods, and was assumed to be the case in Africa as well. However, recent work has undermined this pattern in Africa. In eastern Africa many sites have substantial quantities of obsidian, a volcanic glass with outstanding flaking properties that can often be traced by chemical analysis to its point of extraction. Analyses show that some regularly occurs more than 100 km from its source, and some even greater than 300 km. This is not a unique result. At Adrar Bous in the Sahara, Mousterian and Aterian assemblages included a fine green vitric tuff that was procured from a source 280 km distant (Clark 1993). These raw materials occur in reasonable, albeit low, frequencies, suggesting far-flung formal exchange networks.

Bone tools and the production of technologically complex functional designs

Bone tools are a key element of the Mellars Rubicon, and until recently it was argued that bone tools did not occur in the African MSA (Gamble 1994; Klein

2000). Bone tools come in two varieties, defined by the complexity of the production process: expedient and labor-intensive. The latter are often called "formal" bone tools, but we find that term less useful since it depends on a subjective evaluation of what constitutes formality. "Expedient" refers to a production process that is short and lacking in defined steps. In contrast, labor-intensive tools require a significant energy investment and a more complicated plan in the production process. Presumably, this investment has some economic or social payoff. This characterization is more useful as it allows a continuum between the two extremes, and employs measurable criteria. Experimental studies show conclusively that bone projectile points have very high performance (Knecht 1997), and thus the payoff is economic. One could argue that bone tools are a weak measure of behavioral modernity, and are more reflective of labor intensification (Henshilwood and Marean 2003). While this is probably true, some aspects of bone projectile points may bear on behavioral complexity. Bone points are typically aerodynamically sophisticated; their pointed ends often resemble the tip of a bullet. The regular production of this morphology clearly reflects a practical understanding of principles of flight and penetration.

Bone tools do not preserve equally well in all environments, which is a chronic problem in Africa since most caves occur in acidic contexts. Whereas in southwestern France there are large numbers of excavated MP sites with bone preserved, there are 10–15 in all of Africa. Recovery and analytical techniques further affect our knowledge of bone tool representation since expedient ones are typically made on long bone shaft fragments, and bone tools are often found broken. Most MSA sites in Africa were excavated before sediments were regularly screened, and long bone shaft fragments were often thrown out. As a result it is impossible to estimate with confidence the frequency of bone tools in the African sample. However, labor-intensive bone tools have been found in two recently excavated MSA contexts. At Katanda in the Democratic Republic of the Congo several MSA sites have yielded barbed bone points in association with fish remains (Brooks et al. 1995; Yellen et al. 1995). While these points have not yet been described in detail, at a minimum they reflect scraping, notching, and polishing of bone to reach a sophisticated and standardized projectile weapon. Blombos Cave in the South African Cape yielded a bone tool assemblage dated to a minimum of 77 ky. The complete technological process of production has been reconstructed (Henshilwood et al. 2001a) for both expedient and labor-intensive tools (points, Figure 4.4h). Most were made on long bone shafts of antelope that were initially shaped by flaking and scraping. More labor-intensive tools were then carefully ground and polished to a point, producing projectiles similar to those produced by hunter-gatherers observed in ethnographic contexts.

Symbolic behavior

Virtually every author who has discussed the origins of modern human behavior has discussed symbolic behavior. The ability to construct, use, and understand symbols, including language, uniquely characterizes humans. Symbolic behavior takes many forms, including the production of art. Art occurs in a variety of forms in Stone Age societies: paintings and engravings on fixed rocky surfaces and portable objects, decorating functional objects with artistic symbols (e.g., symbols on a bone point), and painting and scarification on bodies. Behaviors that may reflect symbolic activity include burial of the dead, preparation of a human skeleton after death, or shaping functional objects with symbolic (communicative) goals in mind (e.g., expressing group affiliation through the shape of a projectile point). We might therefore recognize three types of evidence for symbolic behavior in the archaeological record: (1) direct evidence – actual symbols found in the record; (2) indirect evidence – evidence for behaviors that reflect symbolic thought; and (3) technological evidence – the technology to produce art.

The Mellars Rubicon recognizes an explosion of symbolic behavior at the MP/UP boundary. There is little direct evidence for symbolic behavior anywhere in the world prior to 40 ky. Indirect evidence is contentious. For example, burial could have a symbolic component to it, or it may have been practiced simply to dispose of a rotting corpse. The technological evidence differs. It is now clear that many MSA sites in southern Africa have vast quantities of ochre, and much of it is clearly selected for its redness, a color that figures prominently in symbolic activity in many hunter-gatherer societies. It is common for pieces to be worked and even shaped into pencils (Watts 2002). In contrast, pigments are rare in Eurasian MP sites, and, when present, occur in small quantities. This pattern of ochre use thus could be technological evidence for symbolic behavior. This interpretation has been strengthened by the discovery of two pieces of decorated ochre at the site of Blombos Cave. Both have complex crosshatched designs similar to those that regularly occur in hunter-gatherer art (Henshilwood et al. 2002).

Faunal exploitation

The ethnographic record documents that modern humans equipped with Stone Age technologies can effectively hunt every living land mammal. This has led researchers to argue that hunting effectiveness is a measure of behavioral modernity. Binford (1981) argued from French and South African data that the earliest humans were scavengers, and this pattern continued up to 60 ky, after which humans began hunting effectively. Thus, he argued for lengthy stasis in faunal exploitation behavior (Binford 1985). His work stimulated debate, analysis, and reanalysis of the data. Several clear competing models emerged (Marean and Assefa 1999): the obligate scavenger model; the opportunistic scavenger model and less effective hunter model; and the fully effective hunter model.

Zooarchaeologists have focused on three classes of data to reconstruct faunal exploitation: the frequency and placement of surface modification on bones (such as stone tool cut marks); the frequency of different skeletal elements of prey animals in archaeological sites; and the ages of prey represented in the sites (mortality profiles). We focus on the first two as debate surrounds the meaning of patterning in mortality profiles (Marean and Assefa 1999).

Bones in the skeleton have three sources of nutrition attached to them: flesh, marrow, and bone grease. Archaeologists have measured the amounts of these three tissues and arrived at a nutritional ranking of body parts (Binford 1978). Figure 4.5a shows the rankings on a typical ungulate skeleton. The basic proposition is that the first feeder at a carcass will take the highest-ranking parts. If we have an archaeological site with only the lowest-ranking parts, then scavenging is indicated. Similarly, if cut marks tend to be located on high-ranking parts, this suggests hunting, and if they are located on low-quality parts, scavenging is indicated.

Binford (1981, 1985) drew on these propositions to construct the obligate scavenger model for MP/MSA behavior (see also Chapter 5). Based on patterns of skeletal part representation and surface modification (cut marks and carnivore tooth marks), Binford argued that effective hunting of large-bodied mammals did not occur before 60 ky in either Eurasia or Africa. He observed that larger ungulates were predominately represented by head and foot parts (low-utility parts) in archaeological sites. Binford also found that cut marks were dominated by heavy chop marks located where bones articulated, suggesting the chopping up of desiccated carcasses. He found few defleshing cut marks, most confined to low-utility foot bones.

More recently, Stiner (1993, 1994) has argued that Neanderthals in coastal Italy practiced both regular hunting and scavenging. She argued that Neanderthals were not obligate scavengers, but tended to scavenge rather than hunt during times when plant foods were abundant. When plant foods were less abundant, Neanderthals hunted regularly. Stiner relied on several types of data to make her point. Like Binford, she argued that a head-dominated pattern suggests scavenging, and she has identified this at several sites. She also examined the age at death of prey animals, and argued that scavengers generally produce mortality patterns dominated by very old animals. Head-dominated skeletal patterns were associated with old-dominated mortality patterns, and interpreted as evidence for scavenging.

Klein (Klein and Cruz-Uribe 1996) has argued that scavenging was not an important component of MSA behavior. MSA hominins were primarily hunters, but less effective ones than modern humans. His insight derived from comparative analysis of faunal data from MSA contexts at Klasies River (Chapter 5) and later LSA sites. Klein argued that MSA sites have lots of eland and few buffalo and bushpig, while LSA sites from similar environmental regimes show more buffalo and bushpig. In environments similar to those reconstructed for the sites, docile eland is rare while more dangerous buffalo and bushpig are more common. Klein argued that during the MSA people were forced to focus on the less dangerous but less abundant eland due to an inability to regularly kill fierce buffalo and bushpig. During the LSA they had the ability to prey upon animals in equal proportions to their natural abundance. At the same time nearly all the buffalo at Klasies River are juveniles while eland show an abundance of prime-age adults. Klein argued that MSA hunters could only kill very young buffalo, but adult eland fell within their

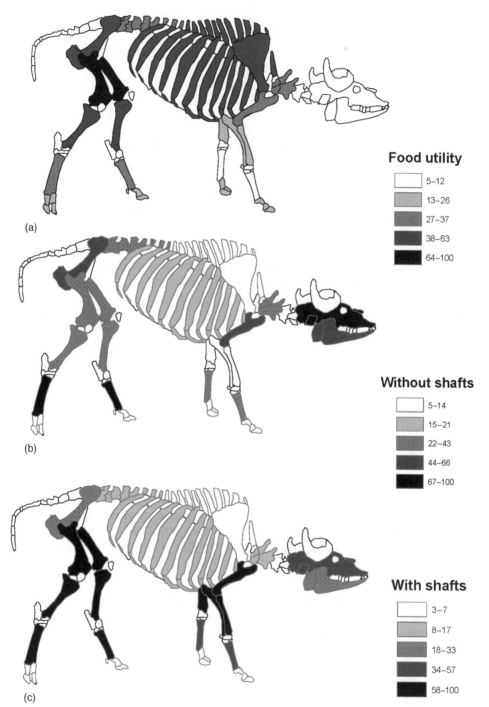

Food utility

☐	5–12
▨	13–26
▦	27–37
▩	38–63
■	64–100

Without shafts

☐	5–14
▨	15–21
▦	22–43
▩	44–66
■	67–100

With shafts

☐	3–7
▨	8–17
▦	18–33
▩	34–57
■	58–100

(a)

(b)

(c)

Figure 4.5. The utility ranking of the major skeletal elements and skeletal element abundance of Die Kelders Cave 1: (a) nutritional ranking of overall food utility on a typical ungulate skeleton (0 = lowest utility, 100 = highest utility); (b) Die Kelders Cave 1 sample with bone shaft fragments excluded; (c) Die Kelders Cave 1 sample with bone shaft fragments included

abilities. A more parsimonious explanation is that these changes in species abundance are the result of an expansion of diet breadth associated with increasing population density (Marean and Assefa 1999). Also, a regression analysis of the faunal data demonstrates that the disparity in the sizes of assemblages accounts for the gross richness differences observed by Klein, and this change is better described as a Holocene/Pleistocene one than an LSA/MSA one (Minichillo 1998).

A fourth model, the fully effective hunter model, was argued for early on (Chase 1988, 1989), based on French MP sites, but was not widely supported. Recently that model has gained increasing support from two areas. Several researchers have reanalyzed assemblages originally studied by Binford and concluded that the data are inconsistent with scavenging and support hunting (Grayson and Delpech 1994; Milo 1998). Other researchers have developed new zooarchaeological approaches and applied them to MSA and MP assemblages (Marean 1998; Marean and Assefa 1999). These approaches directly target a continuing problem in zooarchaeological analyses: bones at archaeological sites do not survive in the precise manner in which they were deposited. However, recent studies of faunal assemblage formation (taphonomy) have produced a general understanding of bone survival, and armed with this understanding, we can better understand patterns in skeletal element survivorship and surface modification.

Assemblages widely interpreted as scavenged have a universal pattern to them: head and foot parts dominate. The primary bones that are missing are the long bones and vertebrae, both of which have high volumes of edible tissue. Long bones are highly patterned in their distribution of dense cortical bone and spongy bone; middle parts of the shaft are denser than the ends and lack spongy bone, while the ends are less dense and contain lots of spongy bone. People typically fragment long bones to remove marrow, leaving two basic types of fragments: isolated shafts that contain no spongy bone with adhering grease; and long bone ends that include greasy, spongy bone. Studies have shown that carnivores typically consume the ends of bones, leaving isolated shafts (Marean and Spencer 1991), and carnivores regularly visit abandoned human sites and ravage bony remains (Blumenschine 1988). They typically completely consume vertebrae, ribs, and other bones where spongy bone is ubiquitous through their interior (Marean et al. 1992). The result is that if we want to reconstruct the relative frequency of bones that were discarded, we must focus on these middle shaft portions. However, these fragments are difficult to identify to skeletal element and prior to the 1970s were often discarded during excavation or not studied by zooarchaeologists when present.

We have recently conducted studies of two MSA sites from Africa and one from Southwest Asia where the excavators kept the shafts, which we identified to skeletal element (Assefa 2002; Marean 1998; Marean and Kim 1998). These new data dramatically impact our understanding of skeletal element abundance. Figures 4.5b and 4.5c illustrate the Die Kelders Cave 1 sample as an example. If we exclude the shafts, as was the case with the scavenged sites reported above, the result is a clear head and foot pattern (Figure 4.5b). However, if we include the shafts, the pattern reverses and the result is that high-utility bones appear abundant (Figure 4.5c), a pattern clearly consistent with hunting. We found a similar result with cut marks.

The shafts of the long bones had high frequencies of cut marks, but removing these shafts from the analysis lowered the cut mark frequencies on high-utility bones relative to low-utility ones. These studies show that hunting was practiced in both Africa and Eurasia, and that the scavenged pattern was a methodological artifact caused by discard, or lack of study, of the fragmented shafts.

Conclusions

It is clear from our review of the empirical record that the MSA represents a significant change from the Acheulean in some key characteristics, yet in others it is either similar or not demonstrably different based on the current sample. The MSA appears to represent a time when people used a wider variety of habitats, and thus may have had a behavior and technology that was both more efficient and more plastic. MSA hunters ranged from the mountains of the Maghreb, to the grasslands of East Africa, to the coastal zones of South Africa, exploiting everything from the largest antelope to marine shellfish, and incorporating freshwater and ocean fish in a highly diverse diet tailored to regional environmental specifics. However, we must realize that the Acheulean record is severely limited relative to the MSA. There are precious few sites with fauna, and even fewer that have been studied with modern techniques. If Acheulean sites were associated with coastal locations and shellfish and fish collection, they are either submerged or eroded away by high sea stands during OIS 5. Thus we must be cautious in drawing a firm line between the behavior of Acheulean and MSA hominins.

In the MSA there appears to have been a greater concern for careful selection of raw materials, perhaps reflecting a desire and need for better tool performance. It was common to exploit raw materials 30–40 km distant, which is well within the typical annual range of most modern hunter-gatherer groups, but is farther than would be typical for raw material decisions based on expediency, and somewhat farther than the typical pattern during the Acheulean. In some situations raw materials were transported vast distances, upwards of 200–300 km. We think it unlikely that raw material transport greater than 100 km was guided by the need for a raw material solely for functional purposes, but likely had aesthetic underpinnings. Both results suggest that MSA relative to Acheulean people were directing greater care toward raw material selection, had developed at least rudimentary exchange networks, and were using these networks to acquire raw materials with social value. The importance of material culture and behaviors with social and symbolic value is further evidenced by the regular use of pigments, and in some cases the shaping of these into pencils, and incising possible symbols onto pieces of pigment.

The MSA also represents a shift in stone tool manufacture, where large bifaces fall from favor and blades and pointed shapes (both retouched and unretouched) become common. The regular occurrence of pointed shapes is a hallmark of the MP in Eurasia as well, but the abundance of lanceolate, foliate, and teardrop bifaces in the African MSA is rather unique. Along with this shift is a diminution in all-lithic classes. This likely represents a shift from hand-gripped tools in the Acheulean

to ones hafted on wooden and bone handles and shafts in the MSA. The introduction of points in the MSA has often been considered an indication of the
increased importance of hunting, but it might just as likely indicate a change in the
way that hunting was accomplished. The faunal remains show us that MSA hunters
effectively hunted even the largest antelope, and in some cases specialized on them,
and may have used advanced tactical strategies for hunting them in open grassland
ecosystems. In some MSA contexts, bone was used to produce labor-intensive
armaments such as harpoons and projectile points, indicating a choice of high performance at the expense of labor. Importantly, these labor-intensive bone tools were
made with complicated production sequences involving numerous steps and various
technologies, signaling a grasp of technological planning.

Along with these basic shifts, we see highly patterned regional and temporal forms of artifact manufacture. Examples include Aterian pedunculates and
Howiesons Poort crescents. Another pattern is the presence, absence, and variability in the production of retouched unifacial and bifacial points. We think that several
patterns have emerged that can be loosely constructed into a continent-wide model
for the occurrence of this technology.

Bifacial point technologies are present throughout the world, but tend to be temporally discontinuous and geographically patchy in distribution. Bifacial technologies that resemble the African MSA ones in size and form are the Clovis period in
North America, the Solutrean in Europe, and the Kimberly point technologies of
Australia. The former two are archaeological, while the latter is ethnographic. Bifacial points of these types are labor-intensive tools that are often, but not always,
made on high-quality raw materials that also required significant investment of labor
to attain. It seems unreasonable to view them as easily discarded tools, such as more
simple flake-based points. If not made too thin, bifacial points have a potential long
use-life because they can be resharpened, and they are durable due to the fact that
their edges tend to be less acute than a flake. Continual resharpening eventually
renders them useless as points, and at that stage they can be converted to knives
and tools for other tasks, effectively recycling them and extending their usefulness.

MSA bifacial points in Africa come in a wide variety of shapes and sizes. Their
shapes generally vary from lanceolate to teardrop. Lupemban and Aterian bifaces
tend to be lanceolate to foliate, Stillbay tend to be foliate, and Bambatan tend to
be teardrop. In all cases they are found in both small and large forms. In some situations, (e.g., Stillbay) extremely thin, refined tools appear too fragile for rigorous
use. Thus, there is a core form that is small to medium in length and robust enough
to be useful, and a more elaborate form that is longer and often very thin. This is
also the case for Solutrean, Clovis, and Kimberly points. It is generally assumed
that most of the longer and thicker points were used as spear tips for hunting, while
there is a general struggle to explain the long and thin types. This still leaves much
unexplained. Hunting was practiced throughout the MSA and LSA, but bifacial
points are uncommon. We need to know what type of hunting strategy is best
accomplished with bifacials, and under what conditions this technology was favored
if we wish to understand bifacial point appearance and significance in the MSA.
The Clovis (North American) and Solutrean (European) adaptations share a

common emphasis on large mammal hunting combined with a highly mobile open habitat adaptation. Similarly, Kimberly points were made to hunt larger animals in open habitats (Mulvany and Kamminga 1999). Under highly mobile conditions, hunters cannot carry heavy loads of raw material for the production of new tools, nor can they easily plan to intersect known sources of raw materials on the landscape. As Kelly (1988) argues, bifacial points represent long use-life tools designed to be part of a reliable technology. We agree, and think that these cases suggest that African MSA bifacial points were likely part of a hunting kit tied to exploitation of open grassland habitats, large mammal hunting, and extreme mobility.

We think that pre-bow and arrow MSA technologies wedded to these conditions often resulted in a bifacial point technology. The Lupemban is likely the earliest bifacial point technology in Africa, and was based in central Africa during OIS 6, a dry, cold period when the thick forests of central Africa were open. When the central African rainforests began to spread with OIS 5, these grassland hunters vacated the forests for the more productive open habitats of northern and southern Africa, bringing the bifacial technologies with them, and blending with *in situ* technologies to form other biface-rich technologies such as the Aterian and Stillbay.

How do we explain the "non-functional" thin and fragile bifaces? The Kimberly case here is instructive. Kimberly bifaces came to be the preferred hunting tool and eventually took on special aesthetic value, such that the production began to emphasize social value (beauty and refinement) over function. These were traded widely, and the function of some shifted away from hunting to social and ritual importance, for example as circumcision knives. They became male prestige items, were hafted as knives, and even decorated. This transmutation of key functional tools by elaboration to social/ritual value is not unusual in human societies – consider cars, clothing, and so on in our society. These elaborate and non-functional bifaces in the African MSA were probably social/ritual elaborations by men of the core item in their hunting kit, the biface.

This brings us back to the question of the origins of modern human behavior. We summarized above how the African record differs from the Eurasian record in a number of key variables widely used as markers of modern human behavior: raw material transport, regular use of pigments, production of labor-intensive bone tools, and so on. The elaborate bifaces of the African MSA also set it off from the contemporary archaeological record in Eurasia. But the key variable here is not the proliferation of functional bifaces designed for hunting, but rather their elaboration and transmutation into non-functional items with ritual and social value. This is one more piece of evidence that the African MSA sees an early expression of symbolic thought unseen in Eurasia at this time.

Clearly, the extension of the Mellars Rubicon to Africa is falsified, suggesting that modern human behavior has its roots in Africa deeper in time than once believed. Alternatively, it may mean that these traits are insensitive to the origins of behavioral modernity, and that we need to develop new methods for recognizing it in the African record. We lean to the former for, in absence of overwhelming empirical evidence, it has a strong theoretical justification. Anatomy and behavior are in most cases intimately linked. Changes in anatomy generally result *from* changes in behavior that place new selection pressures on anatomy. Thus, at the very least, evolution in behavior and anatomy should go hand in hand. An early origin of modern human behavior in Africa should not only date to the same time, it should predate it. However, the archaeology of the MSA in Africa has far to go before we can say we have a confident sample of the range of variation in that record, which makes research in this region a key priority for human evolutionary studies.

REFERENCES

Adams, J. M., and H. Faure, eds., 1997 QEN members: Review and Atlas of Palaeovegetation: Preliminary Land Ecosystem Maps of the World Since the Last Glacial Maximum. Oak Ridge National Laboratory, TN, USA. Electronic Document. <http://www.esd.ornl.gov/projects/qen/adams1.html>, accessed June 2003.

Aiello, Leslie. C., 1993 The Fossil Evidence for Modern Human Origins in Africa: A Revised View. American Anthropologist 95:73–96.

Andrefsky, W., Jr., 1998 Lithics. New York: Cambridge University Press.

Assefa, Zelalem, 2002 Investigations of Faunal Remains from Porc-Epic: A Middle Stone Age Site in Southeastern Ethiopia. Ph.D. dissertation, State University of New York at Stony Brook.

Bailey, Robert. C., Genevieve Head, Mark Jenike, Bruce Owen, Robert Rechtman, and Elzbieta Zechenter, 1989 Hunting and Gathering in Tropical Rain Forest: Is It Possible? American Anthropologist 91:59–82.

Balout, L., 1955 Préhistoire de l'Afrique du Nord. Paris: Arts et Métiers Graphiques.

Barham, Lawrence S., 2001 Central Africa and the Emergence of Regional Identity in the Middle Pleistocene. *In* Human Roots: Africa and Asia in the Middle Pleistocene. Lawrence S. Barham and Kate Robson-Brown, eds. pp. 65–80. Bristol: Western Academic and Specialist Press Limited.

——2002 Systematic Pigment Use in the Middle Pleistocene of South-Central Africa. Current Anthropology 43:181–190.

Bar-Yosef, Ofer, and Bernard Vandermeersch, 1993 Modern Humans in the Levant. Scientific American 268:94–100.

Binford, Lewis R., 1978 Nunamiut Ethnoarchaeology. New York: Academic Press.

——1981 Bones: Ancient Men and Modern Myths. New York: Academic Press.

——1985 Human Ancestors: Changing Views of their Behavior. Journal of Anthropological Archaeology 4:292–327.

Blumenschine, Robert J., 1988 An Experimental Model of the Timing of Hominid and Carnivore Influence on Archaeological Bone Assemblages. Journal of Archaeological Science 15:483–502.

Bordes, François, 1972 A Tale of Two Caves. New York: Harper & Row.

Bräuer, Günter, 1984 The "Afro-European *sapiens* Hypothesis," and Hominid Evolution in East Asia during the Late Middle and Upper Pleistocene. *In* The Early Evolution of Man with Special Emphasis on Southeast Asia and Africa. Peter Andrews and Jens Lorenz Franzen, eds. pp. 145–165. Frankfurt: Courier Forschungsinstitut Senckenberg.

——1989 The Evolution of Modern Humans: A Comparison of the African and Non-African

Evidence. *In* The Human Revolution: Behavioral and Biological Perspectives on the Origins of Modern Humans. Paul Mellars and Christopher Stringer, eds. pp. 123–154. Edinburgh: Edinburgh University Press.

——1992 Africa's Place in the Evolution of *Homo sapiens*. *In* Continuity or Replacement: Controversies in *Homo sapiens* Evolution. Günter Bräuer and Fred H. Smith, eds. pp. 83–98. Rotterdam: A. A. Balkema.

Brooks, Alison S., David M. Helgren, Jon S. Cramer, Alan Franklin, William Hornyak, Jody M. Keating, Richard G. Klein, William J. Rink, Henry P. Schwarcz, J. N. L. Smith, Kathyln Stewart, Nancy Todd, Jacques Verniers, and John E. Yellen, 1995 Dating and Context of Three Middle Stone Age Sites with Bone Points in the Upper Semliki Valley, Zaire. Science 268:548–553.

Butzer, Karl, W., Peter B. Beaumont, and John C. Vogel, 1978 Lithostratigraphy of Border Cave, KwaZulu, South Africa: A Middle Stone Age Sequence Beginning c. 195,000 B.P. Journal of Archaeological Science 5:317–341.

Camps, G., G. Delibrias, and J. Thommeret, 1973 Chronologie des civilisations préhistoriques du nord de l'Afrique d'après le radiocarbone. Libyca 21:65–89.

Chase, Philip G., 1988 Scavenging and Hunting in the Middle Paleolithic. *In* Upper Pleistocene Prehistory of Western Eurasia. Harold L. Dibble and Anta Montet-White, eds. pp. 225–232. Philadelphia: The University Museum.

——1989 How Different was Middle Paleolithic Subsistence? A Zooarchaeological Perspective on the Middle to Upper Palaeolithic Transition. *In* The Human Revolution: Behavioral and Biological Perspectives on the Origins of Modern Humans. Paul Mellars and Christopher Stringer, eds. pp. 321–337. Edinburgh: Edinburgh University Press.

Clark, Amelia M. B., 1999 Late Pleistocene Technology at Rose Cottage Cave: A Search for Modern Behavior in an MSA Context. African Archaeological Review 16:93–119.

Clark, J. Desmond, 1959 The Prehistory of Southern Africa. Baltimore: Penguin Books.

——1964 The Sangoan Culture of Equatoria: The Implications of its Stone Equipment. *In* Miscelanea en homenaje al Abate Henri Brevil (1877–1961), vol. 1. Instituto de Prehistoria y Arqueología, pp. 311–325. Barcelona.

——1982 The Cultures of the Middle Paleolithic/Middle Stone Age. *In* The Cambridge History of Africa: From the Earliest Times to c. 500 BC. J. Desmond Clark, ed. pp. 248–340. New York: Cambridge University Press.

——1988 The Middle Stone Age of East Africa and the Beginnings of Regional Identity. Journal of World Prehistory 2:235–305.

——1993 The Aterian of the Central Sahara. *In* Environmental Change and Human Culture in the Nile Basin and Northern Africa until the Second Millennium B.C. Lech Krzyzaniak, Michal Kobuseiwicz, and John Alexander, eds. pp. 49–67. Poznan: Poznan Archaeological Museum.

——2001 Kalambo Falls Prehistoric Site: The Earlier Cultures, Middle and Earlier Stone Age. New York: Cambridge University Press.

Clark, J. Desmond, and Kyle S. Brown, 2001 The Twin Rivers Kopje, Zambia: Stratigraphy, Fauna, and Artefact Assemblages from the 1954 and 1956 Excavations. Journal of Archaeological Science 28:305–330.

Clark, J. Desmond, Martin A. J. Williams, and Andrew B. Smith, 1973 The Geomorphology and Archaeology of Adrar Bous, Central Sahara: A Preliminary Report. Quaternaria 17:245–297.

Clark, J. Desmond, Kenneth P. Oakley, L. H. Wells, and J. A. C. McClelland, 1947 New Studies on Rhodesian Man. Journal of the Royal Anthropological Society 77:4–33.

Clark, J. Desmond, Kenneth D. Williamson, Joseph W. Michels, and Curtis Marean, 1984 A

Middle Stone Age Occupation Site at Porc-Epic Cave, Dire Dawa (East-Central Ethiopia). The African Archaeological Review 2:37–71.

Clark, J. D., J. de Heinzelin, K. D. Schick, W. K. Hart, T. D. White, G. WoldeGabriel, G. Suwa, B. Asfaw, E. Vrba, and Y. H. Selassie, 1994 African *Homo erectus*: Old Radiometric Ages and Young Oldowan Assemblages in the Middle Awash Valley, Ethiopia. Science 264:1907–1910.

Clarke, David L., 1978 Analytical Archaeology. New York: Columbia University Press.

Cooke, C. K., 1966 The Archaeology of the Mafunabusi Area, Gokwe, Rhodesia. Transactions of the Rhodesian Scientific Association 51:51–78.

Cremaschi, Mauro, Savino di Lernia and Elena A. A. Garcea, 1998 Some Insights on the Aterian in the Libyan Sahara: Chronology, Environment, and Archaeology. African Archaeological Review 15:261–286.

Deacon, Hilary J., and Janette Deacon, 1999 Human Beginnings in South Africa. Cape Town: David Philip.

Deacon, Hilary J., and V. B. Geleijnse, 1988 The Stratigraphy and Sedimentology of the Main Site Sequence, Klasies River Mouth, South Africa. South African Archaeological Bulletin 43:5–14.

Deino, Alan, and Richard Potts, 1990 Single-Crystal 40Ar/39Ar Dating of the Olorgesailie Formation, Southern Kenya Rift. Journal of Geophysical Research 95:8453–8470.

de Maret, Pierre, 1990 Phases and Facies in the Archaeology of Central Africa. *In* A History of African Archaeology. Peter Robertshaw, ed. pp. 109–134. London: James Currey.

Dibble, Harold, 1995 Middle Paleolithic Scraper Reduction: Background, Clarification, and Review of the Evidence to Date. Journal of Archaeological Method and Theory 2(4):299–368.

Evernden, J. F., and G. H. Curtis, 1965 Potassium-Argon Dating of Late Cenozoic Rocks in East Africa and Italy. Current Anthropology 6:343–385.

Ferring, C. Reid, 1975 The Aterian in North African Prehistory. *In* Problems in Prehistory: North Africa and the Levant. Fred Wendorf and Anthony E. Marks, eds. pp. 113–126. Dallas: Southern Methodist University Press.

Gamble, Clive, 1994 Timewalkers: The Prehistory of Global Colonization. Cambridge, MA: Harvard University Press.

Goodwin, A. J. H., and C. van Riet Lowe, 1929 The Stone Age Cultures of South Africa. Annals of the South African Museum 27:1–289.

Grayson, Donald K., and Francois Delpech, 1994 The Evidence for Middle Paleolithic Scavenging from Couche VIII, Grotte Vaufrey (Dordogne, France). Journal of Archaeological Science 21:359–375.

Grün, Rainer, and Peter Beaumont. 2001 Border Cave Revisited: A Revised ESR Chronology. Journal of Human Evolution 40:467–482.

Grün, Rainer, and Christopher B. Stringer, 1991 Electron Spin Resonance Dating and the Evolution of Modern Humans. Archaeometry 33:153–199.

Harpending, Henry, and Alan Rogers, 2000 Genetic Perspectives on Human Origins and Differentiation. Annual Review of Genomics and Human Genetics 1:361–385.

Harpending, Henry C., Stephen T. Sherry, Alan R. Rogers, and Mark Stoneking, 1993 The Genetic Structure of Ancient Human Populations. Current Anthropology 34:481–496.

Henshilwood, Christopher S., and Curtis W. Marean, 2003. The Origin of Modern Human Behavior: A Review and Critique of Models and Test Implications. Current Anthropology 44:627–651.

Henshilwood, Christopher S., Francesco D'Errico, Curtis W. Marean, Richard G. Milo, and Royden J. Yates, 2001a An Early Bone Tool Industry from the Middle Stone Age, Blombos

Cave, South Africa: Implications for the Origins of Modern Human Behavior, Symbolism and Language. Journal of Human Evolution 41:631–678.

Henshilwood, Christopher S., Judith C. Sealy, Royden J. Yates, Kathryn Cruz-Uribe, Paul Goldberg, Frederick E. Grine, Richard G. Klein, Cedric Poggenpoel, Karin van Niekerk and Ian Watts, 2001b Blombos Cave, Southern Cape, South Africa: Preliminary Report on the 1992–1999 Excavations of the Middle Stone Age Levels. Journal of Archaeological Science 28:421–448.

Henshilwood, Christopher S., Francesco D'Errico, Royden Yates, Zenobia Jacobs, Chantal Tribolo, Geoff A. T. Duller, Norbert Mercier, Judith C. Sealy, Helene Valladas, Ian Watts, and Ann G. Wintle, 2002 Emergence of Modern Human Behavior: Middle Stone Age Engravings from South Africa. Science 295:1278–1280.

Imbrie, John, and Katherine P. Imbrie, 1979 Ice Ages: Solving the Mystery. Cambridge, MA: Harvard University Press.

Ingman, Max, Henrik Kaessmann, Svante Pääbo and Ulf Gyllensten, 2000 Mitochondrial Genome Variation and the Origin of Modern Humans. Nature 408:708–713.

Isaac, Glynn Ll., 1977 Olorgesailie: Archaeological Studies of a Middle Pleistocene Lake Basin in Kenya. Chicago: University of Chicago Press.

Keller, Charles M., 1973 Montague Cave in Prehistory. University of California Anthropological Records 28:1–150.

Kelly, Robert L., 1988 The Three Sides of a Biface. American Antiquity 53:717–734.

Klein, Richard G., 1976 The Mammalian Fauna of the Klasies River Mouth Sites, Southern Cape Province, South Africa. South African Archaeological Bulletin 31:75–98.

——1978 The Fauna and Overall Interpretation of the "Cutting 10" Acheulian site at Elandsfontein (Hopefield), Southwestern Cape Province, South Africa. Quaternary Research 10:69–83.

——1995 Anatomy, Behavior, and Modern Human Origins. Journal of World Prehistory 9:167–198.

——1998 Why Anatomically Modern People Did Not Disperse from Africa 100,000 years ago. In Neanderthals and Modern Humans in Western Asia. Takeru Akazawa, Kenichi Aoki, and Ofer Bar-Yosef, eds. pp. 509–521. New York: Plenum Press.

——1999 The Human Career: Human Biological and Cultural Origins. 2nd edition. Chicago: University of Chicago Press.

——2000 Archeology and the Evolution of Human Behavior. Evolutionary Anthropology 9:17–36.

Klein, Richard G., and Kathryn Cruz-Uribe, 1991 The Bovids from Elandsfontein, South Africa, and their Implications for the Age, Palaeoenvironment, and Origins of the Site. The African Archaeological Review 9:21–79.

——1996 Exploitation of Large Bovids and Seals at Middle and Later Stone Age Sites in South Africa. Journal of Human Evolution 31:315–334.

Klein, Richard G., and Katharine Scott, 1986 Re-analysis of Faunal Assemblages from the Haua Fteah and Other Late Quaternary Archaeological Sites in Cyrenaican Libya. Journal of Archaeological Science 13:515–542.

Knecht, Heidi, 1997 Projectile Points of Bone, Antler, and Stone. In Projectile Technology. Heidi Knecht, ed. pp. 191–212. New York and London: Plenum Press.

Lindly, John M., and Geoffrey A. Clark, 1990 On the Emergence of Modern Humans. Current Anthropology 31:59–66.

McBrearty, Sally, 1991 Recent Research in Western Kenya and Its Implications for the Status of the Sangoan Industry. In Cultural Beginnings: Approaches to Understanding Early

Hominid Life-ways in the African Savanna. J. Desmond Clark ed. pp. 159–176. Union Internationale des Sciences Préhistoriques et Protohistoriques, Monograph 19.

McBrearty, Sally, and Alison S. Brooks, 2000 The Revolution That Wasn't: A New Interpretation of the Origin of Modern Human Behavior. Journal of Human Evolution 39:453–563.

McBurney, Charles B., 1960 The Stone Age of Northern Africa. Baltimore: Penguin Books.

——1967 The Haua Fteah (Cyrenaica) and the Stone Age of the Southwest Mediterranean. Cambridge: Cambridge University Press.

Macklin, M. G., I. C. Fuller, J. Lewin, G. S. Maas, D. G. Passmore, J. Rose, J. C. Woodward, S. Black, R. H. B. Hamlin, and J. S. Rowan, 2002 Correlation of Fluvial Sequences in the Mediterranean Basin Over the Last 200 ka and their Relationship to Climate Change. Quaternary Science Reviews 21:1633–1641.

Marean, Curtis W., 1992 Implications of Late Quaternary Mammalian Fauna from Lukenya Hill (South-Central Kenya) for Paleoenvironmental Change and Faunal Extinctions. Quaternary Research 37:239–255.

——1997 Hunter-Gatherer Foraging Strategies in Tropical Grasslands: Model Building and Testing in the East African Middle and Later Stone Age. Journal of Anthropological Archaeology 16:189–225.

——1998 A Critique of the Evidence for Scavenging by Neanderthals and Early Modern Humans: New Data from Kobeh Cave (Zagros Mousterian) and Die Kelders (South Africa Middle Stone Age). Journal of Human Evolution 35:111–136.

Marean, Curtis W., and Zelalem Assefa, 1999 Zooarchaeological Evidence for the Faunal Exploitation Behavior of Neandertals and Early Modern Humans. Evolutionary Anthropology 8:22–37.

Marean, Curtis W., and Soo Y. Kim 1998 Mousterian Large-Mammal Remains from Kobeh Cave: Behavioral Implications for Neanderthals and Early Modern Humans. Current Anthropology 39(Supplement):79–113.

Marean, Curtis W., and Lillian M. Spencer 1991 Impact of Carnivore Ravaging on Zooarchaeological Measures of Element Abundance. American Antiquity 56:645–658.

Marean, Curtis W., Lillian M. Spencer, Robert J. Blumenschine, and Sal D. Capaldo, 1992 Captive Hyena Bone Choice and Destruction, the Schlepp Effect, and Olduvai Archaeofaunas. Journal of Archaeological Science 19:101–121.

Marean, Curtis W., Yoshiko Abe, Carol J. Frey, and Robert C. Randall, 2000 Zooarchaeological and Taphonomic Analysis of the Die Kelders Cave 1 Layers 10 and 11 Middle Stone Age Larger Mammal Fauna. Journal of Human Evolution 38:197–233.

Marks, Anthony E., 1968 The Khormusan: An Upper Pleistocene Industry in Sudanese Nubia. In The Prehistory of Nubia. F. Wendorf ed., pp. 315–391. Dallas: Southern Methodist University Press.

Mason, Reville J., 1988 Cave of Hearths, Makapansgat, Transvaal. Occasional Papers, Archaeological Research Unit, University of the Witwatersrand 21:1–711.

Mehlman, Michael J., 1989 Later Quaternary Archaeological Sequences in Northern Tanzania. Ph.D. dissertation, Department of Anthropology, University of Illinois at Urbana-Champaign.

Mellars, Paul A., 1973 The Character of the Middle–Upper Paleolithic Transition in Southwest France. In The Explanation of Cultural Change. Colin Renfrew ed. pp. 255–276 London: Duckworth.

——1995 Symbolism, Language, and the Neanderthal Mind. In Modeling the Human Mind. Paul Mellars and Kathleen R. Gibson eds. pp. 15–32. Cambridge: MacDonald Institute for Archaeological Research.

——1996 The Neanderthal Legacy: An Archaeological Perspective from Western Europe. Princeton: Princeton University Press.

Merrick, Harry V., and Frank H. Brown, 1984 Obsidian Sources and Patterns of Source Utilization in Kenya and Northern Tanzania: Some Initial Findings. The African Archaeological Review 2:129–152.

Milo, Richard G., 1998 Evidence for Hominid Predation at Klasies River Mouth, South Africa, and its Implications for the Behavior of Early Modern Humans. Journal of Archaeological Science 25:99–133.

Minichillo, Thomas, 1998 Middle Stone Age and Later Stone Age Faunal Assemblages from South Africa: Were Later People More Efficient Hunters? Paper presented at the 63rd Annual Meeting of the Society for American Archaeology.

Mortelmans, G., 1957 La Préhistoire du Congo Belge. Revue de l'Université de Bruxelles 9e année 2–3:119–171.

Mulvaney, John, and Johan Kamminga, 1999 Prehistory of Australia. Washington, DC: Smithsonian Institution Press.

Pearson, Osbjorne M., 2000 Activity, Climate, and Postcranial Robusticity: Implications for Modern Human Origins and Scenarios of Adaptive Change. Current Anthropology 41:569–607.

Pinker, Steven, 1997 How the Mind Works. New York: Norton.

Porat, Naomi, Michael Chazan, Henry P. Schwarcz, and Liora K. Horwitz, 2002 Timing of the Lower to Middle Paleolithic Boundary: New Dates from the Levant. Journal of Human Evolution 43:107–122.

Relethford, John H., 1999 Models, Predictions and the Fossil Record of Modern Human Origins. Evolutionary Anthropology 8:7–10.

Rightmire, G. Philip, 1996 The Human Cranium from Bodo, Ethiopia: Evidence for Speciation in the Middle Pleistocene? Journal of Human Evolution 31:21–39.

Sampson, C. Garth, 1971 The Stone Age Archaeology of Southern Africa. New York: Academic Press.

Sheppard, Peter J., 1990 Soldiers and Bureaucrats: The Early History of Prehistoric Archaeology in the Maghreb. In A History of African Archaeology. Peter Robertshaw, ed. pp. 173–188. London: James Currey.

Shiner, J. L., 1968 Miscellaneous Sites. In The Prehistory of Nubia. Fred Wendorf, ed. pp. 630–650. Dallas: Southern Methodist University Press.

Singer, Ronald, and John Wymer, 1982 The Middle Stone Age at Klasies River Mouth. Chicago: University of Chicago Press.

Smith, Fred H., Anthony B. Falsetti, and S. M. Donnelly, 1989 Modern Human Origins. Yearbook of Physical Anthropology 32:35–68.

Stiner, Mary C., 1993 Modern Human Origins – Faunal Perspective. Annual Review of Anthropology 22:55–82.

——1994 Honor Among Thieves: A Zooarchaeological Study of Neandertal Ecology. Princeton: Princeton University Press.

Stringer, Christopher B., 1990 The Emergence of Modern Humans. Scientific American 263:98–104.

Stringer, Christopher B., and Peter Andrews, 1988 Genetic and Fossil Evidence for the Origin of Modern Humans. Science 239:1263–1268.

Stringer, Christopher, and Günter Bräuer, 1994 Methods, Misreading and Bias. American Anthropologist 96:416–424.

Stringer, Christopher, and Clive Gamble, 1993 In Search of the Neanderthals. New York: Thames & Hudson.

Szabo, B. J., C. V. Haynes, and T. A. Maxwell, 1995 Ages of Quaternary Pluvial Episodes Determined by Uranium-Series and Radiocarbon Dating of Lacustrine Deposits of Eastern Sahara. Palaeogeography, Palaeoclimatology, Palaeoecology 113:227–242.

Thomas, Henry, 1981 La Fauna de la Grotte à Néandertaliens du Jebel Irhoud (Maroc). Quaternaria 23:191–217.

Thorne, Alan, and Milford Wolpoff, 1992 The Multiregional Evolution of Modern Humans. Scientific American 266:76–83.

Tryon, Christian A., and Sally McBrearty, 2002 Tephrostratigraphy and the Acheulian to Middle Stone Age Transition in the Kapthurin Formation. Journal of Human Evolution 42:211–235.

Volman, Thomas P., 1981 The Middle Stone Age in Southern Africa. Ph.D. dissertation, Department of Anthropology, University of Chicago.

——1984 Early Prehistory of Southern Africa. In Southern African Prehistory and Paleoenvironments. R. G. Klein ed. pp. 169–220. Rotterdam: Balkema.

Wadley, Lyn, 1996 The Robberg Industry of Rose Cottage Cave, Eastern Free State: The Technology, Spatial Patterns and Environment. South African Archaeological Bulletin 51:64–74.

Watts, Ian, 2002 Ochre in the Middle Stone Age of Southern Africa: Ritualized Display or Hide Preservative? South African Archaeological Bulletin 57:1–14.

Wayland, E. J., 1924 The Stone-Age in Uganda. Man 124:169–170.

Wendorf, Fred, and Romuald Schild, 1992 The Middle Paleolithic of North Africa: A Status Report. In New Light on the Northeast African Past. F. Klees and R. Kuper eds. pp. 39–80. Köln: Heinrich-Barth-Institute.

Wendorf, Fred, Angela E. Close, and Romuald Schild, 1994 Africa in the period of *Homo sapiens neanderthalensis* and contemporaries. In History of Humanity, vol. 1: Prehistory and the Beginnings of Civilization. Sigfried J. de Laet, Ahmad H. Dani, Jose L. Lorenzo, and Richard B. Nunoo eds. pp. 117–135. New York: Routledge and UNESCO.

Wendorf, Fred, Romuald Schild, and Angela E. Close, 1993 Egypt During the Last Interglacial. New York: Plenum.

Wolpoff, Milford H., 1989 Multiregional Evolution: The Fossil Alternative to Eden. In The Human Revolution: Behavioral and Biological Perspectives on the Origins of Modern Humans. Paul Mellars and Christopher B. Stringer, eds. pp. 62–108. Princeton: Princeton University Press.

Yellen, John E., Alison S. Brooks, Els Cornelissen, Michael J. Mehlman, and Kathlyn Stewart, 1995 A Middle Stone Age Worked Bone Industry from Katanda, Upper Semliki Valley, Zaire. Science 268:553–556.

5

A Late Pleistocene Archive of Life at the Coast, Klasies River

H. J. Deacon and Sarah Wurz

The Late Pleistocene began 125,000 years ago (ky) (Martinson et al. 1987) when the world was as warm or warmer than the present and sea levels were within a few meters of those of today. It was the Last Interglacial and polar ice caps were at a minimum. Warmer oceans meant higher evaporation and generally more precipitation on land. In Africa at that time environments were productive and populations expanded, leaving traces of this expansion in the numbers of Middle Stone Age (MSA) sites (Deacon 2001). However, climates are subject to long-term changes due to orbital forcing and, following a number of oscillations that are best represented in the marine oxygen isotope record (Chapter 4), global climates changed from an interglacial to a glacial mode some 60 ky. Glacials marked by high-latitude ice sheets were registered by increased aridity in African latitudes. With aridity came lower soil moisture levels, reduced productivity of ecosystems, and the contraction of MSA populations in the most affected zones (Deacon and Thackeray 1984; Szabo et al. 1995). This explains why the build up of over 20 m of occupation deposits in the lee of a cliff on the southernmost coast of the African continent near the mouth of the Klasies River (Figure 5.1) ceased some 60 ky. However, the well-stratified deposits and their contents are a valuable archaeological archive of MSA life at the coast during the favorable times of the first half of the Late Pleistocene. The purpose of this chapter is to discuss some of the information gained and the issues raised by the extended investigation of this archive.

Klasies River main site (34.06°S, 24.24°E) has become an icon for the MSA. Its coastal setting is breathtaking and the layers contain impressive finds. There are abundant stone artifacts and hearth features. Middens of shellfish and the remains of other marine animals show early evidence of the systematic use of foods from the sea. Terrestrial animals, mainly bovids, are well represented and there are rare finds of fragmentary human remains.

Reading an archaeological archive depends on accumulating a diverse range of information. Stratigraphy provides essential information on how the deposits

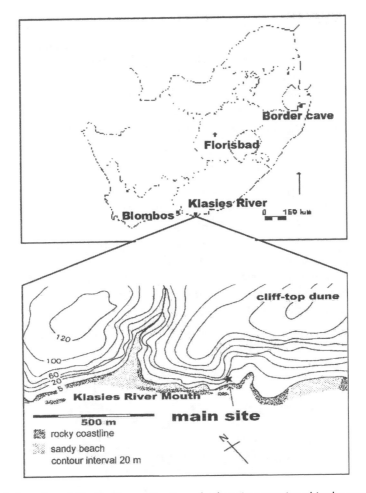

Figure 5.1. Location of Klasies River main site and other sites mentioned in the text

formed and their relative age. But estimating the age of Late Pleistocene deposits is potentially problematic (Chapter 4); biostratigraphy and isotope stratigraphy are used in conjunction with and as a check on age estimates in providing a temporal framework for the archive. It is within this framework that the contents of the main site deposits can be analyzed. As this chapter shows, the long sequence of deposits lends itself to charting changing artifact styles and the turnover of animal species with the rise and fall of sea levels.

The main site archive has generated or contributed to debates on broader issues in archaeology and paleontology. The results of faunal studies on Klasies River materials have been central to debates on distinguishing hunting and scavenging in the archaeological record. In addition the faunal studies have raised questions on how the intensity of resource exploitation may relate to the cognitive skills of prehistoric hunters. The Klasies River archive initiated the debate over whether MSA behavior was like that of ethnographically known hunter-gatherers or more primitive. This has grown into a major debate centered on the African evidence for the emergence of modern humans, modern behavior, and language (Deacon and Deacon 1999; Klein and Edgar 2002; McBrearty and Brooks 2000).

The justification for the investigation of the Klasies River archive over several decades is the detailed information it provides. The information available is a window on the African MSA and it is a resource that is being extended and amplified as interest in the African MSA grows.

Site and Stratigraphy

The main site (Figure 5.2) is a pile of sediments banked up against a sheer cliff. The sediments spill into cave-like openings in the cliff, but this is not properly a cave site. The cliff provides protection, particularly against winter storms, but for the site to be habitable the pile would have been anchored on the seaward side by a back-of-the-beach dune. There are modern analogs in the same section of coast where the frontal dune is stabilized by coastal forest. It was against the cliff and

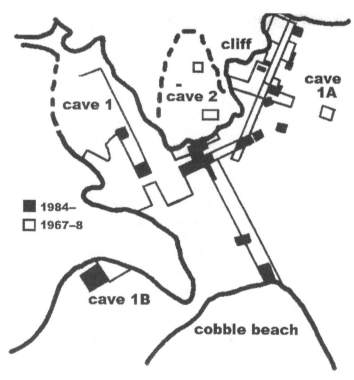

Figure 5.2. Plan of Klasies River main site

behind the dune that the sediment pile grew, and in the process blocked off or filled the openings in the cliff face. The cycles of sediment accumulation started when sea levels fell from their Last Interglacial high, some 118 ky, and ended when sea levels again approached these levels in the mid-Holocene, some 6 ky. The Holocene rise in sea level obliterated all traces of the anchoring frontal dune and undercut the base of the sediment pile, causing a major slump. In the process the greater part of the sediment pile was eroded. The erosion scar forms the surface of the main site, and the extent of the original sediment pile can be traced in remnants cemented to the cliff. Although a considerable volume of deposit was lost through slumping, the erosion provided a natural section through the site. The excavations have been made off this section.

Singer and Wymer (1982:7) originally excavated the site over two seasons in 1967–8 and the results were published in a monograph. In 1984 a program to reha-bilitate collapsed sections and amplify the results by limited excavation was begun and has continued since (Deacon 1995). Apart from sampling the contents of the deposits, these excavations have provided sections for the interpretation of the stratigraphy. The deposits are well stratified and the strata composed of fine layers (termed units) that are a few to some tens of millimeters thick. These units repre-sent occupation deposits and consist of carbonized or humified materials associ-ated with hearth features, shell midden lenses, artifacts, and fauna. They are interbedded with non-occupation units composed of sands. The fineness of layer-ing results from compaction under the sediment load and diagenesis of organic materials. The stratigraphic sequence thus represents a long succession of short-term human occupation events.

In the 1967–8 excavation a number of layers (or spits) were recorded (Singer and Wymer 1982:9). These followed gross stratigraphy and each included numbers of discrete units. The layers were then grouped into larger entities defined on the stone artifact content and labeled from the base upwards as MSA I, MSA II, Howiesons Poort, MSA III, and MSA IV. The labels MSA I–IV were provisional, and only the contents of the Howiesons Poort layers were referred to a named site following the recommendations of the Burg-Wartenstein Conference (Bishop and Clark, eds., 1967). Subsequent research (Wurz 2002) has confirmed that these entities are robust sub-stages within the MSA defined on techno-typological crite-ria. Following convention (Goodwin and van Riet Lowe 1929) each sub-stage should be formally recognized by reference to a named site (as in the case of the Howiesons Poort). However, as a matter of convenience the provisional labels are retained here. The succession of sub-stages describes the culture stratigraphy and the changes in artifact technology and typology through time.

Culture stratigraphy is different from lithostratigraphy, which describes the sequence in terms of accumulated sediments. As underscored in the recommenda-tions of the 1965 Burg Wartenstein Conference (Bishop and Clark, eds., 1967:879) the lithostratigraphy and culture stratigraphy provide different information, and correlation between them is a matter for investigation. The sequence (Figure 5.3) has been divided into a series of lithostratigraphic members (Deacon and Geleijnse 1988) that are from oldest to youngest the LBS, SAS, RF, Upper, and WS members.

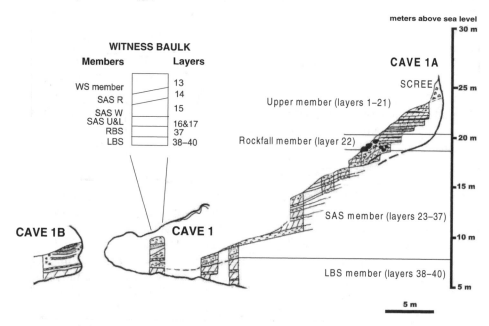

Figure 5.3. Diagrammatic section through Klasies River main site showing the stratigraphy

The layers defined in the original excavations and the units defined in the later excavations can be ascribed to the relevant members.

Dating the Middle Stone Age

The introduction of radiocarbon dating 50 years ago (Vogel 2002) made it possible to obtain age estimates independent of correlations with glacial or pluvial sequences. Initial radiocarbon determinations for MSA sites (J. Deacon 1966) fell between 20 and 40 ky. Although the end of the MSA may date close to 20 ky, the beginnings of the MSA were significantly underestimated because, as the limits of the method are approached, contamination by younger carbon has a significant effect (Beaumont and Vogel 1972; Beaumont et al. 1978). What were initially considered finite age estimates proved to date beyond the limits of radiocarbon resolution. The beginnings of the MSA are still not dated with precision, but may extend to 300 ky or more (McBrearty 2001; McBrearty and Brooks 2000; Tryon and McBrearty 2002; Chapter 4).

Singer and Wymer (1982:189) obtained 27 radiocarbon age estimates for MSA deposits at the main site. These estimates were stratigraphically inverted with finite estimates obtained for samples below samples with infinite ages, an indication that the whole sequence dated beyond the range of radiocarbon. A radiocarbon assay of

>50 ky for the Upper member (Layer 17) provides a minimum age for the top of the sequence (Vogel 2001). Through collaboration with Bada and Deems (1975), amino acid age estimates of 110 ky for the base of the sequence in cave 1 (Layer 38) and 85 ky (Layer 37), 84 ky (Layer 16), and 61 ky (Layer 13) for overlying strata were obtained. These age determinations were made on bone, which is not the preferred material of most analysts. However, the results suggested that all of the MSA deposits at the site dated to more than 60 ky. Shackleton (1982) obtained the most significant age estimate (reported in Singer and Wymer 1982), based on oxygen isotope ratios in turban shell opercula. Operculum from the base of the sequence yielded a range of values, indicating that the shell grew in waters as warm as or warmer than the present, suggesting an association with Marine Isotope Stage (MIS) 5e (Figure 4.1) and an age of 125 ky. Shackleton analyzed selected samples from higher in the sequence, but these results had less readily interpretable implications for dating. These dating results prompted Singer and Wymer (1982:149) to claim that the human remains, notably the most modern-looking mandible from cave 1B, were older than 100 ky.

Uncertainties in the dating of the Howiesons Poort layers remained. Partly on geomorphological considerations and partly on the faunal evidence, Butzer (1982) correlated the Howiesons Poort levels with MIS 5b at ca. 95 ky. The large mammal fauna (Klein 1976) from the Howiesons Poort and MSA III layers indicated an open environment that would be expected in a cooler stadial, when sea levels regressed. If this regression was in MIS 5, the possibilities were 5d or 5b, but a regression in MIS 4 was another possibility (Figure 4.1). Shackleton's suggested age was 50 ky as he correlated the Howiesons Poort levels with MIS 3. These were initial attempts to correlate the oxygen isotope stratigraphy at Klasies River main site with the marine record. However, in the light of remaining uncertainties it was then still possible for Binford (1984) to argue that Howiesons Poort artifacts and the modern-looking human mandible from cave 1B were not significantly older than the European Upper Paleolithic. This made it imperative to improve the resolution of the dating evidence.

The age of the base of the sequence has been confirmed by further isotopic studies (Deacon et al. 1988). The LBS member (Layers 37, 38, and 40 in cave 1) associated with the MSA I is dated to MIS 5e/5d. Support comes from a uranium disequilibrium age of 110 ky (Vogel 2001) and a similar luminescence estimate (Feathers 2002). The associated large mammal fauna (Klein 1976) is consistent with a regressional event, and it would seem that the cave was first occupied after sea levels fell from the high of the Last Interglacial. The SAS member began to accumulate during MIS 5c based on oxygen isotope stratigraphy (Deacon et al. 1988). Uranium disequilibrium dating suggests an age of 100 ky (Vogel 2001) and ESR estimates (Grün et al. 1990) at 93 ky are somewhat younger. ESR dating tends to underestimate the age (Vogel 2001), and for this reason less weight is given to the ESR results. The SAS member is a thick parcel of sediments, which suggests it may have accumulated over a long period. Vogel (2001) has obtained a uranium series age estimate for the top of the member, which suggests these sediments continued to accumulate until after 77 ky. This is the same order of age as estimated for the immediately overlying RF member by luminescence dating (Feathers 2002), but younger than the age indicated by correlation of the RF member with MIS 5b on isotopic measurements (Deacon et al. 1988). The differences in these estimates are an illustration of the level of precision currently achieved, but together the results are a good indication of the order of age.

An age centered on 70 ky (Deacon 1989, 1992) has been argued for the Howiesons Poort layers in the Upper member. This is close to the 65 ky estimate on uranium series dating (Vogel 2001) and is in accord with amino acid dating estimates obtained for the Howiesons Poort horizon elsewhere (Miller et al. 1992; Miller et al. 1999). Luminescence (Feathers 2002) and ESR (Grün et al. 1990) dating provide younger estimates, and in both cases and for different reasons the conditions in this part of the depository may have affected the results.

As the precision of alternative dating methods to radiocarbon improves, archaeology stands to benefit in the kinds of questions that can be answered. For example, the precision of the luminescence estimates can be improved by the analysis of single grains, and a goal of planned future research is to employ this method to measure the duration of the Howiesons Poort sub-stage. The Late Pleistocene is above all a critical period for the study of the emergence and dispersal of modern humans, and this is motivation for the development of existing and new dating methods. Research using a battery of available techniques at Klasies River has shown beyond doubt that the human remains and the MSA artifacts date to the first half of the Late Pleistocene, between 125 and 60 ky.

Human Remains

An aim of the original excavators was to recover well-provenanced and -dated human remains from an MSA context. Later Stone Age remains were related to the indigenous Khoisan, but it was uncertain whether a different and possibly archaic kind of humanity was associated with the MSA. More plausible finds from MSA sites like Florisbad and Border Cave were then not well provenanced or dated. These shortcomings have been rectified by subsequent research (Beaumont 1980; Grün et al. 1996).

The initial search for human remains was successful in that five mandibles, 13 fragments of cranial vault, a frontal and a few post-cranial elements were recovered. Most of the finds were made in the part of the depository labeled cave 1 where the most extensive excavations were undertaken. Subsequent research has obtained further material, but it has been directed at understanding how the human remains accumulated. In this deposit human remains are rare finds but of considerable taphonomic and taxonomic interest.

Two lines of evidence can be used to understand how the human remains accumulated: the skeletal elements present and their stratigraphic position. The remains are very fragmentary and dispersed and not therefore from primary burials. Cranial fragments are best represented and post-cranial elements grossly underrepresented. The predominance of cranial vault elements may reflect the general fragmentary condition of the fauna and selective preservation of more robust elements. It also reflects the initial 1967–8 sampling procedure whereby shaft bone fragments were not collected. In subsequent sampling, small robust elements like phalanges have been found, but they are missing from the older collections. With the exception of human cranial vault bones, which are particularly thick, the type of remains is similar to those of other animals recovered from the site.

White (1987) observed a series of cut marks just below the hairline on the specimen of frontal bone from the site. Adjacent to the cut marks on this specimen is the scar of a tear made when the piece was broken out of the cranium while the bone was still fresh. Heat treatment is evident in spalling on the vault fragments, and some elements including mandibles show charring. Where teeth are preserved in the mandibles, these are the cheek teeth that would have been protected by the masseter muscles. The front teeth are broken out and would have imploded if subjected to heat. Percussion marks and scratches support evidence for the processing of the remains.

This evidence, which is consistent with observations made at the site of Mancos in the American southwest (White 1992), led White to suggest the possibility that cannibalism was involved. Minimally it is strong circumstantial evidence for cannibalism, although on osteological grounds alone some form of mortuary practice cannot be ruled out. The stratigraphic context of the finds provides further information on this point.

The layers with which the original human skeletal finds in cave 1 were associated (Singer and Wymer 1982:30) formed under different depositional regimes. Layers 14 (SAS R) and 15 (SAS W), for example, are steeply dipping foot slope deposits that formed when the entrance to cave 1 had become almost completely blocked and the cave was no longer accessible to people. An articulated leopard skeleton in Layer 15 (Singer and Wymer 1982) shows that carnivores still gained access, but the absence of hearths in these layers shows no primary occupation by people. By contrast the underlying layers, 16 (SAS U) and 17 (SAS L), include hearths and show that at that time human occupation extended into the entrance area of the cave. It seemed unlikely that the fragmentary remains of a number of individuals would be found localized in the entrance area of the cave in both transported and in situ sediments. This encouraged a restudy of the stratigraphic context of the finds.

Although the gross stratigraphic divisions recognized in cave 1 have validity, in not adequately resolving the details, the layer designations given to the 1967–8 finds of human remains can be questioned. More recent excavations in cave 1 (Rightmire and Deacon 2001) suggest that the bulk of these finds came from a single horizon (SAS U) – that is the approximate equivalent of Layer 16 – and would date to some 100 ky. New finds have been recovered from this horizon. The mandible (41815) from cave 1B has been shown to be of the same age (Deacon and Schuurman 1992).

This reinterpretation of the stratigraphic context indicates that the human remains from cave 1 in layers 14–17 and from cave 1B accumulated in the same episode. The new excavations have identified an older occupation in cave 1 associated with human remains. This horizon just above bedrock in the LBS member would have been minimally 10 ky earlier. The finds (Bräuer et al. 1992), a robust and heavily charred maxilla of a young, possibly male individual and a fragment of maxilla of a mature, possibly female individual, were found in a shell midden in the same square meter. The fragments from these two individuals were discarded among the food refuse. The absence of other human remains in the sample of intervening deposits underscores the contention that the remains are not randomly distributed but accumulated at particular times. There are isolated finds from higher in the sequence that may represent further discrete episodes of accumulation. This distribution would not be expected if a mortuary practice was involved. Episodic cannibalism is a more probable explanation.

Episodic cannibalism is well attested in the Late Pleistocene Neanderthal site of Moula-Guercy (Defleur et al. 1999) in France, and other European Middle Paleolithic sites show similar evidence for processing of human remains. Although cannibalism has been documented in older and younger time ranges, it is only in a well-preserved recent prehistoric site in the American southwest that there is biochemical evidence (Marlar et al. 2000) confirming that human tissue was consumed. This example is sufficient to give confidence that the fragmentation, heat treatment, and cut and percussion marking of human remains where documented in a non-burial context are the signature of cannibalism (White 1992). The evidence from the main site is arguably consistent with such criteria.

Few other MSA sites in South Africa have yielded human remains. These are less informative isolated teeth, with the exception of Border Cave (Beaumont 1980). The most complete find from Border Cave, BC 1, is possibly as old as 70 ky, but is unlikely to be younger than 40 ky and therefore can be associated with the MSA (Deacon 1992). Although somewhat younger than the Klasies River material, the completeness of the find suggests cannibalism was not involved and that it may have come from a conscious burial.

All Late Pleistocene finds of human materials from African sites have significance for morphological studies because there are so few and because of their bearing on the out-of-Africa hypothesis (Deacon and Deacon 1999; Klein and Edgar 2002; Chapter 4). The surprise that emerged from the Singer and Wymer (1982) study was that the Klasies River remains included both robust and extremely gracile individuals. As they occur in the same layers it is parsimonious to conclude that they represent a single sexual dimorphic population. The marked dimorphism (Rightmire and Deacon 1991 and references therein) may reflect the absence of nutritional stress because males are more susceptible to nutritional deficiencies and under such conditions dimorphism tends to be reduced. This would not rule out brief episodes of food shortage possibly linked to dietary cannibalism. Although it is impossible to demonstrate in the data available, differences in the diet between males and females may have been a factor. It is conceivable in this situation that the males had greater access to high-quality foods like meat and fat from seals. Whatever explanation is most appropriate, a characteristic of this Late Pleistocene population was its dimorphism.

The main point of discussion about these human remains has been whether they should be assessed as close to modern (Bräuer 1992; Bräuer and Singer 1996;

Bräuer et al. 1992; Rightmire 2001:132; Rightmire and Deacon 1991, 2001) or archaic (Caspari and Wolpoff 1990). The anatomical distinction is a moot one because selection for reduced dimorphism and gracility would have continued to operate over roughly the last 100 ky. The question is rather whether this population was ancestral to the San, or whether it represented an earlier population that predated the differentiation of any ethnographically known populations. Molecular studies show that the genes found in contemporary San are represented in the deepest branches of mitochondrial DNA (mtDNA; Chen et al. 2000; Ingman and Gyllenstein 2001) and Y-chromosome (Semino et al. 2002) phylogenies. These signatures suggest that their ancestry may have included people of the Late Pleistocene MSA. This problem may only be resolved by extracting DNA from the fossil material. Although the prospects of DNA being preserved at main site are low, other Late Pleistocene sites may produce suitable samples.

The Artifact Sequence

When the main site was first excavated there was little knowledge of the MSA aside from Mason's (1962) work at the Cave of Hearths and other sites in the former Transvaal. The artifact succession at Klasies River main site gave a new perspective to these studies. In particular it demonstrated that the Howiesons Poort, a distinctive artifact horizon noted for backed tools classified as segments or trapezes, was in the middle and not at the end of the sequence. Segments, though smaller in size, are a type tool in the Later Stone Age (LSA) Wilton (Chapter 6), and in the absence of any good stratigraphic and dating evidence to the contrary, it was logical to assume that the Howiesons Poort marked the end of the MSA. On the expectation that artifact sequences showed progressive change, the Howiesons Poort, together with the Magosian, had been formally recognized as an intermediate or transitional stage between the MSA and LSA (Clark 1959). The sequence at the main site demonstrated that the Howiesons Poort was not transitional to the LSA because the making of segments did not continue in overlying MSA layers. The Howiesons Poort was also far removed in time from the Holocene Wilton.

In many ways the Howiesons Poort (Wurz 1999) has proved to be the key to understanding the MSA in southern Africa. Once established at the main site that Howiesons Poort was a restricted horizon marker, there was potential to correlate Klasies River with segment-rich occurrences elsewhere. There are typologically similar horizons recognized in sites throughout southern Africa (Deacon 1992) and the dating of a number of these horizons shows them to be penecontemporaneous (Miller et al. 1999). The Howiesons Poort is thus a temporally and spatially bounded phenomenon on a subcontinental scale. It is not the only example in Africa; the Aterian (Caton-Thompson 1946; Cremaschi et al. 1998; Kleindienst 2000; Wrinn and Rink 2003; Chapter 4), with a Sahara-wide distribution, is a similar phenomenon. Such examples indicate the scale on which networks of shared ideas of artifact production operated in Late Pleistocene Africa (for more detailed consideration, see Deacon and Deacon 1999).

There are other ways in which the Howiesons Poort at main site helps us understand the MSA. A techno-typological analysis of Howiesons Poort artifacts shows that blade production dominates. The blades, some 40 mm in length, have small plain platforms and diffuse bulbs of percussion, indicating that they were struck from suitably prepared cores using a soft hammer. Segments were made on whole blade blanks. These technological conventions distinguish Howiesons Poort artifacts from those in the underlying and overlying deposits (Wurz 2002).

Although the significance of the Howiesons Poort horizon has been emphasized here, it is but one of a series of distinctive time-successive sub-stages in the sequence. In the base of the sequence the MSA I is dominated by large blades of up to 100 mm or more in length, similar in relative proportions to those in the Howiesons Poort, but made exclusively in local quartzite. By contrast the MSA II is dominated by levallois-type points (Inizian et al. 1999) with wide faceted platforms and prominent bulbs of percussion that suggest use of a hard hammer for final removals. This sub-stage would best equate with the concept of Goodwin and van Riet Lowe (1929:135) of a Mossel Bay industry. The Howiesons Poort in the overlying strata represents a reversal, in the sense that blade production is again the dominant mode of production, and there is a notable selection for non-local, finer-grained raw materials.

MSA III artifacts occur toward the top of the Upper member where sand intercalations between occupation units become thicker, after which occupation eventually ceased. Use of non-local raw materials decreased but remained significant. Typologically the main formal artifact in MSA III contexts is a knife-like tool on long >100 mm blades (Singer and Wymer 1982:114) retouched along one edge. However, segments are absent. The technological innovation of backing one margin of a blade, presumably to facilitate hafting, was not carried forward in the southern African MSA. Interestingly there appears to have been more continuity in segment manufacture between MSA and LSA in eastern Africa (Mehlman 1989, 1991). There is no evidence for a change in lifeways that might suggest a functional explanation for the disappearance of segments in post-Howiesons layers. It is more plausible to explain their absence in terms of changing symbolic value as the messages they carried became redundant (Cannon 1989).

The sample of MSA III artifacts is too small for a definitive technological analysis. However, there are differences from the Howiesons Poort in the preparation of the core that would be expected at the sub-stage level. The MSA IV was recognized in the WS member in cave 1. This member is a fine sand washed into the back of the cave at a time when the entrance was largely closed. Micro-mammal and cormorant remains attest that small cats, probably viverrids, could still gain access. The artifact sample is small and undiagnostic and inadequate for recognition as a sub-stage.

Singer and Wymer (1982:114) saw the main site sequence as evidence for a long occupation of the site by MSA people that was broken by an invasion of different people during the Howiesons Poort times. There is a potential problem in equating different styles of artifacts with different peoples. This apart, there is a unity to the MSA evident in the shared prepared core technology, and the sub-stages, including the Howiesons Poort, are part of the variability within this whole. The sequence can be seen as reflecting changes in arbitrary conventions of tool-making shaped by local relations but within a subcontinental network of communication. It is difficult to imagine a network operating on this scale outside of an essentially modern capacity for symbolic communication and language (Byers 1999).

Lifeways

The steep offshore profile along the stretch of coast off the mouth of the Klasies River meant that the effects of changing sea levels were mitigated. Even during the MIS 4 regression the coastline is estimated to have been within 11 km of its present position (van Andel 1989). The coastal situation and the convenient access this gave to marine resources may account for people repeatedly returning to this locality over tens of thousands of years. However, the occupants were hunters and gatherers and not solely reliant on marine resources. The evidence is in the bones of the animals discarded at the site and the burnt plant materials surrounding the domestic hearths.

This is a high-energy rocky coast. The dominant shellfish species, past and present, is the brown mussel *Perna perna*. These mussels occur in a broad band in the intertidal zone and are easily harvested. Other species were also harvested, notably *Turbo sarmaticus*, the turban shell, that is exposed at spring low tide. Fish bones are abundant in the site and may have been accumulated through the actions of cormorants that shelter against the cliff in inclement weather and regurgitate the bones of smaller inshore species. There are bones of larger species (von den Driesch, pers. comm. 2002) which other agents like gulls, hyenas, and even humans may have accumulated. The frequency of fish bones is low relative to Holocene LSA deposits associated with fishing equipment like sinkers, and this may argue against active fishing. Other marine resources included penguins and seals. Seals in particular would have been an important source of fat to supplement carbohydrates obtained from plants. The location of penguin colonies and seal rookeries in the past is unknowable; however, wash ups of both animals occur along the coast.

Various species of bovids make up the bulk of the terrestrial fauna. The animals range in size from buffalo to small antelope. The fauna is modern (Klein 1976) with the exception of the buffalo, *Pelorovis antiquus*, which became extinct at the end of the Pleistocene, and the blue antelope, *Hippotragus leucophaeus*, which survived until historic times. The springbok may represent the extinct species *Antidorcus australis*. There are changes in the frequencies of species through time. These changes are plausibly explained by local habitat changes with the rising and falling of sea levels. The frequencies of grazers compared to browsers and mixed feeders is above 60 percent in the LBS member at the base of the sequence, falling to below 40 percent in the SAS member and rising close to 60 percent again in the Upper member (van Pletzen 2000). The isotopic stratigraphy shows that higher frequencies of grazers occurred during regressions in sea level. At such times, cooler, drier climates and the sandy soils on clayey substrates on the exposed coastal margins favored an increase in grassland. The main debates have centered on the interpretation of the large mammal fauna. The original faunal analysis (Klein 1976) provided rich data on the taxa, body part frequencies, and mortality profiles. The pattern that emerged from the body part frequencies was that the ratio of cranial to post-cranial elements increased with bovid size while the ratio of limb to foot elements decreased. Klein argued that only selected parts of the larger animals were brought back to the site, possibly carried in the skins with the foot bones still attached, whereas the whole carcasses of the smaller animals were returned. Selective transport according to body size is the so-called "schlepp effect" (Klein 1976:87). Although the sample from the 1967–8 excavation is large, the fauna was selectively collected and only those elements considered to be identifiable to species were kept. This sampling bias (Deacon 1985; Marean and Kim 1998; Turner 1989) limits the value of the sample as a record of body part frequencies, and the evidence does not demand the operation of the "schelpp effect." In the smaller but less biased sample from the later excavation there is no evidence for this type of patterning (van Pletzen 2000).

Through his publication Binford (1984) made the interpretation of the Klasies River fauna part of the debate over the recognition of scavenging versus hunting in the archaeological record. He used the body part data obtained in Klein's (1976) analysis to argue that scavenging, rather than hunting activities, was the reason for the faunal accumulations at the site. In his reasoning the fauna represented small parcels of food obtained from carnivore kills, food that was consumed but not shared in the safety of the site. The location then was a place of shelter rather than a home base (Rose and Marshall 1996). The numerous domestic hearths throughout the sequence and the large accumulations of shellfish and other food remains make this an implausible scenario (Deacon 1985), and there can be no question that it functioned as a home base. Among the animal remains are those of carnivores like hyenas and leopards, and they would have used the site as a den and accumulated some of the fauna. The damage done to faunal elements by even the larger carnivores is nowhere as significant as that done by humans with hammer stones extracting marrow. The highly fragmented condition of the bones points to people as the main agents of accumulation. This contention is supported by the microscopic study of marks left on the bones (Milo 1998), and cut and percussion marks far outnumber tooth marks. The evidence is consistent with the active hunting and the butchering of all size classes of bovids. This does not exclude opportunistic scavenging by people, or again carnivores using the site as a den and even scavenging human leftovers.

A further point of discussion has been the effectiveness of the MSA people living at main site as hunters. Klein (1976, 1978, 1979) provided age profiles for the different bovids and observed that more docile species (like the eland) were represented by all age classes and showed a catastrophic mortality pattern. By contrast more dangerous animals (like buffalo) showed an attritional mortality pattern and were largely represented by young or old individuals. He inferred that in not hunting prime adults of dangerous game, MSA people showed themselves unable to use potential resources as optimally as later people. This argument has been extended by pointing to the absence of fowling, to shellfish species not being heavily exploited or farmed down in size, and to the MSA inhabitants not timing their visits to the coast when seal pups would have been an abundant source of food (Klein and Cruz-Uribe 1996). This carefully compiled empirical evidence may be interpreted in other ways. The mortality profiles of different bovids in the MSA and later times are similar (van Pletzen 2000), and appear to be species-specific rather than related to competencies of the hunters. The absence of fishing and fowling in the MSA could equally suggest that in those times of more pristine environments these were lower-ranked resources. It is also possible that the appropriate technologies, like fishing lines and bows, were not available. The argument based on Stone Age economics, that MSA people did not maximize the use of resources because they lacked the cognitive abilities to plan ahead, presupposes an innate drive to perform optimally. The degree to which there was intensification in the use of resources would not have depended on conscious decisions but would have been the consequence of the interrelationship between environmental productivity, demographic pressures, and other factors.

The numerous hearths in the main site sequence witness an ability to make fire at will. The associated carbonized surrounds can be interpreted as plant food residues such as accumulated around hearths at better-preserved LSA sites. MSA occupation was not restricted to the coast and occurred on the coastal plain and in the fold mountain range that parallels the coast. Plant foods would have been important in this wide-ranging occupation. Fynbos ecosystems dominate the landscape and the fynbos, a sclerophyllous Mediterranean-type vegetation growing on low nutrient substrates, is rich in geophytes, plants with their buds underground like bulbs, corms, and rhizomes. Geophytes, which are the main edible plants in fynbos, are prolific in the post-fire succession (Deacon 1976). Fire releases nutrients that stimulate the propagation of these plants, which are otherwise a slowly renewing resource in a nutrient-poor environment. Without fire management they would not be a targetable resource. There would have been no reason for MSA and LSA people to venture into the mountain fynbos except to exploit "farms" of geophytes. On the coast and on the coastal plain additional resources would have been available, but everywhere underground plants would have been a primary source of carbohydrates. This is the basis for the arguments that the larger part of the unidentifiable carbonized material around hearths at main site derived from the inedible residues of geophytes and that MSA people practiced fire-stick farming (Deacon and Deacon 1999). The contention is that MSA people were not only hunters, but also gatherers, and that their subsistence strategies can be understood in general terms by reference to the activities of LSA and modern hunter-gatherers (e.g., Owen and Porr 1997).

Living at the Coast

Singer and Wymer (1982:210) concluded that there was virtually no evidence for spiritual activities that may have bound together what they saw as a stable and unchanging society. They noted the presence of ochre with well-rubbed edges and two pieces of bone with a series of scratch marks and serrated edges, but in an obvious reference to the European Upper Paleolithic they considered the absence of art works despite the quantity of bone to be significant. This opens up the specter of a people with a functional existence bereft of religion and art. An even more extreme view of life at the coast in the MSA is that proposed by Binford (1984), with individuals eking out an existence scavenging scraps from carnivore kills. The evidence from the archive is more consistent with a home base where hunter-gatherers lived.

The main debate has been whether the local MSA groups lived like modern hunter-gatherers or whether they lacked the cognitive abilities of modern people. The way in which the archive has grown through successive occupations, with each event marked by small circular domestic hearths with carbonized surrounds and midden heaps of food waste, is the same as the process of site formation at LSA sites. From this it has been inferred that, in the rules for the organization of domestic space and the social structures (Deacon 1995), there was a degree of continuity in lifeways between the MSA, LSA, and the ethnographic present.

The counter-argument stresses differences between the MSA and LSA in the intensity of resource exploitation and in the use of items like personal ornaments. It equates the scale of the transition between the MSA and LSA with that between the Middle and Upper Paleolithic of Eurasia. The argument, set out in full in Klein and Edgar (2002), holds that modern behavior emerged in Africa as recently as 50 ky as the result of mutations affecting human neural networks. The adaptive advantages conferred by rapid genetic changes at this time are given as an explanation for the movement of modern humans out of Africa and the replacement of Neanderthals in Eurasia. On this argument the human remains from Klasies River and other sites dating to the earliest Late Pleistocene in Africa and the Near East represent anatomically modern people who, like the Neanderthals, were not yet modern in their cognition.

This debate on the emergence of modern cognition in Africa was initiated through different readings of the Klasies River archive. It is an important debate because it brings into question the relationship of the African and European Middle and Upper Paleolithic archaeological records (Deacon and Wurz 2001; McBrearty and Brooks 2000; Chapter 4). In particular the conventional wisdom that the Upper Paleolithic represents the earliest archaeological evidence for lifeways rich in symbolic expression, can be seen as Euro-biased. There was no phenomenon comparable to the Upper Paleolithic in Africa, where there was continuity rather than replacement of Late Pleistocene populations. Appreciation that the Upper Paleolithic was not a universal stage in human history is one of the lessons that has been learnt from the better knowledge of African prehistory. A significant contribution of this continuing debate has been to encourage a global perspective on Paleolithic archaeology.

Conclusion

Reading the Klasies River archive has depended on unraveling details of the stratigraphy and dating. From this has come the understanding that the site represents the erosional remnant of what was a large cone of deposition that built up through human occupation in the shelter of the cliff. The long sequence of artifact-rich deposits exposed in this remnant spans the first half of the Late Pleistocene, a time when MSA people were widely distributed in southern Africa. Artifacts in the same style came to be made throughout the subcontinent, and it is for this reason that Klasies River has become the reference site for the southern African MSA.

Interest in the MSA has increased because this stage is associated with the remains of early anatomically modern humans in Africa and because of the priority accorded Africa as a site of modern human evolution under the out-of-Africa hypothesis. The investigation of the Late and Middle Pleistocene in many parts of the continent is still at a reconnaissance level, and at present the full potential of archaeology to contribute to current debates on the origins and dispersals of modern humans cannot be realized. Inhibiting research on a continental scale is the arbitrary distinction drawn between the MSA in sub-Saharan Africa and the Middle Paleolithic in northern Africa. Middle Paleolithic has priority as a stage term and there is no merit in retaining the term Middle Stone Age if it precludes continent-wide comparisons. It is through such comparisons between Pleistocene archives in the different regions of the continent that the understanding of human behavior in the African MSA will progress.

REFERENCES

Bada, J. L., and L. Deems, 1975 Accuracy of Dates Beyond the 14-C Dating Limit Using the Aspartic Acid Racemization Reaction. Nature 255:218–219.

Beaumont, Peter B., 1980 On the Age of Border Cave Hominids 1–5. Palaeontologia Africana 23:21–33.

Beaumont, Peter B., and J. C. Vogel, 1972 On a New Radiocarbon Chronology for Africa South of the Equator. African Studies 31:65–89, 155–182.

Beaumont, Peter B., H. de Villiers, and J. C. Vogel, 1978 Modern Man in Sub-Saharan Africa Prior to 49,000 Years B.P.: A Review and Evaluation with Particular Reference to Border Cave. South African Journal of Science 74:409–419.

Binford, Lewis R., 1984 Faunal Remains from Klasies River Mouth. New York: Academic Press.

Bishop, W. W., and J. Desmond Clark, eds., 1967 Background to Evolution in Africa. Chicago: University of Chicago Press.

Bräuer, Günter, 1992 Africa's Place in the Evolution of *Homo sapiens*. *In* Continuity or Replacement: Controversies in *Homo sapiens* Evolution. Günter Bräuer and Fred H. Smith, eds. pp. 83–89. Rotterdam: A. A. Balkema.

Bräuer, Günter, H. J. Deacon, and F. Zipfel, 1992 Comment on the New Maxillary Finds from Klasies River, South Africa. Journal of Human Evolution 23:419–422.

Bräuer, Günter, and R. Singer, 1996 The Klasies Zygomatic Bone: Archaic or Modern? Journal of Human Evolution 30:161–165.

Butzer, Karl W., 1982 Geomorphology and Sediment Stratigraphy. *In* The Middle Stone Age at Klasies River Mouth in South Africa. R. Singer and J. Wymer, eds. pp. 33–42. Chicago: University of Chicago Press.

Byers, A. M., 1999 Communication and Material Culture: Pleistocene Tools as Action Cues. Cambridge Archaeological Journal 9:23–41.

Cannon, A., 1989 The Historical Dimension in Mortuary Expressions of Status and Sentiment. Current Anthropology 40:437–458.

Caspari, R., and M. R. Wolpoff, 1990 The Morphological Affinities of the Klasies River Mouth Skeletal Remains. American Journal of Physical Anthropology 81:203.

Caton-Thompson, Gertrude, 1946 The Aterian Industry: Its Place and Significance in the Palaeolithic World. Journal of the Royal Anthropological Institute, Huxley Memorial Lecture Volume 76:87–130.

Chen, Y-S., A. Olckers, T. G. Schurr, A. M. Kogelnik, K. Huoponen, and D. C. Wallace, 2000 mtDNA Variation in South African Kung and Khwe – and their Genetic Relationships to other Populations. American Journal of Human Genetics 66:1362–1383.

Clark, J. Desmond, 1959 The Prehistory of Southern Africa. Harmondsworth: Penguin.

Cremaschi, M., S. di Lernia, and E. A. A. Garcea, 1998 Some Insights on the Aterian in the Libyan Sahara: Chronology, Environment, and Archaeology. African Archaeological Review 15:261–286.

Deacon, Hilary J., 1976 Where Hunters Gathered: A Study of Holocene Stone Age People in the Eastern Cape. Monograph 1. Claremont: South African Archaeological Society.

——1985 Review of Binford, L. R.: Faunal Remains from Klasies River Mouth (New York: Academic Press, 1984). South African Archaeological Bulletin 40:59–60.

——1989 Late Pleistocene Palaeoecology and Archaeology in the Southern Cape, South Africa. In The Human Revolution: Behavioural and Biological Perspectives on the Origins of Modern Humans. Paul Mellars and Christopher Stringer, eds. pp. 547–564. Edinburgh: Edinburgh University Press.

——1992 Southern Africa and Modern Human Origins. Philosophical Transactions of the Royal Society, London B, 337:177–183.

——1995 Two Late Pleistocene-Holocene Archaeological Depositories from the Southern Cape, South Africa. South African Archaeological Bulletin 50:121–131.

——2001 Modern Human Emergence: An African Archaeological Perspective. In Humanity from African Naissance to Coming Millennia – Colloquia in Human Biology and Palaeoanthropology. P. V. Tobias, M. A. Raath, J. Muggi-Cecchi and G. A. Doyle, eds. pp. 217–226. Florence: Florence University Press.

Deacon, H. J., and J. Deacon, 1999 Human Beginnings in South Africa: Uncovering the Secrets of the Stone Age. Walnut Creek, CA: AltaMira Press.

Deacon, H. J., and V. B. Geleijnse, 1988 The Stratigraphy and Sedimentology of the Main Site Sequence, Klasies River, South Africa. South African Archaeological Bulletin 43:5–14.

Deacon, H. J., and R. Schuurman, 1992 The Origins of Modern People: The Evidence from Klasies River. In Continuity or Replacement: Controversies in Homo sapiens Evolution. Günter Bräuer and Fred H. Smith, eds. pp. 121–129. Rotterdam: Balkema.

Deacon, H. J., and J. F. Thackeray, 1984 Late Quaternary Environmental Changes and Implications from the Archaeological Record in Southern Africa. In Late Cainozoic Palaeoclimates of the Southern Hemisphere. J. C. Vogel, ed. pp. 375–390. Rotterdam: Balkema.

Deacon, H. J., and Sarah Wurz, 2001 Middle Pleistocene Populations of Southern Africa and the Emergence of Modern Behavior. In Human Roots: Africa and Asia in the Middle Pleistocene. L. Brahma and K. Robson-Brown, eds. pp. 55–64. Bristol: Western Academic and Specialist Press.

Deacon, H. J., A. S. Tama and J. C. Vogel, 1988 Biological and Cultural Development of Pleistocene People in an Old World Southern Continent. In Early Man in the Southern

Hemisphere. J. R. Presto, ed. pp. S23–31. Adelaide: Department of Physics and Mathematical Physics, University of Adelaide.

Deacon, J., 1966 An Annotated List of Radiocarbon Dates for Sub-Saharan Africa. Annals of the Cape Provincial Museums 5:5–84.

Defleur, A., T. White, P. Valence, L. Slick, and É. Crégut-Bonnoure, 1999 Neanderthal Cannibalism at Moula-Guercy, Ardèche, France. Science 286:128–131.

Feathers, J. K., 2002 Luminescence Dating in Less Than Ideal Conditions: Case Studies from Klasies River Main Site and Duinefontein, South Africa. Journal of Archaeological Science 29:177–194.

Goodwin, A. J. H., and C. van Riet Lowe, 1929 The Stone Age Cultures of South Africa. Annals of the South African Museum 27:1–289.

Grün, R., N. J. Shackleton, and H. J. Deacon, 1990 Electron-Spin Resonance Dating of Tooth Enamel from Klasies River Mouth Cave. Current Anthropology 31:427–432.

Grün, R., J. S. Brink, N. A. Spooner, L. Taylor, C. B. Stringer, R. G. Fransiscus, and A. S. Murray, 1996 Direct Dating of Florisbad Hominid. Nature 382:500–501.

Ingman, M., and U. Gyllenstein, 2001 Analysis of the Complete Human mtDNA Genome: Methodology and Inferences for Human Evolution. Journal of Heredity 92:454–461.

Inizian, M., M. Reduron-Ballinger, H. Roche, and J. Tixier, 1999 Technology and Terminology of Knapped Stone. Nanterre: CREP.

Klein, Richard G., 1976 The Mammalian Fauna of the Klasies River Mouth Site, Southern Cape Province, South Africa. South African Archaeological Bulletin 31:75–99.

——1978 Stone Age Predation on Large African Bovids. Journal of Archaeological Science 5:195–217.

——1979 Stone Age Exploitation of Animals in Southern Africa. American Scientist 67:151–160.

Klein, Richard G., and K. Cruz-Uribe, 1996 Exploitation of Large Bovids and Seals at Middle and Later Stone Age Sites in South Africa. Journal of Human Evolution 31:315–334.

Klein, Richard G., and B. Edgar, 2002 The Dawn of Human Culture. New York: Nevraumont.

Kleindienst, Maxine R., 2000 On the Nile Corridor and the Out-of-Africa Model. Current Anthropology 41:107–109.

McBrearty, Sally, 2001 The Middle Pleistocene of East Africa. In Human Roots: Africa and Asia in the Middle Pleistocene. Lawrence Barham and K. Robson-Brown, eds. pp. 81–98. Bristol: Western Academic and Specialist Press.

McBrearty, Sally, and Alison S. Brooks, 2000 The Revolution That Wasn't: A New Interpretation of the Origin of Modern Human Behavior. Journal of Human Evolution 39:453–563.

Marean, Curtis W., and S. Y. Kim, 1998 Mousterian Large-Mammal Remains from Kobeh Cave: Behavioral Implications for Neanderthals and Early Modern Humans. Current Anthropology 39(Supplement):79–113.

Marlar, R. A., B. L. Leonard, B. R. Billman, P. M. Lambert, and J. E. Malar, 2000 Biochemical Evidence of Cannibalism at a Prehistoric Puebloan Site in Southwestern Colorado. Nature 407:74–78.

Martinson, D. G., N. G. Pisias, J. D. Hays, J. Imbrie, T. C. Moore, and N. J. Shackleton, 1987 Age Dating and Orbital Theory of the Ice Ages: Development of a High Resolution 0-to-300,000-year Chronostratigraphy. Quaternary Research 27:1–29.

Mason, R. J., 1962 Prehistory of the Transvaal. Johannesburg: University of the Witwatersrand Press.

Mehlman, Michael J., 1989 Later Quaternary Archaeological Sequences in Northern Tanzania. Ph.D. dissertation, Department of Anthropology, University of Illinois, Urbana-Champaign.

——1991 Context for the Emergence of Modern Man in Eastern Africa: Some New Tanzanian Evidence. *In* Cultural Beginnings. J. Desmond Clark, ed. pp. 177–196. Bonn, Dr. Rudolf Habelt.

Miller, G. H., P. B. Beaumont, A. J. T. Jull, and B. Johnson, 1992 Pleistocene Geochronology and Palaeothermometry from Protein Diagenesis in Ostrich Eggshells: Implications for the Evolution of Modern Humans. Philosophical Transactions of the Royal Society, London B, 337:149–158.

Miller, G. H., P. B. Beaumont, H. J. Deacon, A. S. Brooks, P. E. Hare, and A J. T. Jull, 1999 Earliest Modern Humans in Southern Africa Dated by Isoleucine Epimerization in Ostrich Eggshell. Quaternary Science Reviews, Quaternary Geochronology 18:1573–1548.

Milo, R. G., 1998 Evidence for Hominid Predation at Klasies River Mouth, South Africa, and its Implications for the Behavior of Early Modern Humans. Journal of Archaeological Science 25:99–133.

Owen, L. R., and M. Porr, 1997 Report on the Conference "Ethno-Analogy and the Reconstruction of Prehistoric Artefact Use and Production." Préhistoire Européenne 11:207–211.

Rightmire, G. Philip, 2001 Comparison of Middle Pleistocene Hominids from Africa and Asia. *In* Human Roots: Africa and Asia in the Middle Pleistocene. Lawrence Barham and K. Robson-Brown, eds. pp. 123–133. Bristol: Western Academic and Specialist Press.

Rightmire, G. Philip, and Hilary J. Deacon, 1991 Comparative Studies of Late Pleistocene Human Remains from Klasies River Mouth, South Africa. Journal of Human Evolution 20:131–156.

——2001 New Human Teeth from Middle Stone Age Deposits at Klasies River, South Africa. Journal of Human Evolution 41:535–544.

Rose, Lisa, and Fiona Marshall, 1996 Meat Eating, Hominid Sociality, and Home Bases Revisited. Current Anthropology 37:307–338.

Semino, O., A. S. Santachiara-Benerecetti, F. Falaschi, L. L. Cavalli-Sforza, and P. O. A. Underhill, 2002 Ethiopians and Khoisan Share the Deepest Clades of the Human Y-Chromosome Phylogeny. American Journal of Human Genetics 70:265–268.

Shackleton, N. J., 1982 Stratigraphy and Chronology of the Klasies River Mouth Deposits: Oxygen Isotope Evidence. *In* The Middle Stone Age at Klasies River Mouth in South Africa. R. Singer and J. Wymer, eds. pp. 194–199. Chicago: University of Chicago Press.

Singer, R., and J. Wymer, 1982 The Middle Stone Age at Klasies River Mouth in South Africa. Chicago: Chicago University Press.

Szabo, B. J., C. V. Haynes, and T. A. Maxwell, 1995 Ages of Quaternary Pluvial Episodes Determined by Uranium-Series and Radiocarbon Dating of Lacustrine Deposits of Eastern Sahara. Palaeogeography, Palaeoclimatology, Palaeoecology 131:227–242.

Tryon, C. A., and Sally McBrearty, 2002 Tephrostratigraphy and the Acheulian to Middle Stone Age Transition in the Kapthurin Formation, Kenya. Journal of Human Evolution 42:211–235.

Turner, A., 1989 Sample Selection Schlepp Effects and Scavenging: The Implications of Partial Recovery for the Interpretations of the Terrestrial Mammal Assemblages from Klasies River Mouth. Journal of Archaeological Science 16:1–12.

van Andel, T. H., 1989 Late Pleistocene Sea Levels and the Human Exploitation of the Shore and Shelf of Southern South Africa. Journal of Field Archaeology 16:133–155.

van Pletzen, L., 2000 The Large Mammal Fauna from Klasies River. MA thesis, University of Stellenbosch.

Vogel, J. C., 2001 Radiometric Dates for the Middle Stone Age in South Africa. *In* Humanity from African Naissance to Coming Millennia – Colloquia in Human Biology and Palaeoanthropology. P. V. Tobias, M. A. Raath, J. Muggi-Cecchi, and G. A. Doyle, eds. pp. 261–268. Florence: Florence University Press.

——2002 Secular Variations in Carbon-14 and their Geophysical Implications. South African Journal of Science 98:154–160.

White, T. D., 1987 Cannibalism at Klasies? Sagittarius 2:7–9.

——1992 Prehistoric Cannibalism at Mancos. Princeton: Princeton University Press.

Wrinn, P. J., and W. J. Rink, 2003 ESR Dating of Tooth Enamel from Aterian levels at Mugharet el 'Aliya (Tangier, Morocco). Journal of Archaeological Science 30:123–133.

Wurz, Sarah, 1999 The Howiesons Poort at Klasies River – an Argument for Symbolic Behavior. South African Archaeological Bulletin 54:38–50.

——2002 Variability in the Middle Stone Age Lithic Sequence, 115,000–60,000 Years Ago at Klasies River, South Africa. Journal of Archaeological Science 29:1001–1015.

6

Modeling Later Stone Age Societies in Southern Africa

Peter Mitchell

The hunter-gatherer peoples of southern Africa, collectively called "Bushmen" or "San"[1] by Western researchers, play a central role in both archaeological and anthropological discussions, whether as archetypes of a mobile forager existence or as the source of new understandings of much of the world's rock art (Chapters 2, 9, and 14). Their importance as descendants of some of the first known anatomically modern humans (Chapters 4, 5) and as key players in debates surrounding the involvement of hunter-gatherer peoples with the wider world economy over the past 2,000 years (Chapter 14) are the subject of contributions elsewhere in this book. The focus here falls between the two, the archaeology of "Later Stone Age" hunter-gatherers, with my main concentration the period 12,000–2,000 years ago. Contrary to the term's original definition by Goodwin and van Riet Lowe (1929), we know now that modern human fossils, bone tools, and evidence for art are not associated only with Later Stone Age (LSA) assemblages. Instead, what unites these assemblages in southern Africa is the generally microlithic character of their stone tools and the presence of a wide range of artifacts in both organic and inorganic media that are similar to those of ethnographically known Bushman societies. Examples include rock art, ornamented artifacts, items of personal decoration, specialized hunting and gathering equipment (bows and arrows, digging sticks, bags, nets, fish hooks and sinkers, containers of ostrich eggshell or tortoise shell), and formal burials (J. Deacon 1984a).

I begin by commenting on the historical background of LSA research and then focus on two aspects of work undertaken since the 1960s. Fieldwork initiated in the Cape Fold Mountain Belt and its coastal forelands (Figure 6.1) has been at the forefront of the ecological paradigm that dominated LSA research into the 1980s. Choosing two themes, I examine how archaeologists have explored cultural and environmental change across the Pleistocene/Holocene boundary, and how they

the (1)

artefacts

(1)
the importance of Bushmen/San (South African hunter gatherers) is their similarity
to artefacts of the Latter Stone Age assemblages

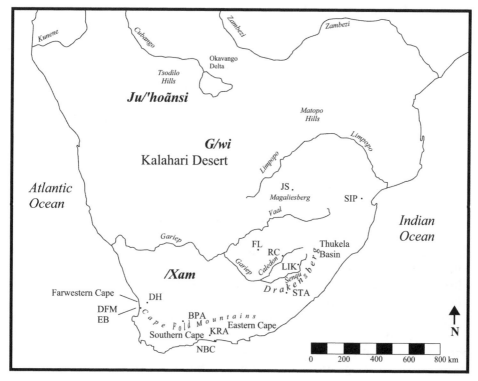

Figure 6.1. Map of southern Africa showing the location of Bushman groups, research areas, and archaeological sites mentioned in the text
Site names are abbreviated as follows: BPA: Boomplaas; DFM: Dunefield Midden; DH: De Hangen; EB: Elands Bay Cave; FL: Florisbad; JS: Jubilee Shelter; KRA: Kangkara; LIK: Likoaeng; NBC: Nelson Bay Cave; RC: Rose Cottage Cave; SIP: Siphiso Shelter; STA: Strathalan

have employed and critiqued notions of seasonal mobility when reconstructing patterns of landscape use. The expanding presence of archaeologists beyond the Cape helped re-evaluate these models, but more crucial has been the change from ecologically oriented inquiries to those interested in the social relations of past hunter-gatherer societies. First introduced into archaeology to help elucidate the meaning of Bushman rock art, this emphasis on ethnographically informed social theory, derived largely from studies of contemporary Kalahari peoples, now incorporates themes as diverse as exchange, gender, and the socio-spatial organization of campsites. How this can best be done, what kinds of analogies should be used, and how archaeological methodologies should alter if these goals are to be attained are among the questions I consider. In addition, the increasing empowerment of Khoisan peoples means that archaeological research can no longer be undertaken in a political vacuum. The implications of this for both archaeologists and Khoisan peoples form the final part of this chapter.

Changing Frameworks of Study

The course of southern African archaeology broadly parallels that of other world areas. Its origins, still insufficiently explored, lie in the mid-19th-century development of a local scientific tradition within Cape colonial society. Connections with leading British scientists were instrumental in encouraging local researchers and in publishing and validating their discoveries. Almost inevitably, Stone Age research in southern Africa thus adopted first the typological and then the culture-historical preoccupations of European Paleolithic archaeology. Only in the 1920s when Goodwin and van Riet Lowe (1929) wrote *The Stone Age Cultures of South Africa* was a uniquely southern African terminology developed. Their Later Stone Age, with its two parallel technological traditions, "Wilton" and "Smithfield," represented the remains of the anatomically modern human inhabitants of the subcontinent. Though raw material and activity differences were recognized as important influences on the archaeological record, work concentrated on "fairly rote filling in of the 'cultural stratigraphic' record" (Parkington 1984a:98), all too often based on single sites or selective samples; migration and diffusion lurked in the background as ultimate explanations of cultural change.

Change came from several quarters, not least the impact of radiocarbon dating as an independent means of establishing prehistoric time scales. The notion of two parallel LSA traditions was successfully challenged, replaced by an evolutionary succession in the Cape of Albany and Wilton Industries (J. Deacon 1972, 1974). Broadly similar assemblages elsewhere in southern Africa were dubbed the Oakhurst and Wilton Complexes, while other excavations firmly located LSA origins in the newly discovered Robberg Industry of late Pleistocene age (Klein 1972; Table 6.1). Recognition that anatomically modern humans have lived in southern Africa long before any of these industries took form (Chapters 4, 5) paralleled redefinition of the LSA as a set of assemblages associated with a suite of artifacts and behaviors historically associated with southern African hunter-gatherers. With Hilary Deacon, Janette Deacon, and John Parkington in the vanguard, LSA archaeology committed itself to emphasizing paleoenvironmental reconstruction and investigating how people adapted to ecological change through time and space, often in the context of larger projects on Quaternary ecosystems (e.g., H. J. Deacon et al., eds., 1983). Institutional growth eventually saw a plethora of such studies emerge beyond the Cape, including some in Lesotho, Namibia and Zimbabwe. Several of these projects, particularly the earlier ones, drew upon theoretical developments beyond southern Africa, among them the paleoeconomy school of Eric Higgs (ed., 1972) and his associates in Cambridge, from which both Parkington (1977) and Carter (1978) derived initial inspiration; systems thinking (H. J. Deacon 1972, 1976); and generalizations about the structure of hunter-gatherer societies taken, in large part, from studies of the subsistence and settlement strategies of Kalahari Bushmen (e.g., Parkington 1972 and references therein). Common to all these studies was an emphasis on developing clear and explicit models of prehistoric behavior, in some cases (most notably Carter 1978)

Table 6.1. Subdivisions of the southern African Later Stone Age

Smithfield ca. a.d. 1200–1870	Either a late continuation of the Wilton tradition or a separate industry found in the Free State and eastern Karoo, characterized by larger endstruck scrapers and a range of distinctive ceramics.
Ceramic Wilton/Post-classic Wilton with pottery ca. 100 b.c. – A.D. 1870	A continuation of the Wilton tradition, with the addition of ceramics and further changes in formal tool morphology and frequencies. In the Northern Cape regional industries are the Swartkops and Doornfontein, and in the Matopo Hills occurrences associated with Bambata (Gwanda) Ware.
Post-classic Wilton ca. 2500 b.c. – a.d. 200	A continuation of the Wilton, but with changes in formal tool frequencies and morphology, notably the gradual supercession of segments by other kinds of backed microliths. Known locally as Amadzimba in the Matopo Hills.
Classic and Early Wilton ca. 2500–7500 b.c.	Microlithic assemblages characterized by a proliferation of small scrapers and backed microliths, as well as by enhanced use of fine-grained rocks. Known locally as Nswatugi in the Matopo Hills.
Oakhurst ca. 6000–10000 b.c.	Non-microlithic assemblages, often emphasizing coarse-grained rocks. Formal tools are few, except for large scrapers, though scrapers with adze-like lateral retouch are common after ca. 7500 B.C. Regional variants are Albany (southern and eastern Cape Fold Belt), Kuruman (Northern Cape), Lockshoek (Free State and Karoo), and Pomongwan (Matopo Hills)
Robberg ca. 7600–19000 b.c.	Microlithic assemblages few formal tools, but rich in unmodified bladelets and bladelet cores, preferentially made in fine-grained rocks.
Early Later Stone Age (ELSA) before 19000 b.c.	Some assemblages predating 19000 B.C. that are microlithic, informal and quartz-dominated, e.g., Boomplaas, Members LP and LPC

with specific reference to the work of David Clarke (ed., 1972), another influential theoretician in the same Cambridge department in which Carter, Parkington, and many other Africanists of the 1960s and 1970s were trained (Clark 1989).

Models are both a boon and a curse. That they simplify complex observations and offer a predictive framework for future work allows those using them to make previously unsuspected connections and to generalize widely beyond a small number of case studies (Clarke 1976:31–34). But these same features can become limiting when they skirt over insufficiencies in the archaeological record, insufficiencies frequently filled in by a sometimes uncritical recourse to ethnographic data that can (literally) put the flesh on archaeological bones. One way in which these difficulties can be addressed is through the continual feedback provided by successive generations of fieldwork and the development of new analytical techniques. Together these may establish a model's limits and offer hitherto unexplored ways of testing its ability to explain old and new evidence alike, as discussion of seasonality issues below will show. More generally, in the case of the southern African LSA there has also been a shift in model emphasis, dissatisfaction with earlier ecologically oriented research contributing to a search for models that stress more "social" and ideological themes. The spark for this change came from the rapid realization that, when applied to Bushman rock art, new quantitative approaches could make little impact, indeed that a narrowly empiricist approach to studying the art was an analytical dead-end. Instead, first Patricia Vinnicombe (1976) and then David Lewis-Williams (1981) turned to Bushman ethnography to develop an anthropologically informed understanding of the art.

Arguing that shamans were central to the social reproduction of Bushman societies in healing the sick, controlling game, and making rain, Lewis-Williams introduced archaeologists to both a wider (non-subsistence-focused) range of Kalahari ethnography and the terminology of structural Marxism. Coupled with emerging unease about an exclusively "people-to-nature" focus in the questions being asked of the past and increasing awareness, given southern Africa's politics, of archaeologists' responsibilities in the present, the result was a sea change in LSA research. Lyn Wadley (1987) in the Magaliesberg Mountains and Aron Mazel (1989) in the Thukela Basin drew heavily on Bushman ethnography to investigate different issues from those emphasized by earlier ecological models: gift exchange, gender relations, and the social consequences of seasonal aggregation and dispersal. Renewed interest was also shown in viewing material culture as the signature of distinct groups of people (e.g., Binneman 1996; S. L. Hall 1990), but, alongside this shift toward asking "people-to-people" questions, cautions have been expressed about how precisely these ideas can be evaluated in the archaeological record. Ethnography has once more been used as a primary means of coloring in the archaeological record, but once again this has been at the expense, at least initially, of exploring variability rather than establishing generalizations. Questions of analytical scale have thus begun to emerge as a major issue, while archaeologists must also now take on board the rapidly changing political context of their work post-apartheid.

The Ecological Paradigm: Cultural and Environmental Change

Meticulously excavating sites with excellent organic preservation in the eastern and southern Cape Fold Belt, Hilary Deacon (1972) borrowed from systems thinking to reconceptualize the Robberg–Albany–Wilton succession as a series of homeostatic adaptive plateaux, characterized by distinctive economies and lifestyles and maintained in largely stable form by feedback between climate, ecology, subsistence strategies, and technology. Change from one plateau to the next was thought to have occurred rapidly. Subsequently, Janette Deacon (1984b) confirmed the integrity of each plateau through detailed study of artifact sequences from three stratified rockshelter sites located in areas in which climatic change had significant environmental impacts: one in the Cape Fold Mountains (Boomplaas); one adjacent to the present coastline (Nelson Bay Cave); and one in a major east/west intermontane valley (Kangkara). Deacon argued that the shift from Robberg to Albany toolkits clearly postdated the onset of late glacial climatic amelioration and could not be explained in narrow functional terms; in her view, changes in artifact assemblages reflected the stress people experienced as they were forced to adjust their lifestyles in changing ecological circumstances. This is an attractive proposition since few stone tools were probably ever employed directly to extract food from the environment (Isaac 1980) and because it emphasizes the individuals who made those artifacts in the first place. But, for all their elegance, both Janette Deacon's argument and the notion of homeostatic plateaux rested uneasily between two quite different analytical poles, those of the site and the subcontinent. Their critique underlines the necessity for archaeologists to consider how best to address processes that operate at diverse rates and scales.

Much of this discussion came to the fore in reaction to Parkington's (1980) essay, "Time and Place." He and several of his commentators raised the possibility that distinctions between Robberg, Albany, and Wilton Industries were reinforced, if not actually produced, by discontinuities in rockshelter occupation. In other words, time gaps in excavated stratigraphic sequences enhanced the differences that archaeologists identified. The practice of sinking smaller stratigraphic units (representing periods of many years or decades) into larger entities (spanning several centuries) in order to create samples large enough for statistical analysis only exacerbated the problem by masking smaller-scale variations. Furthermore, the very notion of homeostatic plateaux was criticized for confining change to the "leaps" between plateaux (or the gaps within excavated sequences). In response, Parkington (1988) eschewed industrial labels, reading his own Elands Bay Cave sequence in terms of successive reschedulings of site use across the Pleistocene/Holocene transition (11,000–5,800 b.c.) from expediently occupied hunting station to home base. Invoking the concept of "place" as "the set of opportunities afforded by (a) location and thus the likelihood of particular activities taking place there" (Parkington 1980:73), he saw people's use of Elands Bay Cave altering in response to changes in its own local situation (from riverine to estuarine to coastal context as sea levels changed), and thus its place within the wider regional settlement system. None of the changes he observed fit neatly within a Robberg–Albany–Wilton succession, nor necessarily led into later Holocene patterns.

Some of these criticisms were clearly misplaced. For one, homeostasis does include the possibility of change at the level of adjustments to the existing system, while the gross succession of Robberg–Albany–Wilton is so widely attested south of the Limpopo River that it must reflect the operation of factors active beyond the level of individual sites (H. J. Deacon 1980). Changes of "place" on their own cannot account for such systematic replacements of one toolkit by another, nor more or less concomitant shifts in subsistence toward a greater emphasis on smaller game, coastal resources, and plant foods. On the other hand, there is value in thinking about these changes in terms of how settlement systems as a whole were organized; no one site can represent the entirety of what people did. For example, drowning of continental shelves at the end of the Pleistocene has undoubtedly destroyed many sites. The subsistence shifts I have just mentioned may be exaggerated by this gap in our data, just as we may seriously misconstrue Robberg lifeways if our sites represent (quite literally in the Cape) no more than the tip of the iceberg of what was once there. Looking in areas where sea-level changes were relatively minor (e.g., KwaZulu-Natal/Lesotho) or irrelevant (Mpumalanga) might provide a sounder grasp of late Pleistocene settlement patterns.

At the root of much of this discussion is the recognition that we must distinguish changes and variables of local and regional importance from those of subcontinental (or wider) significance. Explanations must be sought that take such differences into account, in the expectation that different explanatory processes may be most evident and most useful at different spatiotemporal scales. H. J. Deacon's (1976) suggestion of a specifically eastern Cape Fold Belt "Wilton" entity distinct from any broader, subcontinental usage of the term to denote mid/late Holocene backed microlith/small scraper-rich assemblages was an early recognition of this need. J. Deacon's (1984b) distinction between innovative changes (appearance of new artifacts) and post-innovative changes (shifts in artifact frequency, size, shape) expresses a related concern, as does Wadley's (2000) distinction between inter-regional stylistic and intra-regional activity variability. More thought must be given to how variation in local resource opportunities, ecological constraints, climatic change, cultural histories, and social networks interact and over what time scales, and with what data we can hope to recognize these processes and their effects (Bailey 1983). In so doing we may be better able to explain why, for example, changes in artifact assemblage composition that mark the Robberg–Albany succession are not restricted to the southern Cape; why in some areas (e.g., Lesotho; Mpumalanga) microlithic, bladelet-dominated Robberg toolkits apparently disappeared *without* significant faunal change; why in southeastern Africa this seems significantly to *postdate* their replacement in the Cape Fold Belt (Wadley 1996); and whether, anywhere, such wholesale loss of toolkit components did not have technological and economic, as well as social, causes and consequences (Mitchell 2000).

The Ecological Paradigm: Seasonal Mobility

Addressing these issues has implications for our methodologies that I address later. For now, however, I remain in the Cape to consider a second theme of the ecological paradigm, that of seasonal mobility. Its introduction owed something to surviving oral traditions about how Bushmen had moved across the landscape (e.g., H. J. Deacon 1976), but more to the expectation, derived from the work of Eric Higgs (ed., 1972), that mobile hunter-gatherers maximize their use of the land's carrying capacity by moving seasonally between complementary ecological zones. Carter's (1978) work in the Maloti-Drakensberg Mountains, later elaborated by Cable (1984), and Parkington's (1977) early research in the far western Cape were both motivated by this concern. In the latter area, four decades of fieldwork have located hundreds of sites and produced an impressive suite of excavations (Parkington 1999). The original seasonality model has been refined, debated, and contested, becoming a classic example of how old ideas can be re-evaluated by new fieldwork and methodologies.

Conveniently, Parkington (2001) has recently summarized much of this debate. Empirically, the model was born out of excavations that appeared to provide complementary signatures of late Holocene seasonal occupation at the inland shelter of De Hangen (summer) and the coastal site of Elands Bay Cave (winter), based on estimates of the age of death of two seasonally breeding mammals (seals and rock hyraxes) and the presence of seasonally distinctive resources (grasses with inflorescences, edible underground plant foods, tortoises, etc.). Climatic and ecological contrasts between the mountains and the coast provided the impetus for movement, not least the late Holocene emphasis at Elands Bay Cave on eating mussels that may be made toxic by red plankton blooms in summer. Given the north/south orientation of both shoreline and mountains, integration of seasonally distinct resource sets by east/west movement between them seemed plausible. Stable isotope analysis of human skeletons began to contribute to this discussion in the mid-1980s with the realization that, in this winter rainfall area of southern Africa, marine foods have a different carbon isotope composition from terrestrial foods, and that mixes of the two should be reflected in predictable intermediate values (van der Merwe 1982). This is because marine plants incorporate carbon dioxide into their tissues through photosynthesis through a slightly different chemical pathway than do the trees, shrubs, and temperate grasses that predominate on land. It should therefore be possible to identify the diet of prehistoric individuals by measuring the ratio of ^{12}C to ^{13}C in their bones and teeth (Price, ed., 1989). Sealy and van der Merwe (1988, 1992) examined all relevant human skeletons and interpreted their results as meaning that individuals buried at the coast had eaten quite different foods, often almost entirely marine ones, from those buried inland, apparently refuting the seasonal mobility model. They also argued that environmental constraints identified by Parkington were less restrictive than first proposed, and that neither seal mandible lengths nor rock hyrax tooth eruption patterns were necessarily sensitive to all seasons of the year.

But things are not so clear-cut. Initial analyses used collagen, which reflects protein intake, not total diet. Later work employing the apatite fraction of bone shows that individuals buried at the coast had eaten fats and carbohydrates of both marine and terrestrial origin, as well as marine protein, derived, to judge from excavated evidence, from shellfish, fish, whales, and seals (Lee Thorp et al. 1989). This fits with physiological arguments that a purely marine diet is implausible because of the difficulties that it poses for metabolizing so much protein (Noli and Avery 1988). Other developments include the recognition that isotope readings must be adjusted to take account of changes in atmospheric carbon isotope ratios produced by fossil fuel emissions and that they represent the end-product of dietary intake over a number of years, in other words, an averaged personal history; measures from different parts of the skeleton allow us to explore this because different tissues replace their carbon content at different rates (Sealy et al. 1995).

One important contribution of both isotope studies and the ever-growing body of excavated evidence is the understanding that use of the far western Cape landscape changed repeatedly over the past 13,000 years (Parkington 1999). Virtually all known sites dating to the first millennium b.c., for example, cluster along the coast, many taking the form of huge megamiddens, almost wholly made up of mussel shells (Jerardino 1996). This suggests that regional settlement was overwhelmingly coastal-oriented at this time, though terrestrial foods must still have played an important (Parkington would argue the major) role in people's diets. The argument here partly turns on one's understanding of what megamiddens were: occasionally occupied stations at which shellfish were procured and dried for storage and transport inland (Henshilwood et al. 1994), or base-camps, the domestic signature of which is hidden by necessarily limited excavation and swamped almost beyond recognition by the enormous quantities of shell (Jerardino and Yates 1997)? If the former, where are the inland sites, since recent reanalysis suggests open-air artifact scatters inland that remain undated for want of organic remains should, typologically, be placed before 1000 b.c. (Jerardino 1996)? If the latter, why are known isotope signatures not even more exclusively marine (Parkington 2001)?

One of the key dimensions involved in reconciling the results of isotope analyses with those of archaeological excavations is the recognition that the two measure different things. Isotopes cannot yet differentiate where terrestrial foods are from, nor can they distinguish eating a range of foods at the same time from sequential food consumption at intervals of a few years or less. Excavated plant and animal residues, on the other hand, represent accumulated debris from many people, not the diets of specific individuals (Parkington 2001). Wider issues are also worth considering: Should we expect seasonal mobility to be well defined in all environments? The answer is probably no, as those that are most structured ecologically will probably encourage the most patterned forms of human behavior (Humphreys 1987). Should we imagine whole groups moving *en masse*? Again, looking to Kalahari ethnography, the answer is no, since individuals and their immediate families pursue many diverse residential opportunities during their lives. One expectation from this is that we may be able to approach such individual life histories using stable carbon isotope analysis, for example by comparing male and female signatures, techniques that inform on where people ate, such as strontium analysis, as well as biometric and DNA studies that can examine genetic relationships alongside dietary ones. Together, these data should allow us to consider residence and marriage patterns and gendered access to foodstuffs, alongside issues of landscape use and resource exploitation. The differentiating subsistence strategies already implied by some studies indicate what is possible (Lee Thorp et al. 1989; Sealy and Pfeiffer 2000).

Bushman Ethnography, Social Theory, and the Kalahari Debate

Such topics move beyond a narrowly ecological focus into the broader questions of social relations raised by the paradigm shift in LSA archaeology that began in the mid-1980s. Rock art has played a key role in its development, beginning with Lewis-Williams' (1982) analysis of the part played by shamans in the socio-economic reproduction of Bushman societies. I propose to look at three of the (interrelated) areas in which the quest for social relations has been pursued: aggregation and dispersal; gift exchange; and the identification of the prehistoric alliance networks that linked communities together.

Seasonal patterns of aggregation and dispersal are widespread among hunter-gatherers, including those of southern Africa, but this ecologically grounded behavior takes on clear social aspects when it is recognized that each phase is associated with quite different patterns of ritual activity, exchange, visiting, and gender relations, all with possible implications for the archaeological record. Though partly prefigured in Carter's (1978) study of seasonal patterns of aggregation and dispersal in Lesotho and KwaZulu-Natal, Wadley (1987) was the first archaeologist explicitly to formulate these distinctions and to search for them in her material. Her model (Table 6.2) is most convincing for mid-Holocene sites in the Magaliesberg Mountains, but has proven a popular research tool beyond them. Particularly suggestive is the combination of rock art and "dirt archaeology" in identifying aggregation in late Holocene levels at Rose Cottage Cave through such evidence as bead-making, hunting of large game, formal structuring of space, and paintings relating to the maintenance and vulnerability of social harmony (Ouzman and Wadley 1997).

Rose Cottage also provides evidence for long-distance connections in the form of an Indian Ocean mollusc and paintings of fish that may be native to northern KwaZulu-Natal and areas yet further north. Such long-distance connections have come to be viewed through the prism of *hxaro*, the delayed, reciprocal system of gift exchange recorded for Ju/'hoãnsi Bushmen. Hxaro objects characterize aggregation sites in particular (Yellen 1977), while Wiessner's (1982) classic study shows that people intensify exchange in droughts, concentrating ties on areas with resources reciprocal to their own. As well as insuring against ecological disaster and distributing information and goods, hxaro partnerships also provide ways for parents to find spouses for their children. These ideas have proven popular with archaeologists, who have inferred hxaro in the past from finds of ostrich eggshell beads and bone points. Interpreting the latter as arrow points, these two artifact types are traditionally favored as hxaro items by the Ju/'hoãnsi. Topics explored

Table 6.2. Criteria for the recognition of aggregation and dispersal sites

Evidence	Aggregation phase site	Dispersal phase site
Stone artifacts	Curated, standardized. Many formal tools	Expedient Few formal tools
Lithic raw materials	May include relatively high numbers of exotics	Predominantly local
Spatial patterning	Formal, gender-associated division of space	Absent
Hxaro objects	Manufacturing debris from making ostrich eggshell beads and bone points; finished examples of the same	Very rare or absent
Ritual activity	Portable art objects; rock art; decorated bonework and ostrich eggshell; shamanistic paraphernalia (e.g., quartz crystals, MSA tools); ochre	Very rare or absent
Meat procurement	Fauna includes a wide range of ungulates, many of them hunted	Little evidence for hunting; concentration on snaring small antelope and taking ground game
Seasonality	Variable, but different from disperal phase sites	Variable, but different from aggregation phase sites

Source: after Wadley 1987.

using this approach include: the intensification of exchange in resource-poor conditions to explain the rich material culture of many mid-Holocene Wilton assemblages (Wadley 1987); the proliferation of exchange when colonizing new areas at the start of the Holocene (Mazel 1989); and alternative, non-hierarchical readings of richly ornamented child burials in the southern Cape (Hall and Binneman 1987). Differential patterns of exchange, again assumed to be the result of hxaro, have also been explored in relation to spatial patterning of material culture in order to identify prehistoric interaction networks, what Mazel (1989) has called "social regions." One consequence of correctly identifying such networks would be that we might more reliably be able to link individual sites together within seasonal rounds, rather than just arguing for those linkages on the basis of presumed ecological complementarity between the zones in which the sites occur (Sampson 1988).

These are all laudable goals that have, without doubt, radically transformed the ways in which archaeologists think about their work and the material that they excavate or record. However, they have not gone uncritiqued, with the central issue that of the appropriateness of the connections being made between theory and data.

How can we operationalize these links in order to go beyond what Barham (1992:50) calls "tantalising speculation"? The exchange of views between Barham and Wadley (1992) over how best to characterize the assemblages from their respective mid-Holocene excavations at Siphiso Shelter (Swaziland) and Jubilee Shelter (North West Province) leaves unclear whether and why all, or only some, of the criteria proposed are necessary for establishing whether a site was used as an aggregation focus or a dispersal phase location. Do we place more weight upon bone tools and ostrich eggshell beads and evidence of their production, on the presence of ochre, on site size, or on the organization of space within it? Perhaps more worryingly, this discussion also leaves unresolved what significance should be attached to the quantitative aspects of these criteria: Wadley, for example, argued that the worked bone (one) and ostrich eggshell bead (60) frequencies at Siphiso Shelter were too few to warrant it being termed an aggregation site, but that the numbers of these items (649 and 376 respectively) from Jubilee Shelter were much more compelling. Very likely so, but what then of frequencies an order of magnitude or more greater still from Zimbabwe's Matopo Hills (Walker 1995a)? Alone, numbers mean little and must surely be considered in the context of a local group of contemporary sites, which in turn demands that several such sites are known. But beyond numbers, the size, nature, and duration of occupation all need to be unraveled. One strategy may be to use parameters like settlement area, deposition rate of domestic debris, and deposition rate of items that relate to longer visits (e.g., ostrich eggshell beads that take a long time to make). Though demanding close dating of individual sequences, this might be better than using relative densities of items which necessarily ignore differences in soil matrix composition, such as those produced by differential shellfish collection (Jerardino 1995).

Other concerns include the desirability of a more extensive, systematic set of ethnoarchaeological observations relating to aggregation and dispersal, or the use of material culture to signal social identity; the testing of models not just against the archaeological record of South Africa, but also against that of the Kalahari Bushman peoples from whom the theoretical models derive (Walker 1995b); and a much sounder knowledge of precisely how artifacts were employed. For example, when talking of hxaro, most archaeologists have inferred this process from nothing more than a formal analogy based on present Ju/'hoãn practice regarding the exchange of arrows and beads (on analogy, see Chapter 2). But both items are also used for other purposes, such that their frequency at any one site may not relate to hxaro at all (Walker 1995a). Furthermore, while beads may be readily recognizable as beads, not all bone points were necessarily used as arrow points, and other arrow armatures (notably stone) were also used. More fundamentally, there has been virtually no consideration of the fact that, in most areas, neither bone points nor ostrich eggshell beads can be shown to have moved anywhere at all (but see discussions of this in southeastern southern Africa, from which ostriches seem to have been naturally absent; Mazel 1996; Mitchell 1996). In short, much more empirical documentation of exchange is required, and it is by no means clear from wider considerations of Bushman ethnography that exchange has to take the form of hxaro, or imply particular sets of kinship-based social relations (Kent 1992).

Deepening our knowledge of how and why particular artifacts were made and used is also relevant to other applications of ethnographically informed models of social relations. For example, in KwaZulu-Natal's Thukela Basin, Mazel (1989) defined three mid-Holocene social regions or alliance networks, in part using the proportions of different kinds of backed microliths and the frequencies of different kinds of scraper backing. But for what were these artifacts used? Were backed microliths arrowheads, or, as microwear and residue analyses suggest, elements of composite, multi-purpose cutting tools (Wadley and Binneman 1995; Williamson 1997)? Why should scraper backing reflect social identity, especially if hidden from view when hafted, instead of different patterns of hafting, use, or resharpening (Barham 1992)? Should we expect millennia-long alliance networks to persist, or to be identifiable where so few artifact types are exclusive to one region or the other? And can we reliably infer such networks from small numbers of excavated sites (just one, two and two), as was originally the case? Our lack of ethnography relating to stone tool use and limited acquaintance with microwear and residue studies is one troubling aspect of these debates. Such questions are even more awkward if we wish to argue that particular artifacts were associated with women or men. Since ethnographic studies suggest Bushmen do organize craft activities along gender lines, correct identification of artifact function should allow us to engender a wide set of LSA material culture.

One route to achieving this is by formal analogy from practices recorded ethnographically among Bushman societies. This forms the basis, for example, of Mazel's (1989) argument that increasing quantities of stone adzes and plant food waste demonstrate an enhanced female contribution to subsistence and thus a greater role for women among Thukela Basin hunter-gatherers after 2000 b.c. The links made are between adzes and woodworking, woodworking and the making and repair of digging sticks, digging sticks and plant food exploitation, and plant food-gathering and women. But we also know that adzes and digging sticks had other uses, that less formal stone tools could be used to work wood, and that digging sticks were sometimes employed by men. The underlying assumption that women made their own digging sticks can also be contested (Wadley 1989). At each step along the way more work is needed to establish how far, and under what circumstances, the process of extrapolation is valid. Artifacts may, indeed, be the most difficult realm within which to identify the individual social actors and groups of actors required if we wish to situate the engine of social change in the relations between people, rather than between people and environment. Rock art imagery, some of which can be highly specific and perhaps identifiable to particular artists/shamans, is another avenue. But perhaps the best way of resolving person and gender is through burial and the opportunities that the dead afford us to examine artifact associations, diet, and lifestyle, not least through stable isotope analyses of the kind considered above (Parkington 1998).

There is, however, an underlying difficulty in much of what I have discussed so far. Southern African archaeology most certainly does benefit from an excellent hunter-gatherer ethnography, and physical anthropology, linguistics, social anthropology, and archaeology all demonstrate that there are close associations between the LSA archaeological record and recent and present Bushman peoples (see Barnard 1992; Deacon and Deacon 1999; Mitchell 1997, 2002; Smith et al. 2000; Wadley 1993). But the question is, how close? Ethnohistoric accounts stretch back into the 17th century and took on more coherent form in the late 19th century, but systematic long-term work on Kalahari hunter-gatherers began only after 1950, a period of accelerating, large-scale change. Though ethnographers have studied many other groups, archaeologists continue to draw upon three in particular for analogies to the past: the Ju/'hoãnsi (!Kung) and G/wi of the Kalahari, and the now extinct /Xam of South Africa's Northern Cape Province. Few others elicit much interest. Not only does this mean that we are emphasizing a small, if very well recorded, subsection of the total sample of Bushman ethnography, it also fails to address for the most part the potential impact of two millennia of contact and interaction with farmers and herders, the subject-matter of what has come to be called the "Kalahari debate" (Solway and Lee 1990; Wilmsen and Denbow 1990; Chapter 14). Space does not allow detailed consideration of this here. Suffice it to say that it forms part of the more general critical re-evaluation of ethnographic data provoked by the realization that well before the advent of colonial rule, indeed even before Europe's 15th-century expansion overseas, the world was a much more integrated and interconnected place than was once thought. Discussion of the impact of these connections on Kalahari Bushmen has been heated, though strictly archaeological evidence for their incorporation as a subservient underclass within agropastoralist societies is weak (Sadr 1997).

Nevertheless, it seems likely that some aspects of hunter-gatherer life were altered by contact with food-producers, a proposition central to Jolly's (1996) controversial argument that rock-paintings from Lesotho, which are among the mainstays of a shamanistic understanding of Bushman rock art, reflect instead close involvement with the beliefs and ritual practices of Sotho- and Nguni-speaking farming communities. "Dirt archaeology" has not yet contemplated how far, if at all, some of the social relations of ethnographically known Bushman groups whom it wishes to employ as sources of analogy may have altered over time. There is, indeed, no systematic southern African equivalent to Ann Stahl's direct historical approach that begins with the present and works progressively back in time to track changes away from the ethnographic record. As Stahl (1999:76) writes, "archaeologists interested in a more distant past need to evaluate how historic forces shaped the societies represented in ethnographic sources if they are to avoid importing anachronistic models into a distant African past." For those working in the southern African LSA this highlights three things, beginning with the need to develop a closely argued archaeology of ethnographically known Bushman societies, something already begun for the /Xam (J. Deacon 1996) and in the Tsodilo Hills of Botswana (e.g., Robbins et al. 1996), but something needed elsewhere as well. Second, we need to expand the sample of Bushman societies that we use to include, for example, those who did not practice seasonal aggregation and dispersal or hxaro exchange. The need to "de-!Kung" LSA archaeology is a longstanding call (Parkington 1984b), but there is also a third requirement, to reach beyond the Kalahari in our search for comparative material. Archaeological evidence from areas like the southern (Hall

2000) and far western Cape (Jerardino 1996) document the late Holocene emergence of delayed return economies marked by storage, increased territoriality, more complex burial rituals and, perhaps, widespread production of rock art that points to marked differences with the known Bushman ethnographic record. Archaeological and ethnographic analogs among more "complex" hunter-gatherers may be at least as relevant as Kalahari fieldwork if we are to understand such processes of intensification (S. L. Hall 1990).

Where Now? Possible Directions for Future Research

Both the ecological and social paradigms that I have described have tended to emphasize quite general questions and concepts, sometimes borrowed from a fairly narrow range of ethnographic studies and applied with a concern to integrate disparate data rather than to explore variability within that evidence. To generate the more rigorous and diversified data sets that can be analyzed comparatively in ways that will allow difference, as well as similarity, to be examined, expanded analogical horizons are just one of the directions along which LSA research will need to move. A second direction that deserves emphasis is the growing interest in resolving the archaeological record much more precisely in terms of time, space, and people so as to investigate social relations along the lines indicated above. Parkington (1998) has been at the forefront of this movement, which has two main consequences for archaeological fieldwork. First, rockshelter deposits, while excellent for giving the long view of sequence, are almost inevitably palimpsests of multiple visits and likely to be affected by lateral and vertical displacement of objects. Only rarely will they preserve the highly resolved spatial information that allows individual occupations to be distinguished. This has an obvious bearing on the recognition of aggregation and dispersal phase occupations, for example, which may have alternated within time frames that are impossible for archaeologists to subdivide. One solution is to shift attention to large-scale excavation of short-lived occupations where spatiotemporal resolution may be greater, and social processes like food-sharing and spatial organization easier to recognize. Dunefield Midden, a late Holocene open-air campsite near Elands Bay Cave, is one such site. Combining excellent organic preservation and finely resolved stratigraphy, the bulk of this site represents a single occupation dating to about a.d. 1300 associated with an eland hunt and exploitation of shellfish, ground game, seals, and a beached whale (Parkington et al. 1992). Likoaeng, in Lesotho's highlands, suggests that potentially comparable, if smaller, sites exist inland (Mitchell and Charles 2000), where, indeed, some of Pleistocene age have already been investigated (Brink and Henderson 2001; Opperman 1996).

A complementary solution is to acknowledge the worth of samples smaller than those with which archaeologists have traditionally worked, and to maximize the chronological resolution available within rockshelter sequences. The possibilities of this are illustrated by the 147 individual stratigraphic units identified by Inskeep (1987) in mid/late Holocene levels at Nelson Bay Cave, compared to the 11 such units recognized by Klein (1972) at the same site in the period 3000–8000 b.c.;

both sets of units come from shell-midden situations. Exceptionally careful micros-tratigraphic excavation undertaken on a spatially large scale, married to detailed and sensitive application of radiocarbon dating, may well identify those short-lived phenomena that most closely approximate the decisions of individuals within actual social and environmental contexts. Examples at Elands Bay Cave include a mass stranding of rock lobster (*Jasus lalandii*) ca. 8,000 b.c., intensive exploitation of whelks (*Burnupena* sp.) some 400 radiocarbon years later, and the subsequent inno-vation and use of bone "fish gorges" and *Donax* shell scrapers, patterns restricted at this site to the millennium thereafter (Parkington 1992).

But better dating is not merely a matter of more dates. A signal feature of LSA archaeology is the reluctance to translate radiocarbon determinations into cali-brated dates before about 2,000 years ago. To be sure, the absence of a historic record to which we can seek connections may help explain this, but the free avail-ability of calibration programs and the importance of understanding rates of change in both the archaeological and paleoenvironmental records if we are to grapple with explaining changes in human adaptations should encourage a much more system-atic exploration of this issue. Resolution in time demands calibration, even if fluc-tuations in the calibration curve mean that the ultimate result is more ambiguity, not less. Dating is also important in another respect. Quite rightly, some archaeo-logical research programs have been criticized for not sufficiently incorporating rock art alongside excavated evidence, and most of those which have done so have con-centrated on the last 2,000 years, when images of domestic livestock, agropas-toralists, and European settlers impart some chronological context to paintings and engravings. Integrating rock art's wealth of references to past social relations with excavated evidence can unquestionably offer a richer, more detailed view of the past, but it cannot proceed in a temporal vacuum. Yet unless rock art can be contextualized, chronologically as well as spatially, we shall produce ahistorical, never-changing understandings of the entire archaeological record (Parkington 1998). Recent developments in accelerator radiocarbon dating and the application of Harris matrices (Mazel and Watchman 1997; Russell 2000) indicate some of the ways forward, but much more of the same, linked to studies of pigment composi-tion and style, is needed for rock art and other archaeological materials to become fully integrated.

Of other research strategies one might mention the more thorough application (perhaps of necessity on a site-by-site basis) of detailed studies of artifact function through microwear and residue analyses; the expansion of studies of how stone tools and other artifacts were produced and then reworked while still in use (*chaînes opératoires*; Boëda et al. 1990; Dobres and Hoffman 1994; Schlanger 1996; White 1993); more detailed and commonplace investigations of the taphonomy of archae-ological faunal assemblages to understand their origins and the decisions taken by hunters regarding butchery and transport (cf. Binford 1981; Brain 1981; Brink 1987; Speth 1983; Stiner 1994); and more systematic work on all the formation processes at work on archaeological sites (Chapter 2), something about which we still have much to learn, not least in rockshelter contexts. At a more basic level still, there remain areas of southern Africa in which archaeological research has scarcely begun, or has been done once in a pioneering fashion some decades back but now stands in need of reassessment in the light of more recent work. Within South Africa Mpumalanga, the southeastern Free State, southern KwaZulu-Natal, the former Ciskei and Transkei, and the southern Karoo exemplify this. Further north, and despite the work of Wendt (1972), Kinahan (1991), Walker (1995a), and Robbins et al. (1996, to give but one example), much of Namibia, Botswana, and Zimbabwe, particularly areas where one might try and establish material connections with surviving Bushman communities, falls under the same heading. Attention to open-air sites, rather than just rockshelters, will be critical in all these areas, alongside a more systematic application of probabilistic sampling techniques in field surveys than has been the norm where rockshelters (Mitchell 1996), or total coverage of a landscape (Sampson 1985), have been the focus of study. Recent discoveries of the first mid-Holocene rockshelter occupation in an area as well-studied as the far western Cape (Jerardino and Yates 1996) and of the first ever open-air Pleistocene LSA site (Churchill et al. 2000) reinforce the need for continued survey.

Fieldwork in these and other areas must also consider, more thoroughly than in the past, two final questions. First, if we wish to understand how human societies have coped with southern Africa's fluctuating environments, then archaeologists not only need to maintain their commitment to recovering faunal, botanical, and sedimentological evidence, but also need to seek improved ways of translating what are still impressionistic, often relative, statements about precipitation and temperature into quantitatively more meaningful data that more closely approach real changes in the density, distribution and productivity of the plant, animal, and water resources that people used (cf. Thackeray 1988). Southern Africa's sensitivity to global climatic change makes this much more than a mere academic concern. Second, with both apartheid and a cultural-historical model now superseded, perhaps it is time that archaeologists consider once again evidence for population movements in the LSA past. Walker's (1995b) suggestion that the spread of microlithic assemblages across the Kalahari relates to the expansion of Khoe-speaking groups in the last 2,000–3,000 years is one of the first such examples, but perhaps some aspects of the diffusion of mid-Holocene Wilton microlithic technology could also be profitably be considered in this way. Biometric and DNA studies offer complementary research strategies here, and analysis of the Numic expansion in western North America suggests how such movements may be identifiable in prehistory (Bettinger and Baumhof 1982).

Hunter-Gatherer Archaeology as the Legacy of Khoisan Peoples

Writing over a decade ago, Martin Hall (1990:59) argued that "one of the illusions of southern African archaeology is that the past can be neutral," a point echoed by Lewis-Williams (1993). Despite this, and in contrast to the archaeology of Iron Age societies (not least the Zimbabwe Tradition) or the colonial period, the longstanding economic, social, and political marginalization of hunter-gatherers and people of hunter-gatherer descent arguably made the LSA a safer and politically less charged locus of study for much of the 20th century. And yet the professional establishment of Stone Age archaeology owed much to the scientific and ideological concerns of one of South Africa's most significant political figures, Jan Smuts (Schlanger 2002). Subsequent National Party governments constrained popularization of the results of the archaeological research that they themselves funded, banning the teaching of human evolution from school syllabi and stressing in school textbooks the primitiveness and inevitable post-colonization decline of southern Africa's Khoisan communities (Esterhuysen and Smith 1998; A. Smith 1983). By these and similar falsehoods, all South African citizens were alienated from their past, a process that also long impacted outside South Africa's borders because of the dominance of that country's historiography (Campbell 1998).

The ending of apartheid has brought to the fore the fact that the people whom LSA archaeologists study have millions of living descendants across southern Africa. Through bodies such as the National Khoisan Consultative Conference of South Africa and the Working Group of Indigenous Minorities in Southern Africa, these individuals and the communities to which they belong are increasingly seeking political empowerment and taking a keen interest in reconstructions of their past. In South Africa this has been signaled officially by the use of a rock art motif and a /Xam motto in the new national coat of arms (B. Smith et al. 2000), but such recognition, let alone self-determination and access to traditional lands, remains a pipedream in some other southern African countries (Lee and Hitchcock 1998). Archaeologists' reactions to these recent developments have, on the whole, been positive, offering opportunities for archaeological training to Ju/'hoãn people in Namibia (Smith and Lee 1997; Lee and Hitchcock 1998), building community-based approaches to the presentation and conservation of archaeological resources (Clanwilliam Living Landscape Project 2001), and working with people of Khoisan descent in opening archaeological sites to a wider public (Morris et al. 2001). But it would be unrealistic to pretend that there may be no conflicts of interest, nor that the questions that archaeologists ask, or have asked, are necessarily those of greatest interest to people of Khoisan descent. Calls for reburial of all human skeletons in existing museum collections (Jordan 1999) pose one significant challenge to some forms of archaeological research, although the Southern African Association of Archaeologists has adopted a clear ethical code as one response to the concerns that lie behind these requests, and some recently excavated skeletons have, indeed, been reburied after analysis (Sealy et al. 2000). If southern African archaeology can withstand the challenges to the institutional structures that support it, strengthen its ties with overseas collaborators, and deepen the dialog with its own public, particularly those of Khoisan descent, the future for a third century of LSA research looks bright.

NOTE

1 No term is ideal when referring to southern Africa's indigenous hunter-gatherer peoples. Both "Bushman" and "San" carry potentially pejorative overtones, while "Basarwa" is an

invention of the modern Botswanan government. Nor is there a consensus among surviving communities themselves (Lee and Hitchcock 1998). I use the common English terms "Bushman" and "Bushmen," while rejecting any sexist, racist, or derogatory connotations that others may impute to them.

REFERENCES

Bailey, G. N., 1983 Concepts of Time in Quaternary Prehistory. Annual Review of Anthropology 12:165–192.

Barham, Lawrence S., 1992 Let's Walk Before We Run: An Appraisal of Historical Materialist Approaches to the Later Stone Age. South African Archaeological Bulletin 47:44–51.

Barnard, A., 1992 Hunters and Herders of Southern Africa: A Comparative Ethnography of the Khoisan Peoples. Cambridge: Cambridge University Press.

Bettinger, R. L., and M. A. Baumhof, 1982 The Numic Spread: Great Basin Cultures in Competition. American Antiquity 47:485–503.

Binford, Lewis R., 1981 Bones: Ancient Men and Modern Myths. New York: Academic Press.

Binneman, J. N. F. 1996 The Symbolic Construction of Communities During the Holocene Later Stone Age in the South-Eastern Cape. Ph.D. thesis, University of the Witwatersrand, Johannesburg.

Boëda, E., J.-M. Geneste, and L. Meignen, 1990 Identification de chaînes opératoires lithiques du paléolithique ancien et moyen. Paléo 2:43–80.

Brain, C. K., 1981 The Hunters or the Hunted: An Introduction to African Cave Taphonomy. Chicago: University of Chicago Press.

Brink, J. S., 1987 The Archaeozoology of Florisbad, Orange Free State. Memoirs van die Nasionale Museum, Bloemfontein 24:1–151.

Brink, J. S., and Z. L. Henderson, 2001 A High-Resolution Last Interglacial MSA Horizon at Florisbad in the Context of Other Open-Air Occurrences in the Central Interior of Southern Africa: An Interim Statement. In Settlement Dynamics of the Middle Paleolithic and Middle Stone Age. N. J. Conard, ed. pp. 1–20. Tübingen: Kerns Verlag.

Cable, J. H. C., 1984 Late Stone Age Economy and Technology in Southern Natal. Oxford: British Archaeological Reports.

Campbell, Alec C., 1998 Archaeology in Botswana: Origins and Growth. In Ditswa Mmung: The Archaeology of Botswana. Paul Lane, Andrew Reid, and Alinah K. Segobye, eds, pp. 24–49. Gaborone: The Botswana Society.

Carter, P. L., 1978 The Prehistory of Eastern Lesotho. Ph.D. thesis, University of Cambridge.

Churchill, S. E., J. S. Brink, L. R. Berger, R. A. Hutchison, L. Rossouw, D. Stynder, P. J. Hancox, D. Brandt, S. Woodborne, J. C. Loock, L. Scott, and P. Ungar, 2000 Erfkroon: A New Florisian Fossil Locality from Fluvial Contexts in the Western Free State, South Africa. South African Journal of Science 96:161–163.

Clanwilliam Living Landscape Project 2001. Electronic document. <http://www.cllp.uct.ac.za/home.htm> accessed July 1, 2002.

Clark, J. G. D., 1989 Prehistory at Cambridge and Beyond. Cambridge: Cambridge University Press.

Clarke, David L., ed., 1972 Models in Archaeology. London: Duckworth.

——1976 Analytical Archaeology. 2nd edition. London: Methuen.

Deacon, Hilary J., 1972 A Review of the Post-Pleistocene in South Africa. South African Archaeological Society Goodwin Series 1:26–45.

——1976 Where Hunters Gathered: A Study of Holocene Stone Age People in the Eastern Cape. Claremont: South African Archaeological Society.

——1980 Comment on Time and Place. South African Archaeological Bulletin 35:86–88.

Deacon, Hilary J., and Janette Deacon, 1999 Human Beginnings in South Africa. Cape Town: David Philip.

Deacon, Hilary J., Q. B. Hendey and J. N. Lambrechts, eds., 1983 Fynbos Palaeoecology: A Preliminary Synthesis. Pretoria: Council for Scientific and Industrial Research.

Deacon, Janette, 1972 Wilton: An Assessment After 50 Years. South African Archaeological Bulletin 27:10–45.

——1974 Patterning in the Radiocarbon Dates for the Wilton/Smithfield Complex in Southern Africa. South African Archaeological Bulletin 29:3–18.

——1984a Later Stone Age People and their Descendants in Southern Africa. In Southern African Prehistory and Palaeoenvironments. Richard G. Klein, ed. pp. 221–328. Rotterdam: A. A. Balkema.

——1984b The Later Stone Age of Southernmost Africa. Oxford: British Archaeological Reports.

——1996 Archaeology of the Flat and Grass Bushmen. In Voices from the Past: /Xam Bushmen and the Bleek and Lloyd Collection. Janette Deacon and Thomas A. Dowson, eds. pp. 245–270. Johannesburg: Witwatersrand University Press.

Dobres, M.-A., and C. R. Hoffman, 1994 Social Agency and the Dynamics of Prehistoric Technology. Journal of Archaeological Method and Theory 1:211–258.

Esterhuysen, A. B., and Smith, Andrew B., 1998 Evolution: "The Forbidden Word"? South African Archaeological Bulletin 53:135–137.

Goodwin, A. J. H., and van Riet Lowe, C., 1929 The Stone Age Cultures of South Africa. Annals of the South African Museum 27:1–289.

Hall, Martin, 1990 "Hidden History": Iron Age Archaeology in Southern Africa. In A History of African Archaeology. Peter Robertshaw, ed. pp. 59–77. London: James Currey.

Hall, S. L., 1990 Hunter-Gatherer-Fishers of the Fish River Basin: A Contribution to the Holocene Prehistory of the Eastern Cape. Ph.D. thesis, University of Stellenbosch.

——2000 Burial Sequence in the Later Stone Age of the Eastern Cape Province, South Africa. South African Archaeological Bulletin 55:137–146.

Hall, S. L., and J. N. F. Binneman, 1987 Later Stone Age Burial Variability in the Cape: A Social Interpretation. South African Archaeological Bulletin 42:140–152.

Henshilwood, Christopher, P. Nilssen, and John E. Parkington, 1994 Mussel Drying and Food Storage in the Late Holocene, South-West Cape, South Africa. Journal of Field Archaeology 21:103–109.

Higgs, Eric S., ed., 1972 Papers in Economic Prehistory. Cambridge: Cambridge University Press.

Humphreys, A. J. B., 1987 Prehistoric Seasonal Mobility: What Are We Really Achieving? South African Archaeological Bulletin 42:34–38.

Inskeep, R. R., 1987 Nelson Bay Cave, Cape Province, South Africa: The Holocene Levels. Oxford: British Archaeological Reports.

Isaac, Glynn Ll., 1980 Comment on Time and Place. South African Archaeological Bulletin 35:96–98.

Jerardino, A., 1995 The Problem with Density Values in Archaeological Analysis: A Case Study from Tortoise Cave, Western Cape, South Africa. South African Archaeological Bulletin 50:21–27.

——1996 Changing Social Landscapes of the Western Cape Coast of Southern Africa over the Last 4500 Years. Ph.D. thesis, University of Cape Town.

Jerardino, A., and R. Yates, 1996 Preliminary Results from Excavations at Steenbokfontein Cave: Implications for Past and Future Research. South African Archaeological Bulletin 51:7–16.

———— 1997 Excavations at Mike Taylor's Midden: A Summary Report and Implications for a Re-Characterisation of Megamiddens. South African Archaeological Bulletin 52:43–51.

Jolly, P., 1996 Symbiotic Interactions between Black Farmers and South-Eastern San: Implications for Southern African Rock Art Studies, Ethnographic Analogy and Hunter-Gatherer Cultural Identity. Cultural Anthropology 37:277–306.

Jordan, B., 1999 Row Erupts as Khoisan Call for Return of Old Bones. Sunday Times (South Africa) January 17.

Kent, Susan, 1992 The Current Forager Controversy: Real Versus Ideal Views of Hunter-Gatherers. Man 27:45–70.

Kinahan, J., 1991 Pastoral Nomads of the Central Namib Desert: The People History Forgot. Windhoek: New Namibia Books.

Klein, Richard G., 1972 The Late Quaternary Mammalian Fauna of Nelson Bay Cave (Cape Province, South Africa): Its Implications for Megafaunal Extinctions and Environmental and Cultural Change. Quaternary Research 2:135–142.

Lee, Richard B., and Robert K. Hitchcock, 1998 African Hunter-Gatherers: History and the Politics of Ethnicity. In Transformations in Africa: Essays on Africa's Later Past. Graham Connah, ed. pp. 14–45. Leicester: Leicester University Press.

Lee Thorp, J. A., Judith C. Sealy, and Nicholas J. van der Merwe, 1989 Stable Carbon Isotope Ratio Differences Between Bone Collagen and Bone Apatite, and their Relationship to Diet. Journal of Archaeological Science 16:585–599.

Lewis-Williams, J. David, 1981 Believing and Seeing: Symbolic Meanings in Southern San Rock Paintings. Cambridge: Cambridge University Press.

——1982 The Economic and Social Context of Southern San Rock Art. Current Anthropology 23:429–449.

——1993 Southern African Archaeology in the 1990s. South African Archaeological Bulletin 48:45–50.

Mazel, Aron D., 1989 People Making History: The Last Ten Thousand Years of Hunter-Gatherer Communities in the Thukela Basin. Natal Museum Journal of Humanities 1:1–168.

——1996 Maqonqo Shelter: The Excavation of Holocene Deposits in the Eastern Biggarsberg, Thukela Basin, South Africa. Natal Museum Journal of Humanities 8:1–39.

Mazel, Aron D., and A. L. Watchman, 1997 Accelerator Radiocarbon Dating of Natal Drakensberg Paintings: Results and Implications. Antiquity 71:445–449.

Mitchell, Peter J., 1996 Marine Shells and Ostrich Eggshell as Indicators of Prehistoric Exchange and Interaction in the Lesotho Highlands. African Archaeological Review 13:35–76.

——1997 The Holocene Later Stone Age South of the Limpopo River, 10 000–2000 B.P. Journal of World Prehistory 11:359–424.

——2000 The Organization of Later Stone Age Lithic Technology in the Caledon Valley, Southern Africa. African Archaeological Review 17:141–176.

——2002 The Archaeology of Southern Africa. Cambridge: Cambridge University Press.

Mitchell, Peter J., and R. L. C. Charles, 2000 Later Stone Age Hunter-Gatherer Adaptations in Lesotho. In Human Ecodynamics: Proceedings of the Conference of the Association of

Environmental Archaeology. G. N. Bailey, R. L. C. Charles, and N. Winder, eds. pp. 90–99. Oxford: Oxbow Press.

Morris, D., S. Ouzman, and G. Tlhapi, 2001 Tandjesberg San Rock Painting Rehabilitation Project: From Catastrophe to Celebration. The Digging Stick 18(1):1–4.

Noli, D., and G. Avery, 1988 Protein Poisoning and Coastal Subsistence. Journal of Archaeological Science 15:395–401.

Opperman, H., 1996 Strathalan Cave B, North-Eastern Cape Province, South Africa: Evidence for Human Behaviour 29,000–26,000 Years Ago. Quaternary International 33:45–54.

Ouzman, S., and Lyn Wadley, 1997 A History in Paint and Stone from Rose Cottage Cave, South Africa. Antiquity 71:386–404.

Parkington, John E., 1972 Seasonal Mobility in the Late Stone Age. African Studies 31:223–243.

——1977 Follow the San. Unpublished Ph.D. thesis, University of Cambridge.

——1980 Time and Place: Some Observations on Spatial and Temporal Patterning in the Later Stone Age Sequence in Southern Africa. South African Archaeological Bulletin 35:75–83.

——1984a Changing Views of the Later Stone Age of South Africa. Advances in World Archaeology 3:89–142.

——1984b Soaqua and Bushmen: Hunters and Robbers. In Past and Present in Hunter-Gatherer Studies. Carmel Schrire, ed. pp. 151–174. New York: Academic Press.

——1988 The Pleistocene/Holocene Transition in the Western Cape, South Africa: Observations from Verlorenvlei. In Prehistoric Cultures and Environments in the Late Quaternary of Africa. John Bower and David Lubell, eds. pp. 349–363. Oxford: British Archaeological Reports.

——1992 Making Sense of Sequence at the Elands Bay Cave, Western Cape, South Africa. In Guide to Archaeological Sites in the Western Cape. Andrew B. Smith and B. Mÿtti, eds. pp. 6–12. Cape Town: Southern African Association of Archaeologists.

——1998 Resolving the Past: Gender in the Stone Age Archaeological Record of the Western Cape. In Gender in African Prehistory. Susan Kent, ed. pp. 25–38. Walnut Creek, CA: AltaMira Press.

——1999 Western Cape Landscapes. Proceedings of the British Academy 99:25–35.

——2001 Mobility, Seasonality and Southern African Hunter-Gatherers. South African Archaeological Bulletin 56:1–7.

Parkington, John E., P. Nilssen, C. Reeler, and C. Henshilwood, 1992 Making Sense of Space at Dunefield Midden Campsite, Western Cape, South Africa. Southern African Field Archaeology 1:63–70.

Price, T. D., ed., 1989 The Chemistry of Prehistoric Human Bone. Cambridge: Cambridge University Press.

Robbins, Lawrence H., M. L. Murphy, Alec C. Campbell, and G. A. Brook, 1996 Excavations at the Tsodilo Hills Rhino Cave. Botswana Notes and Records 28:23–45.

Russell, T., 2000 The Application of the Harris Matrix to San Rock Art at Main Caves North, KwaZulu-Natal. South African Archaeological Bulletin 55:60–70.

Sadr, Karim, 1997 Kalahari Archaeology and the Bushman Debate. Current Anthropology 38:104–112.

Sampson, C. Garth, 1985 Atlas of Stone Age Settlement in the Seacow Valley. Memoirs of the National Museum (Bloemfontein) 20:1–116.

——1988 Stylistic Boundaries among Mobile Hunter-Foragers. Washington, DC: Smithsonian Institution Press.

Schlanger, N., 1996 Understanding Levallois: Lithic Technology and Cognitive Archaeology. Cambridge Archaeological Journal 6:231–254.

——2002 Making the Past for South Africa's Future: The Prehistory of Field-Marshal Smuts (1920s–1940s). Antiquity 76:200–209.

Sealy, Judith C., and S. Pfeiffer, 2000 Diet, Body Size and Landscape Use Among Holocene People in the Southern Cape, South Africa. Current Anthropology 41:642–655.

Sealy, Judith C., and Nicholas J. van der Merwe, 1988 Social, Spatial and Chronological Patterning in Marine Food Use as Determined by ^{13}C Measurements of Holocene Human Skeletal Remains from the South-Western Cape, South Africa. World Archaeology 20:87–102.

——————1992 On "Approaches to Dietary Reconstruction in the Western Cape: Are You What You Have Eaten?" – A Reply to Parkington. Journal of Archaeological Science 19:459–466.

Sealy, Judith C., R. Armstrong, and Carmel Schrire, 1995 Beyond Lifetime Averages: Tracing Life Histories through Isotopic Analysis of Different Calcified Tissues from Archaeological Human Skeletons. Antiquity 69:290–300.

Sealy, Judith C., S. Pfeiffer, R. Yates, K. Wilmore, A. H. Manhire, T. M. O'C. Maggs, and J. Lanham, 2000 Hunter-Gatherer Child Burials from the Pakhuis Mountains, Western Cape: Growth, Diet and Burial Practices in the Late Holocene, South African Archaeological Bulletin 55:32–43.

Smith, Andrew B., 1983 The Hotnot Syndrome: Myth-Making in South African School Textbooks. Social Dynamics 9(2):37–49.

Smith, Andrew B., and Richard B. Lee, 1997 Cho/ana: Archaeological and Ethnohistorical Evidence for Recent Hunter-Gatherer/Agropastoralist Contact in Northern Bushmanland, Namibia. South African Archaeological Bulletin 52:52–58.

Smith, Andrew B., C. Malherbe, Mathias Guenther, and P. Berens, 2000 The Bushmen of Southern Africa: A Foraging Society in Transition. Cape Town: David Philip.

Smith, Benjamin, J. David Lewis-Williams, Geoffrey Blundell, and Christopher Chippindale, 2000 Archaeology and Symbolism in the New South African Coat of Arms. Antiquity 74:467–468.

Solway, Jacqueline S., and Richard B. Lee, 1990 Foragers, Genuine or Spurious? Situating the Kalahari San in History. Current Anthropology 31:109–146.

Speth, John D., 1983 Bison Kills and Bone Counts: Decision Making by Ancient Hunters. Chicago: University of Chicago Press.

Stahl, Ann B., 1999 The Archaeology of Global Encounters Viewed from Banda, Ghana. African Archaeological Review. 16:5–81.

Stiner, M. C., 1994 Honour among Thieves: A Zooarchaeological Study of Neanderthal Ecology. Princeton: Princeton University Press.

Thackeray, J. F., 1988 Quantification of Climatic Change During the Late Quaternary in Southern Africa. Palaeoecology of Africa 19:317–324.

van der Merwe, Nicholas J., 1982 Carbon Isotopes, Photosynthesis, and Archaeology. American Scientist 70(6):596–606.

Vinnicombe, Patricia, 1976 People of the Eland. Pietermaritzburg: University of Natal Press.

Wadley, Lyn, 1987 Later Stone Age Hunters and Gatherers of the Southern Transvaal: Social and Ecological Interpretations. Oxford: British Archaeological Reports.

——1989 Gender Relations in the Thukela Basin. South African Archaeological Bulletin 44:122–126.

——1992 Reply to Barham: Aggregation and Dispersal Phase Sites in the Later Stone Age. South African Archaeological Bulletin 47:52–55.

—— 1993 The Pleistocene Later Stone Age South of the Limpopo. Journal of World Prehistory 7:243–296.

—— 1996 The Robberg Industry of Rose Cottage Cave, Eastern Free State: The Technology, Spatial Patterns, and Environment. South African Archaeological Bulletin 51:64–76.

—— 2000 The Wilton and Pre-Ceramic Post-Classic Wilton Industries at Rose Cottage Cave and their Context in the South African Sequence. South African Archaeological Bulletin 55:90–106.

Wadley, Lyn, and J. N. F. Binneman, 1995 Arrowheads or Pen Knives? A Microwear Analysis of Mid-Holocene Stone Segments from Jubilee Shelter, Transvaal. South African Journal of Science 91:153–155.

Walker, N. J., 1995a Late Pleistocene and Holocene Hunter-Gatherers of the Matopos. Uppsala: Societas Archaeologica Upsaliensis.

—— 1995b The Archaeology of the San: The Late Stone Age of Botswana. In Speaking for the Bushmen. A. J. G. M. Sanders, ed. pp. 54–87. Gaborone: The Botswana Society.

Wendt, W. E., 1972 Preliminary Report on an Archaeological Research Programme in South West Africa. Cimbebasia B 2:1–61.

White, Randall, 1993 Technological and Social Dimensions of "Aurignacian-Age" Body Ornaments across Europe. In Before Lascaux: The Complex Record of the Early Upper Palaeolithic. H. Knecht, A. Pike-Tay, and R. White, eds. pp. 277–299. Boca Raton: CRC Press.

Wiessner, Polly, 1982 Risk, Reciprocity and Social Influence on !Kung San Economics. In Politics and History in Band Societies. Eleanor Leacock and Richard B. Lee, eds. pp. 61–84. Cambridge: Cambridge University Press.

Williamson, B. S., 1997 Down the Microscope and Beyond: Microscopy and Molecular Studies of Stone Tool Residues and Bone Samples from Rose Cottage Cave. South African Journal of Science 93:458–464.

Wilmsen, Edwin N., and James R. Denbow, 1990 Paradigmatic History of San-Speaking Peoples and Current Attempts at Revision. Current Anthropology 31:489–524.

Yellen, John E., 1977 Archaeological Approaches to the Present: Models for Reconstructing the Past. New York: Academic Press.

7

Holocene "Aquatic" Adaptations in North Tropical Africa

Augustin F. C. Holl

A plurality of terms is used to refer to the prehistoric societies that left sparse tes-
timonies to their presence in north tropical Africa during the later part of the Pleistocene period. These terms range from Terminal, through Late, to Epipaleolithic
(Aumassip 1986; Barich 1998; Camps 1974; Vermeersch 1992). The terminological situation is even more complex when post-Pleistocene and Early Holocene
forager and herder sites are considered. The terms then range from Mesolithic,
Neolithic of Capsian Tradition (NCT), Neolithic of Sudanese Tradition (NST), and
Saharo-Sudanese Neolithic (SSN), to Aqualithic Civilizations, and (ceramic) Late
Stone Age (LSA).

   All these concepts refer to changing patterns in prehistoric cultural remains (Holl
1989). Late Paleolithic assemblages are differentiated from the preceding Middle
Stone Age (MSA) ones by specific ways of making stone tools (Chapters 4, 6). The
stone blanks are generally obtained from blade cores and later shaped into formal
tools. Stone tools are even smaller during the ensuing post-Paleolithic period.
Microliths, often geometric in shape, are combined to create composite tools
(Chapters 6, 9). Grinding tools are frequent and widespread. Bone tools, ranging
from items of personal adornment to fish hooks and harpoons, are often found in
sites along with evidence for the exploitation of aquatic resources (see Chapter 4
for bone tools in MSA contexts). The specialization of some Early Holocene
communities on the exploitation of wetlands and the intensification of resource-
gathering triggered profound adaptive shifts and new patterns in the material
record. The presence of pottery and grinding equipment was taken by some
researchers (Camps 1980) as indicative of food-producing economies, or, more precisely, of the practice of agriculture. The "Aqualithic Theory" was an important and
interesting attempt to frame a robust and parsimonious explanation for the series
of "events" that led to the expansion of a wetlands lifestyle in north tropical Africa
in areas today encompassed by the Saharan and Sahelian zones.

This chapter explores how early programmatic statements, formulated in advance of significant archaeological evidence, shaped the interpretation of Early to Middle Holocene sites in northern tropical Africa. So-called Saharan-Sudanese Neolithic sites were first interpreted as sites of incipient agriculturalists (Arkell 1949, 1953) and later argued to represent a successful alternative to agriculture (Sutton's "Aqualithic": 1974, 1977). In both scenarios, perceived similarities in material culture were taken to signal cultural connections, and migration assumed to be the mechanism behind shared features. Though early evidence was rather uncritically assimilated to these scenarios, later sections of the chapter explore how that same evidence points to variation and alternative processes of culture change during the Early to mid-Holocene.

misuse of evidence

Arkell, the Mesolithic, and the Origins of Food Production

Arkell (1949, 1953) excavated two sites near the Nile River in the Khartoum area in Sudan that laid the foundations for early understandings of Holocene lifeways in northern tropical Africa. The material from one, Shaheinab, was used to delineate the key characteristics of the "Khartoum Mesolithic" (see Figure 7.1 for site locations). The other, Khartoum Hospital Site, assigned to a later date, was crucial in the characterization of the "Khartoum Neolithic." Though the assemblages from these sites shared a number of characteristics, they differed significantly in others. They had in common evidence of microlithic stone industries; grinding equipment; pottery with characteristic "wavy-line" and "dotted wavy-line" motifs; barbed bone points; and a substantial quantity of wild animal bones with a significant component of fish, crocodile, and hippopotamus bones (Haaland 1992; Sutton 1974, 1977; Yellen 1998). Domestic animal bones, specifically from sheep and goats, were absent from Shaheinab but present at Khartoum Hospital Site. The shared characteristics of these sites suggested a common cultural background for the Early Holocene foragers of the Nile Valley. Some of these foragers later shifted to food production, with small livestock husbandry.

From Arkell's (1949, 1953) perspective, Khartoum "Mesolithic" people adopted livestock husbandry through their links to the ancient Near East. In this period it was believed that the Neolithic revolution took root in the Fertile Crescent, and spread from there to the rest of the Old World (Camps 1980; Childe 1928, 1936; Kuper 1978). The Sudanese sites immediately achieved the status of critical places attesting a north–south and east–west expansion of the new Neolithic life style. As conceived by Gordon Childe (1928, 1936) this new way of life included the practice of agriculture and animal husbandry; heavy food-processing equipment, in this case grindstones and grinders; and sedentary communities living in emerging permanent settlements that later resulted in an urban revolution (Chapters 8, 9, 10, 13).

Later scholars elaborated and extended Arkell's concept of a Sudanese Neolithic based on loose similarities in the patterning of cultural remains. Barbed bone points and pottery decorated with "wavy-line" and "dotted wavy-line" motifs achieved the

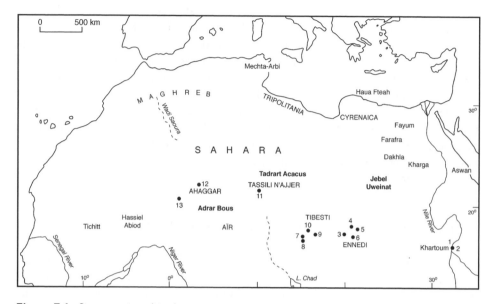

Figure 7.1. Sites mentioned in the text
1. Shaheinab; 2. Khartoum Hospital Site; 3. Delebo; 4. Soro Kezenanga II; 5. Orogourde; 6. Gobe V; 7. Gouro; 8. Aorounga; 9. Fochi; 10. Ounianga Kebir; 11. Ti-n-Hanakaten; 12. Amekni; 13. Meniet

status of type fossils in Africanist archaeology, and came to be used by almost all archaeologists in their effort to understand the dynamics of Early Holocene societies of the Sahara and the Nile (Aumassip 1978; Camps 1978, 1980; Gabriel 1978; Kuper 1978). The Sudanese Nile Valley was considered as the core area from which a new lifestyle spread during the Early Holocene (Haaland 1992). North tropical Africa was divided into two major "cultural zones": (1) the NCT in the north-northwest, in the hinterland Chotts area of Tunisia and Algeria; and (2) the NST in the rest of the Sahara, from the Sudan in the east to Mauritania in the west. According to Camps (1967:286), the NST tradition likely developed in different parts of south and central Sahara during the sixth millennium b.c. It is characterized by a profusely decorated pottery, generally all over the body, spherical in shape, and devoid of handles. Stone tools present a certain amount of variation from area to area. Within the bone and ivory industry, the multiplication of fishing gear, precisely harpoons and fish hooks, can be explained by the frequent clustering of sites along vanished lakes and rivers (Camps 1967:286).

Arkell's Systematics and Saharan Archaeology to the 1980s

Arkell's systematics based on Sudanese Nile material were thus extended through much of the Sahara by a number of researchers from the late 1950s to the early 1980s. In 1956–1957, G. Bailloud (1969) conducted a year-long survey and excavation program in the southwestern part of the Ennedi (Figure 7.1). Surface data, backed by excavated material and radiocarbon dating, were used to outline the chronological succession of pottery decoration styles. Four sites were tested: Delebo, Soro Kezenanga II, Orogourde rockshelter, and Gobe V rockshelter. The deepest level of Delebo cave, termed Zone V, contained the earliest pottery from the Ennedi mountain: "characterized as is the case in Sudan, by a decoration shaped like waves (wavy-line)" (Bailloud 1969:37). Wavy-line pottery was also documented in overlying Zone IV deposits. Dotted wavy-line pottery from Zones III and II was dated to 5230 ± 300 b.c. and 4950 ± 300 b.c. respectively. A similar pottery sequence was recorded at Soro Kezenanga II. According to Bailloud (1969:38–40), the ceramic material from Soro Kezenanga (the upper levels) and Orogourde rock-shelter compared with that from sites like Esh Shaheinab (Sudan) and Meniet in central Sahara. The fauna included large mammals such as antelope, gazelle, large bovids (*Bos* or buffalo), jackal, hyena, wild hog, hippopotamus, as well as ostrich, water tortoise, frog, and fish, especially large amounts of catfish. Cattle, goat, and domestic dog are recorded at Soro Kezananga, "indicating that in this case one may refer to the Neolithic with certainty" (Bailloud 1969:8). Characteristically, and despite the large amount of fish bones recorded from the excavation units, no fishing instruments (i.e., fish hooks or barbed bone points) were documented.

The situation differed in the Borku where J. Courtin (1969) carried out a survey project in 1964–1965. No test excavation was implemented. The relevant archaeo-logical data were collected from surface contexts. The subtlety of Courtin's argument is particularly interesting as it shows how dominant ideas are simply reproduced despite the inadequacy of the database. The material collected during the survey was arranged into chronological groups. "Despite the lack of excavation and consequently of stratigraphies, it is possible to establish a relative chronology of the Borku Neolithic, relying on G. Bailloud's work in the Ennedi and J. Arkell's one in Sudan, as well as our own observations" (Courtin 1969:149). Wavy-line pottery was not represented in the regional samples collected during the survey. Despite the absence of that "critical" diagnostic feature, the author proceeded to argue: "One can assign to the Early Neolithic, pottery of Sudanese type, known at Khartoum, Esh Shaheinab, and in the Ennedi and Tenere. . . . The 'dotted wavy-line', already known at Ounianga (Arkell), on the other hand, is found from the Goz Kerki and east of the Djourab to the eastern limit of the Tibest (Gouro, Aorounga, Fochi)" (Courtin 1969:149). The recorded Neolithic sites were gen-erally located on ancient dunes overlooking closed inter-dunal depressions which were the remains of former small lakes. Few fish bones were collected, and fishing equipment was extremely rare. "In any case, a site located south of Ounianga Kebir had a bi-serial bone harpoon associated with 'dotted wavy-line pottery'" (Courtin 1969:155). Clearly, Courtin's approach to field survey was geared to support Arkell's model.

A. J. Arkell's achievement is remarkable. His influence shaped the terms of debate, and the criteria he devised have been used to fit surface material into neat chronological categories. The circularity of the reasoning is typical of a type-fossil approach. Research conducted in central Sahara, at Ti-n-Hanakaten (Aumassip

1978), Amekni (Camps 1969, 1974, 1980), and Meniet (Hugot 1963), also documented the presence of "wavy-line" and "dotted wavy-line" pottery. Radiocarbon
dating of these sites started to show that some of the central Saharan sites were
older than those from the Nile Valley. As a result, the expression "Neolithic of
Sudanese Tradition" became problematic. According to Camps,

> this Neolithic has been called the *Neolithic of Sudanese Tradition* because its origin had
> been arbitrarily fixed as the banks of the Nile in the region of Khartoum in the Sudan.
> ... At the present time, the oldest manifestations recognized occur to the west of
> the great strip of territory (the Ahaggar) occupied by this group of industries which
> we shall, therefore, henceforth refer to as the *Saharan-Sudanese Neolithic*. (Camps
> 1980:557)

By the mid-1970s, there was considerable evidence for a widespread distribution of spherically shaped pottery, some decorated with wavy-line, dotted wavy-line,
and rocker-stamping, as well as mat impression. Fishing gear was also widespread,
particularly in archaeological sites found near ancient water bodies, including lakes,
rivers, and streams. These shared characteristics were implicitly assumed to signal
a commonality in culture, but scholars before Sutton were preoccupied with
documenting the distribution rather than explaining it. Sutton's (1974, 1977) bold
move consisted in generating a model to account for the distributional patterns of
Early Holocene archaeological sites.

Sutton and the "Aquatic Civilization" of Middle Africa

In the mid-1970s, J. E. G. Sutton published two papers (1974, 1977) dealing with
the archaeological jigsaw that had emerged from fieldwork carried out in north tropical and eastern Africa. In these works, Sutton attempted to encapsulate within a
coherent theoretical framework the phenomena that may have generated and driven
the expansion of the widespread archaeological complex attested in part of north
tropical Africa and the Great Lakes regions of the southeast. For Sutton (1974), all
documented archaeological assemblages with fishing equipment, globular pottery
decorated with wavy-line and dotted wavy-line, and remains of aquatic fauna
belonged to the "Aquatic Civilization of Middle Africa," which he conceived as a
successful alternative to the adoption of agriculture. The "African Aqualithic" paper
(Sutton 1977:25) opened with a bold summary of the issues the article intended
to deal with in four main dimensions: space, time, environment, and archaeological content. A fifth dimension, a historical linguistic one, was added later in the
paper.

In relation to its spatial dimensions, Sutton asserted that:

> during the early post-Pleistocene there flourished right across the middle belt of the
> African continent a highly distinctive way of life intimately associated with the great
> rivers, lakes and marshes. This belt ... comprises the southern Sahara and the Sahel

from the Atlantic to the Nile and there bends up-river to the East African rift valleys and the equator. (Sutton 1977:25)

He sketched out the temporal dimension in few words: "traceable as early as the eighth millennium BC, the zenith of this 'aquatic civilization' was achieved in the seventh millennium" (Sutton 1977:25). The environmental dimension was characterized as, "a time when higher rainfall made rivers longer and more permanent and caused lakes to swell and burst their basins" (Sutton 1977:25). Sutton argued that these climatic circumstances significantly impacted the nature, distribution, and density of resources. The archaeological content of documented sites included, on the one hand, faunal material from food refuse consisting of large quantities of fish, aquatic mammal, and reptile bones; and on the other, cultural remains, with barbed bone points, fish hooks, and "pottery of a common tradition" (the "wavy-line" and "dotted wavy-line" of Arkell; Sutton 1977:25).

After establishing the spatial, temporal, and environmental dimensions of this tradition, Sutton harnessed published material from both West and East Africa to the reconstruction that he had so boldly sketched in the introduction. He suggested that the whole complex may have originated from East Africa, spread northward along the Nile Valley, and finally, westward through the Sahara and Sahel. But "the direction of expansion just suggested–from East Africa to the Nile and the Sahara–is still only one among several possibilities" (Sutton 1977:29). The process of expansion itself was alluded to but not discussed in depth. Possible scenarios ranged from massive demic diffusion triggered by sudden population growth (Sutton 1977:29) to stimulus diffusion, the transfer of material culture items without population movement. As is generally the case in such debates, the author's position was Solomonic: "Almost certainly the truth must lie somewhere between these extremes; and, until better clues on the point of origin are available, the discussion must remain rather hypothetical." The African Aqualithic does "not constitute a 'single culture' . . . but rather a cultural complex" (Sutton 1977:29). The racial affiliation of the bearers of the Aqualithic adaptation was also alluded to when Sutton observed that "very plausibly it helps account for the spread of Negroid peoples north and east of the forest zone" (Sutton 1977:29). The most fascinating and daring aspect of Sutton's paper was his suggestion about the ethnic-linguistic affiliations of "Aqualithic" peoples: "Among the most distinctive features of culture and ethnicity is language. It is necessary, therefore, to test whether the ancient aquatic civilization might bear correlation with any of the known African language-families" (Sutton 1977:30). The distribution of Nilo-Saharan languages was singled out as the most rewarding case to investigate.

Sutton's papers were above all programmatic; research was not advanced enough to address the issues he raised and his discussion was a wonderful exercise in tightrope-walking. It dared to spell out a plethora of issues to be investigated more vigorously in the future. The hypothesis of "Aquatic Civilization of Middle Africa" was successful in initiating an interesting debate that is still in the mainstream of African archaeology (Ehret 2002; Haaland 1992; Yellen 1998). In that respect, it exemplified good science.

The "Aqualithic" Debate

Fundamentally, the "Aqualithic" discussion focuses on the very issue of the transition from foraging to food-producing lifeways. The variables involved in the debate include climatic change and ecosystems dynamics, technological innovation, settlement patterns, and language expansion. Some material elements, such as barbed bone harpoons, fish hooks, and pottery decorated with wavy-line and/or dotted wavy-line motifs, have played a crucial role in the debate. According to Haaland (1992:48), for example, the "invention of pottery and harpoons are . . . critical events in the process which led to the intensification of aquatic resource utilization which is first attested in the Nile Valley around 8500 bp. In the archaeological record, this is manifested technologically in a vast increase of 'Mesolithic' tools, and osteologically in a wide variety of aquatic resources." Haaland arranged the Late and post-Pleistocene transformations of foraging societies into five major phases and asserted that "technological development within each of these phases created preconditions for processes which in turn generated changes leading to the next phase" (Haaland 1992:48). Haaland's analysis was framed by a human ecology perspective and proceeded from a tight deductive system based on a narrow range of considerations: (1) The widespread distribution of wavy-line and dotted wavy-line pottery; and (2) the primacy of the Nile Valley. Dealing with the first consideration, she found it "unlikely that the same type of pottery was independently invented in these areas," and suggests that "this cultural tradition was invented in the Nile Valley and carried to the Sahara/savanna region and East Africa by gradual expansion of people" (Haaland 1992:47). In her perspective, "pottery technology, high population growth, and sedentism based on intensive utilization of aquatic resources and (sorghum) probably constituted the key preconditions which led to the third phase when cultivation was begun" (Haaland 1992:50). The widespread expansion of "Aqualithic People" (Haaland 1992:54, 58) was prompted by higher population growth rates and diffusion to neighboring groups. The process thus involved both demic and stimulus diffusion. The issue of language was dealt with in the last section of the article, with speakers of Nilo-Saharan languages as the most likely "Aqualithic People."

In contrast to Sutton's 1974 and 1977 programmatic papers, Haaland's article presented a wealth of archaeological data; however, she dealt with the historical process in quasi-teleological terms. Circumstances in each phase created preconditions for processes that generated changes resulting in the next phase. This type of argument rests on a logical fallacy: the "affirmation of the consequence."

Barbed bone points are an important diagnostic element of the Aquatic civilization of Middle Africa. They are generally assumed to have been used in fishing activities and the exploitation of other aquatic resources. But in one case at least, at Daima, a harpoon was found in the skeleton of a buried individual dated to the middle of the first millennium b.c. (Connah 1981:117). "One thing is certain: archaeologists working on African prehistory should question very seriously the assumption sometimes made that bone harpoons were merely intended for fishing" (Connah 1981:117). Yellen (1998) addressed one of the issues raised by Arkell (1949, 1953) and Sutton (1974, 1977) through a discussion of barbed bone points found in the Sahara and sub-Saharan Africa. Yellen's discussion dealt with several dimensions of the archaeological material under investigation. First, with the geographic range of harpoons, which have been documented from Botswana to Morocco. Second, with the chronological range of known specimens, which stretches from 90000 b.p. at Katanda in MSA contexts in the western Rift Valley (Chapter 4), to 20000 b.p. for Ishango toward the end of the first millennium a.d. And third, a techno-typological analysis centered on eight attributes that addressed two questions (Yellen 1998:182): (1) are there enough commonalities between documented Holocene harpoons to support the idea of an African tradition? and (2) are temporal and/or regional patterns discernible from the Holocene material at hand?

Based upon a broader comparison with material from other parts of the world (West European Magdalenian, Middle Eastern Natufian, and North America), Yellen (1998:183) concluded that "the similarities among these African specimens are great enough to justify incorporation within a single tradition." However, the examination of African material "in the broadest perspective permits several conclusions and speculations. First, the data clearly show that this tradition does not map on to any tightly defined linguistic or biological group and does not serve as a marker for any 'cultural' entity as defined by common anthropological usage of the term" (Yellen 1998:195).

The "Aqualithic" debate is clearly a discussion about the dynamics of culture change. A single model with minor variations dominated the scene from an early period. Arkell's (1949, 1953) inferences were based almost exclusively on archaeological finds set in diffusion scenarios; that distinct way of dealing with change in the archaeological record was expanded by Aumassip (1978), Bailloud (1969), Camps (1967, 1969, 1974, 1978, 1980), Courtin (1969), and Hugot (1963), among others. Sutton (1974, 1977) added a historical linguistic dimension to the interpretive mix, as did Haaland (1992). This approach was stretched to its limit by Ehret (2002), who used the taxonomy of African languages to structure his reconstruction of the African prehistory from 18000 b.p. to A.D. 1800.

Yellen (1998) offers a sober and more precise grasp of the evidence, in this case, barbed bone points. Keding (1996) did a comparable study of the distribution of wavy-line and dotted wavy-line pottery in her discussion of the material from Wadi Howar. The geographic distribution of barbed bone points and wavy-line/dotted wavy-line decorated pottery overlaps, but does not match in all the cases. Such a match has to be expected if the spread of the material record under investigation resulted from demic diffusion from a core area. Sutton (1974, 1977) located the cradle of the "Aqualithic civilization" somewhere in the hinterland of eastern Africa. Haaland (1992) located this core area along the Nile Valley in central Sudan. For Camps (1980) on the other hand, the central Sahara was a distinct and independent cultural zone.

Wetlands Adaptation: Demic Diffusion, Parallelism, and Convergence

The crucial issue is, then, that of cultural adaptation to changing climatic circumstances linked to an attempt to understand the significance of certain patterns of similarities and differences of the material record. In the "explanatory tradition" represented by Arkell, Sutton, Haaland, and many others, certain classes of similarity in material attributes are more likely a product of common origin. Demic diffusion is well documented in different parts of the world (Levy and Holl 2002). The expansion of early mixed farming societies of the Danubian (Bandkeramik) culture from the Balkans to central and western Europe is a very well investigated example (Sherratt 1990). The archaeological record indicates strong similarities in almost all the components of cultural products. Houses are long and trapeze-shaped. They are flanked on both longitudinal sides by elongated construction pits in which domestic refuse has been dumped. The pottery is decorated with linear bands of two-teeth comb impressions. Wheat and barley are the main agricultural products. Cattle, sheep/goats, and pigs are the most frequent domestic animals. Settlements are generally located on loessial soil along major river courses. Closer in time and in Africa, Fulani expansion from the Futa Jalon in Senegal in the westernmost part of West Africa to Ethiopia in the east in less than 500 years is also a good reminder of the scope of migrations.

The over-reaction against the excesses of diffusionist theories resulted in an anti-migration twist. "It has become unpopular to suggest the movement of peoples as a mechanism for culture change, and most recent research is endogenously oriented in this respect. But the pendulum may have swung far towards the opposite extreme" (Bar Ilan 1998:300). Long-term cultural change can be shaped by multiple structural elements, including migrations, the formation, growth, and demise of cultural entities, and shifts in settlement patterns at local, regional, and supra-regional scales. The problem is not the existence or non-existence of migrations from one part of north tropical Africa to another, but rather archaeologists' ability to discern population movements in the archaeological record. More precisely, what criteria have to be used to achieve high-resolution differentiation of distinct cultural identities (Levy and Holl 2002:84)? Lumping together different categories of archaeological remains and assuming that they were part of the same linguistic package does not properly address the question raised above. The very idea that archaeologists can reconstruct past linguistic entities is still very controversial (cf. Ehret 2002).

The emphasis on demic diffusion has diverted attention from alternative evolutionary scenarios. For example, we need to consider the possibility of parallel evolution with random similarities between completely unconnected populations; the intensification in the exploitation of aquatic and marine resources all over the world during the Early Holocene global warming is a paradigmatic case. Convergence in evolutionary pathways is another option that may operate when different societies devise comparable solutions to more or less similar problems.

An Early Holocene wetlands adaptation was triggered by the radical warming up of the world climate at the end of the Pleistocene. Intensification in the exploitation of marine and aquatic resources is well documented worldwide. The accumulation of shell-middens (*kokkjenmoddings*) along sea coasts and rivers, in estuaries, and on lakes shores is an unmistakable indication of shifts in dietary patterns. These new and intensive food-procurement strategies were part of the "Mesolithic broad spectrum revolution" (Flannery 1969). The Epipaleolithic Capsian of North Africa documented in the Chotts area of the Tunisian/Algerian hinterland is a relatively well investigated case of wetlands adaptation (Lubell et al. 1984). This shift was characterized by greater reliance on smaller-size prey and systematized exploitation of labor-intensive r-selected resources (Winterhalder and Goland 1997; Winterhalder and Smith 2000), which have a high reproduction rate but are available for a relatively short time.

The toolkit may vary from one group to the next; but in general one would expect fishing tools and aquatic resource-processing equipment to be well represented in sites located in wetlands environments. In north tropical Africa, the early Holocene climate was generally wet despite significant fluctuations (Barich 1998; Hassan 1998; Neumann 1989; Petit-Maire, ed., 1991; Petit-Maire and Riser, eds., 1983; Wendorf and Schild 1998). The Saharan desert shrank significantly in size. Major rivers, including the Tilemsi (Gaussen and Gaussen 1988), Azawagh (Bernus et al. 1999), Tefassasset, and Wadi Howar (Keding 1996), as well as shallow to deep lakes, were found in almost every significant portion of the Sahara (Cremacshi and di Lernia, eds., 1999; di Lernia, ed., 1999; di Lernia and Manzi, eds., 1998).

Though the Capsian case in northern Africa (Balout 1955; Camps 1974; Lubell et al. 1984) shows an intensive exploitation of aquatic resources without the introduction of ceramic technology, the invention and/or adoption of pottery amplified the consequences of a narrower wetland adaptation. The manufactured containers were presumably used for processing, cooking, and eating aquatic resources and wild grain collected in different parts of the landscape. According to Pavlu (1996:73), "the comparison of environments at the locations of the earliest pottery appearance, however chronologically remote, enables a generalization of the relations between these events. We can observe that pottery started to be adopted later on different continents under similar environmental conditions." The shapes of the earliest pottery samples include a narrow range of globular to open forms. At Tagalagal in Niger for example, three basic variants of simple shapes are attested: shallow bowls/dishes; medium bowls with in-curving rims; and finally medium to large more or less necked jars (Pavlu 1996). Vessel shapes appear to have been limited to a small number of variants during the early stage of pottery adoption, suggesting (both) parallel and convergent developments. The documented shapes of the earliest ceramic vessels vary within a narrow margin; "the coastal assemblages contain a relatively small number of pottery forms, often only variants on one basic globular form. . . . In desert or inland regions, after a short period of simple forms, the sets of forms quickly developed into a complex variety of three basic forms: dish, bowl, and jar, that compose whole sets mainly used for drinking and eating" (Pavlu 1996:73). The wavy-line and dotted wavy-line decoration found on many of the earliest African ceramic vessels may be another case of parallelism. Thus, the eastern Sahara and Nile Valley on the one hand, and central Sahara on the other, appear to have witnessed parallel and contemporaneous development in pottery manufacturing and decoration techniques.

Conclusion

The "Aqualithic Model" elaborated by Sutton (1974, 1977) is an interesting case of scientific debate. It follows the patterns outlined by K. Popper (1985), according to which science is structured by conjecture and refutation. In the case of the Aqualithic, the conjecture was essentially programmatic, and endeavored to articulate within an encompassing model multiple components of the archaeological landscape. Migrations were assumed to have been the force driving the expansion of the new complex that was hypothesized to have originated from the Great Lakes region of eastern African. Haaland (1992) reproduced this model, but situated its origins in the Sudanese Nile Valley. Yellen's refutation (1998) is based on an analysis of African barbed bone points. The critical evaluation of the "Aqualithic Model" is carried further in this chapter. The superimposition of present-day linguistic families on the archaeological evidence (Ehret 2002) appears to solve the research problem without addressing it properly. In his recent book, Ehret (2002) extends the possibility of linguistic reconstruction as far back as 16,000 years, and transforms the four major African macro-linguistic families into "civilizations." Territories, societies, customs, religions, and ritual practices of the "Afrasans" (Afro-Asiatic), "Nilo-Saharans," "Khoisans," and "Niger-Congo" from 10,000 to 16,000 years ago are reconstructed without any clue on the methodology that informs those reconstructions (Ehret 2002:35–550). In fact, evidence selected from contemporary African cultural practices are pushed backward in a straightforward equation between language and material culture. The reconstruction of word-roots is a sound scientific practice developed by historical linguists (Chapter 12). But the reconstruction of a whole cultural universe from a handful of reconstructed word-roots for time periods as remote as the Late Pleistocene and the Early Holocene is clearly too far-fetched and unsubstantiated.

REFERENCES

Arkell, A. J., 1949 Early Khartoum. London: Oxford University Press.
——1953 Shaheinab. London: Oxford University Press.
Aumassip, G., 1978 In Hanakaten-Bilber einer Ausgrabung. In Sahara: 10000 Jahren zwischen Weide und Wusten. R. Kuper, ed. pp. 208–213. Cologne: Museen der Stadt.
——1986 Le Bas-Sahara dans la préhistoire. Paris: Éditions du CNRS.
Bailloud, G., 1969 L'Évolution des styles céramiques en Ennedi (République du Tchad). In Actes du 1er Colloque International d'Archéologie Africaine. J. P. Lebeuf, ed. pp. 31–45. Fort Lamy.

Balout, L., 1955 Préhistoire de l'Afrique du Nord. Paris: Arts et Métiers Graphiques.

Barich, Barbara E., 1998 People, Water, and Grain. Rome: "L'Erma" di Bretschneider.

Bar Ilan, D., 1998 The Dawn of Internationalism – The Middle Bronze Age. In The Archaeology of Society in the Holy Land. T. E. Levy, ed. pp. 297–319. London: Leicester University Press.

Bernus, E., P. A. Cressier, F. Paris Durand, and J.-F. Saliège, 1999 Vallée de l'Azawagh (Sahara du Niger). Paris: Sepia.

Camps, Gabriel, 1967 Extension territoriale des civilisations epipaléolithiques et néolithiques de l'Afrique du Nord et du Sahara. In Actes du Sixième Congrès Panafricain de Préhistoire. H. J. Hugot, ed. pp. 284–287. Chambéry.

—— 1969 Amekni: Néolithique ancien du Hoggar. Paris: Mémoires du CRAPE.

—— 1974 Les Civilisations préhistoriques de l'Afrique du Nord et du Sahara. Paris: Doin.

—— 1978 Amekni und die neolithische Sahara. In Sahara: 10000 Jahren zwischen Weide und Wusten. R. Kuper, ed. pp. 182–188. Cologne: Museen der Stadt.

—— 1980 Beginnings of Pastoralism and Cultivation in North-West Africa and the Sahara: Origins of the Berbers. In The Cambridge History of Africa, vol. 1. J. Desmond Clark, ed. pp. 548–623. Cambridge: Cambridge University Press.

Childe, V. Gordon, 1928 New Light on the Most Ancient East. New York: The Norton Library.

—— 1936 Man Makes Himself. New York: New American Library.

Connah, Graham, 1981 Three Thousand Years in Africa: Man and his Environment in the Lake Chad Region of Nigeria. Cambridge: Cambridge University Press.

Courtin, J., 1969 Néolithique du Borkou, Nord-Tchad. In Actes du 1er Colloque International d'Archéologie Africaine. J. P. Lebeuf, ed. pp. 147–159. Fort Lamy.

Cremacshi, M. and S. di Lernia, eds., 1999 Wadi Teshuinat: Paleoenvironment and Prehistory in South-Western Fezzan (Libyan Sahara). Florence: Edizioni all' Insegna del Giglio.

di Lernia, S., ed., 1999 The Uan Afuda Cave: Hunter-Gatherer Societies of Central Sahara. Florence: Edizioni all' Insegna del Giglio.

di Lernia, S., and G. Manzi, eds., 1998 Before Food Production in North Africa. Forli: ABACO.

Ehret, Christopher, 2002 The Civilizations of Africa: A History to 1800. Charlottesville: University Press of Virginia.

Flannery, Kent, 1969 Origins and Ecological Effects of Early Domestication in Iran and the Near East. In The Domestication and Exploitation of Plants and Animals. Peter J. Ucko and G. W. Dimbleby, eds. pp. 73–100. Chicago: Aldine.

Gabriel, B., 1978 Gabrong-Achttausendjahrige Keramik im Tibesti-Gebirge. In Sahara: 10000 Jahren zwischen Weide und Wusten. R. Kuper, ed. pp. 189–196. Cologne: Museen der Stadt.

Gaussen, J., and M. Gaussen, 1988 Le Tilemsi préhistorique et ses abords: Sahara et Sahel Malien. Paris: Éditions du CNRS.

Haaland, Randi, 1992 Fish, Pots and Grain: Early and Mid-Holocene Adaptations in the Central Sudan. The African Archaeological Review 10:43–64.

Hassan, Fekri A., 1998 Holocene Climatic Change and Riverine Dynamics in the Nile Valley. In Before Food Production in North Africa. S. di Lernia and G. Manzi, eds. pp. 43–52. Forli: ABACO.

Holl, Augustin 1989 Social Issues in Saharan Prehistory. Journal of Anthropological Archaeology 8:313–354.

Hugot, H. J., 1963 Recherches préhistoriques dans l'Ahaggar Nord-Occidental (1950–1957). Paris: Arts et Métiers Graphiques.

Keding, B., 1996 Djabarona 84/3: Untersuchungen zur Besiedlungsgeschichte des Wadi Howar. Cologne: Heinrich Barth Institut.

Kuper, R., 1978 Vom Jager zum Hirten – Was ist das Sahara-Neolithikum? *In* Sahara: 10000 Jahren zwischen Weide und Wusten. R. Kuper, ed. pp. 60–69. Cologne: Museen der Stadt.

Levy, Thomas E., and Augustin F. C. Holl, 2002 Migrations, Ethnogenesis, and Settlement Dynamics: Israelites in Iron Age Canaan and the Shuwa-Arabs in the Chad Basin. Journal of Anthropological Archaeology 21:83–118.

Lubell, David, Peter Sheppard, and Mary Jackes, 1984 Continuity in the Epipaleolithic of Northern Africa with Emphasis on the Maghreb. *In* Advances in World Archaeology, vol. 3. Fred Wendorf and Angela E. Close, eds. pp. 143–192. New York: Academic Press.

Neumann, Katharina, 1989 Vegetationsgeschichte des Ostsahara im Holozan: Holzkohlen aus prähistorischen Fundstellen (mit einem exkurz über die Holzkohlen von Fachi- 2122 Dogonboulo/Niger). *In* Forschungen zur Umweltgeschichte der Ostsahara. R. Kuper, ed. pp. 13–181. Cologne: Heinrich Barth Institut.

Pavlu, I., 1996 Pottery Origins: Initial Forms, Cultural Behavior and Decorative Styles. Praha: Karolinum.

Petit-Maire, Nicole, ed., 1991 Paleoenvironnements du Sahara: Lacs Holocenes à Taoudenni (Mali). Paris: Éditions du CNRS.

Petit-Maire, Nicole, and J. Riser, eds., 1983 Sahara ou Sahel? Quaternaire récent du bassin de Taoudenni (Mali). Marseilles: CNRS.

Popper, Karl R., 1985[1963] Conjectures et refutations: La Croissance du savoir scientifique. Paris: Payot.

Sherratt, Andrew, 1990 The Genesis of Megaliths: Monumentality, Ethnicity, and Social Complexity in Neolithic North-West Europe. World Archaeology 22:147–167.

Sutton, John E. G., 1974 The Aquatic Civilization of Middle Africa. Journal of African History 15:527–546.

——1977 The African Aqualithic. Antiquity 51:25–34.

Vermeersch, P. M., 1992 The Upper and Late Palaeolithic of Northern and Eastern Africa. *In* New Light on the Northeast African Past. F. Klees and R. Kuper, eds. pp. 99–154. Cologne: Heinrich Barth Institut.

Wendorf, Fred, and Romuald Schild, 1998 Nabta Playa and its Role in Northeastern African Prehistory. Journal of Anthropological Archaeology 17:97–123.

Winterhalder, Bruce G., and G. Goland, 1997 An Evolutionary Ecology Perspective on Diet Choice, Risk, and Plant Domestication. *In* People, Plants and Landscapes: Studies in Paleoethnobotany. K. J. Gremillion, ed. pp. 123–160. Tuscaloosa: University of Alabama Press.

Winterhalder, Bruce G., and E. A. Smith, 2000 Analyzing Adaptive Strategies: Human Behavioral Ecology at Twenty-Five. Evolutionary Anthropology 9:51–72.

Yellen, John, 1998 Barbed Bone Points: Tradition and Continuity in Saharan and Sub-Saharan Africa. African Archaeological Review 15:173–198.

8

Pastoralism and its Consequences

Diane Gifford-Gonzalez

When, from the tenth century on, Arab and European travelers recorded their impressions of Africa, they reported impressive herds of domestic cattle, camels, sheep, and goats. Throughout the continent foreigners encountered African peoples whose livelihoods depended on pastoral livestock. Arab writers probably saw such peoples with eyes accustomed to Bedouin and other pastoral groups known in the Muslim world. To this day scholars have turned to Southwest Asian cases to understand African pastoralism, its nature and origins. However, we are beginning to appreciate that African pastoralism may have emerged under different circumstances and followed an appreciably different path than pastoral economies in the Near and Middle East. Recent DNA evidence suggests a still controversial independent domestication of cattle in Africa, and many now believe that, contrary to the Southwest Asian pattern, African pastoralism emerged before plant domestication and settled farming – and certainly in the absence of states.

This chapter outlines what is known of the emergence of pastoral economies in Africa and current debates in the literature. Opening sections identify three central issues in the study of African forms of domestic animal use, define key concepts, and present an overview of Holocene climatic and environmental changes. A review of evidence for the emergence of pastoralism in Africa, organized temporally and regionally, begins with the earliest occurrences in the Sahara-Sahel. The conclusion offers observations on Africa's unique trajectory toward food production and the implications of African evidence for purportedly universal theories of the origins and nature of pastoralism.

Central Issues in the History of Domestic Animal Use in Africa

Three unique aspects to the history of domestic animal use in Africa merit close attention. First, reliance on cattle, sheep, and goats emerged as a stable and widespread way of life long before the first evidence for either domestic plants or settled village farming communities (Marshall and Hildebrand 2002; Chapter 10). Emergence of pastoralism without farming is so unique in the Old World that scholars working in other regions, and some Africanists, have not been willing to accept the implications of the evidence as it stands (see also Chapters 9, 10). Second, the earliest pastoralist societies of the Sahara-Sahel continued the truly unusual early Holocene pattern of stylistic homogeneity in artifacts over enormous expanses of the region (Chapter 7). Since producing and maintaining homogeneity is an active rather than a passive process, these artifactual patterns have social implications. Third, in contrast to the apparently steady spread of Southwest Asian domestic livestock into greater Eurasia as part of food production systems, their expansion into sub-Saharan Africa was marked by independent but comparable delays and loss of species, notably cattle, in eastern and southern African contexts. These areas were home to thriving pastoralist and agropastoralist economies at the time of colonial contact, so the near-thousand-year "stutter" in development of cattle-based economies bears some scrutiny.

What is a Pastoralist?

Here, pastoralists are defined as groups who depend primarily on the products of their hoofed domestic animals, and who organize their settlement and mobility strategies to suit the dietary needs of their livestock. They include agropastoralists like the historic Dinka of Sudan, who combined cultivation of domestic crops with keeping of substantial herds. They also include so-called "pure pastoralists" of the historic era, such as the Maasai of East Africa, who place ideological emphasis on consuming only the products of their herds and flocks. Though such a diet was characteristic of the warrior age-grade, Maasai in fact exchanged animal products for agrarian and forest produce with symbiotic farmers and foragers (Kjekshus 1977).

Pastoral groups can meet the needs of their herds by moving whole residential units seasonally as the foraging range is depleted in one area and others open for grazing. Where local forage and watering conditions permit, pastoral groups may keep most of their livestock at one settlement year-round, only shifting to another locale after several years, as was the habit of Maasai herders in Kenya and Tanzania. Where forage is not located near potable water or cultivable land, pastoralists may logistically organize into labor groups according to age and gender, some carrying on activities at a residential encampment while others take livestock to far-flung areas of good forage, as did the Nuer of Sudan. In all cases, a segment of such groups devotes considerable labor to moving and protecting livestock, which is in turn conditioned at least in part by net productivity (Johnson 2002).

Pastoralism imposes a set of requirements on herd managers and households in the social and economic realm. Successful pastoralists need labor, for they have too many animals for their immediate household members to manage; to mobilize labor, they must activate varied social relations, from kindred to clients to friend-ships. Unsuccessful pastoralists need allies, for they must replenish their herds though loans, calling in old debts, and other long-dormant social relations that form herders' insurance against disaster (Dahl and Hjort 1976). When we think of pas-toral groups moving through ever-variable savannas, we should recall they con-stantly have in play the social strategies of affiliation and information-gathering typical of such groups (Galaty 1991).

This chapter concentrates on the archaeological vestiges of groups considered to fit the definitions of pastoralism offered above. It focuses therefore on sites in grassland and wooded savanna regions in Early to Middle Holocene times. The very mobility that characterizes pastoral life presents an archaeological challenge. Pastoralists normally carry their homes with them, curate their tools, and reside in one area for short periods, all of which contributes to their low archaeo-logical visibility (MacDonald 2000; Smith 1992). Moreover, pastoralists preferentially situate their camps away from areas liable to flooding (Gifford 1978). This virtually assures that faunal remains discarded in such sites will be more liable to destruction through weathering than to preservation through rapid deposition by water-borne sediments. Rockshelters offer samples of such ways of life, though they are probably not typical situations for pastoral encampments (Klein 1984). Thus, the subsistence and mobility patterns of pastoralists interact to leave few unambiguous traces of their activities on land surfaces (though see Shahack-Gross et al. 2002 on possibilities for discerning manure accumulations).

Taxonomic Issues

African archaeological categories have often been forced into systems of classifica-tion that developed in Europe and Southwest Asia. Stahl (1999) and others (Sin-clair et al. 1993) have argued that this is more than a trivial problem of naming. "Age/Stage" categories such as the "Neolithic" go back to a time in the 19th century when it was assumed that all peoples in the world moved through similar evolu-tionary stages of development marked by diagnostic artifacts.

This problem affects studies of early pastoralism in Africa, where the presence of pottery was thought to distinguish "Neolithic" traditions (Chapters 9, 10). In Southwest Asia, specialized pastoralism emerged as a secondary development, after establishment of settled village life, mixed farming and animal husbandry (Smith 1995), and perhaps as the reaction of mixed food producers to impositions of state-level societies (Bar-Yosef and Khazanov, eds., 1992; Harris 1996). It is thus assumed that non-cultivating pastoralists only emerged after sedentary farming, yet African pastoralism presents an alternative that is not widely understood or accepted outside the Africanist community (see also Chapter 10).

Though this review of necessity draws on existing terminology, we need to recognize its limitations and reject the traditional evolutionist scheme that inspired it.

Holocene Saharan Climate and Early Pastoralism

African pastoralism emerged in what is now the Sahara desert and adjacent Sahelian grasslands. This region has undergone major pulses of greening and desertification from the last glacial maximum through the post-glacial period, according to changes in both temperature and rainfall (Chapter 7). Environmental rhythms in these climatically sensitive zones likely played a major role both in the development of early pastoralism and in impelling later movements of herding peoples into western and eastern Africa.

Saharan climate has been affected by the interaction of two major weather systems, the Mediterranean winter rains and the Intertropical Convergence Zone (ITCZ), a low-pressure belt where moisture from northern (Tropic of Cancer) and southern (Tropic of Capricorn) areas converge. Today the ITCZ monsoonal system moves north in June–July, bringing rains to equatorial regions, and south in November–April, during which equatorial regions are drier. During the Terminal Pleistocene, the ITCZ was weaker and much further south than at present, and continental African temperatures were generally about 5°C lower than today.

At the last glacial maximum, pollen evidence indicates a retreat of tropical forests, resulting in the near-extirpation of tropical hardwood forests in West Africa (Maley 1993). The Sahara was hyper-desiccated and dune systems were active across what is now the Sahelian vegetation zone, as far as 500 km south of the present-day Sahara. Rainfall over the tributaries of the Blue and White Niles was minimal, reducing the Nile's flow to low and even intermittent levels (Hassan 2000). West Africa's Senegal and Niger rivers and portions of the Nile were intermittently blocked by dunes (Grove 1993). Lake cores indicate that Lake Victoria dried up about 13000 b.p. (Johnson et al. 1996).

Beginning about 14000 b.p., rainfall patterns changed radically, with a northward movement and greater moisture load of the ITCZ. Rainfall from central Sahara to south of the equator was at least 140–330 mm/year higher than today (Grove 1997:37). Lake Chad, which today seasonally fluctuates from 2,000 to 26,000 km², spread over 320,000 km², linking to the Benue River. Present-day non-outlet lakes of eastern Africa were 100 to 200 m higher than their present levels, and many had high-stand links to other bodies of water, for example, Lake Turkana joined the Nile (Grove 1993). Fed by higher than modern rainfall, the Nile filled its valley completely. This so-called "wild Nile" phase (cf. Grove 1980) interrupted a long history of human settlement and probably prompted emigration to lake complexes outside the valley (van Neer and Uerpmann 1989).

This early Holocene "greening" of northern Africa was interrupted by the colder, drier conditions of the Younger Dryas (12700–11700 b.p.), which undoubtedly affected groups who had begun exploiting well-watered areas during the previous millennia (Hassan 2000). Moist conditions returned ca. 11700–7500 b.p., followed by a brief but strong dry phase which is thought to have impelled cattle-herding groups in the eastern Sahara to enter the Nile Valley and negotiate residence there with semi-sedentary foragers (Hassan 1988). The final desiccation of the Sahara was underway by at least 5500 b.p., with rainfall reduced to a third of former levels by 4500 b.p. Numerous authors have noted the cline of dates for first appearances of domestic livestock in areas southwest and southeast of the Sahara during this period. As pastoralists and their herds moved into disparate regions of sub-Saharan Africa, differences in ecology and social relations with resident groups created divergent regional histories (see below).

Though a cline of dates charts the appearance of pastoral economies in time and space, it says nothing about the social and economic processes involved in such shifts. Was this demic diffusion (Chapter 7), or the assimilation by local groups of livestock and the complex practices involved in managing them? What might have stimulated demic diffusion, and what was the nature of contact with aboriginal groups? Whereas early research assumed that mere contact with food producers would prompt local hunter-gatherers to convert to farming or animal husbandry, 20th-century studies of foragers have shown them to be more successful than previously supposed (Chapter 9). An ongoing debate over the "encapsulation" of San-speaking hunter-gatherers by Bantu-speaking agropastoralists in southern Africa (Chapter 14) has raised issues of power and competition as an element of intergroup relations; however, the archaeology and ethnohistory of sub-Saharan Africa demonstrate that foraging peoples coexisted symbiotically with food producers for centuries (Chapter 16). This suggests that historic power relations may not have held for the earliest arrivals of herding peoples in various parts of sub-Saharan Africa.

African Pastoralism as a Dry-Land Adaptation

Milk pastoralism and a focus on herd growth is an adaptive strategy well suited to fluctuating savanna-steppe environments. Dramatic and unpredictable variations of rainfall and productivity of grasslands (Pratt and Gwynne 1977) mean that livestock owners follow short-term tactics to enable rapid herd recovery in the long term. Cattle-based pastoral systems in sub-Saharan Africa can sustain losses of over 70 percent during prolonged and severe drought cycles (Dahl and Hjort 1976). Herds grow rapidly during moist cycles so long as the majority of the remnant herd is female. Thus, a pastoral system that aims for recovery from natural climatic cycles emphasizes female survival.

This strategy has two consequences for herd management: (1) most males are culled early in their lives; and (2) herders rely on cows' milk for food. Among modern pastoralists, male calves are killed (or allowed to die of malnutrition) at younger ages in more arid environments than in better-watered ones (Dahl and Hjort 1976; for exceptions see Almagor 1978; Evans-Pritchard 1940). Permitting significant numbers of male castrates to live to full growth, a strategy followed in prehistoric Europe, is relatively rare in African pastoral systems.

Consuming the "secondary product" of cows' milk (Sherratt 1983) is a straightforward means of feeding off an animal without killing it. Milk is the only animal food to provide carbohydrates as well as protein and fat (Oftedal 1984). Presently, we lack proof of dairying in early Saharan pastoralism, but it is noteworthy that rock art representations of cattle from the area emphasize females' full udders. Some scenes, such as the widely circulated image from Station Tissoukaï, Tassili-n-Ajjer (Lhote 1976) of cows being led in to a settlement with calves tied to a picket line may depict the moment before milking. Among modern pastoralists, calves are restrained from nursing by picketing or penning until milking is over. Recently developed stable isotopic analyses of lipid residues in ceramics can distinguish milk from other animal fats (Copley et al. 2003), and may help us to discern whether milk was used by these early pastoralists.

East African pastoralists bleed cattle, both males and females whose milk has failed. The blood is eaten alone in liquid or clotted form, or mixed with milk. Like milking, this permits people to draw nourishment from an animal without killing it. It is especially used when other sources of animal and plant food fail, during dry seasons and droughts (Dahl and Hjort 1976). The technology and practices of bleeding livestock appear to be conservative across major linguistic and ethnic boundaries. A leather tourniquet is tightened around an immobilized animal's neck, and a blunt-headed arrow shot at close range from a small bow into the jugular vein; blood is collected in a container. The bow-and-arrow method for safely bleeding livestock is present among pastoral groups who lack any knowledge of bows as hunting or offensive weaponry, suggesting that this technical practice moved across major geographic, social, and technological boundaries with little change.

These methods of livestock use suggest that African pastoralists selected for herd survival, and hence human survival, through major drought episodes. This is consonant with the known long-term patterns of desiccation of the Saharan region as well as with the decadal and century-scale rainfall fluctuations typical of modern climate regimes.

Pastoral Species in Africa

Radiocarbon dates and more recent DNA studies indicate that goats (*Capra aegagrus* f. hircus) and sheep (*Ovis orientalis* f. aries) were domesticated from Southwest Asian wild progenitors and introduced into northern Africa (Luikart et al. 2001). The term "caprine," subsuming both sheep and goats, will be used in this chapter. These closely related species are difficult to distinguish based on fragmentary osteological remains. "Caprine" is derived from the zoological subfamily Caprinae, and is preferable to "ovicaprid" which suggests a nonexistent family Ovicapridae.

Domestic caprine species were introduced into Africa by one or more routes (Smith 1984): from the Levant via the northern coast of Africa, as part of maritime trade; into the Nile delta from the Sinai; or by boat from the Arabian peninsula based on early dates for goats in the Red Sea Hills of Egypt (Vermeersch et al. 1994). Sheep and goats appear in greater numbers than cattle in the Khartoum region of the Sudanese Nile and in a few sites in north Africa, suggesting that their history in Africa may differ from that of bovines in timing and spread.

Donkeys (*Equus africanu*s f. asinus), ubiquitous beast of burden and emergency food source among pastoralists, are almost certainly an African domesticate, but their scarceness in archaeological sites renders concrete discussion of their history difficult (Clutton-Brock 1997). The introduction of the camel (*Camelus dromedarius*) was relatively late and details are as yet not well understood, and will not be discussed here (see Rowley-Conwy 1988).

The origins and even the proper taxonomic classification of African cattle are still strongly debated. Gautier (1988) settled earlier debates about the variety of wild African *Bos* species prior to domestication, arguing that a number of supposed species are simply regional varieties, or male and females of one species. Present controversy centers on whether cattle were independently domesticated in Africa. Wild cattle remains (usually called *Bos primigenius*, but see below) have been recovered from Pleistocene and Holocene archaeological and paleontological localities in northern Africa as far south as the Nile Valley in northern Sudan westward across north Africa (Churcher 1972, 1983; Gautier 1987b, 1988). With the southward shift of Mediterranean flora at the onset of the Holocene, cattle and other fauna inhabiting such zones likely penetrated areas now part of the Sahara proper. Yet it is unclear how different African wild cattle were from their Southwest Asian and European cousins in environmental preferences and physique. Grigson (2000) notes that wild African cattle *may* (her emphasis) have been slightly smaller than those from the Levant, but small sample size prevents a definitive statement. At the same time, early domestic cattle in northern Africa, while relatively tall, are more linear and gracile than domestic cattle in Southwest Asia. This suggests an adaptation to heat tolerance, which might antedate the domestication process (see below).

Were Cattle Domesticated in Africa?

The traditional viewpoint is that cattle were domesticated in Southwest Asia and later introduced from the Levant into northern Africa. This view was based on dates of first appearance and anatomy: the earliest archaeological instances of cattle in African sites were straight-backed (Carter and Clark 1976; Smith 1986) like Southwest Asian cattle and unlike humped indicine, or zebu, cattle that were separately domesticated around the Indus Valley. Furthermore, the breeds of modern African cattle most tolerant of sleeping sickness (i.e., the N'Dama) and considered products of a long selective history in the tsetse zone of West Africa are also straight-backed.

The widespread humped cattle breeds of Africa, often called "Sanga" (Epstein 1971), were, according to traditional views, a product of more recent cross-breeding of the earliest Southwest Asian introductions with zebu cattle (*Bos primigenius* f. indicus) from South Asia. Zebu were introduced by the British into Sudan and other parts of East Africa in the 19th century, but Epstein (1971) argued that humped indigenous cattle breeds probably derived from an earlier admixture of indicine and taurine stocks, perhaps during the Islamic Indian Ocean trade.

Genetic comparisons of African, South Asian, Southwest Asian, and European cattle breeds have shed new light on cattle domestication, suggesting three independent domestication events, including one in Africa. However, inferences drawn from genetics are not universally accepted among Africanist archaeologists; their reception is complicated by two pre-existing lines of argument, each drawn from a different database. The first centers on controversial assertions of the presence of domestic cattle in the tenth millennium b.p. in Egypt. The second entails comparative osteology of African versus Southwest Asian cattle from later archaeological sites.

Tenth millennium cattle domestication?

Starting in the 1980s, Wendorf, Gautier, and their associates argued for the presence of domestic cattle in the tenth millennium b.p. in sites from the Bir Kiseiba area of the Egyptian Western Desert (Close 1990; Gautier 1984b; Wendorf and Schild 1998; Wendorf et al. 1987). These dates would make African cattle domestication an independent and older event than in Southwest Asia. The osteological remains in question were sparse and not identifiable beyond the designation "large bovid." The main reason for arguing their domestic status was their association with remains of desert-adapted wild species (hares, gazelles, hartebeests), with which *Bos primigenius* is not normally associated. Their presence in an inferred desert environment was thought to reflect human intervention, bringing tamed cattle into arid zones to serve as a source of food and liquids, since cows convert water undrinkable by humans into milk or blood. Gautier and van Neer (1982) further proposed that large bovid bone fragments from the Ti-n-Torha East Cave in Libya (8490–7920 b.p.) could also be of domestic cattle. Again, evidence is sparse and not highly diagnostic.

Grigson (2000) discounts association of putative *Bos* with hartebeest and gazelle as compelling evidence for the artificial (hence domesticated) appearance of cattle in this environmental context. More widely accepted evidence appears by about 7700 b.p. in the Nabta-Kiseiba region (MacDonald 2000). Gautier (1987a, 1987b; Gautier and van Neer 1982) in fact later retracted definitive identifications of *Bos* for both the earliest Egyptian and the Ti-n-Torha East samples.

Comparative osteology

Comparative osteological study of African and Southwest Asian cattle led Grigson (1991) to suggest that African cattle were distinct in cranial and postcranial morphology and that zooarchaeologists should re-examine their assumed derivation from Near Eastern stock. She argued that early African cattle from Egyptian and Saharan sites were tall, straight-backed, and linear, with slender, lyre-shaped horns in cows, and more outward-curved, semi-circular horns in bulls. African cattle have longer and more parallel-sided frontals and flatter faces side to side than *Bos taurus* of Southwest Asia and Europe. She proposed that North African aurochs, *Bos primigenius mauritanicus* (or *Bos primigenius opisthonomus*) was a likely candidate for the ancestor of the humpless domestic African cattle found earliest in African sites. She proposed "*Bos africanus*" as the name for the domestic variant. Grigson (2000) continues to argue for an African domestication event, based both on the new genetic data and the distinctive osteology of African cattle.

Genetic evidence

Comparisons of mitochondrial (mtDNA) and y-chromosome DNA of living domestic cattle (Bradley et al. 1996; Bradley and Loftus 2000; Loftus et al. 1994; MacHugh et al. 1997) from Europe, India, and Africa have yielded several new findings regarding African cattle domestication. Among the most surprising, and directly relevant to Grigson's hypothesis, is that the mtDNA (maternal lineage) of indigenous African cattle breeds are all taurine, whether or not the breeds were straight-backed or humped. Y-chromosome DNA evidence shows that humped cattle derived from an indicine paternal line.

In another study of genetic variation, MacHugh et al. (1997) demonstrated that a haplotype common in African cattle occurs in very low frequencies in both the Levant and the Iberian peninsula, then falls off to nil with increasing distance from Africa. This pattern is expected if the haplotype originated in an African population and spread east and west through low rates of interbreeding of African stock with Levantine and Iberian cattle.

Despite new evidence, cattle domestication in Africa should not be treated as an either/or question, with cattle either domesticated in Africa or introduced from Southwest Asia. Evidence from Merimda in Egypt suggests that this area received caprines, pigs, and Near Eastern domestic plants as a "package" by the fifth millennium b.p., and Grigson (2000) notes that the Merimda cattle measurements (von den Driesch and Boessneck 1985) are nearly identical to those from the Levant. This suggests that cattle may have been introduced to some areas a part of a Southwest Asian "package," especially those closest to that region, but not in other areas. There is no a priori reason for excluding one possibility based on evidence for the other in another area.

In sum, the eastern Saharan osteological evidence from 9000 to 8000 b.p. is too tenuous to establish unequivocally where, when, and how domestic cattle first appeared in Africa. However, several independent lines of genetic evidence offer more substantial evidence that African cattle derive in part from aurochs native to northern Africa.

Current Views on the Origins of African Pastoralism

Current researchers differ in whether they see links between adoption of domestic cattle and caprines. Hassan (2000) proposed that cattle were tamed by foragers in the arid Egyptian Sahara at 8500–9000 b.p. as a risk-reduction strategy to cope with climatic instability and then spread to the central Sahara by 6500 b.p. In Hassan's scenario, caprines were introduced by 7500–7000 b.p. from Southwest Asia by two routes, from the Mediterranean coast (where they appear before cattle) and from the Red Sea Hills. Kevin MacDonald (2000) notes that definite domestic cattle remains exist by 7700 b.p. The earliest evidence for cattle domestication in Southwest Asia is in Anatolia ca. 8000–7000 b.p., while evidence for eighth-millennium domestic cattle in areas closer to the Sinai and northeastern Africa is more equivocal. This suggests that independent domestication events may have been virtually simultaneous.

Smith (e.g., 1986), while agreeing to the general scenario from about the seventh millennium b.p. onward, accepts neither the Early Holocene Egyptian evidence for early domesticates nor the indigenous origins of cattle. Smith contends that cattle and caprines appear together in nearly all places, suggesting that a "Neolithic package" was introduced from Southwest Asia; when a taxon appears in isolation, it reflects specialized use of cattle or caprines in different environmental zones, rather than a temporal order of appearance (Smith 1989). Based on ethnographic sources (e.g., Ingold 1980), Smith argues that a shift to pastoralism would probably be rare, because of social and ideological barriers to its development among hunter-gatherers with an ethos of meat-sharing. He asserts that this difference poses a major barrier to the transition from foraging to food production based on ownership of herds (Smith 1992).

Sadr and Plug (Sadr 2002; Sadr and Plug 2001) have proposed that the line between stock-owning and hunting-gathering is not as stark as depicted by Smith, given archaeological evidence for mixed hunting-herding economies in both South Africa and the Sudanese "Neolithic." South African sites of the Thamaga rock-shelter complex suggest a sequence in which San-speaking foragers originally subsisted solely as hunter-gatherers but, with the arrival of iron-using immigrants in their region, adopted small stock and ceramics and dropped hunting smaller animals, while continuing to hunt larger game. While these foragers ultimately made a full shift to food production, the sequence appears to reflect a gradual transition rather than either resistance or a wholesale "revolution" in subsistence.

Marshall and Hildebrand (2002) stressed that hunter-gatherer economies and ideologies vary, and that so-called delayed-return foragers may have been predisposed to accepting the consequences of ownership that food production brings. Delayed-return foragers invest time and energy in food-getting artifacts, facilities, or storage at one point in their yearly cycle, anticipating a later return on their investment. They have concepts of ownership of the means to produce and the products themselves (Meillasoux 1972; Woodburn 1986). Marshall and Hildebrand argue Early Holocene moist phase communities were delayed-return foragers depending on profuse wild grain harvests (Chapter 7). Climatic change increased unpredictability of this plant food base and led some groups in the eastern Sahara to intensify management of cattle, a process enabled by pre-existing, socially sanctioned forms of non-communal ownership of plant products. Taming cattle that might otherwise disperse lowered prey search time to zero, but only if groups opted for higher mobility than during the earlier moist phase. Marshall and Hildebrand argue that such pastoral mobility may have enhanced the ability to locate now scattered but locally dense wild grain stands under unpredictable rainfall regimes (Chapter 10).

Debates on the origins of African pastoralism tend to focus on cattle. We tend to think of caprines as insignificant "small change," but Saharan rock art and Nilotic iconography reflect the high regard in which goats and sheep were held by African peoples (Le Quellec 1998), and archaeologists need to consider how caprine introductions affected human populations. Sheep and goats were alien species, already domesticated, reproductively successful under human handling, and probably amenable to milking. They would have been a truly novel component in a forager way of life, offering a new food source and lowering search time for smaller prey, but perhaps at the cost of decreasing residential mobility (Stahl 1993; Chapter 9), and certainly requiring a revamping of notions of ownership and entitlement.

Point 1: The Fact of Pastoralism before Farming

Africanist scholars are converging on acceptance of a long pre-agricultural history of the pastoral way of life in Africa. Reliance on cattle, sheep, and goats was a stable and widespread way of life by 6400 b.p., thousands of years before the first appearance of domestic plants or settled village farming communities (Chapter 10). Why the existence of pastoralism without farming has been so hard for many to accept will be taken up in the final section of this chapter. The second unique aspect of early African pastoralism, its technological homogeneity, will be discussed at the end of the section on the North African evidence.

North African Archaeological Evidence

North Africa may be divided into three regions, each of which appears to have its own pastoral trajectory: (1) the northwestern region, or Maghreb, on or close to the shores of the Mediterranean; (2) the Nile Valley and its immediately adjacent dry hinterlands, and (3) the Sahara proper, stretching from west of the Nile to the Atlantic Ocean.

The Maghreb

Much of far North Africa appears to have been a discrete set of cultural provinces through much of the Holocene, tied more to developments in the Mediterranean basin than the Sahara. The Terminal Pleistocene Iberomaurusian, Capsian, and later Neolithic of Capsian Tradition all reflect the geographically distinct aspect of the region (Lubell et al. 1984).

This said, some of the earliest dates for caprines in Africa and early dates for cattle derive from North Africa. Analysis of fauna from the deeply stratified site of Haua Fteah, on the Cyrenaican coast of Libya, suggests that caprines were present early in the seventh millennium b.p. (Higgs 1967; Klein and Scott 1986). The Capelletti Cave in the Aurès Mountains of Algeria (Roubet 1979) shows the early presence of caprines and cattle at 6500 b.p., with cattle increasing in proportion to caprines through the next two millennia, ultimately representing nearly 25 percent of the total identifiable elements at about 4250 b.p. Some have suggested that domesticates, especially caprines, entered North Africa from Sicily and Malta, while others have argued for their spread as part of the active trade along the Mediterranean littoral (see Smith 1992).

The Nile

During the "wild Nile" phase of the Terminal Pleistocene, the hinterlands of Egypt and Sudan had large playa lakes and streams, and even in the ninth and eighth millennia b.p. were more hospitable than present conditions suggest. Sites in oases and around now defunct lakes testify to foraging and, later, to the use of domestic cattle and small stock. The earliest uncontroversial dates for domestic ungulates in Africa are for cattle in the Nabta-Kiseiba region, attributed to the "Middle Neolithic" phase (7700–6500 b.p.). These are not numerous, either in terms of site samples or numbers of specimens. The Nabta-Kiseiba record reflects a period when cattle were not integrated with caprines. Caprines first appear with cattle from ca. 6300 b.p., and perhaps as early as 7000 b.p. on the Bir Kiseiba Scarp, but in culturally "Late Neolithic" contexts (Gautier 1984b). Caprines occur in the Red Sea Hills east of the Nile between 7000 and 6700 b.p. (Vermeersch et al. 1994). Close (2002) has argued that caprines could have crossed the Red Sea to Africa without arriving as part of a farming "package."

In Dakhleh Oasis, near the center of the Egyptian Western Desert, a similar pattern of sedentary foraging is evident from the ninth millennium b.p., with no sign of domestic animals. About 7000 b.p., both cattle and caprines appear in the sites. With increasingly dry conditions after 6500 b.p., pastoral exploitation of the oasis area and its hinterlands continued, with evidence of continuation into Dynastic times (McDonald 1998). Gautier (1976) confirmed that the Kom W assemblage of the Fayûm A complex, originally excavated by Caton-Thompson and Gardner (1934) in the Fayûm Depression, contained wild animals and small stock, but no cattle remains. Other Fayûm A sites dating to ca. 5800 b.p. yielded smaller cattle than *Bos primigenius* from Terminal Paleolithic sites.

Cattle appear later in the Nile Valley. Between 6500 and 6000 b.p., domestic cattle appear in the Nile Delta at Merimda-Benisalama (von den Driesch and Boessneck 1985), along with Near Eastern domestic plants and caprines. Contrary to earlier Egyptological interpretations, Hassan (1988) sees Merimda and other early Predynastic sites not as farming communities, but rather continuations of the long Nilotic tradition of sedentary, intensive foraging, with crops and domestic animals used to reduce risk of food shortfalls (Table 8.1).

The area around Khartoum, Sudan, has long been known for evidence of late tenth- and ninth-millennium b.p. pottery-making sedentary foragers who exploited plants and river animals (Arkell 1949; Haaland 1992). Wavy-line and, later, dotted wavy-line ceramic styles were ubiquitous along the Nile, and associated with diverse lithic traditions (Garcea 1998; Marks et al. 1968; Chapter 7). Though a temporal hiatus may separate Early and Late Khartoum phases, the Late Khartoum type site, Esh Shaheinab, displays similar exploitation of river resources as the Early Khartoum sites (Haaland 1987). Full use of cattle, sheep, and goats begins ca. 6000–5000 b.p. (Barich 1998; Marshall 1998). Researchers have argued that cattle entered the Nubian Nile with immigrating pastoralists during a Saharan dry phase. Garcea (1998) notes that entry of Saharan groups into Nubia is supported by the regional replacement of incised wavy-line by rocker-stamped dotted wavy-line pottery, which first appeared in the Acacus, Hoggar, and Aïr regions.

Krzyzaniak (1978), Haaland (1987, 1992), and Sadr (2002) argue that the sixth-millennium b.p. Late Khartoum saw a regional system of seasonal movements and specialized production timed to the Nile floods. Large, Nile-focused settlements such as Esh Shaheinab were complemented by groups in the drier hinterlands east of the Nile where livestock production dominated, such as Kadero (Gautier 1984a; Krzyzaniak 1978; Sadr 2002), Kedada (Gautier 1986), Umm Direiwa (Haaland 1987), and Zakiab (Tigani el Mahi 1988). Late fourth-millennium b.p. Nubian societies (e.g. Kerma kingdom) and the third-millennium b.p. Meroitic civilization depended heavily on livestock for subsistence and trade. Kerma especially used cattle and sheep in funerary rituals (Chaix 1993, 1994). Sadr (1991) sees later pastoralism in the Sudan's Atbai region as similar to Southwest Asia's, integrated with and responsive to regional states.

The Sahara

The Sahara displays diverse topography including sand seas (ergs) and mountainous regions (Figure 8.1). Early in the Holocene, sand seas were lakes and, later, well-watered marshes or savannas that facilitated human movement by watercraft or served as well-watered avenues for seasonal migrations of wild and domestic ungulate herds. Similar ceramic motifs distributed from the Nile to the Atlantic testify to the greater ease of human communication (Garcea 1998).

The Lake Chad basin is key to understanding communication through the Saharan region (Figure 8.1). This centrally located lake is today distant from the highlands arcing around the south-central Sahara and other major bodies of water. During its Early Holocene high stands, however, it linked via the Benue River to the Niger drainage, and its northeastern margins were much nearer to Jebel Marra and the Ennedi (Grove 1980). Inhabitants of its eastern shores were thus much closer to the Nile, via the Wadi Howar, sometimes called the "Yellow Nile" (Keding

Table 8.1. Dates for early cattle and caprines in the Nile Valley and immediately adjacent areas

Site name	Country	^{14}C yrs.	Dom. cattle	Dom. caprines	Sources
Merimda-Benisalama	Egypt	5830 ± 60 5440 ± 75	x	x	von den Driesch and Boessneck 1985
Fayûm A	Egypt	5860 ± 115	x	x	Wendorf and Schild 1976
Nabta/E-75-8	Egypt	7120 ± 150 6240 ± 70	??	–	Wendorf and Schild 1980
Kharga/E-76-7, E-76-8	Egypt	7890 ± 65 5450 ± 80	??	–	Wendorf and Schild 1980
Bir Kiseiba	Egypt	9000 ± 100 8150 ± 70 8740 ± 95 8740 ± 70	??	–	Close, ed., 1984
Gilf el Kebir	Egypt	6980 ± 80	x	–	Gautier 1980
Shaqadud	Sudan	7500 3500	x	x	Peters 1992
El Kadada	Sudan	4790 ± 110 4630 ± 80 4830 ± 50 4730 ± 80 4840 ± 70 5170 ± 110	x	x	Gautier 1986
Kashm el Girba	Sudan	5000 2000	x	x	Peters 1992
Kadero	Sudan	5630 ± 70	x	x	Gautier 1984a
El Zakiab	Sudan	5350 ± 90 5660 ± 80	x	x	Tigani el Mahi 1988
Um Direiwa	Sudan	4950 ± 880 5600 ± 110 6010 ± 90	x	x	Tigani el Mahi 1988
El Nofalab	Sudan	5290 ± 100 5520 ± 130	x	x	Tigani el Mahi 1988
Laqiya	Sudan	3500 4000	x	x	Van Neer and Uerpmann 1989
Wadi Howar	Sudan	5200 5000 3000	x	x	Van Neer and Uerpmann 1989

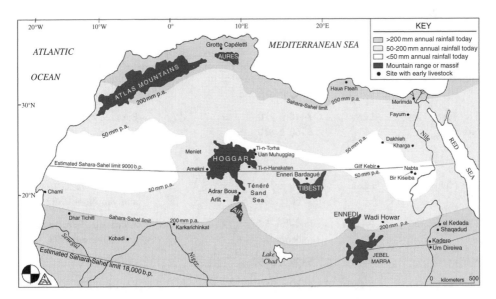

Figure 8.1. Map of North Africa showing physical features; estimated 200 mm rainfall isohyets at 18,000, 9,000, and present; archaeological sites with early domesticates mentioned in text. The 200 mm rainfall isohyet is widely recognized as the border between Sahara (desert) and Sahel (savanna) *Source*: Marshall and Hildebrand 2002:108. Physical and isohyet map by Elisabeth Hildebrand, following Banks 1984, Gautier 1987b, Goudie 1996, and Petit-Maire 1989. Additional sites added by the author.

1998) that flows east to the Dongola reach. Westward-flowing streams from Jebel Marra flowed into Lake Chad, while those on its southeastern side fed the Bahr-el-Arab/Bahr-el-Ghazal complex, ending at the White Nile and Sobat rivers confluence, in turn linked to Lake Victoria and Lake Turkana (Grove 1980).

Because much of the relevant faunal material west of Egypt is preserved in highland rockshelters and caves rather than in open sites, we may have a skewed understanding of when and where livestock herders first colonized ancient Saharan savannas. The Sahara is dotted with hearth-rings and stone concentrations with large, waisted "tethering stones," often interpreted as hobbles for cattle and thus remnants of pastoral sites (Gabriel 1987). Although some such sites yielded materials datable to the span of pastoralism in the Sahara, some sites date from 10500 b.p. Pre-pastoral Saharan rock art shows wild animals as giraffes with a foot caught in wheel-like radial traps moored to similar waisted stones (Le Quellec 1998). It is therefore not possible to diagnose all these so-called *Steinplätze* as pastoral camps. Whatever the impacts of this preservational bias, dates suggest first appearances are earliest in the east, from ca. 7500 b.p., and are distributed throughout the Sahara by a millennium later (Table 8.2).

The Uan Afuda Cave in the Acacus region of Libya, and possibly other sites dating to the ninth millennium b.p., provide intriguing evidence for management

Table 8.2. Dates for early domesticates in the greater Sahara and adjacent regions

Site name	Country	^{14}C yrs.	Dom. cattle	Dom. caprines	Sources
Ennedi Bardagué (), i	Chad	7455 ± 180 bp on animal bone	x	?	Gautier 1987b
Ti-n-Torha Cave North	Libya	7440 ± 220 5260 ± 130	x	x	Barich 1987a, 1987b; Barich et al. 1984; Gautier and van Neer 1982
Uan Muhuggiag	Libya	4730 ± 310 3700 ± 200	x		Gautier 1996; Gautier and van Neer 1982
Ti-n-Hanakaten	Algeria	mid-8th–6th millennia	x	x	Aumassip 1986; Aumassip and Tauveron 1993
Meniet	Algeria	5400 ± 3000	??		Gautier 1987a
Grotte Capeletti	Algeria	6530 ± 250	x	x	Roubet 1979
Haua Fteah	Libya	7000, 6400	x	x	Klein and Scott 1986
Adrar Bous	Niger	4910 ± 140 5760 ± 500 6200 ± 250 6325 ± 300	x	–	Carter and Clark 1976; Paris 2000; Roset 1987
Arlit	Niger	5200 ± 140 2640 ± 100	x		Smith 1980
Karkarichinkat North	Mali	3670 ± 80 3760 ± 85 4000 ± 90	x	x	Guerin and Faure 1983; Smith 1980
Karkarichinkat South	Mali	3360 ± 110 3690 ± 100 4010 ± 160	x	x	Guerin and Faure 1983; Smith 1980
Kobadi	Mali	3335 ± 100 2880 ± 120 2415 ± 12-	x		Raimbault et al. 1987
Dhar Tichitt	Mauritania	3850 ± 250	x	x	Holl 1986
Chami	Mauritania	4000 1500	??	–	Bouchud et al. 1981; Gautier 1987b
Kintampo 6	Ghana	3600 3200?	x	x	Gautier 1987b
Ntereso	Ghana	3600 3200	–	x	Gautier 1987b

Sources: as listed, and Chenal-Vélardé 1997.

of aoudads, or Barbary sheep (*Ammotragus lervia*). Aoudads were the dominant food animal in the Early Holocene/Early Acacus phase. Uan Afuda appears to have been used during the rainy season, and after 8900 b.p. has ample grinding equipment and comb-impressed ceramic vessels (di Lernia 1999, 2001). The presence of layers of caprine dung but the absence of the Southwest Asian caprines from the Early Acacus sequence leads di Lernia (2001) to infer corralling of aoudads, which would not enter a cave on their own. Di Lernia sees penning aoudads, coinciding with a broadening of animal species taken and increased used of wild hard-seeded plants, as adaptations to climatic deterioration. He stresses that, although *Ammotragus* was never brought under domestication, their penning and deferred use imply a social system with delayed-consumption strategies amenable to adopting the use of livestock.

Not far west, in the Tassili-n-Ajjer, ninth-millennium b.p. moist phase occupations exploiting fish and wild grains (Amekni, Camps, ed., 1969), were followed by mid-eighth- to sixth-millennium b.p. pastoral occupations (Ti-n-Hanakaten), associated with intensified harvest of acacia, a tree legume (Aumassip 1986; Aumassip and Tauveron 1993). This may have been aimed at satisfying human nutritional needs, while acacia pods would also have been fodder for livestock.

A thriving pastoral economy focused on cattle thrived in the central Sahara during the seventh to sixth millennia b.p., associated with the Tenerian lithic industry (Carter and Clark 1976; Paris 2000; Roset 1987; Tixier 1962). At Adrar Bous, which is in the process of another round of radiocarbon dating, the Tenerian fauna is almost exclusively cattle, with no caprines, no fish, and some hartebeest (*Alcelaphus*), and gazelle species. The Tenerian is marked by special handling of cattle remains. At Adrar Bous, cattle body segments were reassembled after meat was consumed, and/or bones burned well beyond the stage expected in simple roasting (Gifford-Gonzalez n.d.; Paris 2000). In other cases entire animals, usually young cows, were interred (Paris 2000). The well-known young cow from Adrar Bous (Carter and Clark 1976) was interpreted as a natural death based on its position and lack of a discernible pit. However, interment of young cows has also been noted in the "Late Neolithic" of Nabta Playa in the Egyptian Eastern Desert, where a heifer was found buried under a megalithic construction (Applegate et al. 2001; Wendorf and Schild 1998); other localities have interred body segments. Some Predynastic sites also have cow interments (F. Hassan, pers. comm. 1997), a practice that continues in association with temple construction into the Dynastic era. Applegate et al. (2001) summarize special handling of cattle over a wide range of the central to eastern Sahara, suggesting common practices through this expansive region. Similarities in tool forms and ceramics across a wide region similarly suggest extensive networks of shared knowledge and practice (Garcea 1998). Underlying similarities in artistic convention of rock art also suggest communication over great distances (Smith 1986). Hassan (1993) has argued that rock art played a critical role in the maintenance of pastoral society through the climatic fluctuations of the Early to Middle Holocene (cf. Holl 1995).

Point 2: Stylistic Homogeneity of Early Saharan Pastoralism as a Social Product

Variations in lithic traditions from 6500 to 4500 b.p. suggest that four distinct pastoralist culture areas existed in the Sahara: (1) one stretching from the Aïr and Ténéré Desert to the Nile; (2) the Hoggar highlands (including Tassili); (3) the Tanezrouft drainage off Adrar-des-Iforas in Mali; and (4) the northward bend of the Niger River, not far from Timbuktu. However, communication networks were even broader than these "culture areas," as noted with regard to artistic representation. In addition, amazonite beads from Tibesti are found from the Atlantic coast to the Nile, and a fine-grained green vitric tuff suitable for the elegant stoneworking typical of much of Sahara pastoral assemblages was exchanged from near Adrar Bous into Tassili (Clark 1970).

Early pastoral societies of the Sahara-Sahel thus continued the truly unusual Early Holocene pattern of stylistic homogeneity in artifacts over enormous expanses of the region (Chapter 7). Most research on these ceramic and lithic similarities has concentrated on mapping artifact style and raw materials, without explicit attention to the social practices that sustained such similarities over several millennia in a vast area. This is not necessarily a "natural" phenomenon, since other areas (e.g., the Levant) saw localized lithic industries in the Early to Middle Holocene. Thus, broad similarities in artifact form, art, and wide circulation of special objects and raw materials must have been actively maintained (Bender 1985). Though recent pastoralists have had their former ranges circumscribed by modern nation-states, they maintain geographically extensive networks of affiliation, exchange, and mutual aid. These are generally but not always coterminous with linguistic entities and supported by an ideology of common membership in a loose and flexible association (Galaty 1991; Stenning 1959). The Saharan evidence may reflect the first of such extensive networks, resembling in some ways the footprint of the Fulani expansion from the Fouta Djalon of Senegal to Sudan in the last five centuries. Archaeologists might usefully explore these widespread similarities as the products of socially and ideologically structured action within an "interaction sphere" (cf. the Hopewell interaction sphere, 200 B.C.–A.D. 400; Binford 1965).

The End of Early Saharan Pastoralism

Aridification from 5500 to 4500 b.p. was associated with abandonment of the central Sahara and appearance of livestock and/or pastoralist economies between 4000 and 2500 b.p. in regions south and west (Figure 8.2). Smith (1992) proposed that the southward movement of pastoralists in Central and West Africa was also enabled by drying of more southern zones formerly infested by tsetse flies hosting trypanosomiasis (sleeping sickness), harmful to livestock and humans. Pastoralist settlement in the Sahel (e.g., Karkarichinkat in the Lower Tilemsi Valley) was possible once rainfall fell below the 500 mm/yr minimum that sustains tsetse.

Figure 8.2. Map of Africa showing sub-Saharan sites with early domesticates mentioned in text

One of the best-documented cases of southward movement of pastoralist peoples is the Gajiganna Phase in the mid-fourth to mid-third millennia b.p. in the western Chad basin (Breunig et al. 1996). This clay plain was exposed by retreat of the lake; the first sites are interpreted as pastoralist settlements with little evidence of farming or of domestic morphology grains. Gajiganna Phase ceramics display similarities to Aïr pottery, suggesting a southward movement of peoples when Aïr became too arid to sustain herding. About the same time, caprines (goats, when identified to species) are found among predominantly foraging groups in the forest margin zone of West Africa, as at Kintampo 6 Rockshelter and other sites of the Kintampo Complex in Ghana (Anquandah 1993; Stahl 1993). Here, evidence points to incorporation of caprines into a local tradition rather than to immigrating pastoralists. To the north-west in Mauritania, the sites of Dhar Tichitt (Holl 1985; Munson 1976), display a range of strategies aimed at assuring production of plant and animal foods, including early domestic pearl millet and livestock by the early fourth millennium b.p. (Chapter 10). It is clear that in the fourth and third millennia b.p. a wide variety of subsistence strategies focused on collection and management of wild plants, and hunting animals began to incorporate domesticates typical of the savannas of the Sahara/Sahel in diverse subsistence strategies.

In sum, by the eighth to sixth millennia b.p., animal husbandry based on a combination of domestic sheep, goats, and cattle coalesced in the Sahara, probably supplemented by the gathering of wild grains. Rock art and the special handling of cattle bones suggest that cattle played a central role in ideology. Widespread artifactual similarities suggest mobility but also far-flung networks of communication. Radiocarbon determinations for sites with livestock in western and eastern Africa suggest movements of pastoral peoples east and south from the Saharan zone in two pulses, one along the Nile during the seventh millennium b.p. arid phase, the other during the final desiccation of the Sahara in the fifth millennium b.p. after which a diversity of local hunter-gatherers began incorporating livestock into their economies, often as part of a general intensification in food procurement strategies.

East African Archaeological Evidence

The Saharan triad of cattle, sheep, and goats appears earliest in eastern Africa around 4000–4500 b.p., in the Lake Turkana basin (Barthelme 1985; Marshall et al. 1984), often in association with remains of fish and aquatic reptiles, grindstones, ceramics, and bone harpoons (Barthelme 1985; Phillipson 1977; Robbins 1980). These sites are associated with Nderit- and Ileret-style pottery (Barbour and Wandibba 1989), which has also been recovered from the Jaragole Pillar Site, one of at least five megalithic pillar sites in the Lake Turkana basin (Koch 1994; Nelson 1993). Excavations here yielded cremated human remains, broken large Nderit pots, fired clay figurines of domestic cattle and wild animals, shells and lithics from distant sources, and as yet unanalyzed mammal bone. Pastoral peoples in the Lake Turkana basin were engaged in possibly seasonal social activities similar but not identical to those testified to in the "Late Neolithic" of Nabta Playa (Wendorf and Schild 1998), as well as among more recent pastoral groups in Sudan.

Nderit-style pottery is also found in south-central Kenya and northern Tanzania; however, in these regions the ceramics are not associated with elaborate funerary practices or ceramic figurines. Furthermore, sites with Nderit ceramics south of Lake Turkana are dominated by wild fauna. At Enkapune ya Muto Rockshelter in central Kenya, Ambrose (1998) found Nderit ceramics associated with Eburran Phase 5 lithics by 4860 ± 70 b.p., contemporaneous with dates from the Lake Turkana basin. The long-lived Eburran lithic tradition is associated with a hunting-gathering lifestyle (Chapter 16). Dates on other stratified sites associated with domestic caprines and Nderit pottery are controversial (Bower and Nelson 1978; Bower et al. 1977; Gifford-Gonzalez 1998; Gifford-Gonzalez and Kimengich 1984), though direct dating of bones (e.g., Ambrose 1998; Sealy and Yates 1994,

1996) could elucidate the age of such specimens. Nderit ceramics have also been recovered farther south in Kenya at Lukenya Hill and on the Serengeti plains, Tanzania, associated with a local and long-lived lithic tradition at Nasera Rock (Bower 1991; Mehlman 1977, 1989) and with an exclusively wild fauna at the Gol Kopjes site on the Serengeti (Bower 1991; Bower and Chadderdon 1986). Thus, fifth-millennium b.p. sites south of Lake Turkana yielded a ceramic tradition known for its association with cattle, caprines, and elaborate funerary ritual around Lake Turkana but associated with few domesticates and without elaborate funerary practices in the south (Table 8.3).

A change occurred around 3000 b.p., when archaeological sites testify to dense and geographically extensive pastoralism by stone-using peoples (Ambrose 1984; Bower 1991; Marshall 2000), who adopted iron tools by 1300 b.p. Some groups were perhaps immigrants, although opinion on this differs (Ambrose 1984; Bower 1991; for an extended discussion of the mosaic of adaptations that emerged, see Chapter 16). Fourth-millennium East African sites offer compelling evidence for the economic centrality of livestock, especially cattle. Most faunas comprise 90–100 percent domestic species; sites are located on the open, sloping soil and vegetation zones favored by contemporary pastoralists; and a few have yielded concentrations of manure (Ambrose 1984; Bower 1991; Robertshaw 1988, 1990; Western and Dunne 1979). Cattle outnumber sheep and goat at most savanna sites, though not necessarily in the smaller, closed-country rockshelter sites (Gifford-Gonzalez 1998). They are larger than the average modern East African cattle, but not larger than breeds of great antiquity in Africa, such as the Ankole of Central Africa (Marshall 1986). There is no evidence for cultivation of Sahelian domestic grains, although smaller, readily portable grindstones are present in both Elmenteitan and Savanna Pastoral Neolithic sites (Marshall 1998).

Marshall (1990) has proposed that the beginning of specialized pastoralism in East Africa coincides with the onset of the modern bimodal rainfall regime of East Africa, which permitted a more productive pastoral cycle. Other "Pastoral Neolithic" sites in more wooded zones may be those of local foragers, who used ceramics from their pastoralist neighbors or were in the process of adopting pastoralism.

The nearly millennium-long delay in the establishment of pastoral economies in East Africa remains a widely recognized explanatory challenge, one made more intriguing by the later case of only caprines entering South Africa.

Southern African Archaeological Evidence

The course of development of southern African pastoralism remains shrouded in mystery. The few sure data points leave much room for speculative interpretation and disagreement. Again, taphonomic problems may contribute to the obscure history of southern African pastoralism (Klein 1984). Most domestic animal remains have been recovered from caves and rockshelters, though these are not necessarily typical locales for pastoralist encampments. Because archaeological

Table 8.3. Occurrences of Nderit ceramics and/or domestic animals in eastern Africa

Site name	Location	^{14}C yr. b.p.	Ceramics	Lithics	Dom. cattle	Dom. caprines	Other	Sources
Gdji1, Lopoy	W. Lake Turkana, Kenya	1100 ± 80	Nderit-Turkwel	LSA	–	–	bone harpoon. fish	Robbins 1972, 1980
Gdji2, Aipa	Kangatotha, W. Lake Turkana, Kenya	4800 ± 100	Nderit-Turkwel	LSA	??	??	indeterminate bovids	Robbins 1972, 1980
Geji9 Lothagam Pillar Site	near Kerio River, W. Lake Turkana, Kenya	–	Nderit	unknown	??	??		Koch 1994
Kalakol Pillar Site a.k.a Namoratunga II	W. Lake Turkana, Kenya	–	Nderit	unknown	??	??		Koch 1994
FxJj12 North	Ileret, E. Lake Turkana, Kenya	3245 ± 155	Nderit-Ileret, other decorated	LSA	–	–	bone harpoon	Barthelme 1985
GaJi2, Koobi Fora Ridge	Koobi Fora Ridge, E. Lake Turkana, Kenya	3970 ± 60 4160 ± 110	Nderit	LSA	x	x	fish	Barthelme 1985
GaJi4, Dongodien	Koobi Fora Ridge, E. Lake Turkana, Kenya	3890 ± 60 3945 ± 135 4100 ± 125	Nderit-Ileret	LSA one stone bowl	x	x	fish, wild ungulates	Barthelme 1985; Marshall et al. 1984
GaJi23 Il Lokeridede	E. of Koobi Fora Ridge, E. Lake Turkana, Kenya	–	Nderit	LSA			exotic stone and ostrich eggshell beads	Koch 1994

Site	Location	Date	Pottery tradition	LSA/stone bowl			Fauna/artifacts	Reference
Gbjj1, Jaragole Pillar site	E. of Allia Bay, E. Lake Turkana, Kenya	–	Nderit-Ileret	LSA stone bowl	??	??	zoomorphic, anthropomorphic figurines, cowries, exotic stone ornaments	Koch 1994; Nelson 1993
Gbjj4, unnamed	E. of Allia Bay, E. Lake Turkana, Kenya	–	Nderit	unknown	??	??	zoomorphic, anthropomorphic figurines	Koch 1994
Gtjj12, Enkapune ya Muto	Mau Escarpment, Central Rift Valley, Kenya	4860 ± 70 [first ceramics]; 3390 ± 70; 3990 ± 70	Nderit-Ileret. Salasun/Suswa	Eburran 5	– / –	x / x	wild ungulates	Ambrose 1998
Gujj13, Salasun	Mt. Suswa, Central Rift Valley, Kenya	7255 ± 225	Nderit, Salasun/Suswa	Eburran 5	–	x	wild ungulates	
Gvjm44, Vaave Makongo	Lukenya Hill, Athi Plains, Kenya	3290 ± 145 [Horizon 1]	Nderit [Horizon 1]	local LSA	??	–	wild ungulates	Bower and Nelson 1977; Nelson pers. comm. 1990
Nasera	N. Serengeti Plains, Tanzania	<5000	Nderit	Olmoti, local LSA	–	–	wild ungulates	Mehlman 1989
HbJd1, Seronera	Serengeti Plains, Tanzania	70 ± 115 BC	Nderit [SE 2, SE 3]	LSA	??	??	wild ungulates questionable domesticates	Bower 1973; Bower and Gogan Porter 1981
HcJe1,	Serengeti Plains, Tanzania	7215 ± 250,	Nderit	LSA	–	–	wild ungulates	Bower 1991
Gol Kopjes	Tanzania	6920 ± 530						

Table 8.4. Associated (charcoal) versus direct AMS radiocarbon dates on caprine bones from southern African sites, from northwest to southeast

South African site	Associated ^{14}C yrs. b.p.	Direct bone ^{14}C yrs. b.p.
Wonderwerk	1890 ± 50	480 ± 120
Spoegrivier	1920 ± 40	2105 ± 65
Kasteelberg A	1860 ± 60	1630 ± 60
—— ——	1790 ± 60	1430 ± 55
Die Kelders	1960 ± 85	1325 ± 60
—— ——	1960 ± 95	1290 ± 60
Byneskranskop	1880 ± 50	1370 ± 60
Blombos Cave	–	1960 ± 50
		1880 ± 55
Nelson Bay Cave	1930 ± 60	1100 ± 80

Sources: Sealey and Yates 1994, 1996; Henshilwood 1996.

evidence is limited, linguistic and historical sources have been used to estimate the timing and routes of entry of domestic livestock into southern Africa.

Sheep are earliest domestic animal in southern Africa, appearing in coastal Namibia and southwestern South Africa in the early to late first millennium a.d., without cattle or goat remains (see Smith 2000:226). Layers of caprine dung and sheep hair are found in Mirabib and Geduld (Namibia), Boomplaas A (Southern Cape), and Die Kelders (Southern Cape), suggesting repeated penning of sheep flocks in the shelters. Rock paintings suggest the presence of both fat- and thin-tailed varieties.

The appearance of sheep alone has been called a "puzzle" by those aware of the much greater antiquity of the sheep-goat-cattle triad in the Sahara and other parts of Africa. There are circumstantial reasons to believe that the Saharan triad underwent attenuation in the face of multiple disease challenges in savanna environments. Though dates on associated charcoal suggested that sheep appeared across the western coast within a short period around 2000 b.p., recent direct dating of sheep remains from some of these sites has indicated a nearly millennium-long north–south cline of dates (Table 8.4), with Spoegrivier in the north dated oldest and coastal Nelson Bay Cave youngest (Sealy and Yates 1994). According to Sealy and Yates (1994), sheep bones are rare in nearly all the putatively earliest contexts and may have descended from overlying deposits into predominantly older Later Stone Age strata. They also question whether the appearance of pottery the Western Cape region is coeval with that of domestic sheep. However, a direct date of sheep remains from Blombos Cave on the Southern Cape at about 2000 b.p. has added complexity to this pattern (Henshilwood 1996). In any case, the latest of these early dates for sheep overlap with those for cattle in the Eastern Cape.

Where the sheep came from originally, and by whom they were introduced into the Western Cape region, is still under debate. On linguistic grounds, Elphick

(1977) suggested that the languages spoken by historic Khoekhoen herders derived from northern Botswana, with a later divergence into two streams, one following the Orange River to the Atlantic coast and the other moving south through the Karoo region. Smith (2000) built on this model, positing an earlier movement of herding peoples from Cameroon down the western side of Africa, ultimately making contact with Khoisan-speakers in Angola/Botswana, who gradually moved south. Unfortunately, the key area for assessing this model with archaeological data includes the Democratic Republic of Congo, Angola, and northern Namibia, where civil unrest and war have for decades precluded extensive archaeological field research (Chapter 17). Thus archaeological evidence cannot at present speak to the likelihood of either model.

Whatever the route and manner of introduction, San-speaking sheep herders and Bantu-speaking agropastoralists did not move into empty territory, but rather one long occupied by San-speaking foragers (Chapters 6, 14). Hunter-gatherers appear to have been circumscribed by their herding neighbors, but not without various coping strategies on their part (Smith 2000). Klein (1984) stressed the general continuities of lithic tradition and overall hunter-gathering habits despite the first appearance of sheep in the Western Cape region. Evidence from some sites suggests an emphasis on herding and transhumance between coast and inland highlands (Balasse et al. 2002), while evidence from other sites is interpreted as local hunter-gatherers who exchanged or stole the occasional domesticate from herders (Deacon and Deacon 1999; Klein and Scott 1986; Sadr 2002). Still other sites suggest gradual transition to clientship and herding by some foragers (Sadr and Plug 2001; Chapter 14).

Documentary sources show that, by the late 15th century A.D., the Western Cape was inhabited by Khoisan-speaking herders, generically known as Khoekhoen, who owned vast herds of cattle as well as sheep (Smith 2000). The Eastern Cape and Kwazulu/Natal were by then inhabited by Bantu-speaking agropastoralists who moved into the area by 1200 b.p. These groups had cattle, goats, and sheep, and were involved to differing degrees in the Indian Ocean trade (Voigt 1982, 1983; Voigt and Robinson 1970). Cattle had entered the western parts of southern Africa by the mid-second millennium a.d., but under what circumstances it is not clear. Recent genetically based modeling by Hanotte et al. (2000) suggests that indigenous breeds found the Western Cape region derived from an eastern, rather than from another northern, source. The case of caprines preceding cattle by some centuries leads to a discussion of factors that may have delayed the development of cattle-based pastoralism in eastern and southern Africa.

Point 3: What Caused the "Stutter" in the Spread of Cattle-Based Pastoralism?

Ambrose (1984, 1998) suggested that Holocene East African climate and vegetation changes alternately inhibited and enabled pastoral immigration through the narrow Central Rift Valley of Kenya, the main avenue of entry from Lake Turkana to the plains of southern Kenya and northern Tanzania. Central Rift lakes rose to overflow levels during the Terminal Pleistocene to Early Holocene wet phase (Butzer et al. 1972; Hamilton 1982; Isaac et al. 1972), which would have blocked southward movements of people with livestock Tsetse/sleeping sickness habitat would have expanded with expansion of forest and bush, creating a disease barrier to southward pastoral movement until at least the mid-sixth millennium b.p. (Ambrose 1998). By 3000 b.p., the climate and biotic communities of southern Kenya approached modern conditions (Richardson 1972; Richardson and Richardson 1972), coinciding with virtually simultaneous pastoral occupation.

However, Nderit ceramics and caprines appear in south-central Kenya and northern Tanzania earlier, 4000–3000 b.p. Ambrose (1998) suggests the arid phase, while permitting some pastoralist immigration, may have made south-central Kenya less hospitable to food producers, while permitting indigenous Eburran 5 foragers to adopt a limited set of domesticates and pottery. However, Saharan pastoralists successfully dealt with comparable shifts in climate and vegetation by mobility. What prevented the pastoralists who brought Nderit-style ceramics into south-central Kenya from doing the same? Why are there caprines in these sites but no cattle? Other processes may have created the "stutter" in pastoral expansion into East Africa.

Novel animal disease challenges associated with the sub-Saharan grasslands may have stalled pastoral expansion into the region (Gifford-Gonzalez 2000). Even away from the tsetse-infested bush, sub-Saharan savanna environments present livestock with new disease challenges. These diseases have especially grave effects on cattle and could have led to serious reduction, even extirpation, of cattle from immigrating pastoralist herds. Two diseases in particular are likely to have challenged the sustainability of bovine herding in East Africa. Rift Valley fever (RVF), a tick-borne protozoan parasite infesting African buffalo, kills up to 15 percent of calves a year in modern Africa. Malignant catarrhal fever (MCF), a herpes virus transmitted to cattle from very young wildebeest, is 99 percent fatal to modern cattle within two weeks of exposure.

In recent times, African buffalo are distributed no farther north than the 14th parallel, which marks the southern Lake Chad basin and the Bahr-el-Ghazal, but during the drier phase of the fifth to third millennia b.p., their habitats may have been farther south. Wildebeest existed prehistorically in the Central Rift of Kenya (Gifford et al. 1980), but not in the Lake Turkana basin. Buffalo were reported in extraordinary densities in the savannas around Lake Baringo in early historic times (Percival 1924, 1928; von Höhnel 1968). Thus, pastoralists moving south of Lake Turkana would have simultaneously encountered two virulent cattle diseases. Since buffalo and wildebeest have very similar water and grazing requirements to cattle, it is inevitable that cattle would be exposed these savanna diseases. Modern Maasai, who generally tolerate wild ungulates in their livestock's foraging areas, scrupulously drive out wildebeest because they link the species to MCF. The Central Rift, which had wildebeest at about 1200 b.p., had none when Europeans entered the region in the 19th century, perhaps a testimony to Maa pastoralists' efforts at extirpation

(Gifford-Gonzalez 2000). Caprines are more resistant to these and other diseases carried by East and Central African wild bovids.

It would have been much harder for pastoralists whose grazing grounds in the Lake Turkana basin were vanishing to recover from loss of cattle than it would be among modern pastoralists. The safety net of far-flung livestock loans, marriage alliances, and other obligations for mutual aid would have been thin to absent along such an expanding front. Thus, in contrast to recent pastoralists, early livestock owners who lost their cattle would have been disadvantaged relative to local foragers. If the first pastoralists to enter eastern and southern Africa were practicing the now nearly vanished economy of animal husbandry plus wild plant-gathering rather than agropastoralism, they would not have been able to fall back on farming to make up nutritional shortfalls. Motivation to integrate with local populations of foragers through marriage, clientship, or exchange of products would have been high, as a logical way to enable immigrant to stabilize their food base through increased knowledge of wild foods. Nderit pottery-making pastoralists, if they lost their cattle, may have integrated into forager societies, bringing with them some caprines as a risk-reduction mechanism and the nutritional advantages of ceramic technology (Lupo and Schmitt 1997). No direct evidence for this scenario exists at present, but the animal disease data at least suggest why many foragers in Kenya until recently spoke Cushitic rather than click-based languages (Cronk 1991; Stiles 1981).

The band of sub-Saharan savanna bovid-based epizootics extends nearly entirely across south-central Africa (Gifford-Gonzalez 2000). Were livestock introduced into southern Africa via an independent western route, as is argued by one model, a similar but geographically distinct challenge may also account for this second and geographically separate "stutter" in the diffusion of livestock into southern Africa. Alternately, if Khoisan speakers in Central Africa obtained livestock from foragers in Tanzania, they might have had access only to an attenuated set as the result of the original, East African bottleneck.

Conclusion

Growing evidence suggests that pastoralism in Africa emerged in the absence of settled village farming or state-level tribute systems, and that it emerged as a functional system well in advance of plant domestication (McDonald 1998; Marshall and Hildebrand 2002). In fact, a pastoralist/gathering system with limited hunting and fishing appears to have been extraordinarily successful and resilient in what is now the Sahara and Sahel, ebbing and flowing with climatic fluctuations until the final drying of the Sahara in the fifth to fourth millennia b.p. and continuing in the Lake Chad and Lake Turkana basins for at least another millennium.

Only in the third millennium b.p., especially ca. 2800–2000 b.p., did the Sahelian pastoralist system appear to collapse and transform into other, intensified forms of food production, specialized commodity production, and, by the end of this period, domestication of plant foods and complementary specialized pastoral and agricultural lifeways (Chapter 10). Farther south, divergent forms of pastoralism emerged, partly in response to accommodations with indigenous foragers, perhaps to novel infectious disease challenges to livestock, and ultimately, to the expansion of Bantu-speaking cultivators and other iron-using peoples from the Sahel.

Pastoralism in Africa attests a history of initiatives, defeats, and new initiatives akin to delays and challenges in agricultural colonization of northern Europe (Zvelebil 1986; Zvelebil and Rowley-Conwy 1984). Stasis or even retreat runs counter to ingrained archaeological expectations that major innovations – new species, technologies, economies – inevitably spread, shaped by the idea that "progress" was directional, cumulative, and – especially in the case of technological innovation – undefeatable. Yet innovations never move into neutral space. They expand through complex interactions with salient features of a local setting, evolve into new forms, or become extinct.

Because the African path toward food production departs so profoundly from the "script" for the domestication process in Southwest Asia, it has been profoundly misunderstood for a very long time. Framed by preconceptions and negative evidence (Holl 1997; Sinclair et al. 1993), the absence of sedentary villages in connection with evidence for pastoral livestock, the lack of domestic grains until millennia after the appearance of domestic animals, and the seeming reversal in sedentarization trajectories from lesser to greater mobility in the Sahara, made little sense in light of preconceived scenarios.

This "lack of sense" stems from viewing African facts through lenses colored by hidden assumptions of the Southwest Asian sequence: sedentism is irreversible; intensively harvesting wild grains rapidly produces domestic morphologies; animal domestication occurs in systems based on cultivation; pastoralism emerges only secondarily to settled village farming; and true pastoralism develops as an eco-political accommodation to archaic states. Like Mesoamerica and Andean South America, Africa offers incontrovertible contrasts to the Southwest Asian sequence (itself more diverse and complicated than usually portrayed) calling into question universal models for the origins of food production. Replacing inherited, universalizing models with such critical insights and more sophisticated, actualistically based modeling will permit us to study the record of pastoralism in Africa as another unique trajectory in human history.

REFERENCES

Almagor, Uri, 1978 Pastoral Partners. Affinity and Bond Partnership Among the Dassanetch of Southeastern Ethiopia. Manchester: Manchester University Press.

Ambrose, Stanley H., 1984 The Introduction of Pastoral Adaptations to the Highlands of East Africa. In From Hunters to Farmers: The Causes and Consequences of Food Production in Africa. J. Desmond Clark and Steven A. Brandt, eds. pp. 212–239. Berkeley: University of California Press.

——1998 Chronology of the Later Stone Age and Food Production in East Africa. Journal of Archaeological Science 25:377–392.

Anquandah, James, 1993 The Kintampo Complex: A Case Study of Early Sedentism and Food Production in Sub-Sahelian West-Africa. *In* The Archaeology of Africa: Foods, Metals, and Towns. Thurstan Shaw, Paul Sinclair, Bassey Andah, and Alex Okpoko, eds. pp. 255–260. London: Routledge.

Applegate, Alex, Achilles Gautier, and Steven Duncan, 2001 The North Tumuli of the Nabta Late Neolithic Ceremonial Complex. *In* Holocene Settlement of the Egyptian Sahara, vol. 1: The Archaeology of Nabta Playa. Fred Wendorf, Romuald Schild, and Associates. pp. 468–488. New York: Kluwer Academic/Plenum Publishers.

Arkell, A. J., 1949 Early Khartoum. London: Oxford University Press.

Aumassip, Ginette, 1986 Le Bas-Sahara dans la préhistoire. Paris: Éditions du Centre National de la Recherche Scientifique.

Aumassip, Ginette, and Michel Tauveron, 1993 Le Sahara central a l'Holocène. *In* L'arte e l'ambiente del Sahara prehistorico: dati e interpretazioni. pp. 63–80. Memorie della Società Italiana di Scienze Naturali e del Museo Civico di Storia Naturale di Milano 26. Milan.

Balasse, Marie, Stanley H. Ambrose, Andrew B. Smith, and T. Douglas Price, 2002 The Seasonal Mobility Model for Prehistoric Herders in the South-Western Cape of South Africa Assessed by Isotopic Analysis of Sheep Tooth Enamel. Journal of Archaeological Science 29:917–932.

Banks, Kimball, 1984 Climates, Culture, and Cattle: The Holocene Archaeology of the Eastern Sahara. Dallas: Institute for the Study of Earth and Man, Southern Methodist University.

Barbour, Jane, and Simiyu Wandibba, 1989 Kenyan Pots and Potters. Nairobi: Oxford University Press.

Barich, Barbara E. 1987a Archaeology and Environment in the Libyan Sahara: The Excavation in the Tadrart Acacus, 1978–1983. BAR International Series, 368. Oxford: British Archaeological Reports.

——1987b The Uan Muhuggiag Rock Shelter. *In* Archaeology and Environment in the Libyan Sahara. Barbara E. Barich, ed. pp. 12–61, BAR International Series, 368. Oxford: British Archaeological Reports.

——1998 People, Water, and Grain: The Beginnings of Domestication in the Sahara and the Nile Valley. Rome: "L'Erma" di Bretschneider.

Barich, Barbara E., G. Belloumini, F. P. Bonadonnna, M. Alessio, and L. Manfra, 1984 Ecological and Cultural Relevance of the Recent New Radiocarbon Dates from Libyan Sahara. *In* Origin and Early Development of Food Producing Cultures in North-Eastern Africa. Lech Krzyzaniak and M. Kobusiewicz, eds. pp. 411–417. Poznan: Polish Academy of Sciences.

Barthelme, John W. 1985 Fisher-Hunters and Neolithic Pastoralists in East Turkana, Kenya. BAR International Series, 254. Oxford: British Archaeological Reports.

Bar-Yosef, Ofer, and Anatoly Khazanov, eds., 1992 Pastoralism in the Levant: Archaeological Materials in Anthropological Perspectives. Madison, WI: Prehistory Press.

Bender, Barbara, 1985 Prehistoric Developments in the American Midcontinent and in Brittany, Northwest France. *In* Prehistoric Hunter-Gatherers: The Emergence of Cultural Complexity. T. Douglas Price and James A. Brown, eds. pp. 21–57. New York: Academic Press.

Binford, Lewis R., 1965 Archaeological Systematics and the Study of Culture Process. American Antiquity 31:203–210.

Bouchud, J., P. Brebion, and R. Saban, 1981 Études de faunes holocènes provenant de la zone aride du Sahara atlantique. *In* Préhistoire africaine: Mélanges en homages au doyen Lionel Balout. C. Roubet, H. J. Hugot, and G. Souville, eds. pp. 237–244. Paris: ADPF.

Bower, John R. F., 1973 Seronera: Excavations at a Stone Bowl Site in the Serengeti National Park. Azania 8:78–104.

——1988 Evolution of Stone Age Food-Producing Cultures in East Africa. *In* Prehistoric Cultures and Environment in the Late Quaternary of Africa. John Bower and David Lubell, eds. pp. 91–113. Cambridge Monographs in African Archaeology. BAR International Series, 405. Cambridge: British Archaeological Reports.

——1991 The Pastoral Neolithic of East Africa. Journal of World Prehistory 5:49–82.

Bower, John R. F., and Thomas J. Chadderdon, 1986 Further Excavation of Pastoral Neolithic Sites in Serengeti. Azania 21:129–133.

Bower, John R. F., and Anna Gogan-Porter, 1981 Prehistoric Cultures of the Serengeti National Park. Iowa State University Papers in Anthropology no. 3. Ames: Iowa State University.

Bower, John R. F., and Charles M. Nelson, 1978 Early Pottery and Pastoral Cultures of the Central Rift Valley, Kenya. Man 13:554–566.

Bower, John R. F., Charles M. Nelson, A. F. Waibel, and Simuyu Wandibba, 1977 The University of Massachusetts' Later Stone Age/Pastoral Neolithic Comparative Study in Central Kenya: An Overview. Azania 12:119–146.

Bradley, Daniel G., and Ronan Loftus, 2000 Two Eves for *taurus*? Bovine Mitochondrial DNA and African Cattle Domestication. *In* The Origins and Development of African Livestock. Archaeology, Genetics, Linguistics, and Ethnography. Roger M. Blench and Kevin C. MacDonald, eds. pp. 244–258. London: University College London Press.

Bradley, Daniel G., David E. MacHugh, Patrick Cunningham, and Ronan T. Loftus, 1996 Mitochondrial Diversity and the Origins of African and European Cattle. Proceedings of the National Academy of Sciences, USA 93(10):5131–5135.

Breunig, Peter, Katharina Neumann, and Wim van Neer, 1996 New Research on the Holocene Settlement and Environment of the Chad Basin in Nigeria. African Archaeological Review 13:111–145.

Butzer, Karl W., Glynn Ll. Isaac, J. L. Richardson, and C. K. Washbourne-Kamau, 1972 Radiocarbon Dating of East African Lake Levels. Science 175:1069–1076.

Camps, Gabriel, ed., 1969 Amekni, Néolithique ancien du Hoggar. Paris: Mémoires du Centre des Recherches Anthropologiques, Préhistoriques, Ethnographiques.

Carter, P. L., and J. Desmond Clark, 1976 Adrar Bous and African Cattle. *In* Proceedings of the Pan-African Congress of Prehistory and Quaternary Studies. B. Abebe, J. Chavaillon, and J. E. G. Sutton, eds. pp. 487–493. Addis Ababa: Provisional Military Government of Socialist Ethiopia Ministry of Culture.

Caton-Thompson, Gertrude, and E. W. Gardner, 1934 The Desert Fayum. London: Royal Anthropological Institute of Great Britain and Northern Ireland.

Chaix, Louis, 1993 Les Moutons décorés de Kerma (Soudan): Problèmes d'interprétation. *In* L'arte e l'ambiente del Sahara prehistorico: dati e interpretazioni. pp. 161–164. Memorie della Società Italiana di Scienze Naturali e del Museo Civico di Storia Naturale di Milano 26. Milan.

——1994 Das Rind. Eine wichtige und allgegenwartige Komponente der Kerma-Kultur (N. Sudan, zwischen 3000–1500 v. Chr.). *In* Beitrage zur Archäozoologie und Prähistorischen Anthropologie. M. Kokabi and J. Wahl, eds. pp. 163–167. Stuttgart: Kommissionsverlag Konrad Theiss Verlag.

Chenal-Vélardé, Isabelle, 1997 Les Premières Traces de boeuf domestique en Afrique du Nord: État de la recherche centré sur les données archéozoologiques. ArchaeoZoologia IX:11–40.

Churcher, C. S., 1972 Late Pleistocene Vertebrates from Archaeological Sites in the Plain of Kom Ombo, Upper Egypt. Life Sciences Contribution, Royal Ontario Museum 82.

——1983 Dakhleh Oasis Project Paleontology: Interim Report on the 1982 Field Season. Journal of the Society for the Study of Egyptian Antiquities 13(3):178–187.

Clark, J. Desmond, 1970 The Prehistory of Africa. London: Thames & Hudson.

Close, Angela E., 1990 Living on the Edge: Neolithic Herders in the Eastern Sahara. Antiquity 64:79–96.

——2002 Sinai, Sahara, Sahel: The Introduction of Domestic Caprines in Africa. In Tides of the Desert-Gezeiten der Wüste. Contributions to the Archaeology and Environmental History of Africa in Honour of Rudolph Kuper. Tilman Lenssen-Erz, et al., eds. pp. 459–469. Africa Praehistorica 14. Cologne: Heinrich Barth Institut.

Close, Angela, ed., 1984 Cattle-Keepers of the Eastern Sahara: The Neolithic of Bir Kiseiba. Dallas: Institute for the Study of Earth and Man, Southern Methodist University.

Clutton-Brock, Juliet, 1997 Animal Domestication in Africa. In Encyclopedia of Precolonial Africa: History, Language, Cultures, and Environments. J. O. Vogel, ed. pp. 418–424. Walnut Creek, CA: AltaMira Press.

Copley, M. S., R. Berstan, S. N. Dudd, G. Docherty, A. J. Mukherjee, V. Straker, S. Payne, and R. P. Evershed, 2003 Direct Chemical Evidence for Widespread Dairying in Prehistoric Britain. Proceedings of the National Academy of Science 100:1524–1529.

Cronk, Lee, 1991 Wealth, Status, and Reproductive Success among the Mukogodo of Kenya. American Anthropologist 93:345–360.

Dahl, Gudrun, and Anders Hjort, 1976 Having Herds: Pastoral Herd Growth and Household Economy, vol. 2. Stockholm: Department of Anthropology, University of Stockholm.

Deacon, Hilary J., and Janette Deacon, 1999 Human Beginnings in South Africa. Uncovering the Secrets of the Stone Age. Walnut Creek, CA: AltaMira Press.

di Lernia, Savino, 1999 Delayed Use of Resources: Significance of Early Holocene Barbary Sheep Dung. In The Uan Afuda Cave. Hunter-Gatherer Societies of Central Sahara. S. di Lernia and M. Cremaschi, eds. pp. 209–222. Arid Zone Archaeology Monographs 1. Rome: All' Insegna del Giglio.

——2001 Dismantling Dung: Delayed Use of Food Resources among Early Holocene Foragers of the Libyan Sahara. Journal of Anthropological Archaeology 20:408–441.

Elphick, J., 1977 Kraal and Castle. New Haven: Yale University Press.

Epstein, H., 1971 The Origins of Domestic Animals in Africa. New York: Africana.

Evans-Pritchard, Edward Evan, 1940 The Nuer: A Description of the Modes of Livelihood and Political Institutions of a Nilotic People. Oxford: Clarendon Press.

Gabriel, B., 1987 Palaeoecological Evidence from Neolithic Fireplaces in the Sahara. The African Archaeological Review 5:93–104.

Galaty, John G., 1991 Pastoral Orbits and Deadly Jousts: Factors in the Maasai Expansion. In Herds, Warriors, and Traders. Pastoralism in Africa. J. G. Galaty and P. Bonte, eds. pp. 171–198. Boulder: Westview Press.

Garcea, Elena A. A., 1998 From Early Khartoum to the Saharan Neolithic: Ceramics in Comparison. In Actes de la VIIIe Conférence Internationale des Études Nubiennes. pp. 91–105. Cahier des Recherches de l'Institut de Papyrologie et d'Égyptologie de Lille, vol. 3: Études. Lille: Université Charles de Gaulle.

Gautier, Achilles, 1976 Animal Remains from Archaeological Sites of Terminal Palaeolithic to Old Kingdom Age in the Fayum. In Prehistory of the Nile Valley. Fred Wendorf and Romuald Schild, eds. pp. 369–381. New York: Academic Press.

——1980 Contributions to the Archaeozoology of Egypt. In Prehistory of the Eastern

Sahara. Fred Wendorf and Romuald Schild, eds. pp. 317–344. New York: Academic Press.

——1984a The Fauna of the Neolithic site of Kadero (Central Sudan). *In* Origin and Early Development of Food-Producing Cultures in North-Eastern Africa. Lech Krzyzaniak and M. Kobusiewicz, eds. pp. 43–56. Poznan: Polish Academy of Science.

——1984b Archaeozoology of the Bir Kiseiba Region, Eastern Sahara. *In* Cattle-Keepers of the Eastern Sahara. Fred Wendorf, Romuald Schild, and Angela E. Close, eds. pp. 49–72. Dallas: Southern Methodist University.

——1986 Le Faune de l'occupation néolithique d'El Kadada. Archéologie du Nil Moyen 1:59–111.

——1987a The Archaeozoological Sequence of the Acacus. *In* Archaeology and Environment in the Libyan Sahara. The Excavations in the Tadrart Acacus. B. Barich, ed. pp. 283–312. BAR International Series, 368. Oxford: British Archaeological Reports.

——1987b Prehistoric Men and Cattle in North Africa: A Dearth of Data and a Surfeit of Models. *In* Prehistory of Arid North Africa. Essays in Honor of Fred Wendorf. Angela Close, ed. pp. 163–187. Dallas: Southern Methodist University Press.

——1988 The Final Demise of *Bos ibericus*? Sahara 1:37–48.

Gautier, Achilles, and Willem van Neer, 1982 Prehistoric Faunal from Ti-n-Torha (Tadrart Acacus, Libya). Origini XI:87–127.

Gifford, Diane P., 1978 Ethnoarchaeological Observations on Natural Processes Affecting Cultural Materials. *In* Explorations in Ethnoarchaeology. Richard A. Gould, ed. pp. 77–101. Albuquerque: University of New Mexico Press.

Gifford, Diane P., Glynn L. Isaac, and Charles M. Nelson, 1980 Evidence for Predation and Pastoralism at Prolonged Drift, a Pastoral Neolithic Site in Kenya. Azania 15:57–108.

Gifford-Gonzalez, Diane, 1998 Early Pastoralists in East Africa: Ecological and Social Dimensions. Journal of Anthropological Archaeology 17(2):166–200.

——2000 Animal Disease Challenges to the Emergence of Pastoralism in Sub-Saharan Africa. African Archaeological Review 18:95–139.

——n.d. The Fauna from Adrar Bous. *In* Adrar Bous Archaeology of a Volcanic Ring Complex in Niger. J. D. Clark, E. A. A. Garcea, D. Gifford-Gonzalez, A. B. Smith, and M. A. J. Williams, eds. Tervuren: Annales in Archaeology, Royal Africa Museum.

Gifford-Gonzalez, Diane, and J. Kimengich, 1984 Faunal Evidence for Early Stock-Keeping in the Central Rift of Kenya: Preliminary Findings. *In* The Development and Spread of Food-Producing Cultures in Northeastern Africa. Lech Krzyzaniak, ed. pp. 457–471. Poznan: Polish Academy of Science.

Goudie, A. S., 1996 Climate: Past and Present. *In* The Physical Geography of Africa. W. M. Adams, A. S. Goudie, and A. R. Orme, eds. pp. 34–59. Oxford: Oxford University Press.

Grigson, Caroline, 1991 African Origin for African Cattle? Some Archaeological Evidence. The African Archaeological Review 9:119–144.

——2000 *Bos africanus* (Brehm)? Notes on the Archaeozoology of the Native Cattle of Africa. *In* The Origins and Development of African Livestock. Archaeology, Genetics, Linguistics, and Ethnography. Roger M. Blench and Kevin C. MacDonald, eds. pp. 38–60. London: University College London Press.

Grove, A. T., 1980 Geomorphic Evolution of the Sahara and the Nile. *In* The Sahara and the Nile. M. A. J. Williams and H. Faure, eds. pp. 7–16. Rotterdam: A. A. Balkema.

——1993 Africa's Climate in the Holocene. *In* The Archaeology of Africa: Foods, Metals, and Towns. Thurstan Shaw, Paul Sinclair, Bassey Andah, and Alex Okpoko, eds. pp. 32–42. London: Routledge.

—— 1997 Pleistocene and Holocene Climates and Vegetation Zones. *In* Encyclopedia of Pre-colonial Africa. Joseph O. Vogel, ed. pp. 35–39. Walnut Creek, CA: AltaMira Press.

Guerin, Claude, and Martine Faure, 1983 Mammifères. *In* Sahara ou Sahel? Quateraire récent du Bassin de Taoudenni (Mali). N. Petit-Maire and J. Riser, eds. pp. 16–44. Marseilles: Laboratoire de Géologie du Quaternaire du CNRS.

Haaland, Randi, 1987 Socio-Economic Differentiation in the Neolithic Sudan. BAR International Series, 350. Oxford: British Archaeological Reports.

—— 1992 Fish, Pots, and Grain: Early and Mid-Holocene Adaptations in the Central Sudan. The African Archaeological Review 10:43–64.

Hamilton, A. C., 1982 Environmental History of East Africa. London: Academic Press.

Hanotte, O., C. L. Tawah, D. G. Bradley, M. Kokomo, Y. Verjee, J. Ochieng, and J. E. O. Rege, 2000 Geographic Distribution and Frequency of a Taurine *Bos taurus* and an Indicine *Bos indicus* Gamma Specific Allele amongst Sub-Saharan African Cattle Breeds. Molecular Ecology 9(4):387–396.

Harris, David R., ed. 1996 The Origins and Spread of Agriculture and Pastoralism in Eurasia. Washington, DC: Smithsonian Institution Press.

Hassan, Fekri A., 1988 The Predynastic of Egypt. Journal of World Prehistory 2(135–185):1–16.

—— 1993 Rock Art. Cognitive Schemata and Symbolic Interpretation: A Matter of Life and Death. L'arte e l'ambiente de sahara preistorico: dati e interpretazioni. pp. 269–282. Memorie della Società Italiana di Scienze Naturali e del Museo Civico di Storia Naturale di Milano 25. Milan.

—— 2000 Climate and Cattle in North Africa: A First Approximation. *In* The Origins and Development of African Livestock: Archaeology, Genetics, Linguistics, and Ethnography. Roger M. Blench and Kevin C. MacDonald, eds. pp. 61–86. London: University College London Press.

Henshilwood, Christopher, 1996 A Revised Chronology for Pastoralism in Southernmost Africa: New Evidence of Sheep at c. 2000 b.p. from Blombos Cave, South Africa. Antiquity 70:945–949.

Higgs, Eric S., 1967 Domestic Animals. *In* The Haua Fteah (Cyrenaica). Charles B. M. McBurney, ed. pp. 313–319. Cambridge: Cambridge University Press.

Holl, Augustin F. C., 1985 Subsistence Patterns of the Dar Tichitt Neolithic, Mauritania. The African Archaeological Review 3:151–162.

—— 1996 Économie et Société néolithiques du Dhar Tichitt (Mauritanie). Paris: Éditions Recherche sur les Civilisations.

—— 1995 Pathways to Elderhood. Research on Past Pastoral Iconography. The Paintings from Tikadourine (Tassili-n-Ajjer). Origini Preistorica e Protostoria delle Civiltà Antiche 18:69–113.

—— 1997 Holocene Settlement Expansion in the Chadian Plain. *In* Dynamics of Populations, Movements and Responses to Climatic Change in Africa. Barbara E. Barich and M. C. Gatto, eds. pp. 28–40. Rome: Bonsignori Editore.

Ingold, T., 1980 Hunters, Pastoralists, and Ranchers. Cambridge: Cambridge University Press.

Isaac, Glynn L, Harry V. Merrick, and Charles M. Nelson, 1972 Stratigraphic and Archaeological Studies in the Lake Nakuru Basin, Kenya. Paleoecology of Africa 6:225–232.

Johnson, Amber Lynn, 2002 Cross-Cultural Analysis of Pastoral Adaptations and Organizational States: A Preliminary Study. Cross-Cultural Research 36(2):151–180.

Johnson, Thomas C., Christopher A. Scholz, Michael R. Talbot, Kerry Keits, R. D. Ricketts, Gideon Ngobi, Kristina Beuning, Immaculate Ssemmanda, and J. W. McGill, 1996 Late

Pleistocene Desiccation of Lake Victoria and Rapid Evolution of Cichlid Fishes. Science 273:1091–1093.

Keding, Birgit, 1998 The Yellow Nile: New Data on Settlement and the Environment in the Sudanese Eastern Sahara. Sudan & Nubia 2:2–12.

Kjekshus, Helge, 1977 Ecology Control and Economic Development in East African History. Berkeley: University of California Press.

Klein, Richard G., 1984 The Prehistory of Stone Age Herders in South Africa. *In* From Hunters to Farmers: The Causes and Consequences of Food Production in Africa. J. Desmond Clark and Steven A. Brandt, eds. pp. 281–289. Berkeley: University of California Press.

Klein, Richard G., and K. Scott, 1986 Re-analysis of Faunal Assemblages from the Haua Fteah and Other Late Quaternary Archaeological Sites in Cyrenaican Libya. Journal of Archaeological Science 13:515–542.

Koch, Christopher P., 1994 The Jaragole Mortuary Tradition: New Light on Pastoral Neolithic Burial Practices: Presented at the South Africa Archaeological Association Annual Meetings.

Krzyzaniak, L., 1978 New Light on Early Food Production in the Central Sudan. Journal of African History 19:159–172.

Le Quellec, Jean-Loïc, 1998 Art Rupestre et préhistoire du Sahara. Le Messak Libyen. Paris: Éditions Payot et Rivages.

Lhote, Henri, 1976 Vers d'autres Tassilis. Paris: Arthaud.

Loftus, Ronan T., David E. MacHugh, L. O. Ngere, D. S. Balian, A. M. Badi, Daniel G. Bradley, and R. Patrick Cunningham, 1994 Evidence for Two Independent Domestications of Cattle. Proceedings of the National Academy of Sciences of the United States of America 91(7):2757–2761.

Lubell, David, Peter Sheppard, and Mary Jackes, 1984 Continuity in the Epipaleolithic of Northern Africa with Emphasis on the Maghreb. *In* Advances in World Archaeology, vol. 3. Fred Wendorf and Angela E. Close, eds. pp. 143–192. New York: Academic Press.

Luikart, Gordon, Ludovic Gielly, Laurent Excoffer, Jean-Denis Vigne, Jean Bouvet, and Pierre Taberlet, 2001 Multiple Materials Origins and Weak Phylogeographic Structure in Domestic Goats. Proceedings of the National Academy of Sciences 98(10):5927–5932.

Lupo, Karen D., and Dave N. Schmitt, 1997 Experiments in Bone Boiling: Nutritional Returns and Archaeological Reflections. Anthropozoolgica 25–26:137–144.

MacDonald, Kevin C., 2000 The Origins of African Livestock: Indigenous or Imported? *In* The Origins and Development of African Livestock: Archaeology, Genetics, Linguistics, and Ethnography. Roger M. Blench and Kevin C. MacDonald, eds. pp. 2–17. London: University College London Press.

McDonald, Mary M. A., 1998 Early African Pastoralism: View from Dakhleh Oasis (South Central Egypt). Journal of Anthropological Archaeology 17(2):124–142.

MacHugh, David E., Mark D. Shriver, Ronan T. Loftus, Patrick Cunningham, and Daniel G. Bradley, 1997 Microsatellite DNA Variation and the Evolution, Domestication, and Phylogeography of Taurine and Zebu Cattle (*Bos taurus* and *Bos indicus*). Genetics 146:1071–1086.

Maley, J., 1993 The Climatic and Vegetational History of the Equatorial Regions of Africa during the Upper Quaternary. *In* The Archaeology of Africa: Foods, Metals, and Towns. Thurstan Shaw, Paul Sinclair, Bassey Andah, and Alex Okpoko, eds. pp. 43–60. London: Routledge.

Marks, Anthony E., Joel L. Shiner, and T. R. Hays, 1968 Survey and Excavations in the Dongola Reach, Sudan. Current Anthropology 9:319–323.

Marshall, Fiona B., 1986 Aspects of the Advent of Pastoral Economies in East Africa. Ph.D. dissertation, Department of Anthropology, University of California, Berkeley.

——1990 Origins of Specialized Pastoral Production in East Africa. American Anthropologist 92:873–894.

——1998 Early Food Production in Africa. The Review of Archaeology 19(2):47–59.

——2000 The Origins and Spread of Domestic Animals in East Africa. In The Origins and Development of African Livestock: Archaeology, Genetics, Linguistics, and Ethnography. Roger M. Blench and Kevin C. MacDonald, eds. pp. 191–221. London: University College London Press.

Marshall, Fiona B., and Elisabeth Hildebrand, 2002 Cattle before Crops: The Beginning of Food Production in Africa. Journal of World Prehistory 16:99–143.

Marshall, Fiona B., John W. Barthelme, and Kathlyn Stewart, 1984 Early Domestic Stock at Dongodien. Azania 19:120–127.

Mehlman, Michael J., 1977 Excavations at Nasera Rock, Tanzania. Azania 12:111–118.

——1989 Late Quaternary Archaeological Sequences in Northern Tanzania. Ph.D. dissertation, Department of Anthropology, University of Illinois, Urbana-Champaign.

Meillasoux, Claude, 1972 On the Mode of Production of the Hunting Band. In French Perspectives on African Studies. P. Alexandre, ed. pp. 39–58. Oxford: Oxford University Press.

Munson, Patrick J., 1976 Archaeological Data on the Origins of Cultivation in the Southwestern Sahara and their Implications for West Africa. In Origins of African Plant Domestication. Jack R. Harlan, Jan M. J. de Wet, and Ann B. L. Stemler, eds. pp. 187–209. The Hague: Mouton.

Nelson, Charles M., 1993 Towards Understanding Trade and Social Structure in an Early Pastoral Neolithic Community in the Lake Turkana Basin. World Archaeological Congress Intersession, Mombasa, Kenya, 1993.

Oftedal, Olav T., 1984 Milk Composition, Milk Yield, and Energy Output at Peak Lactation: A Comparative Review. Zoological Society of London Symposia 1984:33–86.

Paris, François, 2000 African Livestock Remains from Saharan Mortuary Contexts. In The Origins and Development of African Livestock. Archaeology, Genetics, Linguistics, and Ethnography. Roger M. Blench and Kevin C. MacDonald, eds. pp. 111–126. London: University College London Press.

Percival, Arthur Blayney, 1924 A Game Ranger's Note Book. London: Nisbet.

——1928 A Game Ranger on Safari. London: Nisbet.

Peters, Joris, 1992 Late Quaternary Mammalian Remains from Central and Eastern Sudan and their Palaeoenvironmental Significance. Palaeoecology of Africa and the Surrounding Islands 23:91–115.

Petit-Maire, Nicole, 1989 Interglacial Environments in Presently Hyperarid Sahara: Palaeoclimatic Implications. In Paleoclimatology and Paleometeorology: Modern and Past Patterns of Global Atmospheric Transport. M. Leinen and M. Sarnthein, eds. pp. 637–661. Dordrecht: Kluwer Academic.

Phillipson, David W., 1977 Lowasera. Azania 12:1–32.

Pratt, D. J., and M. D. Gwynne, 1977 Rangeland Management and Ecology in East Africa. London: Hodder & Stoughton.

Raimbault, M., C. Guerin, and M. Faure, 1987 Les Vertébrés du gisement de Kobadi (Mali). ArchaeoZoologia I(2):219–238.

Richardson, J. L., 1972 Paleolimnological Records from Rift Lakes in Central Kenya. Palaeoecology of Africa 6:131–136.

Richardson, Jonathan L., and A. E. Richardson, 1972 The History of an East Africa Rift Lake and its Paleoclimatic Implications. Ecological Monographs 42:499–534.

Robbins, Lawrence H., 1972 Archaeology in the Turkana District, Kenya. Science 176: 359–366.

——1980 Lopoy and Lothagam. Publications of the Michigan State University Museum, vol. 3, nos. 1 and 2. East Lansing: Michigan State University.

Robertshaw, Peter T., 1988 Environment and Culture in the Late Quaternary of Eastern Africa: A Critique of Some Correlations. In Prehistoric Cultures and Environment in the Late Quaternary of Africa. John Bower and David Lubbell, eds. pp. 115–126. Cambridge Monographs in African Archaeology. BAR International Series, 26. Cambridge: British Archaeological Reports.

——1990 Early Pastoralists of South-Western Kenya. Nairobi: British Institute in Eastern Africa.

Roset, Jean-Pierre, 1987 Néolithisation, néolithique et post-néolithique au Niger nord-oriental. Bulletin de l'Association Française pour l'Étude du Quaternaire 24(32):203–214.

Roubet, Colette, 1979 La Faune consommée dans la Grotte Capeletti. In Économie pas-torale préagricole en Algérie orientale: Le Néolithique de Tradition Capsienne, exemple: l'Aurès. C. Roubet, ed. pp. 383–520. Études d'Antiquités Africaines. Paris: Éditions du Centre National de la Recherche Scientifique.

Rowley-Conwy, Peter, 1988 The Camel in the Nile Valley: New Radiocarbon Accelerator (AMS) Dates from Qasr Ibrim. Journal of Egyptian Archaeology 74:245–248.

Sadr, Karim, 1991 The Development of Nomadism in Ancient Northeast Africa. Philadel-phia: University of Pennsylvania Press.

——2002 Ancient Pastoralists in the Sudan and in South Africa. In Tides of the Desert-Gezeiten der Wüste. Contributions to the Archaeology and Environmental History of Africa in Honour of Rudolph Kuper. Tilman Lenssen-Erz, et al., eds. pp. 471–484. Africa Praehistorica 14. Cologne: Heinrich Barth Institut.

Sadr, Karim, and Ina Plug, 2001 Faunal Remains in the Transition from Hunting to Herding in Southeastern Botswana. South African Archaeological Bulletin 56(173 and 174):76–82.

Sealy, Judith, and Royden Yates, 1994 The Chronology of the Introduction of Pastoralism to the Cape, South Africa. Antiquity 68:58–67.

————1996 Direct Radiocarbon Dating of Early Sheep Bones: Two Further Results. South African Archaeological Bulletin 51(164):109–110.

Shahack-Gross, Ruth, Fiona B. Marshall, and Steve Weiner, 2002 Geo-Ethnoarchaeology of Pastoral Sites: The Identification of Livestock Enclosures in Abandoned Maasaid Settle-ments. Journal of Archaeological Science 29:1–21.

Sherratt, A., 1983 The Secondary Exploitation of Animals in the Old World. World Archae-ology 15(1):90–104.

Sinclair, Paul, Thurstan Shaw, and Bassey Andah, 1993 Introduction. In The Archaeology of Africa: Foods, Metals, and Towns. Thurstan Shaw, Paul Sinclair, Bassey Andah, and Alex Okpoko, eds. pp. 1–31. London: Routledge.

Smith, Andrew B., 1980 Domesticated Cattle in the Sahara and their Introduction into West Africa. In The Sahara and the Nile: Quaternary Environments and Prehistoric Occupa-tion in Northern Africa. Martin A. J. Williams and H. Faure, eds. pp. 489–501. Rotter-dam: Balkema.

——1984 Origins of the Neolithic in the Sahara. In From Hunters to Farmers: The Causes and Consequences of Food Production in Africa. J. Desmond Clark and Steven A. Brandt, eds. pp. 84–92. Berkeley: University of California Press.

——1986 Review Article: Cattle Domestication in North Africa. The African Archaeologi-cal Review 4:127–203.

——1989 The Near Eastern Connection: Early to Mid-Holocene Relations between North

African and the Levant. *In* Late Prehistory of the Nile Basin and the Sahara. L. Krzyza-niak and M. Kobusiewicz, eds. pp. 69–77. Poznan: Polish Academy of Science.

——1992 Pastoralism in Africa: Origins and Development Ecology. London: Hurst.

——2000 The Origins of the Domestic Animals of Southern Africa. *In* The Origins and Development of African Livestock. Archaeology, Genetics, Linguistics, and Ethnography. Roger M. Blench and Kevin C. MacDonald, eds. pp. 222–238. London: University College London Press.

Smith, Bruce D., 1995 The Emergence of Agriculture. New York: W. H. Freeman.

Stahl, Ann B., 1993 Intensification in the West African Late Stone Age: A View from Central Ghana. *In* The Archaeology of Africa. Food, Metals and Towns. Thurstan Shaw, Paul Sinclair, Bassey Andah, and Alex Okpoko, eds. pp. 261–273. New York: Routledge.

——1999 Perceiving Variability in Time and Space: The Evolutionary Mapping of African Societies. *In* Beyond Chiefdoms: Pathways to Complexity in Africa. Susan Keech McIntosh, ed. pp. 39–55. Cambridge: Cambridge University Press.

Stenning, Derrick J., 1959 Savannah Nomads: A Study of the Wodaabe Pastoral Fulani of Western Bornu Province, Northern Region, Nigeria. London: Oxford University Press.

Stiles, Daniel, 1981 Hunters of the Northern East African Coast: Origins and Historical Processes. Africa 51:848–862.

Tigani el Mahi, A., 1988 Zooarchaeology of the Middle Nile Valley. A Study of Four Neolithic Sites near Khartoum. BAR International Series, 418. Oxford: British Archaeological Reports.

Tixier, Jacques, 1962 Le "Ténéréen de l'Adrar Bous III. *In* Mission Berliet Ténéré-Tchad. H. J. Hugot, ed. pp. 333–348. Paris: AMG.

van Neer, Wim, and Hans-Peter Uerpmann, 1989 Palaeoecological Significance of the Faunal Remains of the B.O.S. Missions. Africa Praehistorica 2:308–341.

Vermeersch, P. M., P. van Peer, J. Moyersons, and Willem van Neer, 1994 Sodmein Cave, Red Sea Mountains (Egypt). Sahara 6:31–40.

Voigt, Elizabeth, 1982 Ivory in the Early Iron Age of South Africa. Transvaal Museum Bulletin 18:17–20.

——1983 Mapungubwe: An Archaeological Interpretation of an Iron Age Community, vol. 1. Pretoria: Transvaal Museum.

Voigt, Elizabeth A., and K. R. Robinson, 1970 Faunal Remains from the Iron Age Sites of Matope Court, Namichimba and Chiku Faunal Remains from the Iron Age Sites of Matope Court, Public no. 8, 1970. Blantyre: Malawi Department of Antiquities.

von den Driesch, Angela, and Joachim Boessneck, 1985 Die Tierknochenfunde aus den neolithischen Siedlung von Merimde-Benisalame. Munich: Institut für Palänatomie, Domestikationsforschung und Geschichte der Tiermedizin der Universität München.

von Höhnel, Ludwig, 1968 Discovery of Lakes Rudolf and Stefanie: Frank Cass & Co. Ltd.

Wendorf, Fred, and Romuald Schild, 1976 Prehistory of the Nile Valley. New York: Academic Press.

——1980 Prehistory of the Eastern Sahara. New York: Academic Press.

——1998 Nabta Playa and its Role in Northeastern African Prehistory. Journal of Anthropological Archaeology 17(2):97–123.

Wendorf, Fred, Angela E. Close, and Romuald Schild, 1987 Early Domestic Cattle in the Eastern Sahara. *In* Palaeoecology of Africa. J. A. Coetzee, ed. pp. 441–448. Rotterdam: A. A. Balkema.

Western, David, and T. Dunne, 1979 Environmental Aspects of Settlement Site Decisions among the Pastoral Maasai Models, Analogies, and Theories. Human Ecology 31: 328–350.

Woodburn, James, 1986 African Hunter-Gatherer Social Organization: Is it Best Understood as a Product of Encapsulation? *In* Hunters and Gatherers: History, Evolution and Social Change. T. Ingold, D. Riches, and J. Woodburn, eds. pp. 31–65. New York: Berg.

Zvelebil, Marek, 1986 Mesolithic Societies and the Transition to Farming: Problems of Time, Scale and Organisation. *In* Hunters in Transition. Mesolithic Societies of Temperate Eurasia and their Transition to Farming. M. Zvelebil, ed. pp. 167–188. Cambridge: Cambridge University Press.

Zvelebil, Marek, and Peter Rowley-Conwy, 1984 Transition to Farming in Northern Europe: A Hunter-Gatherer Perspective. Norwegian Archaeological Review 17(2):104–128.

9

Holocene Occupations of the Forest and Savanna

Joanna Casey

The Holocene (from ca. 10000 b.p.) was a time of increasing diversity among the peoples of West and Central Africa. Although many populations shared a recognizably "Late Stone Age" (LSA) technology (Chapter 6), differences in the presence, absence, and proportions of tools, and the variety of environments in which they lived, speak of a multiplicity of lifestyles and subsistence strategies in shifting social and physical environments. Archaeologists have a tendency to regard these LSA peoples as in transition, poised between a prehistoric foraging existence and a commitment to farming characteristic of modern peoples. Regarding this era as a "phase" is detrimental to our understanding of West African prehistory because it perpetuates the "ages and stages" approach to culture change that dichotomizes foraging and farming as mutually exclusive categories of human existence. This has led to a fixation with establishing how close to "neolithic" any particular "transitional" culture may be. Direct evidence for domesticates has been extremely rare (Chapter 10), but researchers have assumed that a "neolithic package" of ground-stone tools, microliths, and ceramics signals the presence of farming. What is being missed in this rush to "neolithicize" the Holocene is the opportunity to investigate a lifeway in which the management of domesticated resources is only one of many options and does not inevitably, predictably, and irrevocably lead to a commitment to large-scale agriculture with everything that implies (Chapters 8, 10).

Our ideas about the African LSA are framed by assumptions about the nature of foraging and farming societies and how the move to food production took place. Our knowledge is based on hypotheses drawn from incomplete databases, and our interpretation shaped by shifting political and ideological orientations (Stahl 1999; Trigger 1989). Consequently, our ideas must be periodically reassessed as new information, and, more critically, new perspectives illuminate the archaeological record. Earlier hypotheses for the origins of agriculture were revolutionary in their day because they forced archaeologists and the wider populace to think differently about the implications of farming. Similarly, information about how foragers actu-

ally live was received as a revelation, changing forever the way in which we interpret hunter-gatherers in the past. Yet we perceive farming and foraging as mutually
exclusive categories, and, more insidiously, as points on an evolutionary continuum
which then guide interpretation (David and Sterner 1999). The archaeological
record does not always corroborate what we think we understand about the way
the world works, and the archaeological record of West and Central Africa presents
a particular challenge to these entrenched ideas. Although researchers have tended
to fit the data into the prevailing paradigm, the Holocene record of West and Central
Africa offers the opportunity to explore social and economic arrangements that defy
expectations based on what we know of the contemporary world, particularly those
in which foraging and farming coexist within complex economic strategies.

Frames of Reference: The Neolithic Revolution

Our understanding of the transition from hunting and gathering to farming has
largely been informed by research on Southwest Asian agricultural origins (Chapters 8, 10). The progressivist paradigm that dominates our ideas about the relationship between foraging and farming is rooted in the work of V. Gordon Childe
(1928, 1934, 1936), who envisioned the transition to farming in revolutionary
terms, and emphasized the quantum leap in human achievement that was possible
with an agricultural base. Childe's work prompted considerable research into agricultural origins world-wide, and his views informed numerous hypotheses directed
at explaining this revolutionary transition. Two theoretical positions have dominated
the subject (Stahl 1984a). The first, with roots in Childe, views agriculture as a
good idea that, as soon as "invented," spread rapidly as foragers became aware of
its possibilities (also Braidwood and Braidwood 1950, 1953; Ehrenberg 1989;
Kenyon 1960; MacNeish 1950, 1964; Mellaart 1958, 1962; Sauer 1952). The
second approach, which became popular between the 1960s and 1980s, took the
position that agriculture was a difficult, labor-intensive, and precarious existence
that people were forced into. Researchers looked to changes in the environment or
to ecological systems to explain the shift (Binford 1968; Cohen 1977; Flannery
1968, 1969; Hayden 1981; Rindos 1984). Although these positions differ in their
views regarding the costs and benefits of farming, they share the perspective that,
ultimately, everyone commits to agriculture whether by enlightenment or through
environmental pressures. Both scenarios assume that foraging ceases to be a viable
subsistence strategy – that foragers simply cease to be.

These hypotheses were supported by archaeological data from prehistoric
Europe and Southwest Asia, where the shift from the Paleolithic to the Neolithic
(via the Mesolithic or Epipaleolithic) coincided with the shift from hunting and
gathering to agriculture, and was associated with a predictable pattern in the development of technology. The smaller, more diverse toolkit of broad-spectrum hunter-
gatherers gave way to groundstone tools, grinding stones, and pottery associated
with agriculture. Agriculture developed from hunting and gathering in Southwest
Asia and spread to Europe in a series of migrations and diffusions. At some point

in this scenario, the Mesolithic/Epipaleolithic hunter-gatherers disappeared, wiped out by marauding farmers or converted to agriculture (Price, ed., 2000; Whittle 1996).

The use of ethnographic analogy has also contributed to the polarization of foragers and farmers. The "Man the Hunter" conference held in 1965 and subsequently published in 1968 (Lee and DeVore, eds., 1968) came at a moment when archaeologists were becoming more concerned with ecological relationships and evolutionary processes. The conference defined hunter-gatherers as a legitimate object of study, and archaeologists came to regard them as unproblematic representatives of a distant past characterized by clearly defined attributes. Archaeologists who studied the residues of hunter-gatherers were interested in ecological relationships, adaptation, and evolutionary processes, and they used the ethnographic record as their analogical base (Chapters 2, 6). The !Kung San of the Kalahari were consistently used as the template for the hunter-gatherer lifestyle because they were regarded as being among the most pristine of the foragers, and there was a vast literature on them (Chapter 14). Other researchers were concerned with the consequences of farming: population increase; trade relationships; social hierarchies; and innovations in material culture. Consequently the perceived gap between foragers and farmers exists in our reading of both the ethnographic and archaeological records, and is perpetuated by our research designs (see David and Sterner 1999; Stahl 1999).

Ironically, although the Man the Hunter conference was instrumental in entrenching the dichotomy between foraging and farming, participants at the conference repeatedly cautioned against the uncritical use of modern hunter-gatherers as analogs for prehistoric human behavior (Binford 1968; Clark et al. 1968). Modern hunter-gatherers live in marginal environments, whereas the archaeological remains of prehistoric hunter-gatherers are found in more optimal environments occupied today by modern farmlands and urban centers. Conference participants also made the point – one later made more eloquently in the often cited but rarely heeded paper by Wobst (1978) – that the archaeological record is the product of many kinds of sociocultural arrangements for which there are no modern analogs (David and Sterner 1999). These arrangements can only be known archaeologically, yet archaeologists appeal to uniformitarian principles of human behavior drawn from an incomplete record.

More recent literature focused the search for the causes of culture change on factors internal to the cultural system under investigation. Hypotheses regarding agriculture are less likely to emphasize circumstances beyond human control, and are more likely to consider the myriad social, political, and historical factors that contribute to subsistence decisions. Agriculture is not seen as inevitable, but rather the result of conscious choices made by human beings operating within social environments (Bender 1981; Hayden 1989; Hodder 1990; Marshall and Hildebrand 2002). Within this framework foraging and farming become points on a continuum, and the chasm between the two subsistence strategies populated by socially diverse peoples with varying relationships to wild and domestic resources (Chapters 8, 10).

The archaeological and ethnographic records are replete with examples of cultures situated somewhere between the poles of foraging and farming, including the aboriginal inhabitants of the northwest coast of North America the Archaic peoples of the American Southeast, and the Natufians of Southwest Asia. These societies displayed many of the social and material features that we consider characteristic of farmers long before they adopted domesticated plants and animals. Conversely, the ethnographic record abounds with examples of peoples who cultivate a limited number of crops or possess domestic animals, and rely extensively on wild resources (Linares 1976). Further blurring the boundary between foragers and farmers is the fact that most contemporary foragers live in contact with farmers and herders in relationships that are likely to be of considerable antiquity (Hart and Hart 1986; Headland and Reid 1989). Initially, these forager–farmer relationships were thought to have developed recently (Bailey and Headland 1991; Headland 1987), but new research and changing perspectives suggest that such arrangements are not unusual. In the Inland Niger Delta of Mali, fishers, pastoralists, and farmers long coexisted in a tripartite symbiotic subsistence arrangement (McIntosh 1997; McIntosh and McIntosh 1983; Sundström 1972), an arrangement foreshadowed millennia earlier when pastoralists entering the Méma region of Mali coexisted with fishers rather than vanquishing or amalgamating them (MacDonald and VanNeer 1994). The coexistence of people who possess domesticates with people who do not undermines absolutist perspectives on the origins of agriculture. Recent ethnoarchaeological studies aimed at illuminating the complex relationships between domestic and wild resources (e.g., D'Andrea et al. 1999; Marshall 2001; Marshall and Hildebrand 2002) are beginning to offer insights with important implications for the interpretation of archaeological sites. Agriculture clearly does not trump foraging every time, and evidently there was some escape from the environmental trap that forced people into farming against their will.

Recent research in Europe and Southwest Asia is demonstrating that the simplistic scenario for agricultural origins has masked the considerable complexity in the transition to farming. A closer reading of the archaeological record in Europe suggests that, far from disappearing, Mesolithic peoples were instrumental in the emergence of farming, and that during the transition, the European landscape supported, not always peacefully, a variety of communities with different commitments to hunting, gathering, and agriculture (e.g., Gronenborn 1999; Price, ed., 2000).

Central to this more nuanced approach to the relationship between foraging and farming is the concept of intensification. Intensification was originally conceived by Boserup (1965) in terms of increased inputs of capital, labor, and skills in order to increase the productivity of land so as to alleviate resource stress due to population pressure, and archaeologists have used the concept to model the origins of agriculture (Morrison 1994). Through time archaeologists have applied the term more broadly to mean visible increases in productivity and/or production, which may or may not be associated with agriculture (Bender 1981; Kaiser and Voytek 1983; Stahl 1989, 1993). An increase in productivity may be recognizable as an increase in attention to the facilities and tools that aid in the subsistence quest, evidence for increased trade relationships, increases in population, or elaboration of social roles. Such changes may signal the desire to assure the reliability of economic activities, or to increase production for social or other reasons. Intensification is a useful way to conceptualize the cultural forms that we see in the Mesolithic, Archaic, Epipaleolithic, and LSA because there is nothing inevitable about any outcome. The concept leaves room for a variety of cultural forms and orientations, only some of which lead to intensified relationships with domestic plants and animals. Other forms of intensification could be aimed at strengthening social relationships with neighboring groups to enhance economic ties, or at increasing the harvest and storage of wild plants to support larger populations, or to support small populations for longer periods of time. This approach encourages a more complex view of the archaeological record, enabling us to see it as diverse populations acting in terms of differing socio-political agendas and in response to different opportunities. Most importantly, it enables us to view such cultures as legitimate life ways in their own right rather than viewing them as in transition between two "less ambiguous" lifestyles.

The Neolithic Trinity

There has been considerable discussion about the use of the term "neolithic" as it applies to Africa (for a good summary see Sinclair et al. 1993). Though "neolithic" originally applied to the advent of the grinding as opposed to chipping technology (McCurdy 1924:156), Childe irrevocably wedded the Neolithic to agriculture when he coined the term "Neolithic Revolution." Since then it has taken on many shades of meaning and an ambiguity that has complicated our understanding of the transition to agriculture (e.g., Price, ed., 2000; Sinclair et al. 1993; Whittle 1996). The use of the term has largely been abandoned in West Africa with preference given to the term "Ceramic Late Stone Age" (McIntosh and McIntosh 1983; Shaw 1978–79; Sinclair et al. 1993; Chapter 7), but the ideas associated with it still persist – most significantly in the perception that particular tool types can be used as signs that agriculture was present.

In Anglophone West Africa, groundstone tools, microliths, and ceramics are markers of the "neolithic" (Ellis 1980:124). Holocene archaeological sites are often classified in terms of their presence or absence, implying a direct connection between these tool types and the advent of farming. There is nothing about any of these tools that is inherently linked to agriculture, and it is not farming so much as reduced mobility that increases the need and opportunity for, and the visibility of, these items. It is imperative, therefore, that we decouple the tool types from our ideas about a commitment to agriculture. Significantly, in Francophone West Africa, the term "neolithic" refers only to changes in technology and therefore does not have the same "revolutionary" implications as it does in Anglophone West Africa (Sinclair et al. 1993). Rather, the French emphasize the process of adopting food production, and the technological changes that accompany the process are not seen as singular. Consequently, technological change is seen as neither driving nor indicating the move toward food production (Camps 1974; Roubet 1968, 1979).

Ever since groundstone tools came to imply the presence of farming, researchers have sought to explain them and their associations with other artifacts in terms of agriculturally related activities. The most diagnostic tool is the groundstone ax – a tool with a ground blade typically made from metamorphosed volcanic material. Ground stone tools occur in many parts of the world where farming never developed, and they often predate farming in areas where it did (Hayden 1989). The significant association appears to be between groundstone tools and woodworking (Hayden 1989), so the presence of groundstone tools likely signifies an increased need for fuel, or the production of perishable wooden artifacts such as watercraft, weirs and architectural components. Sedentism and farming may increase the need for fuel and items made of wood, and consequently increase the numbers of groundstone tools in the archaeological record, but the tools themselves are not restricted to agricultural applications. While some groundstone tools were most certainly used for felling trees (Tessman 1923, cited in Lavachery 2001), ethnographic and use-wear studies of bladed groundstone tools from around the world indicate that they are versatile tools that can be used in a variety of ways (Semenov 1985) and it is likely that they fulfilled multiple functions (Casey 2000). MacDonald (1998) links the appearance of tiny groundstone axes, or *hachettes*, to the appearance of pastoralists in the Sahara and suggests that these items functioned more as currency or durable expressions of cattle wealth.

Geometric microliths come in a variety of shapes, but they have at least one sharp edge, with the opposite edge or edges steeply backed by retouching (Chapter 6). In northern Africa and Southwest Asia they are made from blades, are highly standardized, and often appear in such profusion that the percentages of different types are used to define archaeological complexes (Bar Yosef 1981; Henry 1982; Sheppard 1987). They are thought to have been used primarily as parts of composite tools – hafted singly or in sequence in wood or bone handles and used as projectiles or cutting implements (e.g., Clark and Prince 1978; Mitchell 1988; Phillipson 1980). Many specimens from Southwest Asia display sickle gloss, which has been taken to indicate intensive harvesting of grasses with sickles (e.g., Henry 1989), with important implications for the origins of farming.

Microliths appear very much earlier in Africa than they do in Europe and Asia. The earliest known appearance is around 40,000 years ago (ky) at Matupi Cave in Central Africa (Van Noten 1977, 1982), around 30 ky at Shum Laka in Cameroon (Cornelissen 1996, 2003) and around 18 ky at Ishango in the Democratic Republic of Congo (Brooks and Smith 1987; Brooks et al. 1995). Geometric microliths in sub-Saharan West Africa are less standardized than their northern counterparts due in part to the lithic raw materials from which they are made (Phillipson 1993). Quartz only rarely lends itself to the manufacture of blades, while microliths made from fine-grained materials are often made on smaller chips and chunks from flaking small nodules and tabular pieces (Casey 2000). Sickle gloss has only rarely been found on sub-Saharan West African microliths (Shaw and Daniels 1984), but the grain crops that are currently the most important in West and Central Africa

are not harvested with sickles. Whole seed heads are broken off, often over a relatively blunt instrument. It is likely that geometric microliths had many purposes
besides grass seed harvesting (McIntosh and McIntosh 1983:236; Stahl 1993), and
that in sub-Saharan Africa their presence should not been seen as a precursor to
farming.

Pottery is the third component of the African Neolithic trinity. Ceramics are
certainly useful in agricultural contexts because they facilitate the preparation
and storage of grains. Where they are made and used, ceramic vessels of all shapes
and sizes perform a multiplicity of functions and, with their propensity to break
and their resistance to decay, ceramic sherds dominate the remains of farming
peoples. However, the manufacture and use of ceramics is not restricted to farming
peoples (Chapter 7). Farming predates the appearance of ceramics in Southwest
Asia, and in many parts of Africa ceramics are present millennia before evidence
for farming. The more compelling association worldwide is between ceramics and
sedentism. In Africa ceramics appear first in the Sahara around 9.5 ky (Barich 1987;
Roset 1987), and they are used extensively throughout the Holocene by many
peoples for whom food production has never been demonstrated (Muzzolini 1993;
Chapter 7). When people settle into semi-permanent communities they have an
increased ability and need to take advantage of technologies such as ceramics.
Pottery enables people to boil foods for long periods of time to soften them, rid
them of toxins, or otherwise render them palatable, and they can also be used to
prepare wet foods such as sauces, soups, stews, and porridges. All of this must have
dramatically increased the subsistence base of foragers and given them access to a
wide variety of nutrients (Stahl 1984b, 1989, 1993, 1994). Such a technological
advance is likely one of the things that made sedentism possible by enabling people
to stay longer after first-choice foods had been exploited, and encouraging the collection of resources that could be stored and processed later.

Much of what I have discussed to this point has been based on ethnographic
sources or working assumptions about the nature of hunting, gathering, and agriculture. The archaeological evidence does not necessarily fit expectations drawn
from these narrowly focused sets of observations and ideas. Rather, it challenges us
to think more broadly about the relationships between people, plants, and animals.

Archaeological Evidence

Relatively few Holocene sites in West and Central Africa have been thoroughly
investigated or published, so the generalizations offered here are necessarily tentative. The evidence that is emerging indicates a complex series of events that makes
it difficult to define the period on the basis of technology beyond a general incli-
nation toward smaller chipped stone industries, but there are exceptions even to
this. With so few sites investigated we cannot know how individual sites relate to
whole complexes. For example, small sites and rockshelters may indicate special-
purpose loci whose artifacts and organic remains do not necessarily represent the
wider complex (Chapter 6).

The environmental changes that occurred at the end of the Pleistocene and throughout the Holocene had a significant impact on the opportunities for human occupation in many parts of Africa, and they also shape the way that archaeologists operating under ecological or adaptationist paradigms read the archaeological record. Contemporary West African vegetation ranges from rainforests through drier types of forests and savannas up to the edge of the Sahara. The changes that occurred in West Africa during and after the last glaciation were complex, and varied in intensity throughout the region (see Chapter 8 for details). Climatic events in the Sahara are of interest to West and Central African prehistory because during the arid phases people appear to have evacuated the Sahara, and sub-Saharan Africa is one logical destination. There is no evidence for a large-scale migration out of the Sahara at any point in prehistory, although the Jos Plateau in Nigeria (Soper 1965) and the Grassfields region of Cameroon (Lavachery 2001) have been proposed as refugia during periods of aridity. Similarities in ceramic and lithic styles in later periods suggest affiliations between the desert and areas south of the Sahara, but it is the perceived nature of this relationship that is critical to our understanding of these events (Chapter 10).

The conventional view is that there was little human occupation in West or Central Africa prior to the Late Holocene. Potential Early and Middle Stone Age materials have been found primarily in surface and/or undated contexts (Casey 2003). Sites that can be verified are few and far between, giving the impression that only scattered bands of intrepid, mobile hunter-gatherers were capable of braving the challenges of the sub-Saharan environments – and then, only for short periods during the Pleistocene. There is considerably more evidence during the Holocene, but sites are predominantly small, again suggesting temporary occupation by small, mobile bands. Endemic diseases have been suggested as detrimental to human occupation (Shaw 1977, 1981), as has the impenetrability of the rainforests prior to the advent of ironworking and/or farming (Bailey and Headland 1991; Davies 1964, 1967; Headland 1987; Shaw 1978).

In West Africa, stratified sites dated between 13 and 5 ky contain flaked stone and microliths overlaid by industries with microliths, groundstone tools, and ceramics after 5 ky. The best known of these sites are: Rim (Andah 1979) and Maadaga (Breunig and Wotzka 1993), both in Burkina Faso; Rop (Eyo 1972), Iwo Eleru (Shaw and Daniels 1984), Afikpo (Andah and Anozie 1980; Hartle 1980), Dutzen Kongba (Federal Department of Antiquities Nigeria 1974; York 1978), and Mejiro Cave (Willett 1962) in Nigeria; and Kourounkorokalé (MacDonald 1997) in Mali (Figure 9.1). Elsewhere in West Africa, sites similar to the upper levels of these stratified sites contain numerous small flakes, flake tools, and/or microliths and are usually associated with groundstone tools, and/or ceramics. Bosumpra in central Ghana is the best known of these (Shaw 1944). It has a microlithic quartz industry with ceramics dating to 5330 ± 100 b.p. (Smith 1975). In Sierra Leone, Yengema, Yagala, and Kamabai contain a similar industry without microliths (Atherton 1972; Coon 1968); Sopie and Kokasu in Liberia contain quartz microliths and pottery, but no groundstone tools (Gabel 1976). Other sites include Sumpa in Cameroon (David 1980); Agarade Rockshelter in Togo (de Barros 1992);

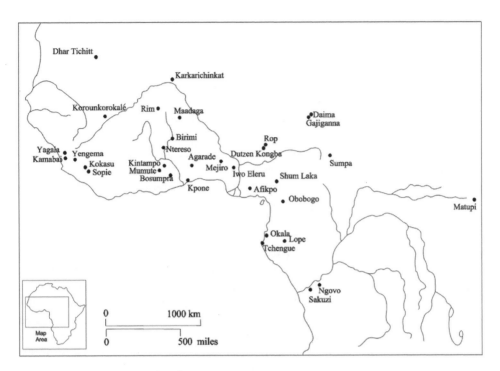

Figure 9.1. Sites mentioned in the text

Kpone in Ghana (Dombrowski 1977; Nygaard and Talbot 1977); and a series of sites on the coast of Côte d'Ivoire (Chenorkian 1983).

In Central Africa there has been less research, so patterns are even more difficult to discern; however, a main difference between Central and West Africa is that ceramics are always associated with settlements in Central Africa (Eggert 1993). Eggert (1993) suggests that ideas about the Bantu expansion, which supposedly brought ceramics, settlement, farming, and ironworking as a package to Central and southern Africa, have confused the issue by encouraging researchers to interpret settlements with pottery as part of that widespread complex (Chapter 12). Prior to the appearance of settlements, Central Africa had an extremely long LSA sequence, beginning with an early microlithic presence (see also Mercader 2003; Mercader and Marti 2003). Shum Laka, located on the border of what is conventionally considered to be West and Central Africa, has produced a continuous sequence of seven occupations from 30 ky through the Iron Age (Cornelissen 1996, 2003; de Maret 1996; Lavachery 1996, 2001; Moeyersons et al. 1996). Unlike the sequence in West Africa, lithics at Shum Laka increased in size through time. Blades and waisted axes made from basalt became more common (Lavachery 1996, 2001). This macrolithic (MacDonald and Allsworth-Jones 1994) trend, dating to between 5500 and 3500 b.p., has also been found at nearby sites such as Abeke (de Maret et al. 1987), Mbi Crater, and Fiye Nkwi (Asombang 1988) in Cameroon, and Ezi-Ukwu Ukpa (Hartle 1980) in Nigeria. Lavachery (2001) suggests that this is a regional development that may be related to an influx of migrants due to the onset of aridity in the Sahara.

Central Africa appears to move from the Pleistocene to the Iron Age without passing through a "neolithic" stage of either complex hunter-gatherers or incipient farmers (Mercader and Brooks 2001). The term "Stone to Metal Age" (SMA) has been proposed as a temporary label for this period in order to avoid the implications of the term "neolithic" (Lavachery 1996). Clist (1986) has been particularly critical of using groundstone tools to imply a "neolithic" lifestyle, demonstrating that these tools are found in LSA contexts, and that they continue into the Iron Age (Eggert 1993). Ground stone tools and pottery, without evidence for food production or ironworking, appear at several sites in Central Africa: Obobogo (Clist 1986) in Cameroon; Okala, Lopé, and Tchengué in Gabon (Clist 1987, 1989; Peyrot and Osisly 1986, 1990); and Ngovo and Sakuzi in the Democratic Republic of Congo (de Maret 1986). All these sites date to around 2400 to 2100 b.p., considerably later than their West African counterparts.

At Shum Laka, ceramics appear around 7 ky in association with a macrolithic technology and chipped stone axes with ground blades between 4000 and 3000 b.p. (Cornelissen 1996; Lavachery 2001). The earliest ceramics at Shum Laka consist of only four sherds, but stylistic and stratigraphic evidence argues against their having been intrusive. Ceramics are rare in all levels at Shum Laka, suggesting that the site was only ever occupied on a short-term basis (Lavachery 2001). Although they are considerably earlier than the majority of ceramic LSA sites, they are in line with dates on ceramics in the Sahara, and there are several sub-Saharan sites – notably the Punpun Phase levels at K6 rockshelter in Ghana (Stahl 1985) and Konduga in northern Nigeria (Breunig et al. 1996) – that contain ceramics dating to between 8 and 6 ky.

Subsistence information is lacking at most sites, but where present indicates a reliance on local wild resources. The exploitation of the oleaginous (oil-producing) plants oil palm (*Elaeis guineensis*) and *Canarium schweinfurthii* is of considerable antiquity in West and Central Africa, and they have often been cited as possible candidates for early plant management (Shaw 1976). Oil palm is currently an important resource in West Africa, where it is grown on plantations primarily for its oil. Oil palms require light, so their appearance in archaeological sites in the forest suggests that people may have been clearing land or otherwise encouraging their growth in open areas in the rainforest (Harlan et al. 1976). The sudden, dramatic rise in oil palm pollen at around 3000 b.p. seen in cores from Lake Bosumtwi in Central Ghana and on the Niger delta in Nigeria (Sowunmi 1981, 1985; Talbot et al. 1984) has lent support for the idea of incipient arboriculture. It must be remembered, however, that natural phenomena such as landslides and tree falls can open large areas in the canopy and provide a suitable environment for oil palm seeds that could have been brought into the area in the digestive tracts of animals, or by human activity. *Canarium schweinfurthii* also occurs at many of these sites, often appearing earlier than oil palm. Its requirements are somewhat more flexible and it thrives under many more kinds of conditions. *Canarium* has been dated as far back as 10 ky at archaeological sites in the Ituri rainforest, where modern for-

agers continue to exploit it today, along with oil palm (Mercader 2003). At Shum
Laka *Canarium* occurs first in a layer dated to 7000–6000 b.p., but increases dramatically in importance in the ceramic LSA and Iron Age deposits while hunting
declines (Lavachery 2001). Although archaeologists have become very excited
about the potential of these plants for indicating the management and control of
resources, the long history of their use and their continued use by modern foragers
also points out their importance as a resource for non-farming peoples. Both are
found most frequently in rockshelters (e.g., K6, Bosumpra, Sopie, Kokasu, Shum
Laka, Lopé, Ngovo) where optimal preservational conditions have certainly been a
factor in their recovery, but it is also worth considering that these were good
resources for people on the move (see also Eggert 1993). Rockshelters are often
repeatedly occupied, temporary accommodations rather than permanent sites;
therefore, it is likely that the plant and animal remains recovered from them represent the exploitation of local resources. Rather than conceiving of management
and control over resources as leading inexorably to settlement and agriculture,
perhaps it is useful to consider alternative approaches to resource management that
would permit the enhancement of local resources without significantly altering successful subsistence routines. For example, simple strategies such as avoiding wild
stands of particular plant species before they are fully ripe, doing minor clearing
around species that could potentially be damaged by bush fires, or starting bush
fires to encourage the growth of new leaves could enhance secondary resources and
add significantly to the resource base without causing undue stress on a system
aimed at the procurement of other, preferred resources. In the case of rockshelters,
which may be occupied annually or at regular intervals, there would be a distinct
advantage to manipulating the flora in the immediate vicinity in order to insure the
presence of useful species (Marshall and Hildebrand 2002).

The first evidence for decreased residential mobility in sub-Saharan West Africa
occurs between 4 and 3 ky, associated with what we now know as the Kintampo
complex. The Kintampo complex is known only from Ghana, although some
Kintampo artifacts have been found in the neighboring countries of Togo and Côte
d'Ivoire. Dates for the Kintampo Complex range from around 4000 b.p. to around
2000 b.p., but most cluster around 3500 b.p. (Stahl 1985). Kintampo has the complete "neolithic" package – groundstone tools, ceramics, and often microliths.
Kintampo has a distinctly ceramic LSA artifact assemblage, but as Stahl (1985,
1986, 1993, 1994) has pointed out, it differs from its predecessors and contemporaries in several significant ways. Larger sites with evidence for permanent or semi-
permanent structures indicate a decrease in residential mobility. Interregional trade
networks are evident in the form of exotic materials, and there is decorative art
including figurines, beads, and bracelets. The presence of domesticates, an increase
in wild fauna associated with cleared areas and settlements, and an increase in the
variety and amount of ceramics and grinding stones indicate changes in subsistence
and processing activities. Kintampo presents an almost classic case for intensification (Stahl 1993).

Initially, Kintampo appeared to stand alone in West Africa, separated in time and
space from anything remotely resembling it. Its appearance coincided with the final

desiccation of the desert, and Kintampo ceramics and lithics bore similarities to those known from the Sahara. Oliver Davies, who first discovered the "Kintampo Neolithic," and apparently operated under a Childean paradigm, pronounced it a migrant culture from the Sahara (Davies 1962, 1980). Although domestic plant and animal remains were not immediately apparent, their presence was assumed because the rest of the "neolithic" package was there.

Prior to the appearance of Kintampo, the Sahara was populated by hunter-gatherer-fishers settled around permanent water sources (Chapter 7). Pastoralists appeared around 6 ky (Clutton-Brock 1993; Gautier 1987; Smith 1992; Chapter 8). Cattle-keeping people at Dhar Tichitt in Mauritania and Karkarichinkat in Mali apparently increased their reliance on wild and later domestic millet coincident with the onset of aridity shortly after 4 ky (Amblard and Pernès 1989; cf. Holl 1985; Munson 1976; Smith 1980). The appearance of Kintampo so soon after the abandonment of Dhar Tichitt and Karkarichinkat led to the interpretation that these events were linked. This is not to imply that the people of Dhar Tichitt fled directly to Ghana, but that the pressures that encouraged them to turn to agriculture and ultimately to flee would have been experienced by everybody living in the Sahara at the time and may have prompted similar solutions and possibly resulted in movement toward the south (Smith 1980).

Most researchers have never really been happy with the suggestion that Kintampo is a product of straightforward migration from the north. At some sites there is evidence for continuity with previous phases, such as between Kintampo and the underlying Punpun Phase at the stratified rockshelters, K1 and K6 in central Ghana (Flight 1976; Stahl 1985). New dates continually push Kintampo farther back in time and bring non-Kintampo LSA sites throughout West Africa closer into its range. One of the most characteristic features of Kintampo was its versatility. Although initially thought to have been adapted to the forest/savanna ecotone (Davies 1962; Flight 1976; Posnansky 1984), Kintampo sites have been found in a variety of environments, and the people appear to have been very successful at exploiting local resources, suggesting an in situ development (Stahl 1985). Those material features that Kintampo appears to share with its Saharan counterparts are spread over a wide temporal and geographic area and are part of a vast, ceramic LSA manifestation (Muzzolini 1993; and see Chapter 7 for a similar argument regarding the so-called "Aqualithic" of the Sahara). In that sense, the ceramic and lithic styles that constitute evidence of shared origins are of a somewhat generalized nature. Influences from the Sahara are certainly likely, but the evidence for a wholesale migration is not clear.

Domestic plants and animals are present at very few Kintampo sites. The only hard evidence for domestic plants comes from Birimi in northern Ghana, where domestic millet has been found in a Kintampo context dating to between 3500 and 3000 b.p. (D'Andrea and Casey 2002; D'Andrea et al. 2001). Here, flotation samples were dominated by grains of pearl millet (*Pennisetum glaucum*) and possible pearl millet (cf. *P. glaucum*), with small quantities of wild grasses, other wild plants from the pea and nightshade families, and a quantity of unidentifiable broken seeds and seed fragments. The material argues for domestic millet cultivation at the site rather than having been brought in by trade because millet is the dominant grain at the site, and the low proportion of wild grass and weed seeds suggests that the millet came from uniform fields rather than stands of mixed grasses. The purity of the sample also suggests that the millet was harvested, as it is today, by breaking off individual compact seed heads rather than by harvesting en masse with a sickle (D'Andrea and Casey 2002; D'Andrea et al. 2001). This is the only direct evidence for domestic plants during Kintampo, but the likelihood of plants being cultivated during Kintampo times had earlier been suggested on ecological and other bases (Casey 1993, 2000; Davies 1968; Flight 1976; Posnansky 1984; Stahl 1985, 1986, 1993). Further south, speculation has focused on the cultivation of yams, although the low preservation potential of tubers made finding evidence unlikely (Davies 1960, 1962; Flight 1976; Posnansky 1984). The recovery of oil palm (*Elaeis guineensis*) remains from some Kintampo sites suggested that then, as now, people in central Ghana may have enjoyed the nutritional benefits of a diet based on cultivated yams and oil palms, and there has been speculation on the role that Kintampo peoples may have played in the husbandry of these trees (Harlan et al. 1976; Posnansky 1984:150). The recovery of tiny carbonized cowpeas (*Vigna unguiculata*) at K6 initially suggested that these might have been an early domesticate for the Kintampo peoples (Flight 1976), but further analysis (Stahl 1985) concluded that the recovered examples are more likely to be wild.

The best evidence for domestic animals has come from K6, where caprine remains have been recovered (Carter and Flight 1972; Flight 1976; Stahl 1985). As there are no wild progenitors in West Africa, there is no question that these are domestic animal remains. Sheep/goat bones come from three units in Stahl's excavations, but they could all have come from a single individual and could have been the result of a single butchering episode. Flight's excavation units were contiguous with Stahl's and it is possible that some of the bones from his excavations might also be from that same goat. Carter and Flight (1972) do not record the faunal remains by element, nor do they give bone counts or minimum numbers of individuals, but interpretation of their data along with Stahl's could represent a minimum of only two individuals. Carter and Flight (1972:280) reported a "mature mandibular tooth row," while epiphyses reported by Stahl suggested an immature goat. Consequently, two goats – one immature and one mature – are possible. Caprids have also been reported from Ntereso, but Davies (n.d.), indicates that there was so much disturbance at the site that it cannot be known for certain that the caprid bones actually pertain to the Kintampo deposits.

The evidence for domestic cattle is considerably less certain. Cattle bones have been reported at K6, Ntereso, and Mumute, but the wild or domestic status of these remains is in question. Only phlanges were sufficiently complete to enable metric analysis on the cattle bones recovered from K6. Specimens fell below the range for both wild and domestic cattle, and as there were no comparative specimens for African domestic dwarf cattle the results are inconclusive (Carter and Flight 1972; Flight 1976; Stahl 1985). The evidence from Mumute consists of tooth fragments cursorily identified by Andrew Smith as *Bos* of unknown status (Dombrowski 1976), and at Ntereso the only recovered bovid bone was from a disturbed context and provisionally identified as buffalo (*Syncerus*) (Carter and Flight 1972; Davies n.d.:52).

The evidence for domestic animals at Kintampo sites has evoked a surprisingly uncritical response from researchers working in other parts of West Africa (Casey 1998). This meager evidence has established Kintampo's credentials as an agropastoral complex such that Kintampo is entrenched in the archaeological literature as being an early site for the southward movement of domestic cattle (Breunig et al. 1996; Holl 1998; Smith 1992). Apart from this limited evidence, the earliest evidence for cattle south of the Sahara is found at Gajiganna and Daima in northern Nigeria at around 3000 b.p. (Breunig et al. 1996), somewhat later than the appearance of Kintampo. The presence of domestic plants and animals in Kintampo sites is certainly significant, but it is also significant that, wherever plant and animal remains have been recovered, wild species usually dominate. The desire to establish Kintampo as a fully self-sufficient agricultural complex on the basis of the few recovered domesticates deflects attention from some much more interesting questions, such as why the addition of domestic species may have been advantageous, and other questions that might lead us beyond explanations of migration and ecology. Furthermore, an emphasis on the domesticated species encourages us to downplay or even ignore the place of wild species that may have been at least as important, or even more important, in the subsistence regime (Chapter 10).

Today in the wooded savanna where the evidence for domestic millet has been found, it would be very difficult for a sizeable group of people to settle without a storable domestic staple because very little vegetable food is available during the dry season (Casey 1998, 2000). Adding a storable starchy staple to a diet that largely consists of wild foods would not only enable people to settle year-round in one place, but would also enhance foraging activity. The act of clearing fields, whether to encourage stands of wild grains or cultivate domestic grain, promotes the growth of volunteer plants that are today eaten as spinaches, some of which can be dried and stored. It also encourages small animal predators that are today easily caught with sticks, dogs, or traps by children and adults, and larger animals that are hunted, often at night, with arrows, spears, and guns (Casey 2000). The addition of a domestic crop may therefore actually increase foraging activity rather than rendering it obsolete, and may have been a reason why domesticates were adopted there in the first place. The question remains as to why people may have wanted or needed to settle down.

Stahl (1985) has suggested that the addition of livestock to the Kintampo economy may have reduced mobility and encouraged settlement; however, it is likely that a reduction in mobility came first. In the savanna environment, it is the presence of a storable staple that would have enabled settlement, not the addition of domestic animals. Animal protein is not a problem during the dry season, but carbohydrates are; consequently there would be little advantage to adding stock in the absence of a reliable dry season food. Pastoralists, of course, use their livestock to overcome periodic shortfalls in seasonal environments (Bernus 1979; Goldschmidt 1979; Swift 1981; White 1986), but they require a critical herd size in order to accomplish this (White 1986), and the evidence from Kintampo does not point to a true pastoralist lifestyle (Chapter 8) in any sense of the word.

Regardless of the status of the cattle bone in Kintampo sites, the addition of cattle to the economy is no small matter. Cattle are in direct competition with humans for their primary food source when humans rely on grains; consequently considerable effort must be made to insure that cattle are kept away from growing and ripening crops. Large herds of cattle would surely require some form of societal adjustment. Small numbers of cattle and small stock such as sheep and goats may be more manageable at the level of a small village, but one must ask what possible advantage there may be to keeping such potentially troublesome beasts. The standard answer is that livestock increases the subsistence base, but as killing animals quickly depletes a small herd, it is unlikely that small numbers of livestock would have been kept for their meat. Milk and cow's blood may also have been significant additions to village nutrition. The fact that neither of these products is used today in traditional sub-Saharan West Africa does not mean that they were not in the past, but does make one question why people stopped using them if they ever were. Today small stock are eaten on special occasions, but the primary advantage of keeping livestock both large and small is as a liquidatable asset that can be traded, sold, or given in times of need. Animals are one of the few resources that can increase in numbers and are therefore a good investment.

More interesting is to ask what kinds of social and political factors would have made the addition of animals to the economy either viable or desirable. One answer might be trade. The appearance of exotic materials and artifacts in Kintampo sites and similarities in projectile point and ceramic styles across a wide area probably signal robust trade and communication networks rather than loci of origin. Livestock may have been a critical resource in this trade, but the numbers found at Kintampo sites are so small that the possibility exists that, rather than Kintampo peoples keeping animals themselves, they may have obtained them in trade either whole or in parts, alive or preserved.

Although it has been established that Kintampo peoples had domestic plants and animals, this in no way allows us to project upon them all our clichéd assumptions about the "neolithic." Finding domestic plants and animals encourages us to become complacent about what we think we know about the "neolithic" rather than to examine what is really going on within the Kintampo area and its surrounding regions. There are much more interesting questions to be asked if we consider the diversity among Kintampo sites, and the similarities that they share with earlier, contemporaneous, and later sites throughout West Africa. Although domestic millet has been found at one Kintampo site, we do not yet know whether sites in other ecological zones oriented their subsistence activities around this or any other domestic crop. Given the ambiguous evidence at other sites, it is likely that there are much more interesting questions to be addressed concerning the variety of subsistence and economic strategies in which domesticates may have played different kinds of roles – even roles that transcend their nutritive properties. There are clear resonances between Kintampo and the Sahara, but questions regarding the nature of the relationship and its implications for robust communication networks and the social and political structures that they enable are considerably more compelling than simple assumptions about migration or deterministic environmental circumstances.

The tendency to conceptualize foraging and farming as separate steps on the evolutionary ladder has encouraged researchers to concentrate on establishing whether Holocene peoples were at one stage or another, rather than taking advantage of an opportunity to investigate lifeways with no modern parallel. Rather than atypical, David and Sterner (1999) encourage us to think of societies that do not fit the expected unilineal pattern as separate evolutionary lines – as evidence of types that may have once been common. The Holocene was undoubtedly a time of diversity, with changes in technology and subsistence creating new possibilities for social arrangements. Consequently it is imperative that we try to understand the archaeological data as we find them, and to recognize that the appearance of any particular technology will have different meanings and applications to people with different backgrounds and opportunities.

Diane Gifford-Gonzalez (2000) recently wrote that archaeologists expect major innovations to spread based on an assumption that their ubiquity in the present implies superiority over all precursors. This applies particularly to the origins of farming. Innovations never expand into blank spaces, and complex interactions occur between new phenomena and local strategies, such that the success of a new idea or technique depends on a variety of factors (Chapter 8). The appearance of livestock and domestic crops during the Kintampo period needs to be thought of in these terms. Ideas about farming were clearly circulating long before we have actual evidence for domestic crops, but the ways in which domesticates were or were not incorporated into existing LSA systems throughout West and Central Africa is the real subject for study. Kintampo offers an opportunity to investigate a complex socio-economic system of which domesticates were a part, but one in which hunting, gathering, fishing, and trade were also significant factors.

REFERENCES

Amblard, Sylvie, and Jean Pernès, 1989 The Identification of Cultivated Pearl Millet (*Pennisetum*) amongst Plant Impressions on Pottery from Oued Chebbi (Dhar Oualata, Mauritania). The African Archaeological Review 7:117–126.

Andah, Bassey, 1979 The Later Stone Age and Neolithic of Upper Volta Reviewed in a West African Context. West African Journal of Archaeology 9:85–117.

Andah, Bassey, and F. Anozie, 1980 Preliminary Report on the Prehistoric Site of Afikpo (Nigeria). West African Journal of Archaeology 10:83–102.

Asombang, Raymond, 1988 Bamenda in Prehistory: The Evidence from Fiye Nkwi, Mbi Crater and Shum Laka Rockshelters. Ph.D. dissertation, Institute of Archaeology, University of London.

Atherton, John H., 1972 Excavations at Kamabai and Yagala Rockshelters, Sierra Leone. West African Journal of Archaeology 2:39–74.

Bailey, R., and T. Headland, 1991 The Tropical Rainforest: Is It a Productive Environment for Human Foragers? Human Ecology 19(2):261–285.

Bar Yosef, Ofer, 1981 The Epi-Paleolithic Complexes in the Southern Levant. *In* Préhistoire du Levant. J. Cauvin and P. Sanlaville, eds. pp. 389–408. Paris: Éditions du CNRS.

Barich, Barbara, 1987 Archaeology and Environment in the Libyan Sahara: The Excavations in the Tadrart Acacus, 1978–1983. BAR International Series, 368. Oxford: British Archaeological Reports.

Bender, Barbara, 1981 Gatherer-Hunter Intensification. *In* Economic Archaeology. A. Sheridan and G. Bailey eds. pp. 149–157. BAR International Series, 96. Oxford: British Archaeological Reports.

Bernus, E., 1979 Le Contrôle du milieu naturel et du troupeau par les éleveurs touaregs sahéliens. *In* Pastoral Production and Society. L'Équipe, Écologie et Anthropologie des Sociétés Pastorales, ed. pp. 67–74. Cambridge: Cambridge University Press.

Binford, Lewis R., 1968 Methodological Considerations of the Archaeological Use of Ethnographic Data. *In* Man the Hunter. Richard B. Lee and Irven DeVore, eds. pp. 268–273. Chicago: Aldine.

Boserup, Ester, 1965 The Conditions of Agricultural Growth: The Economics of Agrarian Change Under Population Pressure. Chicago: Aldine.

Braidwood, R. J., and L. Braidwood, 1950 Jarmo: A Village of Early Farmers in Iraq. Antiquity 24:189–195.

————1953 The Earliest Village Communities in Southwest Asia. Journal of World History 1:278–310.

Breunig, Peter, Katharina Neumann, and Wim van Neer, 1996 New Research on the Holocene Settlement and Environment of the Chad Basin in Nigeria. African Archaeological Review 13:111–145.

Breunig, P., and Wotzka, H.-P., 1993 Archäologische Forschungen im südosten Burkina Fasos 1989/90: Vorbericht über die erste Grabungskampagne des Frankfurter Sonderforschungsbereiches 268 "westafrikanische savanne" Beiträge sur allgemeinen und vergleichenden Archäologie 11:145–187.

Brooks, Alison S., and Catherine C. Smith 1987 Ishango Revisited: New Age Determinations and Cultural Interpretations. The African Archaeological Review 5:65–78.

Brooks, Alison S., D. M. Helgren, J. S. Cramer, A. Franklin, W. Hornyak, J. M. Keating, Richard G. Klein, W. J. Rink, H. Schwarz, J. N. Leith Smith, K. Stewart, N. E. Todd, J. Verniers, and John E. Yellen, 1995 Dating and Context of Three Middle Stone Age Sites with Bone Points in the Upper Semliki Valley, Zaire. Science 268:548–552.

Camps, Gabriel, 1974 Les Civilisations préhistoriques de l'Afrique du Nord et du Sahara. Paris: Doin.

Carter, P. L., and Colin Flight, 1972 A Report on the Fauna from the Sites of Ntereso and Kintampo Rock Shelter Six in Ghana with Evidence for the Practice of Animal Husbandry during the Second Millennium BC. Man 7:277–282.

Casey, Joanna, 1993 The Kintampo Complex in Northern Ghana: Late Holocene Human Ecology on the Gambaga Escarpment. Ph.D. dissertation, Department of Anthropology, University of Toronto.

————1998 The Ecology of Food Production in West Africa. *In* Transformations in Africa: Essays on Africa's Later Past. Graham Connah, ed. pp. 46–70. London: Leicester University Press.

————2000 The Kintampo Complex: The Late Holocene on the Gambaga Escarpment, Northern Ghana. BAR International Series, 906. Oxford: Archaeopress.

————2003 The Archaeology of West Africa from the Pleistocene to the Mid-Holocene. *In* Under the Canopy. The Archaeology of Tropical Rainforests. Julio Mercader, ed. pp. 35–63. New Brunswick, NJ: Rutgers University Press.

Chenorkian, Robert, 1983 Ivory Coast Prehistory: Recent Developments. The African Archaeological Review 1:127–142.

Childe, V. Gordon, 1928 The Most Ancient East. London: Routledge & Kegan Paul.

——1934 New Light on the Most Ancient East: The Oriental Prelude to European Prehistory. London: Kegan Paul.

——1936 Man Makes Himself. London: Watts.

Clark, J. Desmond, and G. R. Prince, 1978 Use-Wear on Later Stone Age Microliths from Laga Oda, Haraghi, Ethiopia and Possible Functional Interpretations. Azania 13:101–110.

Clark, J. Desmond, Irven DeVore, F. Clark Howell, and Colin Turnbull, 1968 Discussion – The Use of Ethnography in Reconstructing the Past. In Man the Hunter. Richard B. Lee and Irven DeVore, eds. pp. 287–289. Chicago: Aldine.

Clist, Bernard 1986 Le Néolithique en Afrique centrale: État de la question et perspective d'avenir. L'Anthropologie 90:217–232.

——1987 Fieldwork in Gabon. Nyame Akuma 28:6–9.

——1989 Archaeology in Gabon. The African Archaeological Review 7:59–95.

Clutton-Brock, J., 1993 The Spread of Domestic Animals in Africa. In The Archaeology of Africa: Food, Metals and Towns. Thurstan Shaw, Paul Sinclair, Bassey Andah, and Alex Okpoko, eds. pp. 61–70. London: Routledge.

Cohen, Mark Nathan, 1977 The Food Crisis in Prehistory. New Haven: Yale University Press.

Coon, Carleton S., 1968 Yengema Cave Report. Philadelphia: University of Pennsylvania Museum.

Cornelissen, Els, 1996 Shum Laka (Cameroon): Late Pleistocene Deposits and Early Holocene Deposits. In Aspects of African Archaeology: Papers from the 10th Congress of the Pan-African Association for Prehistory and Related Studies. G. Pwiti and R. Soper eds. pp. 257–264. Harare: University of Zimbabwe Publications.

——2003 On Microlithic Quartz Industries at the End of the Pleistocene in Central Africa: The Evidence from Shum Laka (NW Cameroon). African Archaeological Review 20: 1–24.

D'Andrea, A. C., and Joanna Casey, 2002 Pearl Millet and Kintampo Subsistence. African Archaeological Review 19:147–172.

D'Andrea, A. C., M. Klee, and Joanna Casey, 2001 Archaeobotanical Evidence for Pearl Millet (Pennisetum glaucum) in Sub-Saharan West Africa. Antiquity 75:341–348.

D'Andrea, A. C., Diane Lyons, M. Haile, and A. Butler, 1999 Ethnoarchaeological Approaches to the Study of Prehistoric Agriculture in the Highlands of Ethiopia. In The Exploitation of Plant Resources in Ancient Africa. M. van der Veen, ed. pp. 101–122. Dordrecht: Kluwer Academic/Plenum Press.

David, Nicholas, 1980 History of Crops and Peoples in North Cameroon to AD 1900. In West African Culture Dynamics. B. K. Swartz, Jr. and Raymond E. Dumett, eds. pp. 139–182. The Hague: Mouton.

David, Nicholas, and Judy Sterner, 1999 Wonderful Society: The Burgess Shale Creatures, Mandara Polities, and the Nature of Prehistory. In Beyond Chiefdoms: Pathways to Complexity in Africa. Susan Keech McIntosh, ed. pp. 97–109. Cambridge: Cambridge University Press.

Davies, Oliver, 1960 The Neolithic Revolution in Tropical Africa. Transactions of the Historical Society of Ghana 4(2):14–20.

——1962 Neolithic Cultures of Ghana. In Actes du IV Congrès Panafricain de Préhistoire et de l'Étude du Quaternaire, Section III, Pré- et protohistoire. G. Mortlemans and J. Nenquin, eds. pp. 291–302. Tervuren: Musée Royal de l'Afrique Centrale.

——1964 The Quaternary in the Coastlands of Guinea. Glasgow: Jackson, Son & Co.

—— 1967 West Africa Before the Europeans. London: Methuen.

—— 1968 Mesoneolithic Excavations at Legon and New Todzi (Ghana). Bulletin de l'IFAN 30 series B no. 3:1147–1194.

—— 1980 The Ntereso Culture in Ghana. In West African Culture Dynamics. B. K. Swartz, Jr. and Raymond Dumett, eds. pp. 205–225. The Hague: Mouton.

—— n.d. Excavations at Ntereso, Gonja, Northern Ghana. Final Report. Unpublished manuscript (1973).

de Barros, Philip, 1992 Preliminary Report on Excavations at Agarade Rockshelter, Togo, West Africa. Unpublished paper presented at the 11th Biennial Society of Africanist Archaeologists Conference. March 26–29, 1992. Los Angeles, California.

de Maret, Pierre, 1986 The Ngovo Group: An Industry with Polished Stone Tools and Pottery in Lower Zaire. The African Archaeological Review 4:103–133.

—— 1996 Shum Laka (Cameroon): General Perspectives. In Aspects of African Archaeology. Papers from the 10th Congress of the Pan-African Association for Prehistory and Related Studies. Gilbert Pwiti and Robert Soper, eds. pp. 275–280. Harare: University of Zimbabwe Publications.

de Maret, Pierre, Bernard Clist, and W. van Neer 1987 Résultat des premières fouilles dans les abris de Shum Laka et d'Aeke au nord-ouest du Cameroun. L'Anthropologie 91(2):559–584

Dombrowski, Joanne C., 1976 Mumute and Bonoase – Two Sites of the Kintampo Industry. Sankofa 2:64–71.

—— 1977 Preliminary Note on Excavations at a Small Midden near Tema, Ghana. Nyame Akuma 10:31–34.

Eggert, Manfred K. H., 1993 Central Africa and the Archaeology of the Equatorial Rainforest: Reflections on Some Major Topics. In The Archaeology of Africa: Food, Metals and Towns. Thurstan Shaw, Paul Sinclair, Bassey Andah, and Alex Okpoko, eds. pp. 289–329. London: Routledge.

Ehrenberg, M., 1989 Women in Prehistory. Norman: University of Oklahoma Press.

Ellis, David V., 1980 Comments on the Advent of Plant Cultivation in West Africa. In West African Culture Dynamics. B. K. Swartz, Jr. and Raymond E. Dumett, eds. pp. 123–137. The Hague: Mouton.

Eyo, Ekpo, 1972 Rop Rock Shelter Excavations 1964. West African Journal of Archaeology 2:13–16.

Federal Department of Antiquities Nigeria (Archaeology Division), 1974 Excavations at Dutsen Kongba near Jos, Nigeria (Preliminary Notice). Nyame Akuma 4:7–20.

Flannery, Kent V., 1968 Archaeological Systems Theory and Early Mesoamerica. In Anthropological Archaeology in the Americas. Betty J. Meggers, ed. pp. 67–87. Washington, DC: Anthropological Society of Washington.

—— 1969 Origins and Ecological Effects of Early Domestication in Iran and the Near East. In The Domestication and Exploitation of Plants and Animals. Peter J. Ucko and G. W. Dimbleby, eds. pp. 73–100. London: Duckworth.

Flight, Colin 1976 The Kintampo Culture and its Place in the Economic Prehistory of West Africa. In Origins of African Plant Domestication. Jack R. Harlan, Jan M. J. DeWet, and Ann B. L. Stemler, eds. pp. 211–221. The Hague: Mouton.

Gabel, Creighton, 1976 Microlithic Occurrences in the Republic of Liberia. West African Journal of Archaeology 6:21–35.

Gautier, Achilles, 1987 Prehistoric Men and Cattle in North Africa: A Dearth of Data and a Surfeit of Models. In Prehistory of Arid North Africa. Angela E. Close, ed. pp. 163–187. Dallas: Southern Methodist University Press.

Gifford-Gonzalez, Diane, 2000 Animal Disease Challenges to the Emergence of Pastoralism in Sub-Saharan Africa. African Archaeological Review 17:95–139.

Goldschmidt, W., 1979 A General Model for Pastoral Social Systems. In Pastoral Production and Society. L'Équipe, Écologie et Anthropologie des Sociétés Pastorales, ed. pp. 15–27. Cambridge: Cambridge University Press.

Gronenborn, Detlef, 1999 A Variation on a Basic Theme: The Transition to Farming in South Central Europe. Journal of World Prehistory 12:123–210.

Harlan, Jack R., Jan M. J. DeWet, and Ann B. L. Stemler, 1976 Plant Domestication and Indigenous African Agriculture. In Origins of African Plant Domestication. Jack R. Harlan, Jan M. J. DeWet, and Ann B. L. Stemler, eds. pp. 3–19. The Hague: Mouton.

Hart, T., and J. Hart, 1986 The Ecological Basis of Hunter-Gatherer Subsistence in African Rainforests: The Mbuti of Eastern Zaire. Human Ecology 14(1):29–55.

Hartle, D. D., 1980 Archeology East of the Niger: A Review of Cultural-Historical Developments. In West African Culture Dynamics. B. K. Swartz, Jr. and Raymond E. Dumett, eds. pp. 195–203. The Hague: Mouton.

Hayden, Brian, 1981 Research and Development in the Stone Age: Technological Transitions among Hunter-Gatherers. Current Anthropology 22:519–548.

——1989 From Chopper to Celt: The Evolution of Resharpening. In Time, Energy and Stone Tools. Robin Torrence, ed. pp. 7–16. Cambridge: Cambridge University Press.

Headland, T., 1987 The Wild Yam Question: How Well Could Independent Hunter-Gatherers Live in a Tropical Rain Forest Ecosystem? Human Ecology 15:463–491.

Headland, T., and L. Reid 1989 Hunter-Gatherers and their Neighbors from Prehistory to the Present. Current Anthropology 37:43–66.

Henry, D. O., 1982 The Prehistory of Southern Jordan and Relationships with the Levant. Journal of Field Archaeology 9:417–444.

——1989 From Foraging to Agriculture: The Levant at the End of the Ice Age. Philadelphia: University of Pennsylvania Press.

Hodder, Ian, 1990 The Domestication of Europe. London: Blackwell.

Holl, Augustin, 1985 Subsistence Patterns of the Dhar Tichitt Neolithic, Mauritania. The African Archaeological Review 3:151–162.

——1998 Livestock Husbandry, Pastoralisms and Territoriality: The West African Record. Journal of Anthropological Archaeology 17:143–165.

Kaiser, Timothy, and Barbara Voytek, 1983 Sedentism and Economic Change in the Balkan Neolithic. Journal of Anthropological Archaeology 2:323–353.

Kenyon, K. M., 1956 Jericho and its Setting in Near Eastern Prehistory. Antiquity 30:184–195.

——1960 Jericho and the Origins of Agriculture. The Advancement of Science. 66:118–120.

Lavachery, Philippe, 1996 Shum Laka Rockshelter Holocene Deposits: From Stone to Metal (Northwestern Cameroon). In Aspects of African Archaeology: Papers from the 10th Congress of the Pan-African Association for Prehistory and Related Studies. Gilbert Pwiti and Robert Soper, eds. pp. 265–274. Harare: University of Zimbabwe Publications.

——2001 The Holocene Archaeological Sequence of Shum Laka Rock Shelter (Grasslands, Western Cameroon). African Archaeological Review 18:213–247.

Lee, Richard B., and Irven DeVore, eds., 1968 Man the Hunter. Chicago: Aldine.

Linares de Sapir, O. 1976 "Garden Hunting" in the American Tropics. Human Ecology 4:331–349.

McCurdy, G. G., 1924 Human Origins: A Manual of Prehistory. New York: Appleton.

MacDonald, Kevin C., 1997 Korounkorokalé Revisited: The Pays Mande and the West African Microlithic Technocomplex. African Archaeological Review 14:161–200.

—— 1998 Before the Empire of Ghana: Pastoralism and the Origins of Cultural Complexity in the Sahel. *In* Transformations in Africa. Graham Connah, ed. pp. 71–103. London: University of Leicester Press.

MacDonald, Kevin C., and P. Allsworth-Jones, 1994 A Reconsideration of the West African Macrolithic Conundrum: New Factory Sites and an Associated Settlement in the Vallée du Serpent, Mali. The African Archaeological Review 12:73–104.

MacDonald, Kevin C., and W. van Neer, 1994 Specialized Fishing Peoples in the Later Holocene of the Méma Region (Mali). *In* Fish Exploitation in the Past. W. van Neer, ed. pp. 243–251. Annales du Musée Royal de l'Afrique Centrale, Sciences Zoologiques, 274. Tervuren: Musée Royal de l'Afrique Centrale.

McIntosh, Roderick J., 1997 Agricultural Beginnings in Sub-Saharan Africa. *In* Encyclopedia of Precolonial Africa. J. O. Vogel, ed. pp. 409–418. Walnut Creek, CA: AltaMira Press.

McIntosh, Susan K., and R. J. McIntosh, 1983 Current Directions in West African Prehistory. Annual Review of Anthropology 12:215–258.

MacNeish, Richard S., 1950 A Synopsis of the Archaeological Sequence in the Sierra de Tamaulipas. Revista Mexicana de Estudios Antropológicos 11:79–96.

—— 1964 Ancient Mesoamerican Civilization. Science 143:531–537.

Marshall, Fiona, 2001 Agriculture and Use of Wild and Weedy Vegetables by the Piik ap Oom Okiek of Kenya. Economic Botany 55:46–69.

Marshall, Fiona, and Elisabeth Hildebrand, 2002 Cattle Before Crops: The Beginnings of Food Production in Africa. Journal of World Prehistory 16(2):99–143.

Mellaart, James, 1958 Excavations at Hacilar: First Preliminary Report. Anatolian Studies 8:127–156.

—— 1962 Excavations at Çatal Hüyük. Anatolian Studies 12:41–65.

Mercader, Julio, 2003 Foragers of the Congo: The Early Settlement of the Ituri Forest. *In* Under the Canopy: The Archaeology of Tropical Rainforests. Julio Mercader, ed. pp. 93–115. New Brunswick, NJ: Rutgers University Press.

Mercader, J., and A. Brooks, 2001 Across Forest and Savannas: Later Stone Age Assemblages from Ituri and Semliki, Northeast Democratic Republic of Congo. Journal of Anthropological Research 57(2),197–217.

Mercader, Julio, and R. Marti, 2003 The Middle Stone Age Occupation of Atlantic Central Africa: New Evidence from Equatorial Guinea and Cameroon. *In* Under the Canopy: The Archaeology of Tropical Rainforests. Julio Mercader, ed. pp. 64–92. New Brunswick, NJ: Rutgers University Press.

Mitchell, Peter J., 1988 The Early Microlithic Assemblages of Southern Africa. BAR International Series, 538. Oxford: British Archaeological Reports.

Moeyersons, J., Els Cornelissen, Philippe Lavachery, and H. Doutrelepont, 1996 L'Abri sous-roche de Shum Laka (Cameroun Occidental) données climatologiques et occupation humaine depuis 30 000 ans. Geo-Eco-Trop 20(1–4):39–60.

Morrison, K. D., 1994 The Intensification of Production: Archaeological Approaches. Journal of Archaeological Method and Theory 1:111–159.

Munson, Patrick J., 1976 Archaeological Data on the Origins of Cultivation in the Southwestern Sahara and their Implications for West Africa. *In* Origins of African Plant Domestication. Jack R. Harlan, Jan M. J. DeWet, and Ann B. L. Stemler, eds. pp. 189–209. The Hague: Mouton.

Muzzolini, A. 1993 The Emergence of a Food-Producing Economy in the Sahara. *In* The

Archaeology of Africa: Food, Metals and Towns. Thurstan Shaw, Paul Sinclair, Bassey Andah, and Alex Okpoko, eds. pp. 227–239. London: Routledge.

Nygaard, S., and Michael Talbot, 1977 First Dates from the Coastal Sites Near Kpone, Ghana. Nyame Akuma 11:39–40.

Peyrot, B., and R. Oslisly, 1986 Researches récentes sur le paléoenvironnement et l'archéologie au Gabon: 1982–1985. L'Anthropologie 90:201–216.

———— 1990 Sites archéologiques associant pierres taillées, céramiques, coquilles marines et outiles en pierre polie à Tchengué, province de l'Ogooué-Maritime, Gabon. Nsi 7:13–19.

Phillipson, David W., 1980 Some Speculations on the Beginnings of Backed-Microlith Manufacture. Proceedings of the 8th Pan-African Congress of Prehistory and Quaternary Studies, Nairobi, September 1977. Richard E. Leakey and P. Ogot, eds. pp. 229–230. Nairobi: International Louis Leakey Memorial Institute for African Prehistory.

———— 1993 African Archaeology. 2nd edition. Cambridge: Cambridge University Press.

Posnansky, Merrick, 1984 Early Agricultural Societies in Ghana. In From Hunters to Farmers. J. Desmond Clark and Steven A. Brandt, eds. pp. 147–151. Berkeley: University of California Press.

Price, T. Douglas, ed., 2000 Europe's First Farmers. Cambridge: Cambridge University Press.

Rindos, David, 1984 The Origins of Agriculture: An Evolutionary Perspective. Orlando: Academic Press.

Roset, J.-P., 1987 Paleoclimatic and Cultural Conditions of Neolithic Development in the Early Holocene of Northern Niger (Aïr and Ténéré). In Prehistory of Arid North Africa. Angela Close, ed. pp. 211–234. Dallas: Southern Methodist University Press.

Roubet, C., 1968 Le Gisement du Damous el Ahmer. Travaux du Centre de Recherches Anthropologiques, Préhistoriques et Ethnographiques en Algérie. Paris: Arts et Métiers Graphiques.

———— 1979 Économie pastorale, préagricole en Algérie orientale: Le Néolithique de Tradition Capsienne. Paris: CNRS.

Sauer, Carl O., 1952 Agricultural Origins and Dispersals. New York: American Geographical Society.

Semenov, S. A., 1985[1964] Prehistoric Technology. New Jersey: Barnes & Noble.

Shaw, C. Thurstan, 1944 Report on Investigations Carried out in the Cave Known as "Bosumpra" at Abetifi, Kwahu, Gold Coast Colony. Proceedings of the Prehistoric Society 10:1–67.

———— 1976 Early Crops in Africa: A Review of the Evidence. In Origins of African Plant Domestication. Jack R. Harlan, Jan M. J. DeWet, and Ann B. L. Stemler, eds. pp. 107–153. The Hague: Mouton.

———— 1977 Hunters, Gatherers and First Farmers in West Africa. In Hunters, Gatherers and First Farmers Beyond Europe. J. V. S. Megaw, ed. pp. 69–125. London: Leicester University Press.

———— 1978 Nigeria: Its Archaeology and Early History London: Thames & Hudson.

———— 1978–79 Holocene Adaptations in West Africa: The Late Stone Age. Early Man News 3–4:51–52.

———— 1981 The Prehistory of West Africa. In General History of Africa, vol. 1. J. Ki-Zerbo, ed. pp. 611–630. California: Heinemann.

Shaw, C. Thurstan, and S. G. H. Daniels, 1984 Excavations at Iwo Eleru. West African Journal of Archaeology 14:1–269.

Sheppard, Peter J., 1987 The Capsian of North Africa: Stylistic Variation in Stone Tool Assemblages. BAR International Series, 353. Oxford: British Archaeological Reports.

Sinclair, Paul J., Thurstan Shaw, and Bassey Andah, 1993 Introduction. *In* The Archaeology of Africa: Food, Metals and Towns. Thurstan Shaw, Paul Sinclair, Bassey Andah, and Alex Okpoko, eds. pp. 1–31. London: Routledge.

Smith, Andrew B., 1975 Radiocarbon Dates from Bosumpra Cave, Abetifi, Ghana. Proceedings of the Prehistoric Society 41:179–182.

—— 1980 The Neolithic Tradition in the Sahara. *In* The Sahara and the Nile. Martin A. J. Williams and H. Faure, eds. pp. 451–465. Rotterdam: Balkema.

—— 1992 Pastoralism in Africa: Origins and Development Ecology. London: Hurst.

Soper, Robert C., 1965 The Stone Age in Northern Nigeria. Journal of the Historical Society of Nigeria 3(2):175–194.

Sowunmi, M. Adebisi, 1981 Late Quaternary Environmental Changes in Nigeria. Pollen et Spores 23(1):125–148.

—— 1985 The Beginnings of Agriculture in West Africa: Botanical Evidence. Current Anthropology 26:127–129.

Stahl, Ann B., 1984a A History and Critique of Investigations into Early African Agriculture. *In* From Hunters to Farmers. J. Desmond Clark and Steven A. Brandt, eds. pp. 9–21. Berkeley: University of California Press.

—— 1984b Hominid Dietary Selection before Fire. Current Anthropology 25:151–168.

—— 1985 Reinvestigation of Kintampo 6 Rockshelter, Ghana: Implications for the Nature of Culture Change. The African Archaeological Review 3:117–150.

—— 1986 Early Food Production in West Africa: Rethinking the Role of the Kintampo Culture. Current Anthropology 27:532–536.

—— 1989 Plant Food Processing: Implications for Dietary Quality. *In* Foraging and Farming: The Evolution of Plant Exploitation. David R. Harris and Gordon C. Hillman, eds. pp. 171–194. London: Unwin Hyman.

—— 1993 Intensification in the West African Late Stone Age: A View from Central Ghana. *In* The Archaeology of Africa: Food, Metals and Towns. Thurstan Shaw, Paul Sinclair, Bassey Andah, and Alex Okpoko, eds. pp. 261–273. London: Routledge.

—— 1994 Innovation, Diffusion and Culture Contact: The Holocene Archaeology of Ghana. Journal of World Prehistory 8(1):51–112.

—— 1999 Perceiving Variability in Time and Space: The Evolutionary Mapping of African Societies. *In* Beyond Chiefdoms: Pathways to Complexity in Africa. Susan Keech McIntosh, ed. pp. 39–55. Cambridge: Cambridge University Press.

Sundström, L., 1972 Ecology and Symbiosis: Niger Water Folk. Uppsala: Studia Ethnographica.

Swift, J., 1981 Labour and Subsistence in a Pastoral Economy. *In* Seasonal Dimensions to Rural Poverty. R. Chambers, R. Longhurst, and A. Pacey, eds. pp. 80–87. London: Francis Pinter.

Talbot, Michael R., D. A. Livingstone, P. G. Parker, J. Maley, J. M. Melack, G. Delibrias, and S. Gulliken, 1984 Preliminary Results from Sediment Cores from Lake Bosumtwi, Ghana. Paleoecology of Africa 16:176–192.

Trigger, Bruce G., 1989 A History of Archaeological Thought. Cambridge: University of Cambridge Press.

Van Noten, Francis, 1977 Excavations at Matupi Cave. Antiquity 51:35–40.

—— 1982 The Archaeology of Central Africa. Graz: Akademische Druk- und Verlagsanstalt.

White, C., 1986 Food Shortages and Seasonality in Wo Daa Be Communities in Niger. Institute of Development Studies (Sussex), Bulletin 17(3):19–26.

Whittle, Alasdair, 1996 Europe and the Neolithic. Cambridge: Cambridge University Press.

Willett, Frank, 1962 The Microlithic Industry from Old Oyo, Western Nigeria. *In* Actes du V Congrès Panafricain de Préhistoire et de l'Étude du Quaternaire. G. Mortelmans and J. Nenquin, eds. Section XI: pp. 261–271. Tervuen: Musée Royal de l'Afrique Centrale.

Wobst, Martin, 1978 The Archaeo-Ethnology of Hunter-Gatherers or the Tyranny of the Ethnographic Record in Archaeology. American Antiquity 43:303–309.

York, R. N., 1978 Excavations at Dutsen Kongba, Plateau State Nigeria. West African Journal of Archaeology 8:139–163.

10

The Romance of Farming: Plant Cultivation and Domestication in Africa

Katharina Neumann

The emergence of agriculture is a key topic in prehistory. Over the past half-century, numerous explanations have been proposed for the transition from foraging to farming, most of them deductive and "only minimally constrained by available information" (Smith 2001a:215). Africa is no exception. This chapter does not aim to give a comprehensive overview of all theories past and present. Instead, it is "data-focused," written from an archaeobotanist's perspective, and relying mainly on archaeological plant remains which are preserved either charred, desiccated, as phytoliths or in the form of plant impressions.[1] I explore available evidence against the background of earlier perspectives on the transition to food production in Africa. Which explanations have received support during the last two decades? Are the old models still valuable in the light of new data? And in broader perspective: how can Africa contribute to the discussion on the origins of agriculture on a world-wide scale?

From Gathering to Agriculture: Some Definitions

A dualistic concept of hunter-gatherers and food producers as opposite and exclusive is not appropriate for Africa. In diachronic as well as synchronic perspective, Africa presents numerous examples of the "middle ground," the large transitional zone in the continuum between hunter-gatherers on the one end and agriculturalists largely depending on domesticated crops on the other (Harlan et al., eds., 1976; Harris 1989, 1996; Smith 2001b). Traditional land-use systems with little mechanization are still practiced on a large scale, and wild or semi-domesticated plants play a central role in contemporary African subsistence.

In the vast anthropological jungle of inconsistent terminology on the origins of agriculture, the terms "cultivation" and "domestication" have proved to be especially valuable (for a critical discussion see Haaland 1999; Harris 1989; Smith

2001b). Cultivation, in its broadest sense, can be defined as any human activity that increases the yield of harvested or exploited plants. Domestication designates genetic, morphological, and physiological changes of the plants resulting from cultivation and conscious or unconscious human selection (Smith 1998; Zohary and Hopf 2000). Cultivation can be practiced with wild or domesticated plants, but domestication occurs only under cultivation (Harris 1996; Smith 2001a), and the presence of domesticated plants marks a *terminus post quem* in the archaeological record. Their appearance is a safe criterion that cultivation was practiced from at least this moment onwards. This is the reason why the question "domesticated or not" is so crucial for archaeologists.

The biased search for the "oldest" domesticated plants in Africa has often led to a distorted picture of prehistoric economies. The presence of domesticated plants in the archaeological record does not signal reliance on agriculture; a single grain of domesticated sorghum does not justify calling the corresponding human population "farmers." Rather, the status of domesticates must be defined in a broader economic and ecological context, based on complete assemblages of plant remains. Furthermore, the question "domesticated or not" cannot always be answered unequivocally, either because diagnostic features are not preserved, or because morphological differences between wild and domesticated varieties are insufficiently clear. Even in modern African agricultural systems, there are many plants with an intermediate status, e.g. fonio (*Digitaria exilis*) and trees such as the oil palm (*Elaeis guineensis*) and the shea butter tree (*Vitellaria paradoxa*).

From General to Regional Approaches: History of Research

Africa was not a focus of interest when research on the origins of agriculture started in the middle of the last century. Pioneering interdisciplinary studies of the 1950s and 1960s focused on the Near East and Mesoamerica (Smith 1998, 2001b). It was not until the 1970s that Africa became recognized as a place worthy of discussion. Jack R. Harlan, a plant geneticist, was especially interested in African domesticated plants, and he felt that biological investigations alone were not sufficient to explain the enormous genetic, morphological, and ecological changes that African crops underwent in the course of their evolutionary history. A Burg Wartenstein symposium organized by Harlan in 1972 brought together scientists from archaeology, agronomy, palynology, genetics, and plant taxonomy. During the next two decades, the symposium proceedings (Harlan et al., eds., 1976) became the main reference for the origins of African plant domestication.

Most of the overviews on African plant food production published in the two decades after the Burg Wartenstein symposium (e.g., Clark and Brandt, eds., 1984; Harlan 1992, 1995; Shaw et al., eds., 1993; Smith 1998) were either based on indirect archaeological evidence or on information about modern plants, but not on botanical remains from archaeological sites. In his compilation Shaw (1976) listed fewer than 20 archaeological sites for the whole continent which had yielded plant remains. Only a few sites were old enough to contribute to the question of early plant food production, and none had been sampled systematically, the finds being more or less accidental by-products of excavation.

The conspicuous lack of direct evidence excluded Africa from ongoing world-wide discussions on the origins of agriculture. Data from Africa were not considered useful in a general theoretical framework. In recent compilations, Africa is either missing altogether, (Hather, ed., 1994; Harris, ed., 1996; Gebauer and Price 1992; Price and Gebauer, eds., 1995; Smith 2001a), or contributions refer to earlier field studies without adding new data (e.g., Harlan 1989, 1992, 1995; Smith 1998).

In the 1980s systematic archaeobotanical field and laboratory work started in Africa. More archaeologists cooperated closely with the natural sciences, as for example the long-term projects in the eastern Sahara (Kuper 1989; Wendorf et al., eds., 2001), Libya (Garcea 2001; di Lernia, ed., 1999), Ethiopia (Phillipson 2000), or West Africa (Breunig and Neumann 1999, 2002a, 2004). Wide-ranging considerations gave way to more regional or local approaches, and today archaeobotanical data are primarily interpreted within small-scale models. The search for the "origins" of agriculture and the oldest domesticated crop has changed into less spectacular attempts to reconstruct economic systems in all their aspects. Together with zoological, geomorphological, and sedimentological information, botanical data elucidate the role of the environment on human occupation and economy, and allow an assessment of how humans in turn modified their natural environments (e.g., Klee et al. 2000; Wasylikowa 2001).

A lack of basic data still remains the major problem. Figure 10.1 shows the distribution of sites from which archaeobotanical remains relevant to the origins of agriculture have been published. For historical reasons, there is a strong concentration in Egypt. The Sahara and West Africa are represented with a number of studies, and data from East Africa are also available. But the central and southern parts of the continent remain *terra incognita*. Moreover, finds are only rarely described and illustrated. Many controversial discussions of the domesticated status of specific finds might have been avoided had they been documented in detail.

The growing need for basic data and a forum for their discussion resulted in the foundation of a workgroup for African archaeobotany in 1994. Three workshops have been organized: 1994 in Mogilany near Kraków (Poland); 1997 in Leicester (Great Britain); and 2000 in Frankfurt (Germany). The proceedings of these conferences (Neumann et al., eds., 2003; Stuchlik and Wasylikowa, eds., 1995; van der Veen, ed., 1999) are a major source of archaeobotanical data.

Of course some early published hypotheses and conclusions are outdated in the light of new data, but many have not lost their relevance, including: Purseglove (1976) on the geographical origins of crops in Africa; Harris (1976) on traditional systems of plant food production; Harlan and Stemler (1976) on modern races of *Sorghum bicolor*; and overviews on the archaeological background by Stahl (1984) and A. B. Smith (1984). The wealth of personal knowledge expressed in the publications of Jack Harlan and J. Desmond Clark, founders of the modern interdisciplinary approach to early food production in Africa (e.g., Clark 1976; Harlan 1992, 1995), continue to inspire.

Figure 10.1. Archaeological sites and regions mentioned in the text

Diffusion or Independent Invention?

Early research was preoccupied with the question of whether African agriculture developed independently or as a result of diffusion, either by migration or stimulus, from the Near East. A very popular view was that agriculture started with Near Eastern crops in the Nile Valley and northern Africa. During periods of climatic amelioration in the Middle Holocene, people equipped with wheat and barley would have moved into the Sahara. With subsequent desiccation, these populations were forced to move further south, until they reached the ecological limits for cultivation of winter rainfall cultigens, and local sorghum and "millets" would have been domesticated in their place (Clark 1964; for an overview see Stahl 1984: 15).

Today, the general discussion of diffusion or independent evolution has lost much of its intellectual glamour. But a diffusionary heritage which saw Africa as a recipient of cultural innovation is reflected in the concentration of sites with archaeological plant remains in Egypt. Because of its obvious relationship with the ancient civilizations in the "Fertile Crescent," Egypt became a focus of archaeological attention as early as the 19th century, and plant remains from tombs were among the first archaeobotanical samples ever collected (Germer 1985). However, most of these data do not contribute to the question of how agriculture emerged, and only in the last 20 years have sites predating the Dynastic periods been systematically sampled for plant remains (e.g., Barakat and Fahmy 1999; Wasylikowa 1997, 2001).

The influence of Egyptian agriculture on the development of sub-Saharan African agriculture remains to be elucidated. For the Sahara, the question of diffusion has been little discussed in recent years. The earliest evidence of Near Eastern crops in Egypt (mainly emmer wheat and barley in Fayum and Merimde) dates around the middle of the sixth millennium b.c. (Wetterstrom 1993; Zohary and Hopf 2000). Scattered finds of Near Eastern crops in Libya and the Maghreb do not allow us to reconstruct their movement along the northern fringes of the Sahara, or their hypothetical dispersal to the south. In a review of the evidence from Libya, van der Veen (1995) found that oasis agriculture in the northern Sahara based on emmer, barley, bread wheat, date palm, and Mediterranean fruit trees, could only be attested at the site of Zinchecra from the middle of the first millennium b.c. Older sites from the Libyan Sahara in the Acacus mountains yielded rich assemblages of wild plants, mainly of Sahelian affinity (see below), and do not furnish evidence for any type of plant food production, either with temperate or tropical crops.

Ethiopia is the second region where domestication of indigenous plants might have been triggered by the introduction of Near Eastern crops, but the question also remains open. Due to the special ecological conditions of the highlands, the indigenous agricultural systems of Ethiopia include winter rain crops from the Near East as well as indigenous African domesticates, some of which, such as tef (*Eragrostis tef*), the oil plant noog (*Guizotia abyssinica*), and enset (*Ensete ventricosum*), obviously originated there (Edwards 1991; Harlan 1969). Archaeobotanical evidence from Ethiopia is still confined to a handful of sites (D'Andrea et al. 1999). The earliest unequivocal archaeobotanical evidence for domesticated plants, dated around 500 b.c., comes from the sites of Lalibela, and consists only of introduced crops (Dombrowski 1970, 1971). In the archaeobotanical samples from the Aksum area dated to the middle of the first millennium b.c. (Pre-Aksumite), emmer, barley and flax are present together with tef as the only Ethiopian crop (Boardman 1999). Other African crops, such as *Sorghum bicolor*, *Eleusine coracana*, and noog are absent in Pre-Aksumite samples and only appear in Aksumite times, suggesting a later domestication or introduction. Several authors have argued for a much earlier introduction of winter rain crops through cultural contact with northeast Africa (Barnett 1999; D'Andrea et al. 1999:106), but these hypotheses remain unproved in the absence of archaeobotanical evidence.

The Geographical Origins of African Crops

Well-dated archaeological plant remains are the most valuable source of information for the study of early agriculture. Important information can also be obtained from living plants, mainly through studies of geographical distribution and the genetic relations between a crop and its wild ancestors (Zohary and Hopf 2000). African crops were first brought into view by Vavilov (1926) who, based on the diversity of cultivated plants, defined eight centers where agriculture could have emerged. In Africa, Vavilov considered the East African highlands to be a potential cradle of agriculture, where he thought barley (*Hordeum vulgare*), coffee (*Coffea arabica*), sorghum (*Sorghum bicolor*), and pearl millet (*Pennisetum glaucum*) originated. Vavilov's theory was largely dismissed in following decades because it became commonly accepted that a center of crop diversity is not necessarily identical to its area of origin. But Vavilov's idea had an enormously inspiring effect on later research on agricultural origins (Harris 1990, 1996), and at least eight plant species of his original list are commonly accepted as domesticated in Ethiopia (Barnett 1999:60; Edwards 1991).

From botanical and linguistic evidence, Chevalier (1938), Portères (1950, 1962), and Murdock (1959) questioned Vavilov's theory of a single Ethiopian center, favoring instead a West African origin of several cereals, including African rice (*Oryza glaberrima*) and pearl millet (*Pennisetum glaucum*). A milestone was set by J. R. Harlan, who localized the cradle of almost 30 crops in Africa based on the distribution of wild relatives, and presented a map for ten of them (Harlan 1971, 1992). In comparison with similar maps from other continents, Africa's difficulty is obvious and has wide-ranging implications for archaeological work. The search for agricultural origins in the Near East or Mesoamerica is restricted to a small area due to the limited distribution of wild ancestors (Smith 1998); however, no "centers" of African plant domestication can be defined. Instead, the hypothetical domestication areas are very large and only weakly overlap. Harlan termed the large, dispersed distribution areas as "non-centers." His map shows a comparatively well defined area in East Africa, which Harlan believed to be the home of *Eragrostis tef*, *Musa ensete*, *Eleusine coracana*, and *Guizotia abyssinica*. In the large savanna belt between Senegal and the Sudan he localized the origin of *Pennisetum glaucum*, *Brachiaria deflexa*, *Digitaria exilis*, *D. iburua*, *Oryza glaberrima*, *Sorghum bicolor*, and the pulses *Voandzeia subterranea* and *Kerstingiella geocarpa*. The hypothetical domestication area of yams (*Dioscorea rotundata*) was located along the fringes of the rain forest between Côte d'Ivoire and Cameroon. Although Harlan's map is incomplete, it presents a starting point for delimiting the key regions for research on agricultural origins.

In other parts of the world, especially the Near East and Mexico, new molecular and genetic methods have been successfully applied to delimit more precisely the hypothetical domestication areas of "founder crops" (Smith 2001a; Zohary 1996). In some cases, the question of single or multiple episodes of domestication can be tentatively answered from DNA evidence and enzymatic studies (Smith

1998; Zohary 1996). For Africa, such investigations are still rare (e.g., Coulibaly et al. 2002; Hilu et al. 1997; Pasquet et al. 1999). For pearl millet, a recent isozyme study has largely confirmed Harlan's ideas and, in addition, further limited its hypothetical domestication area to northern Senegal and Mauritania (Tostain 1998).

Myths from the Sahara and the Nile Valley: Broad Spectrum Revolution vs. Early Cultivation

From the early days of research on African agricultural origins, the Sahara has been an object of particular attention. First, from a diffusionist viewpoint, it was assumed to be a hypothetical center of early agriculture. Second, based on Harlan's (1971) map of hypothetical domestication areas, one could assume that during the more humid Early and Middle Holocene, the distribution areas of wild *Sorghum* and *Pennisetum* extended further north than the Sahelian zone where they are found today. And third, it was in the Sahara and the Nile Valley where the supposedly oldest remains of domesticated cereals were found.

Scholarly discussions about African agricultural origins were profoundly influenced by the implicit and poorly defined concept of the *Neolithic* which, originally developed for Europe and the Near East, was uncritically transmitted to Africa (Chapters 8, 9). In other world areas, the earliest Neolithic is usually characterized by use of domesticated crops; domesticated animals appear either much later or, at the earliest, contemporaneously (Smith 1998). The implicit equation of the *Neolithic* with plant food production led to the expectation that early polished stone tools, pottery, and cattle in the Sahara should be associated with domesticated plants. This has led to "a great deal of tortuous reasoning" (MacDonald 2000:9) to explain the absence of domesticated crops in Early and Middle Holocene sites – or, conversely, to premature inferences of plant cultivation based on the most meager evidence.

This explains why the sites Amekni, Meniet, and Adrar Bous in the central Sahara (Shaw 1976) continued to be cited as references for early agriculture in the Sahara up to recent times (e.g., Harlan 1992; Smith 1998). In Amekni and Meniet the evidence consisted of pollen grains of hypothetically domesticated cereals (Camps 1969; Hugot 1968). But in contrast to Near Eastern cereals, African domesticated grasses cannot be palynologically distinguished from their wild relatives. In Adrar Bous some plant impressions in pottery studied by the French botanist H. Jacques-Félix were thought to belong to domesticated sorghum. The issue was discussed in letters between J. D. Clark and H. Jacques-Félix (Garcea, letter to the author, July 18, 2002), and even though Clark was very suspicious and never published the results, the hypothetically domesticated sorghum entered as an undoubted fact into Shaw's (1976) compilation, and from there into the secondary literature.

Intensive research on agricultural origins has been conducted in the eastern Sahara. In Wadi Kubbaniya, Egypt grains of domestic barley found in late Paleolithic sites seemed to indicate incipient plant food production 18,000 years ago (Wendorf et al. 1979, 1980). Later it turned out that the grains were uncharred, making preservation through such a long time improbable, and they were directly dated by AMS to a maximum age of 4850 b.p. (Hillman 1989; Wendorf et al. 1984). At Nabta Playa, the presence of barley in the levels dated around 8000 b.p., stated by el Hadidi (1980), has not been confirmed by later careful archaeobotanical investigations at the site (Wasylikowa 2001). Ironically, work at Kubbaniya and Nabta Playa, where archaeobotanical work was oriented toward a search for the earliest domesticates, has produced the best documented evidence for wild plant use in the Late Pleistocene and Early Holocene. In Wadi Kubbaniya, Hillman and colleagues found remains of *Cyperus rotundus* and other tuber plants, as well as evidence for a very high dietary diversity and early infant weaning 18,000 years ago (Hillman 1989; Hillman et al. 1989). At Nabta Playa more than 120 plant taxa have been identified at site E-75–6 (dated around 8000 b.p., 6900 B.C.), including wild grasses, small seeded legumes, fruit and tuber plants, and firewood species (Wasylikowa 1997, 2001; Wendorf et al. 1998). The inhabitants of E-75–6 collected wild sorghum and several grasses from the subfamily Panicoideae. Storage facilities have also been reported and certain grasses, including *Sorghum bicolor*, were gathered separately. The sorghum grains are morphologically wild, and attempts to prove their domesticated status with the help of gas chromatography (Wendorf et al. 1992) have had equivocal results (Biehl et al. 1999). Thus the question remains open if it was gathered or cultivated.

One of the most controversial issues is the domestication of sorghum in the Nile Valley. Based on plant impressions in ceramics and circumstantial archaeological evidence, Abdel-Magid (1989) and Haaland (1995, 1999) claim that sorghum was cultivated from 6000 b.p. (4900 B.C.). The striking fact in this scenario is the absence of domesticated sorghum in all of Africa before the beginning of the Christian era (for a review of the evidence and arguments see Breunig and Neumann 2002a; Neumann 2003; Rowley-Conwy et al. 1997; and Wetterstrom 1998). Abdel-Magid and Haaland argue that harvesting techniques and cross-pollination of the sorghum plant were responsible for delayed domestication. In the light of experimental studies on cereal domestication rates (Hillman and Davies 1990), it is improbable that the domestication process of sorghum would have taken almost 5,000 calendar years, even if a high percentage of 30 percent outcrossing is assumed. It is more parsimonious to infer intensive gathering for the Middle Holocene sites in the Nile Valley.

The intensive use of wild plants is also documented from other sites in Egypt and Libya. Wild grass assemblages comparable to those of Nabta Playa have been described from the Egyptian sites Hidden Valley/Farafra and Eastpans/Abu Ballas, dated between 7100 and 6000 b.p. (5900–4900 B.C.; Barakat and Fahmy 1999). A large range of herbaceous species, grasses from the tribe subfamily Panicoideae, and remains of edible tree fruits were found in the Acacus rockshelters of Ti-n-Torha, Uan Muhuggiag, Uan Tabu, and Uan Afuda, dated between 8800 and 4900 b.p. (7900–3700 B.C.) (Mercuri 2001; van der Veen 1995; Wasylikowa 1992, 1993; Wetterstrom 1998). Unfortunately no data are available from the central and western Sahara, the hypothetical homelands of *Pennisetum*, and it is unknown how long and in which way wild pearl millet was used before its domestication.

From the data of the eastern Sahara, Libya, and the Nile Valley intensive exploitation of wild resources, together with the development of appropriate technology such as large grinding stones and pottery (Barich 1998; di Lernia and Manzi, eds., 1998) was characteristic of the Early to Middle Holocene. This is an impressive example of Flannery's (1969) *broad-spectrum revolution*. Wild grass exploitation was a successful aspect of this new economy for some 6,000 years. Cultivation may have been practiced from time to time, but probably on an irregular and small-scale basis. Domesticated cattle were added to this hunter-gatherer complex by around 6500 b.p. (5400 B.C.), and pastoralism spread throughout the Sahara and Sahel during the next four millennia (Marshall 1998; Smith 1992; Chapter 8). Although information about plant exploitation is missing for most Saharan pastoral sites, it is conceivable that the herders collected wild grasses and fruits. Modern analogs of pastoralism with wild grass harvesting include the Tuareg and Zaghawa societies of the southern Sahara and the Sahel (S. E. Smith 1980; Tubiana and Tubiana 1977).

Climatic Change and the Beginnings of Agriculture in the Southern Sahara: Is There a Causal Relation?

Climatic change, human population dynamics, and technological development are commonly invoked as causes for the origins of agriculture (Bar-Yosef 1998). In Africa, it is evident that the drastic fluctuations between more humid and arid phases, particularly in the Sahara, must have had an enormous impact on human populations and their subsistence patterns. Two lines of argument can be distinguished. The first deals with the climatic "amelioration" in the Early Holocene and the subsequent extension of exploitable resources as a necessary condition for the intensification of plant use which would – some thousand years later – lead to agriculture. Formerly harsh and empty desert changed into a mosaic of lakes and rivers, surrounded by grasslands and savannas which harbored a large variety of exploitable plants and animals (Chapters 7, 8).

The second line of argument concerns the processes and causal relations of a transition from collecting to cultivating. A common idea for the Sahara is that, with the onset of drier conditions, a steep ecological gradient developed between a few well-watered areas with rich resources and their dry surrounding environments which were unsuitable for human exploitation. This would have led to concentrations of populations and an increasing need to develop new subsistence strategies to cope with the challenge of restricted resources (Clark 1976: Smith 1998; Stahl 1984; Stemler 1984). The large seasonal river valleys of the southern Sahara play a crucial role in this scenario.

Stahl (1984:16), in referring to Wagner's (1977) and Harris' (1977) general critique of environmental determinism, has questioned the causal relationship between climatic developments and the origins of agriculture in Africa. Should a correlation exist, it would not explain *per se* why a shift to agriculture occurred and would leave the open question of how such changes affected particular subsistence strategies. But even a simple correlation in time and space between paleoclimatic events and archaeologically traceable cultural developments is difficult to establish in Africa. Often pseudo-paleoclimatic information is deduced from indirect archaeological evidence (i.e., the distribution and frequency of sites) resulting in circular arguments. Only in rare cases are independent paleoenvironmental and archaeological data available from the same region.

Although several studies in Africa have contributed to our knowledge of Holocene paleoclimates and paleoenvironments, their time resolution is usually too coarse to support arguments about causality. At least a century order of precision, or ideally, a quarter of a century level (one human generation) would be necessary (Vernet 2002). This level has obviously not been reached in the southern Sahara, although numerous paleolakes – the main source of paleoecological information – have been studied (Guo et al. 2000; Hassan 1997). Moreover, the knowledge of humid episodes is usually better than that of dry ones, which in most cases are not dated directly.

The data from the Sahara suggest that the humid phase after 9500 b.p. (8800/9100 B.C.) was interrupted by series of dry spells and progressive desiccation after 5000 b.p. (3800 B.C.; Guo et al. 2000). If, as it is generally assumed, the increasing desiccation of the southern Sahel was the driving force for migrations to the south and for innovations including agriculture, it would be important to define accurately the climatic events in the period when this is supposed to have occurred, i.e. the third and second millennia b.c. Unfortunately, there is no general agreement on when to place these dry spells. Guo et al. (2000) have identified a phase of extreme aridity around 4000 b.p. (2500 B.C.) which might have been as dry as the Late Pleistocene. Vernet (2002) and Vernet and Faure (2000) also mention a severe dry episode in the Sahara around 4200–4000 b.p. (2800–2500 B.C.). Hassan (1997:218), in a compilation of African paleoclimates, does not recognize a dry spell around 4000 b.p., but places the period of droughts in the southern Sahara and the Sahel between 3800 to 3600 b.p. (2200–1900 B.C.).

Although not consistent in detail, Maley (1997), Guo et al. (2000), and Vernet (2002) report a return to wetter conditions in the southern Sahara in the fourth millennium b.p., with numerous lacustrine formations and high population densities. Ceramic impressions of domesticated *Pennisetum* are the first signs of cereal cultivation which appear during this period, but the evidence is meager, and no recent archaeobotanical data are available. It is important to mention that the earliest traces of agriculture are not linked to a period of extreme dryness, but, in contrast, to one of climatic amelioration, followed by resettlement of previously uninhabitable areas (Vernet 2002). The dominant economic pattern during this period was pastoralism, and several pastoral complexes have been described, from Mauritania to the Nile Valley (Smith 1992; Chapter 8).

From the key area of pearl millet domestication in the southern Sahara between Lake Chad and the Atlantic, only two sites contribute to our knowledge of early agriculture: Karkarichinkat and Dhar Tichitt. Although no systematic archaeobotanical sampling was done at either site and the evidence is meager and ambiguous (Wetterstrom 1998), they act as a "starting point" for future research and are therefore be described in some detail.

In the lower Tilemsi Valley at Karkarichinkat, A. B. Smith (1974, 1975, 1992) excavated seasonally occupied settlement sites dated between 4000 and 3300 b.p. (2500–1600 B.C.). Botanical and faunal remains suggest a Sahelian riparian environment associated with wooded grassland. The sites were occupied by pastoralists with cattle and small stock, who also practiced fishing, hunting, and collecting of tree fruits. Continued re-occupation led to an accumulation of cultural debris in the form of settlement mounds. Impressions of wild and domesticated *Pennisetum* in potsherds from Karkarichinkat Sud were identified by de Wet (Smith 1992:74, 1984:89). As these sherds were collected from the surface and have not been precisely dated, their interpretive value is quite low. The seasonality pattern reconstructed from fish and fruit remains suggest that the sites were visited during the autumn and winter months. The status of pearl millet in the Karkarichinkat economy cannot be determined from these finds, let alone a development of cultivation practices related to environment change.

The archaeological sites of Dhar Tichitt in Mauritania are unique: along the escarpment of Tichitt and Oualata the oldest villages of Africa, including stone architecture and granaries, were constructed during the period of 3500 to 2500 b.p. (1800–800/400 B.C.). The origins of the Tichitt culture are still not well understood, and the chronological sequence relevant to the development of agriculture is a matter of debate (MacDonald 1998; Wetterstrom 1998). The archaeobotanical evidence consists of grain and chaff impressions in potsherds (Amblard and Pernès 1989; Jacques-Félix 1971). Munson (1971, 1976) claims a shift from gathering to pearl millet cultivation in the period between 3500 to 2800 b.p. (1800–950 B.C.), which he relates to increasing aridity. Amblard rejects Munson's interpretation and claims that pearl millet was cultivated from the beginning of the occupation. Her hypothesis is corroborated by two radiocarbon dates around 3500 b.p. (1800 B.C.), directly obtained from organic material in a potsherd tempered with pearl millet chaff (Amblard 1996). The environmental data from Dhar Tichitt are very sparse. From the occurrence of lacustrine sediments which were still deposited during the period of occupation, Person et al. (1995) conclude that the region of Dhar Tichitt received slightly higher rainfall than today and acted as a refuge in comparison to the surrounding arid regions because of its special geomorphological situation.

The southern part of the eastern Sahara and the adjacent Sahel between Lake Chad and the Nile Valley are the key areas for sorghum domestication. Under slightly more humid conditions prevailing in the third and second millennia B.C., the distribution of wild sorghum might have extended into the region of Wadi Howar where detailed paleoenvironmental and archaeological studies have been conducted (e.g. Hoelzmann et al. 2001; Neumann 1989; Pachur and Kröpelin 1987; van Neer and Uerpmann 1989). Hoelzmann et al. (2001) have demonstrated a relation between climate, paleoenvironment, and settlement patterns in the southern part of the eastern Sahara during the Middle and Late Holocene. A stable, favorable environment with a chain of lakes in western Nubia supported sedentary or semi-sedentary hunter-fisher communities from 5300 B.C. and pastoralists from 4000 B.C. onwards. After 3000 B.C., with increasing desiccation of the lakes, seasonal migrations of pastoral populations increased. The crucial period for the establishment of agriculture might be that after 2500 B.C. when pastoralists were forced to concentrate in the Wadi Howar and Jebel Tageru south of 18°N. However, for the time being there is no evidence for plant cultivation in the Wadi Howar where settlement activities finally ceased around 1000 B.C. In the Nile Valley, no sites are known from 4000 to 2000 b.p. (2500 B.C.–0 B.C./A.D.), and populations might have shifted there to a purely pastoral adaptation (Haaland 1984; Wetterstrom 1998). The first domesticated sorghum appears in the Nile Valley only after the beginning of the Christian era, at the sites Qasr Ibrim, Meroë, and Jebel Tomat (Rowley-Conwy et al. 1997; Wetterstrom 1998). For the time being, there is no conclusive model which would explain the beginning of sorghum cultivation between Lake Chad and the Nile Valley during the first millennium B.C. in relation to climatic change.

Clark (1976) argued that two main subsistence systems existed side by side in the southern Sahara and these reacted in different ways to the challenge of restricted resources. Pastoral groups would have been more reluctant to adopt cultivation because the sedentary or semi-sedentary lifestyle required for effective agriculture conflicted with their nomadic or transhumant lifestyle. Clark suggested instead that the initial steps to cultivation began among hunting-gathering-fishing populations at the edges of the remaining water bodies. Casey (1998), in pointing out seasonality as an important factor for the emergence of agriculture in West Africa, also stresses the dichotomy between herders and fishers. However, the archaeological data from the southern Sahara and the Sahel indicate that more complex subsistence patterns have to be assumed for the second millennium b.c., with pastoralism, hunting, gathering, and facultative cultivation as flexible modules of an economy of diversified risks. Sites like Karkarichinkat, Gajiganna (northeast Nigeria) Wadi Howar, and others in West and Central Africa furnish evidence for pastoralists exploiting fish and other wild resources which were eventually cultivated (Breunig and Neumann 2002a; Keding 1997; Smith 1992; van Neer 2002).

Because longer chronological sequences with occupational, paleoenvironmental, and paleoeconomic information are unavailable for the southern Sahara, the existing models on the emergence of agriculture as an adaptation to more arid climate are largely deductive. Either the evidence for plant cultivation is missing altogether (such as in the Wadi Howar) or, in the case of pearl millet at Dhar Tichitt and Karkarichinkat, it is so weak and ambiguous that we cannot assess whether the crop was introduced or locally domesticated, or the role that cultivation played in the economy. A detailed model for pastoralists as the first cultivators in Africa remains to be developed and poses a challenge to notions that sedentism is a crucial factor in the shift to agriculture (MacDonald 2000; Marshall and Hildebrand 2002; Chapter 8). The southern Sahara between Mauritania and the Nile Valley remains the key area where the origins of pearl millet and sorghum domestication should be sought.

The Spread of Plant Food Production in Africa

Surprisingly, the spread of pearl millet from the southwestern Sahara to West Africa seems to have been rapid. Almost contemporaneously with the finds of Dhar Tichitt around 1800 b.c., domesticated pearl millet is recorded in the archaeological sites of Windé Korodji (Mali), Ti-n-Akof (Burkina Faso), and Birimi (Ghana) (Breunig and Neumann 2002a; D'Andrea and Casey 2002; D'Andrea et al. 2001; MacDonald 1996; Neumann 1999; Vogelsang et al. 1999). The open West African savannas probably favored the distribution of people and ideas, and there were strong population movements from the desiccating Sahara into the Sahel and further south in the second and first millennia b.c.

In the West African Sahel, patterns of occupation and subsistence are comparatively well studied, and archaeobotanical data exist from a number of sites. For Burkina Faso and the Chad basin of northeastern Nigeria, a team from the University of Frankfurt (Germany) has explored an archaeobotanical, paleoenvironmental, and archaeological sequence spanning the period from around 1800 B.C. to modern times (Albert et al. 2000; Breunig and Neumann 2002a, 2002b, 2004; Höhn et al. in press; Klee and Zach 1999; Klee et al. 2000; Neumann et al. 1998; Vogelsang et al. 1999). Based on the data of numerous well-dated sites, Breunig and Neumann (2002b) and Neumann (2003) have presented a two-stage model for agricultural development in the West African savannas, each characterized by specific crops and markedly different technological, social, and economic patterns. In the classical terminology, phase I corresponds to the final period of the Late Stone Age in the second millennium b.c., and phase II to the beginning of the Iron Age in the second half of the first millennium b.c. (Peregrine and Ember, eds., 2001).

In phase I, pearl millet is the only crop recorded so far. The absence of other crops might be due to bad preservation, but Breunig and Neumann (2002b; Neumann 2003) argue that this evidence reflects the comparatively minor role of cultivation in the subsistence systems during the second millennium and the first half of the first millennium B.C. In Gajiganna and Kursakata (Nigeria) pearl millet cultivation was integrated into a mixed economy of sedentary or semi-sedentary populations at least after 1200 B.C., with a strong focus on cattle-keeping, hunting, fishing, and gathering of wild grasses (Klee and Zach 1999; Klee et al. 2000; Neumann et al. 1996). In Burkina Faso and Mali a more mobile way of life can be inferred from scattered pearl millet finds in sites of mobile pastoralists or hunter-gatherers (MacDonald 1996; Vogelsang et al. 1999). Only in Birimi, a northernmost site of the Kintampo culture, might pearl millet cultivation have been a dominant activity for the sedentary population (D'Andrea and Casey 2002; D'Andrea et al. 2001), but interestingly *Pennisetum* is also the only crop recorded so far.

Breunig and Neumann (2002b) claim that dramatic economic, technological, and social changes took place in the West African Sahel during the first millennium bc (phase II) which were eventually correlated with climatic fluctuations. The development of iron technology, social stratification, and larger villages and urban centers, together with a highly diversified Iron Age agriculture, are poorly under-stood. Important crops which became the main components of modern West African agriculture, such as sorghum, African rice (*Oryza barthii*), cowpea (*Vigna unguiculata*), bambara groundnut (*Voandzeia subterranea*), and okra (*Hibiscus esculentus*), appear between 500 B.C. and A.D. 500 (Neumann 2003; Wetterstrom 1998). The roots of the very productive Iron Age subsistence systems in the West African savannas in the first millennium b.c., based on agro-forestry and mixed cropping of cereals and pulses, still remain to be elucidated.

Little progress has been made in recent decades on the origins of agriculture in the humid tropical zones of Africa. Evidence is almost as scarce as in the 1970s, when Coursey (1976) published his ideas on the origins of yam domestication. It is commonly assumed that the emergence of agriculture in the western and central African rain forest areas was stimulated from the north, and that grain crop agri-culture in Africa preceded tuber crop cultivation (Harris 1976), but neither archae-ological nor archaeobotanical data are available which might confirm diffusion between the West African Sahel and the rain forest area. A valuable cultural complex for the study of diffusion processes are sites from the Kintampo complex in Ghana which are distributed from the dry wooded savanna to the margins of the rain forest. The presence of domesticated *Pennisetum* at Birimi around 1800 b.c. (D'Andrea and Casey 2002; D'Andrea et al. 2001) evokes the question of how subsistence at the forest margins was influenced by the introduction of domesticated cereals some hundred kilometers further north. The available archaeobotanical evidence from the southern Kintampo sites in the second millennium B.C. is weak and could be inter-preted in terms of either a hunter-gatherer subsistence or incipient cultivation (Casey 2000; D'Andrea and Casey 2002; Stahl 1986).

Yams, the most important crop of the rain forest complex, are particularly diffi-cult to find in the archaeological record. Attempts have been made to trace yam cultivation indirectly, most often through the presence of oil palm (*Elaeis guineen-sis*) fruit stones or pollen. *Elaeis* is a natural component of forest margin vegetation and a pioneer which colonizes open ground. In a review of the palynological evidence, Sowunmi (1999) states that the distinct increase of *Elaeis* in the pollen profiles of West and West Central Africa after 3000 b.p. (1200 B.C.) indicates cul-tivation. This view has been questioned by Maley and Chepstow-Lusty (2001), who interpret the high oil palm percentages in rain forest pollen profiles as resulting from a dramatic forest decline due to an abrupt climatic crisis which culminated around 2500 b.p. (800/400 B.C.). It has often been stated that bad preservation of plant remains in the rain forest is the main obstacle for the study of agricultural origins in the rain forest. However, charred wood and fruit remains of *Canarium schweinfurthii* and oil palm have often been found in Central African archaeologi-cal sites as well as in Kintampo K6 in Ghana (Eggert 1993; Stahl 1985; Chapter 9) which suggests that the problem lies with lack of appropriate recovery techniques.

Surprisingly, the first and up to now single direct archaeobotanical proof for agri-culture in the rain forest consists of phytoliths of the cultivated banana (*Musa* sp.), a crop introduced from Asia (Mbida et al. 2000; Mbida Mindzie et al. 2001). Its early presence at the site Nkang in the Cameroonian rain forest around 800/400 B.C. raises more questions than it solves. How did the banana cross the Indian Ocean and East Africa before it entered the rain forest? Did the introduction of Asian crops act as a stimulus for the development of indigenous rain forest agriculture? What is the role of the banana in an agricultural system which enabled the occupation of the rain forest in the first millennium B.C.? And last, but not least: is the emergence of agriculture related to climatic change which seriously affected the central African rain forest in the first millennium B.C. (Maley and Brenac 1998; Schwartz 1992)?

There are hardly any new archaeobotanical data on the spread of agriculture to southern Africa. Research on one of the most fascinating problems in African archaeology, the origin and spread of "Bantu" communities from their supposed homelands in West Central Africa all over the continent, is mainly in the hand of linguists and archaeologists working with indirect circumstantial evidence (Chapter 12). The enormous intellectual distance between the indirect approach and concepts based on "hard evidence" is illustrated by Vansina (1994/95:15), who states that "a complex based on grain crops and the herding of domestic stock developed in northeast Africa during the sixth millennium B.C. and spread southward." The gap of 6,000 years between Vansina's "grain crop complex" and the first appearance of domesticated sorghum in the archaeological record reflects the incompatibility and the mutual ignorance of two fundamentally different approaches. Stahl (1984:20) sees the attempt to correlate the spread of ironworking, agriculture, and Bantu-speaking peoples as an "an archaeological cul-de-sac." The surprises that can be expected in the future if plant remains from archaeological sites are interpreted without prejudice are shown in the study of Jonsson (1998) on Iron Age sites in Zimbabwe, dated between 400 and 1600 a.d. Besides domesticates such as sorghum, finger millet, and bambara groundnut, the sites yielded several wild grasses and fruits harvested for food, a further example of a mixed economy already known from western Africa. This has no equivalent in the crop-centered linguistic concepts. Studies from Europe and the Near East have demonstrated how much a generalized picture of agricultural diffusion has to be modified and corrected in the light of new data (Harris, ed., 1996). The archaeobotanical evidence for southern Africa necessary for such a correction remains to be found.

Why So Late?

The most striking pattern in the available archaeobotanical information is the very young age of the indigenous African crops. Of course the absence of evidence does not inevitably mean evidence of absence. We have to admit that for some areas, especially the rain forest and its margins where the origin of tuber crops is assumed, no data are available at all. However, the archaeobotanical assemblages from the Sahara, the Sahel, East Africa, and southern Africa draw a consistent picture of agriculture as a late phenomenon, developing slightly before 1800 b.c. in the southwestern and south-central Sahara, and much later, from the middle of the first millennium b.c. onwards, in other parts of the continent. Comparison of the African data with those from other continents reveals a gap of several thousand years in the appearance of domesticated plants. Even if only the "safe" archaeobotanical finds are considered and controversial older evidence is regarded with caution, the gap between the earliest domesticates in Africa and those from other continents would be at least 1,500 years for America, 5,000 years for China, and 6,000 years for the Near East (Neumann 2003).

Especially striking is the large gap between the emergence of agriculture in Egypt and that in sub-Saharan Africa. At least 3,000 years before pearl millet and 5,000 years before sorghum were domesticated, agriculture based on crops of Near Eastern origin is attested at Predynastic sites dated to the sixth millennium b.c. (Wetterstrom 1993; Zohary and Hopf 2000:219). It has often been argued that the Near Eastern domesticates could not spread to sub-Saharan Africa with its monsoonal climate, because they are long-day plants and must be planted in the winter (Willcox 1992). However, diffusion of the idea of agriculture might well have been possible. Ancient Egypt was not isolated, and it is conceivable that during the periods when its agricultural system flourished, people in the Sahara or the adjacent Sudan might have taken up the idea of cultivation and converted it into the domestication of tropical summer crops. Why did this not occur, or why did it occur so late?

Several lines of argument can be distinguished (Neumann 2003). Unfavorable preservation in tropical soils or taphonomy and site context might be responsible for the missing evidence (Young and Thompson 1999). Stemler (1984), Haaland (1995, 1999), and Abdel-Magid (1989) see cross-pollination and harvesting techniques as the major factor preventing the selection of domestication traits, especially in *Sorghum* and *Pennisetum*. Diamond (1997) also regards cross-pollination in wild grasses as the main obstacle for the domestication process, and holds that Africa was at an environmental disadvantage because it does not possess enough plant species suitable for domestication to compete with other continents.

Claims that agriculture in Africa must be older than attested by archaeobotanical data get their support from the persisting paradox that several African crops appear earlier in India than on their home continent Africa. A recent review has established the reliability of the Indian finds which formerly had been a matter of debate (Fuller 2003). *Sorghum bicolor*, *Pennisetum glaucum*, and *Vigna unguiculata* became available in India during the first half of the second millennium B.C. As the wild ancestors of these crops are distributed in Africa, but not in India, initial domestication must have taken place on the African continent, and the period required for this process would be the end of the third millennium b.c., for which evidence is still completely missing. But even if remains of domesticated sorghum, pearl millet, and cowpea dating to the third millennium b.c. were detected, thus furnishing the "missing link" between Africa and India, this would not generally change the picture, as it would only slightly reduce the time gap between sub-Saharan Africa and the other continents, especially the Near East.

J. D. Clark (1980:59) suggested that the very nature of African ecosystems maintained population densities below the maximum carrying capacity and thus postponed the emergence of agriculture much longer than on the other continents. In this scenario, the savannas play a prominent role. Savannas cover large parts of the continent and extended far into the Sahara during the Early and Middle Holocene. The "Garden of Eden" hypothesis (Neumann 2003) explains the late emergence of agriculture with the special ecological conditions of the savannas which harbor a wealth of wild plants and animals which, however, are unequally distributed in time and space and can be best exploited by mobile populations.

A further reason is Africa's special development of animal domestication. Pastoralism with cattle emerged much earlier than plant cultivation and was a well-established system in the Sahara from at least 5000 B.C. (Chapter 8). Herding of cattle requires a nomadic or transhumant way of life which fits better with a flexible exploitation of abundant wild plant resources than with plant cultivation (Marshall and Hildebrandt 2002). Farming on a larger scale is inevitably connected with a sedentary way of life, and both developed only late in the savanna because mobile economies were so successful.

Conclusion

The use of wild plants was an important element of African subsistence throughout the Holocene and continues to be successful up to modern times. Africa presents the greatest example of the "vast middle ground" in the transitional zone between foragers and agriculturalists. Given the intimate knowledge of wild resources which has a long tradition in Africa dating back to the Pleistocene, it is conceivable that some "low-level food production" (Smith 2001b) was practiced long before domesticates appear in the archaeological record. However, this can only be detected if the biased focus on domesticates is given up in favor of studies on complete plant assemblages. Our understanding of "middle ground economies" can be greatly enhanced by ethnobotanical information on the modern use of semi-domesticates and the management of wild plants as well as on traditional plant cultivation and processing.

Modeling the role of plant cultivation in an economy of diversified risks, including stock-keeping, foraging, fishing, and hunting, is a key issue for studies on the emergence of agriculture in the southern Sahara. A relationship with increasing climatic insecurity during the third and second millennia b.c. can be assumed, but for the time being the paleoenvironmental and archaeobotanical data are too sparse to formulate a conclusive model. The fact that pearl millet remains the only domesticate for more than a millennium may be due to the small number of sites from which plant remains have been studied. But it may equally reflect the minor role that cultivation played in the subsistence systems.

The absence of evidence for agriculture in central, eastern, and southern Africa until the middle of the first millennium b.c. is often put down to preservation, site context, or recovery problems. A gap of 6,000 years or more between the emergence of agriculture in the Near East and Africa seems inconceivable – and may be unacceptable if it is implicitly taken for granted that all continents must have had their "Neolithic revolution" early in the Holocene. Would it not be much more consistent to assume that Africa's way was unique, because of its rich environmental resources, especially in the savannas, and the particular role of mobile pastoralism as two factors postponing agriculture for several millennia?

The first millennium b.c. seems to be of fundamental importance for the development of sedentary agriculture all over Africa. Or is it a mere coincidence that domesticates of all kinds (cereals, pulses, and even introduced Asian crops) show up at the beginning of the Iron Age in West, Central, and East Africa? The relationship between the emergence of iron technology, social complexity, and diversified agricultural systems is almost completely unknown – at least if regarded from a "data-focused" perspective. In my view, the emergence of diversified agricultural systems and the rapid spread of crops all over the continent in the first millennium b.c. is one of the most challenging research topics for the future.

It can no longer be said that evidence is absent because no one looks for the plant remains in African archaeological sites. Numerous studies, mainly from the Sahara and West Africa, have contributed to our knowledge of prehistoric plant use. However, the lack of basic data still remains the major problem in the search for agricultural origins, especially in regard to central and southern Africa. A general experience from archaeobotanical work in Africa is that new data often open the way to surprising insights and lead to a revision of former models. More surprises can be expected in the future.

NOTE

1   A major problem for any discussion of the transition from gathering to plant food production is temporal inaccuracy. The inconsistent use of uncalibrated and calibrated dates in the literature makes direct comparison difficult, especially with older material where the deviation between calibrated and uncalibrated dates can be considerable. Direct AMS dates on plant remains and calibration programs have brought considerable progress. For a better comparison within this chapter, all available b.p. dates have been calibrated with OxCal v3.5 © Bronk Ramsey 2000 (Bronk Ramsey 1995) with atmospheric data from Stuiver et al. (1998). Calibrated dates are expressed as B.C./A.D.

REFERENCES

Abdel-Magid, Anwar, 1989 Plant Domestication in the Middle Nile Basin: An Archaeoethnobotanical Case Study. Cambridge Monographs in African Archaeology 35. BAR International Series, 523. Oxford: British Archaeological Reports.

Albert, Klaus-Dieter, Maya Hallier, Stefanie Kahlheber, and Christoph Pelzer, 2000 Montée et abandon des collines d'occupation de l'Age de Fer au nord du Burkina Faso. Berichte des Sonderforschungsbreichs 268 14:335–351.

Amblard, Sylvie, 1996 Agricultural Evidence and its Interpretation on the Dhars Tichitt and

Oualata, South-Eastern Mauritania. *In* Aspects of African Archaeology. Papers from the 10th Congress of the Pan-African Association for Prehistory and Related Studies. Gilbert Pwiti and Robert Soper, eds. pp. 421–427. Harare: University of Zimbabwe Publications.

Amblard, Sylvie, and Jean Pernès, 1989 The Identification of Cultivated Pearl Millet (*Pennisetum*) Amongst Plant Impressions on Pottery from Oued Chebbi (Dhar Oualata, Mauritania). The African Archaeological Review 7:117–126.

Barakat, Hala, and Ahmed el-Din Fahmy, 1999 Wild Grasses as "Neolithic" Food Resources in the Eastern Sahara: A Review of the Evidence from Egypt. *In* The Exploitation of Plant Resources in Ancient Africa. Marijke van der Veen, ed. pp. 33–46. New York: Kluwer Academic/Plenum Publishers.

Barich, Barbara, 1998 People, Water and Grain. The Beginnings of Domestication in the Sahara and the Nile Valley. Rome: L'Erma di Bretschneider.

Barnett, Tertia, 1999 The Emergence of Food Production in Ethiopia. Cambridge Monographs in African Archaeology 45. BAR International Series, 763. Oxford: Archaeopress.

Bar-Yosef, Ofer, 1998 Introduction. Some Comments on the History of Research. *In* The Transition to Agriculture in the Old World. Ofer Bar-Yosef, ed. The Review of Archaeology 19(2):1–11.

Biehl, Edward, Fred Wendorf, Warren Landry, Asrat Desta, and Leilani Watrous, 1999 The Use of Gas Chromatography and Mass Spectroscopy in the Identification of Ancient Sorghum Seeds. *In* The Exploitation of Plant Resources in Ancient Africa. Marijke van der Veen, ed. pp. 47–53. New York: Kluwer Academic/Plenum Publishers.

Boardman, Sheila, 1999 The Agricultural Foundation of the Aksumite Empire, Ethiopia: An Interim Report. *In* The Exploitation of Plant Resources in Ancient Africa. Marijke van der Veen, ed. pp. 137–147. New York: Kluwer Academic/Plenum Publishers.

Breunig, Peter, and Katharina Neumann, 1999 Archäologische und archäobotanische Forschungen in Westafrika. Archäologisches Nachrichtenblatt 4:336–357.

———2002a From Hunters and Gatherers to Food Producers: New Archaeological and Archaeobotanical Evidence from the West African Sahel. *In* Drought, Food and Culture: Ecological Change and Food Security in Africa's Later Past. Fekri A. Hassan, ed. pp. 123–155. New York: Kluwer Academic/Plenum Publishers.

———2002b Continuity or Discontinuity? The 1st Millennium BC Crisis in West African Prehistory. *In* Tides of the Desert-Gezeiten der Wüste. Contributions to the Archaeology and Environmental History of Africa in Honour of Rudolph Kuper. Tilman Lenssen-Erz, et al., eds. pp. 491–505. Africa Praehistorica 14. Cologne: Heinrich Barth Institut.

———2004 Zwischen Wüste und Regenwald. Besiedlungsgeschichte der westafrikanischen Savanne im Holozän. *In* Mensch und Natur in Westafrika. Klaus-Dieter Albert, Doris Löhr, and Katharina Neumann, eds. 93–138. Weinheim: Wiley–VCH.

Bronk Ramsey, C., 1995 Radiocarbon Calibration and Analysis of Stratigraphy: The OxCal Program. Radiocarbon 37:425–430.

Camps, Gabriel, 1969 Amekni. Néolithique ancien du Hoggar. Mémoires du CRAPE 10. Paris: Centre de Recherches Anthropologiques, Préhistoriques et Ethnographiques.

Casey, Joanna, 1998 The Ecology of Food Production in West Africa. *In* Transformations in Africa. Essays on Africa's Later Past. Graham Connah, ed. pp. 46–70. London: Leicester University Press.

———2000 The Kintampo Complex: The Late Holocene on the Gambaga Escarpment, Northern Ghana. BAR International Series, 906. Oxford: British Archaeological Reports.

Chevalier, A. 1938 Le Sahara, centre d'origine de plantes cultivées. Mémoires de la Société de Biogéographie 6:307–322.

Clark, J. Desmond, 1964 The Prehistoric Origins of African Cultures. Journal of African History 5:161–183.

——1976 Prehistoric Populations and Pressures Favoring Plant Domestication in Africa. *In* Origins of African Plant Domestication. Jack R. Harlan, Jan M. J. de Wet, and Ann B. L. Stemler, eds. pp. 67–105. The Hague: Mouton.

——1980 Early Human Occupation of African Savanna Environments. *In* Human Ecology in Savanna Environments. David R. Harris, ed. pp. 41–71. London: Academic Press.

Clark, J. Desmond, and Steven A. Brandt, eds., 1984 From Hunters to Farmers. The Causes and Consequences of Food Production in Africa. Berkeley: University of California Press.

Coulibaly, S., R. S. Pasquet, R. Papa, and Paul Gepts, 2002 AFLP Analysis of the Phenotypic Organization and Genetic Diversity of *Vigna unguiculata* L. Walp. Reveals Extensive Gene Flow Between Wild and Domesticated Types. Theory of Applied Genetics 104: 358–366.

Coursey, D. G., 1976 The Origins and Domestication of Yams in Africa. *In* Origins of African Plant Domestication. Jack R. Harlan, Jan M. J. de Wet, and Ann B. L. Stemler, eds. pp. 383–408. The Hague: Mouton.

D'Andrea, A. Catherine, and Joanna Casey, 2002 Pearl Millet and Kintampo Subsistence. The African Archaeological Review 19:147–173.

D'Andrea, A. Catherine, Marlies Klee and Joanna Casey, 2001 Archaeobotanical Evidence for Pearl Millet (*Pennisetum glaucum*) in Sub-Saharan Africa. Antiquity 75:341–348.

D'Andrea, Catherine, Diane Lyons, Mitku Haile, and Ann Butler, 1999 Ethnoarchaeological Approaches to the Study of Prehistoric Agriculture in the Highlands of Ethiopia. *In* The Exploitation of Plant Resources in Ancient Africa. Marijke van der Veen, ed. pp. 101–122. New York: Kluwer Academic/Plenum Publishers.

Diamond, Jared, 1997 Guns, Germs and Steel: The Fates of Human Societies. New York: W. W. Norton.

di Lernia, Savino, ed., 1999 The Uan Afuda Cave. Hunter-Gatherer Societies of Central Sahara. Arid Zone Archaeology Monographs 1. Florence: Edizioni all' Insegna del Giglio.

di Lernia, Savino, and Giorgio Manzi, eds., 1998 Before Food Production in North Africa. Forlì: Edizioni ABACO.

Dombrowski, Joanne C. 1970 Preliminary Report on Excavations in Lalibela and Natchabiet Caves, Begemeder. Annales d'Ethiopie 8:21–29.

——1971 Excavations in Ethiopia: Lalibela and Natchabiet Caves, Begemeder Province. Ph.D. dissertation, Boston University.

Edwards, S. 1991 Plants with Wild Relatives Found in Ethiopia. *In* Plant Genetic Resources of Ethiopia. J. Hawkes, J. M. J. Engels, and T. Wordede, eds. pp. 42–74. Cambridge: Cambridge University Press.

Eggert, Manfred K. H., 1993 Central Africa and the Archaeology of the Equatorial Rainforest: Reflections on Some Major Topics. *In* The Archeology of Africa. Food, Metals and Towns. Thurstan Shaw, Paul Sinclair, Bassey Andah, and Alex Okpoko, eds. pp. 289–329. London: Routledge.

el Hadidi, M. Nabil, 1980 Vegetation of the Nubian Desert (Nabta Region). *In* Prehistory of the Eastern Sahara. Fred Wendorf and Romuald Schild, eds. pp. 345–351. New York: Academic Press.

Flannery, Kent V., 1969 Origins and Ecological Effects of Early Domestication in Iran and the Near East. *In* The Domestication and Exploitation of Plants and Animals. P. J. Ucko and G. W. Dimbleby, eds. pp. 73–100. Chicago: Aldine.

Fuller, Dorian Q., 2003 African Crops in Prehistoric South Asia: A Critical Review. *In* Food, Fuel and Fields: Progress in African Archaeobotany. Katharina Neumann, Ann Butler, and

Stefanie Kahlheber, eds. pp. 239–271. Africa Praehistorica 15. Cologne: Heinrich Barth Institut.

Garcea, Elena, ed. 2001 Uan Tabu in the Settlement History of the Libyan Sahara. Arid Zone Monographs 2. Florence: Edizioni all' Insegna del Giglio.

Gebauer, Anne Birgitte, and T. Douglas Price, eds. 1992 Transitions to Agriculture in Prehistory. Monographs in World Archaeology 4. Madison: Prehistory Press.

Germer, Renate, 1985 Flora des pharäonischen Ägypten. Mainz: Philipp von Zabern.

Guo, Zhengtang, Nicole Petit-Maire, and Stefan Kröpelin, 2000 Holocene Non-Orbital Climatic Events in Present-Day Arid Areas of Northern Africa and China. Global and Planetary Change 26:97–103.

Haaland, Randi, 1984 Continuity and Discontinuity: How to Account for a Two-Thousand Year Gap in the Cultural History in the Khartoum Nile Environment. Norwegian Archaeological Review 17:39–51.

——1995 Sedentism, Cultivation, and Plant Domestication in the Holocene Middle Nile Region. Journal of Field Archaeology 22:157–174.

——1999 The Puzzle of the Late Emergence of Domesticated Sorghum in the Nile Valley. In The Prehistory of Food. Chris Gosden and Jon Hather, eds. pp. 397–418. London: Routledge.

Harlan, Jack R., 1969 Ethiopia: A Center of Diversity. Economic Botany 23:309–314.

——1971 Agricultural Origins: Centers and Non-Centers. Science 174:468–474.

——1989 The Tropical African Cereals. In Foraging and Farming. David R. Harris and Gordon C. Hillman, eds. pp. 335–343. London: Unwin Hyman.

——1992 Indigenous African Agriculture. In The Origins of Agriculture, C. Wesley Cowan and Patty Jo Watson, eds. pp. 59–70. Washington, DC: Smithsonian Institution Press.

——1995 The Living Fields: Our Agricultural Heritage. Cambridge: Cambridge University Press.

Harlan, Jack R., and Ann B. L. Stemler, 1976 The Races of Sorghum in Africa. In Origins of African Plant Domestication. Jack R. Harlan, Jan M. J. de Wet, and Ann B. L. Stemler, eds. pp. 465–478. The Hague: Mouton.

Harlan, Jack R., Jan M. J. de Wet, and Ann B. L. Stemler, eds., 1976 Origins of African Plant Domestication. The Hague: Mouton.

Harris, David R., 1976 Traditional Systems of Plant Food Production and the Origins of Agriculture in West Africa. In Origins of African Plant Domestication. Jack R. Harlan, Jan M. J. de Wet and Ann B. L. Stemler, eds. pp. 311–356. The Hague: Mouton.

——1977 Alternative Pathways Towards Agriculture. In Origins of Agriculture. Charles A. Reed, ed. pp. 179–243. The Hague: Mouton.

——1989 An Evolutionary Continuum of People–Plant Interactions. In Foraging and Farming. The Evolution of Plant Exploitation. David R. Harris and Gordon C. Hillman, eds. pp. 11–26. London: Unwin Hyman.

——1990 Vavilov's Concept of Centres of Origin of Cultivated Plants: Its Genesis and its Influence on the Study of Agricultural Origins. Biological Journal of the Linnean Society 39:7–16.

——1996 Domesticatory Relationships of People, Plants and Animals. In Redefining Nature: Ecology, Culture and Domestication. R. Ellen and K. Fukui, eds. pp. 437–463. Oxford: Berg.

Harris, David R., ed., 1996 The Origins and Spread of Agriculture and Pastoralism in Eurasia. London: University College London Press.

Hassan, Fekri A., 1997 Holocene Palaeoclimates of Africa. African Archaeological Review 14:214–230.

Hather, Jon G., ed., 1994 Tropical Archaeobotany: Applications and New Developments. One World Archaeology 22. London: Routledge.

Hillman, Gordon C., 1989 Late Palaeolithic Plant Foods from Wadi Kubbaniya in Upper Egypt: Dietary Diversity, Infant Weaning, and Seasonality in a Riverine Environment. In Foraging and Farming: The Evolution of Plant Exploitation. David R. Harris and Gordon C. Hillman, eds. pp. 207–239. One World Archaeology 13. London: Unwin Hyman.

Hillman, Gordon C., and M. Stuart Davies, 1990 Domestication Rates in Wild-Type Wheats and Barley Under Primitive Cultivation. Biological Journal of the Linnean Society 39:39–78.

Hillman, Gordon C., Ewa Madeyska, and Jonathan Hather, 1989 Wild Plant Foods and Diet at Late Paleolithic Wadi Kubbaniya: The Evidence from Charred Remains. In The Prehistory of Wadi Kubbaniya, vol. 2: Stratigraphy, Paleoeconomy, and Environment. Fred Wendorf, Romuald Schild, and Angela E. Close, eds. pp. 162–242. Dallas: Southern Methodist University Press.

Hilu, K. W., K. M. Ribu, H. Liang, and C. Mandelbaum, 1997 Fonio Millets: Ethnobotany, Genetic Diversity and Evolution. South African Journal of Botany 63(4):185–190.

Hoelzmann, Philipp, Birgit Keding, Hubert Berke, Stefan Kröpelin, and Hans-Joachim Kruse, 2001 Environmental Change and Archaeology: Lake Evolution and Human Occupation in the Eastern Sahara During the Holocene. Palaeogeography, Palaeoclimatology, Palaeoecology 169:193–217.

Höhn, Alexa, Stefanie Kahlheber and Maya Hallier-von Czerniewicz, In press Den frühen Bauern auf der Spur – Siedlungs- und Vegetationsgeschichte der Region Oursi (Burkina Faso). In Mensch und Natur in Westafrika. Klaus-Dieter Albert, Doris Löhr, and Katharina Neumann, eds. Weinheim: Wiley–VCH.

Hugot, H.-J., 1968 The Origins of Agriculture: Sahara. Current Anthropology 9:483–488.

Jacques-Félix, H., 1971 Grain Impressions. In The Tichitt Tradition: A Late Prehistoric Occupation of the Southwestern Sahara. Patrick J. Munson, Ph.D. dissertation, Department of Anthropology, University of Illinois, Urbana-Champaign.

Jonsson, Jimmy, 1998 Early Plant Economy in Zimbabwe. Studies in African Archaeology 16. Uppsala: Uppsala University. Department of Archaeology and Ancient History.

Keding, Birgit, 1997 Djabarona 84/13. Untersuchungen zur Besiedlungsgeschichte des Wadi Howar anhand der Keramik des 3. und 2. Jahrtausends v.Chr. Cologne: Heinrich Barth Institut.

Klee, Marlies, and Barbara Zach, 1999 The Exploitation of Wild and Domesticated Food Plants at Settlement Mounds in North-East Nigeria (1800 cal BC to Today). In The Exploitation of Plant Resources in Ancient Africa. Marijke van der Veen, ed. pp. 81–88. New York: Kluwer Academic/Plenum Publishers.

Klee, Marlies, Barbara Zach, and Katharina Neumann, 2000 Four Thousand Years of Plant Exploitation in the Chad Basin of NE Nigeria 1: The Archaeobotany of Kursakata. Vegetation History and Archaeobotany 9:223–237.

Kuper, Rudolph, ed. 1989 Forschungen zur Umweltgeschichte der Ostsahara. Africa Praehistorica 2. Cologne: Heinrich Barth Institut.

MacDonald, Kevin C., 1996 The Windé Koroji Complex: Evidence for the Peopling of the Eastern Inland Niger Delta (2100–500 BC). Préhistoire et Anthropologie Méditeranéennes 5:147–165.

——1998 Before the Empire of Ghana: Pastoralism and the Origins of Cultural Complexity in the Sahel. In Transformations in Africa. Essays on Africa's Later Past. Graham Connah, ed. pp. 71–103. London: Leicester University Press.

——2000 The Origins of African Livestock. Indigenous or Imported? In The Origins and

Development of African Livestock: Archaeology, Genetics, Linguistics and Ethnography. Roger M. Blench and Kevin C. MacDonald, eds. pp. 2–17. London: University College London Press.

Maley, Jean, 1997 Middle to Late Holocene Changes in Tropical Africa and Other Continents: Palaeomonsoon and Sea Surface Temperature Variations. *In* Third Millennium BC Climatic Change and Old World Collapse. Nüzhet Dalfes, George Kukla, and Harvey Weiss, eds. pp. 611–639. NATO Advanced Science Institut Series I, 49. Berlin and Heidelberg: Springer.

Maley, Jean, and Patrice Brenac, 1998 Vegetation Dynamics, Palaeoenvironments and Climatic Change in the Forests of Western Cameroon During the Last 28000 Years B.P. Review of Palaeobotany and Palynology 99:157–187.

Maley, Jean, and Alex Chepstow-Lusty, 2001 *Elaeis guineensis* Jacq. (Oil Palm) Fluctuations in Central Africa During the Late Holocene: Climate or Human Driving Forces for this Pioneering Species? Vegetation History and Archaeobotany 10:171–120.

Marshall, Fiona, 1998 Early Food Production in Africa. The Review of Archaeology 19(2):47–59.

Marshall, Fiona, and Elisabeth Hildebrandt, 2002 Cattle Before Crops: The Beginnings of Food Production in Africa. Journal of World Prehistory 16(2):99–143.

Mbida, Christophe M., Wim van Neer, Hugues Doutrelepont, and Luc Vrydaghs, 2000 Evidence for Banana Cultivation and Animal Husbandry During the First Millennium BC in the Forest of Southern Cameroon. Journal of Archaeological Science 27:151–162.

Mbida Mindzie, Christophe, Hugues Doutrelepont, Luc Vrydaghs, Ronny L. Swennen, Rudy J. Swennen, Hans Beeckman, Edmond De Langhe, and Pierre de Maret, 2001 First Archaeological Evidence of Banana Cultivation in Central Africa during the Third Millennium Before Present. Vegetation History and Archaeobotany 10:1–6.

Mercuri, Anna Maria, 2001 Preliminary Analysis of Fruits, Seeds and Few Plant Macrofossils from the Early Holocene Sequence. *In* Uan Tabu in the Settlement History of the Eastern Sahara. Elena A. A. Garcea, ed. pp. 189–210. Arid Zone Archaeology Monographs 2. Florence: Edizioni all' Insegna del Giglio.

Munson, Patrick J., 1971 The Tichitt Tradition: A Late Prehistoric Occupation of the Southwestern Sahara. Ph.D. dissertation, Department of Anthropology, University of Illinois, Urbana-Champaign.

——1976 Archaeological Data on the Origins of Cultivation in the Southwestern Sahara and their Implications for West Africa. *In* Origins of African Plant Domestication. Jack R. Harlan, Jan M. J. de Wet, and Ann B. L. Stemler, eds. pp. 187–210. The Hague: Mouton.

Murdock, G. P., 1959 Africa. Its Peoples and their Culture History. New York: McGraw-Hill.

Neumann, Katharina, 1989 Holocene Vegetation of the Eastern Sahara: Charcoal From Prehistoric Sites. The African Archaeological Review 7:97–116.

——1999 Early Plant Food Production in the West African Sahel: New Evidence. *In* The Exploitation of Plant Resources in Ancient Africa. Marijke van der Veen, ed. pp. 73–80. New York: Kluwer Academic/Plenum Publishers.

——2003 The Late Emergence of Agriculture in Sub-Saharan Africa: Archaeological Evidence and Ecological Considerations. *In* Food, Fuel and Fields: Progress in African Archaeobotany. Katharina Neumann, Ann Butler, and Stefanie Kahlheber, eds. pp. 71–92. Africa Praehistorica 15. Cologne: Heinrich Barth Institut.

Neumann, Katharina, Aziz Ballouche, and Marlies Klee, 1996 The Emergence of Plant Food Production in the West African Sahel: New Evidence from Northeast Nigeria and Northern Burkina Faso. *In* Aspects of African Archaeology. Papers from the 10th Congress of the Pan-African Association for Prehistory and Related Studies. Gilbert Pwiti, and Robert Soper, eds. pp. 441–448. Harare: University of Zimbabwe Publications.

Neumann, Katharina, Ann Butler, and Stefanie Kahlheber, eds., 2003 Food, Fuel and Fields. Progress in African Archaeobotany. Cologne: Heinrich Barth Institut.

Neumann, Katharina, Stefanie Kahlheber, and Dirk Uebel, 1998 Remains of Woody Plants from Saouga, a Medieval West African Village. Vegetation History and Archaeobotany 7(2):57–77.

Pachur, Hans-Joachim, and Stefan Kröpelin, 1987 Wadi Howar: Palaeoclimatic Evidence from an Extinct River System in the Southeastern Sahara. Science 237:298–300.

Pasquet, Rémy S., Sonya Schwedes, and Paul Gepts, 1999 Isozyme Diversity in Bambara Groundnut. Crop Science 39:1228–1236.

Peregrine, Peter N., and Melvin Ember, eds., 2001 Encyclopedia of Africa, vol. 1: Africa. New York: Kluwer Academic/Plenum Publishers.

Person, Alain, Nour E. Saoudi, and Sylvie Amblard, 1995 Nouvelles recherches, objectifs et premier résultats sur le paléoenvironnement holocène des sites archéologiques de la région des Dhars Tichitt et Oualata (Mauritanie sud-orientale). Journal des Africanistes 65(2): 9–29.

Phillipson, David W., 2000 Archaeology at Aksum, Ethiopia. 1993–7, vols. 1 and 2. London: The British Institute in Eastern Africa.

Portères, Roland, 1950 Vieilles agricultures africaines avant le XVIème siècle: Berceaux d'agriculture et centres de variation. L'Agronomie Tropicale 5:489–507.

——1962 Berceaux agricoles primaires sur le continent africaine. Journal of African History 3:195–210.

Price, T. Douglas, and Anne Birgitte Gebauer, eds., 1995 Last Hunters – First Farmers. Santa Fe: School of American Research Press.

Purseglove, J. W., 1976 The Origins and Migrations of Crops in Tropical Africa. In Origins of African Plant Domestication. Jack R. Harlan, Jan M. J. de Wet, and Ann B. L. Stemler, eds. pp. 291–309. The Hague: Mouton.

Rowley-Conwy, Peter A., W. J. Deakin, and C. H. Shaw, 1997 Ancient DNA from Archaeological Sorghum (Sorghum bicolor) from Qasr Ibrim, Nubia. Implications for Domestication and Evolution and a Review of the Archaeological Evidence. Sahara 9:23–34.

Schwartz, Dominique, 1992 Assèchement climatique vers 3000 B.P. et expansion Bantu en Afrique centrale atlantique: Quelques réflexions. Bulletin de la Société Géologique de France 163:353–361.

Shaw, C. Thurstan, 1976 Early Crops in Africa: A Review of the Evidence. In Origins of African Plant Domestication. Jack R. Harlan, Jan M. J. de Wet, and Ann B. L. Stemler, eds. pp. 107–153. The Hague: Mouton.

Shaw, C. Thurstan, Paul Sinclair, Bassey Andah, and Alex Okpoko, eds., 1993 The Archaeology of Africa: Food, Metals and Towns. One World Archaeology 20. London: Routledge.

Smith, Andrew B., 1974 Preliminary Report of Excavations at Karkarichinkat, Mali, 1972. West African Journal of Archaeology 4:33–55.

——1975 A Note on the Flora and Fauna from the Post-Paleolithic Sites of Karkarichinkat Nord et Sud. West African Journal of Archaeology 5:201–204.

——1984 Origins of the Neolithic in the Sahara. In From Hunters to Farmers. The Causes and Consequences of Food Production in Africa. J. Desmond Clark and Steven A. Brandt, eds. pp. 84–92. Berkeley: University of California Press.

——1992 Pastoralism in Africa: Origins and Development Ecology. London: Hurst.

Smith, Bruce D., 1998 The Emergence of Agriculture. 2nd edition. New York: Scientific American Library.

—— 2001a The Transition to Food Production. *In* Archaeology at the Millennium: A Source-book. Gary M. Feinman and T. Douglas Price, eds. pp. 199–229. New York: Kluwer Academic/Plenum Publishers.

—— 2001b Low-Level Food Production. Journal of Archaeological Research, 9(1):1–43.

Smith, Susan E., 1980 The Environmental Adaptation of Nomads in the West African Sahel: A Key to Understand Prehistoric Pastoralists. *In* The Sahara and the Nile. Martin A. J. Williams and Hugues Faure, eds. pp. 467–489. Rotterdam: Balkema.

Sowunmi, M. Adebisi, 1999 The Significance of the Oil Palm (*Elaeis guineensis* Jacq.) in the Late Holocene Environments of West and West Central Africa: A Further Consideration. Vegetation History and Archaeobotany 8:199–210.

Stahl, Ann Brower, 1984 A History and Critique of Investigations into Early African Agri-culture. *In* From Hunters to Farmers. J. Desmond Clark and Steven A. Brandt, eds. pp. 9–21. Berkeley: University of California Press.

—— 1985 Reinvestigation of Kintampo 6 Rockshelter, Ghana: Implications for the Nature of Culture Change. The African Archaeological Review 3:117–150.

—— 1986 Early Food Production in West Africa: Rethinking the Role of the Kintampo Culture. Current Anthropology 27:532–536.

Stemler, Ann B. L., 1984 The Transition from Food Collecting to Food Production in North Africa. *In* From Hunters to Farmers, J. Desmond Clark and Steven A. Brandt, eds. pp. 127–131. Berkeley: University of California Press.

Stuchlik, Leon, and Krystyna Wasylikowa, eds., 1995 Acta Palaeobotanica 35(1). Kraków: Polish Academy of Sciences, W. Szafer Institute of Botany.

Stuiver, M., P. J. Reimer, E. Bard, J. W. Beck, G. S. Burr, K. A. Hughen, B. Kromer, G. McCormac, J. van der Plicht, and M. Spurk, 1998 INTCAL 98 Radiocarbon Age Calibration, 24000-0 cal BP. Radiocarbon 40:1041–1083.

Tostain, Serge, 1998 Le Mil, une longue histoire: Hypothèses sur sa domestication et ses migrations. *In* Plantes et paysages d'Afrique: Une histoire à explorer. Monique Chastenet, ed. pp. 461–490. Paris: Karthala.

Tubiana, Marie-José, and Joseph Tubiana, 1977 The Zaghawa from an Ecological Perspec-tive. Rotterdam: Balkema.

van der Veen, Marijke, 1995 Ancient Agriculture in Libya: A Review of the Evidence. Acta Palaeobotanica 35(1):85–98.

van der Veen, Marijke, ed., 1999 The Exploitation of Plant Resources in Ancient Africa. New York: Kluwer Academic/Plenum Publishers.

van Neer, Wim, 2002 Food Security in Western and Central Africa During the Late Holocene: The Role of Domestic Stock Keeping, Hunting and Fishing. *In* Drought, Food and Culture. Ecological Change and Food Security in Africa's Later Past. Fekri A. Hassan, ed. pp. 251–274. New York: Kluwer Academic/Plenum Publishers.

van Neer, Wim, and Hans-Peter Uerpmann, 1989 Palaeoecological Significance of the Holocene Faunal Remains of the B. O. S. Missions. *In* Forschungen zur Umweltgeschichte der Ostsahara. Rudolph Kuper, ed. pp. 307–341. Africa Praehistorica 2. Cologne: Heinrich Barth Institut.

Vansina, Jan, 1994/95 A Slow Revolution: Farming in Subequatorial Africa. *In* The Growth of Farming Communities in Africa From the Equator Southwards. J. E. G. Sutton, ed. pp. 15–26. Azania 29–30. Nairobi: British Institute in Eastern Africa.

Vavilov, Nikolai I., 1926 Studies on the Origin of Cultivated Plants (Russian and English). Leningrad: State Press.

Vernet, Robert, 2002 Climate During the Late Holocene in the Sahara and the Sahel: Evo-lution and Consequences on Human Settlement. *In* Drought, Food and Culture: Ecological Change and Food Security in Africa's Later Prehistory. Fekri A. Hassan, ed. pp. 47–63. New York: Kluwer Academic/Plenum Publishers.

Vernet, Robert, and Hugues Faure, 2000 Isotopic Chronology of the Sahara and the Sahel During the Late Pleistocene and the Early and Mid-Holocene (15.000–6000 BP). Quaternary International 68–71:385–387.

Vogelsang, Ralf, Albert Klaus-Dieter, and Stefanie Kahlheber, 1999 Le Sable savant: Les Cordons dunaires sahéliens au Burkina Faso comme archive archéologique et paléoécologique du Holocène. Sahara 11:51–68.

Wagner, Philip A., 1977 The Concept of Environmental Determinism in Cultural Evolution. *In* Origins of Agriculture. Charles A. Reed, ed. pp. 77–88. The Hague/Paris: Mouton.

Wasylikowa, Krystyna, 1992 Exploitation of Wild Plants by Prehistoric Peoples in the Sahara. Würzburger Geographische Arbeiten 84:247–262.

——1993 Plant Macrofossils from the Archaeological Sites of Uan Muhuggiag and Ti-n-Torha, Southwestern Libya. *In* Environmental Change and Human Culture in the Nile Basin and Northern Africa until the Second Millenium B.C. Lech Krzyzaniak, Michal Kobusiewicz, and John Alexander, eds. pp. 25–41. Studies in African Archaeology 4. Poznan: Poznan Archaeological Museum.

——1997 Flora of the 8000 Years Old Archaeological Site E-75-6 at Nabta Playa, Western Desert, Southern Egypt. Acta Palaeobotanica, 37(2):99–205.

——2001 Site E-75-6: Vegetation and Subsistence of the Early Neolithic at Nabta Playa, Egypt, Reconstructed from Charred Plant Remains. *In* Holocene Settlement of the Egyptian Sahara, vol. 1: The Archaeology of Nabta Playa. Fred Wendorf and Romuald Schild, eds. pp. 544–608. New York: Kluwer Academic/Plenum Publishers.

Wendorf, Fred, Romuald Schild, and associates, eds., 2001 Holocene Settlement of the Eastern Sahara, vol. 1, The Archaeology of Nabta Playa. New York: Kluwer Academic/Plenum Publishers.

Wendorf, Fred, Romuald Schild, and Angela E. Close, 1980 Loaves and Fishes: The Prehistory of Wadi Kubbaniya. Dallas: Southern Methodist University, Department of Anthropology.

Wendorf, Fred, Romuald Schild, Krystyna Wasylikowa, Jeff Dahlberg, John Evans and Ed Biehl, 1998 The Use of Plants during the Early Holocene in the Egyptian Sahara: Early Neolithic Food Economies. *In* Before Food Production in North Africa, Savino di Lernia and Giorgio Manzi, eds. pp. 71–78. Forlì: Edizioni ABACO.

Wendorf, Fred, Angela E. Close, Romuald Schild, Krystyna Wasylikowa, Rupert A. Housley, Jack R. Harlan, and Halina Królik, 1992 Saharan Exploitation of Plants 8000 Years BP. Nature 359:721–724.

Wendorf, Fred, Romuald Schild, M. Nabil el Hadidi, Angela E. Close, Michal Kobusiewicz, Hanna Wieckowska, B. Issawi, and H. Haas, 1979 Use of Barley in the Egyptian Late Palaeolithic. Science 205(9):1341–1347.

Wendorf, Fred, Romuald Schild, Angela E. Close, D. J. Donahue, A. J. T. Jull, T. H. Zabel, Hanna Wieckowska, Michal Kobusiewicz, M Nabil el Hadidi, and B. Issawi, 1984 New Radiocarbon Dates on the Cereals from Wadi Kubbaniya. Science 225:645–646.

Wetterstrom, Wilma, 1993 Foraging and Farming in Egypt: The Transition from Hunting and Gathering to Horticulture in the Nile Valley. *In* The Archaeology of Africa. Food, Metals and Towns. Thurstan Shaw, Paul Sinclair, Bassey Andah, and Alex Okpoko, eds. pp. 165–226. One World Archaeology 20. London: Routledge.

——1998 The Origins of Agriculture in Africa: With Particular Reference to Sorghum and Pearl Millet. *In* The Transitions to Agriculture in the Old World. Ofer Bar-Yosef, ed. The Review of Archaeology 19(2):30–46.

Willcox, George, 1992 Some Differences Between Crops of Near Eastern Origin and those from the Tropics. *In* South Asian Archaeology 1989. C. Jarrige, ed. pp. 291–300. Monographs in World Archaeology 14. Madison, WI: Prehistory Press.

Young, Ruth, and Barbara Thompson, 1999 Missing Plant Foods? Where Is the Archaeobotanical Evidence for Sorghum and Finger Millet in East Africa? *In* The Exploitation of Plant Resources in Ancient Africa. Marijke van der Veen, ed. pp. 63–72. New York: Kluwer Academic/Plenum Publishers.

Zohary, Daniel, 1996 The Mode of Domestication of the Founder Crops of Southwest Asian Agriculture. *In* The Origins and Spread of Agriculture and Pastoralism in Eurasia. David R. Harris, ed. pp. 142–158. London: University College London Press.

Zohary, Daniel, and Maria Hopf, 2000 Domestication of Plants in the Old World. The Origin and Spread of Cultivated Plants in West Asia, Europe, and the Nile Valley. 3rd edition Oxford: Oxford Science Publications.

11
Metallurgy and its Consequences

S. Terry Childs and Eugenia W. Herbert

The archaeology of metallurgy in sub-Saharan Africa is more advanced than in many other parts of the world. This is surprising since archaeology was viewed as difficult in much of the subcontinent because of the intractable environment and political instability. It testifies, however, to the importance of metalworking well into the 20th century, and to the tenacity of researchers from a range of disciplines. Africa is one of the very few places where archaeology and ethnography have complemented and informed each other for decades. Nowhere is this truer than in the field of metallurgy, which has benefited from interdisciplinary collaboration with historians, art historians, material scientists, engineers, and geologists.

Nevertheless, obstacles remain in studying the three stages of prehistoric metallurgical operations: mining, smelting, and forging. Historic and modern mining companies have often obliterated traces of ancient mines. Smelting transforms ore into raw, impure metal (called a "bloom" in the case of iron) through control of temperature and atmosphere in a furnace; under the best of circumstances, all that survives of ancient furnaces are the bowls or foundations, leaving few clues to superstructure (Avery et al. 1988). Forging involves heating and working raw metal into finished objects. Even less survives of forges since they consisted simply of stone or iron anvils situated next to a small fire pit of charcoal. Furthermore, in arid regions, desert winds may wear away surfaces or deposit sands over settlements; trees may become fossilized, making carbon dating confusing – old wood used for fuel may be preserved for centuries. In forest areas, dense vegetation obscures potential sites in a tangle of growth. Torrential rains and thin tropical soils cause strata to collapse in on each other; iron rusts away.

At the same time, our knowledge of African metallurgy is shaped by the questions that archaeologists pose. The most hotly debated has been the question of origins: did the knowledge of metalworking come to Africa from the outside world? If so, when and whence? But archaeologists are also looking at the technology itself to see in what ways it has evolved. Has it changed over time and adapted to local conditions? Are there uniquely African innovations? What impact have metals and metalworking had on individual societies and on the interrelationships between different groups? Did the advent of metals mark a distinct era in human history? Why did African metalworking stop short of making the next leap to industrial production, even in areas where it was a major player in the local economy? With provocative insights from ethnography and ethnoarchaeology, archaeologists are also examining the culture of metals. What were the social, political, and economic contexts of metal production and use? How did they vary across cultures and why? What roles did metals play in trade? Can we decipher the language of materials in which iron, copper, and gold played significant roles in ancient and more recent African cultures?

While archaeology can confirm the existence of metals and metalworking, it struggles to provide details of these technologies, and even more so the social relations and belief systems that underpinned them (e.g., Childs 1989a, 1991a; Collett 1993; Haaland et al. 2002; Killick 1991b; Miller 2001, 2002; Schmidt and Mapunda 1997). Continued use of interdisciplinary methods to probe the sociocultural contexts of metal production and use, combined with focused research on gaps in the time-space coordinates of the archaeometallurgical record should help us reconstruct more of the culture and history of metals in Africa.

Origins

Later African prehistory has been conceived as a simple sequence, encompassed by the Late Stone Age (LSA) through the Iron Age. This sequence built on differences between stone-using hunter-gatherer sites and later settled village sites associated with a mixed economy of agriculture and pastoralism, pottery and iron. Early researchers found little evidence of other metals, except for the early preoccupation with gold at Great Zimbabwe. Although we know more today about the Iron Age, numerous questions remain about the beginnings, development, and spread of metal-using and metal-producing cultures.

European models based on archaeological research in western Asia dominated much of the early speculation about the origins of African metalworking. Metalworking evolved in both the Middle East and China through a long-drawn-out sequence of exploitation, first of native copper, next smelted copper, then copper alloys, and finally smelted iron. The discovery that copper ores could be smelted to produce pure copper probably resulted from the use of copper carbonates to glaze pottery: the heat and reducing atmosphere in kilns used to fire pots accidentally produced metallic copper. Over time, metalworkers experimented with different types of ores, from the more easily smelted carbonates to the complex sulphides. They also learned that alloying copper with other metals enhanced its qualities, hardening it for forging or making it more ductile for casting.

Copper ores can be smelted at lower temperatures and with less control over the mandatory reducing atmosphere than iron, and metallic copper is easier to shape in the forge because it is softer. Hence, it is not surprising that copper and copper alloys were worked before iron. Indeed, most scholars have assumed that it would have been impossible to discover how to work iron, the most complex of the metals to reduce from ore in prehistory, without passing through these intermediate stages of pyrotechnical experience with more easily worked metals. Since copper-smelting furnaces were commonly fluxed with iron oxides, scholars have hypothesized that iron-smelting in the Near East first occurred as an accidental by-product of copper-smelting, and spread out from there. The diffusionist model was no doubt buttressed in some quarters by older assumptions about African backwardness (Chapter 1), but it also seemed to have the weight of logic on its side.

According to this scenario, then, metal technology must have come from outside the continent. But by what routes and when? The debate has raged for decades and is far from resolved. One school held that the most likely path ran south and west from Meroë on the Nubian Nile, while another proposed Phoenician settlements in North Africa as the source from which the technology dispersed southward across the Sahara. Still another suggested that there might have been multiple centers of diffusion. Whatever the source, metalworking would have reached sub-Saharan Africa in the final centuries preceding the present era and gradually spread throughout central and southern Africa as part of Bantu expansion (Chapter 12) in the period 500 b.c. to a.d. 500. A few oppositional voices argued all along, however, against an uncritical acceptance of diffusion, insisting that metalworking could have been invented independently in sub-Saharan Africa (Andah 1979; Schmidt and Avery 1983).

In the absence of written records for most of the continent before the late 15th century, archaeology (and linguistics) held out the only hope for settling the debates about origins and chronology. As more and more sites have been surveyed and excavated since the 1960s, radiocarbon dating has provided an indispensable tool for drawing the timeline of African metalworking. This is due to the fact that wood was the fuel universally employed in both smelting furnaces and forges. Hundreds of radiocarbon dates have been recovered in the past four decades from the Sahel to southern Africa, ranging from the second millennium b.c. to recent times.

The dates that have stirred the greatest interest are the roughly fifty falling within the 800–400 b.c. window and obtained from widely separated parts of the continent (Killick in press). Nevertheless, because they are so widely scattered and because dating is imprecise, it is impossible to track the spread of iron metallurgy from radiocarbon dates alone. Most controversial of all are those from the Termit mountains (eastern Niger) where iron and copper artifacts have been found in sites dated to ca. 1500 b.c. and smelting furnaces dated to ca. 800 b.c. (Figure 11.1). This could be interpreted to mean that metallurgy arrived in two stages: first as metal objects, then as the technology to manufacture them. However, Quéchon argues against this. It is more likely, he maintains, that smelting furnaces are sparse and hard to detect, while metal objects are more plentiful and easier to identify (Quéchon 2002:108ff; also Person and Quéchon 2002). He concludes, therefore, that metallurgy itself dates to the mid-second millennium b.c.

If this negative evidence of iron-smelting technology is accepted, these early dates constitute powerful evidence for the independent invention of ironworking south of

Figure 11.1. Location of sites mentioned in the text

the Sahara. However, iron slag, the non-metallic by-product of iron-smelting, is extremely durable in the archaeological record, much more so than iron objects in most African soils. Why, then, is there more evidence of iron objects rather than smelting by-products if metal production was practiced early on? Another difficulty is that all of the Niger dates earlier than 1000 b.c. appear to come from surface collections where a few iron objects occur together with stone tools and potsherds. Since the dates have been obtained from grass temper baked into the pottery, they are considered reliable as far as the pottery is concerned; the problem is to prove that the iron objects are contemporary with the pottery. Considerably more regional survey work and excavation of undisturbed, stratified settlement and metal-production sites must be undertaken to support Quéchon's hypothesis.

What about the argument that ironworking requires previous experimentation with high-temperature technology? Could a Neolithic society with no experience beyond the firing of pottery in open bonfires (kilns were not used in pottery-making outside the Nile Valley before 1000 b.c. and rarely thereafter), skip directly to iron-working without passing through an age of copper or copper alloys? In most of sub-Saharan Africa, iron was the first metal used or iron and copper are found simultaneously, although there are several exceptions. In Upper Nubia, copper objects have been dated to about 3000 b.c. and copper smelting to 2600 b.c. Iron objects and iron-smelting appear much later, but there is no reason to believe that either technology was developed locally rather than imported from the Middle East via the Nile Valley. Far to the west, near Akjoujt in Mauritania, a few small objects of copper have been found in Neolithic sites dated between 800 and 400 b.c., con-temporaneous with a copper mine and copper-smelting furnaces (Lambert 1983). Some objects are similar to those found in North Africa from the same period and are associated with an artifact of Phoenician origin. Since Akjoujt lies along a route marked with rock-engravings of horse-drawn chariots running from Morocco to Mauritania and south across the Sahara, this seems to be "a classic case of stimulus diffusion, in which traded copper objects stimulated the use of local native copper and copper oxides" (Killick in press). On the other hand, there is no evidence that iron was being smelted at Akjoujt in this period, even though it was being smelted in the Senegal River Valley, 400 km to the south, at about the same time.

Copper-smelting has also been identified in the region west of Agadez in Niger. Dates of 3500–2000 b.c. were initially announced, but these have been discredited as not associated with copper-working at all (Grébenart 1983, 1985, 1988; Killick et al. 1988). However, true copper furnaces have been excavated there and all but one have yielded dates after 1000 b.c. While some of these dates are only a few cen-turies younger, their interpretation has been complicated by the persistence of old wood in this region, wood from trees killed by the gradual drying up of the savanna woodlands in what is now the Sahel in the period 4500–2500 b.c. Other dating methods, such as thermoluminescence used to date fired-furnace ceramics, may eventually be useful to cross-check these dates.

The multitude of dates has resolved some debates, but not all. First, Meroë on the upper Nile can be ruled out as a source for ironworking in sub-Saharan Africa. Iron objects, presumably imports from Egypt, appear in lower Nubia by about the eighth century b.c. and at Meroë, farther south, by the sixth century b.c. (Trigger 1969). However, Meroë's iron-smelting industry, whose scale so impressed early visitors and later archaeologists, appears to have begun no earlier than the third century b.c. (Tylecote 1982). More work needs to be done to better understand the origins and development of the industry and its regional economic and social effects (Shinnie 1985).

Phoenician North Africa also looks less likely. While Phoenicians settled on the coast about the ninth century b.c., limited archaeological research in this area has turned up only a little slag in the ruins of Carthage, dated to about the fifth century b.c. True, Phoenician settlements are deeply buried under the layers of later occu-pation, but the current evidence favors only the diffusion of copper, not iron, and only to the Akjoujt region rather than farther south.

What about independent invention in sub-Saharan Africa? The growing corpus of early calibrated radiocarbon dates for iron-smelting (ca. 800–400 b.c.) from Niger, Nigeria, Gabon, Cameroon, the Central African Republic, and the Great Lakes region strengthens this possibility (Bocoum 2002). But there are still questions to be resolved about the reliability of some dates, the number of dates necessary to accurately date a site, and whether the dates are in fact associated with iron manufacture. We also know little about the history of metals in northeastern Africa and the Arabian peninsula during the crucial centuries of the first millennium b.c. If anonymous African metalworkers did indeed master the art of smelting iron ores without previous experimentation with pyrotechnology, archaeology is unlikely to unravel the mystery of how they did it without considerably more work. This must involve more fieldwork in the little-explored regions of the continent, careful cross-checking of dates by several methodologies, and use of archaeometallurgical lab techniques to understand technical achievements (Echard, ed., 1983; Miller 2001; Miller and van der Merwe 1994).

The connections between Bantu expansion and the spread of metallurgy in Africa are also more complex than they once appeared. In the 1960s and 1970s, it was hypothesized that peoples speaking Bantu languages spread throughout central and southern Africa from their original cradle in the border area of present-day Nigeria and Cameroon (Chapter 12). It was believed that this was due to their mastery of iron and to the military and economic superiority that followed from this. "Bantu expansion" is now regarded as misleading to the extent that it suggests a unidirectional mass migration by a culturally homogeneous group, the "Bantu," confusing a purely linguistic term with a people, a culture, or even a race (Vansina 2001:52 n. 1; Chapter 12). "There was no one great 'Bantu Expansion'. Instead, an immense variety of regional and local histories of agricultural expansion, of cross-cultural encounter, and of social, political, and cultural change lie behind the vast distribution of Bantu speech communities we find today" (Ehret 2001:5).

Furthermore, this process began long before any Bantu-speaking peoples acquired knowledge of metalworking (Klieman in press; Chapter 12). Linguistic sources suggest that, in the initial phases of this dispersion, Bantu-speaking peoples were borrowers rather than innovators; they acquired knowledge of ironworking, seed agriculture, and animal husbandry from their non-Bantu-speaking neighbors. Nevertheless, as they overspread central and southern Africa, their "linguistic dominance . . . was everywhere connected with the ability to manufacture iron tools and weapons" (Oliver 2001:445). By the time this process of migration was complete, the working and use of metals extended to virtually all of sub-Saharan Africa.

Technology

The primary metals worked in sub-Saharan Africa were iron, copper, and gold. The red soil so typical of much of Africa is, in fact, exposed lateritic crust or low-grade iron ore. Copper deposits, by contrast, are relatively scarce in West Africa, with the exception of areas of the southern Sahara in Mauritania, Mali, and Niger, and small deposits in eastern Nigeria. Copper is more plentiful in regions of central and southern Africa.

Gold, in both alluvial and reef form, occurs throughout the continent, more widely than is often realized. While some Iron Age sites contain both iron and copper artifacts, the earliest archaeological finds of gold come from Jenné-jeno (seventh-eighth centuries A.D.) and from elite burials at Mapungubwe near the Limpopo River dated to the 12th century a.d. In southern Africa as in West Africa, the international gold trade stimulated both production and domestic consumption in areas that were incorporated into long-distance trading networks. The first networks were developed with the Indian Ocean and with North Africa and the Mediterranean, then directly with Europe after sea routes were opened from the late 15th century. Elsewhere, the metal seems to have been largely ignored before the colonial era.

Lead occurs occasionally, especially associated with copper as in the Niari-Kwilu Valley of the Congo Republic. Tin was exploited in only a few regions: Rooiberg in northern South Africa (Friede and Steel 1976) and the Bauchi Plateau in Nigeria. Portuguese obsessions to the contrary, there is little silver to be found in Africa. The metal has come into use only recently, except in the Sahara and Sahel (Herbert 1984:20, 122).

The metallurgical *chaîne opératoire* – the "conventionalized, learned sequence of technical operations, tightly imbricated with patterned social relations" (Pfaffenberger 1998:294; cf. Lemonnier 1983) – has three main components: mining, smelting, and fabricating finished objects. Increasingly, insights into these ancient processes and their socio-technological variation across time and space have been achieved by archaeologists and archaeometallurgists through interdisciplinary collaboration with historians, engineers, and material scientists.

Mining

Although the traces of ancient mining have been obliterated in most places by more recent workings, fragmentary archaeological evidence, complemented by later travelers' and ethnographic accounts, allows us to reconstruct the main outlines. Undoubtedly, many ores were collected on or near the surface as well as in bogs and riverbeds. They were identified by telltale staining of the soil or by characteristic vegetation which prospectors (and now archaeologists) learned to associate with minerals. Ironworkers also learned to distinguish lower and higher grades of ore and exploited only oxides, such as hematite, magnetite, and limonite.

Modern geological surveys have shown that virtually all copper deposits in sub-Saharan Africa were identified and worked by indigenous craftsmen before colonial times. The only exception was the Zambian copperbelt, where ores have been only identified with 20th-century prospecting techniques. Indigenous copper miners sought out carbonates, such as malachite, which were found above the water table; in contrast to other parts of the Old World, sulphides were never smelted.

Typically, both iron and copper ores were dug out of shallow pits and shafts with hoes or digging sticks. They were then broken up (often with hammer stones) to get rid of some of the stony matrix and quite often roasted before smelting.

Some of the open-cast copper mines were enormous. What came to be known as the Star of the Congo mine in Katanga (Democratic Republic of the Congo), for example, comprised a pit three-quarters of a mile long, and 600–1,000 feet wide, an excavation comparable to modern pits dug by steam shovel. At Kansanshi, across the border in Zambia, ancient workings covered an area of about 7,000 yards in diameter, from which European surveyors calculated that thousands of tons of malachite had been extracted over the centuries by indigenous miners (Bisson 1976; Herbert 1984:23–25).

Alluvial gold was panned in streams and rivers after the rains, the flecks of gold laboriously separated from sand by swirling and sifting. Nuggets or grains of metal were then pure enough to be melted and cast into desired forms or simply traded as gold dust or lumps of metal. Deeper mining was necessary in hardrock areas such as Nubia, central and southern Africa. In simplest form, miners dug shafts down which they descended by ropes or steps, then passed ore to the surface in baskets (there is no evidence that winches were ever used). Connecting shafts provided ventilation. Most of our information about deeper mining comes from Zimbabwe and South Africa. The extensive ancient copper mine at Umkondo (eastern Zimbabwe), dated to the 17th century a.d., contained shafts sunk to a depth of 60 feet. Hard-rock mining of gold reefs on the Zimbabwean plateau went even deeper: up to 180 feet in the case of open trenches for near-vertical reefs or by shafts and levels for reefs extending diagonally underground (Summers 1969; Swan 1994). Miners used fire-setting to fracture the surfaces, then iron picks and hammer stones to dislodge the ore. Shafts were narrow and winding; timbering was used rarely or not at all. Ore was hauled to the surface in wooden or leather containers, pulverized by stone, and panned like alluvial gold to separate fine ore from rock. Shafts could be sunk only to the depth of the water table since pumps were unavailable. Deep workings could not be ventilated.

Mining of iron, copper, and gold was carried out by men, women, and even children, and was always a dangerous occupation, as human remains found in collapsed workings bear witness.

Smelting

As more and more sites are surveyed and excavated in Africa, the vast scale of precolonial iron-smelting becomes ever more impressive. While some industries produced only for local needs, others engaged in intensive production, often over long periods of time. In West Africa, the best-known areas of large-scale production were the Middle Senegal Valley, Futa Jallon in Guinea, Mema in Mali, Yatenga in Burkina Faso, the Bassar region of western Togo, Hausa-speaking regions in Niger and northern Nigeria, and the Ndop Plain of Cameroon. There were also major centers in Central Africa (the Batéké plateaux of Gabon and Congo); the Great Lakes

Region of Rwanda/Burundi and Tanzania, Malawi; the Shona-speaking region of Zimbabwe; and Phalaborwa in the eastern Transvaal (Dupré and Pinçon 1997; Herbert 1993:6–8; Holl 2000).

Both iron and copper were smelted in bloomery furnaces that achieved temperatures high enough to separate gangue from solid metal (about 1,150–1,200°C) and converted the gangue to liquid slag. This required a reducing atmosphere to eliminate the oxygen from the ores by reacting with the carbon monoxide gas released by the charcoal fuel. The reducing atmosphere had to be more carefully controlled for iron than copper. Further, if the temperature was too low in iron-smelting, masses of slag adhered to the iron "bloom"; if the temperature was too high, cast iron resulted, which was too brittle to work (Gordon and Killick, 1993). Tuyeres or blowpipes, usually made of clay, were connected to bellows to push air into a furnace to increase internal temperatures.

African smelters used a mind-boggling variety of furnace types to produce bloomery iron, steel, and copper (gold was simply melted in crucibles) (Cline 1937; Kense 1983). In some cases the furnace was no more than an open bowl in which a reducing atmosphere was achieved by smothering ore with charcoal. The resulting bloom could be retrieved from the floor of the bowl and slag tapped through a channel to an adjoining pit. More commonly, furnaces consisted of shafts over a bowl into which both charcoal and ore were fed. High temperatures were obtained by using a set of bellows and a tuyere inserted directly into the furnace, or by means of a natural draft. Slag could be tapped through the same holes, or allowed to run out through the bottom of the furnace. Some furnaces were solid structures, meant to be operated over and over again; others were broken open after a single use. Some produced massive blooms, others only modest chunks of metal. It is possible to find, even within a small area, several furnace types. This is especially true at early colonial period sites where the furnace remains are better preserved. Although it is difficult to determine the factors that influenced the choice of particular furnace forms, the local resources, such as ores or charcoal fuels, craft organization, local economic factors, cultural beliefs, or a combination of these and other factors, must all be explored. Technological style (Childs 1991b) and social agency of technological practice also are fruitful avenues for related study.

A peculiarly African innovation is the tall shaft furnace that relies on natural draft. It draws air into a number of holes around the base, thereby dispensing with the intensive labor inputs of bellows operators (Killick 1991a). Outside of Africa, the only known historical example is in Burma. Natural draft furnaces appear to have been used exclusively for smelting iron. Recent research in Yatenga (Burkina Faso) has documented the evolution of this furnace type to ever larger structures – up to 7 m high – that, once set in operation, required no labor at all during the extended smelting period. Not only did these giant furnaces produce larger quantities of bloom, it is also claimed that they produced carbon steel (Martinelli 2002). How far back in time natural draft furnaces may go is not known.

In general, only furnace bowls, quantities of iron slag, and fragments of tuyeres survive in the archaeological record, which makes it difficult to reconstruct the size and form of the chimney. However, some Early Iron Age smelting furnaces, such as in western Tanzania and Rwanda/Burundi, were built of clay coils and bricks, which permit some degree of reconstruction (Schmidt 1997). Also, we know from the ethnographic record that refining furnaces were sometimes used as an intermediate step to purify the bloom of slag and charcoal before making finished objects. This furnace type has not yet been identified in the archaeological record.

It is beyond dispute that African ironworkers produced low to medium carbon steel, at least during the last millennium. Wrought iron is pure iron and is quite soft, though not as soft as pure copper. Steel is an alloy of iron and carbon produced in the reducing atmosphere of the furnace. The higher the amount of carbon, within very specific limits and generally under 1 percent, the harder and stronger the steel becomes (Craddock 1995). Cast iron contains 2–5 percent carbon, but generally cast iron was poorly suited for hand-forging with a hammer because of its brittleness. It is unclear whether African iron-smelters intentionally produced cast iron, except for a Cameroonian case where the iron was then decarburized in a crucible before being forged (David et al. 1989). Cast iron was definitely produced on occasion when temperatures rose above the optimum for smelting bloomery iron or if certain chemical impurities were introduced to the smelt that lowered the temperatures necessary to produce metal.

The types of metal produced during smelting are easily verified by metallographic analysis of multiple samples of blooms and slags from a furnace context. Other aspects of the smelting technology, such as possible sources of ore, fuel, and refractory clay and details of the pryotechnical dynamics within the furnace, may also be gleaned from careful metallographic, petrographic, and chemical analyses of these and other artifact classes (e.g., tuyeres and furnace wall debris). Metallography is the use of reflected light microscopy to determine the microstructures created during a manufacturing process. Wrought iron, steel, copper, and slags, for example, have characteristic structures resulting from smelting, forging, or casting (e.g., Bachmann 1982; Childs 1991c, 1996; Miller 1996). Petrography is the use of polarized light microscopy to identify minerals in ceramic bodies, as well as slags. Petrographic analysis of clay tuyeres, crucibles, and furnace materials is an underutilized but fruitful methodology, especially to examine the refractory qualities of clays used by ancient metalworkers, clay selection, and the formation process of a ceramic body (Childs 1989b). Chemical analyses are effective to determine the source(s) of ore or manufactured objects based on compositional patterns and fingerprints (e.g., Grant 1999).

Reconstructions performed by present-day ironworkers, followed up by laboratory analyses, have also been used to test hypotheses generated by archaeological evidence. The hypothesized ancient practice of consciously preheating a furnace to gain optimum thermal efficiency, for example, is one such hypothesis that remains controversial and requires more testing (Avery and Schmidt, eds., 1996; Killick 1996; Rehder 1996). Others have sought to estimate the amount of ore and fuel used during a smelt from the resulting slag and other furnace remains, or to estimate the size of an iron bloom from the amount of resulting slag (de Barros 1986; Schmidt 1997). These questions can be resolved only when we understand if and how slag was recycled in an area. Slag, for example, was used to temper Late Iron

Age pottery and for house foundations in East African villages (Schmidt 1997:62).

The furnaces used to smelt copper ores were smaller and often less solid than their counterparts used for iron (Cline 1937; Herbert 1984:ch. 3 passim). Since copper-smelting came to an end in most regions before iron, they are in a state of ruin or have vanished altogether, leaving, at best, heaps of slag to mark their former presence. Even these slag heaps are frequently mistaken for iron-smelting slags because of the frequent association of copper and iron oxides and their very similar physical characteristics. Metallographic analysis, however, can identify copper-smelting slags.

From later eyewitness accounts, we can surmise that these furnaces, like iron-smelting furnaces, were frequently built of clay from termite and anthills. In some cases, they were broken down after each use to retrieve the smelted metal, which collected at the bottom of the bowl; others were used repeatedly during a season by running the molten ore out into ingot molds. Copper was also alloyed with tin to form bronze in crucibles. There is evidence of indigenous bronze-making in Nigeria (Craddock et al. 1989; Shaw 1970) and southern Africa (Zimbabwe and South Africa; Caton-Thompson 1931; Stanley 1929), but the abundant amounts of brass (a copper–zinc alloy) found in Africa over the last century were almost certainly imports. All in all, we know very little about prehistoric copper and bronze technologies and their organization across much of Africa (see also Posnansky 1977).

Making finished objects

The final stage in the operational chain was manufacturing finished objects, which involved different techniques depending on the metal and expertise at hand. Iron bloom was forged by repeated heating, hammering, and welding to make tools, weapons, and ornaments. Idiosyncrasies of the bloom, such as high slag or phosphorus content, or production of functional or ornamental details on the final objects, meant that many smiths were highly skilled.

Copper ingots or bars were smithed into an almost infinite number of forms by cold-hammering and heating. Copper and iron wire was made by both hammering, and, over large areas of central and southern Africa, by drawing (Lagercrantz 1989; Lindblom 1939; Steel 1975). Here the craft was practiced over hundreds of years: vises and drawing plates have been uncovered at Ingombe Ilede (Zambia) dating to about 1400 a.d., and drawn wire has been recovered from various sites in Zimbabwe dating to this same time period (Fagan 1969; Herbert 1984:ch. 4 passim). Since little is known about the prehistoric development of wire-drawing or the technical innovations or stylistic differences in the drawing tools used or craft organization, this is an avenue ripe for future exploration.

The art of lost-wax (*cire perdue*) casting reached a remarkable level of perfection throughout West Africa, as far south as the Cameroon Grassfields. This involves making a model of the object to be cast in wax, then enveloping it in clay. When the wax is melted in an oven, the metal is run in to take the exact shape of the "lost" wax (Williams 1974). Although the technique of lost-wax casting dates back to ancient Egypt, African casters adapted their own refinements. Both Akan (Ghana) and Cameroonian artists, for example, often attached crucible to mold when casting smaller objects in order to reduce the build-up of gases and enable the molten metal to flow more quickly and evenly. Most lost-wax casting utilizes copper alloys, such as bronze or brass, because of their lower melting temperature and greater ductility without unwanted gases.

Finds from three small sites at Igbo Ukwu in southeastern Nigeria, dated to the eighth–tenth centuries a.d., include bronze pendants, staff heads, and vessels (Shaw 1970). These objects illustrate the mastery of the technique as well as a virtuoso delight in replicating natural materials in metal. A few centuries later, the heads and torsos from Ife and the huge repertoire of Benin bronzes (actually brasses) continued this casting tradition (Shaw 1978). Some of the classic figures from Ife were cast in pure copper, a technical feat of the first order. In contrast to Igbo Ukwu, neither the Ife nor the Benin objects were found in undisturbed contexts. They have been dated respectively by stylistic affinities with terracottas found in undisturbed contexts and by seriation of stylistic criteria.

The Culture of Metals

The use of metals spread very gradually in Africa and overlapped with the continued use of stone. Its ultimate effect was nonetheless revolutionary, encouraging both greater economic productivity and deadly efficiency in warfare. The socio-cultural impact of iron and other metals was equally profound, if more diverse and harder to evaluate archaeologically and historically. In many cultures, myths of origin refer to the introduction of metalworking as a signal event, while objects of iron, copper, and gold have long figured in political, economic, social, and religious life (Herbert 1984, 1993). Metals also conditioned the image of Africa in foreign eyes: so abundant were its deposits of gold that the continent was for centuries synonymous with the glittering metal, first to the Arab and Indian Ocean worlds, then to Europeans. However, among most Africans, iron has been the primary metal in all spheres of life, from utilitarian to ritual. In many societies, copper was traditionally more highly esteemed than gold (Herbert 1984:xix–xx and *passim*).

Smiths and smelters were invariably male, although women and children provided a great deal of ancillary labor for mining, preparing ores, and making charcoal in many recent cultures. Their involvement in ancient metallurgical operations is very difficult to determine. In some areas a single craftsman both smelted and smithed iron or copper or sometimes both metals. In others, there was greater specialization among smelters and smiths as well as among those who forged tools and those who made ornaments of iron, copper, bronze, or gold. In some areas smelters and smiths were full-time craftsmen; in others, they were also agriculturists. Smiths also functioned as sculptors, diviners, buriers of the dead, amulet makers, circumcisers, and morticians. Their wives were often potters and excisers in female initiation (Herbert 1993:21, chs. 1, 8).

The occupation often was – and still is – hereditary, especially in the western Sudan, the Cameroon highlands, and Ethiopia. While much of the ethnographic literature emphasizes the "otherness" of the African metalworker, this was most characteristic of West African peoples, such as the Mande and their neighbors where smithing was limited to certain endogamous "castes" (McNaughton 1988; Tamari 1991). It also occurred in pastoral societies, such as the Maasai and Tuareg, where smiths were looked down on in part, at least, because they performed manual labor. Where the craft was not hereditary or assigned to a particular lineage or ethnic group, aspirants often had to pay costly apprenticeship and initiation fees, which tended to limit access and to make it hereditary *de facto* if not *de jure*.

The complex and often ambivalent attitudes expressed toward smelters and smiths derived in large measure from the acknowledgment of their power. The rest of society, from farmer and hunter to king and priest, was dependent on their ability to transform inert matter into hoes, spears, emblems of authority and status, and symbols of the spirits – objects that were themselves believed to be endowed with agency. Because they literally "play with fire" (de Maret 1980), metalworkers had to acquire a great store of both technical and ritual knowledge. Ritual was particularly crucial to smelting, the primary act of transformation (Herbert 1993). It usually took place in isolation and involved invocations and offerings to the ancestors and other spirits, strict observance of sexual, menstrual, and other taboos, and ample use of medicines. Comparable rituals might attend the setting up of a new forge or manufacture of a new hammer or anvil (e.g., Rowlands and Warnier 1993).

Smiths, like chiefs, were often feared as potential sorcerers or witches since the power they wielded could be beneficent or dangerous. Like chiefs, they were commonly believed to have control over fertility, metaphorically and even actually (Herbert 1993:ch. 6). Smelting rituals, in particular, frequently invoked the human model of gender and age to explain and insure transformative power. But the supernatural powers ascribed to smiths made them potential competitors with rulers. Throughout Africa, legends, epics, and oral traditions underscore the ambivalent interdependence of king and smith. This could play itself out in many ways. In central Africa, smiths performed a major role in many royal investiture ceremonies and in manufacturing elements of regalia (Childs and Dewey 1996; Kriger 1999; de Maret 1985a). The ancient kingdom of Kongo carried this even farther: here the king was symbolically equated with the smith (Herbert 1993:ch. 6). Variations of the same theme are found in the Great Lakes region of eastern Africa. In fact, excavations of royal tombs in Rwanda revealed two iron anvils at the head of King Rugira (Van Noten 1972).

In the western Sudan, on the other hand, there was at some point a rupture between smithing and kingship, a separation of powers. On the basis of linguistic evidence and oral tradition, one scholar ties this to the creation of the Mande caste system during the Malinke–Sosso wars in the 13th century a.d.. The Sosso king was not a smith in the literal sense but "formed an alliance with divinities associated with ironworking, and thus, iron, ironworking and certain iron objects were for him both symbols of – and means to – mystical and political power" (Tamari 1991:238), as was the magic xylophone he kept in his secret chamber. He was defeated by the epic hero, Sundjiata, and, thereafter, the special relationship of kingship with both metallurgy and music was reinterpreted in the direction of craft specialization to avoid such concentration of power in a single group (Tamari 1991:235–241; also, Herbert 1993:ch. 6).

Metals played an equally important part in the economic life of Africa. Iron tools often coexisted alongside wooden digging sticks and stone hammers, but undoubtedly iron hoes and axes made it easier to clear bush and forest for cultivation. Iron fishhooks, arrow tips, and spears increased the productivity of fishermen and hunters. Since some areas were better endowed with ores than others and some developed centers of skilled craftsmanship, both iron and copper entered networks of trade from the early centuries of the present era, if not before, until the last century. The massive iron slag heaps at Meroë, produced between ca. 300 b.c. and a.d. 300, suggest that the region probably supplied a large portion of the Nile Valley (Killick in press), although archaeological evidence is lacking. Excavations of over 300 burials from five sites in the Upemba Depression (Democratic Republic of the Congo), dating from ca. a.d. 700 to the colonial period, revealed an enormous assortment of well-crafted iron and copper objects for fishing, hunting, agricultural use, personal adornment, and ritual functions (de Maret 1977, 1985a, 1985b, 1992). Trade goods in other materials were also recovered. No contemporaneous metal production sites have been found there to confirm or refute local metal production, although very little regional survey work or non-burial excavations have been accomplished to date.

For later times, the evidence for regional and long-distance trade is more robust. During the 19th century, raw iron from the Bassar region of northwestern Togo was traded extensively, even as far as the coast, either in the form of horseshoe-shaped blooms or discs for hoe blades (de Barros 1988). So plentiful was the metal produced by local smelters that it was sold daily at the Bassar market, where it attracted the renowned blacksmiths of Kabye (de Barros 2000; Goucher and Herbert 1996:41). Across the continent, Barongo smiths, south of Lake Victoria, made a variety of goods such as axes, spears, knives, and agricultural tools, which were widely traded in interior regions well into the 1940s. A century earlier it is probable that Barongo hoes ended up in Uganda and in the market at Tabora, where they were exchanged for slaves and sold to caravans coming up from the coast (Schmidt 1996:80–81).

Gold offers a special case. Its role in international commerce can be documented in written sources (both Arabic and European), in coins, and in exotic trade goods found in archaeological contexts. In West Africa, three primary gold fields were exploited: Bambuk at the headwaters of the Senegal River; Buré at the headwaters of the Niger River; and the Akan fields lying on the savanna/forest margin in present-day northern Ghana. In southern Africa, the main sources were on the Zimbabwean plateau and in the northern Transvaal. While little is known about the early history of West African gold-mining, some historians have argued that Roman mints in North Africa relied on West African gold from the fourth or fifth century a.d. This seems unlikely in the light of trace element analysis, which shows that Roman and early Islamic gold coins from North African mints both used metal from the same sources. Not until the ninth century, soon after Arabic documents first mention the trans-Saharan gold trade, does the chemistry reveal the presence of a new source, namely West Africa (Guerra et al. 1999; Gondonneau and Guerra 2002). From then on, the "golden trade of the Moors" (Bovill 1958) provided legendary quantities of the yellow metal to the Muslim and Mediterranean worlds, and served as a catalyst for European maritime explorers, eager to bypass the Muslim stranglehold and gain direct access to the sources of wealth. Paradoxically, there is little evidence for the indigenous use of gold in West Africa until well after trading connections were established with the Mediterranean and subsequently with Europe.

Gold first appears in historical accounts of the East African coast in the mid-12th century a.d. The Arab writer al-Idrisi mentions "Sofala" as the source of both gold and high-quality iron, which were exported to Arabia and India. Sofala was a generic term for the coastal region between the Sabi and Zambezi rivers and the entrepôts into which were funneled goods bound for Indian Ocean trade. Idrisi's account precedes the earliest certain finds of gold in southern African sites: the gold burials at Mapungubwe on the Limpopo River, dated to about the mid-12th century (Fouché 1937). By this time, gold production was undoubtedly in full swing and the trade in gold would continue to be a leitmotif of accounts of the Swahili coast, just as it was in the case of the trans-Saharan trade. Here, however, the intrusion of Europeans seems to have been more disastrous than in West Africa. While an unknown portion of West African gold was diverted to European trading centers on the coast, the trans-Saharan trade did not immediately collapse. Eventually, the gold trade was overshadowed in both directions by the trade in slaves. On the East African coast, in contrast, the Portuguese attempted to seize the entire trade by force, sending military forces into the interior to locate the actual sources of gold. The net result of their intervention was to kill the goose that laid the golden egg; the combination of Portuguese interference, the breakdown of indigenous political authority, and the rise of the slave trade led to a precipitous decline in indigenous gold production (Miller et al. 2000:91). Production picked up again when European prospectors arrived in the late 19th and early 20th centuries. Their work was made much easier by the remains of "ancient workings."

Foreign trade also brought enormous imports of copper, and later iron. Bulky as they were, copper and copper alloys (especially brass) were staples of the trans-Saharan trade, feeding an insatiable demand in West Africa, which had few native sources of its own. With the opening up of maritime trade with Europe, even greater quantities were imported in the form of bars, bracelets, and basins, each section of the coast having its particular preferences. In time, iron rods joined the list of imports. Massive imports of scrap iron undermined local production by the 20th century, but in earlier colonial times it may simply have augmented the supplies produced by indigenous craftsmen, who themselves may have responded to ever-growing demand by increasing their own output (de Barros 2000; Fowler 1990; Warnier and Fowler 1979).

Iron, copper, and gold all served as currencies, especially valued since they were among the few durable commodities with which one could accumulate wealth. They took many forms in different places and times. Groups in northeastern Congo, for example, used iron spearheads or knives. Elsewhere hoes or iron bars were preferred. Some of these currencies were all-purpose, but others were intended for a single use such as bridewealth. Thus, for example, the Fang of Gabon would accept only bundles of small arrowheads, *bikei*, for bride payments in the late 19th century. Wives were themselves a form of wealth, so that the wealthy could become even wealthier by converting one form of wealth – iron – into another – wives. This reinforces the multiple associations of iron with fertility in many societies (Herbert 1993:112–113), a cultural construct that will be very difficult to discern in the archaeological record.

During the 19th century iron currencies gave way to copper and brass in bridewealth payments in many parts of the Zaïre basin. This did not necessitate a radical revision on the symbolic level, because both copper and brass also carried connotations of fertility in precolonial Africa; in a sense they were synonyms, at least in the context of bridewealth (Herbert 1984:266 et seq.). But copper and brass currencies also came in a bewildering variety of forms: lumps, ingots, rods, bars, wire, rings, basins, knives, bullets, "top hats" (*musuku*), and "golf clubs" (*marale*) (Steel 1975), but almost never as coins. Some of these came as imports in the trans-Saharan and Atlantic trades, but many originated in copper-producing areas within Africa, then were dispersed over wide areas.

Among the best documented archaeologically are the copper crosses of varying sizes found from Katanga (Democratic Republic of the Congo) to the Zimbabwean high veld. A few mold fragments and pieces of ingots have been found on either side of the Congo/Zambia border dating to the fourth through seventh centuries at both mining and smelting sites. Large numbers of crosses have been excavated in various burials to the north in the Upemba Depression. The smallest, most abundant, and most recent in age range from 5 mm to 15 mm; the largest and generally oldest are more than 150 mm. These have been dated from the 15th to the 19th centuries a.d., although a few have been found in earlier graves. Much larger crosses from Ingombe Ilede (Zambia) and Zimbabwe have also been dated to the 15th and 16th centuries. The crosses clearly served as currency since they were of uniform shape with gradations in size, but it is hard to explain the extreme differences. Presumably the smaller ones served as general-purpose currencies, while the very large ones may have functioned only in the prestige sphere (Bisson 2000:115–122; de Maret 1981).

Iron and copper, the two primary metals used in sub-Saharan Africa, have several physical differences: color, malleability, and luminosity. The softness of copper, in particular, seemed to influence its relatively rare use for utilitarian purposes, although copper arrow tips, spear points, needles, fish hooks, knives, and awls have been recovered at sites across the continent. It functioned principally in the overlapping spheres of trade and currency, art, ornamentation and ritual, and as a symbol of social status and power. Iron figured in all these spheres as well as in utilitarian ones. While it is difficult to fully unravel the reasons that dictated the use of one metal over the other (or why both in one object), we may hypothesize that the choices were not arbitrary for most of Africa's history. Metals, like other materials, were used to make statements that were recognizable to people within a culture or even over wide culture areas. Thus one may speak of a language of materials, varying according to locale and changing over time like other forms of language. Ethnography, oral tradition, and material culture have helped to reconstruct this language in more recent times. What can archaeology hope to tell us about the culture of metals in the more distant past?

First of all, it can tell us more about copper and copper alloys than about iron since the former are more resistant to oxidation. Nevertheless, the archaeological record confirms that in many areas of the sub-continent iron and copper were used concurrently for the last two millennia. This was certainly the case at Igbo Ukwu (Shaw 1970), although the iron objects are less well preserved. Both served as prestige items, items of regalia, items of ritual, and as grave goods, but we must examine closely the functional and physical differences, as well as similarities, to tease out the local language of these materials.

Archaeology also shows that copper from indigenous sources was traded over large regions that lacked ores, complemented by imports from international trade. The discovery of 2,085 brass rods scattered on the sands of the western Sahara and dated to about the 12th century supports written sources in Arabic about the importance of copper imports from North Africa and the Mediterranean throughout the centuries of the trans-Saharan trade (Monod 1969). Why was this metal so valued there? Far to the southeast, the finds of trade beads and Chinese ceramics at Mapungubwe and Great Zimbabwe complement written accounts of the export of gold from these regions to the Indian Ocean trade (Fouché 1937; Garlake 1973). Written accounts for all of Africa emphasize the enormous demand for cloth of all kinds, but this does not show up in the archaeological record. Most of the gold produced in Africa was exported, but archaeometallurgists are working on methods to fingerprint sources (Miller et al. 2001), just as lead isotope analysis and other techniques have been used to distinguish sources of the copper-based metals used at Ife and Benin, on the one hand, and Igbo Ukwu on the other (Craddock 1985; Craddock and Picton 1986; Goucher et al. 1976; Willett 1981). These methods will help trace the complexity of routes used to distribute these valuable metals.

More difficult is the task of recovering ancient belief systems and social structures in the archaeological record. Nevertheless, there are enticing clues. Social differentiation of individuals is clearly revealed in the hundreds of burials in the Upemba Depression through the quantity and types of objects interred with them. A number of objects, such as decorated iron axes, have various political, social, and ritual functions today, which inform possible functions in the past (Childs and Dewey 1996; Chapter 17). Intriguing ethnographic evidence also suggests that stylistic differences in the morphological details of certain object types, such as spears, axes, and knives, relate to ethnicity, local age groups, and status. A large sample of such objects must be recovered, however, before such relationships can be hypothesized in the archaeological record.

In many parts of Africa modern-day smelters have inserted pots containing medicines in the bottom of furnace bowls (de Barros 2000:167–168; Herbert 1993:70;

Holl 2000:38, 62, 70). Small ritual pits containing pots and other objects have been found in Early Iron Age furnaces in western Tanzania and Rwanda, dating back as early as the first century a.d. (Schmidt 1997; Schmidt and Childs 1985; Van Noten 1983). The clay brick and coils of some Early Iron Age furnaces in this same area were also decorated with dots, chevrons, and vertical grooves. These may relate to the more recent practice of decorating a furnace as a fertile bride or woman or as a productive cooking pot (Childs and Killick 1993).

At Great Zimbabwe, remains of metalworking have been found within the walled enclosures of the valley and a store of ironstone in a cave within the hilltop "acropolis." Possibly this signifies royal appropriation of metalworking, metalworkers, and metallurgical knowledge (Herbert 1996).

Other Directions for Future Research

If one roughly calculates the total quantities of copper and brass that ended up in sub-Saharan Africa from the beginnings of copper-working in the early first millennium b.c. to the later 19th century a.d., a very conservative estimate would be some 50,000 tons, including imports. The actual figure could, however, be double this amount. Only a tiny fraction of this has been recovered, so that one may safely predict that many tons of copper – and unimaginable quantities of iron – remain to be uncovered by the archaeologist's trowel. Many finished objects will probably be found in grave sites and may help to flesh out the picture of metals as markers of social prestige and political power, as well as products of trade. Also, the social, political, and economic roles of metal craftsmen may be better understood when their characteristic tools, such as forging hammers or molds, are found in graves. It is important, however, that more ancient village sites are found and excavated to better understand the functions of metal objects in a variety of contexts over time and space. Careful laboratory analysis of these objects will provide more information on techniques of manufacture.

Researchers will continue to face the challenge, too, of finding and excavating undisturbed sites where both metal objects and metallurgical processes, especially smelting, can be more accurately dated by various methods. But the need for better dates should not be allowed to obscure other promising areas of research. To begin with, we need more data on the spatial relationship of ancient smelting sites to settlements, which has often been hampered by the presence of contemporary villages on ancient sites. In historical times, smelting commonly took place in isolated spots, away from villages, in order to exclude women and others and to safeguard the secrecy of rituals and techniques from prying eyes. At some Early Iron Age sites in Zambia and one in central Malawi, however, smelting appears to have been carried out within the confines of the village (Killick 1990:76–77). Does this mean that a thousand years ago smelters were not yet concerned that the presence of fertile and menstruating women could cause the process to fail, or that the evil intentions of witches and sorcerers were not feared (Herbert 1993:124)? Or are there other possible interpretations? This might be one way of testing the hypothesis that metal technology has been accompanied by ritual behaviors from the beginning, which, much as they may vary over time and space, express a core set of ancient beliefs.

More exploration is needed into the role of local metal production in the development of socio-political complexity, specifically the rise of chiefdoms and states. We know that production and trade in gold affected local economic and political systems, but what about the production of iron, copper, and bronze? How were resources such as ore and charcoal controlled and how was craft production organized over time? Is there evidence of changing spatial patterns that indicate changes in labor organization? For example, clues of metalworking within royal enclosures might suggest political control over these processes as well as craft specialization. The use of an operational chain model should help to elucidate these questions and draw insights into the changing character and complex history of metallurgical technology in past African societies.

The ecological effects of large-scale and long-term metal industries must have been profound. Thus far only a few archaeologists have looked at deforestation and its implications for affected areas by using such methods as palynology and archaeobotany. The disappearance of slow-burning hardwoods in areas of intense production was a major factor in the decline of iron-smelting, one which has often been overlooked because of assumptions that the ecological history of Africa has been different from that of other parts of the world (Goucher 1981; Haaland 1985:61–72; Schmidt 1997:ch. 11).

It is likely that the trans-Atlantic slave trade brought many African metalworkers to the Americas. Did these craftsmen play a role in the production of metals in the Americas as some preliminary evidence suggests (Goucher 1990)? Did the social, religious, and symbolic roles of iron and copper metals, as well as specific metal object types, survive the crossing? If so, did they change in the new socio-cultural context?

Finally, continued use of metallography and petrography will help decipher the technical aspects of metalworking, contributing to the many issues outlined above. The use of trace elements to source the metals used in objects found at and traded between archaeological sites is also promising, although the practice of mixing and recycling metals may make this difficult (Miller et al. 2001). So far the use of trace elements and lead isotope ratios has proven most useful in grouping objects by similar composition rather than pinpointing the actual sources of metal, which requires a large comparative database. Significant advances in the understanding of metallurgical production and object use have been made from archaeometallurgical research, but this specialty requires extensive training and laboratory facilities with specialized equipment. A number of universities in the United States and Europe, and one in Africa, offered opportunities for such training and research in the 1980s and early 1990s. Unfortunately, these facilities and experts are fast dwindling due to financial and other operational constraints. We must be strong advocates for this research specialty, or future insights into African metallurgy will be severely hampered.

VIDEOS AND FILMS ON AFRICAN METALLURGY

David, Nicholas, Yves le Bléis, and Henri Augé, 1988 Dokwaza: Last of the African Iron Masters. 50 min.

Dewey, William, 1990 Weapons for the Ancestors. 25 min.

Echard, Nicole, 1969 Noces de feu. 16 mm; 32 min.

Huysecom, Eric, and Bernard Augustoni, 1997 Inagina: The Last House of Iron. 52 min.

O'Neill, Peter, Frank Muhly, Jr., and Winnie Lambrecht, 1988 The Tree of Iron. 57 min.

Saltman, Carlyn, with Candice Goucher and Eugenia Herbert, 1986 The Blooms of Banjeli: Technology and Gender in West African Iron Making. 28 min.

REFERENCES

Andah, Bassey, 1979 Iron Age Beginnings in West Africa: Reflections and Suggestions. West African Journal of Archaeology 9:135–150.

Avery Donald H., and Peter R. Schmidt, eds., 1996 Use of Preheated Air in Ancient and Recent African Iron Smelting Furnaces *and* Preheating: Practice or Illusion? *In* The Culture and Technology of African Iron Production. Peter R. Schmidt, ed. pp. 240–246 and 267–276. Gainesville: University Press of Florida.

Avery, Donald H., Nicholas J. van der Merwe, and S. Saitowitz, 1988 The Metallurgy of the Iron Bloomery in Africa. *In* The Beginning of the Use of Metal and Alloys. Robert Maddin, ed. pp. 245–260. Cambridge, MA: MIT Press.

Bachmann, Hans-Gert, 1982 The Identification of Slags from Archaeological Sites. Institute of Archaeology, Occasional Publication 6. London: University of London.

Bisson, Michael, 1976 The Prehistoric Copper-Mines of Zambia. Ann Arbor, MI: University Microfilms International.

——2000 Precolonial Copper Metallurgy: Sociopolitical Context. *In* Ancient African Metallurgy: The Sociocultural Context. Joseph Vogel, ed. pp. 83–145. Walnut Creek, CA: AltaMira Press.

Bocoum, Hamady, 2002 La Métallurgie du fer en Afrique: Un patrimoine et une ressource au service du développement. *In* Aux origines de la métallurgie du fer en Afrique: Un ancienneté méconnue. Afrique de l'Ouest et Afrique Centrale. Hamady Bocoum, ed. pp. 94–103. Paris: Publications UNESCO.

Bovill, E. W., 1958 The Golden Trade of the Moors. London: Oxford University Press.

Caton-Thompson, Gertrude, 1931 The Zimbabwe Culture: Ruins and Reactions. London: Oxford University Press.

Childs, S. Terry, 1989a Clays to Artifacts: Resource Selection in African Early Iron Age Smelting Technologies. *In* Pottery Technology: Ideas and Approaches. Gordon Bronitsky, ed. pp. 139–164. Boulder, CO: Westview Press.

——1989b Petrographic Analysis of Archaeological Ceramics. Materials Research Society Bulletin XIV(3):24–29.

——1991a Iron as Utility or Expression: Reforging Function in Africa. *In* Metals and

Society: Theory beyond Analysis. Robert Ehrenreich, ed. pp. 57–67. Research Papers in Science and Archaeology 8(2). Philadelphia: MASCA.

——1991b Style, Technology and Iron-Smelting Furnaces in Bantu-Speaking Africa. Journal of Anthropological Archaeology 10:332–359.

——1991c Transformations: Iron and Copper Production in Central Africa. *In* Recent Trends in Archaeometallurgical Research. Peter Glumac, ed. pp. 33–46. Research Papers in Science and Archaeology 8(1). Philadelphia: MASCA.

——1996 Continuities and Adaptations of Iron Working in Tanzania: Evidence from the Laboratory. *In* The Culture and Technology of African Iron Production. Peter R. Schmidt, ed. pp. 277–320. Gainesville: University of Florida Press.

Childs, S. Terry, and William J. Dewey, 1996 Forging Symbolic Meaning in Zaire and Zimbabwe. *In* The Culture and Technology of African Iron Production. Peter R. Schmidt, ed. pp. 145–171. Gainesville: University Press of Florida.

Childs, S. Terry, and David Killick, 1993 Indigenous African Metallurgy: Nature and Culture. Annual Review of Anthropology 22:317–337.

Cline, Walter W., 1937 Mining and Metallurgy in Negro Africa. Menasha, WI: George Banta Publishing.

Collett, David P. 1993 Metaphors and Representations Associated with Precolonial Iron-Smelting in Eastern and Southern Africa. *In* The Archaeology of Food, Metals and Towns. Thurstan Shaw, Paul Sinclair, Bassey Okpoko and Alex Okpoko, eds. pp. 499–511. London: Routledge.

Craddock, Paul T., 1985 Medieval Copper Alloy Production and West African Bronze Analysis – Part I. Archaeometry 27:17–41.

——1995 Early Metal Mining and Production. Washington, DC: Smithsonian Institution Press.

Craddock, Paul T., and J. Picton, 1986 Medieval Copper Alloy Production and West African Bronze Analysis – Part II. Archaeometry 28:3–32.

Craddock, Paul, J. Ambers, D. Hook, R. Farquhar, V. E. Chikwendu, A. Umeji, and Thurstan Shaw, 1989 Metal Sources and the Bronzes from Igbo-Ukwu, Nigeria. Journal of Field Archaeology 24:405–429.

David, Nicholas R., R. Heimann, David Killick, and M. Wayman, 1989 Between Bloomery and Blast Furnace: Mafa Iron Smelting Technology in North Cameroon. The African Archaeological Review 7:183–208.

de Barros, Philip, 1986 Bassar: A Quantified, Chronologically Controlled, Regional Approach to a Traditional Iron Production Centre in West Africa. Africa 56:148–174.

——1988 Societal Repercussions of the Rise of Large-Scale Traditional Iron Production: A West African Example. The African Archaeological Review 6:91–113.

——2000 Iron Metallurgy: Sociocultural Context. *In* Ancient African Metallurgy: The Sociocultural Context. Joseph Vogel, ed. pp. 147–98. Walnut Creek, CA: AltaMira Press.

de Maret, Pierre, 1977 Sanga: New Excavations, More Data, and Some Related Problems. Journal of African History 18:321–337.

——1980 Ceux qui jouent avec le feu: La Place du forgeron en Afrique centrale. Africa 50:263–277.

——1981 L'Évolution monétaire du Shaba central entre le 7e et le 18e siècle. African Economic History 10:117–149.

——1985a The Smith's Myth and the Origin of Leadership in Central Africa. *In* African Iron Working: Ancient and Traditional. Randi Haaland and Peter Shinnie, eds. pp. 73–87. Oslo: Norwegian University Press.

——1985b Fouilles archéologiques dan la Vallée du Haut-Lualaba, Zaire–II: Sanga et Katongo, 1974. Tervuren: Royal Museum for Central Africa.

——1992 Fouilles archéologiques dan la Vallée du Haut-Lualaba, Zaire–III: Kamilamba, Kikulu, et Malemba-Nkulu, 1975. Tervuren: Royal Museum for Central Africa.

Dupré, Marie-Claude, and Bruno Pinçon, 1997 Métallurgie et politique en Afrique centrale: Deux mille ans de vestiges sur les plateaux Batéké Gabon, Congo, Zaïre. Paris: Karthala.

Echard, Nicole, ed., 1983 Métallurgies africaines: Nouvelles contributions. Paris: Mémoires de la Société des Africanistes 9.

Ehret, Christopher, 2001 Bantu Expansions: Re-envisioning a Central Problem of Early African History. International Journal of African Historical Studies 34:5–41.

Fagan, Brian, 1969 Excavations at Ingombe Ilede, 1960–62. In Iron Age Cultures in Zambia II. Brian M. Fagan, David W. Phillipson, and S. G. H. Daniels, eds. pp. 55–161. London: Chatto & Windus.

Fouché, L., 1937 Mapungubwe, Ancient Bantu Civilization on the Limpopo. Cambridge: Cambridge University Press.

Fowler, Ian, 1990 Babungo: A Study of Iron Production, Trade and Power in a Nineteenth Century Ndop Plain Chiefdom (Cameroons). Ph.D. dissertation, University of London.

Friede, H. M., and R. H. Steel, 1976 Tin Mining and Smelting in the Transvaal during the Iron Age. Journal of the South African Institute of Mining and Metallurgy 76:461–470.

Garlake, Peter S., 1973 Great Zimbabwe. London: Thames & Hudson.

Gondonneau, A., and M. F. Guerra, 2002 The Circulation of Precious Metals in the Arab Empire: The Case of the Near and Middle East. Archaeometry 44:573–600.

Gordon, Robert B., and David J. Killick, 1993 Adaptation of Technology to Culture and Environment: Bloomery Iron Smelting in America and Africa. Technology and Culture 34:243–270.

Goucher, Candice, 1981 Iron is Iron 'Til It Is Rust: Trade and Ecology in the Decline of West African Iron-Smelting. Journal of African History 22:179–189.

——1990 John Reeder's Foundry in the History of Eighteenth-Century African-Caribbean Technology. Jamaica Journal 25:39–43.

Goucher, Candice, and Eugenia W. Herbert, 1996 The Blooms of Banjeli: Technology and Gender in West African Iron Making. In The Culture and Technology of African Iron Production. Peter R. Schmidt, ed. pp. 40–57. Gainesville: University Press of Florida.

Goucher, Candice, Jehanne Teilhet, Kent Wilson, and Tsaihwa Chow, 1976 Lead Isotope Studies of Metal Sources for Ancient Nigerian "Bronzes." Nature 262:130–131.

Grant, M. R., 1999 The Sourcing of Southern African Tin Artefact. Journal of Archaeological Science 26:1111–1117.

Grébénart, D., 1983 Les Métallurgies du cuivre et du fer autour d'Agadez (Niger) des origines au début de la période médiévale: Vues générales. In Métallurgies africaines: Nouvelles contributions. Nicole Echard, ed. pp. 109–125. Paris: Mémoires de la Société des Africanistes 9.

——1985 La Région d'In Gall-Tegidda n Tesemt (Niger) II: Le Néolithique final et les débuts de la métallurgie. Niamey: Études Nigériennes.

——1988 Les Premiers Métallurgistes en Afrique occidental. Paris: Errance.

Guerra, M. F., C.-O. Sarthre, A. Gondonneau, and J.-N. Barrandon, 1999 Precious Metals and Provenance Inquiries using LA-ICP-MS. Journal of Archaeological Science 25:1101–1110.

Haaland, Gunnar, Randi Haaland, and Suman Rijal, 2002 The Social Life of Iron: A Cross-

Cultural Study of Technological, Symbolic, and Social Aspects of Iron Making. Anthropos 97:35–54.

Haaland, Randi, 1985 Iron Production, its Socio-Cultural Context and Ecological Implications. *In* African Iron Working: Ancient and Traditional. Randi Haaland and Peter Shinnie, eds. pp. 50–72. Oslo: Norwegian University Press.

Herbert, Eugenia W., 1984 Red Gold of Africa: Copper in Precolonial History and Culture. Madison: University of Wisconsin Press.

——1993 Iron, Gender, and Power: Rituals of Transformation in African Societies. Bloomington: University of Indiana Press.

——1996 Metals and Power at Great Zimbabwe. *In* Aspects of African Archaeology: Papers from the 10th Congress of the Pan-African Association for Prehistory and Related Studies. Gilbert Pwiti and Robert Soper, eds. pp. 641–654. Harare: University of Zimbabwe Publications.

Holl, Augustin F. C., 2000 Metals and Precolonial African Society. *In* Ancient African Metallurgy: The Sociocultural Context. Joseph O. Vogel, ed. pp. 1–81. Walnut Creek, CA: AltaMira Press.

Kense, François, 1983 Traditional African Iron Working. African Occasional Papers 1. Calgary, Alberta: Department of Archaeology, University of Calgary.

Killick, David. J., 1990 Technology in its Social Setting: The Ironworkers of Kasungu, Malawi. Ph.D. dissertation, Yale University.

——1991a A Little Known Extractive Process: Iron Smelting in Natural-Draft Furnaces. Journal of Minerals, Metals and Materials 43:62–64.

——1991b The Relevance of Recent African Iron-Smelting Practice to Reconstructions of Prehistoric Smelting Technology. *In* Recent Trends in Archaeometallurgical Research. Peter Glumac, ed. pp. 47–54. Research Papers in Science and Archaeology 8(1). Philadelphia: MASCA.

——1996 On Claims for "Advanced" Ironworking Technology in Precolonial Africa. *In* The Culture and Technology of African Iron Production. Peter R. Schmidt, ed. pp. 247–266. Gainesville: University Press of Florida.

——In press Technology in Africa South of the Sahara. *In* Technology in World History. W. Bernard Carlson, ed. Oxford: Oxford University Press.

Killick, David, Nicholas van der Merwe, Robert B. Gordon, and Daniel Grébenart, 1988 Reassessment of the Evidence for Early Metallurgy in Niger, West Africa. Journal of Archaeological Science 15:367–394.

Klieman, Kairn, In press Toward a History of Pre-Colonial Gabon: Farmers and Forest-Specialists along the Middle Ogooué River, 500 B.C.–A.D. 1000. *In* Culture, Ecology, and Politics in Gabon's Rainforest. Michael C. Read and James F. Burns, eds. Boulder: Westview Press.

Kriger, Colleen E., 1999 Pride of Men: Ironworking in the 19th Century West Central Africa. Portsmouth, NH: Heinemann.

Lagercrantz, Sture, 1989 Wire-Drawing in Africa. Jahrbauch de Museums für Völkerkunde zu Leipzig 38:224–247.

Lambert, Nicole, 1983 Nouvelle contribution à l'étude du Chalcolithique de Mauritanie. *In* Métallurgies africaines: Nouvelles contributions. Nicole Echard, ed. pp. 63–87. Paris: Mémoires de la Société des Africanistes 9.

Lemonnier, P., 1983 L'Étude des systèmes techniques, une urgence en technologie culturelle. Techniques et Culture 1:11–34.

Lindblom, K. G., 1939 Wire-Drawing, Especially in Africa. Stockholm: Ethnographical Museum of Sweden.

McNaughton, Patrick, 1988 The Mande Blacksmiths. Bloomington: Indiana University Press.

Martinelli, Bruno, 2002 Au seuil de la métallurgie intensive: Le Choix de la combustion lente dans la boucle du Niger (Burkina Faso et Mali). *In* Aux origines de la métallurgie du fer en Afrique: Un ancienneté méconnue. Afrique de l'Ouest et Afrique Centrale. Hamady Bocoum, ed. pp. 165–188. Paris: Publications UNESCO.

Miller, Duncan, 1996 The Tsodilo Jewellery: Metalwork from Northwestern Botswana. Cape Town: University of Cape Town Press.

——2001 Indigenous Iron Production in Southern Africa: Archaeological Observations and Interpretations. Mediterranean Archaeology 14:229–234.

——2002 Smelter and Smith: Metal Fabrication Technology in Southern African Early and Late Iron Age. Journal of Archaeological Science 29:1083–1131.

Miller, Duncan, and Nicholas J. van der Merwe, 1994 Early Metal Working in Sub-Saharan Africa: A Review of Recent Research. Journal of African History 35:1–36.

Miller, Duncan, Nirdev Desai, and Julia Lee-Thorp, 2000 Indigenous Gold Mining in Southern Africa: A Review. South African Archaeological Society Goodwin Series 8:91–100.

Miller, Duncan, N. Desai, D. Grigorova, and W. Smith, 2001 Trace-Elements Study of Gold from Southern African Archaeological Sites. South African Journal of Science 97:297–300.

Monod, T., 1969 Le "Ma'aden Ijâfen": Une épave caravanière ancienne dans la Majâbat al-Loubrâ. *In* Actes du Première Colloque International d'Archéologie Africaine, 1966, pp. 286–320. Fort Lamy.

Oliver, Roland, 2001 *Comment on* Bantu Expansions: Re-envisioning a Central Problem of Early African History. International Journal of African Historical Studies 34:43–45.

Person, Alain, and Gérard Quéchon, 2002 Données chronométriques et chronologiques de la métallurgie à Termit: Matériaux graphiques pour l'étude des âges anciens du fer. Aux origines de la métallurgie du fer en Afrique: Un ancienneté méconnue. Afrique de l'Ouest et Afrique Centrale. Hamady Bocoum, ed. pp. 115–22. Paris: Publications UNESCO.

Pfaffenberger, Bryan, 1998 Mining Communities, *Chaînes opératoires* and Sociotechnical Systems. *In* Social Approaches to an Industrial Past. A. Bernard Knapp, Vincent C. Piggott, and Eugenia W. Herbert, eds. pp. 291–300. London: Routledge.

Posnansky, Merrick, 1977 Brass Casting and its Antecedents in West Africa. Journal of African History 18:287–300.

Quéchon, Gérard, 2002 Les Datations de la métallurgie du fer à Termit (Niger): Leur fiabilité, leur signification. *In* Aux origines de la métallurgie du fer en Afrique: Un ancienneté méconnue. Afrique de l'Ouest et Afrique Centrale. Hamady Bocoum, ed. pp. 105–14. Paris: Publications UNESCO.

Rehder, J. E., 1996 Use of Preheated Air in Primitive Furnaces: Comment on the Views of Avery and Schmidt. *In* The Culture and Technology of African Iron Production. Peter R. Schmidt, ed. pp. 234–39. Gainesville: University Press of Florida.

Rowlands, Michael, and J. P. Warnier, 1993 The Magical Production of Iron in the Cameroon Grassfields. *In* The Archaeology of Africa: Food, Metals and Towns. Thurstan Shaw, Paul Sinclair, Bassey Andah, and Alex Okpoko, eds. pp. 512–550. London: Routledge.

Schmidt, Peter R., 1996 Reconfiguring The Barongo: Reproductive Symbolism and Reproduction among a Work Association of Iron Smelters. *In* The Culture and Technology of African Iron Production. Peter R. Schmidt, ed. pp. 74–127. Gainesville: University Press of Florida.

——1997 Iron Technology in East Africa: Symbolism, Science, and Archaeology. Bloomington: Indiana University Press.

Schmidt, Peter R., and Donald Avery, 1983 More Evidence for an Advanced Prehistoric Iron Technology in Africa. Journal of Field Archaeology 10:421–434.

Schmidt, Peter R., and S. Terry Childs, 1985 Innovation and Industry during the Early Iron Age in East Africa: The KM2 and KM3 Sites of Northwestern Tanzania. The African Archaeological Review 3:53–94.

Schmidt, Peter R., and Bertram B. Mapunda, 1997 Ideology and the Archaeological Record in Africa: Interpreting Symbolism in Iron Smelting Technology. Journal of Anthropological Archaeology 16:73–102.

Shaw, Thurstan, 1970 Igbo-Ukwu: An Account of Archaeological Discoveries in Eastern Nigeria. 2 vols. Evanston: Northwestern University Press.

——1978 Nigeria: Its Archaeology and Early History. London: Thames & Hudson.

Shinnie, Peter L., 1985 Iron Working at Méroe. In African Iron Working: Ancient and Traditional. Randi Haaland and Peter Shinnie, eds. pp. 28–35. Oslo: Norwegian University Press.

Stanley, G. H., 1929 Primitive Metallurgy in South Africa: Some Products and their Significance. South African Journal of Science 26:732–748.

Steel, R. H., 1975 Ingot Casting and Wire Drawing in Iron Age Southern Africa. Journal of the South African Institute of Mining and Metallurgy 76(4):232–237.

Summers, R., 1969 Ancient Mining in Rhodesia and Adjacent Areas. Salisbury, Rhodesia: Trustees of the National Museums of Rhodesia.

Swan, Lorraine, 1994 Early Gold Mining on the Zimbabwean Plateau. Uppsala, Sweden: Societas Archaeologica Upsaliensis.

Tamari, Tal, 1991 The Development of Caste Systems in West Africa. Journal of African History 32:221–250.

Trigger, Bruce G., 1969 The Myth of Meroë and the African Iron Age. African Historical Studies 2:23–50.

Tylecote, Ronald F., 1982 Metal Working at Meroë, Sudan. Meroitic Studies 6:29–42.

Van Noten, Francis, 1972 Les Tombes du Roi Cyirima Rujugira et de la Reine-Mère Nyirayuhi Kanjogera. Tervuren: Royal Museum for Central Africa.

——1983 L'Histoire archéologique du Rwanda. Série 8, Sciences Humaines, no. 112. Tervuren, Belgium.

Vansina, Jan, 2001 Comment on Bantu Expansions: Re-envisioning a Central Problem of Early African History. International Journal of African Historical Studies 34:52–53.

Warnier, J.-P., and Ian Fowler, 1979 A Nineteenth Century Ruhr in Central Africa. Africa 49:329–351.

Willett, Frank, 1967 Ife in the History of West African Sculpture. New York: McGraw-Hill.

——1981 The Analysis of Nigerian Copper Alloys. Retrospect and Prospect. Critica d'Arte Africana 46:135–146.

Williams, Denis, 1974 Icon and Image: A Study of Sacred and Secular Forms of African Classical Art. New York: New York University Press.

12

The Bantu Problem and African Archaeology

Manfred K. H. Eggert

In the 1850s the German linguist Bleek discovered a genetic relationship between a large number of languages distributed over the southern half of Africa. He called these languages *Bantu*, after the Zulu term *aba-ntu* ("men"), a term found in etymologically related forms in many Bantu languages. The phenomenon described by Bleek has intrigued researchers ever since because it implied a common origin for these widely distributed languages. As this chapter will show, Bantu historical studies have been largely shaped by linguistic data and assumptions. As soon as archaeological evidence became available, it was considered supportive and fitted in the linguistic frame. Two competing linguistic paradigms worked to account for Bantu language dispersal, and archaeology played an ever-increasing role in both. Before long it became apparent, however, that archaeologists were building their arguments on linguistic assumptions, while linguists used their archaeological colleagues' reasoning in turn as independent confirmation of their own ideas. As will be demonstrated, a pendulum-like pattern between interpretive paradigms and major concepts was characterized by a tendency toward wholesale rejection of previous key issues which, after a while, tended to reappear in more or less modified form.

From Bleek to Guthrie and Beyond: The First Hundred Years of Bantu Linguistics and Culture History

Even today, after almost 150 years of intensive research on the structure and relationship among Bantu languages and their relationship to non-Bantu languages, scholars have yet to agree on even fundamental issues. For example, the question of which criteria are necessary or sufficient for a language to be classified as Bantu is still a matter of debate. Thus, there is no agreement on whether certain languages in the northwestern part of the Bantu area are "real" or "semi"-Bantu. Not surprisingly, figures on the number of Bantu languages vary greatly. Estimates in the 1970s were between 200 and 400 individual languages (e.g., Vansina 1979:291), but more recent ones run to some 600 (Vansina 1995:179, 180; cf. Nurse 1994/95:65–66; 1997:367). As Derek Nurse (2002:1) observed, some estimates run as high as 680 individual languages, but because there is "a cline of linguistic difference between the similar and the dissimilar, and since no one knows exactly where to cut a cline, it is hard to state with accuracy the total of Bantu 'languages'."

Though debates over the number of Bantu languages continue, the fact that the better part of sub-Saharan Africa is settled by people who speak Bantu languages demands an explanation. How did such a vast area come to be occupied by linguistically related speech communities? The "Bantu expansion," as it is commonly called, remains what Jan Vansina (1979:287) termed "a major puzzle in the history of Africa." The intricate story of Bantu research, with all its seeming breakthroughs and vicissitudes, has been recounted several times. For example, in 1979 and 1980 Vansina published a detailed study in which he showed, *inter alia*, how the term *Bantu*, originally coined in a purely technical sense without any non-linguistic connotations, was transformed into a designation referring indiscriminately to language, culture, society, and race.[1] The 1979 part of his paper, which covered the period to the mid-1950s, remains the most penetrating in-depth analysis of the Bantu issue before prehistoric archaeology got involved in the topic. It is sufficient here to briefly review some central points.

As Vansina (1979) made clear, Bantu research was never restricted to linguistics alone, although this constituted its genuine domain. As early as 1886, Harry Johnston, a British colonial administrator and early Bantuist, postulated an ancestral tongue from which all Bantu languages sprang. Thirteen years later the German linguist Carl Meinhof reconstructed this hypothetical ancestral language or, as he called it in German, *Ursprache*, on the basis of regular sound shifts. This constituted a major breakthrough in comparative Bantu linguistics (see Vansina 1979). Already in 1886 Johnston went beyond linguistics when he imagined an original Bantu people somewhere in west Central Africa speaking this putative ancestral language. In hindsight, Johnston's imagining was a first attempt to transfer Bleek's *Bantu* from the purely linguistic to a general anthropological sphere. Thus Johnston was the first to envision the term *Bantu* in an all-encompassing manner, and the legacy of this vision remains part and parcel of Bantu studies to this day.

Key developments in Bantu research over the last five decades were stimulated by the findings of Joseph H. Greenberg and Malcolm Guthrie. Though their work was contradictory, it stimulated discussion within both Bantu linguistics and the wider domain of Bantu studies. The ensuing debate may be ascribed paradigmatic value since the response by archaeologists and historians displayed a pattern which has repeated itself ever since. The debate culminated in the Viviers Conference, "L'Expansion bantoue," organized by the French Centre National de la Recherche Scientifique in April 1977 (Bouquiaux, ed., 1980). Its history has been documented and analyzed in considerable detail elsewhere (see Eggert 1981 and Vansina 1980 for fully referenced treatments).

In the late 1940s, the American linguist Greenberg began publishing a series of articles on the classification of African languages which included two papers of special importance for the Bantu problem (Greenberg 1949a, 1949b). His influential book (Greenberg 1955) is a collection of these and related studies originally published in the *Southwestern Journal of Anthropology*.

Based on a comparison of lexical resemblances in fundamental vocabulary of a large number of western Sudanic and Bantu languages, Greenberg concluded that these two language groups were historically related. For him, Bantu was a subgroup within a subfamily of West Sudanic, which itself belonged to what he called the "Niger-Congo family." The West Sudanic subfamily comprised about 23 languages, all spoken within a restricted area around the Nigeria–Cameroon border. Following the rule that the area of origin of a language is found where the greatest number of closely related tongues are spoken, Greenberg (1955:116) located the "area of Bantu origin" in the central Benue Valley (Figure 12.1b). This outcome was at variance with the commonly held view that the original Bantu speakers had fanned out all over the southern half of the continent from somewhere in the East African Great Lakes region (see Vansina 1979:298, 314, 316, 320).

Greenberg's linguistic thesis was brought to the attention of a wide audience through the publication of George Peter Murdock's *Africa: Its Peoples and their Culture History* (1959). Greenberg's language classification provided the linguistic basis of Murdock's book. But Murdock amplified Greenberg's abstract linguistic differentiations by associating them with a socio-economic and sociocultural background in which the non-specialist reader was most interested. In fact, Murdock acted as a catalyst insofar as the Greenberg–Murdock conception of the Bantu expansion was soon supplemented with, and modified by, archaeological data published by Merrick Posnansky (1961; see Eggert 1981:281–286). Like Murdock, Posnansky stressed the importance of bananas and yams for what he termed "Bantu genesis." To this he added knowledge of ironworking as a significant element in Bantu dispersal, and interpreted specific ceramics in Central, East, and Southeast Africa (so-called "dimple-based" and "channeled" pottery) as witness to a rapid expansion of Bantu people.

Most genetic classifications of Bantu are based on a quantitative method commonly known as "lexicostatistics." Developed by Morris Swadesh in the early 1950s (Swadesh 1951, 1952, 1955), it proceeds on the basis of a word list (the so-called "Swadesh list") of some 100, or more rarely 200 items considered to belong to the "basic" or "core vocabulary" of a language. Core vocabulary is that part of the lexicon which concerns fundamental phenomena of human existence like body parts (e.g., head, nose, mouth, breast, arm), basic biological functions (like drinking, eating, sleeping, and dying), general facts and phenomena of nature (like water, rain, stone, fire, mountains, stars, sun, and moon), flora and fauna (e.g., leaf, tree, fish, dog) and specific concepts such as numerals (e.g., one, two, three), size (e.g., big, small), personal, demonstrative, and interrogative pronouns (e.g., I, we, you, this, what, who) and color (e.g., red, white, black). This vocabulary is labeled "basic" since its referents are believed to represent cultural universals in the sense of being of relevance in all cultures. It is presumed that these terms are more resistant to

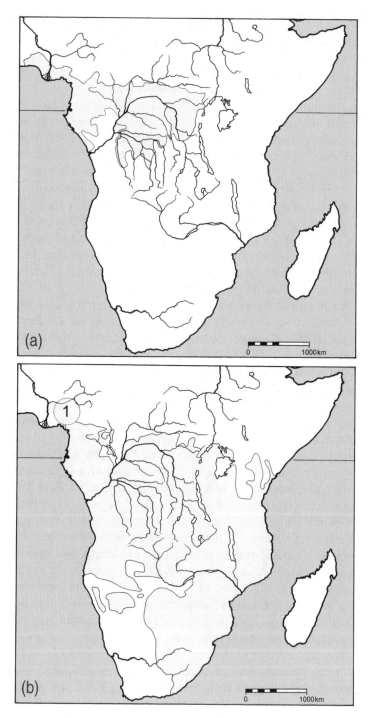

Figure 12.1. (a) The equatorial rainforest. (b) The distribution of Bantu languages and the putative area of origin (1)
Source: Generalized and modified after Nurse 1994/95:76 [fig. 1].

change and to borrowing than others – that there is stable transmission over long periods within a given linguistic community.

Cognates (words of similar meaning and phonetic form or phonological correspondence) are worked out by comparing the word lists of basic vocabulary of different languages. Cognates are interpreted as genetically related, in other words, going back to a common ancestor language. Consequently, cognates are viewed as retentions from this ancestor. The number of cognates in each language pair is used to calculate the "percentage of cognation" between them (Nurse 1997:364). In this manner a statistical measure of the degree of similarity of each language to each other language in the set is generated. The "retention rate" of reflexes of the proto-language in each of these languages is taken as an indicator of relative distance of the language in question from the proto-language. This retention rate is then used to construct tree diagrams as a visual representation of language genealogy.

The tree, family tree, or genealogical tree model of language relationship was devised in the context of Indo-European studies in the 1870s to account for the appearance of new languages. It constitutes a model which, in its orthodox form, postulates that an ancestral or "mother" language splits and develops into two new "daughter" languages, each of which splits again in two languages, and so on. Obviously, this mechanistic concept cannot be taken as reflecting historical reality. As Theodora Bynon (1977:67) observed, it is "impossible to say" to what extent it reflects reality "since it is based on only those languages which have survived into the present or of which we possess written records." Nevertheless, tree diagrams are routinely employed in linguistic classification. They are useful in that they mirror in a convenient way both the inferred relative chronological position of and the relationship between languages.

At about the time that Greenberg's work was attracting attention among non-linguists interested in the roots of Bantu Africa, the British Bantuist Guthrie published several articles on the most important results of his ongoing studies of Bantu languages (Guthrie 1959, 1962a, 1962b). His research culminated in a four-volume monograph entitled *Comparative Bantu* published between 1967 and 1971 (see Flight 1980, 1988). Working on the basis of a word list of 500 items supplemented by major grammatical features, he established an areally oriented referential classification of Bantu into "zones" (see Figure 12.2a). In contrast to the Swadesh list, the glosses were derived partly from core vocabulary and partly from non-core vernacular lexicon, including terms for traditional Bantu cultural inventory. Guthrie isolated more than 2,000 groups of cognate items in over 200 Bantu languages. Considering these current items as "reflexes" of ancestral items and applying the rules of sound shift, he reconstructed "starred forms," i.e., the hypothetical "roots" reflected in contemporary vocabulary. While about 450 reflexes occurred over the whole or most of the Bantu area, approximately the same number showed a predominantly western distribution, while about twice as many were found within the eastern part of Bantu Africa. Guthrie paid special attention to the 450 reflexes that were rather evenly distributed over the Bantu area. He termed the roots of these reflexes "general roots." He then checked the percentage of reflexes of these general roots in 28 test languages chosen from all over Bantu Africa and plotted the cor-

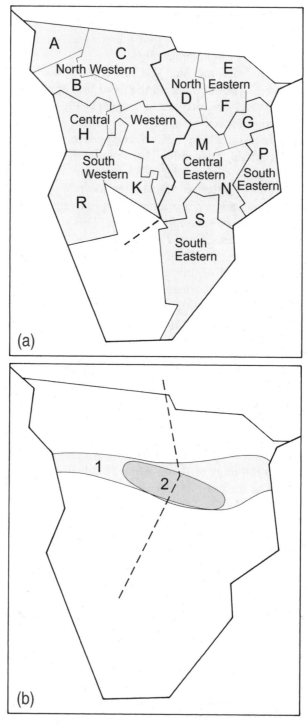

Figure 12.2. (a) Guthrie's Bantu classification in zones and regions. (b) Guthrie's Bantu nucleus (1) and central nucleus area (2) as well as later PB-A and PB-B divide
Sources: (a) after Guthrie 1967 [vol. 1]:65 [map] and 83 [fig. 3]; (b) after Guthrie 1967[vol. 1]:102 [topograms T.1, T.2. and T.3].

responding figures on maps. These topological exercises resulted in a narrow belt of high figures oriented roughly east–west across the Bantu area which Guthrie termed a "nucleus." The highest percentages of reflexes with general roots occurred in a flat ellipse toward the center of this belt – his "central nucleus area" – i.e., in the woodland belt to the south of the equatorial rainforest in what is now the Katanga province of the Democratic Republic of Congo (Figure 12.2b).

Guthrie's interpretation of his findings in terms of the "prehistory of the Bantu languages" (Guthrie 1962a) was straightforward: (1) Because general roots were widely distributed, Guthrie inferred that they belonged to a single ancestral language which he called *Proto-Bantu* or PB-X. (2) The fact that the highest percentages of the reflexes of general roots showed a significant clustering suggested to Guthrie that this ellipsoid cluster indicated the area of origin of Proto-Bantu. (3) The east–west patterning of reflexes and roots led Guthrie to conclude that this mirrored a differentiation into a western and eastern dialect of Proto-Bantu (PB-A and PB-B). Based on additional statistical treatment of the data he argued that the western dialect developed before the eastern one. (4) Guthrie took the overall distribution of the percentages as an indication of a north- and southward dispersion of the respective ancestor languages from the nucleus. (5) On the basis of the cultural vocabulary inferred from the general roots, Guthrie concluded that the speakers of Proto-Bantu worked iron, fished, and possessed canoes.

Oliver's Synthesis and the Rise of Archaeology: Adding Material Substance to the Linguistic Frame

It became immediately obvious that Guthrie's data, findings, and ensuing interpretations were diametrically opposed to Greenberg's. Before long, historians and archaeologists directed their attention toward Guthrie's work and tried to incorporate his results into their own schemes of Bantu history. Roland Oliver, a leading British historian of Africa, presented an influential historical synthesis, which Vansina (1980:297) dubbed "the London paradigm" (Oliver 1966). Oliver's four-stage model of Bantu expansion (Figure 12.3) tried to reconcile Guthrie's and Greenberg's views by interpreting their different areas of origin as successive stages in the dispersal of Bantu speakers (Eggert 1981:288–293; Vansina 1980:297–303). Greenberg's "central Benue Valley" represented the original "homeland," while Guthrie's nuclear area was considered a later secondary center from which Bantu speakers dispersed. At the same time Oliver partly endorsed but also modified Murdock's socio-economic speculations on the history of tropical and subtropical agriculture, and added to the picture any pertinent archaeological information that was available at the time.

Oliver's synthesis was widely acclaimed for its multi-disciplinary thrust and historical imagination. With it came, for a time, general recognition of the importance of Guthrie's findings for any solution to the Bantu problem. As Sutton (1994/95:5–6) observed, Oliver stressed the widely accepted association of Bantu "culture" and ironworking, and thereby reinforced the assumption that the Bantu

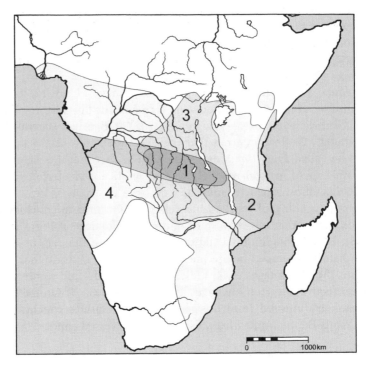

Figure 12.3. Oliver's four-stage model of Bantu expansion. (1) Bantu nucleus; (2) Stage 2; (3) Stage 3; (4) Stage 4
Source: after Oliver 1966:349 [fig. 1].

languages were spread by people who possessed a superior technology. The following years saw papers by two archaeologists whose findings were firmly based on Guthrie's work (Huffman 1970; Posnansky 1968). In the early 1970s, however, under the impact of linguistic studies by Bernd Heine and others, the pendulum swung back again. Heine's (1973) results, based on lexicostatistical analysis of 137 Bantu languages using a 100-item word list adapted from Swadesh, were at odds with Guthrie's, but fitted quite well with Greenberg's conclusions. Guthrie's findings were abandoned and Greenberg found himself restored to his former position within the larger part of the Bantu studies community.

From the late 1960s archaeological research on the Early Iron Age in sub-Saharan African, especially in East Africa and southeastern Africa, progressed at a very rapid pace (see e.g., Robertshaw, ed., 1990; Wotzka 2001a, 2001b). The center of gravity of integrated Bantu studies shifted from what might be labeled a *linguistics cum archaeology* to an *archaeology cum linguistics* stage (see Sutton 1994/95). With archaeology moving rapidly to the fore, the archaeologist David Phillipson (1976a) published a synthesis of archaeological and linguistic data for eastern and southeastern Africa. Because Guthrie had fallen out of favor with his Bantu studies colleagues and Greenberg was of no help for the regions concerned, Phillipson relied to a large extent on the findings of Christopher Ehret, a linguist who at that time specialized in studies of loan words in Eastern Bantu languages. Ehret's speculative reconstructions and results – he postulated that the greater part of eastern and southern Africa was once settled by speakers of Central Sudanic languages before Bantu speakers – posed considerable problems for Phillipson. In his desire to integrate the regional archaeological database with what was available in terms of historical linguistics, Phillipson had to turn, metaphorically speaking, Ehret's reconstructions inside out. Not surprisingly, the outcome was hardly convincing (Eggert 1981:306–310).

A critical reading of archaeological contributions to the Bantu problem of that period will show that archaeologists in general tended to prematurely accept the propositions offered by Bantuists and adapt them to their own point of view. Critical examination of linguistic hypotheses in the light of archaeological evidence was almost absent. Thus, Phillipson represented a common (if somewhat extreme) attitude and practice. His *World Archaeology* paper (1976a) is based on *ad hoc* reasoning; shunning the fundamental theoretical implications of the problem at hand, he accommodated Ehret's linguistic reconstructions almost at will to the archaeological evidence. The linguistic reconstruction served as an overall framework that provided the material evidence (mostly ceramics) with a "historic" outlook of sorts. With its dependency on linguistic hypotheses, this paper fitted squarely with the general pattern displayed by integrated studies of the Bantu problem.

The extent to which archaeologists were willing to trim their sails to the linguistic wind (to paraphrase Posnansky 1976:630), became apparent in the same year in another article on the Early Iron Age in eastern and southern Africa by Phillipson (1976b). He must have learned of Heine's (1973) reclassification of Bantu languages shortly after the first paper was written and became aware of its consequences for their expansion (Figure 12.4a). He immediately adopted its main results and integrated them into another dispersal scenario which was, in important ways, quite different from his "Archaeology and Bantu Linguistics" paper of the same year (also Phillipson 1977). Whereas he had formerly believed in one migration route from a Bantu homeland in the northwest of the present Bantu territory across the savanna belt north of the equatorial forest into East Africa, he now – under the impact of Heine's findings – argued for an additional southward movement at about the same time (Figure 12.4b).

In summary there is no doubt that the cultural-historical interpretation of the Early Iron Age of sub-Saharan Africa through the late 1970s was largely a function of the varying hypotheses favored by linguists to account for the Bantu data (Eggert 1981; Vansina 1980). Although the relationship between archaeology and historical linguistics was strongly biased in favor of linguistics, the flow of information was in no way unidirectional as might be supposed. Archaeological considerations did not fail to leave their imprint on linguistic reasoning as well. An especially telling example is provided by Heine as author and co-author of two very influential articles on the classification and expansion of Bantu languages (Heine 1973; Heine et al. 1977). When he tried to bolster his own as well as fellow-linguist Alick Henrici's (1973) new results on the classification of Bantu, he stated explicitly that they were

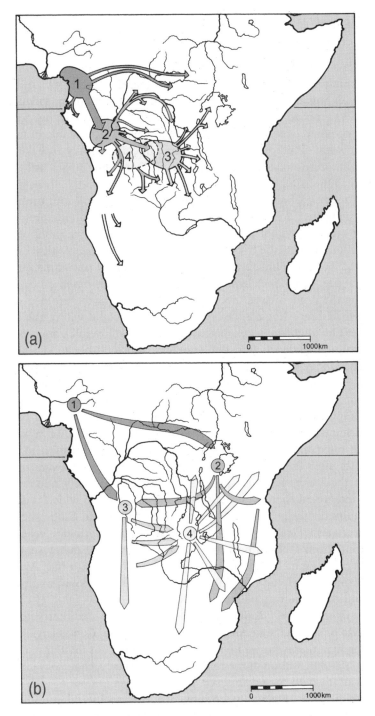

Figure 12.4. (a) Heine's model of Bantu expansion. (1) Proto-Bantu nucleus; (2) Congo nucleus; (3) East Highland nucleus; (4) Kwilu-Kasai convergence area. (b) Phillipson's 1976 and 1977 model of Bantu expansion; numbers indicate successive centers
Sources: (a) after Heine et al. 1977:71; (b) after Phillipson 1977:109.

"in accordance with archaeological findings," citing two key papers by Phillipson (1976a, 1976b) as support. He was not aware, however, that Phillipson's work on archaeology and the Bantu was itself heavily dependent on current linguistic research, not least of which were his own contributions to the Bantu problem.

The 1980s saw few attempts to link Bantu linguistics and archaeology. Archaeologists were more aware of the pitfalls involved in an integrated approach and tried to avoid circular reasoning of the kind summarized above. Thus, Phillipson (1985b:80) explicitly stressed that his new survey of the archaeological evidence was based "exclusively on archaeological data" and made "no use whatsoever of any results derived from linguistic studies." His concluding attempt to relate the rather meager archaeological information on Central Africa to the supposed spread of the Bantu languages from their proposed area of origin into the equatorial forest and beyond was hardly convincing. However, the archaeological data for his *Chifumbaze Complex*, representing the Early Iron Age in eastern and southern Africa (Phillipson 1985a:171), were much better. He interpreted its wide distribution in terms of an "extremely rapid expansion" through the eastern and southern savannas of populations subsisting mainly on food production and practicing pottery manufacture and ironworking (Phillipson 1985b:81). In the process of this large-scale population movement, so he argued, autochthonous people with an exclusively hunter-and-gatherer way of life were marginalized or replaced. Although he now stressed the fact that there were no *a priori* reasons why linguistic change should parallel changes in other domains of culture (Phillipson 1985b:81), he ventured beyond his newly adopted restraint: the rapid dispersal of the Chifumbaze Complex, he argued, could "reflect in a general way the dispersal of the eastern Bantu languages." However, his own admission that "the two processes cannot be said to coincide" (Phillipson 1985b:82) quite clearly indicates how little, if any, common ground there was.

How quickly Phillipson adapted his archaeological perspective to the latest linguistic hypotheses is also evident when one compares the first edition of his *African Archaeology* (1985a) with his paper of the same year (Phillipson 1985b). While in the book he was rather vague as to the route the earliest expansion of Bantu languages from their Nigerian-Cameroonian homeland had taken – it may have been "either through or along the fringes of the equatorial forest" (Phillipson 1985a:179) – he presented a clear answer in his paper: the early Bantu speakers spread in and through the rainforest. Though he stressed the very unsatisfactory state of archaeological research in Central Africa, he outlined his hypothesis with the little archaeological evidence there was (Phillipson 1985b:71–75). The reason for this sudden decision for the "forest option" was simple: After his book manuscript had gone to press he apparently learned of the "three waves" scenario (Vansina 1984:134) of the initial Bantu spread which Vansina had developed in his paper on "Western Bantu Expansion." Phillipson (1985b:71) explicitly acknowledged this paper, which provided, as he put it, "a plausible historico-geographical reconstruction of the expansion of Western Bantu speakers in and through the equatorial forest."

Phillipson (1993:198–199) integrated Vansina's (1984, 1990:49–57) concept of Western Bantu spread into the second edition of this book, where it continued to

serve as a base line for his archaeological reasoning. He thus felt tempted to interpret the archaeological evidence from Central Africa available at that time "as evidence for expansion through the Central African forest by the ancestors of the
recent Bantu-speaking people" (Phillipson 1993:187). The problem with this
approach is that Phillipson probably misjudged the nature of Vansina's conception,
which he thought was based "very largely on lexicostatistical data and classifications, as viewed against the backcloth of the physical environment" (Phillipson
1985b:71). However, while Vansina used the lexicostatistical data of Bastin, Coupez
and de Halleux (1983), his notion of Western Bantu spread represented first and
foremost an integration of linguistic, archaeological, and ecological evidence of dis-
putable overall culture-historical value (Eggert 1992). Thus, when Phillipson considered this a linguistically derived study independent of archaeological evidence,
we were, once again, confronted with a vicious circle.

Vansina's Turnabout or the Rise and Fall of the Migration Paradigm

Vansina's "Western Bantu Expansion" (1984) and the pertinent section in his *Paths
in the Rainforests* (1990:49–57) constituted the most ambitious effort in Bantu historiography of the 1980s and early 1990s. However, his historical narrative was both
selective and unduly general, paying too little attention to both the specific and the
overall context of the relevant archaeological features in the rainforest. For example,
he singled out certain radiocarbon dates without discussing their specific and
regional archaeological context. Likewise, he did not reflect on the validity of treat-
ing radiocarbon dates as "tests" for the adequacy of glottochronological estimations of languages splits (see below). He did not pay due attention to the lacunae
in our knowledge of rainforest archaeology, compensating for the lack of pertinent
archaeological evidence with speculation based on a rather general assessment of
regional ecology and topography (Eggert 1992:7). In this respect one is reminded
of Murdock's (1959) *Africa*, which similarly drew on contemporary phenomena, in
that case ethnographic and ecological patterns and features, to fill in gaps in historical evidence.

  Empirical data rather than armchair reasoning are clearly required in order to
reconstruct the settlement processes associated with the dispersal of Bantu languages. If dispersal was brought about by migratory movements – as the majority
of Bantuists, archaeologists, cultural anthropologists, and historians argued – then
we ought to search for whatever tangible evidence of these migrations might have
survived. With regard to the equatorial rainforest (Figure 12.1a), Vansina's synthesis of where, when, and how Bantu languages came to be spoken, there was far too
little non-linguistic evidence to be convincing.

  Considering Vansina's earlier writing it came as a big surprise when in 1995 he
suddenly used "Bantu expansion" in quotation marks and announced that he no
longer believed in "a single continuous migration" (Vansina 1995:173). He now
considers the traditional "least moves" model of expansion as "patently absurd"
(Vansina 1995:178). The change in his view was motivated by the results of an

imposing comparative study in Bantu lexicostatistics carried out by Bastin and Coupez (data collection and collation) in collaboration with Michael Mann (statistical processing and text). Their work proposed a new subclassification of Bantu based on 542 vocabularies from 440 out of a total of some 600 languages (Bastin et al. 1999). As Vansina (1995:180–183) tells it, the computer, operating on various assumptions and with different statistical techniques, generated seven different family trees of Bantu which were then reduced to four on the basis of plausibility. However, Vansina (1995:175, 183) was alerted to the inflexibility of the tree model which stipulates that every language can be derived from only one ancestor language, excluding the possibility of mixed languages that go back to two or more ancestors. Therefore, he used the computations of the remaining four trees to create a "wave" model (Vansina 1995:184–186). This type of model was developed at about the same time, in the 1870s, as the family tree model in German Indo-European linguistics (*Wellentheorie* in German).

Wave and tree models of language change are based on different assumptions. In a tree model "daughter" languages develop out of "mother" languages through community split and subsequent geographical isolation brought about by emigration of speakers. The wave model, however, assumes that new languages arise out of a common pool of interrelated ancestral dialects, thus allowing for the possibility of mixed languages of multiple "genetic" origins. Languages exist side by side in a given territory and changes brought about at a certain spot may "spread outward like waves in a pond," to quote Vansina's simile (Vansina 1995:175). The linguistic data considered item by item convinced Vansina (1995:186) that "Bantu languages do form a huge dialect continuum," an insight with profound implications for the received understanding of the Bantu problem. According to this model, languages spread whereas people more or less stay put.

Vansina's new model suggested a succession of three main phases of Bantu dispersal. In accordance with the now commonly accepted Greenberg hypothesis, the "original Bantu language" is thought to have developed out of a cluster of Bantoid languages in westernmost Cameroon. According to Vansina (1995:186), it expanded from this area eastwards toward the East African Great Lakes and, on a smaller scale and partly by seaborne travel, toward the lower Ogooué River area in what is now Gabon. The assumption of seaborne travel was inspired by the linguistic and geographic position of the Bubi and Seki languages on the island of Bioko and in the Muni estuary respectively. He speculated that, during the expansion process, dialects on opposite sides of the original Bantu language continuum developed into different languages after western and eastern communities were separated by the vast marsh territory between the Sangha River in Congo-Brazzaville and the Ubangi River. At the same time, according to Vansina (1995:186–187), the original language in the core area differentiated into several language clusters. Thus, under the influence of the Bantoid language block – the so-called "semi" Bantu languages in the northwestern part of the Bantu area – a northwest cluster of Bantu languages began to differentiate internally. Two others – "proto-West" and "proto-East" Bantu – developed into West and East Bantu and became the focus of expansion of the next phase. West Bantu is supposed to have differentiated first in the

Sangha and Likwala-aux-Herbes Rivers marsh area, after which a number of dialects and languages evolved in a process of further differentiation in the inner Congo basin as well as in the savanna region to the south of the rainforest. Finally, in a third phase of dispersal, proto-East Bantu expanded from the forest into southeast Africa to develop into several clusters of East Bantu.

At the core of Vansina's new scenario of Bantu development and dispersal lies the idea of continuous fission and internal differentiation on all major levels of linguistic reality and spatial distribution. He proceeds from a number of implicit, and partly conflicting, assumptions centered on phenomena like language continuum, linguistic borrowing, mixing, and superpositioning as well as geographical isolation and language death. His view of early Bantu history is very dynamic, in that he conceives of the dispersal as characterized by a multitude of overlapping, more or less simultaneous processes within a "huge dialect continuum." If we follow him, only the wave model can adequately account for this very complex situation (Vansina 1995:186). But it is hard to see how the resulting narrative differs from that which is based on the traditional tree model. For example, if one compares his 1995 paper with his "Western Bantu Expansion" of 1984 it is difficult to find any fundamental difference in the overall manner of reasoning. Both are characterized by the same highly generalized and abstract narrative which flows from a database that is only alluded to in the most general terms. As a non-linguist I have profound difficulties in grasping the historical significance of a narrative of this sort. The broad contemporaneity of linguistic evidence is not easily translated into what might pass as a sufficiently detailed and internally consistent historical process. In fact, the potential of doing so appears rather limited indeed. The effort to overcome the limitations inherent in linguistic data far too often leads to speculative narrative rather than an empirically grounded historical account. A general problem in historical linguistics lies in the fact that independent, i.e., non-linguistic, corroborative evidence is usually lacking.

To be sure, Vansina (1995:188) now argues against attempts to identify dispersal routes since, as he maintains, "the dynamics of language differentiation in Bantu do not support a scenario of 'migration' along specific routes." Only in rare cases may it be possible to correlate certain geographical features, such as coasts and rivers, with language spread. He thus deduces from the correspondence of language distribution and rivers in the rainforest that "the languages spread by the major river routes." As in this sentence, the words and manner in which he describes the initial dispersal Bantu languages still seem very close to the traditional concept of migration. Yet he explicitly and strongly rejects the "once-persuasive migration hypothesis" which he now considers "totally discredited" by both the new linguistic data and archaeological evidence (Vansina 1995:190). Using the simile that ripples on a pond's surface caused by a stone thrown into the water create an optical illusion that water is "flowing," he points out that language dispersal can happen in a similar manner: language spreads although communities remain in place and, consequently, no migration of any dimension occurs. While this may happen, the question is whether this possibility fits the Bantu situation with its language distribution of continental dimension. Moreover, Vansina is remarkably vague as to what terms such as "spread" and "dispersal" really mean when, for example, he speaks of "successive spreads of a single language followed by differentiation into new languages, some of which later spread again." When he sets this view against an alleged "usual" conception of a "single continuous migration" (Vansina 1995:190), he overstates the central issue. No Africanist, except perhaps the most devoted adherents of the view that the Bantu speakers spread over almost all of sub-equatorial Africa because of their military and technological might, ever believed, as Vansina (1995:189) contends, that the Bantu expansion constituted "a single migration event." One of the few who held such a view was Christopher Wrigley (1960), but even he did not exclude "two 'waves' of Bantu immigration" into southern Africa, assuming a possible hiatus between them (Wrigley 1960:202). Oliver (1966) was another believer in the Bantu expansion "as a unique, progressive event" (Flight 1988:277); however, he allowed about a millennium for his four-stage model of Bantu expansion to be realized (Oliver 1966:347–351).

Vansina's contention that archaeological evidence militates against the migration hypothesis is also misleading. While he is right that archaeology failed to demonstrate the technological superiority of the Bantu speakers or provide empirical support for overpopulation in the Benue-Cross area (the putative "cradle" of the Bantu languages) this does not disprove the hypothesis. The crucial point is, rather, that archaeology has not come up yet with any convincing material evidence, such as ceramics, linking the "area of origin" with whatever region is thought to have been involved in the dispersal of Bantu. Moreover, we do not possess any firm material (i.e., ceramic) link between these regions themselves, for instance, between the inner Congo basin on the one hand and northwestern Central Africa on the other (e.g., Eggert 2002). But even this does not invalidate the hypothesis that the Bantu languages spread primarily through migration, though of course not by the single mass movement from the Nigeria–Cameroon borderland to southern Africa that Vansina attributes to its defenders. Clearly, reasoning by negative evidence cannot, by its very nature, lead very far. And as every archaeologist interested in Central Africa is aware, the state of regional research is far from satisfactory (Chapter 17). Rather, archaeological fieldwork in Central Africa, especially (but not only) in the equatorial forest, resembles a walk in a pitch-dark night where vision is dependent on the perimeter of the torchlight and the night is boundless (Eggert 2002:521). Incidentally, Vansina's rejection of the migration hypothesis resembles the "pendulum pattern" of reasoning observed earlier.

Vansina (1995:187) stresses that, after the initial differentiation of Bantu, fissioning became the central driving force toward linguistic diversity. Thus, according to him, the same sequence occurred repeatedly: after each fission the outermost dialects developed into separate languages. The dying out of some ancient languages is thought to have left only one single language of a former cluster, creating the illusion that the surviving language differentiated very early and persisted without further dialect differentiation. But how can we assess possibilities and speculations of this sort when linguists do not agree on basic concepts, let alone on the historical significance of specific linguistic data? Given the peculiar nature of linguistic material as historical evidence – it is taken from contemporary languages and dialects and therefore does not qualify as historical in the strict sense of the term – the argument requires support from independent data. Unfortunately, such supporting evidence is rare. The important point here is not one of pragmatics alone, in the sense that empirical archaeological research is wanting. Rather, it is also a matter of theoretical and methodological priority. We have to deal with the question of how far language spread on the magnitude of Bantu can be traced by other than purely linguistic means. If migration was involved, it must have left material traces and we thus turn to archaeology for an answer. The problem is that archaeological evidence for Central Africa – that part of Africa most concerned in the early phases of Bantu dispersal – is very unsatisfactory.

To sum up, Vansina's (1995:193, 194) "tentative scenario" is built around a linguistic construct of at least nine major "diffusions," each of them characterized by the pattern of internal dynamics sketched above. To achieve the present geographical distribution of Bantu languages, he estimates that the whole sequence of diffusion lasted up to two millennia (Vansina 1995:191). Although he does not completely exclude "straightforward migration" (Vansina 1995:194), he appears convinced that this must have been exceptional. While he is certainly right that there are "many possible alternatives between the extreme of large-scale immigration and the other extreme of language shift without any population movement at all" (Vansina 1995:191), his own suggestions do not appear particularly convincing. How are we to qualify his vivid scenario (Vansina 1995:192) of competing Bantu heads of households ("houses") attracting followers of their own kin and autochthonous foragers alike, thereby creating stable points of reference for whole regions and enhancing the prestige of the Bantu language at the expense of the vernacular tongues? What makes this different from mere speculation? Is it the fact that this scenario is based on elements like "house," "village," and "district" which he considers "inherent to the social structure of early Bantu-speaking societies"? Though this sort of speculation may be stimulating, it does not qualify as history. And is it convincing to assume, as Vansina (1995:192) does, that these factors "are responsible for the first dispersal of their language"? While I strongly endorse inspired speculation as a heuristic device, the ingredients of Vansina's "tentative scenario," though perfectly possible in one situation or another, are hardly plausible enough for the concept of migration to be factually dismissed as both an important potential factor of historical reality and, consequently, as a major explanatory device.

Concepts, Methods, and Problems:
Remarks on Historical Linguistics

Not long ago research on the Bantu problem was marked by a lack of critical reflection on underlying concepts and methods. As a result, the literature was characterized by an undue amount of wishful thinking, circular reasoning, and largely uninspired, if not negligent, combining of concepts and data of different disciplines. In hindsight, it is apparent that ongoing research was marred and adequate progress hindered by more than simply mutual ignorance and misunderstanding of the other field's methodology and the epistemological potential of its results. Rather, even within the two academic fields most concerned, linguistics and archaeology, critical assessment of the ways and means of research was uncommon.

In a recent article, Derek Nurse (1997) addressed important issues of comparative and historical linguistics. His contribution was written with the aim of sensitizing historians to the historical potential and pitfalls of linguistic data and methodology. While this was achieved in an exemplary manner, Nurse also succeeded in presenting a coherent picture of traditional and contemporary historical linguistics. He thus rendered a great service to those outside this field for whom its main trends are hard to grasp from original literature (see also Nurse 1994/95).

Of particular importance here is that over the last three decades the general attitude toward language contact and linguistic change has been influenced markedly by developments in general linguistics. Whereas earlier approaches were informed by a mechanistic conception that conceived languages rather than people as actors, more recent ones are informed by sociolinguistic perspectives that emphasize socio-economic and sociocultural conditions in speech communities as important factors of linguistic change (Nurse 1997:383–388). This shift was accompanied by a more dynamic interpretation of the venerable *Stammbaummodell* (family or genetic tree model) developed in late 19th-century Indo-European studies and routinely generated in linguistic classification. Thus, Nurse (1997:375–377) supplements the traditional "migration model" with four other models which, in the final analysis, are all inspired by the impact of sociolinguistics on the comparatively and historically oriented subfields of linguistics. They are respectively the "wave-of-advance model," the "discontinuous-spread model," the "wave model," and, as I propose to call it, the "language-substitution model." These different concepts of language dispersal are not mutually exclusive. For example, Vansina's 1995 "wave model" is in fact a combination of Nurse's discontinuous-spread and wave models: it combines the idea of an initial discontinuous and temporarily extended movement of people with that of a socioculturally induced spreading of linguistic features to adjacent languages. Nurse's models have considerable explanatory power, but their suitability has to be demonstrated in each particular case.

Considering the general trend within linguistics, the "sociological" impact (see Hymes 1977) reached African historical linguistics somewhat belatedly. Nevertheless, Vansina's sudden change of position in the mid-1990s does appear as a turning point, all the more felt because of his undisputable prominence among anthropologically oriented historians of Africa. Yet, similar ideas have been expressed earlier. Ehret, for example, has been advocating concepts like dialect chaining in the context of Bantu history since the early 1980s (Ehret 1982:59). As stated in one of his latest books (Ehret 1998:293–294), he considers the Bantu expansion as "the event that never was" and envisions "a wider and wider establishment of Bantu languages" accompanied by "a long and complex history of the spread of agriculture southward and eastward across the continent." David Lee Schoenbrun (1998:43–45), one of his former students, imagines that the spread of Bantu may have happened partly through dialect chaining and partly through "pulses of expansion" of Bantu communities "interspersed with long periods of slow growth" (Schoenbrun 1998:44).

While the contemporary tendency to replace traditional interpretation of linguistic trees with more subtle, anthropologically derived models of language contact and change will certainly grow in the years to come, there is little reason to hope that this will radically change our insight into early Bantu history. As historical linguists know only too well, the Bantu languages have never been fully analyzed by the "comparative method" (e.g., Nurse 1997:368). Developed in 19th-century Indo-European studies, this method represents the standard analytical procedure of comparative linguistics (e.g., Anttilla 1972:229; Bynon 1977:45–46; Nurse 1997:361–363). It works on the premise that a group of related languages derives from a common ancestor or "proto-language." To demonstrate this, it first and foremost proceeds by a detailed phonological and morphological analysis of the vocabulary of these languages with the aim of establishing sound correspondences. These correspondences can then be shown to operate according to certain principles which are codified as a number of phonological rules.

In contrast to the penetrating studies devoted to Indo-European languages, even the most ambitious attempts to genetically classify Bantu languages failed on the count of broad-scale and in-depth comparison. Guthrie's massive *Comparative Bantu* (1967–71) is a prominent example. For this four-volume study to be realized at all, Guthrie had to practice a rigorous sampling procedure at various levels. He initially chose some 200 languages out of a much larger reservoir and finally concentrated on the proportional distribution of 450 reflexes in 28 test languages out of a total of 2,000 reflexes worked out at the outset. Considering this, it does not appear particularly surprising when Nurse (1997:364 n. 13) states that the classic division of Bantu into Western and Eastern Bantu and, moreover, virtually all historical classifications of Bantu, rest on a "shaky foundation." Consequently, he warns against putting much trust in current interpretations of early Bantu history (see also Nurse 1994/95).

As indicated above, genetic classifications of Bantu usually rest on lexicostatistics, which aims to devise a *relative* chronology of the languages and dialects concerned. In contrast, glottochronology is intended as a means of fixing their temporal position in *absolute* terms. Whereas the majority of historical linguists subscribe to Dixon's (1997:35–37, 49) dictum of the "chimera of glottochronology" (Nurse 1994/95:66–67, 1997:366; for an early critique see Bergslund and Vogt 1962), some continue to believe in the viability of this method (e.g., Renfrew 2000:xi). In doing so they apparently subscribe to what Dixon (1997:36) calls in question, namely "that one can infer genetic relationships from lexicon alone; that the lexicon of all languages is always replaced at a constant rate; and that core vocabulary always behaves in a different way from non-core." A key question for both glottochronology and lexicostatistics is the idea of a "linguistic threshold" (Renfrew 2000:x), a borderline in time beyond which similarities between languages of common descent can no longer be differentiated from those generated by random chance. The linguistic community is far from agreeing on how many millennia – eight, nine, ten thousand years or more? – might be needed before that cut-off is reached. But, if we follow Dixon (1997:48), there is not even a definitive answer to the question of dating any proto-language. In his words: "Surely, the only really honest answer . . . is 'We don't know'. Or, one might venture something like 'probably some time between 5,000 and perhaps 12,000 BP'."

Despite critiques of lexicostatistics since its inception by Swadesh (e.g., Hoijer 1956; Hymes 1960; Teeter 1963; on the current situation see Embleton 2000), we must recognize that it was "widely used with African languages during the 1970s and 1980s, mainly with Niger-Congo and Bantu" (Nurse 1997:364; for an early summary see Heine 1972), and remains the most important method employed in Bantu language classification. The massive comparative Bantu study of the Tervuren group (Bastin et al. 1999) used lexicostatistics based on a word list of 92 glosses reproduced in Table 12.1.[2] However, we should recall that, as Dixon (1997:10) stressed, there is "no universal principle" according to which core vocabulary "is less likely to be borrowed than non-core items."

More important than the linguistic status of core vocabulary for our purposes is its historical significance. What historical insights can we derive from the Tervuren word list beyond the immediate purpose of providing information on the genetic classification of the 440 Bantu languages treated and their relative temporal position? Because of its "universal" character, core vocabulary cannot reflect historically relevant details of bygone populations. Once again, we may turn to Vansina's 1995 reflections on the "Bantu expansion" as an example. As soon as one takes into account that the substance of his narrative is based on the Tervuren word list, it becomes clear why it is marked by generalities and abstraction. Exactly the same applies to his 1984 "Western Bantu Expansion" based on a slightly different word list. What little there is of a vivid historical account in both papers is essentially derived not from historically imbued linguistic evidence, but from speculation.

Historical Linguistics and Archaeology: Concluding Remarks on a Common Field

Dixon asserted that archaeologists, geneticists, and anthropologists are happy to be presented with a "clear-cut linguistic hypothesis, about where and when a proto-language was spoken and exactly how it split and spread" to anchor their theories (Dixon 1997:43–44). But this relationship is not unidirectional. Rather, there has been circular reasoning on both sides, i.e., historical linguists on one side and archaeologists, historians, and anthropologists on the other (Eggert 1981; Vansina 1980). Dixon (1997:47) also questioned why a particular proto-language should be related to a particular material culture, and not to some other. Though his remarks were directed at proto-Indo-European reconstructions, the question can equally be posed with regard to proto-Bantu. The important point for archaeologists is not whether a language or proto-language is associated with a particular material culture, but whether a given linguistic entity is concomitant with a specific material expression at all. It is through material configurations that archaeologists approach a bygone reality of whatever dimension and temporal distance. They feel

Table 12.1. The Tervuren word list

all/tous	hair (of head)/cheveu	round (as ball)/rond (comme une boule)
arm/bras	head/tête	
ashes/cendres	hear/entendre	sand/sable
bark n/écorce	heart/coeur	say/dire
belly/ventre	horn/corne	see/voir
big/grand (≠ long)	kill/tuer	seed n/semence (graine mise en terre)
bird/oiseau	knee/genou	
bite/mordre	know/savoir	sit/assis
black/noir	leaf/feuille (d'arbre)	skin (human)/peau (humaine)
blood/sang	leg/jambe	sleep n/sommeil
bone/os	lie (down)/couché	small/petit
breast/sein	liver/foie	smoke n/fumée
burn intr/brûler (être en feu)	long/long (≠ grand)	stand/debout
cloud/nuage	louse/pou	star/étoile
cold (weather)/froid (temps)	man/homme (être humain masculin)	stone/pierre
come/venir		sun/soleil
die/mourir	many/beaucoup (nombreux)	swim/nager
dog/chien	meat/viande	tail/queue
drink v/boire	moon/lune	tongue/langue (corps)
dry/sec	mountain/montagne	tooth/dent
ear/oreille	mouth/bouche	tree/arbre
eat/manger	nail/ongle	two/deux
egg/oeuf	name/nom	walk/marcher
eye/oeil	neck/cou	warm (weather)/chaud (temps)
fat n/graisse (animale)	new/nouveau	
feather/plume	night/nuit	water/eau
fire/feu	nose/nez	what?/quoi?
fish n/poisson	one/un (nombre)	white/blanc
fly v/voler (oiseau)	path/chemin	who?/qui?
full/plein	person/personne (être humain)	woman/femme (être humain féminin)
give/donner		
good/bon	rain n/pluie	
ground (on the ~)/terre (par terre)	red/rouge	
	root/racine	

Source: after Bastin et al. 1999:5, table 2.1.1.

uneasy, therefore, when confronted with a kind of "history" which hinges on nothing but word lists devoid of any specific cultural content (Chapter 7). I am reminded of what A. R. Radcliffe-Brown (1952:3), in the context of social anthropology, called "pseudo-historical speculations," in his words, "a kind of historical study," where anthropologists, due to the lack of empirical historical evidence, "fall back on conjecture and imagination." Throughout his long career Radcliffe-Brown was much interested in the difference between what he called "the historical and the generalising methods" (Radcliffe-Brown 1958:50), and he never weakened in his fight against "conjectural or hypothetical history" which has haunted cultural and social anthropology for quite some time (see Radcliffe-Brown 1958:26, 46–55). With respect to Bantu studies, it is hard to escape the conclusion that many historically intended studies based primarily on comparative data from core vocabulary fall within this Radcliffe-Brownian category.

This critique from an archaeologist's point of view should not be read as an attack on historical linguistics as such. Schoenbrun's (1998) recent volume concentrates on the cultural world of Bantu-speaking peoples in the Great Lakes region of East Africa from about 1000 b.c. to A.D. 1500. He does so by making use of the methodological arsenal of comparative linguistics supplemented with a very rich corpus of ethnographic data. Although the chronology of this work, based as it is on glottochronology (Schoenbrun 1998:39–41, with fig. 1.1), is open to criticism, Schoenbrun did not restrict his use of lexicostatistics to core vocabulary. Rather, his linguistic database consists of a varied cultural vocabulary, detailed analysis of which was presented in an article and a monograph (Schoenbrun 1994, 1997). Even if one remains skeptical with regard to the methodological tool of glottochronology and his distinction between "instrumental" and "creative" power (Schoenbrun 1998:12–13), the author succeeds in presenting a fascinating account of "the dialectical historical interplay of environment, agriculture, and social practices in shaping historical experience and consciousness" (Schoenbrun 1998:17).

Though Schoenbrun's study demonstrates the historical potential of varied linguistic analyses, archaeologists of Bantu Africa should stick to their material evidence and try to contribute to an ever more closely knitted archaeology of Bantu language territory. With rare exceptions (i.e., parts of East Africa), we are unable to even sketch the broadest outlines of Bantu territory archaeology. With this in mind, it is hardly adequate to prematurely link, as has been so frequently done, archaeological finds and features with linguistic phenomena and to suggest possible routes of language diffusion of whatever nature.

The obligation to first clear up one's own methodological and empirical difficulties before joining forces starts, of course, with one's own field. By way of example, equatorial rainforest archaeology, i.e., the archaeology of a specific biotope of almost transcontinental expansion which linguistically almost exclusively belongs to the Bantu sphere (cf. Figures 12.1a and 12.1b), has not yet linked the oldest and stylistically rather differentiated pottery of the interior Congo basin to ceramics of other regions within and outside the forest (Eggert 2002; Wotzka 1995:257–269, 2001b:66–67). Until archaeology can solve this specific problem, archaeologists should not actively participate in any debate on "Western Bantu expansion." Still, rainforest archaeologists need to familiarize themselves with the ongoing discussions on the dispersal of Bantu languages and use their expertise and intellect to critically assess as far as possible the various concepts involved.

Thus, I am not convinced that Vansina's wave-model-inspired "turnabout" has contributed anything of lasting importance to the explanation of how Bantu languages came to be distributed over most of the southern half of Africa. Convincing as his case may be at first glance, it rests on Vansina partly reviving – and beating – a dead horse. That he is not alone in first creating and then fighting against "the event that never was," to quote Ehret (1998:293), is of little comfort for those who know that but a tiny minority of Africanists visualized the distribution of Bantu languages in terms of one "single continuous expansion" or "migration event" (Vansina 1995:189, 190). Reducing a specific conception of an evidently exceedingly complex historical development for the sake of argumentative expediency to a straw man position does not contribute to scientific progress, but rather impedes it. It may help to visualize the Bantu problem as what it is – a phenomenon of nearly continental dimension. Keeping this in mind, it appears strange that a putative mechanism and, indeed one of the most plausible ones, is dismissed without substantive evidence. May we reassure ourselves with the fact that, as discussed above, the baby so rudely and ostentatiously thrown out with the bathwater through the front door is welcomed again at the rear one (cf. Anthony 1990, 1992)?

Be this as it may, it will take some time for archaeology to legitimately raise its voice in the debate of how Bantu languages came to be distributed over most of sub-Sahelian Africa. When the appropriate moment has come, its message will be thoroughly substantiated by empirical evidence. I suspect that in this process there will the opportunity will once again arise to recall the pendulum metaphor: migration will probably have been restored to its former position as an important interpretive concept. This does not mean, however, that archaeology will be able to present the evidence needed for retracing the routes taken by Bantu speakers on the move. Rather, it will simply offer evidence of material relations between more or less distant points in space, which in spite of the difficulties connected with an "archaeological proof of migration" (Burmeister 2000), perhaps would be best explained by invoking that concept. Whether or not it appears probable that the migrants in question might have spoken a Bantu language will then be debated – languages, as we all know only too well, do not leave material traces except for writing.

It is evident that the current distribution of Bantu languages still represents one of the major problems in the linguistic and cultural history of sub-Saharan Africa. Considering the time-depth involved, there is no academic field but archaeology which disposes of genuine historical evidence reaching back that far – i.e., evidence which in its materiality was once part of the past in question. It follows from this that archaeology must contribute whatever it can to the solution of the Bantu problem. On the other hand, it must also be careful not to be absorbed by the "question of origins." Intriguing and important as origins are, there is always the danger that more immediate concerns are being neglected in the search for origins. In Central Africa we have barely begun to investigate basic issues such as settlement, economy, and social organization through time (on farming, for example, see Vansina 1994/95). In a sense, sub-Saharan archaeology has been preoccupied with questions of origin. Now we have clearly reached the point where it is time to pause and look ahead: it is through intensive and systematic fieldwork in transdisciplinary projects integrating archaeology, paleo-ethnobotany, archaeozoology, physical geography, and ecology that we will contribute most to the historical agenda which constitutes the heart of archaeology. Having pursued this for some time on the basis of carefully designed regional research programs, we will also be in much better position than we are today to deal with intricate questions like the one reviewed here.

NOTES

1 Vansina (1979:288) suggested that Bleek, in borrowing the term Bantu from the vocabulary of autochthonous languages, "reified the similarity" between these languages "into an ethnic label," if unwittingly so (also Vansina 1979:321).
2 The Tervuren list was reduced from Swadesh's 100-word list by omitting glosses that were, for example, climatically inappropriate and by adding precision to others (Bastin et al. 1999:5).

REFERENCES

Anthony, David. W., 1990 Migration in Archeology: The Baby and the Bathwater. American Anthropologist 92:895–914.

—— 1992 The Bath Refilled: Migration in Archeology Again. American Anthropologist 94:174–176.

Anttilla, Raimo, 1972 An Introduction to Historical and Comparative Linguistics. New York: Macmillan.

Bastin, Yvonne, André Coupez, and B. de Halleux, 1983 Classification lexicostatistique des langues bantoues (214 relevés). Bulletin des Scéances de l'Académie Royale des Sciences d'Outre-Mer 27:173–199.

Bastin, Yvonne, André Coupez, and Michael Mann, 1999 Continuity and Divergence in the Bantu Languages: Perspectives from a Lexicostatistic Study. Musée Royal de l'Afrique Centrale, Annales, Sciences Humaines 162. Tervuren: Musée Royal de l'Afrique Centrale.

Bergsland, Knut and Hans Vogt, 1962 On the Validity of Glottochronology. With Comments and a Reply. Current Anthropology 3:115–153.

Bouquiaux, Luc, ed., 1980 L'Expansion bantoue. Actes du Colloque International du CNRS, Viviers (France) 4–16 avril 1977. Paris: SELAF.

Burmeister, Stefan, 2000 Archaeology and Migration: Approaches to an Archaeological Proof of Migration. With Comments and a Reply. Current Anthropology 41:539–567.

Bynon, Theodora, 1977 Historical Linguistics. Cambridge Textbooks in Linguistics. Cambridge: Cambridge University Press.

Dixon, R. M. W., 1997 The Rise and Fall of Languages. Cambridge: Cambridge University Press.

Eggert, Manfred K. H., 1981 Historical Linguistics and Prehistoric Archaeology: Trend and Pattern in Early Iron Age Research of Sub-Saharan Africa. Beiträge zur Allgemeinen und Vergleichenden Archäologie 3:277–324.

—— 1992 The Central African Rain Forest: Historical Speculation and Archaeological Facts. World Archaeology 24:1–24.

—— 2002 Southern Cameroun and the Settlement of the Equatorial Rainforest: Early Ceramics from Fieldwork in 1997 and 1998–99. In Tides of the Desert / Gezeiten der Wüste: Contributions to the Archaeology and Environmental History of Africa in Honour of Rudolph Kuper. Tilman Lenssen-Erz, Ursula Tegtmeier, Stefan Kröpelin, et al., eds. pp. 507–522. Africa Praehistorica 14. Cologne: Heinrich Barth Institut.

Ehret, Christopher, 1982 Linguistic Inferences about Early Bantu History. In The Archaeological and Linguistic Reconstruction of African History. Christopher Ehret and Merrick Posnansky, eds. pp. 57–65. Berkeley: University of California Press.

——1998 An African Classical Age: Eastern and Southern Africa in World History 1000 BC to AD 400. Charlottesville: University Press of Virginia.

Embleton, Sheila, 2000 Lexicostatistics/Glottochronology: From Swadesh to Sankoff to Starostin to Future Horizons. In Time Depth in Historical Linguistics 1. Colin Renfrew, April McMahon and Larry Task, eds. pp. 143–165. Papers in the Prehistory of Languages. Cambridge: McDonald Institute for Archaeological Research.

Flight, Colin, 1980 Malcolm Guthrie and the Reconstruction of Bantu Prehistory. History in Africa 7:81–118.

——1988 The Bantu Expansion and the SOAS Network. History in Africa 15:261–301.

Greenberg, Joseph H., 1949a Studies in African Linguistic Classification: I. The Niger-Congo Family. Southwestern Journal of Anthropology 5:79–100.

——1949b Studies in African Linguistic Classification: III. The Position of Bantu. Southwestern Journal of Anthropology 5:309–317.

——1955 Studies in African Linguistic Classification. New Haven: Compass.

Guthrie, Malcolm, 1959 Problèmes de génétique linguistique: La Question du Bantu commun. Travaux de l'Institut de Linguistique de l'Université de Paris 4:83–92.

——1962a Some Developments in the Prehistory of the Bantu Languages. Journal of African History 3:273–282.

——1962b Bantu Origins: A Tentative New Hypothesis. Journal of African Languages 1:9–21.

——1967–71 Comparative Bantu: An Introduction to the Comparative Linguistics and Prehistory of the Bantu Languages, vols. 1–4. Farnsborough: Gregg.

Heine, Bernd, 1972 Historical Linguistics and Lexicostatistics in Africa. Journal of African Languages 11:7–20.

——1973 Zur genetischen Gliederung der Bantu-Sprachen. Afrika und Übersee 56:164–185.

Heine, Bernd, Hans Hoff, and Rainer Vossen, 1977 Neuere Ergebnisse zur Territorialgeschichte der Bantu. In Zur Sprachgeschichte und Ethnohistorie in Afrika: Neue Beiträge afrikanistischer Forschungen. Wilhelm J. G. Möhlig, Franz Rottland, and Bernd Heine, eds. pp. 57–72. Berlin: Reimer.

Henrici, Alick, 1973 Numerical Classification of Bantu languages. African Language Studies 14:82–104.

Hoijer, Harry, 1956 Lexicostatistics: A Critique. Language 32:49–60.

Huffman, Thomas N., 1970 The Early Iron Age and the Spread of the Bantu. South African Archaeological Bulletin 25:3–21.

Hymes, Dell, 1960 Lexicostatistics So Far. With Comments. Current Anthropology 1:3–44.

——1977[1974] The Scope of Sociolinguistics. In Foundations in Sociolinguistics: An Ethnographic Approach. Dell Hymes. pp. 193–209. London: Tavistock.

Murdock, George Peter, 1959 Africa: Its Peoples and their Culture History. New York: McGraw-Hill.

Nurse, Derek, 1994/95 "Historical" Classifications of the Bantu Languages. In The Growth of Farming Communities in Africa from the Equator Southwards. John E. G. Sutton, ed. Special Volume. Azania 29/30:65–81.

—— 1997 The Contributions of Linguistics to the Study of History in Africa. Journal of African History 38:359–391.

—— 2002 A Survey Report for the Bantu languages. SIL International 2001. Electronic document. <http://www.sil.org/silesr/2002/016/SILESR2002-016.htm>, accessed November 2002.

Oliver, Roland, 1966 The Problem of the Bantu Expansion. Journal of African History 7:361–376.

Phillipson, David W., 1976a Archaeology and Bantu linguistics. World Archaeology 8:65–82.

—— 1976b The Early Iron Age in Eastern and Southern Africa: A Critical Re-appraisal. Azania 11:1–23.

—— 1977 The Spread of the Bantu Language. Scientific American 236:106–114.

—— 1985a African Archaeology. Cambridge: Cambridge University Press.

—— 1985b An Archaeological Reconsideration of Bantu Expansion. Muntu 2:69–84.

—— 1993 African Archaeology. 2nd edition. Cambridge: Cambridge University Press.

Posnansky, Merrick, 1961 Bantu Genesis. Uganda Journal 25:86–93.

—— 1968 Bantu Genesis – Archaeological Reflexions. Journal of African History 9:1–11.

—— 1976 Review of Africa in the Iron Age: c. 500 B.C. to A.D. 1400, by Roland Oliver and Brian M. Fagan. Cambridge University Press (1975). Journal of African History 17:629–631.

Radcliffe-Brown, A. R., 1952 Structure and Function in Primitive Society: Essays and Addresses. London: Cohen & West.

—— 1958 Method in Social Anthropology. Selected Essays. M. N. Srinivas, ed. Chicago: University of Chicago Press.

Renfrew, Colin, 2000 The Problem of Time Depth. In Time Depth in Historical Linguistics 1. Colin Renfrew, April McMahon, and Larry Task, eds. pp. ix–xiv. Papers in the Prehistory of Languages. Cambridge: McDonald Institute for Archaeological Research.

Robertshaw, Peter, ed., 1990 A History of African Archaeology. London: Currey.

Schoenbrun, David Lee, 1994 Great Lakes Bantu: Classification and Settlement Chronology. Sprache und Geschichte in Afrika (SUGIA) 15:91–152.

—— 1997 The Historical Reconstruction of Great Lakes Bantu Cultural Vocabulary: Etymologies and Distributions. SUGIA vol. 9. Cologne: Köppe.

—— 1998 A Green Place, a Good Place: Agrarian Change, Gender, and Social Identity in the Great Lakes Region to the 15th Century. Portsmouth, NH: Heinemann.

Sutton, J. E. G., 1994/95 The Growth of Farming and the Bantu Settlement on and South of the Equator: Editor's Introduction. In The Growth of Farming Communities in Africa from the Equator Southwards. John E. G. Sutton, ed. Special Volume. Azania 29/30:1–14.

Swadesh, Morris, 1951 Diffusional Cumulation and Archaic Residue as Historical Explanations. Southwestern Journal of Anthropology 7:1–21.

—— 1952 Lexico-Statistic Dating of Prehistoric Ethnic Contacts: With Special Reference to North American Indians and Eskimos. Proceedings of the American Philosophical Society 96:452–463.

—— 1955 Towards Greater Accuracy in Lexicostatistic Dating. International Journal of American Linguistics 21:121–137.

Teeter, Karl V., 1963 Lexicostatistics and Genetic Relationship. Language 39:638–648.

Vansina, Jan, 1979 Bantu in the Crystal Ball, I. History in Africa 6:287–333.

—— 1980 Bantu in the Crystal Ball, II. History in Africa 7:293–325.

—— 1984 Western Bantu Expansion. Journal of African History 25:129–145.

—— 1990 Paths in the Rainforests: Toward a History of Political Tradition in Equatorial Africa. Madison: University of Wisconsin Press.

——1995 New Linguistic Evidence and "the Bantu Expansion." Journal of African History 36:173–195.

——1994/95 A Slow Revolution: Farming in Subequatorial Africa. *In* The Growth of Farming Communities in Africa from the Equator Southwards. John E. G. Sutton, ed. Special Volume. Azania 29/30:15–26.

Wotzka, Hans-Peter, 1995 Studien zur Archäologie des zentralafrikanischen Regenwaldes: Die Keramik des inneren Zaïre-Beckens und ihre Stellung im Kontext der Bantu-Expansion. Africa Praehistorica, 6. Cologne: Heinrich Barth Institut.

——2001a Central African Neolithic. *In* Enyclopedia of Prehistory 1. Africa. Peter N. Peregrine and Melvin Ember, eds. pp. 46–58. New York: Kluwer Academic/Plenum.

——2001b Central African Iron Age. *In* Enyclopedia of Prehistory 1. Africa. Peter N. Peregrine and Melvin Ember, eds. pp. 59–76. New York: Kluwer Academic/Plenum.

Wrigley, Christopher, 1960 Speculations on the Economic Prehistory of Africa. Journal of African History 1:189–203.

13

The Archaeology of Sub-Saharan Urbanism: Cities and their Countrysides

Adria LaViolette and Jeffrey Fleisher

The archaeology of urbanism has played out largely in world areas outside of Africa, most notably Southwest Asia and Mesoamerica. Images of Africa as a place of tribal societies and city-less states made it seem irrelevant to the study of urbanism, which was taken as a key marker of progress in the narrative of world prehistory. African cities with roots more ancient than the colonial period were presumed to be foreign implants grafted onto less complex societies, with little power to inform on the origins of social complexity or urbanism. City inhabitants were viewed as operating independently from a faceless surrounding countryside. Nonetheless, as early as the 1930s, archaeologists began documenting and excavating large-scale settlements in sub-Saharan Africa, and have done so almost continuously since the 1950s when professional archaeology became established on the subcontinent.

We now know that such settlements came into being in sub-Saharan Africa in the first millennium a.d., in the context of settled, iron-using, mixed farming societies. Archaeologists have made urbanism an explicit research agenda only since the 1980s. The lure of doing archaeology in the ruins of large centers resulted in reconstructions of elite life, but rarely in an understanding of the broader societies in which people lived. After independence, locally based archaeological scholarship also focused on urban sites that could counter colonial views of the African past as unprogressive, a concern shaped by modern nation-building.

Two major agendas have shaped ancient African urban studies: the continued influence of trait-list thinking by archaeologists, which draws on Eurocentric ideologies; and the related issue of classifying African urban origins as foreign or indigenous. Many archaeologists who conduct research on complex societies link urbanism to the state: in this view, states might exist without cities, but cities will not come into existence in the absence of a centralized state polity (H. Wright 1977; cf. R. McIntosh 1991; Smith 2003). Here, we focus primarily on ancient African cities as the unit of analysis, but attempt also to address the larger contexts in which the cities operated. We have chosen three case studies – the West African savanna, the Zimbabwe plateau, and the Swahili coast – because they provide evidence not just for ancient urbanism in sub-Saharan Africa, but for three strikingly different types of urbanism and relationships to states on the continent. The Inland Niger Delta of West Africa is characterized by multiple examples of heterarchical urban clustering from the early first millennium A.D., and seems to lack physical mani-festations of hierarchy generally, both within the urban system and in any larger political context. Great Zimbabwe was the political and economic capital, and ritual center, of an enormous state, and its architecture has a monumentality rare in sub-Saharan Africa. And the Swahili coast provides examples of scores of roughly coeval but politically independent urban centers – some say city-states – sharing numer-ous cultural characteristics. Swahili society developed with explicit attention to "foreign" influences, from Islam to components of material culture, which chal-lenges us to consider the ways in which archaeologists handle the exotic in the context of African complex societies. These examples sample the richness of African urbanisms, which have much to contribute to understanding the diversity of urban forms globally.

Pressing Problems: Defining Urbanism and Africa's Place in Urbanism Theory

Urbanism in archaeology

"Urbanism" has been studied by geographers, sociologists, anthropologists, and archaeologists for much of the 20th century (O'Connor 1993; Wheatley 1972). Two broad approaches can be distilled from this literature with direct application to our concerns (Fleisher 2003; Marcus 1983). The first, a trait-list approach, identifies criteria that settlements must exhibit to be considered urban. This approach defines what a city "is" (S. McIntosh 1997). It is rooted in a sociological definition of cities developed by Louis Wirth (1938) and the archaeological modeling of V. Gordon Childe (1950, 1957), and follows Lewis Henry Morgan's approach to progressive stages of social development (Wheatley 1972:611). Excavation of materially rich cities in ancient Mesopotamia, Classical Greece, and Rome, viewed as precursors to Euro-American civilization, led Western scholars to elevate these ancient soci-eties above others. Despite the historical specificity of each example, they came to represent universal prototypes of urban living (Chapter 1).

For archaeologists, Childe's (1950:9) prescriptive view of urban settlements described cities based on required traits: a socially stratified, large, dense popula-tion; central appropriation of surplus food; monumental public architecture; liter-acy and writing; and sciences, including math and astronomy. Despite its historical specificity, the items on Childe's list became the criteria against which archaeolo-gists worldwide, sometimes implicitly, defined or defended ancient centers and societies as urban, the associated traits defining the parameters of urbanity and civ-ilization (e.g., Frankfort 1951). The thousands of ancient societies outside these traditions received intellectual attention only much later, and were placed in a lower-order tier of human achievement.

Mesopotamia and its perceived legacy – the Classical Mediterranean – became the defining tradition of the so-called Old World. Mesopotamian states and cities were considered "primary," i.e., emerging independently as the first such societies. Ancient Mesoamerica, although not seen by Western scholars as contributing to the Western tradition, was eventually elevated to "primary" status, because it, too, produced cities and states, evidencing many traits on the Mesopotamian trait-list earlier than any other region of the New World. All other cities and states in the ancient world were thus "secondary," emerging in contexts in which older societies had established the framing paradigms of achievement. Cross-cultural comparisons between other parts of the world and Mesopotamia and/or Mesoamerica continue to be framed by such criteria (Adams 1966; Schwartz and Falconer, eds., 1994).

Trait-lists are powerful in their exclusivity, but are descriptively static. They foreclose analytical understanding of the settlement or society, or changes over time and space (see Smith 2003). What we call a functionalist approach to urbanism arose in response to this shortcoming and addresses a different set of concerns. It focuses on the role of institutions within urban centers with respect to both urban and rural populations. Archaeological proponents of this approach followed sociologists such as Weber (1958) and Sjoberg (1960) in explicitly linking urbanism, modern or ancient, to urban/rural interdependence. Cities thus served as central places within articulated systems. Functionalism built upon the trait-list approach by examining how traits integrated a complex system, emphasizing relationships and political economy over particularisms such as "writing."

The historiography of sub-Saharan African urbanisms has been shaped by these larger debates. Weber's (1958) definition of the city provided a foundation of functionalist modeling. Cities, Weber argued (1958:66–67), were where local people, including rural dwellers, could meet their daily material needs in local markets. An urban "community" (Weber 1958:80–81), however, was one that was primarily commercial but included a fortification, system of laws and a court. Thus, for Weber, urban communities were based on a particular economic strategy as well as the control of autonomous political functions. While he argued that such communities were found only in Western contexts (Eickelman 1981:266–267; Fox 1977), his model is significant in linking the functional responsibilities of a city toward a local urban and rural population.

These functional concerns were paralleled by work in geography that sought to describe and explain the spatial organization of human settlement (e.g., Garner 1967; Haggett 1965). In the landmark volume *Man, Settlement, and Urbanism* (Ucko et al., eds., 1972), which brought functional studies of urbanism to the forefront of Americanist and British archaeology, Trigger (1972:577) made his influential statement that "whatever else a city may be it is a unit of settlement which performs specialized functions in relationship to a broad hinterland." This is our most basic working definition of a city. In mid-20th-century anthropological archaeology, a spatial or locational approach to urbanism accorded well with settlement archaeology, one of the dominant theoretical and methodological approaches of the time

(Trigger 1989:279ff) that was applied extensively in Mesopotamia and Meso-america (e.g., Adams 1966; Willey 1953; see Billman and Feinman, eds., 1999; Vogt and Leventhal, eds., 1983; H. Wright 1977). Archaeologists had come to see the value in connecting individual sites with their larger landscapes. Some of this work followed Steward's (1955) ecological approach, seeking to understand how emerging regional systems were related to their environmental setting, while later work drew on systems theory and locational geography to understand how settlement patterns revealed administrative systems (Flannery 1972). All of these settlement approaches sought to answer similar questions about distributions of different-sized sites in a regional landscape, and marked a shift from researching how life looked in the past, to how it worked.

The trend toward functional analysis of ancient urban systems emphasized the dynamic relationships among different components of a society, a "systems" approach (e.g., Blanton 1976; Clarke, ed., 1977; Hodder and Orton 1976). In these models, society is likened to an organism or system in which different parts work together in integrated fashion. This idea was made famous by 19th-century sociologist Herbert Spencer (1974), who elaborated his organic analogy comparing human societies to biological organisms. In similar ways, Émile Durkheim (1997) focused on how solidarity was achieved in different societies. For him, the solidarity of more complex societies was "organic," with people forming a collective conscience for society to function. The "organic solidarity" of industrialized societies thus relied on economic and occupational cooperation to function, rather than on kinship, which was seen as holding together less complex societies. It was this interdependence that led to balanced and cohesive society. Several ideas are implicit in these works: that social formations should always be working toward homeostasis; that societies evolve from less to more complex forms; and that more complex societies require hierarchical political and economic mechanisms to manage them. Following this line of thinking, it is not difficult to see how cities – as management or administrative centers – might be viewed as the "natural" outcome of emerging complex societies.

These ideas influenced archaeological approaches to urbanism. First, urbanism was believed to be a universal process, the "natural" outcome of increasing social complexity. This had both positive and negative repercussions for theorizing urbanism. On the positive side, it led to fruitful cross-cultural studies of urbanism (e.g., Adams 1966). On the negative, the evolutionary framework in which these models were developed meant that places without hierarchically ordered urban systems were deemed less complex and primitive. Second, urban systems became synonymous with hierarchical social formations, the latter viewed as necessary for managing increasingly complex societies. Archaeologically, hierarchy was sought in obtrusive symbols of authority – temples, palaces – but also in the number of administrative levels within an urban system. Settlement pattern studies provided data crucial to questions of hierarchy, such as site sizes and the distances between sites. Archaeologists used these data to construct settlement tiers that reflected administrative and political organization.

Functional approaches to urbanism move discussion away from what an urban system is (the trait-list approach) to what it does. But we recognize that this theoretical paradigm carries with it problematic assumptions. One is the assumption that urbanism evolves because of shared interests: the smooth operation of the society at large. This perspective tends to erase the negotiations and fractures within cities. While we reject the evolutionary implications of functional urban models, as well as the presumption that hierarchy is the natural organizing principle of urban regions, we are interested in understanding what cities *do* in their regional contexts. This, we believe, is a crucial first step in establishing baseline data for urban regions in Africa. However, we believe that urban studies need to be cognizant of dissonances within African urbanism, drawn along the lines of (minimally) class, gender, and faction (Brumfiel 1992). The voices that we emphasize most strongly are those of rural and non-elite urban people, and the way they may have participated in, resisted, exploited, or ignored the emergence of cities and urbanism.

Operationalizing these principles requires archaeological sampling of all the parts of a center and its hinterlands, work which to date has been limited to only a few projects on the subcontinent. Hinterland studies and settlement pattern research require systematic survey, test excavations, and larger-scale excavations at many sites, a major expense and time commitment under the best of circumstances (see Bower 1986; Curtis and Walz 2001; Fleisher and Lawson 2001). Although such approaches have come to dominate archaeological studies of urbanism worldwide, in practice this has only been somewhat successful in Africa, to which we now turn.

Approaching African cities and urbanism

The African subcontinent has been largely excluded from discussions of early cities and urbanism (S. McIntosh 1997, 1999b). Trait-list definitions of urbanism drawn from other world areas excluded all potential cases in Africa based on insistence that literacy, science, or monumental architecture were key features of urban forms (Childe 1950; Sjoberg 1960). Because African cities outside the Nile Valley appeared several millennia later than in Mesopotamia, Africa was viewed as having no "primary" or "archaic" states (e.g., Clark 1962; Feinman and Marcus, eds., 1998), and therefore by extension, cities (cf. Smith 2003). Urban settlements like Great Zimbabwe or Swahili coastal towns were dismissed because they were seen as foreign in inspiration (J. D. Clark 1962:29; see also Morton-Williams 1972).

For Clark and other anthropologists of the time, urbanism was unimaginable in sub-Saharan Africa because of the continent's favorable climate for agriculture, unlimited land, and the nature of its subsistence economies, a situation which removed incentive for the development of social complexity (J. D. Clark 1962:29; see Winters 1983). As Sinclair et al. (1993a:23) pointed out, the idea that individuals in African societies were unable to accumulate wealth or capital, either through control over land or production, was believed to restrict the development of hierarchical societies (e.g., Fortes and Evans-Pritchard 1940). An Africa-centered perspective could have provided alternative possibilities, for example: that "permanent" building materials, especially stone, are not available in many parts of the continent; that agricultural efficacy promoted the movement of settlements, even cities, often enough to make tremendous investment in architecture undesirable; that monumentality of place, and its correlate – high archaeological visibility – is not valued in all societies, even hierarchical and centralized ones (Connah 1987:214ff.; S. McIntosh 1997:462); and that for some societies social wealth, "wealth-in-people," is a far more potent source of power and its reproduction than the accumulation of material goods – again, with repercussions for the material record upon which we depend (e.g., Fortes and Evans-Pritchard 1940; Guyer 1995; S. McIntosh 1999b). It should come as no surprise, then, that none of the "primitive states" highlighted in Fortes and Evans-Pritchard's (1940) volume on African political systems was believed to contain cities. Similarly, attempts to examine the locational aspects of African societies (Taylor 1975) were all based on "middle-range" societies not thought to contain "urban" settlements at all (see Wenke 1989 and O'Connor 1993 for debates about urbanism in ancient Egypt).

Reaction to such claims has been strong, and perhaps most forcefully articulated by R. McIntosh and S. McIntosh (1984, 1993; R. McIntosh 1991, 1999; S. McIntosh 1997). Their work on West African urbanism stresses the interdependence of urban centers and their hinterlands. They, more than anyone else, set the functionalist agenda in African urban studies (S. McIntosh and R. McIntosh 1984:77).

S. McIntosh (1997:463) argues that cities function as marketplaces and provide the mechanism for "circulation of commodities essential to subsistence (food, iron used to produce food)." Echoing Trigger (1972), she writes, "Whatever else a city may be, it is a unit of settlement that performs specialized functions in relation to a broader hinterland ... Urbanism thus represents a novel kind of relationship among sites in a region and involves the emergence of specialization and functional interdependence" (S. McIntosh 1997:463).

We argue that a functional approach is a more productive avenue for understanding the character of African urban formations; however, understanding the countryside is not just important in defining a city's functions. As Yoffee states, "the evolution of cities entails also the evolution of the countryside, ruralization being the counterpart of urbanization" (1997:260). Our position is not meant to devalue research based in urban centers alone; indeed, some of the richest sub-Saharan archaeology falls into this category (e.g., Chittick 1974; Horton 1996; Munro-Hay 1991). But in such cases functional urbanism cannot be addressed.

The issue of origins in African urbanism

A conventional wisdom thus emerged in African archaeology that those few large ancient centers that did appear on the continent did so at the instigation or through the inspiration of foreign agents. Few questioned this assumption until recently. Gertrude Caton-Thompson stood virtually alone when in 1931 she took the position that Great Zimbabwe was indigenously conceived, built, and governed; few believed her then, and most ignored her. For many people at the time (see Kuklick 1991:152), and for decades thereafter, the idea of indigenous, complex African societies was anathema and threatening. Caton-Thompson's evidence-based approach to determining the origins of the Zimbabwe phenomenon did not lead to a wave of other researchers following suit at the time. This example has broader implications for the context in which studies that challenged conventional wisdoms about African history were taking place.

Each of the three areas we feature below – the Inland Niger Delta, the Zimbabwe plateau, and the eastern African coast – has witnessed familiar debates about the foreign origins of medium- and large-scale societies there. Cities of the western Sudan such as Jenné-jeno and Timbuktu were considered North African Arab trading colonies placed on the far side of the desert to help control the trans-Saharan trade (e.g., Ajayi and Crowder 1976; Bovill 1995). Europeans believed the stone capitals of the Zimbabwe plateau to be indisputable evidence of Mediterranean colonialism in southern Africa (Garlake 1982; Kuklick 1991; Sinclair 1987). Nineteenth-century colonists saw no connection between these and the modern people living in what was to become Southern Rhodesia and adjacent colonial states. Stone ruins of deserted Swahili centers were attributed to legions of Arab colonizers who were pictured as coming to the coast to control Indian Ocean trade with the African interior. Here they married local women and produced the Swahili, people "between two worlds" racially, culturally, and geographically (e.g., Kirkman 1964; Le Guennec-Coppens 1991).

The important thing here is the pernicious weight of the assumptions made in these interpretations. Europeans attempted to dominate political and economic life across the African continent from the late 19th until the mid-20th century. From the time of the Atlantic slave trade, the West constructed Africa as a place of inferior people, institutions, and accomplishment (Robertshaw 1990). Anything considered extraordinary in Africa was assigned to some other, non-African origin (Trigger 1989:129ff). Ancient Egypt had long been assigned to the Classical world (Bernal 1987); Nubia was "African," but strongly influenced by its "Classical" neighbor to the north (Connah 2001). Sub-Saharan African cities were assigned to foreign origins or influence, whether considered ancient or not.

Undeniably, this climate affected the intellectual vigor of African archaeology as well as studies of urbanism. Perhaps most importantly, by separating (foreign) cities from (indigenous) countrysides, there was no possibility or motivation to examine the countrysides at all, whereas it was precisely the study of countrysides that was becoming a focus of urbanism studies in places such as Mesoamerica and Mesopotamia. Why seek the larger systems in which cities were articulated, when the countrysides were considered African, and the cities deemed anything but (e.g., Burton 1967; Kirkman 1959:175)?

Three Case Studies in Sub-Saharan Urbanism Research

The Inland Niger Delta

The Inland Niger Delta (IND) is a mosaic floodplain environment crisscrossed with seasonally inundated channels that had enormous potential for subsistence production in prehistory. It was settled about 250 B.C. by rice and millet/sorghum farmers, fishers, and livestock raisers who made and used pottery (S. McIntosh and R. McIntosh 1980; S. McIntosh 1999a; S. McIntosh, ed. 1995). The premier example of an urban center in the IND is Jenné-jeno, which began as a seasonal village at this time in an area of concentrated settlement probably founded by migrants from the north (see Figure 18.1). The settlement measured 12 hectares by A.D. 100, and grew into a permanent village of daubed pole-and-mat houses, occupying 25 hectares by A.D. 400. In these first centuries iron ore and ground stone were brought from outside the IND from up to 50 km away, as well as a small number of glass beads that came into the region from the Mediterranean. The settlement reached its greatest physical extent – 33 hectares – from A.D. 400 to 900, and was characterized by round, coursed earth houses. Extrapolating cautiously from different ethnographically derived examples, the population of Jenné-jeno itself has been estimated to have been between 3,200 and 6,400 at this time, and of the Jenné-jeno settlement cluster from 6,700 to 13,400 (S. McIntosh 1999a:73). Subsistence remained largely the same over these centuries except for a decrease in wild species use; however, changes in the economy and interaction spheres can be seen in the presence of copper (from at least 300 km away) and gold (from minimally 600 km away). A massive wall was built to encircle the 33-hectare center near the end of this period, around A.D. 900, made from sun-dried cylindrical bricks. Jenné-jeno's growth was echoed by an increase in the surrounding region's population, with the number of hinterland villages at its peak around A.D. 900, including those clustered closely about the center itself.

Conventional wisdom saw centers such as Jenné-jeno as the result of trans-Saharan trade and the direct influence of North African traders who needed outposts from which to exploit trading possibilities far from home. However, the McIntoshes showed that Jenné-jeno originated long before such trade was a force in West Africa, was later a magnet for that long-distance trade, but had grown smaller by A.D. 1000 when trans-Saharan trade began to flourish. Involvement in that trade was evidenced by quantities of imported glass, spindle whorls, and brass at Jenné-jeno. The beginning of the second millennium A.D. also marked the introduction of rectilinear houses made of the same cylindrical bricks (S. McIntosh 1999a). Jenné-jeno itself was abandoned by around A.D. 1400. The city of Jenné today, 3 km from Jenné-jeno, is considered its successor – it is the largest center in the area, and part of a settlement cluster – although recent work at Jenné has shown that its settlement history overlaps that of the older site (R. McIntosh et al. 1996). The urban system of the area never collapsed, but rather deflated beginning in the 15th century, a trend signaled by settlement abandonment and declining population generally, a decline abetted by a pan-regional drying trend which made the local economic base more tenuous. This decline was also affected by shifts in long-distance trade routes in West Africa that accompanied world-systems changes; while the trans-Saharan trade never ended, the most important commercial routes shifted west and south to the Atlantic coasts.

The McIntoshes have argued that the settlements surrounding Jenné-jeno by the early second millennium A.D. should be considered an "urban cluster," a group of settlements working in heterarchical tandem, and providing economic and social functions for a broad hinterland (R. McIntosh and S. McIntosh 2003:104). Heterarchy is a perspective first articulated in the archaeological literature by Crumley (1987; see also Ehrenreich et al., eds., 1995), which challenges the notion that social complexity must be founded on the coincidence of economic, political, and religious hierarchies. Instead, Crumley (1987:158) argues, social structures can be heterarchical, where "each element [in a social system] is either unranked relative to other elements or possesses the potential for being ranked in a number of different ways." Such a perspective forces reconsideration of the assumption that economic complexity must be linked to political or religious hierarchies, an assumption that requires the coincidence of economic and political central places in order to have "true" complex societies (Brumfiel 1995:126). Recent research detailing socially complex, heterarchical formations in many parts of the world suggest that hierarchy cannot be taken as the *de facto* organizational structure of large population aggregates (e.g., Ehrenreich et al., eds., 1995; Feinman 2000). As the McIntoshs' work at Jenné-jeno has shown, the coordination of large populations can be accomplished through corporate organization and does not necessitate an economic or political hierarchy. Archaeological studies applying the concept of heterarchy have begun breaking down monolithic approaches to what "complexity" means, and instead of asking "How complex were social systems?" have begun asking "How were they complex?" (Nelson 1995:614; Rautman 1998).

So what is the content of this particular example of an early African urban system – the large-scale urban cluster? "[A] cluster comprises a large, central settlement mound of up to 10 meters in height and 20–80 hectares in area, surrounded by intermediate and smaller mounds at distances of 200 meters or less" (S. McIntosh 1999a:66). What the McIntoshes have identified at Jenné-jeno are "aggregation, population growth, increasing scale, and specialization," functional processes widely associated with urbanization, but not "subsistence intensification, highly visible ranking or stratification, [or] imposing public monuments" (R. McIntosh and S. McIntosh 2003:104). The inhabitants of the urban cluster, they suggest, were,

> segmented communities of specialists or distinct corporate groups that voluntarily come together to take advantage of the services of others and a larger market for their products, but that make a demonstrable effort to preserve their separate identity by strategies of physical distinctiveness. The clustered city was a stable solution to . . . life within a rich environment, but one marked by rain and flood regimes of high . . . variability . . . We suggest that the solution hit upon by the inhabitants to combat unpredictability was to develop increasingly specialized artisan and subsistence producers linked into a generalized economy. (R. McIntosh and S. McIntosh 2003:111)

Related research on urban clusters from the Méma region of Mali, east of the central IND, provides complementary data for complex social differentiation but a lack of obvious hierarchy (Bedaux et al. 2001; R. McIntosh and S. McIntosh 1987; Togola 1996). The clustering pattern seems to correspond to the later tendency toward separation of specialists we see in a large region of West Africa (e.g., Conrad and Frank 1995); however, the difficulty of controlling the full range of materials and the activities they represent within deeply stratified component sites of every urban cluster makes this a challenging argument to substantiate thoroughly (see Baloian and Hietala 2002; M. Clark 2003).

Yet it remains a tantalizing possibility that in the region's deep-time urban formations one might be seeing the roots of the later ethnic and specialist florescence that famously characterizes this area (R. McIntosh 1998; R. McIntosh and S. McIntosh 2003). The McIntoshs' model reaches beyond strictly archaeological data for the kinds of cognitive systems that might have spawned such an urban form and then held it together. They see in the region's current, complex ethnographic and linguistic make-up, its multiple, carefully maintained strategies of sharing power among ethnic and other corporate groups, and its widespread oral traditions concerning the deep histories of these and other relationships, possible homologs for the origins of the ancient clustering seen archaeologically (R. McIntosh 1998; Chapter 18).

The western Sudan produced societies contemporary with that at Jenné-jeno which did not seem to share the heterarchical ideology implied by urban clustering. For example, the states and eventual empires of Ghana, Mali, and Songhai, better known from Arabic documentary sources than from archaeological ones, were described as ruled by kings of great power and wealth (Delafosse 1912). Although the purported capitals and some major towns of these states were excavated before the 1970s (de Barros 1990), archaeologists did not excavate below the Islamic levels, such that knowledge of the settlements' earliest manifestations remains elusive (but see Arazi 1999; Insoll 1999; and S. McIntosh and R. McIntosh 1986 for relevant work which goes beyond archaeological validation of Islamic documents).

For the moment, the urban clusters identified archaeologically in the IND region are striking in their scale and longevity, and yet have no archaeologically recovered manifestations of hierarchical wealth and control. Here researchers have provided evidence of a particular form of urbanism, one which questions the validity of using traits like monumental public architecture (R. McIntosh 1991; R. McIntosh and S. McIntosh 1993), centralization of craft production (LaViolette 2000a; R. McIntosh 1993), hierarchical stratification or ranking, and subsistence intensification (S. McIntosh 1999a, 1999b) as definitive indicators of city life.

The Zimbabwe plateau

The 13th- to 15th-century site of Great Zimbabwe (Figure 15.1), located in south-central Zimbabwe, has been extensively studied yet remains under-theorized in the debates we are discussing here (cf. Sinclair 1987). It and other major centers of the Zimbabwe plateau region – Mapungubwe before it, Khami, Torwa, and Mutapa after – have been considered major centers, even capitals, of chiefdoms or states, prime movers in cycles of state formation since European attention was drawn to them in the early 20th century (Chapter 15). The explicit urban function of any of the settlements, nonetheless, remains ambiguous (cf. Pikirayi 2001; Sinclair et al. 1993a). States, and certainly chiefdoms, can exist without urban centers (see e.g., Adams and Nissen 1972; H. Wright 1977), and the polities on the Zimbabwe plateau, however extensive, need not have had urban centers in their hierarchical structures – but it is a question that begs to be explored further.

Sophisticated research on the nature of the larger polities has indeed taken place. While undertaking archaeological investigations of Great Zimbabwe's origins in the 1920s, Caton-Thompson (1970) conducted excavations at smaller, Zimbabwe Tradition stone settlements up to several hundred kilometers from Great Zimbabwe that she posited were regional centers under the capital's rule. The defining archaeological characteristic of the Zimbabwe Tradition, centered on the plateau, was its curvilinear granite-block architecture whose origins are in first-millennium a.d. settlements associated with cattle-keeping and farming (Hall 1990; Pikirayi 2001). This stone architecture, identified at some 200 sites based on surface remains (Kuklick 1991), suggests the probable extent of the Zimbabwe Tradition polities. The earlier architecture is curvilinear but made from coursed earth or *daga* (Hall 1990). Although building in stone gained momentum in the late first, early second millennium a.d. (Sinclair 1987), it never replaced daga as the architecture of the majority. Daga is important to our discussion, because the archaeology of stone architecture greatly outpaced that of daga buildings and settlements. This has affected how archaeologists talk about the function of larger centers and their local contexts.

Mapungubwe is considered the first capital – and implicitly perhaps the first urban center – of the Zimbabwe Tradition polities and the immediate predecessor to Great Zimbabwe. Located in the Limpopo Valley, and dated to the 11th–13th centuries a.d. (Pikirayi 2001), most excavation has focused on the stone structures of the elite tradition built into the rocky hilltop. Yet the greater part of the settlement comprises daga buildings around the base of the hill which remain unexcavated (Hall 1990). Huffman (1982) and others conducted research at several smaller stone-built settlements in the region, at distances of 10, 40, and 85 km away, which allowed them to posit Mapungubwe as the center of a hierarchical system of settlements organized along state lines. Evidence suggests that Mapungubwe played a role in extensive economic networks which existed before the town's own rise (Chapter 15).

One of the truisms about Zimbabwe Tradition polities is that at any time there was but one capital and a series of lower-echelon settlements. This is consistent with conceptualizing the major sites as state centers rather than as cities *per se*. Great Zimbabwe, 300 km north, replaced Mapungubwe as the capital, dominating the Zimbabwe plateau politically from the later 13th century until its decline by the early 15th century (Pikirayi 2001). The scale and number of stone structures at Great Zimbabwe was vast, making it the largest ever of the Zimbabwe Tradition centers and one of the largest precolonial settlements in sub-Saharan Africa. It included: the hilltop complex, granite structures built amidst boulders on a dominating hill; buildings to the south and below the hill, around the famous elliptical Great Enclosure; another web of structures to the east of the Great Enclosure called the valley complex; other peripheral stone structures; and a mass of daga buildings throughout the area. Perimeter (though not defensive) walls were constructed at least twice during the settlement's history (Garlake 1973; Pikirayi 2001). A tradition of carved stone sculptures combining human and animal features, mounted at various locations around the site and echoed in a tradition of monolithic rough stone spires, has been interpreted as relating to leadership and ancestral power (Huffman 1984, 1996; Matenga 1998).

Daga houses sit amidst the stone walling on the hilltop and below, and surface survey and sub-surface testing reveal extensive daga housing in large expanses without stone. Archaeological research suggests class differences can be discerned among these daga houses, in greater spacing between structures inside the enclosures than those outside, and greater material consumption inside as well (Thorp 1995; see e.g., Caton-Thompson 1970; Garlake 1973; Randall-MacIver 1906). Daga structures took up an area many times that of the stone precincts, allowing suggested population figures for the entire center (720 hectares at its maximum size) of 10,000–18,000 (Pikirayi 2001; Sinclair 1987; Sinclair et al. 1993b). Great Zimbabwe has scale, monumental public architecture, long-distance trade relations with the Swahili coast, elite residences, sculptural traditions related to spiritual power, and was apparently the capital of an ancient state. It is a polity that has been used to invigorate nationalist ideology in a modern African nation perhaps more than any other example in Africa (see Kuklick 1991).

What can we posit about Great Zimbabwe according to our functionalist definitions? Archaeologists have hypothesized three prime functions for the settlement – management of long-distance trade, administration of local production, and a role as a religious center (see Sinclair 1987:156ff.) – based on research primarily at the site itself, but drawing also from work at smaller regional centers. Evidence for Great Zimbabwe's role in trade, particularly with the Swahili world, is seen in nearby gold and copper mining presumed to be under the center's control, the presence of copper ingots at the site, and in the imported goods obtained from contact with the coast (Huffman 1972; Sinclair et al. 1993b; Chapter 15). Imports have also been found at some smaller centers (e.g., Caton-Thompson 1970; Lindahl, ed., 2000). Domestic economy was based heavily on cattle transhumance, agriculture, and mining of stone and ores (Hall 1990; Sinclair et al. 1993b), and management of lineage-based holdings of agricultural land and herds is considered key to the building of the elite class that came to dominate (Hall 1987). The site has long been seen as having religious significance as well, as it symbolizes physically the state's guiding spiritual ideologies (Garlake 1973; Huffman 1984; Pikirayi 2001). All of these functions could certainly have been at work; expectations are that Great Zimbabwe also functioned as a political and administrative center for a large network of smaller regional polities of the Zimbabwe Tradition.

Sinclair et al.'s (1993b) ecologically minded discussion of "urban trajectories" in the area focuses on the possibility of the settlement's primary function as a manager of the local and regional economy, which would place it squarely within functional urban models. However, the kind of systematic settlement pattern studies

– the kind Pikirayi (1993) has carried out for the later Mutapa state – that would test that model for Great Zimbabwe have not yet been conducted. They would need to target daga settlements and daga portions of stone settlements in order to speak to issues of urbanism. Strictly economic models for the site will probably never suffice to tell its full story. For example, Huffman's (1984) analysis of the function of the Great Enclosure as a ritual center, where state ideologies based on such qualities as gender and age were reproduced through the regular teaching of young women from the countryside, is evocative, although his dependence on ethnohistorical evidence and oral traditions has been considered too uncritical by some (Beach 1998; Pikirayi 2001:137; Chapter 2). Zimbabwe's current political and economic crises have curtailed the pace of research; however, with the ongoing commitment of the modern state to its past, details about Zimbabwe urbanism are hopefully not far out of reach.

The Swahili coast

The Swahili coast encompasses the narrow coastline and offshore islands stretching 2,500 km from Somalia to Mozambique, including northern Madagascar, and the Comoro and Zanzibar archipelagos. We find here the remains of towns and villages dated from the eighth to 18th centuries A.D. (Figure 15.1). Many of these sites, called stonetowns, have standing mortared-limestone ruins of mosques, elaborate above-ground tombs, multi-storied domestic structures, and, in some cases, town walls. Such abandoned settlements have extensive scatters of locally made artifacts, as well as imported ceramics, glass, beads and other objects from as far as Egypt and southern and eastern Asia, that suggest the stonetowns were at their efflorescence from the 13th to 15th centuries A.D.

Through archaeological and historical research, and analogies drawn from descendant populations (Middleton 1961, 1992; Prins 1971), scholars commonly argue that Swahili stonetowns functioned as economic centers (e.g., Horton and Middleton 2000; Kusimba 1999), and characterize Swahili society as "mercantile" (Horton and Middleton 2000; Middleton 1992; Prins 1961, 1971). The acceptance of stonetowns as urban centers during the late 1970s and early 1980s must be understood in relation to a changing political climate. Scholars in newly independent eastern African nations were interested in foregrounding the richness of their nation's prehistory and reasserting the greatness of the precolonial past. Research on Swahili followed suit, and many researchers rejected what became a colonial model of Swahili origins, whereby Arab colonists were thought to have founded, built, and controlled coastal towns, beginning in the tenth century A.D. (e.g., Ingrams 1967; Kirkman 1964; Pearce 1967).

More recently, Swahili urban development has been attributed to the increasing participation of some coastal dwellers in long-distance trade during the ninth to 11th centuries, who later became "middlemen elites," managing commerce and local production for the Indian Ocean trade system. Through wealth accumulation, these elites established stratified and centralized political systems, with integrated and functionally differentiated economies. In this view, the main function of Swahili stonetowns was brokering long-distance trade between distant African hinterlands, the surrounding countrysides, and far-flung ports on the Indian Ocean rim. Although other stonetown roles are imagined, such as providing locales for Islamic education and religious ritual, control over the political economy has been viewed as their primary function.

This model portrays Swahili middlemen merchants coordinating and controlling trade relations with four groups of people: merchants of their fellow sub-clan; overseas traders; trade partners in the coastal hinterland; and rural populations in the surrounding countrysides (Horton and Middleton 2000:92, 112). Based on excavations and ethnohistoric research on particular stonetowns, we have learned much about the first two socio-economic relationships, and we have a clearer picture of the integral connections between stonetowns and the hinterland areas behind the coastal corridor (Abungu and Mutoro 1993; Curtis and Walz 2001; Helm 2000; Kusimba and Kusimba 2000; D. Wright 2002). However, as the image of Swahili society has built steadily out from the towns, we have only begun to know about rural Swahili (e.g., Fleisher 2003). Villages have been portrayed as part of the agricultural and productive economy that supported and allowed for the extension of city-based elite activities (Kusimba 1999; Wilson 1982; H. Wright 1993). Although some attributes of urbanism – stonetowns with multiple economic classes, powerful merchants alongside political rulers, and centralized religious rituals – are evident from research at these sites, the relationship between cities and their surrounding communities has been largely presumed rather than tested.

Swahili stonetowns included populations regularly in excess of 5,000, with a number of centers such as Kilwa and Mombasa larger than 15,000. Many northern stonetowns were surrounded by town walls (Takwa, Pate, Gede), representing either real protective features or symbolic markers that defined "cultured" spaces. All stonetowns contained elite architecture and mosques, as well as unique pillar tombs commemorating political and religious figures. Beginning in the 12th century, these striking features dominated many towns on the northern Swahili coast (north of the current Tanzania–Kenya border). In contrast, most towns on the southern coast contained few stone buildings that were scattered among much larger earth-and-thatch neighborhoods. These distinctions may have much to do with the way power was negotiated by town-based elites. Towns with large, dense stone sectors surrounded by small wattle-and-daub neighborhoods may have been structured around a more horizontally differentiated power base, with numerous leaders (merchant, religious, political) vying for position of "first among equals." In contrast, towns with few elite structures surrounded by extensive wattle-and-daub may have been organized around a small-scale, ranked hierarchy, whose leader ruled through custom and consent.

Most researchers agree that long-distance trade was a crucial factor in the development of Swahili urban centers (Horton 1987:91; Horton and Middleton 2000:12; Kusimba 1997:512; Spear 1984:303), and that stonetowns were not bound together in an integrated state system (Horton and Middleton 2000; H. Wright 1993). The towns remained largely autonomous but interconnected through social and economic relationships. However, there are at least three models for the development of Swahili urban centers, each representing distinctive ideas about how trade and regional development led to urban forms. The first argues that Swahili stonetowns developed to administer a complex settlement hierarchy of functional centers, and produce goods crucial for long-distance trade (Kusimba 1999). The second imagines stonetowns as relatively independent mercantile cities that functioned as production and market centers (Horton 1996; Horton and Middleton 2000; Sinclair and Håkansson 2000). And the third argues that such centers formed due to competitive relationships between coastal elites, who melded the community ritual of Islam with the power of exotic goods to create centers of power and authority (H. Wright 1993). In each model, the city is a functional center that controlled either territory, production, and markets or ritual life.

Kusimba (1999:123–124) argued that Swahili stonetowns managed economic relationships between town and country, and that agricultural goods, raw materials, and finished products came from countrysides to support stonetown dwellers. Stonetown elites thus sat atop a settlement hierarchy, managing a system of small towns and villages to create an efficient network for the movement of goods. This regional picture, developed from Wilson's (1982) study of settlement patterns along the Kenyan coast, is similar to that of settlement hierarchies in other urbanized state societies (Marcus and Feinman 1998; Wright and Johnson 1975).

Sinclair and Håkansson (2000) have presented the clearest argument for viewing stonetowns as city-states or mercantile cities (also Horton 1987; Horton and Middleton 2000). For them, stonetowns are entrepôts and/or production centers, functioning in a string of settlements (the "Swahili Corridor") that serviced the commodity needs of Muslim Indian Ocean merchants (Horton 1987; Kleppe 1995, 2001) and the surrounding countryside populations.

Such urban/rural models rely heavily on ethnographic data from 19th- and 20th-century coastal populations (Horton and Middleton 2000; Middleton 1961, 1972, 1992; Middleton and Campbell 1965). It is from such data that we draw a binary image of Swahili regions composed of "stonetowns" and "country-towns." In Middleton's model (1992:58), country-towns were places of small-scale craft and food production, where goods were consumed locally and traded to nearby centers. Country-towns were relatively self-sufficient, in contrast to stonetowns, dependent on goods produced in villages and other stonetowns (Middleton 1992:56; also Kusimba 1999:133, 142). In exchange for these goods, country-town residents received other products from hinterland and overseas ports, and military protection. In this view, supra-local interactions were key to Swahili stonetowns, as found in other city-state systems, and the stonetowns were not administrative but market and production centers (Horton 1996:412). If such ethnographic and ethnohistoric descriptions of town–country relationships are an accurate representation of ancient ones, then the economic organization of Swahili stonetowns functioned in ways quite similar to mercantile cities or city-states (Fox 1977:92ff; Nichols and Charleton 1997; Trigger 1993). That surplus goods moved from rural communities to stonetowns through trade rather than taxation indicates the relative economic autonomy of the countrysides. What tied them all together was not administration, but the demand in the countrysides for goods and services obtainable only in the stonetowns, leaving villages largely self-sufficient.

Wright (1993:671–672) has criticized the reliance on trade as the primary causative agent in the transformation of Swahili society. He argued that there can be no *direct* correlation between increasing trade and the development of hierarchical stonetowns because of ample evidence that coastal villagers had been participating in long-distance trade long before the appearance of urban centers or structured hierarchies. Instead, he suggests the introduction of imported goods may have been used by certain people to reinforce elite statuses at villages, but that the rise of hierarchy was the result of interaction and competition between coastal groups, not simply the introduction of foreign goods, increases in wealth, and greater control over the surpluses of others.

Wright's proposition rules out administrative or mercantile urban systems as the earliest manifestations of Swahili town development. Instead, Islam, alongside trade, is crucial: "Islamic institutions would have been made central in community life only in order to stabilize relations among the emerging elites of the larger communities, and subsequently extended to bind villages and smaller centers more closely to emerging towns" (H. Wright 1993:671–672). This challenges the notion of Swahili towns as mercantile centers in their original foundation. He argues that emerging coastal towns had a more ritual basis. The crucial element in drawing populations to emerging centers may have depended on the establishment of centralized, communal rituals, as found in Islamic practice.

In this formulation, it would be a mistake to label the earliest Swahili towns "entrepôts," since that reduces their Islamic element to a commercial function, when it may, in fact, have been the reverse. One useful way of thinking about this distinction is what scholars have discussed as the "Islamic city" (Abu-Lughod 1987; Eickelman 1981:261–288; Hourani and Stern, eds., 1970; Lapidus 1969). As theorized, the "Islamic city" was an attempt to construct an urban model that held for population aggregates in the Middle East that, like urban forms in Africa, were systematically excluded from literature on urbanism. In order to escape the trait-lists that described Western cities, these models stressed the particular functional attributes of an Islamic city, where the urban community was coterminous with the religious one. As Wheatley (1972:622) argued, "for the traditional Muslim the city was necessary as the only locale in which the life prescribed by the Book of God and the Tradition of the Prophet could be lived out to the full, and the features predicated of his city were a Friday mosque, with its adjunct of the public bath, and a permanent market." These physical structures created the three-dimensional landscape most desired by practitioners, functional attributes which distinguished centers from smaller settlements.

Research into the political-economic relationship between an eighth- to 16th-century Swahili stonetown called Chwaka and its hinterland is underway in northern Pemba Island, Tanzania, a center that followed the southern-coast pattern of a small number of stone buildings surrounded by a much larger earth-and-thatch-dwelling urban community (Fleisher 2003; LaViolette 1999; LaViolette et al. 2003). Archaeological evidence comes from excavations in Chwaka itself, both the stone and earth-and-thatch sectors, and survey data from approximately 30 shorter-lived village sites in Chwaka's surrounding countryside, inhabited for one to two centuries each while Chwaka was a dominant settlement in that region. So far, data on the consumption of imported goods, production, and subsistence suggest that Chwaka was not in economic or political control of the countryside population. The rural settlements show evidence of iron and pottery production in numerous places, and appear to be independent in terms of subsistence. Evidence for production at Chwaka of iron and cloth, and possibly pottery, is distributed throughout the stone and earth-and-thatch sectors, suggesting that household-level production characterized the town's domestic economy throughout its history. Imported goods, including Far Eastern and Middle Eastern glazed ceramics, glass vessels, stone and glass beads, and small copper-alloy objects, while strikingly more numerous at Chwaka than in the countryside, are nevertheless found in a variety of rural settings, including at villages with no evidence of stone building. While even preliminary analysis of these data reveals differences in class (architecture, quantity of consumption, subsistence patterns) within Chwaka and between Chwaka and its rural neighbors, there is no evidence yet for Chwaka acting as an administrative center to its hinterland (Fleisher 2003; LaViolette et al. 2003).

We can envision people drawn to emergent Swahili towns because of burgeoning symbols of power and community organization, which had a powerful effect on the earliest Muslim elite residents, who not only controlled international trade relations but, more importantly, community ritual. Though town development may have led to greater coordination of craft production or control over non-elite labor, these cannot be seen as the "determinants" of urbanism, any more than can the control or wealth of merchants.

African Urbanisms in the Wider World: Emerging Research Directions

Our three case studies highlight different manifestations of African urbanism. From this alone, we must see that "ancient African urbanism" is a multifaceted institution – not surprising, given the vastness of the subcontinent and its multitude of physical and cultural environments. Can we be mindful of the differences we see in these particular cases, and also connect them to urbanisms in other parts of the world?

The urban clustering of the Inland Niger Delta and adjacent Méma region of Mali provides the earliest documented example of sub-Saharan urbanism thus far, and a pattern not yet seen in any other African locales. The population boom associated with the peak period of urban clustering did not correspond to recognizable evidence for social or political hierarchy in the society, including architectural monumentality, which is often seen as supporting elite structures of power. This led R. McIntosh (1991) to draw parallels from the IND to ancient China. He argued that in each case social complexity in the form of urbanism can be seen emerging in a landscape absent of centralized, hierarchical power structures such as one associates with a state (Smith 2003). Possehl (1998) has made a similar case for the Mature Harappan phase of Indus Valley civilization, where he argues there were both cities and a state, but no monumentality associated with either.

In contrast to these examples, Great Zimbabwe's monumentality conjures a sense of tremendous power and hierarchy in the modern viewer. Indeed, it conjures this so thoroughly that the issue of whether urbanism was at work has never been questioned, or tested archaeologically. A recurrent question in the study of major centers on the Zimbabwe plateau has been whether their ritual functions were as important as, or even more important than, their political and economic roles. Richard Fox's (1977:39–57) cultural anthropological work on regal-ritual cities provides compelling ways to look at places such as Great Zimbabwe. In his formulation, regal-ritual cities (as opposed to administrative or mercantile cities) consist of "simply the social arrangements of the king's court or the priest's temple . . . no other municipal government exists" (Fox 1977:53). Fox's own comparisons are to the Swazi state, the Rajputs, and the Carolingian state, but they have also been applied to Bronze Age China and some Mesoamerican centers (Marcus 1983; Sanders and Webster 1988). Fox's discussions encourage the kind of cross-cultural comparison we would like to see take place vis-à-vis African examples.

The Swahili cities, or city-states, provide another alternative urban configuration, distinguished from the IND and Zimbabwe examples by the large number of relatively independent urban centers, explicitly not organized into a unified state system. Even the most powerful places, such as Kilwa Kisiwani (Figure 15.1) during the 13th–15th centuries A.D., likely exhibited only limited influence over neighboring stonetowns. What is striking about Swahili urbanism is the balance that stonetowns struck between autonomy and interdependence. Though stonetowns varied in internal organization they were entwined in supra-local relationships that defined regional interaction spheres. These commonalities are similar to what Webster (1997:141) has described for the Maya Lowlands as a "Classic Maya Great Tradition" that involved "common ideological conventions" in realms such as art and ritual. This supra-city-state ideology was the framework that allowed for the interaction of politically independent polities (Freidel 1986). The recognition of common ritual and ideological ties must be seen as crucial parts of the emergence of Swahili urbanism, occurring alongside and enabling merchant functions. The study of villages and commoner contexts within urban sites has resulted in a more multidimensional understanding of life on the Swahili coast. As archaeologists continue to study ancient African cities, we look forward to developing comparative insights into the political economy that links centers to smaller centers and countrysides; the inclusion of the still barely visible villagers and urban-dwelling commoners into urban landscapes; and the domestic economies overlooked in the pursuit of prime-mover explanations for urbanization such as long-distance trade. This direction is a crucial step in constructing multi-scalar approaches to African urban forms. The scales most commonly investigated have been at the level of the city itself, and the much larger world-systems level. This ultimately excludes a great majority of the populations that were integral to, and affected by, emergent urban systems.

The study of regions not only broadens the contexts in which we can understand urban centers, but can also reveal intra-regional variability (Horton 1994; LaViolette et al. 2003; Marcus 1983; Schmidt and Curtis 2001). We should expect significant differences in the ways in which urban systems were formed and maintained within culture areas commonly viewed monolithically (such as the Swahili coast). Rather than seeking to model urban systems narrowly, we should seek patterns but remain open to variability (Fox 1977; Marcus 1983). The increasingly higher profile of cultural resource management in Africa may play a welcome role in this, as survey for archaeological sites becomes more commonly linked to development projects and other infrastructural ventures (see MacEachern 2001).

Establishing the varied indigenous processes that shaped urbanization on the subcontinent has helped us re-envision ancient Africa. Perhaps the greatest test of our liberation from the colonialist models of foreign origins would be scholarly open-mindedness to the full array of cultural influences that come together in African urban systems, whether "indigenous" or "foreign" (Connah 2001; Chapter 15). The cosmopolitan nature of many ancient African cities and states suggests the openness of those societies to global crosscurrents: religious, material, artistic. There is no longer any doubt that urbanism is an African phenomenon, born in great variety in numerous places. There is also no doubt that many African societies – long before the colonial domination of Africa by Europe – were open to visitors, immigrants, and the long-distance exchange of ideas. For modern researchers to close the door on those possibilities archaeologically is to overlook significant aspects of what made such societies unique.

We wish to end by returning to our hope that the household and the commoner grow more important in the study of African urbanism. Cities and their hinterlands have households as their building blocks. Household archaeology, which focuses on one of the smallest-scale units archaeologists study, is directly tied analytically to what we can say about whole settlements and settlement networks (Blanton 1994). The majority of urban archaeology still takes place at individual centers. The inclusion of both ends of the analytical continuum – households on the one hand, regions on the other – locates settlements in their place between these levels of analysis, rather than suspending them in analytical mid-air. A commitment to households – elite and common, urban and rural – brings us finally to the archaeology of daily life, an effort to add more humanistic approaches to the modeling of ancient societies (Fleisher and LaViolette 1999; Kent, ed., 1998; Lane 2000; LaViolette 2000b; Meskell 2002; Stahl 1999). Research into African urbanism that does not go beyond studying the elite keeps us distant from the men, women, and children whose lives made up the majority of African history we want to tell.

REFERENCES

Abu-Lughod, Janet L., 1987 The Islamic City: Historic Myth, Islamic Essence, and Contemporary Relevance. International Journal of Middle Eastern Studies 19:155–176.

Abungu, George H. O., and Henry W. Mutoro, 1993 Coast-Interior Settlements and Social Relations in the Kenya Coastal Hinterland. *In* The Archaeology of Africa: Food, Metals and Towns. Thurstan Shaw, Paul Sinclair, Bassey W. Andah, and Alex Okpoko, eds. pp. 694–704. New York: Routledge.

Adams, Robert. Mc C., 1966 The Evolution of Urban Society. Chicago: Aldine.

Adams, Robert Mc C., and Hans J. Nissen, 1972 The Uruk Countryside: The Natural Setting of Urban Societies. Chicago: University of Chicago Press.

Ajayi, J. F. Ade, and Michael Crowder, 1976 History of West Africa, vol. 1. 2nd edition. New York: Columbia University Press.

Arazi, Noemie, 1999 An Archaeological Survey in the Songhay Heartland of Mali. Nyame Akuma 52:25–43.

Baloian, Mary C., and Harold J. Hietala, 2002 Complexity from the Periphery: A Spatial Analytic Approach to Understanding Settlement Organization at Nucleated Site Clusters, Inland Niger Delta, Mali. Paper presented at the Biennial Meeting of the Society for Africanist Archaeologists, Tucson.

Beach, David, 1998 Cognitive Archaeology and Imaginary History at Great Zimbabwe. Current Anthropology 39:47–72.

Bedaux, Rogier M., K. MacDonald, A. Person, H. Polet, K. Sanogo, A. Schmidt, and S. Sidibé, 2001 The Dia Archaeological Project: Rescuing Cultural Heritage in the Inland Niger Delta (Mali). Antiquity 75:837–848.

Bernal, Martin, 1987 Black Athena: The Afroasiatic Roots of Classical Civilization. London: Free Association Books.

Billman, Brian R., and Gary M. Feinman, eds., 1999 Settlement Pattern Studies in the Americas: Fifty Years Since Virú. Washington, DC: Smithsonian Institution Press.

Blanton, Richard E., 1976 Anthropological Studies of Cities. Annual Review of Anthropology 5:249–264.

——1994 Houses and Households: A Comparative Study. Interdisciplinary Contributions to Archaeology. London: Plenum.

Bovill, Edward William, 1995[1958] The Golden Trade of the Moors: West African Kingdoms in the Fourteenth Century. Princeton: Marcus Wiener Publishers.

Bower, John, 1986 A Survey of Surveys: Aspects of Surface Archaeology in Sub-Saharan Africa. The African Archaeological Review 4:21–40.

Brumfiel, Elizabeth M., 1992 Breaking and Entering the Ecosystem: Gender, Class, and Faction Steal the Show. Distinguished Lecture in Archeology. American Anthropologist 94:551–567.

——1995 Heterarchy and the Analysis of Complex Societies: Comments. *In* Heterarchy and the Analysis of Complex Societies. R. M. Ehrenreich, C. L. Crumley, and J. E. Levy, eds. pp. 125–131. Archaeological Papers of the American Anthropological Association, 6. Washington, DC: American Anthropological Association.

Burton, Sir Richard F., 1967[1872] Zanzibar: City, Island, and Coast, vol. 1. London: Johnson Reprint Company Ltd.

Caton-Thompson, Gertrude, 1970[1931] The Zimbabwe Culture: Ruins and Reactions. New York: Negro Universities Press.

Childe, V. Gordon, 1950 The Urban Revolution. The Town Planning Review 21:3–17.

——1957 Civilization, Cities and Towns. Antiquity 31:36–38.

Chittick, H. Neville, 1974 Kilwa: An Islamic Trading City on the East African Coast. Memoir 5. Nairobi: British Institute in Eastern Africa.

Clark, J. Desmond, 1962 Africa South of the Sahara. *In* Courses Toward Urban Life. Robert J. Braidwood and Gordon R. Willey, eds. pp. 1–33. Chicago: Aldine.

Clark, Mary E., 2003 Archaeological Investigations at the Jenné-jeno Settlement Complex, Inland Niger Delta, Mali, West Africa. Ph.D. dissertation, Southern Methodist University.

Clarke, David L., ed., 1977 Spatial Archaeology. London: Academic.

Connah, Graham, 1987 African Civilizations: An Archaeological Perspective. Cambridge: Cambridge University Press.

——2001 African Civilizations: An Archaeological Perspective. 2nd edition. Cambridge: Cambridge University Press.

Conrad, David C., and Barbara E. Frank, 1995 Status and Identity in West Africa: Nyamakalaw of Mande. Bloomington: Indiana University Press.

Crumley, Carole L., 1987 A Dialectical Critique of Hierarchy. In Power Relations and State Formation. T. C. Patterson and C. W. Gailey, eds. pp. 155–159. Washington, DC: American Anthropological Association.

Curtis, Matthew C., and Jonathan R. Walz, 2001 Regional Approaches to the Archaeology of East Africa and the Horn: From Past to Present. Paper presented at the Annual Meeting of the American Anthropological Association, Washington, DC.

de Barros, Philip, 1990 Changing Paradigms, Goals & Methods in the Archaeology of Francophone West Africa. In A History of African Archaeology. Peter Robertshaw, ed. pp. 155–172. London: James Currey.

Delafosse, Maurice, 1912 Haut-Sénégal-Niger. Paris: Larose.

Durkheim, Émile, 1997[1893] The Division of Labor in Society. W. D. Halls, trans. New York: Free Press.

Ehrenreich, Robert M., Carole L. Crumley, and Janet E. Levy, eds., 1995 Heterarchy and the Analysis of Complex Societies. Archaeological Papers of the American Anthropological Association, 6. Arlington, VA: American Anthropological Association.

Eickelman, Dale, 1981 The Middle East: An Anthropological Approach. Englewood Cliffs: Prentice-Hall.

Feinman, Gary M., 2000 Corporate/Network: New Perspectives on Models of Political Action and the Puebloan Southwest. In Social Theory in Archaeology. Michael B. Schiffer, ed. pp. 31–51. Salt Lake City: University of Utah Press.

Feinman, Gary M., and Joyce Marcus, eds., 1998 Archaic States. Santa Fe: School of American Research.

Flannery, Kent V., 1972 The Cultural Evolution of Civilizations. Annual Review of Ecology and Systematics 3:399–426.

Fleisher, Jeffrey B., 2003 Viewing Stonetowns from the Countryside: An Archaeological Approach to Swahili Regions, AD 800–1500. Ph.D. dissertation, Department of Anthropology, University of Virginia.

Fleisher, Jeff, and Adria LaViolette, 1999 Elusive Wattle-and-Daub: Finding the Hidden Majority in the Archaeology of the Swahili. Azania 34:87–108.

Fleisher, Jeff, and Amy Lawson, 2001 A "Survey of Surveys" Revisited: The Last Fifteen Years in Africa. Paper presented at the Annual Meeting of the American Anthropological Association, Washington, DC, December.

Fortes, Meyer, and E. E. Evans-Pritchard, 1940 African Political Systems. London: Oxford University Press.

Fox, Richard G., 1977 Urban Anthropology: Cities in their Cultural Surroundings. Englewood Cliffs: Prentice-Hall.

Frankfort, Henri, 1951 The Birth of Civilization in the Near East. Bloomington: Indiana University Press.

Freidel, David, 1986 Maya Warfare: An Example of Peer-Polity Interaction. In Peer Polity

Interaction and Socio-Political Change. Colin Renfrew and John F. Cherry, eds. pp. 93–108. Cambridge: Cambridge University Press.

Garlake, Peter S., 1973 Great Zimbabwe. London: Thames & Hudson.

——1982 Prehistory and Ideology in Zimbabwe. Africa 52(3):1–19.

Garner, B. J., 1967 Models of Urban Geography and Settlement Location. *In* Socio-Economic Models in Geography. R. J. Chorley and P. Haggett, eds. pp. 303–360. London: Methuen.

Guyer, Jane I., 1995 Wealth in People, Wealth in Things – Introduction. Journal of African History 36:83–90.

Haggett, Peter, 1965 Locational Analysis in Human Geography. New York: St. Martin's Press.

Hall, Martin, 1987 Archaeology and Modes of Production in Pre-Colonial Southern Africa. Journal of Southern African Studies 14:1–17.

——1990 Farmers, Kings and Traders: The People of Southern Africa 200–1860. Chicago: University of Chicago Press.

Helm, Richard M., 2000 Conflicting Histories: The Archaeology of the Iron-Working Farming Communities in the Central and Southern Coast of Kenya. Ph.D. dissertation, University of Bristol.

Hodder, Ian, and Clive Orton, 1976 Spatial Analysis in Archaeology. Cambridge: Cambridge University Press.

Horton, Mark, 1987 The Swahili Corridor. Scientific American 257(3):86–93.

——1994 Closing the Corridor: Archaeological and Architectural Evidence for Emerging Swahili Regional Autonomy. *In* Continuity and Autonomy in Swahili Communities. David Parkin, ed. pp. 15–21. London: School of Oriental and African Studies.

——1996 Shanga: the Archaeology of a Muslim Trading Community on the Coast of East Africa. Memoir 14. London: British Institute in Eastern Africa.

Horton, Mark, and John Middleton, 2000 The Swahili: The Social Landscape of a Mercantile Society. London: Blackwell.

Hourani, A. H., and S. M. Stern, eds., 1970 The Islamic City. Philadelphia: University of Pennsylvania Press.

Huffman, Thomas N., 1972 The Rise and Fall of Great Zimbabwe. Journal of African History 13:353–366.

——1982 Archaeology and Ethnohistory of the African Iron Age. Annual Review of Anthropology 11:133–150.

——1984 Where You Are the Girls Gather to Play: The Great Enclosure at Great Zimbabwe. *In* Frontiers: Southern African Archaeology Today. Martin Hall, Graham Avery, D. M. Avery, M. L. Wilson, and A. J. B. Humphreys, eds. pp. 252–265. Cambridge Monographs in African Archaeology, 10. Oxford: British Archaeological Reports.

——1996 Snakes and Crocodiles: Power and Symbolism in Ancient Zimbabwe. Johannesburg: Witwatersrand University Press.

Ingrams, W. H., 1967[1931] Zanzibar: Its History and its People. London: Frank Cass.

Insoll, Timothy, 1999 Preliminary Results of Excavations in Timbuktu, September 1998. Nyame Akuma 51:41–44.

Kent, Susan, ed., 1998 Gender in African Prehistory. Walnut Creek, CA: AltaMira Press.

Kirkman, James S., 1959 Excavations at Ras Mkumbuu on the Island of Pemba. Tanganyika Notes and Records 53:161–178.

——1964 Men and Monuments on the East African Coast. London: Lutterworth.

Kleppe, Else Johansen, 1995 To Blow Trade: Medieval Zanzibar and the Indian Ocean Trade. AmS-Varia 24:65–70.

——2001 Archaeological Investigations at Kizimkazi Dimbani. *In* Islam in East Africa: New Sources. Biancamaria Scarcia Amoretti, ed. pp. 361–384. Rome: Herder.

Kuklick, Henricka, 1991 Contested Monuments: The Politics of Archeology in Southern Africa. *In* Colonial Situations: Essays on the Contextualization of Ethnographic Knowledge. George Stocking, Jr., ed. pp. 135–169. History of Anthropology, 7. Madison: University of Wisconsin.

Kusimba, Chapurukha M., 1997 Swahili and the Coastal City-States. *In* Encyclopedia of Precolonial Africa. Joseph O. Vogel, ed. pp. 507–513. Walnut Creek, CA: AltaMira Press.

——1999 The Rise and Fall of Swahili States. Walnut Creek, CA: AltaMira Press.

Kusimba, Chapurukha M., and Sibel Barut Kusimba, 2000 Hinterlands and Cities: Archaeological Investigations of Economy and Trade in Tsavo, Southeastern Kenya. Nyame Akuma 54:13–24.

Lane, Paul, 2000 Hearth and Home in the Iron Age of Eastern Africa: Ethnographic Models, Historical Linguistics and the Archaeological Evidence. Paper presented at the Biennial Meeting of the Society of Africanist Archaeologists, Cambridge.

Lapidus, Ira M., 1969 Muslim Cities and Islamic Societies. *In* Middle Eastern Cities: A Symposium on Ancient, Islamic, and Contemporary Middle Eastern Urbanism. Ira M. Lapidus, ed. pp. 47–79. Berkeley: University of California Press.

LaViolette, Adria, 1999 Swahili Archaeology on Pemba Island, Tanzania: Pujini, Bandari ya Faraji, and Chwaka, 1997–'98. Nyame Akuma 53:50–63.

——2000a Ethno-Archaeology in Jenné, Mali: Craft and Status among Smiths, Potters and Masons. BAR International Series, 838. Oxford: British Archaeological Reports.

——2000b Daily Life, Sacred Space in the Swahili Palace of Pujini. Paper presented at the Biennial Meeting of the Society of Africanist Archaeologists, Cambridge.

LaViolette, Adria, Jeff Fleisher, and Bertram B. B. Mapunda, 2003 Preliminary Report: Pemba Archaeological Project, First Season, June–August 2002. Zanzibar: Department of Archives, Museums, and Antiquities.

Le Guennec-Coppens, Françoise, 1991 Les Swahili entre Afrique et Arabie. Paris: Karthala.

Lindahl, Anders, ed., 2000 Ceramics, Metal Craft and Settlement in South-Eastern Zimbabwe since ca 1400 AD. Lund: Laboratory for Ceramic Research, Dept. of Quaternary Geology.

MacEachern, Scott, 2001 Cultural Resource Management and Africanist Archaeology. Antiquity 75:866–871.

McIntosh, Roderick J., 1991 Early Urban Clusters in China and Africa: The Arbitration of Social Ambiguity. Journal of Field Archaeology 18:199–212.

——1993 The Pulse Model: Genesis and Accommodation of Specialization in the Middle Niger. Journal of African History 34:181–220.

——1998 The Peoples of the Middle Niger. Oxford: Blackwell.

——1999 Western Representations of Urbanism and Invisible African Towns. *In* Beyond Chiefdoms: Pathways to Complexity in Africa. Susan K. McIntosh, ed. pp. 56–65. Cambridge: Cambridge University Press.

McIntosh, Roderick J., and Susan Keech McIntosh, 1987 Prospection archéologique aux alentours de Dia, Mali: 1986–1987. Nyame Akuma 29:42–45.

——— 1993 Cities Without Citadels: Understanding Urban Origins along the Middle Niger. *In* The Archaeology of Africa: Food, Metals and Towns. Thurstan Shaw, Paul Sinclair, Bassey Andah, and Alex Okpoko, eds. pp. 622–641. London: Routledge.

——— 2003 Early Urban Configurations on the Middle Niger: Clustered Cities and

Landscapes of Power. *In* The Social Construction of Ancient Cities. Monica L. Smith, ed. pp. 103–120. Washington, DC: Smithsonian Institution Press.

McIntosh, Roderick J., Paul Sinclair, Téréba Togola, Michael Petrèn, and Susan Keech McIntosh, 1996 Exploratory Archaeology at Jenné and Jenné-jeno (Mali). Sahara 8:19–28.

McIntosh, Susan Keech, 1997 Urbanism in Sub-Saharan Africa. *In* Encyclopedia of Precolonial Africa. Joseph O. Vogel, ed. pp. 461–465. Walnut Creek, CA: AltaMira Press.

——1999a Modelling Political Organization in Large-Scale Settlement Clusters: A Case Study from the Inland Niger Delta. *In* Beyond Chiefdoms: Pathways to Complexity in Africa. Susan Keech McIntosh, ed. pp. 66–79. Cambridge: Cambridge University Press.

——1999b Pathways to Complexity: An African Perspective. *In* Beyond Chiefdoms: Pathways to Complexity in Africa. Susan Keech McIntosh, ed. pp. 1–30. Cambridge: Cambridge University Press.

McIntosh, Susan Keech, ed., 1995 Excavations at Jenné-jeno, Hambarketolo, and Kaniana (Inland Niger Delta, Mali), the 1981 Season. Berkeley: University of California Press.

McIntosh, Susan Keech, and Roderick J. McIntosh, 1980 Prehistoric Investigations in the Region of Jenné, Mali. 2 vols. Cambridge Monographs in African Archaeology, 2. Oxford: British Archaeological Reports.

——————1984 The Early City in West Africa: Towards an Understanding. The African Archaeological Review 2:73–98.

——————1986 Archaeological Reconnaissance in the Region of Timbuktu, Mali. National Geographic Research 2(3):215–258.

Marcus, Joyce, 1983 On the Nature of the Mesoamerican City. *In* Prehistoric Settlement Patterns: Essays in Honor of Gordon R. Willey. Evon Z. Vogt and Richard M. Leventhal, eds. pp. 195–242. Albuquerque: University of New Mexico.

Marcus, Joyce, and Gary M. Feinman, 1998 Introduction. *In* Archaic States. Gary M. Feinman and Joyce Marcus, eds. pp. 3–13. Santa Fe: School of American Research.

Matenga, Edward, 1998 The Soapstone Birds of Great Zimbabwe: Symbols of a Nation. Harare: African Publishing Group.

Meskell, Lynn, 2002 Private Life in New Kingdom Egypt. Princeton: Princeton University Press.

Middleton, John, 1961 Land Tenure in Zanzibar. Colonial Research Studies, 23. London: HMSO.

——1972 Patterns of Settlement in Zanzibar. *In* Man, Settlement and Urbanism. Peter J. Ucko, Ruth Tringham, and George W. Dimbleby, eds. pp. 285–292. London: Duckworth.

——1992 The World of the Swahili. New Haven: Yale University Press.

Middleton, John, and Jane Campbell, 1965 Zanzibar, its History and Politics. London: Oxford University Press.

Morton-Williams, P., 1972 Some Factors in the Location, Growth and Survival of Towns in West Africa. *In* Man, Settlement and Urbanism. Peter J. Ucko, Ruth Tringham, and George W. Dimbleby, eds. pp. 883–890. London: Duckworth.

Munro-Hay, Stuart, 1991 An African Civilisation: The Aksumite Kingdom of Northern Ethiopia. Edinburgh: Edinburgh University Press.

Nelson, Ben A., 1995 Complexity, Hierarchy, and Scale: A Controlled Comparison between Chaco Canyon, New Mexico, and La Quemada, Zacatecas. American Antiquity 60:597–618.

Nichols, Deborah L., and Thomas H. Charleton, 1997 The Archaeology of City-States: Cross-Cultural Approaches. Washington, DC: Smithsonian Institution Press.

O'Connor, David, 1993 Urbanism in Bronze Age Egypt and Northeast Africa. *In* The

Archaeology of Africa: Food, Metals and Towns. Thurstan Shaw, Paul Sinclair, Bassey Andah, and Alex Okpoko, eds. pp. 570–586. London: Routledge.

Pearce, Maj. F. B., 1967[1920] Zanzibar: The Island Metropolis of Eastern Africa. London: Frank Cass.

Pikirayi, Innocent, 1993 The Archaeological Identity of the Mutapa State: Towards an Historical Archaeology of Northern Zimbabwe. Uppsala: Societas Archaeologica Upsaliensis.

——2001 The Zimbabwe Culture: Origins and Decline of Southern Zambezian States. Walnut Creek, CA: AltaMira Press.

Possehl, Gregory L., 1998 Sociocultural Complexity without the State: The Indus Civilization. In Archaic States. Gary M. Feinman and Joyce Marcus, eds. pp. 261–291. Santa Fe, NM: School of American Research.

Prins, A. H. J., 1961 The Swahili-Speaking Peoples of Zanzibar and the East African Coast: London, International African Institute.

——1971 Didemic Lamu: Social Stratification and Spatial Structure in a Muslim Maritime Town. Groningen: Instituut voor Culturele Antropologie der Rijksuniversiteit.

Randall-MacIver, David, 1906 Medieval Rhodesia. London: Macmillan.

Rautman, Alison E., 1998 Hierarchy and Heterarchy in the American Southwest: A Comment on McGuire and Saitta. American Antiquity 63:325–334.

Robertshaw, Peter, 1990 A History of African Archaeology: An Introduction. In A History of African Archaeology. Peter Robertshaw, ed. pp. 3–12. London: James Currey.

Sanders, William T., and David Webster, 1988 The Mesoamerican Urban Tradition. American Anthropologist 90:521–546.

Schmidt, Peter R., and Matthew C. Curtis, 2001 Urban Precursors in the Horn: Early 1st-Millennium BC Communities in Eritrea. Antiquity 75(290):849–859.

Schwartz, Glenn M., and Steven E. Falconer, eds., 1994 Archaeological Views from the Countryside: Village Communities in Early Complex Societies. Washington, DC: Smithsonian Institution Press.

Sinclair, Paul J. J., 1987 Space, Time and Social Formation: A Territorial Approach to the Archaeology and Anthropology of Zimbabwe and Mozambique c. 0–1700 AD. Uppsala: Societas Archaeologica Upsaliensis.

Sinclair, Paul J. J., and Thomas Håkansson, 2000 The Swahili City-State Culture. In A Comparative Study of Thirty City-State Cultures. Mogens H. Hansen, ed. pp. 463–482. Copenhagen: The Royal Danish Academy of Sciences and Letters.

Sinclair, Paul J. J., Thurstan Shaw, and Bassey Andah, 1993a Introduction. In The Archaeology of Africa: Food, Metals and Towns. Thurstan Shaw, Paul Sinclair, Bassey Andah and Alex Okpoko, eds. pp. 1–31. London: Routledge.

Sinclair, Paul J. J., Innocent Pikirayi, Gilbert Pwiti, and Robert Soper, 1993b Urban Trajectories on the Zimbabwean Plateau. In The Archaeology of Africa: Food, Metals and Towns. Thurstan Shaw, Paul Sinclair, Bassey Andah, and Alex Okpoko, eds. pp. 705–731. London: Routledge.

Sjoberg, Gideon, 1960 The Preindustrial City. Glencoe, IL: Free Press.

Smith, Monica L., 2003 Introduction: The Social Construction of Ancient Cities. In The Social Construction of Ancient Cities. Monica L. Smith, ed. pp. 1–36. Washington, DC: Smithsonian Institution Press.

Spear, Thomas, 1984 The Shirazi in Swahili Traditions, Culture, and History. History in Africa 11:291–305.

Spencer, Herbert, 1974 The Evolution of Society: Selections from Herbert Spencer's Principles of Sociology. Robert L. Carneiro, ed. Chicago: University of Chicago Press.

Stahl, Ann B., 1999 Perceiving Variability in Time and Space: The Evolutionary Mapping of

African Societies. *In* Beyond Chiefdoms: Pathways to Complexity in Africa. Susan K. McIntosh, ed. pp. 39–55. Cambridge: Cambridge University Press.

Steward, Julian, 1955 Theory of Culture Change. Bloomington: University of Indiana Press.

Taylor, Donna, 1975 Some Locational Aspects of Middle-Range Hierarchical Societies. Ph.D. dissertation, City University of New York.

Thorp, Carolyn R., 1995 Kings, Commoners and Cattle at Zimbabwe Tradition Sites. Memoir 1 (NS). Harare: National Museums and Monuments of Zimbabwe.

Togola, Téréba, 1996 Iron Age Occupation in the Méma Region, Mali. African Archaeological Review 13:91–110.

Trigger, Bruce G., 1972 Determinants of Urban Growth in Preindustrial Cities. *In* Man, Settlement, and Urbanism. Peter Ucko, Ruth Tringham, and George W. Dimbleby, eds. pp. 575–600. London: Duckworth.

——1989 A History of Archaeological Thought. Cambridge: Cambridge University Press.

——1993 Early Civilizations: Ancient Egypt in Context. Cairo: American University in Cairo.

Ucko, Peter, Ruth Tringham, and George W. Dimbleby, eds., 1972 Man, Settlement, and Urbanism. London: Duckworth.

Vogt, Evon Z., and Richard M. Leventhal, eds., 1983 Prehistoric Settlement Patterns: Essays in Honor of Gordon R. Willey. Albuquerque: University of New Mexico Press.

Weber, Max, 1958 The City. New York: Free Press.

Webster, David, 1997 City-States of the Maya. *In* The Archaeology of City-States: Cross Cultural Approaches. D. Nichols and T. H. Charlton, eds. pp. 135–154. Washington, DC: Smithsonian Institution Press.

Wenke, Robert J., 1989 Egypt: Origins of Complex Societies. Annual Review of Anthropology 18:129–155.

Wheatley, Paul, 1972 The Concept of Urbanism. *In* Man, Settlement and Urbanism. Peter. J. Ucko, Ruth Tringham, and George W. Dimbleby, eds. pp. 601–637. London: Duckworth.

Willey, Gordon R., 1953 Prehistoric Settlement Patterns in the Virú Valley, Perú. Bulletin 155. Washington, DC: Bureau of American Ethnology.

Wilson, Thomas H., 1982 Spatial Analysis and Settlement on the East African Coast. Paideuma 28:201–220.

Winters, Christopher, 1983 The Classification of Traditional African Cities. Journal of Urban History 10(1):3–31.

Wirth, Louis, 1938 Urbanism as a Way of Life. American Journal of Sociology 44(1):1–24.

Wright, David, 2002 Filling in the Gaps: The Pastoral Neolithic of Tsavo. Paper presented at the Biennial Meeting of the Society of Africanist Archaeologists, Tucson.

Wright, Henry T., 1977 Recent Research on the Origins of the State. Annual Review of Anthropology 6:379–397.

——1993 Trade and Politics on the Eastern Littoral of Africa, AD 800–1300. *In* The Archaeology of Africa: Food, Metals and Towns. Thurstan Shaw, Paul Sinclair, Bassey Andah, and Alex Okpoko, eds. pp. 658–672. London: Routledge.

Wright, Henry T., and Gregory A. Johnson, 1975 Population, Exchange, and Early State Formation in Southwestern Iran. American Anthropologist 77:267–289.

Yoffee, Norman, 1997 The Obvious and the Chimerical: City-States in Archaeological Perspective. *In* The Archaeology of City-States: Cross-Cultural Approaches. D. L. Nichols and T. H. Charlton, eds. pp. 255–263. Washington, DC: Smithsonian Institution Press.

14

Interaction, Marginalization, and the Archaeology of the Kalahari

Andrew Reid

The picture is evocative. A man (invariably a man) stands in a slightly stooped pose, body taut, arrow slung and bow drawn, concentrating intently on an unseen prey. He stands in a flat, scrubby environment, dotted perhaps with an occasional bush, and invariably with sand underfoot. The man is clad only in a skin loincloth. He may wear a few ornaments, but he bears no signs of modern life as we know it. This image of man in nature suggests a timeless quality, one unencumbered by the concerns and vagaries of agricultural routines, political regimes, financial targets, or labor markets. This is man stripped bare, reduced to his most basic components. In him we may imagine our inner, biological core.

This stereotypical image of life in the Kalahari belongs to the world of the tourist postcard and is constantly reaffirmed in popular culture. Peruse tourist brochures for destinations in Botswana, Namibia, and South Africa and you will see that these unpatented stereotypes are worth millions (e.g., Buntman 1996). Valuable though they may be to national economies in terms of tourism revenue, the stereotypical image is also used by governments to validate the systematic marginalization and denial of basic rights to the peoples on whom the image was based. All of these uses of the stereotype rely on assumptions regarding the archaeological past, an assumption created without recourse to archaeological evidence. The stereotype assumes that these populations lived undisturbed and unchanged in the Kalahari for thousands of years. Most importantly, the stereotype is not simply manufactured in popular culture; it has been, and to some extent is still, cherished by academics. Anthropologists and archaeologists rely on such images to create their frameworks for understanding past societies, using these images of hunter-gatherers as the foundation on which to build understandings of global prehistory (Shott 1992). If Africa was the epitome of the barbaric "other" (Chapter 2), the hunter-gatherer populations of the Kalahari provided the foundation on which this image was constructed. While this volume makes abundantly clear that archaeologists no longer subject Africa to this degradation, the first peoples of the Kalahari continue to be perceived as remnants of a distant past. Thus, investigations of early hominids routinely make direct reference to modern hunter-gatherer populations, from the Kalahari and elsewhere, in attempts to understand what happened in the past (e.g., Bartram et al. 1991; Binford 1988; Brain 1981; Bunn 1983; Freeman 1981; Monahan 1998; O'Connell et al. 1988; cf. Schrire 1984; Shott 1992). In some cases there is a clear implication that these peoples are in some way inferior to postmodern urban society. Explicitly or not, these modern populations have long been considered to be living relics of the past. Clearly such views are dehumanizing and insulting. In the context of the Kalahari it would also appear that they are highly inaccurate.

Recent interest in Kalahari hunter-gatherer populations originated in the 1950s. Popular interest was encouraged by people such as Laurens van der Post (e.g., 1958), who claimed to have discovered unknown peoples. Academic interest in the Kalahari was stimulated by the film-making and ethnography of the Marshalls in the 1950s (e.g., Marshall 1956). Interest flowed from a belief that these societies were a throwback to the ancient human hunter-gatherer past. These initial encounters sparked an interest which ultimately led to *Man the Hunter* (Lee and DeVore, eds., 1968), one of the most fundamental contributions to recent anthropology and archaeology, a volume that enshrined the specific importance of Kalahari populations within anthropological inquiry. Of particular significance was the idea that hunter-gatherer lifestyles were relatively easy to sustain because of the diverse resource base they could access. Hunter-gatherer societies were shown to be broadly egalitarian and often dependent on gathering and fishing rather than hunting, which revealed a greater role for women in basic living strategies. This was a novel perception, which contrasted markedly with the generally perceived notion that male-dominated hunter-gatherer societies lived an extremely difficult life, constantly struggling to acquire food and avoid starvation, with no leisure time in which to create culture (Sahlins 1968:85). Hence, *Man the Hunter* demonstrated the inadequacy of previous understandings of human society which assumed that farming would automatically replace hunting and gathering because of its obvious benefits. It was out of this background that the Harvard Kalahari Research Group emerged, involving individuals such as Richard Lee, John Yellen, and Polly Wiessner, promoting what might be called an evolutionary ecological model of the Kalahari. These, and other scholars working independently in the 1970s, explored a range of different aspects of Kalahari societies (e.g., Lee, 1979, 1984; Lee and DeVore 1976; Silberbauer 1981; Wiessner 1983; Yellen 1976, 1977); however, the initial motivation for each project appears to have been the same, if not always openly stated as such. Here were populations who replicated past lifeways and needed to be studied as quickly as possible before they were swamped by modernity. In some instances, this motive was explicitly stated:

> even nowadays many still live a life of hunting and gathering away from the influences of modern civilisation, relying on "Stone Age" subsistence techniques. . . . The fact that a group of people with a population of several thousand is still living in the same fashion as human societies of almost 10 000 years ago is a miracle, although it can also

illustrate the disadvantages of living in the Kalahari Desert, fit neither for cultivation of plants not for domestication of animals. This kind of San existence offers important information about the daily life of early man, and can be an aid in the reconstruction of his society and the evolution of human society. (Tanaka 1980:xi–xii)

Lee (1982:55) subsequently explored the internal dynamics of !Kung society, emphasizing that their productive and political systems represented a form of "primitive communism." As one of his informants, /Twi!gum, stated when discussing decision-making, "we are all headmen" (Lee 1982:50). Nevertheless, this focus on "primitive communism" betrayed a continuation of the notions that underwrote the initial research – it provided the most basic counterpoint to capitalism. Thus, at least implicitly, there was an emphasis on what modern society had become since it stopped being hunter-gatherer, and the specific histories of Kalahari societies were in some way coincidental to the main purpose of study.

In the late 1970s one strand of anthropological research in the Kalahari in conjunction with archaeology produced a new model for the historical development of Kalahari societies, known as the Revisionist school (e.g., Gordon and Douglas 2000; Wilmsen 1989; Wilmsen and Denbow 1990). This revision required viewing the Kalahari and its inhabitants in terms of political economy. Hunter-gatherer societies were not isolated by absence of contact, but rather were marginalized by political processes which had been operating in the broader region over many centuries. As a result of their writings, an acrimonious and undignified academic confrontation occurred, generally termed the Kalahari debate (e.g., Lee and Guenther 1991, 1995; Solway and Lee 1990; Wilmsen 1993; Wilmsen and Denbow 1990; and see also Kuper 1993; Shott 1992). This chapter reviews the substance of the Kalahari debate and considers some of its ramifications for academics and for the inhabitants of the Kalahari and its margins. In particular, the chapter explores archaeological views implicitly assumed and/or generated by academic discourse.

The Empty Kalahari

The Kalahari is a vast expanse of sand which stretches from northwestern parts of South Africa, through most of Botswana and eastern Namibia, into southernmost Angola (Figure 14.1). It is by no means the most extreme of deserts; in geographical terms it is designated semi-arid, having a mean annual rainfall of 200 mm. However, ubiquitous flat sands mean that surface water is fleeting after rains. Hence, the name "Kgalagadi" in Setswana, which means the great dryness, or thirst.

The initial premise upon which much of the original anthropological and ethnoarchaeological work was based was that the Kalahari represented an untouched island inhabited by populations who had not encountered modernity. For anthropologists, here was human society at its most basic: from a socio-evolutionary perspective the bottom rung of the ladder, the "basic human adaptation" (Leacock and Lee 1982:5); from Marxian perspectives the "original affluent society" (Sahlins 1968:85) before ownership, personal status, and greed. Decision-making was

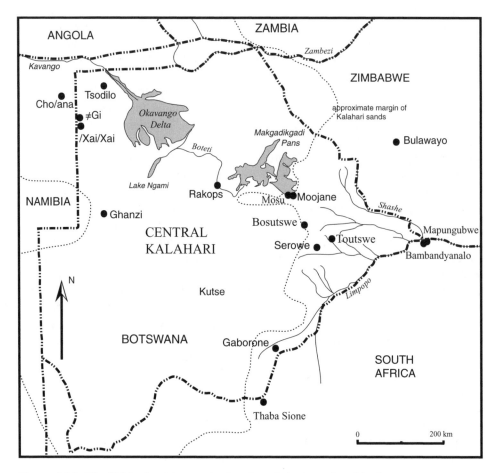

Figure 14.1. The Kalahari and its margins: location of sites mentioned in the text

communal, meat from hunting was shared, and they depended heavily on female food-collection strategies. They represented an ideal and unproblematic world, which, as an opposition, informed and fed perceptions of how modern societies constructed themselves. Thus, Leacock and Lee (1982:1) began *Politics and History in Band Societies* by declaring that the book "deals with a set of questions which are vital to our understanding of ourselves as human beings." As they subsequently suggested, anthropologists, in challenging the assumption that

> the behavior patterns of Western culture reflect basic "human nature" . . . have been particularly interested in learning more about the behavior of peoples in societies that are structured along cooperative lines, by contrast with the competitive structure of capitalism. That people have lived and therefore can live cooperatively contradicts a common assertion that humans are innately too aggressive and competitive to be capable of socialism. (Leacock and Lee 1982:2)

Ethnoarchaeological research on these populations (Lane 1998) was inspired by a similar premise. Motivated by developments in archaeological theory in the 1960s, archaeologists recognized the need for ethnographically grounded models as aids in interpreting archaeological remains (e.g., Binford 1967, 1968; Yellen 1977; Yellen and Harpending 1972). While Kalahari populations were not necessarily regarded as historical relics in this view, they were believed to share common processes and forms of behavior with past archaeological communities.

The means of verifying the connection and the strength of inference that could be made from studying contemporary foraging societies was considered to be potentially problematic. To counter this Yellen sought to combine his ethnoarchaeological insights with Brook's archaeological investigations in northwestern Botswana to establish a direct comparison. Thus at =Gi they could claim to be able to test their ethnoarchaeological models against long-term human habitation of the Kalahari.

> The Dobe group were used to develop a testable model of the relationship between activity organization in space and archaeological site formation for foraging groups. This model was then tested against the archaeological record of more than 80 000 years of occupation in the northwest Kalahari area. (Brooks and Yellen 1987:66)

Within this essentially evolutionary approach they also employed a short-term historical perspective to consider hunter-gatherer campsites, using informants to identify habitations abandoned over the previous 50 years (Brooks 1978, 1984). However, in this and other anthropological and ethnoarchaeological writing, the Kalahari populations were clearly treated as timeless object rather than historical subject. In other words Kalahari populations were incidental to the overall research theme. The significance of these studies was never to understand or investigate these populations in themselves, but to use them to tell us more about the general human condition, as constructed by Western academic traditions.

In sum, everything that makes hunter-gatherers historically distinct was to be ignored. Anthropological and archaeological inquiry was premised on a notion of a Kalahari empty but for hunter-gatherer populations. This may explain why some scholars have so vociferously defended the integrity of these populations – that is their validity as a general object of study which can be used to inform on hunter-gatherers in distant times. As Vansina (1990:516) noted, the revisionist critiques of the Kalahari "undermine the basis of any comparative anthropology, based on sociocultural evolutionary theory, and force us to reconsider the premises on which a sound comparative anthropology must be built." Similar concerns had been raised by Lévi-Strauss as early as 1966 at the *Man the Hunter* conference: "we cannot consider them as belonging to a semi-animal condition of mankind. Yet at the same time, I noticed a strong temptation to call upon recent studies of primates – monkeys and apes – or even studies of lesser animals such as rodents to explain, for example, the existence of a territorial instinct in Australian aborigines" (Lévi-Strauss 1968:349). Lévi-Strauss concluded that "certainly we should not try to use these recent hunter gatherers to reconstruct events and conditions in the prehistory of mankind" (1968:350). Missing from the above examples were attempts to place these populations in broader contexts of time, change, and history. Even where dating was discussed, the perception was one of timelessness and a lack of change. A perceived need for historical perspectives drove new strands of research on the Kalahari and demanded the historical incorporation of Kalahari peoples.

Peoples of the Kalahari

In the absence of archaeological evidence, archaeologists writing about the region sustained the notion of the empty Kalahari. Phillipson (1969:35) noted that "the available evidence suggests that most of Botswana was occupied largely, if not exclusively, by hunting gathering peoples of Late Stone Age stock until very recent times." In retrospect, this position was hardly surprising. By 1970, only two sites had been excavated in Botswana, a country almost the size of Texas (Campbell 1998). Fewer than 200 sites were known in the country at this time. Interpretations of this archaeological record were therefore largely extensions of phenomena seen in neighboring countries, particularly South Africa and what was then Rhodesia (now Zimbabwe) (e.g., Cooke 1979). It was in the context of an assumed and/or borrowed archaeology that concerted archaeological research began in Botswana in the 1970s and, in part, the revisionist model of the Kalahari emerged from this work. The new model also arose from the general theoretical demand for greater circumspection and critique of historical constructs. It was recognized that, while European expansion and the development of global systems greatly influenced the course of recent history, this necessarily meant that other, non-Western histories needed to be recognized and generated (Wolf 1982). As Wilmsen (1989:xii) observed, "No peoples – no matter how far they may seem removed from the rest of the world – have been so remote as to have escaped participation in the economic forces swirling around them." For Wilmsen the diverse human contexts of the Kalahari "have been treated in ethnographies as if they had only tenuous ties to each other. Those whom anthropologists have labeled hunter-gatherer or forager ('Bushman' or San in the southern African context) have been further removed in administrative and academic placement, assigned to a subperipheral sphere barely visible from any center" (Wilmsen 1989:xii).

The revisionist model, therefore, essentially contended that all Kalahari hunter-gatherer societies were the product of historical relationships in which they were increasingly marginalized (Wilmsen, 1989). In the mid- to late 19th century, European mercantile capital penetrated deep into the Kalahari. Dominant agropastoralist communities, particularly Tswana polities, benefited from this and strengthened their influence across the Kalahari. While this economic situation persisted, there were certain advantages in practicing a hunter-gatherer lifestyle and providing the raw materials for the trade – which was principally in animal products. When this trade collapsed, however, at the end of the 19th century, the hunter-gatherer lifestyle was difficult to sustain. Therefore, in the revisionist view, the 20th-century hunter-gatherer societies subject to such extensive ethnographic study were seen as the product of late 19th- and early 20th-century interactions, which forced them to choose between servitude as herders at Tswana cattle posts or fleeing to the central Kalahari where they could only survive in the sands of the Kalahari by hunting and gathering. On account of these processes it became necessary to question the forager mode of production models produced by Kalahari ethnographies. Furthermore, Wilmsen (1989:158–271) believed that these societies were considerably less egalitarian than previously assumed.

Far from being discovered in the 1950s, the peoples of the Kalahari had long been known to Europeans. Related societies had been encountered at the Cape of Good Hope when the Portuguese first passed on their way to the Indies in 1498. Archaeology at the Cape has explored the early stages of interaction between Europeans and the indigenous population (Schrire 1988, 1995; Smith 1993). From these early times the indigenous populations were constructed as the "other" (see Butchart 1998). Human subjects drawn from southern Africa were publicly displayed and studied, first live, but increasingly in autopsies of the dead. In the early 19th century Sara Baartman, "the Hottentot Venus," was publicly displayed in London and Paris while she was alive; after her death she was dissected and her body parts displayed until very recently in the Musée de l'Homme, Paris (Strother 1999). Her body was finally returned to South Africa for burial in May 2002. Another indigenous southern African, El Negro of Banyoles, was an unidentified man whose body was stolen from his grave immediately after burial around 1830 by French anatomists, and then sold, stuffed, and displayed in Banyoles, Spain, until it was taken to Botswana for burial in October 2000 (Parsons and Segobye 2002). From the early 19th century, intellectuals in Europe were therefore clearly aware of the people of the Kalahari and its margins (Barnard 1999; Wilmsen 1989:12–22) and indeed this process of classification and display stimulated the socio-evolutionary constructs of the likes of Spencer, Tylor, and Morgan which are still so influential today (Chapter 1).

Certainly in the broadest terms it could be argued that these evolutionary views differ little from the disciplinary foundations of the Kalahari research of the 1960s and 1970s (Barnard, 1999). Such Victorian attitudes increasingly colored the way in which living populations were perceived by academics and by members of general society who created and molded government policy. One colonial official in Uganda with a keen anthropological interest described living populations as "leading an existence no higher in culture than that of the predatory carnivorous man in the lowest Stone Age" (Johnston 1902:214).

It was in the context of these socio-evolutionary perspectives and racial science that the South African Museum in Cape Town embarked on a process of taking casts of living people who represented "nearly extinct races" (Davison 2001). These casts were made of "Bushmen," often prison inmates, between 1907 and 1924. The figures produced from the casts were then displayed without context or discussion, and indeed became a major attraction for tourists and schoolchildren alike. Hence, by the 1950s, far from being isolated, these indigenous populations of southern Africa had been robbed of their land, hunted, captured, killed, displayed, measured, dissected, marginalized, and disparaged for over 300 years (Gordon and Douglas 2000; Wilmsen 1989).

But who exactly might we be talking about? Naming these populations has been intentionally avoided, so as not to lead the reader. Much of the terminology used to refer to so-called hunter-gatherers is problematic or inappropriate (see Wilmsen 1989:26–32; Chapter 6). Indeed, it can be argued that the very search for an appropriate nomenclature is part of the process whereby ethnography "authenticates the creation of a 'primitive' opposition to our 'civilized' world" (Wilmsen 1989:xiii). No single name is recognized by all the different, formerly hunter-gatherer, peoples that we are trying to subsume here. "Bushmen" from Dutch, "San" in Nama, and "Basarwa" in Setswana are all derogatory terms. Various attempts have been made to rehabilitate and ennoble "San" and "Bushmen," but these terms have not been unanimously taken up, either by the people themselves or by academics. As this problem with nomenclature suggests, there are other populations in the Kalahari who have had an important bearing on matters. And archaeological evidence has established that these other societies have long been present on the margins of the Kalahari. This is in marked contrast to the image of the empty Kalahari in which Bantu-speaking peoples (Chapter 12) were believed to have only settled on the margins in the last few hundred years. In part this perception was linked to colonial notions of the late arrival of Bantu-speaking peoples in southern Africa (Gawe and Meli 1990; Lane et al. 1998; Marks 1980).

Archaeological research from the late 1970s has established that the margins of the Kalahari were, over a long period of time, far from empty. On the eastern margins of the Kalahari, Denbow (1979) recognized that ancient middens, associated principally with what archaeologists labeled the Toutswe tradition, were colonized by a single grass type, which then showed up as distinctive light patches on aerial photographs. Hence, Denbow (1984a) was able to document several hundred sites, trebling the number of known sites in the whole of Botswana in a very short period of time. Denbow suggested that the middens were cattle dung formations, and that midden size would indicate numbers of cattle and, by association, political status. The latter association drew on ethnographic and anthropological studies of the Central Cattle Pattern in southern African societies, in which cattle ownership was manipulated to heighten status through acquisition of wives, patron–client arrangements, and gifts (Huffman 1990, 1998; Kuper 1982). Denbow then defined a hierarchical pattern of site distribution, with many small, short-lived settlements, a few medium-sized regional centers, and three major sites (Denbow 1984a, 1986). While the clarity of this hierarchical structure has been shown to be much less pronounced than Denbow originally suggested (Reid and Segobye 2000), there are certainly marked population concentrations and centers on the eastern margins of the Kalahari between A.D. 900 and 1300. These centers were clearly linked to major towns further east at the confluence of the Limpopo and Shashe Rivers (Chapter 15). First Bambandyanalo (K2) and then Mapungubwe were the original centers for the trade in gold and other commodities between the interior and the Indian Ocean coast. Toutswe tradition sites contain small amounts of pottery from these centers, as well as imported glass beads obtained through the Indian Ocean trade, though in much smaller quantities than the centers of the Limpopo–Shashe confluence. Toutswe Tradition sites cannot, however, simply be seen as offshoots of

Limpopo-Shashe society, and their success must also have been linked to their ability to access resources in the west. Certainly livestock would have been important, and the location of Toutswe sites would have enabled them to make use of the grassy Kalahari sands during the wet season, conserving the rocky terrain of the east for the dry winters. But livestock are unlikely to have been the only factor.

It is important to recognize that the Kalahari is not all sand (Thomas and Shaw 1991). In its northern reaches a finger of sandstone extends westwards, creating perennial springs from the water that it catches, and enabling safe movement of people and stock into the Kalahari. This finger acts as a barrier to an even more amazing phenomenon – water flowing from the sand in the west. Rainfall in far-away Angola flows into the Kavango River, which disperses into the flat sands of the Okavango Delta, a huge expanse of shallow water within the Kalahari itself. Before greatly increased groundwater exploitation began around 1980, the surge from each new rainy season in Angola, would, several months later, lead to over-flow in the Okavango and flooding in the Thamalakane and Boteti channels. In the latter case, the water surged on, creating a "miraculous landscape" as described by Passarge in 1896 (Wilmsen, ed., 1997:47) encompassing "the light green masses of reed, the blue strip of water inhabited by countless waterfowl such as sandpipers, herons, ducks, and geese, enlivened from time to time by the canoes of black fishermen or the black heads of playing hippopotamuses lifting in and out of the water."

The waters of the Boteti, constrained by the flat landscape and the sandstone finger emanating from the east, eventually fan out into the basin of the Makgadikgadi paleoloake and evaporate. There is, therefore, a relatively straightforward route across the northern wastes of the Kalahari. It is perhaps not surprising, then, that evidence for farming communities has been found around the eastern and southern margins of the Makgadikgadi Pans (Denbow 1999; Reid and Segobye 2000), at the southern margins of the Okavango Delta (Denbow 1990), and as far west as the Tsodilo Hills (Denbow 1990, 1999). The latter, which in 2001 became Botswana's first designated World Heritage Site, is a series of four prominent hills surrounded by the sands of the Kalahari and situated some 50 km from the Kavango River. Archaeological research has documented a seemingly continuous 70,000-year occupation of the hills until recent times by hunter-gatherer societies (Robbins et al. 1994). The walls of the hills feature more than 4,000 individual rock art images, most of which suggest a preoccupation with a hunter-gatherer lifestyle (Walker 1998). Most importantly, there are also several farming sites dating to between the seventh and 12th centuries A.D. (Denbow 1990). These are not simply dispersed and isolated settlements. There are glass beads present, attesting participation in the Indian Ocean trade. These communities also manufactured metalwork, particularly jewelry, in copper and iron (Miller 1996; Miller and van der Merwe 1994). The copper had to have come from at least 200 km away, the nearest source of copper ore being in Zambia (Denbow 1990). Thus, by as early as perhaps the eighth century, there was a major network of farming communities extending deep into the Kalahari. Denbow (1990) produced a very interesting graphic model of trade systems into the Kalahari featuring an array of different commodities, although it is based on little actual archaeological evidence.

Besides this floruit towards the end of the first millennium A.D., recent archaeological research has also established the presence of early farming communities
dating from around the fifth century in southeastern (Campbell et al. 1996), eastern
(Denbow 1986), and northeastern Botswana (Denbow and Wilmsen 1986). After
the Toutswe tradition (ending ca. a.d. 1300), there is some evidence of decline in
population, but Zimbabwe Tradition occupation (Chapters 13, 15) occurred in the
later phases at Bosutswe (Denbow 1999) and is also present in the Makgadikgadi
Pans (Denbow 1999; Reid and Segobye 2000). From around a.d. 1700 onwards
there appears to have been a significant increase in populations on the eastern
margins of the Kalahari, culminating in the major Tswana polities of the 19th
century (Reid et al. 1997). These Tswana communities had gradually developed a
network of agricultural settlements and livestock posts extending out into the Kalahari, making use of seasonally available resources. On account of these connections,
Tswana communities were therefore well placed to profit from increased European
commercial interest in the Kalahari, acting as middlemen between Kalahari hunters
and European traders. The former could be cajoled into providing products and
the latter needed little encouragement not to have to venture into the Kalahari
themselves. The principal commodities were ivory and ostrich feathers. Ostrich
feathers may not immediately conjure up the same emotive images as ivory, and
they are unlikely to survive as archaeological debris, but they were nonetheless
significant and were evidently supplied in great quantity both from southern Africa
and in trans-Saharan trade (Newbury 1966). As an example of their consumption,
for instance, US Infantry dress hats for all ranks in the mid-19th century featured
ostrich-feather brocades (Todd 1980:62).

Politics of the Kalahari

By the late 19th century a number of European travelers, missionaries, and traders
had penetrated deep into the Kalahari along several well-established routes in addition to the Makgadikgadi–Boteti corridor. Notably, from Livingstone's accounts
(e.g., 2001[1857]) onwards, the Kalahari is a place where people were encountered
with surprising regularity. Accounts from this period shed some light on the
societies they encountered and underscore the dire plight of San or Bushmen
communities.

> The contest for the possession of certain villages of Bakalahari or Bushmen is a fruit-
> ful source of strife in Bechwana towns. . . . When one Bechwana tribe attacks another,
> the Bushmen and Bakalahari belonging to both are placed in the same category with
> cattle and sheep – they are to be "lifted" or killed as opportunity offers. (Mackenzie
> 1883:62–63)

These communities had become servants of Tswana overlords, men either used
to keep Tswana cattle, or sent off to secure hunted products to be given as tribute,
with women retained as concubines. When the missionary Hepburn visited the

Tswana in northwestern Botswana in 1886 and requested permission to preach to the underclass, their chief, Moremi, declared in anger that God "do what He would, should never prevent them from killing Masarwa and Makoba forever" (Hepburn, quoted in Landau 1995:144). Masarwa is the singular form of Basarwa, and the use of the singular implies people who have no status; people who are not people.

By the end of the 19th century therefore, the remnants of the hunter-gatherer populations living in the Kalahari were reviled by Europeans, whose science saw them as the lowest form of humanity, and by fellow Africans, who regarded them as objects for exploitation. Into the 20th century this picture hardly improved, and these populations were disregarded as a people heading for socio-evolutionary oblivion (e.g. Makin 1929:278). Hence, the hunter-gatherer communities studied from the 1950s could hardly be regarded as newly discovered or pristine. Indeed, this point has been recognized by some of those individuals involved in the research.

> But these things we ignored, relatively speaking, because we didn't come all the way round the world to see them. We could have stayed near home and seen people behaving as rural proletariat, while nowhere but the Kalahari and a few other remote locations allow a glimpse of "the hunting and gathering way of life." So we focus upon bush camps, upon hunting, upon old fashioned customs, and although we remind each other once in a while not to be romantic, we consciously and unconsciously neglect and avoid the !Kung who don't conform to our expectations. (Howell, quoted in Wilmsen 1989:35–36)

In Place of Stereotypes

Arguably, one of the problems with both models of Kalahari life presented above is that they imply singular patterns of identity, interaction, and activity. Yet these populations have no sense of common identity, and there are marked distinctions between different hunter-gatherer societies (Kent 1992, 1996), as indeed there are between different farming communities. It seems entirely likely that, given the geographical dispersal, time depth, and diversity of populations, there have been different forms of interaction between hunter-gatherers and farmers over time.

Opponents of the Revisionist model of the Kalahari have argued that the model assumes only one form of interaction between farmers and hunter-gatherers: encapsulation (Kent 1998:16; Sadr 1997). These detractors have rather simplistically argued that Denbow and Wilmsen believe that the presence of a few exotic items in a hunter-gatherer assemblage is adequate proof that the population has entirely forsaken its cultural repertoires and values and has adopted elements of the dominant society. This argument has generated some interesting lines of enquiry, which have helped move the Kalahari debate on from its original dogma. In particular, Sadr (1997), working from the view that encapsulated societies should display a marked transformation in material culture, has reviewed the archaeological evidence from a range of sites with LSA technologies across Botswana over the last 2,000 years. He argues that there are no marked changes in stone tool assemblages until perhaps the 17th century. Although Sadr was reluctant to draw this conclusion, this time frame correlates reasonably with the establishment of Tswana polities in Botswana.

Smith and Lee (1997) undertook a novel research strategy to identify non-encapsulated hunter-gatherer populations. Focusing on the NyaeNyae-Dobe area of Namibia in which Lee had previously worked, a dual archaeological and ethno-historical perspective was adopted. Interviews with informants in the area today helped to identify potential long-standing archaeological habitation locations and to reconstruct local Ju/'hoãnsi history. Documents of 19th-century travelers who had passed nearby were consulted to establish where they had gone, what they had been doing, and whom they had seen. Finally excavation was undertaken at Cho/ana, a location known to be important in living memory for *hxaro*, long-distance, kinship-based, reciprocal exchange transactions (Chapter 6). Perhaps not surprisingly, they concluded that there was no evidence of direct contact with agriculturalists or encapsulation in this area. Hence, it can be argued that some populations in isolated locations within the Kalahari have been free to determine their own lifestyle, have chosen to be hunter-gatherers, and are, therefore, representative of pristine hunter-gatherer lifestyles.

Despite these innovative developments and new perspectives on the Kalahari, a number of points of disagreement remain. These are: the significance and integrity of cattle teeth found at /Xai/Xai and whether these can be taken to represent the presence of herders in the NyaeNyae-Dobe area 1,000 years ago (Wilmsen 1988; Yellen and Brooks 1988, 1990); the impact of an obvious dichotomy between "Stone Age" and "Iron Age" archaeologists, how this mitigates against the recognition of interaction between hunting and farming populations, and the significance of "Iron Age" archaeologists' not having attempted an archaeological survey in the remotest locations of the Kalahari (Denbow 1999; Wilmsen and Denbow 1990); the exact coverage of European traders/travelers and of trade networks across the northwestern Kalahari in the late 19th century; and the precise processes of interaction and their likely archaeological manifestations. Of more general concern is that archaeologists who accept the Revisionist stance work in "Iron Age" contexts, while those who reject it work on the "Stone Age" (cf. Chapter 6).

The overriding focus on encapsulation by critics of the revisionist model of the Kalahari has served to entirely overlook the very important issue of interactions that have taken place at least on the fringes of the Kalahari over the last 2,000 years (Denbow 1984b). In the difficult conditions of the Kalahari, populations must have been highly mobile and capable of identifying and moving to available resources. In this context, it is inconceivable that hunter-gatherers would have no form of contact, direct or indirect, with societies on the margins of the Kalahari. The emphasis on encapsulation and its archaeological manifestations makes the unfortunate suggestion that material objects are more important than ideas and social systems, an interpretation that does not sit well in the context of recent developments in archaeological theory. Another important lesson to be learned from the above debates is how archaeologists subconsciously order and categorize the archaeological record based on the material they encounter. As Denbow (1999) notes, it is all too easy for archaeologists to slip into the assumption that sites dominated by stone tools were inhabited by hunter-gatherer peoples and that sites with pottery were occupied by farmers. Subconsciously a leap can then be made to ethnicize these economic activities. Clearly, from a general theoretical perspective, there is no *a priori* reason why such a dichotomy should be assumed.

This ambiguity was well illustrated by work conducted by the University of Botswana in the Mosu area in 1998 (Reid and Segobye 1999, 2000). One site featured a series of walled enclosures stretching more than a kilometer along a hidden river valley, 5 km south of Sowa pan. The settlement included vitrified dung middens and assumed grain bin platforms, indicating a full-fledged farming community. Tswana informants in the general area identify this broad location as the birth place of Khama III, probably the most important Tswana political figure in the late 19th and early 20th centuries, who molded the shape of modern Botswana. Our investigations began the process of surveying and excavating the site to confirm this designation. As part of this process, oral interviews were conducted, and it was suggested that a nearby Khoisan-speaking community might be able to help us. These informants pointed out that this was not a Tswana settlement, but rather a location occupied by their ancestors together with a community of Kalanga farmers who were fleeing aggressive Kololo incursions further to the east, suggesting a mid-19th-century date. The place became known as Moojane, meaning "What shall we eat?" in iKalanga and indicating the contribution that the Khoisan-speaking community made in helping the Kalanga community to identify food resources in the strange pan-edge environment. At the same time, once the settlement was established, the Kalanga community taught the Khoisan speakers to farm and to keep livestock. This occupation was expressed in idyllic terms, in deliberate contrast to subsequent events. The Bangwato, the most powerful Tswana polity, pushed its dominance into this area in its continuous search to identify and control new sources of pasture, water, and arable land on the margins of the Kalahari. The multi-ethnic community at Moojane was broken up, the Kalanga being chased further west to Rakops, from which they were subsequently removed in the 1940s and 1960s. The Khoisan-speaking community at Moojane was forced onto Bangwato cattle posts, around which they remain today, unpaid and under-privileged.

The example of Moojane could be used in various ways to support different viewpoints within the entrenched Kalahari debate, but that is not the concern here. Moojane quite clearly indicates that archaeologists must take care to consider the possibility of multi-ethnic populations within the sites that they investigate, and need to consider means by which multiple ethnicities might be recognized. A potentially useful step along these lines has been the identification of distinct patterns of ostrich eggshell bead sizes at different sites, and particularly combinations of sizes at large settlements (Reid and Segobye 2000; Tapela 2001).

Elsewhere Khoi herders were known to dominate the Boteti/Lake Ngami area in the 18th and 19th centuries (Reid et al. 1998). However, it also needs to be recognized that shifts in activity need not only have been from hunter-gatherer to farmer, simple to complex. In the Makgadikgadi area Livingstone describes "our old friends the Bushmen" being "at least six feet high, and of a darker colour than the Bushmen of the south" (Livingstone 2001:190). Farming populations could therefore change to hunting and gathering, and there was no necessary correlation between physical appearance and economic activity. Perhaps all that we can safely say is that, certainly by the 18th and 19th centuries, and quite possibly earlier, an incredibly complex range of interactions was taking place between different populations in and around the Kalahari. Archaeology and anthropology must endeavor to explore this complexity. While more nuanced approaches to the archaeology of the Kalahari have been developed, the attraction of simplistic analogy remains. One recent research initiative has ignored the historical context of the Kalahari to use contemporary populations around the major town of Serowe as a model for farmer–forager interactions in the Early European Neolithic (Fewster 1999).

Current Representations of Archaeology

The Kalahari debate has highlighted the interaction and marginalization of Kalahari populations. Yet this debate has been centered in Western academia without engaging people in southern Africa. As a consequence, inadequacies in the treatment of hunter-gatherer populations have continued; preconceptions regarding the "primitive" nature of these populations were merely confirmed by the work of the 1960s and 1970s. In Botswana, hunter-gatherers are presently considered by the urban Tswana population an embarrassment who should be forced to live like other people. "How can you have a Stone Age creature continue to exist in the age of computers?" commented Festus Mogae, shortly before he became president of Botswana in 1997: "if the Bushmen want to survive, they must change or otherwise, like the dodo, they will perish" (Daley 1996). This perception is perhaps encouraged among the general public for political ends. These peoples have long been actively denied basic land rights. The Tribal Grazing Land Policy was used to create designated pastures, but heavily favored the major Tswana polities (Biesele and Royal-/O/oo 1999; Hitchcock 1999a; Hitchcock and Ebert 1989; Tanaka and Sugawara 1999). This policy denied land rights to hunter-gatherers since they were perceived to have no land needs: they moved in an open range. They were considered to be mobile, and the lands which they exploited in their annual range were perceived to be unused. No attempt was made either to allow these societies to change their lifestyle or to explore how hunter-gatherers regulate range use. Subsequently, they were allocated the Central Kalahari Game Reserve as their own personal concern, since it was perceived to have no value, being barren, sand-filled land.

The vast array of anthropological and ethnoarchaeological work that took place in the 1960s and 1970s had further important impacts. The Botswana government perceived, understandably so, that there was an unnecessary focus by anthropologists working within the country on these hunter-gatherer populations, who represent a small minority within the country. The nature of this focus is demonstrated by a bibliography of all archaeological publications on Botswana, published before 1999 (van Waarden 1999). Archaeological publications featuring Botswana date back as early as 1892, but were initially sporadic, averaging one or two publications per decade. Publications greatly increased from the late 1960s, and particularly in the 1980s and 1990s, as archaeology was established as a discipline within Botswana. A significant 13 percent of all the archaeological publications produced about Botswana are ethnoarchaeological, and all of those publications focus entirely, or in part, on hunter-gatherer peoples who make up around 3 percent of the national population. This is an unusually high focus and one that has had considerable ramifications for practicing archaeological research in Botswana. In general research in Botswana is encouraged and, indeed, for national institutions it is considered to be part of their general remit which requires no permission. Archaeology, on the other hand, is considered to fall under the Anthropological Research Act 1967, which requires all research proposals, national or international, to be submitted to, and cleared by, the Office of the President. In part this is related to fears concerning the promotion of ethnicity which pervaded early independence policy in Botswana, politicians being worried about the impact that such a focus might have on the fledgling nation. Similar concerns led to the lack of government support for the National Museum in Gaborone in its first six years of existence between 1968 and 1974 (Pule 1998). Subsequently, however, it has become clear that politicians have been using this reticence toward anthropological research and considerations of ethnicity in general to mask the unequal distribution of wealth that emerged as the Botswana economy rapidly developed over the past 30 years. Power and wealth is concentrated in select hands, particularly the elite of the main Tswana polities. Power has led to the control of land rights, favoring certain individuals and elite polities over more marginalized communities. Since Kent (pers. comm., 1997) was refused permission to continue work at Kutse in the late 1990s, there has been a proliferation of court cases involving individual cattle-owners encroaching on the Kutse area and also fencing off key water sources. Indeed the sensitivity towards further investigations of these populations was such that, in the 1990s, it was perceived that any archaeological proposal that showed a concern with modern hunter-gatherer populations would not be given research clearance. Hence, the anthropological and ethnoarchaeological work, and to a certain extent the Kalahari debate, have all had a major negative impact on the development of archaeology as a discipline within Botswana.

A final problem is that archaeological research has had little impact on generally held notions of the archaeological past. Despite the active participation of archaeologists from South Africa and Botswana in the last decade, general perceptions of the archaeological past have largely remained the same. Mazel (1993) has shown how perceptions of hunter-gatherer populations in KwaZulu Natal over the last 200 years changed from extermination, through denial, to romance. Extinct populations, of course, offer little threat and it is perhaps in this context that a now extinct Khoisan language, /Xam, has been incorporated, together with a modified rock art image, into the new South African coat of arms (Smith et al. 2000). There are still, however, localized situations in South Africa where populations are still at odds, such as Tswana resistance around Schmidtsdrift to the resettlement of Khoisan-speaking communities who had served with the South African military in

Angola and Namibia (Ouzman 1995). In this context, authorship of rock art images at Thaba Sione, some of which were almost certainly made by hunter-gatherer populations, was appropriated by Tswana populations in generating contemporary politics and access to land.

The "Bushmen" casts at the South African Museum, mentioned above, have become the source of a major debate (Davison 2001). Faced with changing perspectives on hunter-gatherer society emerging from the 1950s, some of the castes were incorporated into a diorama, purporting to represent a campsite, complete with ethnographic artifacts. Subsequently, slight changes were made, for instance clothing the individuals and giving them an early 19th-century date, as a reaction to increasing criticism of the diorama. After the end of apartheid, the efficacy of the diorama itself has been questioned (Lane 1996; Skotnes, ed., 1996). Objectors point to the location of the diorama (along with material relating to other African societies) in the Natural History Museum rather than the South African Cultural History Museum, which was for "white" culture. It is only "Bushmen" who were subjected to public display in the form of casts, perpetuating 19th-century stereotypes of their social segregation. However to underscore the ambiguities and difficulties behind resolving the representation of indigenous pasts, indigenous groups support retaining the diorama in order to raise public awareness of their issues (Davison 2001). In April 2001 the diorama was boarded up pending a process of consultation whereby relevant interest groups would be involved in planning its future and how, if at all, appropriate use could be made of the diorama and its contents.

Meanwhile, in Botswana, the general perception is still that the Kalahari was essentially empty prior to the arrival of the Tswana polities (Lane et al. 1998). Indeed, one development resulting from the growth in archaeological practice in Botswana has been to suggest that Tswana populations in the past may have appropriated imagery and symbolism from neighboring regions, especially Zimbabwe, and hence distinct cultural traditions can be claimed to be Tswana, thus establishing an earlier Tswana presence in the landscape (Tsheboeng 2001). At the same time the government of Botswana disarms the term indigenous by arguing, not unreasonably, that all African populations in Botswana are indigenous to the country and so no population can be granted special status. This apparent homogeneity in visions of the past and present serves to mask the unequal distribution of resources in the country.

New Uses of Archaeology

Clearly, Khoisan-speaking populations have been an object rather than a subject of academic interest. But archaeological perspectives are now, at last, being used by former and current hunter-gatherer populations to represent their own interests. In the 1990s the Botswana government reversed its previous policies of settlement in the Central Kalahari Game Reserve, arguing instead that these populations should be provided with settlements in areas where resources, such as water, health, and education could be made available (Hitchcock 1996, 1999b; Tanaka and Sugawara 1999). Forced movements have ensued as water supplies to Central Kalahari communities have been withdrawn and there have been physical threats and beatings. Besides the promise of a better location and of the gift of livestock at the new settlement, none of which seem to have been forthcoming, the Botswana government has argued that these populations now pose a threat to wildlife. This partly reflects the recent shift in exploiting the Central Kalahari as a tourist destination, but it is widely believed that the overriding factor is the discovery of diamonds within the Central Kalahari. By forcing populations to move, the government can avoid paying compensation for mineral exploitation. In fighting these trends, these communities and their supporters have begun to incorporate archaeological perspectives in their rhetoric.

> The San Bushmen – the indigenous people of southern Africa – are Africa's oldest inhabitants, having lived in the region for over twenty-five thousand years. Throughout history they thrived in one of the most hostile environments in the world, living as semi-nomadic hunter gatherers in the arid areas of Angola, Botswana, Namibia and South Africa. Well known for their rich legacy of rock art that can be found leaping off the walls of mountain ranges across the continent, the San have strong cultural traditions that until recently remained relatively untouched. (Sanscapes 2003)

The website for the Working Group for Indigenous Minorities of Southern Africa (WIMSA) similarly proclaims that "the San are the aboriginal people of Southern Africa. Their distant hunter-gatherer culture stretches back over 20 000 years" (Working Group for Indigenous Minorities of Southern Africa 2003). In addition to such generalized stances, there are also more specific statements tying these communities to the Central Kalahari itself, and importantly these have been adopted by the people themselves.

> My name is Kuela Kiema. I come from the western part of Botswana, from the Ghanzi District. Our forefathers have been living for thousands of years in the eastern part of the Ghanzi District. . . . I was living in the Kalahari Desert where life was free for us until we were told it was a game reserve. (Singleton 2003)

It is unfortunate that no archaeological (as opposed to ethnoarchaeological) investigation has been undertaken in the Central Kalahari to support this assertion. In large part this has been for the very good reason that it would appear to be a huge expanse of barren sand, in which any sites that may have existed would be rapidly buried. These statements completely ignore the notion of interaction and change in and around the Kalahari and are also factually in error. But perhaps we should endorse the essence of these statements as they represent uses of the past by people most closely associated with that past.

> They say it is our ancestors who made the many rock paintings all over southern Africa. I believe it, although I have seen only some of these many paintings. The ones that I have seen illustrate things that I know so well from our culture. Yes, I believe the San

made it. *I feel it in my body. I do not see myself as just another artist. Being an artist is my heritage.* (DADA (Coex'ae Qgam) 2000)

The Kalahari, then as now, was not empty and has been contested for more than a thousand years. But perhaps the important point to highlight is that the populations of the Kalahari have now become the subject of discussion rather than mute objects. Also these statements discussing antiquity of tradition are semantically rooted in the present: rather than "*still* living" as past societies did (Tanaka 1980:xi), in these recent statements these societies "*are* Africa's oldest inhabitants" and, as Kuela Kiema above says, "our forefathers *have been* living for thousands of years" in the Kalahari (emphasis added throughout).

The Future of the Kalahari's Past

The Kalahari debate has exposed a number of problems in the way anthropology operates. A fundamental difficulty is that any attempt to generate cross-cultural models of human societies necessarily places Kalahari hunter-gatherers towards, if not at, the bottom of the scale. This is because they are hunter-gatherers and because hunting and gathering is the earliest economic strategy displayed by anatomically modern humans. Archaeologists considering a cross-cultural approach need to decide whether this invalidates the whole initiative or whether it is possible to maneuver theoretically around such an issue. In considering the Kalahari debate, both arguments hold merit and have their strengths as well as weaknesses. It is instructive to look at the comments presented by two leading academics. Trigger (1990), well known for his exposition of historical materialism, is committed to an evolutionary view of society that enables the explanation of cultural variation. He is clearly unnerved by what he considers the prospect of returning to a historical particularist stance which the work of the 1960s and 1970s had rejected. On the other hand, Vansina (1990), an African historian with deep linguistic and anthropological roots, is dismissive that anything other than the "evident truth" of a historicized account can adequately explain the present-day position of Kalahari, or any other, forager societies. Perhaps more important than this academic discourse is the point that neither argument in the Kalahari debate, despite some novel approaches to engagement, has actually managed to include indigenous populations in its discourse or change the perception of such societies by ruling political elites. It is indeed troubling that such extensive literary efforts should have had virtually no obvious relevance to their host populations.

The cyclical nature of anthropological theory and the changing relationship between archaeology and ethnology over the last 200 years has been noted and solutions have been suggested on how to break this cycle within Western academic traditions (e.g., Shott 1992; Trigger 1990). Indeed, it is ironic that Lee himself referred to his own writing as "a 'revisionist' account" (1979:433) countering extant preconceptions regarding hunting and gathering societies. However, Barnard (1999:382) does not believe such cycles will ultimately be broken until foragers themselves can enter the academic debate: "when the day comes that foragers, or their grandchildren, read the works of Hobbes, Rousseau, and Marx, which, if any, will they cite?"

The future must clearly see the incorporation of Kalahari societies into the direction of these debates. Archaeology can make a significant contribution in ensuring a more interactive and inclusive vision of the past. To do this archaeologists must recognize the need for much more sensitive considerations of ethnicity and political interactions within settlements. Clearly, culture-historical emphasis on material culture will not suffice, but the whole nature of investigation and the strategies undertaken will need to be changed and investigated. A multi-ethnic approach also needs to be adopted in the public dissemination of research within the region. We can hope that the declaration of the Tsodilo Hills as Botswana's first World Heritage Site (in 2001) will be used to promote an appropriately multi-ethnic perspective on the Kalahari. Such a perspective must encourage the inhabitants of the Kalahari today to recognize the multitude of cultural influences on their past, but that can only be done if they are offered equable status and rights within nation-states. Archaeology has a great potential role in developing understanding and communication between communities, but the process by which this might be achieved is by no means straightforward. The more that populations can be encouraged to engage with archaeology, and in particular with current academic understandings, the more readily it should become evident that compromise is necessary. And one of the biggest jobs now is to get general anthropology and archaeology to recognize the damage they do by continuing to perpetuate static stereotypes. The Kalahari is surely an outstanding case study whereby Western academic traditions have failed to intertwine their research initiatives with the needs of indigenous populations. The past in the Kalahari must be a rich weave of different hunter-gatherer, herder, and farmer populations in the different niches of the Kalahari and the different political systems that have extended their influence across the sands.

Postscript – A Vision of the Future

As this chapter was being completed an intriguing and somewhat ironic story was developing which may point the way to future perceptions of the peoples of the Kalahari (Mangold 2003). South African scientists analyzed the Hoodia, a cactus-like desert plant, after learning that Kalahari populations consume it in order to suppress hunger during long hunting trips. The scientists discovered a molecule which convinces the brain to stop eating. Clinical tests are now under way to see if this can be used to treat obesity in Western societies, and it has belatedly been recognized that royalties should be paid to South African San communities should commercial production result. Thus can the West benefit by recognizing and respecting the value of indigenous knowledge systems, while Kalahari communities may be able to alleviate their poverty. Rather than alienating Kalahari societies in opposition to Western society, the peoples of the Kalahari should be recognized as sources of alternative and compatible knowledge systems.

REFERENCES

Barnard, Alan, 1999 Images of Hunters and Gatherers in European Social Thought. *In* The Cambridge Encyclopedia of Hunters and Gatherers. R. B. Lee and R. Daly, eds. pp. 375–383. Cambridge: Cambridge University Press.

Bartram, Laurence E., Ellen M. Kroll, and Henry T. Bunn, 1991 Variability in Camp Structure and Bone Food Refuse Patterning at Kua San Hunter-Gatherer Camps. *In* The Interpretation of Archaeological Spatial Patterning. Ellen M. Kroll and T. Douglas Price, eds. pp. 77–148. New York: Plenum Press.

Biesele, Megan, and Kxao Royal-/O/oo, 1999 The Ju/'hoãnsi of Botswana and Namibia. *In* The Cambridge Encyclopedia of Hunters and Gatherers. Richard B. Lee and Richard Daly, eds. pp. 205–209. Cambridge: Cambridge University Press.

Binford, Lewis R., 1967 Smudge Pits and Hide Smoking: The Use of Analogy in Archaeological Reasoning. American Antiquity 32:1–12.

—— 1968 Methodological Considerations of the Archaeological Use of Ethnographic Data. *In* Man the Hunter. Richard B. Lee and Irven DeVore, eds. pp. 268–273. Chicago: Aldine.

—— 1988 Fact and Fantasy about the Zinjanthropus Floor: Data, Arguments and Interpretations. Current Anthropology 29:123–135.

Brain, C. K., 1981 The Hunters or the Hunted? An Introduction to African Cave Taphonomy. Chicago: University of Chicago Press.

Brooks, Alison S. 1978 A Note on the LSA Features at =Gi: Analogies from Historic San Hunting Practices. Botswana Notes and Records 10:1–3.

—— 1984 San Land-Use Patterns Past and Present: Implications for Southern African Prehistory. *In* Frontiers: Southern African Archaeology Today. Martin Hall, Graham Avery, D. M. Avery, M. L. Wilson, and A. J. B. Humphreys, eds. pp. 40–52. BAR International Series, 207. Oxford: British Archaeological Reports.

Brooks, Alison S., and John E. Yellen, 1987 The Preservation of Activity Areas in the Archaeological Record: Ethnoarchaeological and Archaeological Work in Northwest Ngamiland, Botswana. *In* Method and Theory for Activity Area Research: An Ethnoarchaeological Approach. Susan Kent, ed. pp. 63–106. New York: Columbia University Press.

Bunn, Henry T., 1983 Comparative Analysis of Modern Bone Assemblages from a San Hunter-Gatherer Camp in the Kalahari Desert, Botswana, and from a Spotted Hyaena Den near Nairobi, Kenya. *In* Animals and Archaeology, vol. 1: Hunters and their Prey. Juliet Clutton-Brock and Caroline Grigson, eds. pp. 143–148. BAR International Series, 163. Oxford: British Archaeological Reports.

Buntman, B., 1996 Bushman Images in South African Tourism Advertising: The Case of Kagga Kamma. *In* Miscast: Negotiating the Presence of the Bushmen. Pippa Skotnes, ed. pp. 271–279. Cape Town: University of Cape Town Press.

Butchart, Alexander, 1998 The Anatomy of Power: European Constructions of the African Body. London: Zed.

Campbell, Alec C., 1998 Archaeology in Botswana: Origins and Growth. *In* Ditswa Mmung: The Archaeology of Botswana. Paul J. Lane, Andrew Reid, and Alinah K. Segobye, eds. pp. 24–49. Gaborone: Pula Press/Botswana Society.

Campbell, Alec C., Catrien van Waarden, and Grunilla Holmberg, 1996 Variation in the Early Iron Age of Southeastern Botswana. Botswana Notes and Records 28:1–22.

Cooke, Cran K., 1979 The Stone Age in Botswana: A Preliminary Survey. Arnoldia 8:1–32.

DADA (Coex'ae Qgam), 2000 Kuru Kalahari. Electronic document, <www.africaserver.nl/kuru/english/index2.html>, accessed June 27, 2003.

Daley, Suzanne, 1996 Botswana Is Pressing Bushmen To Leave Reserve. New York Times, July 14, sect. 1, p. 3.

Davison, Patricia, 2001 Typecast. Representations of the Bushmen at the South African Museum. Public Archaeology 2:3–20.

Denbow, James R., 1979 Cenchrus ciliaris: An Ecological Indicator of Iron Age Middens Using Aerial Photography in Eastern Botswana. South African Journal of Science 75:405–408.

——1984a Cows and Kings: A Spatial and Economic Analysis of a Hierarchical Early Iron Age Settlement System in Eastern Botswana. In Frontiers: Southern African Archaeology Today. Martin Hall, Graham Avery, D. M. Avery, M. L. Wilson, and A. J. B. Humphreys, eds. pp. 24–39. BAR International Series, 207. Oxford: British Archaeological Reports.

——1984b Prehistoric Herders and Foragers of the Kalahari: The Evidence for 1500 Years of Interaction. In Past and Present in Hunter-Gatherer Studies. Carmel Schrire, ed. pp. 175–194. Orlando: Academic Press.

——1986 A New Look at the Later Prehistory of the Kalahari. Journal of African History 27:3–28.

——1990 Congo to Kalahari: Data and Hypotheses about the Political Economy of the Western Stream of the Early Iron Age. The African Archaeological Review 8:139–176.

——1999 Material Culture and the Dialectics of Identity in the Kalahari: AD 700–1700. In Beyond Chiefdoms: Pathways to Complexity in Africa. Susan Keech McIntosh, ed. pp. 110–123. Cambridge: Cambridge University Press.

Denbow, James R., and Edwin N. Wilmsen, 1986 Advent and Course of Pastoralism in the Kalahari. Science 234:1509–1515.

Fewster, Kathryn J., 1999 Basarwa and Bamangwato Interaction: A View from Above. In Making Places in the Prehistoric World: Themes in Settlement Archaeology. J. Brück and M. Goodman, eds. pp. 178–197. London: Routledge.

Freeman, Leslie G., 1981 The Fat of the Land: Notes on Palaeolithic Diet in Iberia. In Omnivorous Primates: Gathering and Hunting in Human Evolution. Robert S. O. Harding and Geza Teleki, eds. pp. 104–165. New York: Columbia University Press.

Gawe, Stephen, and Francis Meli, 1990 The Missing Past in South African History. In The Excluded Past: Archaeology in Education. Peter Stone and Robert Mackenzie, eds. pp. 98–108. London: Unwin Hyman.

Gordon, Robert J., and Stuart S. Douglas, 2000 The Bushman Myth: The Making of a Namibian Underclass. 2nd edition. Colorado: Westview Press.

Hitchcock, Robert K., 1996 Botswana's Decision to Relocate People of the Central Kalahari Game Reserve: Consumers or Genocide? Indigenous Affairs 3(96):44–47.

——1999a The Tyua of Northeastern Botswana and Western Zimbabwe. In The Cambridge Encyclopedia of Hunters and Gatherers. Richard B. Lee and Richard Daly, eds. pp. 225–230. Cambridge: Cambridge University Press.

——1999b A Chronology of Major Events Relating to the Central Kalahari Game Reserve. Botswana Notes and Records 31:105–117.

Hitchcock, Richard K., and James I. Ebert, 1989 Modeling Kalahari Hunter-Gatherer Subsistence and Settlement Systems: Implications for Development Policy and Land Use Planning in Botswana. Anthropos 84:47–62.

Huffman, Thomas N., 1990 Broederstroom and the Origins of Cattle-Keeping in Southern Africa. African Studies 49(2):1–12.

——1998 The Antiquity of Lobola. South African Archaeological Bulletin 53:57–62.

Johnston, Sir Harry H., 1902 The Uganda Protectorate. London: Hutchinson.

Kent, Susan, 1992 The Current Forager Controversy: Real versus Ideal Views of Hunter Gatherers. Man 27:45–70.

—— 1996 Cultural Diversity among African Foragers: Causes and Implications. *In* Cultural Diversity among Twentieth-Century Foragers: An African Perspective. Susan Kent, ed. pp. 1–18. Cambridge: Cambridge University Press.

—— 1998 Gender and Prehistory in Africa. *In* Gender in African Prehistory. Susan Kent, ed. pp. 9–21. Walnut Creek, CA: AltaMira Press.

Kuper, Adam, 1982 Wives for Cattle: Bridewealth and Marriage in Southern Africa. London: Routledge & Kegan Paul.

—— 1993 Post-modernism, Cambridge and the Great Kalahari Debate. Social Anthropology 1:57–71.

Landau, P. S., 1995 The Realm of the Word. London: James Currey.

Lane, Paul J., 1996 Breaking the Mould? Exhibiting Khoisan in Southern African Museums. Anthropology Today 12(5):3–10.

—— 1998 Ethnoarchaeological Research – Past, Present and Future. *In* Ditswa Mmung: The Archaeology of Botswana. Paul J. Lane, Andrew Reid, and Alinah K. Segobye, eds. pp. 177–205. Gaborone: Pula Press/Botswana Society.

Lane, Paul J., Andrew Reid, and Alinah K. Segobye, 1998 Introduction. *In* Ditswa Mmung: The Archaeology of Botswana. Paul J. Lane, Andrew Reid, and Alinah K. Segobye, eds. pp. 13–19. Gaborone: Pula Press/Botswana Society.

Leacock, Eleanor, and Richard B. Lee, 1982 Introduction. *In* Politics and History in Band Societies. Eleanor Leacock and Richard B. Lee, eds. pp. 1–20. Cambridge: Cambridge University Press.

Lee, Richard B., 1979 The !Kung San: Men, Women and Work in a Foraging Society. Cambridge: Cambridge University Press.

—— 1982 Politics, Sexual and Non-Sexual, in an Egalitarian Society. *In* Politics and History in Band Societies. Eleanor Leacock and Richard B. Lee, eds. pp. 37–60. Cambridge: Cambridge University Press.

—— 1984 The Dobe !Kung. New York: Harcourt Brace.

Lee, Richard B., and Irven DeVore, eds., 1968 Man the Hunter Chicago: Aldine.

—— 1976 Kalahari Hunter-Gatherers: Studies of the !Kung San and their Neighbors. Cambridge, MA: Harvard University Press.

Lee, Richard B., and Mathias Guenther, 1991 Oxen or Onions? The Search for Trade [and Truth] in the Kalahari. Current Anthropology 32:592–601.

—— 1995 Errors Corrected or Compounded? A Reply to Wilmsen. Current Anthropology 36:298–305.

Lévi-Strauss, Claude, 1968 The Concept of Primitiveness. *In* Man the Hunter. Richard B. Lee and Irven DeVore, eds. pp. 349–352. Chicago: Aldine.

Livingstone, David, 2001[1857] Missionary Travels and Researches in Africa. Santa Barbara: Narrative Press.

Mackenzie, John, 1883 Day Dawn in Dark Places. London: Cassel.

Makin, William J., 1929 Across the Kalahari Desert. London: Arrowsmith.

Mangold, Tom, 2003 Sampling the Kalahari Cactus Diet. Electronic document, <http://news.bbc.co.uk/1/hi/programmes/correspondent/2947810.stm>, accessed June 10, 2003.

Marks, S., 1980 South Africa. "The Myth of the Empty Land." History Today 30(1):7–12.

Marshall, John, 1956 The Hunters [16 mm film]. Cambridge, MA: Film Study Center of the Peabody Museum, Harvard University.

Mazel, Aron, 1993 Changing Fortunes: 150 Years of San Hunter-Gatherer History in the Natal Drakensberg, South Africa. Antiquity 66:758–767.

Miller, Duncan E., 1996 The Tsodilo Jewellery: Metal Work from Northern Botswana. Cape Town: University of Cape Town Press.

Miller, Duncan E., and Nicholas J. van der Merwe, 1994 Early Iron Age Metal Working at the Tsodilo Hills, Northwestern Botswana. Journal of Archaeological Science 21:101–116.

Monahan, Christopher M., 1998 The Hadza Carcass Transport Debate Revisited and its Archaeological Implications. Journal of Archaeological Science 25:405–424.

O'Connell, James F., Kristen Hawkes, and Nicholas Blurton-Jones, 1988 Hadza Hunting, Butchering and Bone Transport and their Archaeological Implications. Journal of Anthropological Research 44(2):113–161.

Newbury, C. W., 1966 North Africa and Western Sudan Trade in the Nineteenth Century: A Re-evaluation. Journal of African History 7:233–246.

Ouzman, Sven, 1995 Spiritual and Political Uses of a Rock Engraving Site and its Imagery by San and Tswana-Speakers. South African Archaeological Bulletin 50:55–67.

Parsons, Neil, and Alinah K. Segobye, 2002 Missing Persons and Stolen Bodies: The Repatriation of "El Negro" to Botswana. In The Dead and their Possessions: Repatriation in Principle, Policy and Practice. Cressida Fforde, Jane Hubert, and Paul Turnbull, eds. pp. 245–255. London: Routledge.

Phillipson, David W., 1969 Early Iron Using Peoples of Southern Africa. African Societies in Southern Africa. L. Thompson, ed. pp. 24–49. London: Heinemann.

Pule, Tickey, 1998 Archaeology and Museums. In Ditswa Mmung: The Archaeology of Botswana. Paul J. Lane, Andrew Reid, and Alinah K. Segobye, eds. pp. 240–248. Gaborone: Pula Press/Botswana Society.

Reid, Andrew, Paul J. Lane, Alinah K. Segobye, Lowe Borjeson, Nonofo Mathibidi, and Princess Sekgarametso, 1997 Tswana Architecture and Responses to Colonialism. World Archaeology 28(3):96–118.

Reid, Andrew, Karim Sadr, and Nicholas Hanson-James, 1998 Herding Traditions. In Ditswa Mmung: The Archaeology of Botswana. Paul J. Lane, Andrew Reid, and Alinah K. Segobye, eds. pp. 81–100. Gaborone: Pula Press/Botswana Society.

Reid, Andrew, and Alinah K. Segobye, 1999 The Archaeology of the Makgadikgadi Pans, Botswana. Unpublished paper presented at the 4th World Archaeological Congress, Cape Town.

——— 2000 Politics, Society and Trade on the Eastern Margins of the Kalahari. In The Limpopo Valley – The Last 2000 Years. Mary Leslie and Tim Maggs, eds. pp. 58–68. Goodwin Series, 8. Cape Town: South African Archaeological Society.

Robbins, Lawrence H., Michael L. Murphy, Kathlyn M. Stewart, Alec C. Campbell, and George A. Brook, 1994 Barbed Bone Points, Paleoenvironment, and the Antiquity of Fish Exploitation in the Kalahari Desert, Botswana. Journal of Field Archaeology 21:257–264.

Sadr, Karim, 1997 Kalahari Archaeology and the "Bushman Debate." Current Anthropology 38:104–112.

Sahlins, Marshall, 1968 Notes on the Original Affluent Society. In Man the Hunter. Richard B. Lee and Irven DeVore, eds. pp. 85–89. Chicago: Aldine.

Sanscapes, 2003 Sanscapes – Bushman Tribal Rhythms Meet Urban Grooves. In Aid of the Bushmen of Southern Africa. Electronic document, <http://www.melt2000.com/projects/sanscapes/san_history.html>, accessed June 27, 2003.

Schrire, Carmel, 1984 Wild Surmises on Savage Thoughts. In Past and Present in Hunter Gatherer Studies. Carmel Schrire, ed. pp. 1–25. Orlando: Academic Press.

——— 1988 The Historical Archaeology of the Impact of Colonialism in 17th-Century South Africa. Antiquity 62:214–225.

——1995 Digging Through Darkness: Chronicles of an Archaeologist. Charlottesville: University of Virginia Press.

Shott, Michael J., 1992 On Recent Trends in the Anthropology of Foragers: Kalahari Revisionism and its Archaeological Implications. Man 27:843–871.

Silberbauer, George, 1981 Hunter and Habitat in the Central Kalahari Desert. Cambridge: Cambridge University Press.

Singleton, Iona 2003 Tribal Voices: The Bushmen of the Kalahari. Electronic document, <www.kindredspirit.co.uk/articles/5740_kalahari.asp>, accessed June 27, 2003.

Skotnes, Pippa, ed., 1996 Miscast: Negotiating the Presence of the Bushmen. Cape Town: University of Cape Town Press.

Smith, Andrew B., 1993 Different Facets of the Crystal: Early European Images of the Khoikhoi at the Cape, South Africa. In Historical Archaeology in the Western Cape. Martin Hall and A. Markell, eds. pp. 8–20. Goodwin Series, 7. Cape Town: South African Archaeological Society.

Smith, Andrew B., and Richard B. Lee, 1997 Cho/ana: Archaeological and Ethnohistorical Evidence for Recent Hunter-Gatherer/Agropastoralist Contact in Northern Bushmanland, Namibia. South African Archaeological Bulletin 52:52–58.

Smith, Benjamin, J. David Lewis-Williams, Geoffrey Blundell, and Christopher Chippendale, 2000 Archaeology and Symbolism in the New South African Coat of Arms. Antiquity 74:467–468.

Solway, Jacqueline S., and Richard B. Lee, 1990 Foragers, Genuine or Spurious? Situating the Kalahari San in History. Current Anthropology 31:109–146.

Strother, Z. S., 1999 Display of the Body Hottentot. In Africans on Stage. Studies in Ethnological Show Business. Bernth Lindfors, ed. pp. 1–61. Bloomington: Indiana University Press.

Tanaka, Jiro, 1980 The San Hunter Gatherers of the Kalahari. D. Hughes, trans. Tokyo: Tokyo University Press.

Tanaka, Jiro, and Kazuyoshi Sugawara, 1999 The /Gui and //Gana of Botswana. In The Cambridge Encyclopedia of Hunters and Gatherers. Richard B. Lee and Richard Daly, eds. pp. 195–199. Cambridge: Cambridge University Press.

Tapela, Milton, 2001 An Archaeological Examination of Ostrich Eggshell Beads in Botswana. Pula: Botswana Journal of African Studies 15(1):70–81.

Thomas, David S. G., and Paul A. Shaw, 1991 The Kalahari Environment. Cambridge: Cambridge University Press.

Todd, F. P., 1980 American Military Equipage 1851–1872. New York: Scribners.

Trigger, Bruce, 1990 Comment on "Foragers, Genuine or Spurious? Situating the Kalahari San in History" by Jacqueline S. Solway and Richard B. Lee. Current Anthropology 31:134–135.

Tsheboeng, Alfred, 2001 Late Iron Age Human Responses and Contribution to Environmental Change in the Shashe-Limpopo River Basin, North Eastern Botswana. In People, Contacts and the Environment in the African Past. Felix Chami, Gilbert Pwiti, and Chantal Radimilahy, eds. pp. 124–128. Dar es Salaam: DUP.

van der Post, Laurens, 1958 The Lost World of the Kalahari. London: Hogarth.

Vansina, Jan, 1990 Comment on "Paradigmatic History of San-Speaking Peoples and Current Attempts at Revision" by Edwin N. Wilmsen and James R. Denbow. Current Anthropology 31:516.

van Waarden, Catrien, 1999 The Prehistory and Archaeology of Botswana: An Annotated Bibliography. Gaborone: Botswana Society.

Walker, Nicholas, 1998 Botswana's Prehistoric Rock Art. In Ditswa Mmung: The Archaeology of Botswana. Paul J. Lane, Andrew Reid, and Alinah K. Segobye, eds. pp. 206–232. Gaborone: Pula Press/Botswana Society.

Wiessner, Polly, 1983 Style and Social Information in Kalahari San Projectile Points. American Antiquity 48:253–276.

Wilmsen, Edwin N. 1988 The Antecedents of Contemporary Pastoralism in Western Ngamiland. Botswana Notes and Records 20:29–39.

—— 1989 Land Filled With Flies. Chicago: University of Chicago Press.

—— 1993 On the Search for (Truth) and Authority: A Reply to Lee and Guenther. Current Anthropology 34:715–721.

Wilmsen, Edwin N., ed., 1997 The Kalahari Ethnographies (1896–1898) of Siegfried Passarge. Gaborone: Botswana Society.

Wilmsen, Edwin N., and James R. Denbow, 1990 Paradigmatic History of San-Speaking Peoples and Current Attempts at Revision. Current Anthropology 31:489–524.

Wolf, Eric R., 1982 Europe and the People without History. Berkeley: University of California Press.

Working Group for Indigenous Minorities of Southern Africa, 2003 Home of the Southern African San. Electronic document, <http://www.san.org/za/>, accessed June 27, 2003.

Yellen, John E. 1976 Settlement Patterns of the !Kung: An Archaeological Perspective. In Kalahari Hunter-Gatherers: Studies of the !Kung San and their Neighbors. Richard B. Lee and Irven DeVore, eds. pp. 47–72. Cambridge, MA: Harvard University Press.

—— 1977 Cultural Patterns in Faunal Remains: Evidence from the !Kung Bushmen. In Experimental Archaeology. Daniel Ingersoll, John E. Yellen, and William MacDonald, eds. pp. 271–331. New York: Columbia University Press.

Yellen, John E., and Alison Brooks, 1988 The Late Stone Age Archaeology of the !Kangwa and /Xai/Xai Valleys, Ngamiland. Botswana Notes and Records 20:5–27.

—— —— 1990 The Late Stone Age Archaeology in the /Xai/Xai Region: A Response to Wilmsen. Botswana Notes and Records 22:17–19.

Yellen, John. E., and Henry Harpending, 1972 Hunter-Gatherer Populations and Archaeological Inferences. World Archaeology 4(2):244–253.

15

Southern Africa and the East African Coast

Gilbert Pwiti

This chapter examines the evidence for early contact and relations between south-ern Africa and the East African coast, and the impact of such relations on the com-munities of southern Africa. The period to be surveyed begins about a.d. 700, as it is from about this time that we begin to have evidence of contacts between south-ern Africa and the coast, and ends at about the 18th century A.D. During this period, southern African communities, particularly on the Zimbabwean plateau, witnessed a number of important cultural developments, including the rise and decline of complex state systems. The period covered falls within what has been termed the Iron Age in southern and eastern Africa, a technological term which has generally been used to describe a culture system characterized not only by the use of iron for various purposes, but also the building of semi-permanent villages, the making of similarly decorated ceramic vessels (at least before a.d. 1000) and an economic system based on agriculture and the herding of domestic animals. After about a.d. 700 a new element in the economy is seen in the form of participation in external trading networks.

The Archaeological Background

The evidence that has accumulated over several years of research in southern Africa strongly suggests that the Iron Age, which is associated with the establishment of settled farming communities in the region, dates from around the second century a.d. (Hall, 1987; Huffman 1970; Phillipson 1976, 1977, 1985; Soper 1971, 1982). Most researchers now accept that this new cultural system, which seems to be intrusive among the Late Stone Age societies of the region, can be explained most convincingly in terms of population movements from further north (Collett 1982; Huffman 1970; Maggs 1984; Phillipson 1977, 1985; Soper 1971, 1982), though disagreement and uncertainty remain on the nature of the movements or indeed their area of origin. Some have even gone so far as to question whether there were any population movements at all. For example, Chami (1999) has argued that the migrationist model is faulty and reminiscent of what Garlake (1982) labeled a settler colonialist paradigm in the interpretations of the African past. However, it is not the intention of this chapter to engage in the debate on the origins of Iron Age cultures of southern and eastern Africa, but rather to note that, from the time at which this culture system becomes evident in the archaeological record, the communities associated with it underwent a number of social, economic, political, and cultural changes. In this chapter, I examine how these changes took place and how they can be explained in the context of relations between the region and the East African Indian Ocean coast.

It should be noted from the outset that due account must be taken of the limitations of available evidence. Archaeological research has been unevenly distributed in southern Africa, both in time and space, a problem that confronts the researcher throughout the African continent. At present, although there has been an upsurge of archaeological research in southern Africa, most of the relevant evidence comes from the Zimbabwe plateau, the Limpopo valley in South Africa, the southern Mozambique coast and, to some extent, the southern parts of Zambia (see Figure 15.1). It is not clear whether available evidence in these areas should be seen as reflecting a genuine picture of what happened in prehistory or as simply a result of research coverage. In view of the large amount of research carried out in Zimbabwe and South Africa, it is tempting to adopt the former assumption, but it is perhaps best for the moment to be cautious and take the latter. For one thing, far more archaeologists have worked in these areas than, for example, in Botswana, Malawi, Zambia, Angola, and Namibia. However, the early research efforts of Fagan et al. (1969) in Zambia, and, more recently, Denbow (1984) and the various authors in Lane et al. (1998) in Botswana must be acknowledged (Chapter 14). With the exception of the recent work of John Kinahan (1991) and Jill Kinahan (2000) in Namibia, meaningful research for the period under consideration has yet to be undertaken in the western part of the region.

Nevertheless, whatever the spatial and chronological gaps in our knowledge, there now exists in southern Africa a sufficient body of archaeological evidence to enable us to reconstruct something about the economies of these societies and the processes of change affecting them during the first and second millennia a.d. On the basis of available data, the early village communities of southern Africa, dating between a.d. 100 and 900, appear to have been composed of subsistence farmers engaged in crop cultivation, mainly of millets and sorghum, and the herding of domestic stock. The initial emphasis was on small stock (sheep and goats), although cattle were also present. Over time, however, cattle began to increase in the faunal assemblages. Hunting also appears to have been important (Plug 1997), although its importance and contribution to the diet seem to decrease with time (Voigt 1981). Mining activities were largely limited to the production of iron ore for the manufacture of agricultural and hunting implements, as well as some jewelry (Maggs 1984; Phillipson 1985). The amount of waste from iron-processing at most sites suggests that production was mostly geared toward satisfying local village needs.

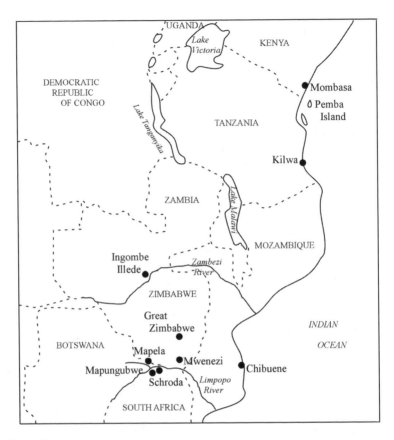

Figure 15.1. Sites mentioned in the text

Through time, however, there are indications in some areas that such production may have become more specialized to meet the needs of areas beyond the individual village (Hall 1987; Maggs 1984; Mulindwa 1993).

In terms of socio-political organization, some archaeologists (e.g., Sinclair 1987), have suggested that the early iron-using farming communities appear to have been at a relatively simple level of organization, fitting within the tribal level of organization as defined by Friedman and Rowlands (1977). The evidence for this is found in, for example, the uniformity of residential structures within the villages, which lack the differentiation expected of stratified societies. Although comparatively little evidence on this is available, it has been suggested that burial data also point to this conclusion (Sinclair 1987).

It is not possible at present to say much about the relationships among these early farming community villages, whether they were in contact with each other and, if so, the nature of such contact. Generally, researchers have argued that each village was probably self-sufficient and clearly isolated from any contacts with the outside world. This appears to be the general picture up to about the seventh to eighth centuries a.d., when a number of alterations observable in the archaeological record give sufficient indication that some major changes were in progress, changes which appear to be, in part, related to economic developments resulting from contact with the East African coast and the introduction of external trading relations.

The earliest evidence for contact and the establishment of trading relations between southern Africa and the outside world via the East African coast has been recovered mostly in the form of glass beads of various types and colors which have been shown to have originated from sources outside southern Africa. In later times, from about the 13th century onwards, ceramics of various types were imported into the region from outside. Glass beads appear as a new class of material culture at a number of excavated sites and are associated dates clustering around the seventh and eighth centuries a.d. Although this chapter is more concerned with the archaeological evidence, the archaeological dates for the appearance of this evidence correspond with some of the earliest written records of contacts between southern Africa, the East African coast, and the Arab world. As will be shown later, such contacts seem to have extended further south along the Indian Ocean to the Mozambican coast. The most often cited of these records include the mariner's guide, the *Periplus of the Ethyrean Sea* (Huntingford 1980), written in the first century of the Christian era, and Ptolemy's *Geography* of the second century A.D. Much later are the writings of two Arabs, al Masudi and al Idrisi (ninth century A.D.), who compiled information on the East African coast and, more relevant to this discussion, made reference to some of the products obtained there, for example ivory and animal skins. Although it is not entirely certain which places they particularly refer to, it is clear that the East African coastal settlements through which imports entered the southern African interior are included.

Returning to the archaeological evidence, we should note that the majority of the bead types that have been recovered from archaeological sites of early and later iron-using farming communities in southern Africa are of Indian and Persian origin, and the same is true of the ceramics which, however, also include vessels from as far afield as China. When this evidence is linked with the admittedly insufficient and vague early written records referred to above, it would appear that the agents responsible for the appearance of these exotic goods in southern Africa were Arab and, later, Swahili traders (Kusimba 1999). The Swahili are now recognized as a distinct culture that developed on the East African coast as a result of interaction and intermarriage between the Arab traders and the African coastal populations (Chami 2002; Chapter 16). Thus, the region's earliest direct trading contacts with the outside world were with the Eastern world. It is not until much later, around the late 15th century A.D., that Europeans, especially the Portuguese, appeared on the East African coast. It may be that some products from southern Africa indirectly found their way to Europe as, similarly, some items of European origin may also have found their way into southern Africa. For these early years, however, the evidence for any form of contact between Europe and southern Africa is virtually non-existent. The possibility of European goods filtering down to the region via North Africa and the Mediterranean world has yet to be demonstrated archaeologically. For East Africa, however, Juma (1996) and, more recently, Chami (1999) have recovered evidence of very early trading links between the East African coast and the Indian Ocean islands such as Zanzibar and Mafia, as well as with the Graeco-Roman world. The dates for these early trading links range from the last two centuries b.c. to around the fourth century a.d.

The Nature of the Evidence

Having provided an outline of the channels of trade and contacts between the region and the outside world in the form of Arab and Swahili traders, I turn now to some of the important sites where the evidence has been recovered, and to the nature of the evidence itself. The earliest types of imported glass beads that have been found in southern Africa are believed to have been manufactured in India and Persia in the early centuries of the Christian era (Hall 1987; Sinclair 1982; van der Sleen 1955, 1967). These include the blue, green, and yellow segments of blown canes of glass, and, later, Indian red beads. These have been recovered from such sites as Makuru in southern Zimbabwe dating from the seventh century a.d. (Huffman 1973), and Schroda in the Limpopo valley in South Africa with a date for the lower occupation horizons of a.d. 815 ± 50 (Hanisch 1981). More recently, research in southeastern Zimbabwe has also yielded evidence of imported glass beads from the lower occupation levels of the sites of Malumba and Mwenezi farm dated to the seventh century a.d. (Manyanga 2001; Manyanga et al. 2000). On the Mozambique coast, Sinclair's research work has revealed similar evidence at the site of Chibuene, where the lower level of occupation has been dated to the eighth century a.d. Some of the sites have local ceramic vessels that fit within the basic Gokomere-Zhizo Tradition associated with the early iron-using farming communities in southern Africa (see Maggs 1984 for a summary of the ceramic traditions of southern Africa) Although detailed studies have not yet been undertaken, Sinclair (1987) has drawn attention to the similarity between the beads found at Chibuene and those from the sites of Makuru, Schroda, and other Zhizo Tradition sites in the interior. The evidence has been used to support the suggestion that the coastal site of Chibuene was the point of entry of exotic goods into the southern African interior at this period, before links were established with coastal Swahili settlements further north.

By the tenth century, and a little later, more bead types had been introduced. Also, as is evident particularly at Chibuene, Islamic/Persian ceramic vessels had also been introduced, including tin-glazed ware with splashed painted decoration and light-blue glazed "Sassanian Islamic" ware. Both types are similar to imported ware from the early phases of the occupation of the major East African coastal town site of Kilwa dated from the ninth century. Important sites in the interior dating from the second millennium include the sites of Leopard Kopje's and Mapela in Zimbabwe, the sites of K2, and, perhaps more important for this discussion, Mapungubwe in the Shashe–Limpopo valley in South Africa. The quantities and types of imported beads at these sites, including sites such as Ingombe Ilede, as far away as the interior of southern Zambia (Phillipson 1977), show two things in connection with contacts between this region and the Swahili world. Firstly, we observe that, by the end of the first millennium a.d., southern Africa had become integrated into the Indian Ocean commercial network. Secondly, it is also clear that the quantities of imports involved and spatial extent of the trading contacts in the interior had increased considerably over time. It remains to be shown what the southern African interior contributed toward the trading networks by way of exports. Evidence for exports is not as clear as for imported goods. It is comparatively easy to demonstrate the presence of durable imports such as glass beads and ceramics. Also, they are clearly not indigenous and in some cases have been sourced to their area of origin (Wood 2000). However, at some sites it has been possible to show that there was a shift in production activities from the basic subsistence-oriented economy of earlier times to the additional production of commodities with exchange value on an external market. This is more clearly discernible from the evidence of ivory-working at sites like Schroda, where slivers from ivory-trimming have been recovered (Voigt 1981). Although it is evident that some of the ivory was consumed locally in the form of items of personal adornment such as bangles and beads, it is clear that most of it was destined for the outside market. It would also appear from the archaeological evidence that skins of animals such as leopards were exported (Hall 1987; Voigt 1981). Support for this interpretation of the bone remains from Schroda also comes from Arab writings which refer to elephant-hunting, and to ivory and animal skins from the East African coast as items of exchange. Somewhat later, shortly after the beginning of the second millennium a.d., we also see the beginnings of gold-mining in the Shashe–Limpopo valley (Miller, Desai and Lee-Thorpe 2000) and especially on the Zimbabwe plateau (Swan 1994), principally to satisfy the demand for this metal on the outside market. As with ivory, it is clear that, although some of the gold was for local use, most of it was destined for export to the Arab world and beyond.

Thus, the general picture discernible is one where, from around the seventh century a.d., societies in southern Africa, both along the coast and in the interior, began receiving goods from outside sources. To obtain these goods, the societies embarked on the exploitation of new products such as ivory, gold, and animal skins that were in demand in the world outside Africa. The archaeological evidence clearly indicates that there was a gradual increase through time in the scale of participation in external long-distance trade. By the 13th century A.D., especially with the emergence of centers such as Mapungubwe and later Great Zimbabwe, the region had become part of an important trading network involving the East African Indian Ocean coast and beyond.

The Indian Ocean Trade, Indigenous Economies, and the Development of Complexity

Having shown some of the archaeological evidence for the establishment of contacts between southern Africa and the outside world, particularly relating to long-distance trade, I turn to the issue of how such trading connections affected societies

in the region. The role of external trade has frequently been cited as the major stimulus to the growth of societies on the African continent in the precolonial period.
As Lonsdale (1981:171) has commented, "The most popular explanation for the
rise of state power was the growth of long distance trade, the Pirenne thesis of
medieval Africa." Although Garlake has since shifted his position, in writing on
African kingdoms in 1978, for example, he made the categorical statement that
"centralized authority grew from a monopoly of foreign trade" (Garlake 1978a:24).
Such interpretations of the African past face two main problems. In most cases,
writers have cited external or long-distance trade as being important without adequately or clearly explaining its possible effects or considering the possible local and
indigenous factors which may have made a contribution to, and in some cases may
have been more important in, the growth and development of these societies. This
way of thinking about the African past was grounded in a settler colonialist paradigm which tended to attribute all change in the continent's past to external stimulus. Examples include the origins of agriculture (Chapter 10), the development of
metallurgy (Chapter 11), and, in this case, the development of complex systems
(Chapter 13). What I wish to do here is to show that the establishment of external
trade affected southern African societies, and to look at the possible ways in which
the growth of trade affected them. At the same time, however, it should be borne
in mind that the African societies themselves were already in a state of growth prior
to this new development.

It has already been noted that the economies of the early iron-using farming
communities of southern Africa were basically subsistence-oriented, and production was probably at the local level for local needs. It has also been noted that
the villages of these societies show little of the differentiation indicative
of elaborate large-scale political organization; and it also appears that there is no
evidence for social stratification, except probably by age and sex. However, from
the time at which the evidence for external trade becomes available, parts of
the sub-region witnessed the growth of new economic, social, and political
organizations, and the coincidence between the two is quite striking. The relevant
sites in this connection are Mapungubwe, K2, Mapela, Leopard's Kopje, and,
later, Great Zimbabwe. The evidence from these sites shows that, although the basic
agricultural crop economy remained qualitatively unchanged, there was increased
participation in long-distance trade on the one hand, and the local exploitation
of gold and ivory on the other. At the same time, at sites like K2, Mapungubwe,
Leopard's Kopje and Great Zimbabwe, the growing importance of cattle as an
economic resource is also evident. Apart from their economic value, cattle
seem to acquire ideological significance (Huffman 1993, 1996a). This evidence is
accompanied for the first time by indications of social and economic differences
in society. At Mapungubwe and Mapela for example, there are differences in
residential structures, with some, presumably those belonging to people higher
on the social and economic scale, enclosed within stone walls and located on
hilltops, while more ordinary settlements are in open and lower locations. It has
been argued that this differential residential pattern establishes the association

between royalty and mountains or high places, which has been characteristic of some southern Bantu societies (Hall 1987; Huffman 1981, 1986, 1996a). Such a settlement system is thought to be a symbolic expression of differential status in society.

To demonstrate further that social, economic, and political differences existed in these societies, evidence can be cited from Mapungubwe, where a number of human burials have been recovered in association with gold objects (Gardner 1963). It is clear that Mapungubwe was a center of considerable economic and political importance, to the extent that archaeologists now agree that it was the center of the region's first state system, developing from the 11th century and collapsing some time during the early part of the 13th century A.D. It is also noted that evidence for craft specialization, sometimes cited as one of the criteria of state systems (Renfrew 1972), is present at Mapungubwe in the form of spindle whorls used for spinning cotton. There is also evidence for manufacture of gold and ivory beads as well as bangles. Furthermore, although it is not clearly demonstrated, the spatial evidence suggests a site hierarchy consistent with a state system. The smaller site of Mapela, 85 km away and contemporary with Mapungubwe, is assumed to have fallen within the hierarchical settlement patterning of the state structure. The development of Mapungubwe and Great Zimbabwe, its presumed successor (Hall 1987; Huffman 1981; Maggs 1984), can thus be used as case studies to show the development of early state systems in the region and how this relates to external trade and other factors.

Mapungubwe as a state center clearly developed from amongst the local indigenous farming populations. There is no evidence of any new population movements into the area that initiated this development. This being so, the question to be asked is how such communities grew into such large settlements and political units. The answer seems to lie partly in the indigenous economies as well as in the new opportunities that the possession of exotic goods provided. The archaeological evidence has shown that large herds of cattle were of major importance amongst societies of the Iron Age in southern Africa. Faunal remains from major sites such as Mapungubwe and Great Zimbabwe have shown how dominant cattle were (Barker 1978; Brain 1974; Garlake 1978b; Hall 1987; Thorp, 1984, 1995; Voigt 1981). It seems clear, therefore, that possession of large herds of cattle was a source of status and power, and the ability to command a following in society was in part based on this. For example, the evidence at Great Zimbabwe, now generally agreed to have been the center of one of southern Africa's largest and most successful states in prehistory, suggests some kind of state or elite control of this resource (Thorp 1995). Thus the growth of social complexity and state formation in southern Africa in part owed its origin to increased wealth in the form of cattle held by some individuals. However, as has already been noted, there is a striking coincidence between the development of socio-political complexity and the increase in the volume of external trade in the region, to the extent that a link between the two can be accepted. But to demonstrate the correlation between the transformation of southern African communities resulting from their participation in external trade and possession of imported goods is one thing; to explain how this new branch of production led to this socio-political transformation is another.

A number of hypotheses have been put forward. Some archaeologists of southern Africa (e.g., Hall 1987; Huffman 1972, 1981) have argued that the development of complexity and the eventual emergence of state systems in the region could not have resulted simply from the increase of wealth through cattle. It has been argued that cattle are a "democratic" resource that is renewable, whereas imported trade goods such as glass beads and ceramics are not. Under favorable conditions, they argue, any individual with suitable breeding stock could accumulate herds of cattle (Hall 1987). How, then, did the possession of trade goods translate into power and lead to a hierarchical society and statehood as it is argued to have done in the case of Mapungubwe? The answer to this question is that the value of imported commodities lay in their rarity and that they provided an avenue to power because they represented a form of wealth that could be stored and distributed differently from cattle. Some scholars, for example Kipp and Schortman (1989), have referred to exotic goods as "preciousities." Such goods may not always have economic or practical value. Their rarity could be used for social or political ends where rulers or the emerging elite used them to maintain and reinforce their power, for example by restricting access. Kipp and Schortman have further argued that goods obtained from distant sources are often distributed on a selective basis to reproduce a system of rank, status or offices within a polity. The key to power and state formation lay in elite control of the products used in external trade. By controlling gold production, for example, the emergent elite then also controlled the acquisition of exotic goods that had prestige value and represented a new form of wealth. Such an elite could control the external trade through their possession of the wealth needed to sponsor the exploitation of the products for exchange. The differential distribution of the products of external trade then reinforced the hierarchical relations among the elite, as well as the position of the elite in relation to their dependents. Such imported goods could then be used to reinforce power and command a following by redistribution. We can infer that such a situation existed based on the differential recovery of exotic items from different parts of sites such as Great Zimbabwe. Further, in the historically documented Mutapa state in northern Zimbabwe, Portuguese records dating from the 16th century show us that the state rulers used herds of cattle to sponsor gold-mining among their dependents and that the metal was then used to acquire exotic goods (Mudenge 1988; Pikirayi 1993, 2000). One 16th-century Portuguese source tells us that, "When the Monomatapa wants gold he sends a cow to those of his people who are to dig, and it is divided among them according to their labour and the number of days they are required to work" (Monclaro 1569, cited in Randles 1979:86)

From this, it becomes fairly clear that an indigenous branch of production in the form of cattle-herding represented a source of wealth used to procure the precious metal that was in turn used to acquire exotic goods on the external market. In the final analysis, the picture that emerges is one that illustrates how complex systems resulted from an interplay of different variables. In order to appreciate the impact of the East African coastal trade on southern African societies, one should try to trace the prehistory of the region from the establishment of iron-using farming communities up to the first few centuries of the second millennium. Taking such an approach, four stages can be identified. In the first stage, the farming communities were characterized by communities living in scattered villages which show no evidence of outside connections or of a hierarchically organized society. The second stage, which can be dated from about the seventh century, coincides with the introduction of external trade when we see a shift in production toward goods with exchange value. The third stage, from about the tenth century, saw an increase in the volume of trade and was characterized by villages which began to show evidence of social differentiation. The fourth and last stage saw the establishment of state structures such as Mapungubwe, and social stratification that is in part evident from residence structures. These developments reached a climax with the establishment of the Zimbabwe state that was centered at the major site of Great Zimbabwe, the successor to Mapungubwe. A further illustration of the relationship between the establishment of contact between eastern Africa and the development of state systems can be seen in the coincidence between the demise of Mapungubwe and the rise of the Zimbabwe state. The two have been seen as related developments linked to the growing importance of gold in the Indian Ocean trade. The shift in the center of power from Mapungubwe to Great Zimbabwe is explained by a greater abundance of goldfields on the Zimbabwe plateau compared to the Limpopo Valley. Furthermore, the coincidence between the rise of the coastal city of Kilwa and Great Zimbabwe has also been noted (Garlake 1973). It is now generally accepted that the two benefited from each other, Kilwa being the entry point of exotic goods destined for Zimbabwe and Zimbabwe being the interior supply center of the local products destined for the external market. Thus the development of Great Zimbabwe, not only as a major urban center but also as a state capital, must have been linked to the coastal trade. Similarly the collapse of Great Zimbabwe in the latter half of the 15th century seems related to a similar development at Kilwa.

Conclusion

While the role of external trade in the transformation of southern Africa is quite clear, it should be noted that the addition of this new element in the economy was not the only factor in the process. Such developments in the southern African interior should not be seen merely as responses to external trade. The process of growth was also internally stimulated. It has to be emphasized that not all complex systems in southern Africa necessarily developed as a result of external stimuli through participation in external trade. A good example is the 13th-century a.d. Toutswe state in eastern Botswana, with its capital at the hilltop site of Toutswemogala. The archaeological evidence clearly shows that it developed without a significant external trade input but through local wealth such as cattle (Denbow 1984; Lane et al. 1998; Chapter 14). The importance of cattle at Great Zimbabwe has also been demonstrated (Garlake 1978b, 1982, 1983; Thorp 1995). To further demonstrate this position, we can also appeal to the historical record, where it is clear that major 19th-century political systems in southern Africa, such as the Zulu state under Shaka and the Ndebele state under Lobengula, developed into very powerful systems with an economy that was based on large-scale cattle-herding. Trade was an insignificant part of their economies (Chanaiwa 1980; Cobbing 1976).

I have argued elsewhere (Pwiti 1996a, 1996b) that the processes of socio-political transformation in southern Africa should not be seen in monocausal terms, but within a multicausal framework that considers the interplay and interaction of different factors. Such a framework should consider the indigenous economies, long-distance trade, and ideological change. Possibilities of climatic as well as environmental change (see Huffman 1996b; Tyson and Lindesay 1992) should also not be overlooked in the overall scheme of things. In the final analysis, I argue that southern African communities were already in a process of growth that was then accelerated by their participation in external trade. To this extent, the relationship that was established between the region and the East African coast was an important one in terms of building up on a process that was already underway.

REFERENCES

Barker, G., 1978 An Investigation of the Manekeni Zimbabwe, Mozambique. Azania 13:71–100.

Brain, C. K., 1974 Human Food Remains from the Iron Age at Great Zimbabwe. South African Journal of Science 70:303–309.

Chami, F., 1999 Graeco-Roman Trade Link and the Bantu Migration Theory. Anthropos 94:1–3.

——2002 Kaole and the Swahili World. In Southern Africa and the Swahili World. F. Chami and Gilbert Pwiti, eds. pp. 1–11. Dar es Salaam: Dar es Salaam University Press.

Chanaiwa, D., 1980 The Zulu Revolution: State Formation in a Pastoralist Society. African Studies Review 23:23–29.

Cobbing, J. D., 1976 The Ndebele under the Khumalos, 1820–96. Ph.D. dissertation, University of Lancaster.

Collett, David, 1982 Models of the Spread of the Early Iron Age. In The Archaeological and Linguistic Reconstruction of African History. Christopher Ehret and Merrick Posnansky, eds. pp. 182–198. Berkeley: University of California Press.

Denbow, James, 1984 Cows and Kings: A Spatial and Economic Analysis of a Hierarchical Early Iron Age Settlement System in Eastern Botswana. In Frontiers: Southern African Archaeology Today. Martin Hall, Graham Avery, D. Avery, M. Wilson, and A. Humphreys, eds. pp. 24–39. BAR International Series, 207. Oxford: British Archaeological Reports.

Fagan, Brian, David W. Phillipson, and S. G. Daniels, 1969 Iron Age Cultures in Zambia. London: Chatto.

Friedman, Jonathan, and Michael Rowlands, 1977 Notes Towards an Epigenetic Model of Evolution of Civilization. In The Evolution of Social Systems. J. Friedman and M. Rowlands, eds. pp. 1–76. London: Duckworth.

Gardner, G. A., 1963 Mapungubwe, vol. 2. Pretoria: Van Schaik.

Garlake, P., 1973 Great Zimbabwe. London: Thames & Hudson.

—— 1978a Kingdoms of Africa. Oxford: Elsevier-Phaidon.

—— 1978b Pastoralism and Zimbabwe. Journal of African History 19:479–493.

—— 1982 Great Zimbabwe Described and Explained. Harare: Zimbabwe Publishing House.

—— 1983 Prehistory and Ideology in Zimbabwe. In Past and Present in Zimbabwe. J. D. Peel and Terence O. Ranger, eds. pp. 1–19. Manchester: Manchester University Press.

Hall, Martin, 1987 The Changing Past: Farmers, Kings and Traders in Southern Africa, 200–1860 AD. Cape Town: David Phillip.

Hanisch, E., 1981 Schroda: A Zhizo Site in Northern Transvaal. In A Guide to Archaeological Sites in Northern and Eastern Transvaal. E. Voigt, ed. pp. 1–6. Pretoria: Transvaal Museum.

Huffman, Thomas N., 1970 The Early Iron Age and the Spread of the Bantu. South African Archaeological Bulletin 25:3–21.

—— 1972 The Rise and Fall of Zimbabwe. Journal of African History 13:353–366.

—— 1973 Test Excavations at Makuru, Rhodesia. Arnoldia 5:1–21.

—— 1981 Snakes and Birds: Expressive Space at Great Zimbabwe. African Studies 40:131–150.

—— 1986 Iron Age Hierarchies and the Origins of Class Distinction in Southern Africa. Advances in World Archaeology 5:291–338.

—— 1993 Broederstroom and the Central Cattle Pattern. South African Journal of Science 89:220–226.

—— 1996a Snakes and Crocodiles: Power and Symbolism in Ancient Zimbabwe. Johannesburg: Witwatersrand University Press.

—— 1996b Archaeological Evidence for Climatic Change during the Last 2000 Years in Southern Africa. Quaternary International 33:55–60.

Huntingford, G. W., 1980 The Periplus of the Ethyrean Sea. London: Hakluyt Society.

Juma, A., 1996 The Swahili and the Mediterranean World: Pottery of the Late Roman Period from Zanzibar. Antiquity 70:148–154.

Kinahan, Jill, 2000 Cattle for Beads: The Archaeology of Historical Contact and Trade on the Namib Coast. Uppsala: Department of Archaeology/Windhoek: Namibia Archaeological Trust.

Kinahan, John, 1991 Pastoral Nomads of the Central Namib Desert. Windhoek: Namibia Archaeological Trust.

Kipp, L., and E. Schortman, 1989 The Political Impact of Trade in Chiefdoms. American Anthropologist 91:370–385.

Kusimba, C., 1999 The Rise and Fall of Swahili States. Walnut Creek, CA: AltaMira Press.

Lane, Paul, Andrew Reid, and Alinah Segobye, eds., 1998 Ditswa Mmung: The Archaeology of Botswana. Gaborone: Pula Press and the Botswana Society.

Lonsdale, J., 1981 States and Social Processes in Africa: A Historiographical Survey. African Studies Review 24:139–225.

Maggs, T. O., 1984 The Iron Age South of the Zambezi. In Southern African Prehistory and Palaeoenvironments. Richard Klein, ed. pp. 329–395. Rotterdam: Balkema.

Manyanga, M., 2001 Choices and Constraints: Animal Resource Exploitation in South-Eastern Zimbabwe c. AD 900–1500. Uppsala: Department of Archaeology.

Manyanga, M., Innocent Pikirayi, and W. Ndoro, 2000 Coping with Dryland Environments: Preliminary Results from Mapungubwe and Zimbabwe Phase Sites in the Mateke Hills, South Eastern Zimbabwe. In African Naissance: The Limpopo Valley 1000 Years Ago. Mary Leslie and Tim Maggs, eds. pp. 69–77. Goodwin Series 8. Cape Town: South African Archaeological Society.

Miller, Duncan, N. Desai, and J. Lee-Thorpe, 2000 Metals, Ideology and Power: The Manufacture and Control of Materialized Ideology in the Area of the Limpopo–Shashe Confluence, c. AD 900–1300. *In* African Naissance: The Limpopo Valley 1000 Years Ago. Mary Leslie and Tim Maggs, eds. pp. 100–111. Goodwin Series 8. Cape Town: South African Archaeological Society.

Mudenge, S. G., 1988 A Political History of Munhumutapa c. 1400–1902. Harare: Zimbabwe Publishing House.

Mulindwa, D. K., 1993 The Iron Age People of East-Central Botswana. *In* The Archaeology of Africa: Food, Metals and Towns. Thurstan Shaw, Paul Sinclair, Bassey Andah, and Alex Okpoko, eds. pp. 386–390. London: Routledge.

Phillipson, David W., 1976 Prehistory of Eastern Zambia. Memoir 6. Nairobi: British Institute in Eastern Africa.

——1977 The Later Prehistory of Eastern and Southern Africa. London: Methuen.

——1985 African Archaeology. Cambridge: Cambridge University Press.

Pikirayi, Innocent, 1993 The Archaeological Identity of the Mutapa State: Towards an Historical Archaeology of Northern Zimbabwe. Uppsala: Societas Archaeologica Upsaliensis.

——2000 The Zimbabwe Culture: Origins and Decline of Southern Zambezian States. Walnut Creek, CA: AltaMira Press.

Plug, Ina, 1997 Early Iron Age Buffalo Hunters on the Kadzi River, Zimbabwe. African Archaeological Review 14:85–105.

Pwiti, Gilbert, 1996a Continuity and Change: An Archaeological Study of Farming Communities in Northern Zimbabwe, AD 500–1700. Uppsala: Department of Archaeology.

——1996b Peasants, Chiefs and Kings: A Model of the Development of Cultural Complexity in Northern Zimbabwe. Zambezia 23:31–52.

Randles, L. G., 1979 The Empire of Munhumutapa. Gwelo: Mambo Press.

Renfrew, Colin, 1972 The Emergence of Civilisation. London: Methuen.

Sinclair, Paul, 1982 Chibuene: An Early Trading Site in Southern Mozambique. Paedeuma 28:149–164.

——1987 Space, Time and Social Formation: A Territorial Approach to the Archaeology of Mozambique and Zimbabwe. Uppsala: Societas Archaeologica Upsaliensis.

Soper, Robert, 1971 A General Review of the Early Iron Age in the Southern Half of Africa. Azania 6:5–37.

——1982 Bantu Expansion into Eastern Africa: The Archaeological Evidence. *In* The Archaeological and Linguistic Reconstruction of African History. Christopher Ehret and Merrick Posnansky, eds. pp. 223–244. Berkeley: University of California Press.

Swan, L., 1994 Early Gold Mining on the Zimbabwean Plateau. Uppsala: Societas Archaeologica Upsaliensis.

Thorp, Carolyn, 1984 Faunal Remains as Evidence of Social Stratification. Master's Thesis, University of the Witwatersrand, Johannesburg.

——1995 Kings, Commoners and Cattle at Zimbabwe Tradition Sites. Memoir 1. Harare: National Museums and Monuments of Zimbabwe.

Tyson, P., and R. Lindesay, 1992 The Climate of the Last 2000 Years in Southern Africa. Holocene 2:271–278.

van der Sleen, N., 1955 Zimbabwe Beads and Ribbed Ware. South African Archaeological Bulletin 10:61–62.

——1967 A Handbook on Beads. Liege: Musée du Verre.

Voigt, Elizabeth, 1981 The Faunal Remains from Schroda. *In* Guide to Archaeological Sites in the Northern and Eastern Transvaal. Elizabeth Voigt, ed. pp. 55–60. Pretoria: Transvaal Museum.

Wood, M., 2000 Making Connections: Relationships Between International Trade and Glass Beads from the Shashe–Limpopo Area. *In* African Naissance: The Limpopo Valley 1000 Years Ago. Mary Leslie and Tim Maggs, eds. pp. 78–90. Goodwin Series 8. Cape Town: South African Archaeological Society.

16

Mosaics and Interactions: East Africa, 2000 b.p. to the Present

Chapurukha M. Kusimba and
Sibel B. Kusimba

Archaeologists refer to the last 2,000 years in East Africa as the Iron Age, though metal technology during this period was by no means ubiquitous. For a long time, the appearance of the Iron Age was conceived as a rapid transition from a stone-tool-using forager way of life to that of the iron-using agriculturalist, associated with a population movement that swept sub-Saharan Africa, bringing in many areas "a wholly new way of life . . . in a single process of Bantu expansion" (Oliver and Fagan 1975:93; Holl 2000; but see Clark 1970:216; Chapter 12). Underscoring the idea of a single population expansion, John Iliffe wrote, "It is likely that the Bantu languages were carried by colonists who also took agricultural skills into regions where they were often hitherto unknown. Descendants of these colonists still possess considerable genetic as well as linguistic homogeneity" (Iliffe 1995:17, cited in Schoenbrun 2001:1).

More recent approaches based on accumulating archaeological evidence show rather that the spread of Bantu language, pottery, food production, and metallurgy throughout central, eastern and southern Africa was more likely the result of several much more gradual and often separate processes of immigration, diffusion, invention, and admixture (Ehret 2001; Vansina 1995; Chapter 12). For example, in the Early Iron Age of southwestern Tanzania, three different early ironworking techniques coexisted, and may have been practiced by different language communities (Mapunda 2000). Domesticates like chicken and bananas came from Indian Ocean trade, and probably reached East Africa long before Bantu languages (Chami 2001; De Langhe et al. 1994–95). Furthermore, Bantu speakers may be associated with Later Stone Age occupations of East Africa (Chami 2001). Indeed, widespread Bantu oral traditions tell of the Mbonelakuti, a pre-Bantu, short people with iron and domestic cattle who inhabited East and South Africa before the Bantu (Mac-Donald and Allsworth-Jones 1994; Schadeberg 1999). Archaeological and linguistic studies (Chami 1999; Denbow 1990; Ehret 1998; Kiyaga-Mulindwa 1993; Mapunda 2003; Vansina 1995) show that iron technology, domestic cattle, pottery, and the Bantu languages had separate trajectories of appearance and spread over southern Africa during the last millennium, rather than having spread recently and as a package as part of a migration or "expansion."

As a consequence of this variability, when the lens is fixed on particular regions, such as East Africa, the picture that emerges is one of interaction among peoples of diverse origins practicing and inventing different ways of life, with different levels of political complexity, and different economic and ritual specializations. Over the last 2,000 years, East Africa's most populated areas were complex multi-ethnic, multi-economic regions which we call mosaics. Mosaics typically included several communities practicing different economies, religions, inventions, and vocations, bound together by friendships and clientships, alliances, knowledge, and concepts of personal and social identity. Guyer and Belinga (1995:117) have emphasized kinship, status, space and demography, and specialized knowledge as the most important dimensions of the mosaic. Conflict and competition, however, were often part of the mosaic as well. Archaeologists can arm themselves with such ethnographic concepts when uncovering the history of African cultures. Over the last 2,000 years, food production spread, but foraging persisted, and a diversity of farming and pastoral techniques were practiced. Furthermore, pottery and other stylistic indicators show that symbolic boundaries existed, even as trade contacts developed among different groups. Overlapping distributions of different kinds of material culture make the understanding of mosaics one of the most difficult undertakings in African archaeology.

Some of the most important facts of modern Africa – especially the dynamics of ethnicity and social and political power – are rooted in Iron Age interactions. Furthermore, the Iron Age mosaic is important to us not just as grist to the archaeologist's mill, but also as a reservoir of potential for East Africa's pluralistic future. This chapter will examine the history of perspectives on the last 2,000 years (or so) in East Africa. We discuss the history of interpretations of this period with regard to three geographical areas: Kenya's Central Rift Valley, the Great Lakes region, and the Taita-Tsavo area of southeastern Kenya (Figure 16.1).

Approaches to Mosaics: A History

European colonization has influenced the way archaeologists have approached the study of mosaics in Africa. Anthropology shared in the colonial task of labeling and describing African cultural diversity as a patchwork of bounded ethnic groups or tribes (see Hobsbawm and Ranger 1983; Southall 1970). An ethnic group was confidently assigned a set of descriptors: a language family affiliation, a social system, an ecology, an economy, a religion, and a legal system. Through such labels, African cultures became known to the European world. African archaeology has reinforced these perspectives by focusing on normative patterns in the ways of life of discrete peoples (MacEachern 1994), and by linking archaeological patterns to the ethnographic present by identifying the archaeological ancestors of modern-day ethnic groups.

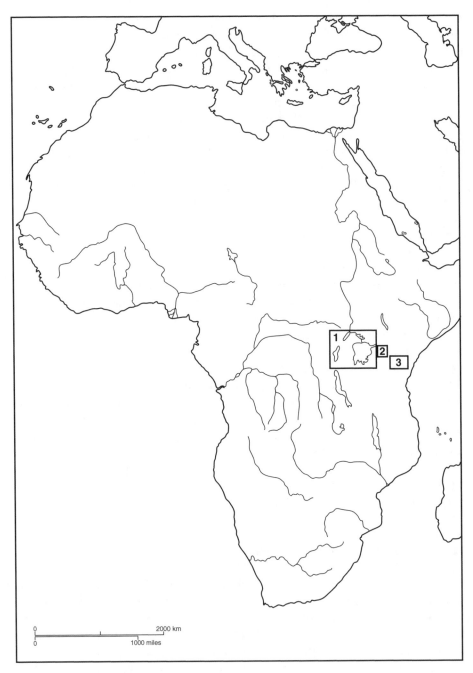

Figure 16.1. Location of East African mosaics: (1) the Great Lakes; (2) Central Rift; (3) Taita-Tsavo

In defining ethnic groups, archaeologists have been concerned with two major attributes: language affiliation and economy. Historical linguistics has examined change in every aspect of culture that is mirrored in word histories of African languages, identifying inheritance and borrowing through cognate words, and reconstructing the prototypes of modern languages and their dates of origin (Ehret 1997, 2002). Archaeologists have used this historical linguistic information on dating, geographic location, pottery style, and economy to match archaeological occurrences to proto-language families. For example, much of modern-day Kenya, now inhabited by speakers of Bantu and Nilotic languages, was formerly occupied by speakers of Southern Cushitic languages, who have been linked to the Pastoral Neolithic stone-tool-using pastoralists (see Chapters 8 and 12 for more on links between linguistics and archaeology).

Another way social units have been identified archaeologically is through data on subsistence economies. For many anthropological schools, the principal classification of human societies has been by their mode of subsistence – hunting and gathering, pastoralism, horticulture, or agriculture – assuming that the way in which food is procured or produced has significant effects on other aspects of culture. For example, hunting and egalitarian organization are thought to co-occur (Roscoe 2002). The economic and linguistic approach to labeling archaeological units has been particularly common in East Africa because sites often produce considerable evidence about ecology and economy.

In addition to establishing the language and economy of the people living on ancient sites, these approaches have also tried to understand interaction across ethnic boundaries. Barth (1969) developed an ecological analogy for understanding ethnic mosaics. For Barth, the ecological diversity of a region set the range of possibilities and the boundaries for social groups and their relationships. He described four types of relationships: symbiosis, where groups develop a mutually beneficial relationship; conflict, where the parties contest claims to a resource; avoidance, where one of the parties moves away to avoid both competition and cooperation; and segmentary opposition, where closely related but competing groups erect strong cultural boundaries in order to prevent interaction (Barth 1969:11). Most often, the situation in a mosaic is some complex combination of all of these, often played out and negotiated in day-to-day practice. Barth argued that ethnic identities were themselves a by-product of interaction in these mosaics, and that ethnicity is a consequence of a group's believing itself distinct vis-à-vis others (Barth 1969:11). This outlook has had some influence in African anthropology and archaeology, suggesting that ethnic identity has less to do with cultural content than with the signaling of negotiable distinctions. The alternative hypothesis is that ethnicity emerges internally within a culture as people create beliefs and practices (see Bravman 1998). Obviously, both internal and external sources of ethnicity are important. Furthermore, interacting groups necessarily share at least some aspects of their culture or communication would be impossible. The groups in a mosaic may have a "reservoir of symbols, myths and beliefs . . . [which they access] in order to extract, craft, and visually display . . . tradition" (McIntosh 1989:77).

A Barthian perspective on regional distributions of material culture has been influential in East African archaeology. As the case studies below demonstrate, ethnic, and especially linguistic, boundaries have been read in pottery style distributions and plant and animal remains of prehistoric economies. The dominant approach to mosaics has been to match archaeological groupings to the major linguistic/ethnic categorizations of 20th-century East Africa.

Our intention in the following case studies is not to deny the usefulness of this approach, but rather to point out some shortcomings and continued anomalies of the approaches we examine. The main problem is that archaeological cultures or traditions are found over much larger areas than are usually occupied by modern ethnic or linguistic groups (MacEachern 1994). What, then, is the meaning of the cultural units that archaeologists have recognized? We can go a step further and ask if we can expect to find an Iron Age "match" for ethnographically known social groupings. Indeed, historical studies of social identity in many parts of Africa have shown that ethnic groups had different social meanings and social roles before the colonial period, and that historically, as today, ethnic boundaries are porous and situational (Ambler 1988; de la Gorgendière et al. 1996). In northern Cameroon, for example, precolonial individuals identified primarily with a territorial lineage group (MacEachern 2001:81), usually a patrilineally related group but including many others not related to the patriline, and associated with a physical area, such as a rocky prominence or plateau. Similarly, in East Africa, though precolonial ethnic and linguistic divisions sometimes coincided broadly with those of the present day, people primarily identified with a much smaller group, usually including their families, kin, and local area. Individuals and families cultivated contacts and alliances beyond this local group which included people of different language groups. By the same token, common language could obscure significant cultural differences. Certain individuals and clans could move from one group to the other because of their ritual or other specialized knowledge (David et al. 1988; Guyer and Belinga 1995). Individuals had flexible, expandable networks of association far and near, both within and beyond their kin and language groups. It was, as Ambler (1988:32) calls it, "a complex world of overlapping, layered, and shifting associations."

Another potential problem is the conceptualization of distinct categories of "agriculturalist," "hunter-gatherer," and "pastoralist." Theoretically, the separation of forager from food producer relies on discerning "domestic" from "wild" resources, which has proven a quagmire (S. Kusimba 2003; Smith 2001; Chapters 9, 10). Identifications of "hunter-gatherers" versus food producers are often based on a simple assessment of site contents, such as proportions of wild to domestic cattle (Mapunda 2000; Schrire 1992; Schrire and Deacon 1989). Most "Neolithic" and Iron Age economies were significantly less specialized than ethnographic ones, and probably exchanged foodstuffs as well. Schrire (1992) for example, has pointed out that many regional site inventories form a continuum when proportions of wild to domestic fauna, pottery, lithic artifacts, and other artifact types are considered.

Another caveat may be raised with regard to use of the ethnographic record. Prehistoric economies and strategies were often very different from those of the ethnographic present, and the direct historical approach can lead to a misuse of analogy (Stahl 2001; Chapter 2). One good example is the site of Engaruka in south-central Kenya (a.d. 1400–1700), where irrigation agriculture was practiced on a grand scale in one of the most arid areas of East Africa. Irrigation agriculture of sorghum was also combined with stall-feeding of small cattle and goats (Sutton 1998a). Ornaments of shell and bone, cowrie shells, glass beads, and copper objects attest trade with the East African coast, around 200 km to the east. There is evidence of iron-forging only, perhaps of bloom received from another group, guild, or clan of smelters. In an area almost uninhabited today, Engaruka's population exceeded 5,000 people in seven villages on a hilltop above the complex maze of irrigation fields. Just two centuries before colonialism, then, East African lifeways were dramatically different from those inscribed in ethnographic texts.

Finally, a problem that remains to be resolved is the assumption that pottery styles encode symbolic information. Many studies have sought to understand the relationship between artifact industries and styles and ethnicity (Conkey and Hastorf 1990; David et al. 1988). Although pottery styles can indeed mark ethnic boundaries, archaeologists are only beginning to explore how diversity in pottery may relate to individual artisans, functional differences, trade wares, gender differences, prestige wares linked with certain clans, social groups or social meanings, or specialized technologies such as ironworking (Herbich 1987; Hodder 1991; Stahl and Cruz 1998; Stewart 1993). The future challenge will be to develop ways to tease this information out from analysis of pottery. In some cases, for example, sourcing studies and ethnohistorical information may tell us more about pottery life history.

Three Case Studies

We present three case studies – the Central Rift Valley of west-central Kenya, the Great Lakes region, and the Taita-Tsavo region of southeastern Kenya – in order to explore the ways archaeologists can understand the social interactions of mosaics. The first area we consider is the Central Rift Valley, including the Nakuru, Naivasha, and Elmenteita Lake basins and the highlands of the Mau and Aberdare ranges that rim the lake basins. Today, the lake basins are about 1,600 m in altitude and include Acacia grasslands with some trees. As one ascends the highland slopes one passes through distinct zones of bushland and montane forest (Ambrose 1986:15). Altitudinal differences contribute to the formation of a varied ecological stage typical of a cultural mosaic.

The second area is the Great Lakes region, including the eastern Rift Valley and the Lake Victoria basin. This area also includes rainforest, woodland, scrub forest, and semi-evergreen bushland and thicket, crosscut by a variety of water bodies – which served not only as reservoirs of resources but also as conduits for trade goods and communication (Schoenbrun 1998; White 1983:46, 180). It has abundant resources and high rainfall. It also seems to have acted as a refuge during the cold, dry periods of the Pleistocene (Hamilton 2000).

Our third case study is the area of southeastern Kenya encompassing the Taita Hills and the Tsavo grasslands, about 100 km inland from the Kenya coast. Because of its relatively harsh ecology, hunter-gatherers have been important denizens of this area, although they too interacted with often peripatetic food producers. The Tsavo region includes low-relief, low-elevation plains of arid bushlands, uplands with better-watered large hills and inselbergs greater than 2,000 m in altitude, ephemeral streams and associated riparian woodlands, and arid, open to dense bushlands. In general the low-lying areas received only about 300 mm of rain per year and were home to tsetse fly (vector of sleeping sickness, or trypanosomiasis), while higher altitudes received as much as 1,000 mm of rainfall and were tsetse-free (Geological Map of Kenya 1987; Ojany and Ogendo 1973; Wijngaarden and van Engelen 1985).

The Central Rift Valley

The first inhabitants of the Central Rift were, of course, hunter-gatherers. The Eburran Industry (Ambrose 1984) is found at several sites in the Central Rift and consists of backed blades of obsidian; it is associated with wild faunal remains. Over the course of the Holocene, Eburran peoples hunted and gathered in the basin of the Rift Valley lakes, preferring to camp in moderate altitudes on the boundaries between lowland grasslands and upland forest areas. Most likely, they exploited resources in both areas – game on the plains, and forest game and honey in the montane forests.

As early as 4000 b.p. (Marean 1992), the technology of food production, specifically sheep and goats, was introduced into the area, and was followed a thousand years or more later by cattle pastoralists (Chapter 8). Use of sorghum and millets by these early pastoralists is inferred from linguistic reconstructions or bone chemistry studies (Ambrose and DeNiro 1986; cf. Chapter 10). Wild fauna, however, have been found at most Pastoral Neolithic sites after 3000 b.p., showing the continued importance of hunting. Faunal assemblages from numerous sites in the Central Rift Valley indicate that animal husbandry was practiced alongside hunting and fishing (Barthelme 1984, 1985; Hivernel 1978; Karega-Munene 1996; Marshall 1991, 2000; Marshall et al. 1984; Onyango-Abuje 1977a, 1977b; Phillipson 1993; Robertshaw and Collett 1983; Stewart 1991). These early food-producing economies were thus broad-spectrum (see Chapters 9 and 10).

Exceptions are found at Maringishu in the Central Rift (Bower et al. 1977; Chapter 8) and Lemek North-East and Sambo Ngige in south-western Kenya (Marshall 1991, 2000), where herding was more specialized. The absence of wild animals, except equid, in the faunal samples from Lemek North-East and Ngamuriak could indicate the development of specialized pastoralism by 3000 b.p. (Marshall 1991), although other cases of specialized Neolithic pastoralism are yet to be found.

Shortly after this period, a complex array of pottery styles, lithic artifacts, and economic remains is found on sites around the Central Rift, a pattern that characterizes contemporaneous sites in the Great Lakes region, especially around Lake Victoria. Interpretations of this diversity vary. Karega-Munene (2002) recently summarized the history of investigation into these complex patterns; our discussion relies heavily on his historical survey. The first attempts (in the 1960s) to synthesize Pastoral Neolithic cultures, as well as most of those that followed, were based on pottery. Early on the pottery from several sites was classified into three categories, Classes A, B, and C (Sutton 1964). Class A consisted of Elmenteitan Ware pottery as represented at Gambles Cave II, Njoro River Cave, Naivasha Railway Rockshelter, and Long's Drift. Class B included Gumban and Hyrax Hill pottery, and Class C all roulette-decorated pottery, including Lanet Ware. Class A was considered to be the oldest because it was presumably created by hunter-gatherers, and Class C the youngest because of its apparent association with sedentary communities who had knowledge of ironworking (Sutton 1964). In spite of contemporaneous variation in pottery styles, there was an attempt to order pottery wares along a chronological trajectory. The chronological scheme that was proposed for the pottery (Class A, followed by Class B and Class C) was not based on chronometric evidence (Karega-Munene 2002).

In the 1970s, Wandibba (1977, 1980) made a more careful attempt to classify Pastoral Neolithic pottery from Rift Valley sites using attributes like firing, decorative techniques and motifs, vessel shapes, and features like lugs, handles, spouts, and knobs (Wandibba 1977, 1980). Wandibba recognized five wares named after their respective type sites: Nderit Ware, Narosura Ware, Remnant Ware (Elmenteitan), Maringishu Ware, and Akira Ware. *Nderit Ware* was characterized by carinated or narrow-mouthed bowls decorated on both surfaces. External decoration consisted of closely set cuneiform impressions and, on the internal surface, scores or grooves, line incisions, or jabs. *Narosura Ware* was characterized by comb-stamping or line incisions which were occasionally delimited with horizontal lines or divided by zigzag reserved bands on open- and narrow-mouthed bowls, bowls with slightly everted rims and beaker-like vessels. *Maringishu Ware* included many ovoid beakers, and was characterized by broad, undulating horizontal ridges filled with small linear impressions, punctations, or very fine cord roulette impressions. *Akira Ware* was characterized by thin-walled vessels with highly burnished surfaces, the decoration consisting of panels of very fine incised lines. Narrow bands of applied decoration occurred on some vessels. *Remnant (Elmenteitan) Ware* was generally undecorated, but sometimes had panels of punctations on some vessels. Common vessel types included open-mouthed bowls, large open-mouthed cauldron-like vessels, platters and carinated cups; other significant features included lugs, handles, and spouts on some vessels (Wandibba 1977, 1980). These wares are represented at several sites in northern and southwestern Kenya, the Kenyan Central Rift Valley, and northern Tanzania.

The chronological relationships among these wares have never been clear. To Wandibba (1977, 1980; see Karega-Munene 2002, 2003) Nderit Ware appeared to be the oldest, followed by Narosura Ware, Remnant Ware (Elmenteitan), Akira Ware, and Maringishu Ware. Onyango-Abuje's (1980) scheme was similar, except that Akira Ware and Maringishu Ware were thought to be contemporaneous. A scheme proposed by Bower et al. (1977) ordered the pottery as follows, beginning with the oldest: Nderit Ware, Kansyore Ware, Narosura Ware, Akira Ware, and Maringishu Ware. Karega-Munene (2003) criticizes these schemes for (1) how they assigned pottery collections to wares, and (2) for how radiocarbon dates were interpreted (Karega-Munene 2002). For example, Onyango-Abuje (1980) lumped Elmenteitan Ware (Remnant) pottery from Njoro River Cave with Narosura Ware pottery from the type site, because they dated to about the same period, while the scheme of Bower et al. (1977) excluded Elmenteitan Ware.

Perhaps the best way out of the confusion is to examine the pottery in relation to other evidence. Ambrose (1984) examined the mosaic of Central Rift sites in terms of economy, chronology, pottery, lithic artifacts, and geographic distribution. Exploration of the relationship between chronology, material culture, and subsistence activities led him to delineate three broadly contemporaneous groups: the Savanna Pastoral Neolithic (SPN), Elmenteitan, and Eburran (Ambrose 1984). The SPN consisted of two sub-groups, Lowland SPN and Highland SPN, distinguished by dating, geographic distribution, and elevation. Sites belonging to the former sub-group date to about 5200–3300 b.p. and are restricted to the low-lying areas of northern Kenya, while highland SPN sites are found in central Kenya and northern Tanzania, and are dated to about 3300–1300 b.p. The Eburran Neolithic Phase 5 is the most recent of the Eburran phases and dates to ca. 2900–1900 b.p. The Elmenteitan group is made up of sites that are restricted to the western side of the Rift Valley, the adjacent Mau Escarpment and the Loita Plains to the west of the Mau Escarpment (Ambrose 1982, 1984). Ambrose's scheme was one of the first to use multiple lines of evidence, not just pottery, in defining the cultural boundaries of the mosaic. Issues of diet can be approached not only through linguistic and faunal studies but, when human skeletal evidence is available, the estimation of proportions of animal to plant foods in human diet from bone chemistry (Price 1989). These studies have shown that diets of people buried at SPN sites were rich in the milk and blood of grazing animals, while Elmenteitan peoples ate more plant foods and more animal flesh, possibly from hunted animals (Ambrose and DeNiro 1986).

To most scholars the pottery wares, regardless of how they are identified, represent distinct cultural entities which can be correlated with specific linguistic and/or ethnic groups. These associations are suggested by historical linguistic hypotheses about the movement of past populations in the region. The hypotheses suggest that the region was occupied by hunter-gatherers (ancestors of southern African Khoisan speakers) during the "pre-Neolithic" period, and that these groups were displaced or absorbed by Southern Cushitic-speaking pastoralists from Ethiopia. Subsequent migrations to the region involved Southern Nilotes, who are also thought to have been food producers (Ehret 1967, 1968, 1971, 1974). The hunter-gatherers have been associated with Kansyore Ware; Southern Cushites (ancestors of the Alagwa, Aramanik, Asa, Burungi, Dahalo, Gorowa, and Iraqw of Kenya and

Tanzania) with Akira Ware, Narosura Ware, Nderit Ware, and Maringishu Ware; and Southern Nilotes (ancestors of the Barabaig and Kalenjin of Tanzania and Kenya) with Elmenteitan Ware (Ambrose 1982, 1984).

Problems in understanding the Central Rift mosaic are ongoing. Although correlations between linguistic reconstructions and the archaeological record continue to be provocative, some data patterns cannot be explained by these correlations. Chief among these patterns is that some wares are found in the same deposits at the same sites (Karega-Munene 1996, 2002). At Seronera in Tanzania, for example, Kansyore Ware pottery was associated with Nderit Ware (Bower 1973); at Nyang'oma and Chole in the same country, Kansyore Ware was found in the same deposits with Iron Age pottery (Soper and Golden 1969); and at Gogo Falls in western Kenya Kansyore Ware was found in the same deposits with Elmenteitan Ware, Akira Ware, and Urewe Ware (Karega-Munene 1996, 2002; Robertshaw 1991). Conventionally, this phenomenon is explained as depositional mixing of deposits from successive site occupations by different linguistic and/or ethnic groups through time. However, other reasons need to be examined. For example, ethno-archaeological work has demonstrated that artisans within a community will often develop different styles (Herbich 1987). Wandibba (2003) provides effective evidence that, as Karega-Munene (2002) points out, no easy correlations exist between ethnicity and pottery "wares" as archaeologically defined; nevertheless, certain aspects of production method and style are broadly uniform within an ethnic group. Distinguishing such "community indicators" archaeologically, perhaps with the aid of ceramic sourcing studies, may hold the key to untangling cultural interaction in East African archaeology.

Transport and exchange are other processes whereby stylistic boundaries among groups can become blurred. Provenience studies (Merrick and Brown 1984a, 1984b; Merrick et al. 1990), have demonstrated significant trade in obsidian, and pottery too may have been traded. Ideas about alternative explanations of the definition and distribution of pottery wares are being developed. Karega-Munene (2002) in particular, has disputed the association between pre-Neolithic hunter-gatherers and Kansyore Ware at Gogo Falls in western Kenya, where the pottery was found with skeletal remains of sheep/goats and cattle in deposits dated to 3400 b.p. (Karega-Munene 2002).

Instead of clear-cut succession from one pottery ware to another, some have argued that pottery wares in fact overlap in time and space (Bower 1991; see Karega-Munene 2002, 2003). Kansyore Ware dates, for instance, fall between 2400 and 8200 b.p.; those of Nderit Ware are from 1500 to 7000 b.p.; Narosura Ware dates from 1400 to 2700 b.p.; Maringishu Ware to 1700 b.p.; Remnant Ware (Elmenteitan) from 1300 to 3300 b.p.; and Akira Ware from 1200 to 1900 b.p. While these dates suggest that Kansyore is the earliest known pottery and that it probably had the longest life-span, they also indicate that Nderit, Narosura, and Elmenteitan Wares may have been created contemporaneously. Karega-Munene rightly argues that Kansyore pottery may not necessarily be older than other wares when they are found together (Karega-Munene 2003). In sum, then, the problem of pottery diversity in the Central Rift continues to hinder our understanding of social interaction. Social phenomena other than language or ethnic affiliation may have conditioned pottery diversity, including function, manufacturing technique, artisanal creativity, and association with a clan, artisanal, gender, or other social grouping.

The Great Lakes mosaic

The Great Lakes region, dominated by Lake Victoria and its basin, is a highly diverse region of forests, woodlands, grasslands, mountains, and swamps crosscut by numerous rivers. Prehistorically and today, the region's lakes and rivers served not only as reservoirs of resources but also as conduits for communication and trade goods, including pots, iron as ore, bloom, or smelted iron, fish and other foodstuffs, bark cloth, and salt. Production, trade, and consumption of food, goods, iron, and salt formed overlapping webs of interregional trade, especially in raw materials for artisans.

As in the Central Rift, economic specializations sometimes developed here around fish, cattle, or agriculture (Schoenbrun 1998; Sutton 1989). East Africa's earliest ironworking civilizations date to 600 b.c. in Tanzania west of Lake Victoria and in Burundi and Rwanda as well (Schmidt 1997). Later, unlike the Central Rift Valley, the area also saw the development of complex, stratified societies or chiefdoms where social power was closely linked to knowledge of ironworking (Schmidt 1998). Initially, these societies were small, short-lived city-states; after a.d. 1000, larger, more permanent political elites were established.

MacLean (1994–95) and Schoenbrun (1994–95) have constructed the following picture of communities west of Lake Victoria over the last 2,000 years. As in the Central Rift, there is an uncomfortable but intriguing fit between linguistics and archaeology. Before 2,000 years ago, foragers occupied the largest part of the area, especially rockshelters on hill slopes. Their archaeological signature includes lithic tools and, according to MacLean (1994–95), sites with Kansyore pottery. Along the shores of Lake Albert (Mwitanzige), stone-tool-using hunter-gatherer-fishers were the main occupants until a.d. 1000 (Connah 1996). Fishing and possibly farming communities lived closer to Lake Victoria and near larger, permanent rivers. They were apparently associated with Kansyore pottery as well, at sites such as Gogo Falls in western Kenya. According to linguistic evidence, Cushitic and Sudanic speakers who herded cows and goats and farmed sorghum were also present, especially southeast of Lake Victoria. Bantu speakers from Central African lowlands came to the region, judging from sites including polished stone axes in the Kivu area, around 2,000 years ago. They originated from Central Africa, and cleared valley bottoms to plant root crops, and, according to linguistic evidence, they also fished, farmed, hunted, and gathered (Schoenbrun 1998). The early Bantu speakers sometimes lived amidst the fishing people using the Kansyore pottery.

Slightly later, around 600 b.c., sites show evidence of iron-smelting, often containing Urewe or Dimple-based pottery, especially in places of good soil and adequate rainfall. Linguistic evidence suggests that these Bantu people learned cattle-keeping, grain agriculture, and ironworking from Central Sudanic speakers (Ehret 1998; Schoenbrun 1990). Exact archaeological confirmation of the earliest ironworkers' linguistic picture is lacking; indeed, sites of the Early Iron Age are rare (MacLean 1994–95).

Regardless of the specific linguistic affiliation of Great Lakes peoples, ethnic symbioses, or mutually beneficial interactions between or among social groups, played themselves out. The demand for firewood and needs of shifting agriculture caused a gradual expansion from the Kivu Rift east to the western shores of Lake Victoria, branching then to the north and to the south. The lakes and rivers also facilitated the spread of farming and metallurgy. Early agriculturalists cleared not only to plant but to smelt iron, and in so doing created areas, called *caka in the early Great Lakes Bantu language, that were free of thick bush, tsetse flies, and ticks and suitable for cow pastoralism. Southern Cushite cow-herders near the area moved into the areas Bantu speakers had cleared and made possible the development of pastoralist specialization in the Great Lakes around a.d. 800. In this way, the human mosaic modified the ecological mosaic.

Cow pastoralism in the Great Lakes is marked by the appearance of rouletted pottery and an expansion of agropastoralism and iron-using away from the wetter regions near rivers and lakes to upland areas and areas below ridge tops. The shifting agriculture practiced by people who used rouletted pottery, combined with the heavy fuel demands of smelting, contributed to their rapid expansion. Sites dating to after a.d. 800 contain abundant cattle bones, grindstones, and sorghum, and demonstrate an agropastoral economy that emphasized either pastoralism or herding depending on the site.

After a.d. 1000, economic specializations (such as salt at Kibiro; Connah 1996) operated within a regional economy. Sites like Bigo and Ntusi (Sutton 1998c) demonstrate substantial population aggregations with large cattle herds, pottery and ivory artifact production, and, at Bigo, substantial earthworks consisting of an inner cluster of small enclosures and mounds, and an outer boundary, constructed in several phases of settlement, mound accumulation, ditching, and embanking. The purposes of these earthworks were manifold, but defense was a likely component of the structures (Sutton 1998c:63). At sites like Bigo and Munsa, elaborate earthworks may have been defensive in nature; large cattle herds were kept at both of these sites. Only 15 km south of Bigo, the site of Ntusi, over 100 hectares in size, appears to represent an agriculturalist site. Sutton (1998c) argues that contact between Bigo and Ntusi was probably much more significant than among historically known agriculturalists and pastoralists, who formed two distinct communities. On the contrary, Robertshaw (1994, 1997) argues that the economies at these sites are as poorly known as the interactions between them. Oddly, too, cowries and other evidence of coastal trade are common at Ntusi but rare at the earthworks sites. The relationship between Bigo and Ntusi – contemporaneous, neighboring, yet very different settlements – has yet to be understood.

Taita-Tsavo, southeast Kenya

The third mosaic, the Taita-Tsavo area, is less well known archaeologically than those we have just reviewed. However, based on eyewitness accounts of explorers, missionaries, and colonial officials, this region was an important interaction sphere. It is located 100 km from the Kenya coast where Iron Age city-states developed after a.d. 1000 (Figure 16.2; Chapter 13). The Taita-Tsavo area's abundance of highly lucrative resources, such as ivory, rhinoceros horns, rock crystals, skins, and beeswax, made it an important trading partner for the coastal cities (C. Kusimba and S. Kusimba 1998–2002; Chapters 13, 15). The Taita-Tsavo case study not only demonstrates the responses of African communities to long-distance trade, but also shows the devastating effects of slave trade and colonialism.

Oral traditions have formed the groundwork for our archaeological research and have helped us identify and understand the major components of the Taita-Tsavo mosaic. Ethnohistorical interviews have also helped us understand how people defined their own social groups and those of others over time. Oral traditions collected from local groups tell of migration, settlement, intermarriages, alliances, fictive relationships, interregional trade and co-dependence, and warfare by various peoples whose descendants claim Tsavo as their homeland. The groups who lived in Tsavo were so interconnected and relationships constantly shifting that the term mosaic seems far too static to adequately describe intergroup relationships. Nevertheless, ethnic boundaries remained, even if they were not the primary personal affiliation for every social context.

Ethnic groups in the area included the Waata (primarily foragers), the Oromo (nomadic pastoralists), and Wataita and Wakamba (agriculturalists; French-Sheldon 1891; Lewis 1966; Stiles 1979, 1980, 1981, 1982). Akamba, Taita, and Waata traditions claim that the first inhabitants of Tsavo were hunter-gatherer dwarves who lived in caves and rockshelters, forged iron tools, and hunted elephants with poisoned arrows. Taita oral traditions say that food producers moved in around 2,000 years ago (Lamphear 1970; Merritt 1975). Since that time, several social groups have inhabited the Tsavo area.

According to oral traditions, the Oromo arrived from Ethiopia by the 15th century. Swahili and Mijikenda ethnohistories recall Oromo supremacy on the coast and hinterland as far south as Pangani in Tanzania (Hobley 1912; C. Kusimba 1999; Spear 1997). The oral traditions of the agropastoralist Wataita indicate that they arrived in the area during the 15th century (Allen 1993; Spear 1981). The ancestors of the Wataita peoples settled in the plains of Tsavo and gradually colonized the slopes of Sagalla, Taita, and Kasigau Hills where they can still be found (Bravman 1998; Kitson 1931; Merritt 1975).

Wataita and Oromo pastoralist groups were organized into patrilineal corporate groups, in which elder males attempted to have strong influence over younger men and women. Although these societies lacked ranking, significant authority was held by elder males, who sought to accumulate and control distribution of cattle and land. Consequently, intergroup conflict over wealth-building resources, such as cattle, coexisted with alliances for exchange of goods, information, and ritual power

(Bravman 1998; Herlehy 1984; C. Kusimba and S. Kusimba 1998–2002; Merritt 1975). Like other Tsavo peoples, Wataita claim to have participated in the coast–hinterland trade as suppliers of ivory and skins to traders visiting the markets from the coast. They maintained the inland markets in their areas by ensuring that they were accessible and secure. These inland markets (i.e., Rukanga and Bungule) were located along permanent perennial streams and could have supplied fresh water, vegetables, fruits, and other services to long-distance caravan traders. They could also have served as collection centers for traders further inland. During the late 18th century and the 19th century the Taita were captured by Arab and Swahili slave traders.

Waata foragers, referred to pejoratively by their neighbors as Walyankuru (those who eat pig), spoke a Southern Cushitic language (Hobley 1895, 1912; Parker and Amin 1983:24; Stiles 1980; Thorbahn 1979). Waata were adept in the use of bows and poisoned arrows for hunting. Waata poison was one of the most desirable trade items among East African groups and was traded far and wide. The Wataa relationship with their numerically and politically more powerful Oromo neighbors was one of patron–client. Thus, "If they shoot an elephant one tusk is given to the Galla (Oromo) Chief" (Hobley 1895:557).

During the height of the ivory trade in eastern Africa, many groups bought Wataa poison or tried to replicate the techniques of making that poison. Some became professional poison makers as well as elephant hunters. Some hunters abandoned foraging in favor of a more comfortable lifestyle in the numerous towns that had emerged on the coast, while those from other communities became involved in trade. In any case, trade allowed individuals to develop a personal network of contacts across many lineages and language groups, in which they were sometimes subordinate but nevertheless maintained social power. Hunter-gatherer relationships with their Wataita neighbors in the hilly and mountainous regions of Tsavo were based upon blood brotherhoods, fictive kinships that could be inherited. In this sense, blood brotherhoods enabled the exchange of ideas and knowledge, eased tensions arising from competition for resources, and allowed the exchange of technical and sacred knowledge. Thus, through alliances and clientships, individuals, especially those involved in the ivory trade, were welcome in several communities as technicians or "transformers" (David et al. 1988). Some forms of technical and practical knowledge, such as hunting techniques, poison-making, and animal tracking, were so prized that blood brotherhoods and secret societies controlled the spread of this sacred information (C. Kusimba and S. Kusimba 1998–2002).

In contrast to the Central Rift Valley and the Great Lakes region, where linguistic and pottery evidence has been useful in creating a culture-historical framework out of an abundance of archaeological diversity, the Taita-Tsavo region has not yet yielded enough archaeological evidence to forge strong fits between styles of pottery, beadwork, or other artifacts and social identities. However, historical evidence coupled with excavation of site clusters and radiocarbon dates does provide some clues to how the mosaic worked. Based on archaeological surveys, preliminary excavations of select sites, radiocarbon dates, and oral traditions collected in the area since 1998, we have developed a culture-historical outline of the Taita-Tsavo area

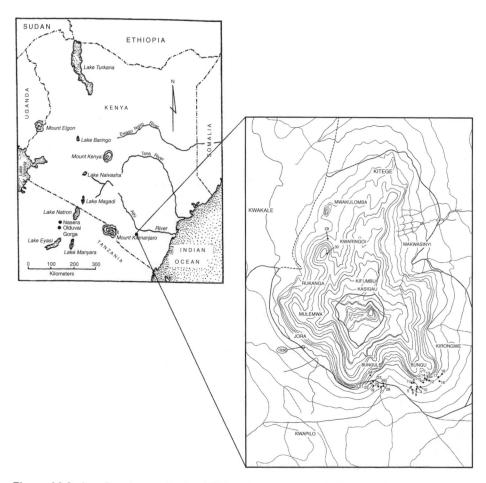

Figure 16.2. Iron Age sites on Kasigau Hill listed in Tables 16.2 and 16.3

(Table 16.1). Our archaeological surveys and radiocarbon dates illustrated in Tables 16.1 and 16.2 have identified six site cluster types that characterized the cultural mosaic of Taita-Tsavo, from which a number of patterns emerge (see Table 16.3 for typical finds). First, contemporaneous sites clearly bear out the area's economic and cultural diversity. Evidence of herding, contact with the coast, and technological specialization varies among contemporaneous habitations. Second, sites with dramatically different characteristics and contents are found very close to each other. Site clusters at the southern end of Mount Kasigau (Figure 16.2), for example, include sites associated with specialized occupations such as stock-keeping (associated with goat and cow pens of dry stonework), iron-smelting, and iron-forging, as well as residential and mortuary sites.

All these sites are likely the components of a single ethnic group, yet they are dramatically different in their situation and contents. There are clear separations

Table 16.1. Historical sequence at Taita-Tsavo area

Years before present	Predominant technology	Subsistence economies	Residences	Contact with neighbors
10000–5000	Late Stone Age	Foraging	Open sites, rockshelters	Interperson/intergroup trade
5000–3000	Late Stone Age Pastoral Neolithic	Foraging, herding	Rockshelters, pastoral villages	Interperson/intergroup trade
3000–2000	Pastoral Neolithic–Early Iron Age	Foraging, herding, gardening(?)	Rockshelters, agrarian/pastoral villages	Interperson/intergroup trade
2000–1000	Early Iron Age, Late Iron Age	Foraging, gardening, herding; craft specialists?	Rockshelters, terraced hillslope villages, pastoral villages and camps	Regular markets in the interior communities; interperson/intergroup trade; coastal contact
1000–500	Late Iron Age–Colonial period	Specialized foraging, farming, nomadic and sedentary (pen-feeding) herding	Rockshelters, stonework fortified rockshelters, open villages and camps	Regular markets in the interior communities; interperson/intergroup trade; coastal contact
500–100	Colonial period	Specialized foraging, farming, nomadic pastoralism and sedentary (pen-feeding) herding	Fortified rockshelters and caves, migration to hill tops	Decreased trade and collapse of traditional market systems, abandonment of terraced farming, tensions and inter-community warfare; blood brotherhoods and alliances
100–0	Colonial and Post-colonial	Specialized foraging, agrarian, pastoral, agropastoral	Villages, manyattas, individual farmsteads	Inter-community trade, European colonial economy

Table 16.2. Site clusters of the Taita-Tsavo interaction sphere

Site cluster type	Features	Sites	$^c14$ dates (RCY B.P.)
Hillslope agropastoralist villages	Dry stonework terracing and irrigation canals, burial cairns. cranial display niches, rockshelters with dry stone work cattle/ goat pens, hearths and food-grinding areas, iron and pottery production sites	Bungule 1 28, 29, 30, 31; Sungululu 1, Makwasinyi 1, Jora 1	170 ± 70–380 ± 70
Forager–food producer rockshelter occupations	Pottery, metals, lithic artifacts, Indian and European beadwork, coastal shells and shell beads, sheet metal and smelted iron artifacts and arrowheads, domestic and wild fauna	Kisio, Muasya, Bungule 1, 9, Kirongwe 1, 2, 7	100 ± 25–1000 ± 25 380 ± 70–5330 ± 70
Plains mound settlements	White coral burial mound clusters, collapsed houses. Burials: European trade beads, attributed to Wambisha and Orma pastoralists	Konu Moju	No data
Inselberg trading posts	Prominent inselbergs – lithic scatters, grinding hollows, faunal remains, meat-drying and trade areas, aggregation sites	Mudanda Rock, Rukanga and Bungule markets	No data
Fugitive stockade settlements	Hillside and mountain rockshelters and caves in inaccessible locales with defensive offset doors and dry stonework fortifications	Bungule 20, Rukanga 1	207 ± 40–300 ± 70
Specialized intensive economic activity sites	Goats, sheep and cattle pens, ironsmithing sites, agricultural terraces, salt mines, grinding shallows and hollows	Bungule 1, 28, 31, Kirongwe 1–7, Saghala 1	Early Iron Age, 170 ± 70–240 ± 70

Table 16.3. Finds at Taita-Tsavo sites

Site	Type	Finds
Bungule 1	Rockshelter	Iron slag, tuyeres, pottery, lithics, shell, glass, and bone beads, worked cowrie shell, dung, wild and domestic fauna, carbonized seeds, dry stonework
Bungule 7	Rockshelter	Domestic and wild fauna, shell beads, dung
Bungule 9	Rockshelter	Stone tools, pottery, shell, glass, and bone beads, worked cowrie shell, dung, wild and domestic fauna, carbonized seeds
Bungule 20	Rockshelter	Dung piles, fortifications, storage gourds, dry stone work
Bungule 28	Cave	Dry stone work, dung piles, domestic and wild fauna, ostrich eggshell beads
Bungule 29	Village	Pottery, metal artifacts, whisky bottles, glass, iron artifacts
Bungule 31	Cave	Dry stone work, dung piles, domestic fauna
Kirongwe 1	Rockshelter/smithing site	Dry stone work, domestic fauna, wild fauna, glass, shell, and bone beads, iron artifacts, tuyeres, forge, pottery
Kirongwe 2	Rockshelter	Dry stonework, pottery
Kirongwe 7	Iron-smelting site	Iron-smelting furnaces, tuyeres, pottery

between domestic sites and specialized economic sites. For example, goat/cow pens are usually several meters from domestic spheres, a pattern similar to that found at Hyrax Hill and other Iron Age pastoralist sites (Sutton 1998b). Site economic specialization may be a result of coastal contact in this area, but probably reflects a common store of cultural knowledge from which this region's inhabitants forged economic and cultural ties (S. Kusimba 2003). Three major types of residential patterns are dominant: terraced hillslope villages, rockshelter and cave sites, and open plains settlements. Certainly, large-scale ecological boundaries seem to be associated with particular economic activities – pastoralists lived on the flat plains, while agriculture was undertaken on the hillslopes. On the other hand, within an area such as the well-watered, secure, and tsetse-free Mount Kasigau zone, a diversity of economic and subsistence activities were undertaken, including foraging, farming, hunting, herding, and trading. An extensive ironsmithing and smelting site, Kirongwe 1-7, was no doubt crucial to the regional economy. On the other hand, our surveys have located evidence of strife as well – especially territoriality in the form of highly visible regionally specific mortuary practices. On the Taita, Kasigau, and Sagalla Hills, burial cairns up to 1 m in diameter and constructed from black igneous stones mark homesteads. Precolonially, persons were disinterred from cairns and their skulls displayed in a rockshelter shrine along with others of the patrilineage. The ancestral shrines validated a patrilineage's identity and established its claims to land. Similarly, the open plains of Tsavo East are dotted with large cairns of white stone attributed to Oromo pastoralists, which served as highly visible markers of shifting territorial boundaries.

The Taita-Tsavo area contains important archaeological evidence of the fate of mosaic communities in the wake of slave trade and colonialism – a fate well explored by historians as well (Ambler 1988; Robertson 1997). Throughout the Kasigau area, just south of Tsavo National Park and 80 km from the coast, village sites on the hill's apron were abandoned in the 16th century. Villagers moved up the hills into rocky, bushy terrain and converted rockshelters into fortified "maroons" (Morton 1990). Several of these fortified sites are still intact on the south side of Kasigau Hill. Our surveys termed them B1, B20, B28, B29, and B31.

The largest, most intact of the Kasigau rockshelters is B20, which is reached by a one-hour walk up the hill's steepest face. It has a formidable appearance, with impressive dry stone architecture around a large, enclosed space. The site originally had two enclosures: one with dry stone architecture; the other a wooden frame structure on a dry stone foundation. Although the shelter was located on a steep cliff, a clay and stone foundation 2 m thick was constructed to create a causeway into the shelter, which itself was protected by a dry stonework wall.

The enclosure is faced with dry stone wall reaching nearly 2 m in height. The wall is supported by vertical wooden frame. The doorway is a tunnel at least 1.5 m long under the wall and is lined with vertical slabs supporting at least four heavy beams which in turn support the meter of rocks above. The doorway emerges into an area protected by a wooden partition which runs parallel to the wall. The entire front portion of the shelter was reserved for human use and still preserved grass bedding, a hearth, ceramics, and gourds. Behind the partition, piles of fossilized dung dominated the shelter's ovicaprid pen. The dung extended under the front wall to the paths outside and a clear sheltered area adjacent to the enclosure.

The fortress walls were 2 m thick at base and 14 m long, held up by a wooden superstructure that was constructed before the dry stones were piled up. The entrance to the enclosure was large enough for use by humans and livestock, most probably ovicaprids. The size of the enclosure is approximately 11 m long, 6 m wide, and 1.75 m high. The surface of the enclosure was a thick deposit of fossilized animal dung reaching 80 cm thick in some areas. A small partitioned area reserved for people had an intact grass bed, a hearth, a few broken but originally whole pots, and gourds.

The exterior partially enclosed section covers the western half of the site. This section was 7 m long and 6 m wide, with a 1.5–4 m high ceiling. Two distinct activity areas characterized the outside enclosure. The inner sub-section had been cordoned off and a low wall constructed, leaving only the entrance. This section was reminiscent of a modern pastoralist's calf- or goat-pen in corrals. This area contained thick deposits of fossil dung. They also contained a great deal of recent goat dung, yet some sections, especially the southern and western sub-sections, were surprisingly clean, exhibiting no dung, and had remains of fence posts running along the length of the rockshelter to prevent people and animals from accidentally falling down the steep cliff. Three samples obtained from the vines and wood holding the dry stone wall were dated 207 ± 40, 290 ± 70, 300 ± 70 b.p., placing the date of construction of the dry wall in the late 17th century and 18th century a.d.

This period in East Africa was punctuated by ivory and slave trade financed by European, Indian, and Arab slave and ivory merchants. Slave raiding caused widespread insecurity, fear, famine, disease, and the collapse of farming and pastoral societies, chiefdoms, and states in East Africa (C. Kusimba 1999). Elephant overhunting also accompanied a reversion of open savanna to woodland and forest and a return of the tsetse fly, a vector of sleeping sickness among people and of trypanosomiasis in cattle and wildlife. Declining ecosystem quality was one factor that forced people and their wildlife to retreat to the hills and other tsetse fly-free habitats (C. Kusimba 2004).

The investment in the architecture of the rockshelter refugia provides evidence that the rockshelter enclosures of Kasigau were defensive structures. Dry stone architecture specifically for penning animals, is not widely practiced among African pastoralists. However, the data show that all rockshelters served partly as animal pens, and the labor, time, and materials invested in their construction and maintenance was extensive. The evidence is compelling enough to conclude that the Kasigau enclosures were built for purposes of protecting the animals and people from rustlers and slave raiders. The structural design and internal use of space in the enclosures suggest the use of cooperative strategies that took advantage of the landscape to effectively respond to an uncertain and threatening future. The walls of the shelters were so thick they would have required considerable effort to break. Such walls were not necessary for the safety of only goats. It is remarkable that the community would have had the resources and time to expend on such huge private and "public" constructions at a time when it was under relentless attack.

Oral traditions recount that, when slave raiding and cattle rustling intensified in the Tsavo region, people abandoned their settlements in the valleys and plains for the safety of the hilltops, caves, and fortified rockshelters (C. Kusimba and S. Kusimba 1998–2002). These oral narratives are bolstered by the fact that many unprotected rockshelters were not used during this period, nor were the villages in the plains and the base of the hills. Tsetse fly infestation in the plains could also have contributed to the shifting of homesteads to cooler hillside and hilltop residences, but oral stories emphasize the terror of slave raiders and cattle rustlers. Oral stories we collected also told of brave parties descending into the plains to collect grasses, a practice also observed in 1883 by Thomson, who saw:

> two hundred natives of Rombo returning from the outer plains laden with neatly made-up bales of grass, which they feed to their cattle, as there is little pasturage on the mountain, and they dare not let them be seen outside their huts. They were evidently in great terror as suddenly seeing us, and would have pitched their loads and fled, but for our kind words. (Thomson 1887:67)

The Kasigau evidence is a poignant reminder of the disintegration of many East African cultural mosaics in the face of the slave trade. The evidence also underscores the considerable upheavals African societies experienced during the colonial period. Ethnographic accounts, a frequent source of ethnographic analogy for the precolonial past, thus reflect societies already profoundly transformed in the interim period (Stahl 2001). This evidence further underscores the important role archaeology can play in reconstructing later history in Africa and providing historical context for the ethnographic present. Questions of historical identity remain seminal to the present-day task of nation-building in East Africa.

Conclusion

Colonization in Africa enlisted anthropology in the task of labeling and describing cultural diversity. An ethnic group was confidently assigned a set of descriptors and social system, ecology, economy, religion, and legal system. African cultures became known to the European world through these labels. Similarly, archaeology in East Africa has taken its primary goal as the description of normative patterns in the ways of life of discrete peoples. Over time, archaeologists have realized that the easiest way to identify people is by their economy. Bones and biotic remains often yield a great deal of information about prehistoric subsistence patterns. Since economy is one of the chief ways of differentiating modern East African groups, it has been another way of labeling prehistoric peoples as hunters, pastoralists, or hunter-gatherers. Correspondences have been constructed between ethnicity, economy, pottery type, and linguistic affiliation to allow the neat assortment of groups into appropriate pigeonholes. Linguistic data have been linked to these descriptions of lifeways, which have then been anchored to the past using pottery styles. This has opened the way to speculations about economies and social systems that rely, whether implicitly or explicitly, on ethnographic analogy (Ambrose 1982; Ehret 1998; Freeman-Grenville 1958; Huffman 1982, 1984, 1986; Nurse and Spear 1985; Phillipson 1970, 1977, 1993).

All these understandings of African peoples have, however, come to be revised. First of all, it is becoming clear that ethnicity is not the boundary it was thought to be. Intermarriage and shifting alliances of exchange and conflict make ethnicity an ever-changing stage. Similarly, we now understand just how variable subsistence practices still are. The rigid mosaic has become an ever-shifting kaleidoscope. Taking the kaleidoscope back into the past means coming to grips with diversity and flexibility, and attempting to model the constraints and freedoms around and through which people have acted.

The later prehistory of Africa cannot be fully understood and appreciated without the use of a holistic perspective that critically interrogates and integrates methodologies and approaches from the humanities and the social and natural sciences. Without incorporating data from history, ethnohistory, and oral traditions with archaeology, our attempts as prehistorians to reconstruct the African precolonial experience will continue to be hamstrung. Indeed, disciplinary isolationism and rigidity have largely contributed to the linear evolutionary model common in anthropological parlance – hunter-gatherer-pastoralist-agrarian subsistence strategies – which are often conceived of as rigid, hierarchical, and oppositional rather than flexible and complementary to one another.

Earlier understandings in East African archaeology hoped to reinforce the coincidence of economy, language, and material culture, especially pottery distributions. However, we should not confuse these identifications with the much smaller scale of ethnic and community identities that prevailed precolonially as reconstructed from ethnohistory. Furthermore, trade and interaction will necessarily introduce overlapping material culture distributions. In the East African mosaics we have examined, alliances and blood brotherhoods and sisterhoods that crosscut ethnic identities have been particularly important. Intercommunity and interethnic networks of alliances enabled resource- and information-sharing and shaped the symbolic reservoir (Herlehy 1984). Alliances meant access to specialized ritual knowledge, and kept ethnic boundaries fluid, minimized competition and conflicts, and impacted both the cultural and ecological landscape of the region. Perhaps the major challenge awaiting the archaeology of mosaics will be to develop archaeological ways of recognizing these crosscutting alliances and interactions that persisted in spite of ethnic boundaries, and in so doing helped define ethnic identities themselves.

REFERENCES

Allen, J. De V., 1993 Swahili Origins. Athens: Humanities Press.

Ambler, Charles H., 1988 Kenyan Communities in the Age of Imperialism: The Central Region in the Late Nineteenth Century. New Haven and London: Yale University Press.

Ambrose, Stanley H., 1982 Archaeological and Linguistic Reconstructions of History in East Africa. In The Archaeological and Linguistic Reconstruction of African History. Christopher Ehret and Merrick Posnansky, eds. pp. 104–157. Berkeley: University of California Press.

——1984 The Introduction of Pastoral Adaptations to the Highlands of East Africa. In From Hunters to Farmers: The Causes and Consequences of Food Production in Africa. J. Desmond Clark and Steven A. Brandt, eds. pp. 212–239. Berkeley: University of California Press.

——1986 Hunter-Gatherer Adaptations to Non-Marginal Environments: An Ecological and Archaeological Assessment of the Dorobo Model. Sprache und Geschichte in Afrika 7:11–42.

Ambrose, Stanley H., and Michael J. DeNiro, 1986 Reconstruction of African Human Diet Using Bone Collagen Carbon and Nitrogen Isotope Ratios. Nature 319:321–324.

Barth, F., 1969 Introduction. In Ethnic Groups and Boundaries: The Social Organization of Culture Differences. F. Barthes, ed. pp. 9–15. Bergen: Universitets Forlaget.

Barthelme, John W., 1984 Early Evidence for Animal Domestication in Eastern Africa. In From Hunters to Farmers: the Causes and Consequences of Food Production in Africa. J. Desmond Clark and Steven A. Brandt, eds. pp. 200–205. Berkeley: University of California Press.

——1985 Fisher-Hunters and Neolithic Pastoralists in East Turkana, Kenya. BAR International Series, 254. Oxford: British Archaeological Reports.

Bower, John R. F., 1973 Early Pottery and Other Finds from Kisii District, Western Kenya. Azania 8:131–140.

——1991 The Pastoral Neolithic of East Africa. Journal of World Prehistory 5:49–82.

Bower, John R. F., C. M. Nelson, A. F. Waibel, and S. Wandibba, 1977 The University of Massachusetts' Later Stone Age/Pastoral Neolithic Comparative Study in Central Kenya: An Overview. Azania, 12:119–143.

Bravman, B., 1998 Making Ethnic Ways: Communities and their Transformations in Taita, Kenya, 1800–1950. Portsmouth: Heinemann.

Chami, F., 1999 Graeco-Roman Trade Link and the Bantu Migration Theory. Anthropos 94:205.

——2001 A Response to Christopher Ehret's "Bantu Expansions." International Journal of African Historical Studies 34:647–651.

Clark, J. Desmond, 1970 The Prehistory of Africa. London: Thames & Hudson.

Conkey, Meg, and Christine Hastorf, eds. 1990 The Uses of Style in Archaeology. Cambridge: Cambridge University Press.

Connah, Graham, 1996 Kibiro: The Salt of Bunyoro Past and Present. Memoir 13. London: British Institute in Eastern Africa.

David, Nicholas, Judy Sterner, and K. Gavua, 1988 Why Pots Are Decorated. Current Anthropology 29:365–389.

De Langhe, E., R. Swennen, and D. Vuylsteke, 1994–95 Plaintain in the Early Bantu World. Azania 29–30:147–160.

de la Gorgendière, L., K. King, and S. Vaughan, 1996 Ethnicity in Africa: Roots, Meanings, and Implications. Edinburgh: Centre of African Studies, University of Edinburgh.

Denbow, James, 1990 Congo to Kalahari: Data and Hypotheses about the Political Economy of the Western Stream of the Early Iron Age. The African Archaeological Review 8:139–176.

Ehret, Christopher, 1967 Cattle-Keeping and Milking in Eastern and Southern African History: The Linguistic Evidence. Journal of African History 8:1–17.

——1968 Sheep and Central Sudanic Peoples in Southern Africa. Journal of African History 9:213–221.

——1971 Southern Nilotic History: Linguistic Approaches to the Study of the Past. Evanston: Northwestern University Press.

——1974 Ethiopians and East Africans: The Problem of Contacts. Nairobi: East African Publishing House.

——1997 Historical Linguistics. In Encyclopedia of Africa South of the Sahara, vol. 2. John Middleton, ed. pp. 579–580. New York: Charles Scribner's Sons.

——1998 An African Classical Age: Eastern and Southern Africa in World History, 1000 BC to AD 400. Charlottesville: University of Virginia Press.

——2001 Bantu Expansions: Re-envisioning a Central Problem of Early African History. International Journal of African Historical Studies 34:5–43.

——2002 The Civilizations of Africa: A History to 1800. Charlottesville: University Press of Virginia.

Freeman-Grenville, G. S. P., 1958 Some Recent Archaeological Work on the Tanganyika Coast. Man 58:106–111.

French-Sheldon, Mrs. 1891 Customs Among the Natives of East Africa, from Teita to Kilimengilia, with Special Reference to their Women and Children. Journal of the Royal Anthropological Institute of Great Britain and Ireland 21:358–390.

Geological Map of Kenya, 1987 Government Printer, Nairobi.

Guyer, Jane, and Samuel M. Eno Belinga, 1995 Wealth in People as Wealth in Knowledge.

Accumulation and Composition in Equatorial Africa. Journal of African History 36:91–120.

Hamilton, A. C., 2000 History of Forests and Climate. In The Conservation Atlas of Tropical Forests: Africa. J. A. Sayer, C. Harcourt, and N. Collins, eds. pp. 17–25. New York: Simon & Schuster.

Herbich, Ingrid, 1987 Learning Patterns, Potter Interaction and Ceramic Style among the Luo of Kenya. The African Archaeological Review 5:193–204.

Herlehy, T. J., 1984 Historical Dimensions of the Food Crisis in Africa: Surviving Famines along the Kenya Coast, 1880–1980. Boston: African Studies Center, Boston University.

Hivernel, Françoise M. M., 1978 An Ethnoarchaeological Study of Environmental Use in the Kenya Highlands. Ph.D. dissertation, Institute of Archaeology, University of London.

Hobley, C. W., 1895 Upon a Visit to Tsavo and the Taita Highland. Geographical Journal 5:545–561.

——1912 The Wa-lungulu or Araingulu of the Taru Desert. Man 12:18–21.

Hobsbawm, Eric, and Terence Ranger, eds. 1983 The Invention of Tradition. Cambridge: Cambridge University Press.

Hodder, Ian, 1991 Gender Representation and Social Reality. In The Archaeology of Gender. Proceedings of the Twenty-Second Annual Chacmool Conference of the Archaeological Association of the University of Calgary. Dale Walde and Noreen D. Willows, eds. pp. 11–16. Calgary: Archaeological Association of the University of Calgary.

Holl, Augustin, 2000 Metals and Precolonial African Society. In Ancient African Metallurgy: The Sociocultural Context. Joseph Vogel, ed. pp. 1–81. Walnut Creek, CA: AltaMira Press.

Huffman, Thomas N., 1982 Archaeology and Ethnohistory of the African Iron Age. Annual Review of Anthropology 11:133–150.

——1984 Leopard's Kopje and the Nature of the Iron Age in Bantu Africa. Zimbabwea 1:28–35.

——1986 Iron Age Settlement Patterns and the Origins of Class Distinction in Southern Africa. Advances in World Archaeology 5:291–338.

Karega-Munene, 1996 The East African Neolithic: An Alternative View. African Archaeological Review 13:247–254.

——2002 Holocene Foragers, Hunters and Fishers of Western Kenya. Cambridge Monographs in African Archaeology, 54. Cambridge: Cambridge University Press.

——2003 The East African Neolithic: A Historical Perspective. In East African Archaeology: Foragers, Potters, Smiths, and Traders. Chapurukha M. Kusimba and Sibel Kusimba, eds. pp. 17–32. Philadelphia: University of Pennsylvania Museum Publications.

Kitson, E., 1931 A Study of the Negro Skill with Special Reference to the Crania from Kenya Colony. Biometrika 23:271–314.

Kiyaga-Mulindwa, D., 1993 The Iron Age Peoples of East-Central Botswana. In The Archaeology of Africa: Food, Metal, and Towns. Thurstan Shaw, Paul Sinclair, Bassey Andah, and Alex Okpoko, eds. pp. 386–390. London: Routledge.

Kusimba, Chapurukha M., 1999 The Rise and Fall of Swahili States. Walnut Creek, CA: AltaMira Press.

——2004 Archaeology of Slavery in East Africa. African Archaeological Review. In press, scheduled for June 2004.

Kusimba, Chapurukha M., and Sibel Kusimba, 1998–2002 Field Notes, Tsavo Archaeological Research Project. Chicago: Field Museum of Natural History.

Kusimba, Sibel, 2003 African Foragers: Environment, Technology, Interactions. Walnut Creek, CA: AltaMira Press.

Lamphear, J., 1970 The Kamba and the Northern Mrima Coast. *In* Precolonial African Trade. R. Gray and D. Birmingham, eds. pp. 75–101. London: Oxford University Press.

Lewis, H. S., 1966 The Origins of the Galla and Somali. Journal of African History 7:27–46.

MacDonald, Kevin C., and P. Allsworth-Jones, 1994 A Reconsideration of the West African Macrolithic Conundrum: New Factory Sites and an Associated Settlement in the Vallée du Serpent, Mali. The African Archaeological Review 12:73–104.

MacEachern, Scott, 1994 "Symbolic Reservoirs" and Inter-Group Relations: West African Examples. The African Archaeological Review 12:205–224.

——2001 Setting the Boundaries: Linguistics, Ethnicity, Colonialism, and Archaeology South of Lake Chad. *In* Archaeology, Language, and History: Essays on Culture and Ethnicity. John Edward Terrell, ed. pp. 79–101. Westport, CT: Bergin & Garvey.

McIntosh, Roderick J., 1989 Middle Niger Terracottas before the Symplegades Gateway. African Arts 22:74–83, 103–104.

MacLean, M. R., 1994–95 Late Stone Age and Early Iron Age Settlement in the Interlacustrine Region: A District Case Study. Azania, 29–30:296–302.

Mapunda, B. B., 2000 Ironworking. Journal of African History 41:487–529.

——2003 Fipa Iron Technologies and their Implied Social History. *In* East African Archaeology: Foragers, Potters, Smiths, and Traders. Chapurukha M. Kusimba and Sibel Kusimba, eds, pp. 71–86. Philadelphia: University of Pennsylvania Museum Publications.

Marean, Curtis W., 1992 Hunter to Herder: Large Mammal Remains from the Hunter-Gatherer Occupation at Enkapune ya Muto Rockshelter, Central Rift Valley, Kenya. The African Archaeological Review 10:65–127.

Marshall, Fiona, 1991 Origins of Specialized Pastoral Production in East Africa. American Anthropologist 92:873–894.

——2000 The Origins of Domesticated Animals in Eastern Africa. *In* The Origins and Development of African Livestock: Archaeology, Genetics, Linguistics, and Ethnography. Roger M. Blench and Kevin C. McDonald, eds. pp. 191–221. London: University College London Press.

Marshall, Fiona B., K. Steward, and John W. Barthelme, 1984 Early Domestic Stock at Dongodien in Northern Kenya. Azania 19:120–127.

Merrick, H., and F. H. Brown, 1984a Obsidian Sources and Patterns of Source Utilization in Kenya and Northern Tanzania: Some Initial Findings. The African Archaeological Review 2:129–152.

————1984b Rapid Chemical Characterization of Obsidian Artifacts by Electron Microprobe Analysis. Archaeometry 26:230–236.

Merrick, H., F. H. Brown, and M. Connelly, 1990 Sources of the Obsidian at Ngamuriak and Other Southwestern Kenyan Sites. *In* Early Pastoralists of South-Western Kenya. P. Robertshaw, ed. pp. 173–181. Memoir 11. Nairobi: British Institute in Eastern Africa.

Merritt, H., 1975 A History of the Taita. Ph.D. dissertation. Ann Arbor: University Microfilms.

Morton, F., 1990 Children of Ham: Freed Slaves and Fugitive Slaves on the Kenya Coast 1873 to 1907. Boulder, CO: Westview Press.

Nurse, Derek, and Thomas Spear, 1985 The Swahili: Reconstructing the History and Language of an African Society, 800–1500. Philadelphia: University of Pennsylvania Press.

Ojany, F. F., and R. B. Ogendo, 1973 Kenya: A Study in Physical and Human Geography. Nairobi: Longman.

Oliver, Roland, and Brian Fagan, 1975 Africa in the Iron Age. Cambridge: Cambridge University Press.

Onyango-Abuje, J. C., 1977a A Contribution to the Study of the Neolithic in East Africa with Particular Reverence to Nakuru-Naivasha Basins. Ph.D. dissertation, Department of Anthropology, University of California, Berkeley.

—— 1977b Crescent Island: Preliminary Report on Excavations at an East African Neolithic Site. Azania 12:147–159.

—— 1980 Temporal and Spatial Distribution of Neolithic Cultures in East Africa. *In* Proceedings of the 8th Pan-African Congress of Prehistory and Quaternary Studies. Richard E. Leakey and B. A. Ogot, eds. pp. 289–292. Nairobi: The International Louis Leakey Memorial Institute for African Prehistory.

Parker, I., and M. Amin, 1983 Ivory Crisis. London: Chatto & Windus.

Phillipson, David W., 1970 The Prehistory of Eastern Zambia. Memoir 6. Nairobi: The British Institute in Eastern Africa.

—— 1977 The Later Prehistory of Eastern and Southern Africa. New York: Homes & Meier.

—— 1993 African Archaeology. 2nd edition. Cambridge: Cambridge University Press.

Price, T. Douglas, 1989 The Chemistry of Prehistoric Bone. Cambridge: Cambridge University Press.

Robertshaw, Peter, 1991 Gogo Falls: Excavations at a Complex Archaeological Site East of Lake Victoria. Azania 26:63–195.

—— 1994 Archaeological Survey, Ceramic Analysis, and State Formation in Western Uganda. The African Archaeological Review 12:105–131.

—— 1997 Munsa Earthworks. Azania 32:1–20.

Robertshaw, Peter, and David Collett, 1983 The Identification of Pastoral Peoples in the Archaeological Record: An Example from East Africa. World Archaeology 15:67–78.

Robertson, C., 1997 Trouble Showed the Way: Women, Men, and Trade in the Nairobi Area, 1890–1990. Bloomington: University of Indiana Press.

Roscoe, P., 2002 The Hunters and Gatherers of New Guinea. Current Anthropology 43:153–162.

Schadeberg, T., 1999 Batwa: The Bantu Name for the Invisible People. *In* Challenging Elusiveness: Central African Hunter-Gatherers in Multidisciplinary Perspective. K. Biesbrouck, S. Elders, and G. Rossel, eds. pp. 21–40. Netherlands: Universitat Leiden Research School CNWS.

Schmidt, Peter R., 1997 Iron Technology in East Africa: Symbolism, Science, and Archaeology. Bloomington: Indiana University Press.

—— 1998 Reading Gender in the Ancient Iron Technology of Africa. *In* Gender in African Prehistory. Susan Kent, ed. pp. 139–162. Walnut Creek, CA: AltaMira Press.

Schoenbrun, David L., 1990 Early History in East Africa's Great Lakes Region: Linguistic, Ecological and Archaeological Approaches, ca. 500 B.C. to ca. A.D. 1,000. Ph.D. thesis, University of California, Los Angeles.

—— 1994–95 Social Aspects of Agricultural Change Between the Great Lakes: AD 500 to 1000. Azania 29–30:270–282.

—— 1998 A Green Place, A Good Place: Agrarian Change, Gender, and Social Identity in the Great Lakes Region to the Fifteenth Century. Portsmouth, NH: Heinemann.

—— 2001 Representing the Bantu Expansions: What's at Stake? International Journal of African Historical Studies 34:1–4.

Schrire, Carmel, 1992 The Archaeological Identity of Hunters and Herders at the Cape over the Last 2000 Years: A Critique. South African Archaeological Bulletin 47:62–64.

Schrire, Carmel, and Janette Deacon, 1989 The Indigenous Artifacts from Oudepost 1, a Colonial Outpost of the VOC at Saldanha Bay, Cape. South African Archaeological Bulletin 44:105–113.

Smith, B., 2001 Low-Level Food Production. Journal of Archaeological Research 9:1–43.

Soper, R., and B. Golden, 1969 An Archaeological Survey of Mwanza Region, Tanzania. Azania 4:15–79.

Southall, Aidan, 1970 The Illusion of Tribe. Journal of Asian and African Studies 5:28–50.

Spear, Thomas, 1981 Kenya's Past: An Introduction to Historical Method in Africa. New York: Longman.

——1997 Mountain Farmers: Moral Economies of Land and Agricultural Development in Arusha and Meru. Berkeley: University of California Press.

Stahl, Ann B., 2001 Making History in Banda: Anthropological Visions of Africa's Past. Cambridge: Cambridge University Press.

Stahl, Ann B., and Maria D. Cruz, 1998 Men and Women in a Market Economy: Gender and Craft Production in West Central Ghana c. 1775–1995. In Gender in African Archaeology. Susan Kent, ed. pp. 205–226. Walnut Creek, CA: AltaMira Press.

Stewart, K., 1991 Fish Remains from Gogo Falls. Appendix III. In Gogo Falls: Excavations at a Complex Archaeological Site East of Lake Victoria. P. Robertshaw, ed. Azania 26:179–180.

——1993 Iron Age Ceramic Studies in Great Lakes Eastern Africa: A Critical and Historiographical Review. The African Archaeological Review 11:21–37.

Stiles, Daniel, 1979 Hunters of the Northern East African Coast. Africa 51:848–862.

——1980 Archaeological and Ethnographic Studies of Pastoral Groups in Northern Kenya. Nyame Akuma 17:20–24.

——1981 Hunters of the Northern East African Coast: Origins and Historical Processes. Africa 51:848–862.

——1982 A History of Hunting Peoples on the Northern East African Coast. Paideuma 28:165–174.

Sutton, John E. G., 1964 A Review of Pottery from the Kenya Highlands. South African Archaeological Bulletin 19:27–35.

——1989 History of African Agricultural Technology and Field Systems. Azania, 24:1–122.

——1998a Engaruka: An Irrigation Agricultural Community in Northern Tanzania before the Maasai. In Archaeological Sites of East Africa: Four Studies. John E. G. Sutton, ed. Azania 33:1–37.

——1998b Hyrax Hill and the Later Archaeology of the Central Rift Valley of Kenya. In Archaeological Sites of East Africa: Four Studies. John E. G. Sutton, ed. Azania 33:73–112.

——1998c Ntusi and Bigo: Farmers, Cattle-Herders and Rulers in Western Uganda, AD 1000–1500. In Archaeological Sites of East Africa: Four Studies. John E. G. Sutton, ed. Azania 33:39–72.

Thomson, J., 1887 Through Masai Land: A Journey of Exploration among the Snowclad Volcanic Mountains and Strange Tribes of Eastern Equatorial Africa. London.

Thorbahn, P., 1979 Precolonial Ivory Trade of East Africa: Reconstruction of a Human–Elephant Ecosystem. Ph.D. dissertation, University of Massachusetts, Amherst.

Vansina, Jan, 1995 New Linguistic Evidence and the Bantu Expansion. Journal of African History 36:173–195.

Wandibba, S., 1977 The Definition and Description of Ceramic Wares of the Early Pastoralist Period in Kenya. Ph.D. dissertation, Kenyatta University College, Nairobi.

——1980 The Application of Attribute Analysis to the Study of Late Stone Age/Neolithic Pottery Ceramics in Kenya. In Proceedings of the 8th Pan-African Congress of Prehistory and Quaternary Studies. Richard E. Leakey and B. A. Ogot, eds. pp. 283–285. Nairobi: The International Louis Leakey Memorial Institute for African Prehistory.

——2003 Ceramic Ethnoarchaeology: Some Examples from Kenya. In East African Archaeology: Foragers, Potters, Smiths, and Traders. Chapurukha M. Kusimba and Sibel Kusimba, eds. pp. 59–70. Philadelphia: University of Pennsylvania Museum Publications.

White, F., 1983 The Vegetation of Africa: A Descriptive Memoir to Accompany the UNESCO/AETFA/UNSO Vegetation Map of Africa, UNESCO Natural Resources Research, vol. 20. Paris: UNESCO.

Wijngaarden, W. V., and V. W. P. van Engelen, 1985 Soils and Vegetation of the Tsavo Area. Nairobi: Geological Survey of Kenya.

17

From Pottery Groups to Ethnic Groups in Central Africa

Pierre de Maret

Expressing interest in the archaeology of Central Africa over the last 2,000 years is usually met with polite disbelief: "Is there anything to be found?" This question, posed by Africans and Westerners alike, reflects the prejudices and misinformation that prevail over the area. More than a century ago, Joseph Conrad, in his famous novel *Heart of Darkness*, captured well the stereotypes of the equatorial rainforest in the center of the continent:

> Going up that river was like travelling back to the earliest beginnings of the world, when vegetation rioted on the earth and the big trees were kings. An empty stream, a great silence, an impenetrable forest. . . . We penetrated deeper and deeper into the heart of darkness. It was very quiet there. . . . But suddenly, as we struggled round a bend, there would be a glimpse of rush walls, of peaked grass-roofs, a burst of yells, a whirl of black limbs, a mass of hands clapping, of feet stamping, of bodies swaying, of eyes rolling, under the droop of heavy and motionless foliage. The steamer toiled along slowly on the edge of a black and incomprehensible frenzy. The prehistoric man was cursing us, praying to us, welcoming us – who could tell? We were cut off from the comprehension of our surroundings; we glided past like phantoms, wondering and secretly appalled, as sane men would be before an enthusiastic outbreak in a mad-house. We could not understand because we were too far and could not remember, because we were travelling in the night of first ages, of those ages that are gone, leaving hardly a sign – and no memories. (Conrad 1950:102–105)

If these recent cultures were "prehistoric," they could not have produced significant archaeological remains, and even if they did, how could one expect to recover something in such a jungle?

The Natural, Cultural, and Political Setting

"Mysterious," "primitive," "wild" – perhaps more than any other part of the continent, Central Africa is associated with such imagery. Indeed, since independence,

the states of the region, often under the rule of megalomaniac dictators, manipulated by the West or the Eastern bloc in the context of the Cold War, have
without exception, suffered *coups d'état*, prolonged civil wars, and even genocide.

So, despite, or maybe because of, its great natural wealth (in diamonds, gold,
uranium, copper, tin, timber, and vast hydroelectric potential), the countries of
Central Africa are among the poorest on earth, with all that this implies in non-
existent or dilapidated infrastructure. It is estimated that since independence, over
90 percent of the road system in the Congo has reverted to forest. If one adds that
Central Africa is home of some of the most lethal outbreaks of diseases like
AIDS and Ebola fever, it is not an understatement to say that those factors have
combined over the last 40 years to make this vast area the least attractive in the
continent for archaeological research. The ten countries generally considered
part of Central Africa (Cameroon, southern Chad, the Central African Republic,
Equatorial Guinea, Gabon, Congo-Brazzaville, the Democratic Republic of Congo,
Rwanda, Burundi, Angola) cover a vast territory, about the size of the United States
west of the Mississippi River (Figure 17.1). In the center of this vast region flows
the Congo River, the second most powerful river in the world. The Congo and its
navigable tributaries provide a vast transportation network. The river is navigable
in stretches between cataracts from the start of the Upemba depression moving
downstream for 500 km to Kongolo, and for 1,700 km from Kisangani to the
Malebo Pool, a large, circular expanse of water just above the last series of rapids
leading to the estuary. The capital cities of Kinshasa and Brazzaville are located at
its outlet. The Pool has long been the hub of long-distance trade, its markets being
the exchange place for goods coming downstream from the Congo basin and from
the Atlantic Coast by caravans (Vansina 1973:247–281). The volume of water flow
at Kinshasa varies widely, from as low as 21,400 m^3/second in July to an all-time
recorded maximum of 74,000 m^3/s in November. Though imagery of the Congo
stresses the ubiquity of tropical forest vegetation, its basin is bordered on the north
and south by plateaus covered by savanna vegetation, and to the east by a tall volcanic mountain range.

Less than half of Central Africa is covered by rainforest. Yet this block of
rainforest is second only to the Amazon in size. Contrary to common belief, the
"rainforest" encompasses a wide diversity of habitats, flora and fauna. Over 14 different forest vegetation types characterize what appears in most atlases as a uniform
green spot. Conrad's "green hell" is better characterized as a "biodiversity paradise"
whose host of habitats is grossly oversimplified on a general map. Western myth
paints the rainforest as impenetrable, hostile to man. In reality, once the green wall
created by sunlight at the edge of any clearing (river banks, roads, fields) has been
crossed, one can move quite easily. In addition, the abundant precipitation responsible for the rainforests creates a dense hydrological network of streams, rivers, and
lakes that connect with the Atlantic coastline, thus providing easy communication.
Forest people are well aware of the many opportunities provided by such a mosaic
of biotopes, even at the local level. Underestimating the forest's diversity and over-
estimating its isolation leads to a flawed understanding of the interaction between
forest dwellers and their habitats (Vansina 1990:41). Indeed, the Congo basin is

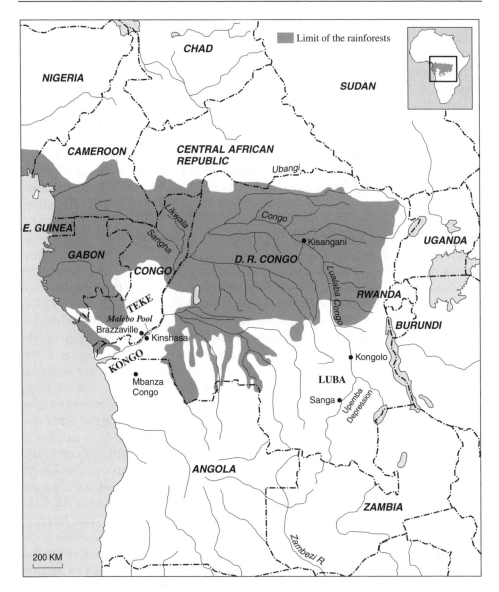

Figure 17.1. Central African sites mentioned in the text

arguably a vast crossroads where western Africa meets eastern and southern Africa, the Congo River basin connecting the Niger/Benue, the Nile, and the Zambezi basins.

Even though the term "savanna" is less misleading as a general description than "rainforest," one should not underestimate the diversity of savanna resources. The vast area of savanna north and south of the central basin varies not only according to latitude, altitude, rainfall, and soils, but also as a result of the actions of man and fire (Nicolaï et al. 1996). The flora is extremely variable and supports many large mammals emblematic of the wild game of Africa. As a whole the flora and fauna offered many opportunities for hunting and gathering.

In many ways the cultural diversity of Central Africa parallels its natural diversity. More than 850 different languages are spoken in this region of Africa, representing the four primary linguistic families of the continent. Central Africa also offers, side by side, not only examples of major kingdoms, such as the Kongo or the Luba, and autonomous villages with collective leadership, but also a wide range of intermediate political systems. This provides a rare opportunity to go from simple to complex systems and vice versa and to test various models of political transformation (Vansina 1989).

To grasp the reality of Central Africa one must combine the complexities of the natural, cultural, and political mosaic. Their interaction provides many research opportunities for the future, especially if one adds the time dimension and tries to understand how this complex array of societies evolved and developed. This can best be attempted by linking archaeology to comparative linguistics and comparative ethnography. But, despite this tremendous ethno-linguistic diversity, there are strong elements of commonality among the diverse peoples who make up the population of this African crossroads.

Many of these commonalities stem from a common linguistic origin, at the proto-Bantu (Chapter 12), or even before, at the proto-Benue Congo level. They not only share many similar words, but also beliefs concepts, mythology, rituals, and ideology (de Heusch 1972, 1982; Schoenbrun 1997, 1999; Vansina 1990). Some cultural elements have been transmitted and dispersed from generation to generation from their common ancestry, while other cultural traits have diffused across environmental, cultural, or linguistic borders. This provides the anthropologist, as well as the archaeologist and linguist, with a very wide and challenging area for the comparative study of the dynamics of diachronic process and cultural variability.

For example, this is an area where the banana, originating in Southeast Asia, has become a major food staple, but with more cultivars than anywhere else in the world (De Langhe and de Maret 1999). Similar symbols of power, like leopard skins, iron anvils, and double iron bells, have been used throughout the area (de Maret 1985a). Often the myths speak of a cultural hero, a great hunter, coming from the east with the sun, who is the founder of the various kingdoms.

Changing Archaeological Perspectives on Central Africa's Past

Considering the many research opportunities provided by its amazing natural and cultural diversity, and how crucial Central Africa is in understanding the past of the continent, it is even more frustrating to acknowledge the limited extent of our archaeological knowledge. Provocatively one can say that over the last 30 years our archaeological knowledge of the last 2,000 years in this area has decreased – that we know less today than we thought we did three decades ago. There are several reasons for this counterintuitive claim. First, as Eggert (Chapter 12) has argued, early archaeological scenarios were often based on speculative schemes derived from contemporary language distributions and ethnographic traits. These schemes were not assessed in relation to independent archaeological evidence. Second, we have become more aware of the amazing cultural diversity of the area, and thus of its great potential for comparative research. The process of diversification from a common cultural and/or linguistic ancestor through adaptation to local environmental conditions and interaction with autochthonous populations has few parallels worldwide. Even within a given ethnolinguistic group, there is variability among subsistence practices, flexibility of political entities, and even relativity of some ethnonymes (Petit 1996). Anthropological observations of present-day populations have greatly contributed to a more nuanced perspective of many basic social or economic categories. Yet one wonders about the capacity of archaeology to grasp in the past categories that appear so elusive in the present.

Recent scholars have documented a complex mosaic of overlapping subsistence and social strategies, especially in the rainforest (Bahuchet et al. 2001; Hladik et al. 1993), which provide models for analyzing the character of such mosaics in the past. The few systematic excavations that have been conducted in this region have demonstrated the wealth of remains that can be retrieved. Local archaeological sequences of the recent past usually provide a more complex view than the one derived from oral tradition, where the historical past blends after a few generations into the mythical past. Each time a significant amount of archaeological data have been obtained they have complicated the usually very schematic scenarios about the distant past drawn from linguistic or ethnographic sources.

For even more distant periods, archaeological evidence has shown that the origins of food production, pottery, and iron metallurgy were not systematically linked in Central Africa, contrary to the very circular explanation that had prevailed for many years about the "Bantu expansion" (Chapters 9, 12). For example, in recent years, more detailed linguistic studies combined with new archaeological evidence have undermined the link between two central themes in the archaeology of Central Africa: the Bantu expansion and the origins of iron metallurgy (Chapter 11), both of which now appear to predate the last 2,000 years. Where archaeological surveys have been possible, they have yielded many promising sites, making us even more conscious of the need to excavate more sites before attempting to propose generalizations about the course of Central Africa's past (Assoko 2001; de Maret 1992; Eggert 1993; Zangato 1991).

The "decrease" in archaeological knowledge described above leaves us with a void in the period covered by this chapter, as there is very little evidence for the first ten, if not fourteen, centuries of our era in west Central Africa! Few excavated sites fall in this time period. The reason for this gap in the archaeological record has been a source of controversy. Is it due to a demographic downturn, a lack of visibility of the remains, a change in the nature of the sites, or a lack of interest on the part of archaeologists? Nobody knows for sure, but the answer is probably a mix of the above explanations. Areas of Central Africa which have been subject to systematic excavations have usually yielded some radiocarbon dates and remains in this time bracket, but just enough to prove that the area was not abandoned. This meager evidence nevertheless contrasts with the more substantial record recorded for the last millennium b.c. (Chapter 9) and the last millennium a.d.

In some ways what could be nicknamed the Middle Iron Age is also a "muddle in the middle," like the so-called Middle Stone Age (Chapter 4). Research in both periods has suffered from a frenzy among archaeologists for the "earliest": the earliest hominid, stone tool, or settlement in the MSA, or the earliest food producer, iron-smelting, or ethnic-linguistic expression at the other end of the time scale.

During the last 20 years, major progress has been made in the knowledge of the early food producers in the western part of Central Africa, from Cameroon to Congo (Chapter 9). We know that this part of the rainforest was populated by various farming communities between 1000 and 500 b.c. In sharp contrast, in the savanna south of the rainforest, we have no evidence of farming communities, usually considered as Early Iron Age, before the start of the first millennium a.d., except perhaps in Lower Congo (de Maret 1986). But here also, with few exceptions where systematic archaeological research has been conducted in Central Africa, the earliest stage of the Iron Age is better known than the long phase stretching from then to the recent ethnographically documented past.

The goal of archaeology in Central Africa during colonial times was to specify Africa's place in world prehistory. As a result, collections and excavations centered almost exclusively on the Stone Age, and there was a general lack of interest in the past of the many ethnic groups (de Maret 1990). Ethnographers working for the various colonial institutions and museums did not resort to archaeology to probe the past of the groups they were studying. This probably reflects the goal of gaining a good knowledge of the various "tribes" in order to rule them efficiently, rather than the division/compartmentalization between archaeology and social anthropology that characterized that period. The only exception came from the famous French ethnologist Marcel Griaule who, with Jean-Paul Lebeuf, carried out pioneering excavations during their 1936 expedition to the region south of Lake Chad in order to understand the past of local people and to check oral traditions. Their discovery of the so-called "Sao Civilization" (Chapter 18) had considerable impact at that time and inspired new research on the archaeology of African peoples. It also generated interest in ethnoarchaeology which, following the tradition established by Marcel Mauss, was combined with a marked interest in material culture (Griaule 1943; Lebeuf 1937).

Aside from this work the only colonial-period excavations undertaken on the recent past were directed at documenting early European influence. Several excavations were conducted with the aim of studying the first evangelization of the Kongo Kingdom, and, more specifically, to collect evidence of the martyrdom of a Flemish Capuchin who had been slain in 1652, in order to press for his canonization. Thirty-five tombs in an old church ruin were excavated in 1938 and 1942 by missionaries, under the partial supervision of a Belgian archaeologist, Maurits Bequaert. The excavations yielded an interesting mixture of Kongo potteries and pipes with European objects: religious medals, crosses, iron weapons, glass bottles, decorated nail heads, and tombstones (Vandenhoute 1973). These materials provided a rare glimpse into the past of the famous Kongo Kingdom, yet this research was discontinued when excavators failed to locate the one burial place that interested them. The promise of such research to yield important insights into the character of African–European relations has been borne out in recent decades in other areas of Africa (e.g., DeCorse 1998, 2001; Kelly 1997, 2001). Even after the Second World War, Bequaert, one of only three full-time (if not professionally trained) archaeologists in Central Africa, was not interested in finding out more about a kingdom which had given its name to the whole country. In applying for funding to the Minister of Colonies he listed what he considered the outstanding problems to be studied in the Congo and Rwanda-Burundi pre- and protohistory (de Maret 1990). Out of 46 topics of interest, only six were not strictly related to the Stone Age, among them the project to carry out the study of Christian burial in the Lower Congo or look for traces of European penetration of the ancient capitals of the Kuba king, which was another major topic of interest for colonial ethnography.

A Dutch missionary, Hendrik van Moorsel, though also primarily interested in the Stone Age, nevertheless collected pots and potsherds around the city of Kinshasa. He was the first to excavate an Iron Age site there in 1948, but once again his primary interest was to correlate it with the description of a town visited in the 17th century by a Capuchin missionary. Thus, in the colonial context, even one of the most famous kingdoms of Africa was insufficient to spark the interest of archaeologists. The paradox is that one of the best-known kingdoms of the continent from a historical and ethnographic point of view (Hilton 1985; Thornton 1983) is virtually unknown from the archaeological perspective.

The Kongo Kingdom was located south of the Congo River estuary and came to the attention of European explorers at an early time. When the leader of the first expedition, the Portuguese navigator Diogo Cao, landed in 1483 in the Congo estuary, he was astonished to discover a centralized political state, what he perceived as an African replica of the Portuguese kingdom (Randles 1968; Vansina 1966). The king of Kongo was baptized in 1491 by the Portuguese, who gave him the name of their king, João (John). Under his successor, Afonso, Christianity spread even further throughout the kingdom. However, instead of becoming a religion of the masses, it was adopted by a small ruling elite who made it a royal cult, reinforcing their political authority. One of Afonso's sons was even ordained a bishop as early as 1518. The missionaries were mainly Jesuits and Capuchins; the traders and officials left behind a vivid description of the development of the kingdom which permitted a detailed reconstruction of the daily lives of its inhabitants at a time when their civilization was as its peak (Balandier 1965). Their highly centralized political structure allowed them to rule over an area of 150,000 km^2 stretching south and east of the Congo estuary. They acquired a mastery of metallurgy, weaving, and textiles. The art of the Kongo remains, even today, one of the most elaborate in Africa, making use of wood, cloth, terracotta, and even stone. Kongo not only survived contact with the Portuguese, but continued to expand and develop into a centralized state until the start of the civil war in the late 17th century A.D. (Hilton 1985; Thornton 1979, 1983).

Among the most prestigious of the Bantu kingdoms, Kongo had a far-reaching impact, for around it and through it a network of trade with all of Central Africa was established. Later on, Kongo was the threshold for the vast Belgian colonial penetration of Central Africa, hence the colonial designation, Belgian Congo. In time Kongo also gave its name to both modern independent republics of Congo. Many slaves were shipped to the New World from the Kongo Kingdom, and one can still find traces of this Congo diaspora in Brazil, the Caribbean islands, and the United States (de Heusch 2000; Thompson 1981). The memory of this magnificent kingdom which proclaimed very early the achievements of African civilization is still present in the minds of many intellectuals and leaders of Africa today, which made possible the significant oral historical work undertaken by Vansina and his students, not only on Kongo, but on many other famous kingdoms of the savanna south of the rainforest (Vansina 1966).

There is considerable interest within contemporary archaeology in early complex societies and related phenomena, such as the function of sacred kingship, the development of long-distance trade, and the origins of urbanism. Until recently, very little research on these topics had been done in Africa (McIntosh, ed., 1999). Available evidence is scarce thus far, with some notable exceptions in western and eastern Africa (Huffman 1996; McIntosh and McIntosh 1980, 1993; Pikirayi 1993; Pwiti 1996; Shaw et al., eds., 1993; Sinclair 1987; Chapter 13). The Kongo Kingdom provides an excellent case study whose cities were unique in Africa south of the equator. However, the Kongo Kingdom has never been subject to systematic archaeological research, and this remains an important research priority for future. Prior to the Portuguese arrival in the late 15th century, we do not know much about the antiquity of the Kongo Kingdom. Its emergence is generally dated to the 14th century on the basis of the known list of Kongo kings, but its origins could be much older than suggested by evidence based on oral traditions collected during the 16th and 17th centuries. Linguistic evidence relating to a specific trend of word-shortening, to a set of political titles, and to terms designating clapperless bells (authority emblems throughout Central Africa: de Maret 1985a; Vansina 1969) indicates that the Kongo, and the neighboring Tio principalities, originated well before the start of the 13th century. Unfortunately from the archaeological point of view, although there is evidence of various pottery groups on the coast and in the lower stretches of the Congo Valley from at least the fourth century b.c. to the fifth century a.d., there is a virtual gap in our knowledge of dated records from the fifth to the 11th centuries a.d.

Because the Kongo Kingdom was considerably more centralized than other kingdoms in the region, the best investigative strategy would be to start by excavating the site of the Kongo capital, Mbanza Kongo, now São Salvador in northern Angola, and its various provincial capitals there and in the Democratic Republic of Congo. While this has been on the archaeological agenda since the early 1970s, the prolonged political and economic crises in both countries, combined with the concern about fueling Kongo tribalism, has made such work almost impossible so far (in 1973 I surveyed Mbanza Nsundi and was shown a graveyard, but due to local conflict between rival clans I was not allowed to test it).

More recently (1980), in Angola, the Laboratorio Nacional de Anthropologia conducted a survey of the Soyo Province of the former kingdom and test-excavated its capital, Mbanza Soyo, and the related cemetery next to the estuary of the Congo River (Abranches 1991). Skeletons, potsherds, and Christian crosses were collected, but the material has never been studied in detail or published. In the kingdom's capital, Mbanza Kongo, road work revealed the foundations of various stone structures. This confirms the great potential of the site, which is presently at risk due to urbanization. Europeans visitors to Mbanza Kongo in the 17th century described the city as a large agglomeration of as many as 40,000 inhabitants. Though centered on the royal enclosure and several churches, it nonetheless resembled an oversized village with separate houses surrounded by gardens and hedges.

Adaptive Research Strategies in Key Areas and their Results

When, in the 1970s, thanks to a lull in armed conflicts and an improvement in the economic situation, the National Museums Institute of Congo (then Zaire) was created, systematic archaeological research was planned in close cooperation with the Royal Central African Museum in Belgium. While training local archaeologists, a research strategy was devised to produce a first general chronology of the main areas of the Democratic Republic of Congo by known major stratified sites and burial grounds, and by systematic surveys of unknown areas or sites relevant to periods which had not yet raised interest. This section provides an overview of the results achieved with limited means by the creative design of surveys and excavations in difficult terrain. This overview is organized as if one was going up the Congo River from the coast.

Surveys and test excavations through the lower portion of the Congo Valley, on both sides of the river between the Atlantic coast and the Malebo Pool, Kinshasa, and Brazzaville, have yielded much archaeological evidence over the last 50 years. Erosion is fierce, mingling artifacts of various periods to the point that it was once believed to be a genuine archaeological culture (the Tumbian: Menghin 1925) that was "identified" in many other parts of Africa and the world (de Maret 1990; Menghin 1949).

In order to find objects in primary context, surveys concentrated on rock-shelters, caves, and open-air sites, and on pits and furnaces for iron or copper smelting. Many pottery groups have been identified throughout the area, first by Mortelmans in two caves while he was preparing field trips for the 1958 Pan-African Congress on Prehistory (Mortelmans 1962). Initially, he ordered them from I (the oldest) to VI (most recent) on the basis of decreasing mineral crust thickness. As the first group had some dimple bases, they were related to the famous "dimple-based pottery" which was at that stage starting to be associated in the Great Lakes region of eastern Africa with Bantu migration (Leakey et al. 1948). The very elaborate decoration of Group II pottery was reminiscent of well-known Kuba decorative motifs. As the Kuba live much further east, did a broader distribution of these motifs attest an earlier migration? But Group II decoration could also be linked to Kongo motifs, suggesting that this pottery could be contemporary with the Kongo Kingdom, dated between the 14th and 16th centuries A.D. Groups III, IV, and V were represented by a few potsherds. The thick, coarse, and sparsely decorated Group VI pottery was not encrusted, and was tentatively dated to the second half of the 17th century (Mortelmans 1962). In the 1950s, before radiocarbon techniques were widely applied, pottery typologies such as this were usually the basis of archaeological chronology.

In order to find Mortelman's various pottery groups in stratigraphy, and in the hope of being able to radiocarbon-date associated charcoal, test pits were excavated in the same two caves. During the 1970s they produced evidence that the Group VI pottery was associated with the last centuries b.c. (de Maret 1975), and was thus not the most recent. Even if chronologically invalid, Mortelman's groups were further revised and expanded on the basis of the study of old collections stored in the Royal Central African Museum in Tervuren, Belgium, especially those from Becquaert's fieldwork in the Lower Congo in 1937–38 and 1950–52, and of new surveys and test excavations (Clist 1982; de Maret 1972). Besides Group VI, which is by far the oldest and has been renamed the Ngovo Group (de Maret 1986), the other groups seem to date roughly from the same period (the second half of the last millennium b.c.). In addition to some newly created groups, they continue to serve as a basis for classification.

Group II pottery has been radiocarbon-dated in several instances to the 18th century through the Lower Congo up to the Pool. Like other ceramic groups, its distribution seems to correspond to the trade routes of the Kongo Kingdom. The Congo River ceases to be navigable due to the formidable rapids at the outlet of the Pool, thus closing access to the thousands of miles of waterways of the inner Congo basin. As a result, the Pool is of great commercial importance. In that region, around Kinshasa and Brazzaville, several sites yielding pottery from at least Groups I and II from downstream have been found in conjunction with a very fine white ware which was produced further upstream and has been named Group X (de Maret and Stainier 1999). It confirms that the area was a major commercial center where the Atlantic trade connected with the flow of goods and slaves coming from the central basin. This exchange culminated in the 19th century, forming what has been described in the historical literature as the "Great Congo Trade" that was under the control of the Tio (or Teke) Kingdom, north of the Kongo (Vansina 1973:247–281).

This kingdom is probably as old as Kongo, but we have no direct description of it before the late 19th century. Archaeological evidence is relatively abundant but scattered through the area: iron and copper furnaces; sometimes very large slag heaps dated to the fifth century; and thick layers of potsherds along the bank of the river and the Pool. This occupation seems to culminate around the 13th–14th centuries. At the same time, in the south of the Teke area, copperworking underwent a significant growth, maybe in connection with the extension of new political systems, as copper was used as currency (Chapter 11) and also for the imposing necklaces worn as a symbol of power.

Around the 15th century archaeological evidence seems to support oral traditions of a transfer of the center of power from the Congo River banks to the plateau further inland and to the west (Pinçon 1991). Here also a more systematic excavation program aimed at corroborating the very detailed reconstruction of the recent history of that kingdom outlined by Vansina (1973) would be most interesting.

Upstream from Kongo and Teke territories the center of the inner Congo basin remained virtually unknown archaeologically until a systematic waterborne exploration of its major river banks was conducted between 1977 and 1987 by a team of German archaeologists led by Eggert (1993; Wotzka 1995). A central focus of this research was the question of Bantu origins, since the grassfields of northwestern Cameroon and the Nigerian border were accepted as the Bantu homeland from which early waves of Bantu speakers dispersed to the south and the east (Chapter 12). It was, therefore, crucial to know if, as seemed likely, they had crossed the forest and, in that case, how and when. As the waterways were the most logical routes through the forest, a survey using the same strategy was devised. It proved a very effective means of exploring a large part of the central basin in a short time.

More than 11,000 pieces of pottery from more than 190 localities were collected by systematic excavation, surface collecting, and ethnoarchaeological studies of contemporary potters for the south of the Congo River and assigned to 35 different style groups comprising six traditions by Wotzka (1995). The six traditions are, from the oldest to the most recent: Imbonga (radiocarbon-dated 400–100 b.c.); Inganda (200 b.c.–a.d. 80); Lusako (a.d. 1–650); Bokuma/Lingonda (a.d. 1–650); Longa (a.d. 500–1000); Bekongo (no date available); Bondongo (a.d. 1000–1400); and, Bokone (after a.d. 1600). The Imbonga Tradition is the most detailed and complex, encompassing 21 different style groups in a sequence starting with the Imbonga horizon, associated with the initial settlement dated around 400 b.c., and ending with the Ikenge horizon made of pots produced at the time of the survey.

Though some of the proposed groups are less firmly defined and dated than others, Wotzka has been able to develop a continuous 2,500-year sequence. The early forest settlers started from a limited stretch of the Congo River where it crosses the equator, then slowly colonized the major tributaries. The whole process took at least a millennium and a half and occurred in successive waves of upstream expansion into the central part of the basin.

The German team's survey of the Ubangi, the Likwala-aux-Herbes, and the Sangha rivers to the north and the east led to the identification of two other traditions, a North and a Northeast tradition, whose origin differs from the six traditions that fanned out from the Congo River eastward. Surprisingly the Northern and Northeastern traditions are earlier in time. How this whole sequence of events fits with the developments taking place before and during the same period further west and north, and with the so-called "Bantu expansion," is far from clear.

The German River Reconnaissance Project succeeded in establishing a basic spatial and chronostratigraphic framework for what was previously a major gap in our knowledge. Based primarily on test pit excavation, it provides only limited information on settlement patterns, lifestyle, and subsistence strategies. So far, there is no conclusive evidence of iron production before a.d. 1000, except on the northeast of the Likwala-aux-Herbes river. There, a bowl-like structure containing slag was excavated and dated between 106 b.c. to a.d. 420 (Eggert 1997). It is so far the oldest furnace from the inner Congo basin.

The progress achieved in ten years in our knowledge of the inner basin is remarkable, and demonstrates the great potential of further studies. Unfortunately, the 1990s brought no progress in terms of archaeological fieldwork, there or in other parts of the Congo.

The limited state of our archaeological knowledge is even more frustrating when considered in relation to the seminal work on the region published in 1990 by Vansina entitled *Paths in the Rainforests: Toward a History of Political Tradition in Equatorial Africa*. Vansina draws on a wide range of evidence to offer a synthesis of the political, social, and economic history of the whole forest area. His use of the "words and things" technique allows him to link linguistic evidence with objects and concepts, and to set them in a chronological framework, leading to a new interpretation of tradition. Given the archaeological potential of this terrain, it will be extremely interesting to test the many conclusions and hypotheses that Vansina offers by devising systematic archaeological excavation programs (cf. Chapter 12).

Much further upstream, after Kisangani, the Congo River is known as the Lualaba. Starting in the south, at the border with Zambia, the Lualaba crosses a savanna area and flows through a 150 mile-long depression – the Upemba depression – and then flows toward the forest. This depression is a vast floodplain dotted with lakes and marshes. It is rich with fish and wildlife, and its soil is fertile thanks to the loam deposited by regular flooding. The variety and number of food sources contrast with the surrounding savannas, and thus the area has attracted a dense human population for many centuries, leaving a rich archaeological record. The rare places in the Upemba depression floodplain that were suitable for the establishment of villages were the high grounds on the shores of the numerous lakes and streams. These sites have often been in continuous use for various purposes since the Early Iron Age – as fields, settlements, refuse pits, or graveyards.

Though early colonial administrators and missionaries made note of the abundant archaeological materials in this area, it was not until the end of the colonial period that, at the request of an ethnographer, an initial archaeological excavation was started at Sanga, on the shore of Lake Kisale (Hiernaux et al. 1971; Nenquin 1963). These excavations revealed a very large graveyard. Although graves provide only partial information on lifestyle and subsistence, they are a valuable source of archaeological insight into social organization. If numerous enough to be statistically significant, they may be used to identify ritual patterns in conjunction with circumstances of death or social differentiation according to rank, gender, age, and their evolution through time. Grave goods are often better preserved than artifacts in settlement layers. Because they were deposited simultaneously, and are thus contemporaneous, they provide useful elements for chronology-building. Three ceramic wares were recognized among the Sanga material: Kisalian, Mulongo, and Red Slip.

Nenquin, the first excavator, thought that these wares formed a successive chronological sequence: first Kisalian, then Mulongo, and finally Red Slip. His insight was
based on pottery typology in relation to mortuary context, particularly overlapping
graves. But additional excavation during the following year, supervised by
Hiernaux, yielded a mixture of the three pottery groups in three graves. This led
Hiernaux to question Nenquin's chronology and to suggest instead that the three
groups were contemporary: that Mulongo and Red Slip had been either imported
by the producers of the Kisalian ware, or that the pottery was associated with
members of a minority living side by side with a Kisalian majority. Of the 145
burials excavated, only two, one with atypical Kisalian pottery, the other with no
pottery, were radiocarbon-dated to the seventh–ninth centuries a.d.

Nenquin had noted that the shapes of certain Mulongo group potteries were
reminiscent of Kisalian, that many forms of the Red Slip Ware group were similar
to Mulongo pottery, and that at least one type was very like modern Luba pottery.
Thus Nenquin raised the problem of the relationship of the Sanga archaeological
finds with what was known from oral traditions about the history of the famous
Luba empire, which centered around lakes Kisale and Upemba. But because it was
not considered possible to go back any further than the 16th century with the Luba
state, it did not seem possible to Nenquin (1963:272) to correlate his discoveries,
dated to the ninth century at the latest, with what was known of the Luba state at
that time (Verhulpen 1936). Even a very careful ethnohistorical study of the Luba
state could not convincingly trace the Luba origins much further than the end of
the 17th century (Reefe 1981).

Once again it was difficult to relate pottery to the history of a specific ethnic
group. On one side were the traditions of one of the most prestigious savanna kingdoms, whose aura was such that, by the 19th century, many kingdoms further south
traced their origin to the Luba dynasty; on the other hand was a major archaeological site, dated ten centuries earlier and associated with three distinct groups of
pottery.

In the mid-1970s, new surveys and systematic excavations of five additional sites
(out of the more than 50 discovered in the Upemba depression) were carried out
in an attempt to link the archaeological evidence with its historical and anthropological counterparts. More than 150 new graves were excavated, providing evidence
to establish a complete chronology of the settlements and graveyards. This sequence
is confirmed by over 50 radiocarbon and thermoluminescence dates (de Maret
1977, 1979, 1982, 1985b; Ghey and de Maret 1982). Extending from the 17th
century a.d. to the present, this sequence bridges the gap between the archaeological record and the Luba, so well documented by history, anthropology, and
linguistics.

The long cultural continuity which links the Luba of the last century to the first
food-producing, iron-using communities in the Upemba back to the seventh
century a.d. is methodologically interesting for both archaeology and social anthropology. There are few instances where it has been possible, in Africa or elsewhere,
to link the remote archaeological past to the ethnographic present. Thus, little attention has been paid so far to how archaeological insight changes our understanding

of a major ethnic group, and conversely, how what we know about that group can be used to illuminate the archaeological record (Chapter 18).

Such a degree of continuity remains truly exceptional and allows for a credible, although debatable, use of ethnographic data to interpret excavated occurrences. Without some ethnographic data on Luba practices and beliefs, the use of certain objects or certain aspects of the burial rituals would have been much harder to interpret. Of course, there is no proof that they have not evolved through time, but it permits a more focused set of interpretations.

The opportunity to link the archaeological record to art history, ethnography, history and linguistics is very fruitful but also leads to the much-discussed issue of ethnicity, identity, and related problems of change and continuity. The term Luba itself is very ambiguous and has been put to many uses since the last century (Petit 1996). Projecting it as such in the past does not make much sense, and one should refrain from using present-day vocabulary and categories to describe past realities, as this will be anachronistic. And yet, there is empirical evidence in the archaeological sequence of both continuity and change. Some aspects of the material culture and ritual practice change while some others endure; some change together, while others do not. It is thus a matter of appreciation to decide if we are dealing with the same population, and to what extent archaeological evidence could be used to literally ground ethnicity in the past.

Of course this issue has important political implications in view of ongoing ethnic conflicts and wars. Many groups, and not only the Luba, claim some sort of legitimacy by asserting their autochthony. Archaeological evidence, especially if collected by outsiders, has been, and will be, manipulated in order to prove it.

Using the previously recognized pottery groups as a base, but adding some groups, and correlating them with changes in rituals, several phases can be recognized in the archaeological sequence of the Upemba depression. They are as follows: after some scant evidence of Late Stone Age occupation, the Iron Age begins in the seventh century a.d. with the Kamilambian. Associated pottery is related to the Zambian copperbelt Early Iron Age tradition further south, but so far no copper artifacts have been found in the only grave and the related thick occupation layer from that period that have been excavated. Consistent with the Zambian pattern, there is no evidence of trade. Judging from the scarcity of Kamilambian remains throughout the Upemba, the density of population was still low at this stage. The shapes of the few Kamilambian iron implements and weapons are related to the ones of subsequent periods. They were the only grave goods of the single excavated Kamilambian grave.

The following Early Kisalian phase is dated from the eighth to the ninth centuries. Excavated occupation layers and graves are not numerous, suggesting that population density was increasing but still relatively low compared to Classic Kisalian that followed. Two iron hoes were found, confirming that farming was practiced. The Early Kisalian pottery group displays most of the very distinctive characteristics of Kisalian Ware, but with some archaic traits that link it as well to the previous Kamilambian group. The presence of a few copper beads on an iron necklace, and of copper bangles, suggests that the area was slowly incorporated into the widening trade networks that distributed copper from further south. Large iron machetes, typical of the Kisalian, are also present. Two elaborate ceremonial axes, their handles decorated with iron nails, were retrieved from Kisilian graves. It is certainly not a coincidence that out of 161 Kisalian graves (both Early and Classic), one of the two graves with a ceremonial ax was also the only one with an iron anvil.

In Central Africa ceremonial axes were often a status symbol, and this is well documented among the present-day inhabitants. We know that the Luba used iron nails to adorn the shafts of their axes. Those nails had the shape and name of an iron anvil, though they were much smaller (Childs and Dewey 1996; Dewey and Childs 1996). This is not surprising as there are many symbolic and ritual connections between forging and leadership in this part of the world (Chapter 11). Iron anvils were used as regalia by Luba chiefs, and a crucial part of the enthronement process was even called "striking the anvil" (Womersley 1975:82–83). There was a very important homology between the practical and the symbolic functions of the smith and those of the chiefs and kings (de Maret 1980, 1985a; Herbert 1993). The symbolic parallel goes even further as the iron anvil in the Kisalian grave was placed next to the skull, in a position that is identical to that of anvils found in an Iron Age grave in Zambia, as well as in the grave of a Rwandese king (Van Noten 1972), confirming their use as symbol of power (de Maret 1985a). This evidence suggests that ceremonial axes and anvils were elaborate symbols of power manipulated since the Early Kisalian phase by local leaders for their own legitimization. It probably marks the start of the major political, economic, and cultural process that culminated with the famous Luba kingdoms.

Around the tenth century, the Early Kisalian evolved into the Classic Kisalian, which lasted until the end of the 13th century. The great increase in the size and the number of sites from this phase indicates a sharp demographic increase. The wealth and the beautiful state of preservation of the various grave goods from Classic Kisalian contexts provide a unique set of evidence on the nature and the range of economic and ritual activities, like farming, fishing, hunting, smithing, pottery-making, and trading (de Maret 1982, 1992, 1999). The masterful execution of artifacts in clay, iron, copper, ivory, bone, and shell indicates the presence of skilled, specialized artisans. Several hundred vessels, often intact, were recovered from Classic Kisalian graves. They display highly characteristic shapes, delicate decoration, and unusual spouts or handles. Many pots were produced in series and were never used except as grave goods as they show no sign of use-wear. Some miniatures were made for interment with children, and, more generally, there is a strong correlation between the average size of pottery in grave and the age of death.

Blacksmiths displayed a mastery of highly sophisticated techniques (Childs 1991). Welding of different grades of iron was used for blades, and wire-drawing of iron and copper was used to produce elaborately woven necklaces, belts, and pendants. Copper ornaments abound, indicating close trade links with copper-mining areas to the south.

Although the Upemba depression is more than 1,500 km from either ocean coast, cowries from the Indian Ocean were found in graves of this Classic Kisalian period, indicating at least indirect long-distance contacts. Mortuary evidence suggests that imported objects of value were appropriated by the wealthiest, probably in order to display their power. We find them in the graves with the more numerous, unusual, and probably valuable objects. Membership in the rich minority was apparently inherited, as several of the wealthiest tombs belonged to children.

Around the 13th century, Kisalian gave way after a brief, and poorly documented, period of transition to the Kabambian phase. The reasons for the change remain obscure, but one notes a very different pottery, different funerary rituals, and the appearance of cast-copper cross ingots as grave goods. Although Kabambian grave goods are usually less abundant, a few graves revealed a wealth of goods but almost no power symbols. This suggests that the nature of power had changed. Long-distance trade is attested during that period by the presence of cowries and glass beads. The presence of small, cruciform-shaped copper ingots typical of Kabambian graves links the Upemba with the copperbelt further south, suggesting that regional trade was expanding. During the course of the Kabambian, the crosses diminished in size, became more standardized and more numerous, and their position in relation to the skeleton shifted from the chest toward the hands and the hips. This evolution may well reflect their initial use as a special-purpose currency or a prestige good restricted to social and ritual exchanges, and their gradual development into a multi-purpose currency used in various transactions (de Maret 1981, 1985a).

At the same time, around the 16th century, grave goods were reduced to a few vessels, often covered with a thick red slip, and with shapes often anticipating recent Luba pottery. This corresponds to the Kabambian B that lasted until the 18th century, when this pottery group and the corresponding ritual is replaced by ethnographically identifiable "Luba" practices. By that time the Luba state had emerged as a vast political and economic entity well documented by various historical and ethnographic sources (Reefe 1981). In recent years, scholars have envisioned that this famous kingdom rested more on symbolic than on military power. Power took a variety of forms and meanings. By manipulating them, the crafting of a wide array of polities was achieved (McIntosh, ed., 1999; Schoenbrun 1999). Its strength rested in its capacity to manipulate a rich array of regalia, emblems, myths, and rituals to incorporate and legitimize the power of a constellation of chiefs, officeholders, and societies in relation with the king. The prestige of the Luba Kingdom extended far as chiefs and kings in distant regions claimed Luba origins. This evidence suggests that models of social and political organization may differ significantly from those inspired by recent European history. The Western vision of a "state" has much to do with the "nation-states" of our modern history. African history provides several examples of "states" built on different foundations (Chapters 13, 18).

Are the changes outlined for the Upemba archaeological sequence due to growing exterior contacts, to population movements, or to the influence of new rulers? We do not know, but there is clear continuity, despite change, in some aspects of the pottery, iron weapons, and implements. One notices also a lesser degree of cultural homogeneity in artifacts and rituals over time. In later periods, the river probably did not play the same unifying role that it did during Kisalian times. Was it because the Kabambian groups were progressively subdued by a larger political structure centered outside the depression? Present evidence suggests certain continuities in the Upemba from the Early Iron Age to present-day Luba through a 1,300-year sequence. Due to the size of the sites inside the depression and thus the density of local Kisalian population, which must have contrasted with the drier and less populated surrounding plateaus, it would be surprising if the arrival of new populations annihilated autochthones. However, only systematic excavation programs in the savannas surrounding the Upemba will provide more detailed insight into the sources of change that exist within these continuities.

The archaeological record shows that the Luba ethnic group is the result of a complex cultural process spanning the whole Iron Age. It is likely that the past of the many other ethnic groups could be documented in much the same way, linking the pottery groups from the past to the ethnic groups from the present. This will be of major interest for them.

Central Africa is one of the least known regions of the world from an archaeo-logical perspective. It is not only a very challenging area in which to conduct archae-ological research, but the emphasis through the colonial period has been on Stone Age archaeology, which fit at that time with the interest in world prehistory. Our knowledge of the last 2,000 years is thus very limited. This is in sharp contrast with the detailed historical works on Central Africa kingdoms produced in the 1960s and 1970s. Yet archaeology has much empirical data to contribute to the origin of those kingdoms. The lack of a critical mass of archaeological data has encouraged speculative scenarios not only about the origin of those states, but about the deeper past and the history of the settlement of present-day populations. Grand explana-tory schemes have been devised and combined, on the basis of comparative lin-guistics, ethnographic traits, and oral tradition, in connection with the origin of food production, iron metallurgy, and Bantu expansion. They have generated a lot of interest and debate for over 40 years, but only a sound archaeological database will allow us to assess them. In a limited number of areas along the Congo River innovative survey strategies and excavations have yielded, with limited means, during a brief period of peace in the 1970s and 1980s a host of data that shed some interesting light on the complexity of the process in the past.

The archaeological study of Central Africa offers many opportunities, not only to contribute to ongoing theoretical discussions on a wide variety of topics in our own discipline, but also to devise creative links with other scientific fields such as ethnography, linguistics, and history, as well as conservation, agronomy, and envi-ronmental sciences. But one should not overlook the need for today's inhabitants of Central Africa simply to have a better understanding of their past, and to take pride in the accomplishments of their ancestors, as in any other part of the world. Even more important is the contribution archaeology can make in relativizing eth-nicity and autochthony and its many manipulations that fuel hate and exclusion, instead of stressing the common background shared by most.

REFERENCES

Abranches, Henrique, 1991 Sobre of Basolongo Arqueologia da tradição oral. Brussels: Fina Petroleos de Angola.

Assoko Ndong, Alain, 2001 Archéologie du peuplement Holocène de la réserve de faune de La Lopé, Gabon. Ph.D. dissertation, Université Libre de Bruxelles.

Bahuchet, Serge, Pierre de Maret, Françoise and Pierre Grenand, 2001 Des forêts et des hommes: Un regard sur les populations des forêts tropicales. Brussels: Éditions de l'Université Libre de Bruxelles.

Balandier, Georges, 1965 La Vie quotidienne au Royaume de Kongo du XVIe au XVIIIe siècle. Paris: Hachette.

Childs, S. Terry 1991 Transformations: Iron and Copper Production in Central Africa. *In* Recent Trends in Archaeometallurgical Research. Peter Glumac, ed., pp. 33–46. Research Papers in Science and Archaeology, 8(1). Philadelphia: MASCA.

Childs, S. Terry, and W. J. Dewey, 1996 Forging Symbolic Meaning in Zaire and Zimbabwe. *In* The Culture and Technology of African Iron Production. Peter. R. Schmidt, ed. pp. 145–171. Gainesville: University of Florida Press.

Clist, Bernard, 1982 Étude archéologique du matériel de la mission Maurits Bequaert de 1950–1952 au Bas-Zaïre. MA thesis, Université Libre de Bruxelles.

Conrad, Joseph, 1902 [1950] Heart of Darkness. New York: New American Library.

DeCorse, Christopher R., 1998 Culture Contact and Change in West Africa. *In* Studies in Culture Contact: Interaction, Culture Change and Archaeology. James G. Cusick, ed. pp. 358–377. Occasional Paper 25. Carbondale: Southern Illinois University, Center for Archaeological Investigations.

DeCorse, Christopher R., ed. 2001 West Africa during the Atlantic Slave Trade: Archaeological Perspectives. London: Leicester University Press.

de Heusch, Luc, 1972 Le Roi ivre ou l'origine de l'État. Paris: Gallimard.

——1982 Rois nés d'un cœur de vache. Paris: Gallimard.

——2000 Le Roi Kongo et les monstres sacrés. Paris: Gallimard.

De Langhe, Edmond, and Pierre de Maret, 1999 Tracking the Banana: Its Significance in Early Agriculture. *In* The Prehistory of Food: Appetites for Change. Chris Godsen and Jon G. Hather, eds. pp. 377–396. London: Routledge.

de Maret, Pierre, 1972 Étude d'une collection de céramiques protohistoriques du Bas-Zaïre. MA thesis, Université Libre de Bruxelles.

——1975 A Carbon-14 Date from Zaïre. Antiquity 49:133–137.

——1977 Sanga: New Excavations, More Data and Some Related Problems. Journal of African History 18:321–337.

——1979 Luba Roots: A First Complete Iron Age Sequence in Zaïre. Current Anthropology 20:233–235.

——1980 Ceux qui jouent avec le feu: La Place de forgeron en Afrique Centrale. Africa 50:263–279.

——1981 L'Évolution monétaire du Shaba Central entre le 7ème et le 18ème siècle. African Economic History 10:117–149.

——1982 New Survey of Archaeological Research and Dates for West Central and North-Central Africa. Journal of African History 23:1–15.

——1985a The Smith's Myth and the Origin of Leadership in Central Africa. *In* African Iron Working: Ancient and Traditional. Raandi Haaland and Peter Shinnie, eds. pp. 73–87. Bergen: Bergen University Press.

——1985b Fouilles archéologiques dans la vallée du Haut-Lualaba, Zaïre–II Sanga et Katongo 1974. 2 vols. Tervuren: Musée Royal de l'Afrique Centrale.

——1986 The Ngovo Group: An Industry with Polished Stone Tools and Pottery in Lower Zaïre. The African Archaeological Review 4:103–133.

——1990 Phases and Facies in the Archaeology of Central Africa. In A History of African Archaeology. Peter Robertshaw, ed. pp. 109–134. London: James Currey.

——1992 Fouilles archéologiques dans la Vallée du Haut-Lualaba, Zaïre–II Kamilamba, Kikulu et Malemba-Nkulu, 1975. 2 vols. Tervuren: Musée Royal de l'Afrique Centrale.

——1999 The Power of Symbols and the Symbols of Power through Time: Probing the Luba Past. In Beyond Chiefdoms. Pathways to Complexity in Africa. Susan Keech McIntosh, ed. pp. 151–165. Cambridge: Cambridge University Press.

de Maret, Pierre, and Xavier Stainier, 1999 Excavations in the Upper Levels at Gombe and the Early Ceramic Industries in the Kinshasa Area (Zaire). In Festschrift für Günter Smolla. Günter Smolla, Fritz-Rudolf Herrmann, Ingeborg Schmidt, and Frank Verse, eds. pp. 477–486. Wiesbaden: Selbstverlag des Landesamtes für Denkmalpflege Hessen.

Dewey, William, J., and S. Terry Childs, 1996 Forging Memory. In Memory: Luba Art and the Making of History. Mary Nooters Roberts and Allen F. Roberts, eds. pp. 151–175. New York: The Museum for African Art.

Eggert, Manfred K., 1993 Central Africa and the Archaeology of the Equatorial Rainforest: Reflections on Some Major Topics. In The Archaeology of Africa: Food, Metals and Towns. Thurstan Shaw, Paul Sinclair, Bassey Andah, and Alex Okpoko, eds. pp. 289–329. London: Routledge.

——1997 Equatorial Africa Iron Age. In Encyclopedia of Precolonial Africa. Joseph Vogel, ed. pp. 429–435. Walnut Creek, CA: AltaMira Press.

Ghey, Mebus, and Pierre de Maret, 1982 Histogram Evaluation of 14C Dates Applied to the First Complete Iron Age Sequence from West Central Africa. Archaeometry 24:158–163.

Griaule, Marcel, 1943 Les Sao légendaires. Paris: Gallimard.

Herbert, Eugenia W., 1993 Iron, Gender and Power: Rituals of Transformation in African Societies. Bloomington: Indiana University Press.

Hiernaux, Jean, Emma Maquet, and Jos Debuyst, 1971 Fouilles archéologiques dans la vallée du Haut-Lualaba I Sanga 1958. Tervuren: Musée Royal de l'Afrique Centrale.

Hilton, Anne, 1985 The Kingdom of Kongo. Oxford: Clarendon Press.

Hladik, C. M., A. Hladik, O. F. Linares, H. Pagezy, A. Semple, and M. Hadley, eds., 1993 Tropical Forests, People and Food: Biocultural Interactions and Applications to Development. Paris: UNESCO (Parthenon Publishing).

Huffman, Thomas N., 1996 Snakes and Crocodiles. Power and Symbolism in Ancient Zimbabwe. Johannesburg: Witwatersrand University Press.

Kelly, Kenneth, 1997 The Archaeology of African–European Interaction: Investigating the Social Roles of Trade, Traders, and the Use of Space in the Seventeenth- and Eighteenth-Century Huéda Kingdom, Republic of Bénin. World Archaeology 28(3):351–369.

——2001 Change and Continuity in Coastal Benin. In West Africa during the Atlantic Slave Trade: Archaeological Perspectives. Christopher R. DeCorse, ed. pp. 81–100. London: Leicester University Press.

Lanfranchi, Raymond, 1979 Recherches préhistoriques dans la moyenne vallée du Niari (République populaire du Congo). Ph.D. dissertation, Université Libre de Bruxelles.

Leakey, Mary, D., W. E. Owen, and Louis S. B. Leakey, 1948 Dimple-Based Pottery from Central Kavirondo, Kenya Colony. Nairobi: Coryndon Museum Occasional Papers.

Lebeuf, Jean-Paul, 1937 Rapport sur les travaux de la quatrième mission Griaule. Journal de la Société des Africanistes 7:213–219.

McIntosh, Susan Keech, ed., 1999 Beyond Chiefdoms: Pathways to Complexity in Africa. Cambridge: Cambridge University Press.

McIntosh, Susan Keech, and Roderick J. McIntosh, 1980 Prehistoric Investigations at Jenné, Mali. 2 vols. Cambridge Monographs in African Archaeology, 2. Oxford: British Archaeological Reports.

——1993 Cities without Citadels: Understanding Urban Origins along the Middle Niger. In The Archaeology of Africa: Food, Metals and Towns. Thurstan Shaw, Paul Sinclair, Bassey Andah, and Alex Okpoko, eds. pp. 622–641. London: Routledge.

Menghin, Oswald, 1925 Die Tumbakultur am unteren Kongo und der westafrikanische Kulturkreis. Anthropos 20:516–557.

——1949 El Tumbiense africano y sus correlaciones intercontinentales. RUNA Archivo para las ciencias del hombre 2(1–2):89–125.

Mortelmans, Georges, 1962 Archéologie des grottes Dimba et Ngovo (région de Thysville, Bas-Congo). In Actes du IVe Congrès Panafricain de Préhistoire et de l'Étude du Quaternaire, vol. 1. Georges Mortelmans and Jacques Nenquin, eds. pp. 407–426. Tervuren: Musée Royal de l'Afrique Centrale.

Nenquin, Jacques, 1963 Excavations at Sanga 1957 The Protohistoric Necropolis. Tervuren: Musée Royale de l'Afrique Centrale.

Nicolaï, Henri, Pierre Gourou, and Mashini Dhi Mbita Mulenghe, 1996 L'Espace zaïrois: Hommes et milieux. Paris: l'Harmattan.

Petit, Pierre, 1996 Au coeur du royaume: Réflexions sur l'ethnicité luba. Bulletin des séances de l'Académie Royale des Sciences d'Outre-Mer 42(4):759–774.

Pikirayi, Innocent, 1993 The Archaeological Identity of the Mutapa State: Towards an Historical Archaeology of Northern Zimbabwe. Uppsala: Societas Archaeologica Upsaliensis.

Pinçon, Bruno, 1991 L'Archéologie du royaume teke. In Aux origines de l'Afrique Centrale. Raymond Lanfranchi and Bernard Clist, eds. pp. 243–252. Paris: Sépia.

Pwiti, Gilbert, 1996 Continuity and Change. An Archaeological Study of Farming Communities in Southern Zimbabwe AD 500–1700. Uppsala: Department of Archaeology, Uppsala University.

Randles, W. G. L., 1968 L'Ancien Royaume de Congo, des origines à la fin du XIXe siècle. Paris: Mouton.

Reefe, Thomas Q., 1981 The Rainbow and the Kings: A History of the Luba Empire to 1981. Berkeley: University of California Press.

Schoenbrun, David L., 1997 The Historical Reconstruction of Great Lakes Bantu Culture Vocabulary: Etymologies and Distributions. Cologne: Rüdiger Köppe Verlag.

——1999 The (In)visible Roots of Bunyoro-Kitara and Buganda in the Lakes Region: AD 800–1300. In Beyond Chiefdoms: Pathways to Complexity in Africa. Susan Keech McIntosh, ed. pp. 136–150. Cambridge: Cambridge University Press.

Shaw, Thurstan, Paul Sinclair, Bassey Andah, and Alex Okpoko, eds., 1993 The Archaeology of Africa: Food, Metals and Towns. London: Routledge.

Sinclair, Paul J. J., 1987 Space, Time and Social Formation: A Territorial Approach to the Archaeology and Anthropology of Zimbabwe and Mozambique c. 0–1700 AD. Uppsala: Societas Archaeologica Upsaliensis.

Thompson, Robert Farris, 1981 The Structure of Recollection: The Kongo New World Visual Tradition. In The Four Moments of the Sun: Kongo Art in Two Worlds. Robert Farris Thompson and Joseph Cornet, eds. pp. 141–210. Washington, DC: National Gallery of Art.

Thornton, John K., 1979 The Kingdom of Kongo in the Era of the Civil Wars 1641–1718. Ph.D. dissertation, University of California, Los Angeles.

—— 1983 The Kingdom of Congo: Civil War and Transition 1641–1718. Madison: University of Wisconsin Press.

Vandenhoute, J., 1973 De Begraafplaats van Ngongo Mbata (Neder-Zaïre). Opgravingsverslag en historische situering. MA thesis, Rijksuniversiteit Ghent.

Vansina, Jan, 1966 Kingdoms of the Savanna. Madison: University of Wisconsin Press.

—— 1969 The Bells of Kings. The Journal of African History 10:187–197.

—— 1973 The Tio Kingdom of the Middle Congo 1880–1892. London: Oxford University Press.

—— 1989 Deep Down Time: Political Tradition in Central Africa. History in Africa 16:341–362.

—— 1990 Paths in the Rainforests: Toward a History of Political Tradition in Equatorial Africa. Madison: University of Wisconsin Press.

Van Noten, Francis, 1972 Les Tombes du Roi Cyirima Rujugira et de la Reine-mère Nyirayuhi Kanjogera: Description archéologique. Tervuren: Musée Royale de l'Afrique Centrale.

Verhulpen, Edmond, 1936 Baluba et Balubaïsés du Katanga. Anvers: Éditions de l'Avenir Belge.

Womersley, Harold, 1975 In the Glow of the Log Fire. London: Peniel Press.

Wotzka, Hans-Peter, 1995 Studien des zentral-afrikanischen Regenwaldes. Cologne: Heinrich Barth Institut.

Zangato, Étienne, 1991 Étude du mégalithisme dans le Nord-Ouest de la République Centrafricaine. Ph.D. dissertation, Université de Paris X.

18

Two Thousand Years of West African History

Scott MacEachern

West African societies have repeatedly been transformed over the last two millennia in response to their own internal dynamics and their changing physical and cultural environments. In this, they resemble societies all over the world: two thousand years is a long time. However, the images of West African history held by many have not reflected that dynamism. Archaeologists and historians in western Europe and North America have often interpreted Africa's past through simplifying models, privileging continuity and timelessness over inventiveness and adaptation to changing environments, and obscuring the complexity and diversity of African social, political, and ideological experience (Chapters 1, 2).

In keeping with the evolutionary preoccupations of earlier scholars, West African history was conceived as a particular instance of the unilinear evolution of human cultures across the globe (Chapters 1, 8–10, 13). As a result, scholars envisioned West African societies in the later first millennium A.D. beginning a crucial evolutionary advance from non-state to state forms of sociopolitical organization under diffusionary influence from outside the continent. This transformed the political environment of the subcontinent, now conceived of in terms of political relations between states and (asymmetrically) between states and non-states. This transformation of West Africa into a region of states was not, however, completed at the time of the last progressive transition in its history. This occurred when European contact woke a "precolonial" subcontinent to outside influences, the slave trade and ultimately the colonial period.

This model has been questioned as archaeologists have challenged diffusionary assumptions (Chapter 13) and unilinear evolutionary schema, emphasizing instead the importance of regional environmental variability in structuring cultural change. However, such universal schema still dominate many representations of West African history, as they are disseminated to students and to people outside of the disciplines of history and archaeology. This chapter offers a brief overview of the last 2,000 years of West African history from a perspective at odds with simplistic progressive schemes of cultural evolution. It seeks to evaluate cultural and historical continuities across time and space, taking into account geographical and temporal variability in cultural trajectories through this part of the African continent.

Changing Environments and Human Settlement

By A.D. 1, people had occupied West Africa for many millennia, and a variety of geographical and environmental continuities had affected them (Chapters 7, 9). Perhaps most important was the interplay of global climatic systems that produce the east–west environmental zones across the subcontinent (Chapter 9). The boundaries between these zones varied greatly in the past, as for example when the Sahara virtually disappeared in the Early Holocene (Chapters 7, 8, 10) and then reappeared in the drier conditions that held after 5000 b.c. They continue to vary today.

By 2,000 years ago, the Sahara had expanded roughly to its modern extent, transforming woodlands, grasslands, and river systems into desert and semi-desert in a complex sequence of climatic cycles over thousands of years. Environmental change of this magnitude elicited a variety of different adaptive responses (R. McIntosh 2000), including modifications to the complex systems of seasonal movement that are important elements in the economies of many societies in West Africa. These involve not only mobile pastoral populations (Smith 1992:143–167) but also the farmers with whom they trade and whose harvested fields their herds often graze and fertilize, as well as a variety of different specialist groups (Conte 1991).

In the Inland Niger Delta (IND), the origins of modern social systems can be traced to cyclical population movements and interactions between southern Saharan communities (R. McIntosh 1993, 1998), adapting to environmental changes through the last two millennia b.c. This involved the gradual abandonment of the dying northern tributaries of the Niger, the occupation of hitherto flooded basins along the IND, and the development of a sophisticated economic system in which different ethnic groups specialized in different kinds of production activities. The archaeological traces of similar cultural interactions are found in Mauritania (Vernet 1993), Burkina Faso (Neumann and Vogelsang 1996), Ghana (Davies 1980; Shinnie and Kense 1989; Stahl 1985), and northern Nigeria and Cameroon (Breunig et al. 1996; Connah 1981). Linguistic (Fleming 1983) and genetic (Cruciani et al. 2002) data also indicate the importance and complexity of contacts between North Africa, the Sahara, and West Africa.

The Saharan boundaries of West Africa were thus not impassable barriers to human movement, but rather zones of interaction and cultural innovation. The same was true of the fluctuating boundaries between the savanna and the tropical forest along the Atlantic coast. Important changes in the extent and character of forest environments took place, probably in response to the same processes that affected areas to the north (Maley 1989; Sowunmi 1981). Such variability encouraged the same kinds of population movement (both cyclical and permanent) and economic experimentation as along the southern margins of a variable Sahara. West Africa almost certainly saw population movements and cultural interactions within the tropical forest and from the forest toward the savanna to the north (MacDonald 1998a; Stahl 1985) as well as in the opposite direction. East–west connections were equally important and probably even easier given the relative constancy of environmental zones in those directions. The long-distance migrations of Fulbe and Shuwa Arab populations (Stenning 1957; Zeltner 1979) during the second millennium A.D., eastward from Senegambia and westward from the Nile Valley respectively, provide historical illustration of such processes. Both population movements significantly influenced cultural and political arrangements through the Sudanic zone of West and Central Africa. Similar east–west contacts existed further to the south, in the forests and along the Atlantic coast as well; thus, for example, common elements of ritual and material culture supported Mande-speaking trading networks (McNaughton 1992), while the coastal lagoon system between the Volta and Niger rivers offered an easy avenue for commodity movement and political interaction over hundreds of kilometers (Law 1983).

West African populations had undoubtedly engaged in trade for many millennia, but by the late first millennium b.c. exchange networks broadened to encompass large areas and a wide variety of goods. A number of important sites in different areas of the West African savanna have yielded evidence for such trade. These include the Jenné-jeno site cluster in the IND of Mali, where excavations yielded significant evidence for urban development and long-distance contacts from the late first millennium B.C. until ca. A.D. 1400, and Daima in northeastern Nigeria, where settlement probably began some centuries earlier and ended in the early to mid-second millennium A.D. At Jenné-jeno, iron ore, stone, and copper were imported from substantial distances, probably using the Niger River for transport (S. McIntosh and R. McIntosh 1993a). Food preparation at Daima and other sites on the stoneless *firki* plains of northeastern Nigeria depended upon the import of grindstones and finer stone from sources 100–200 km distant (Connah 1981:139–140). Many of the wheeled vehicles depicted in Mauritanian rock art of the period are being pulled by cattle, not horses – which may indicate use of carts for haulage, rather than chariots in warfare (Vernet 1993:322–324). These communities were, by A.D. 1, enmeshed in a continuous process of adaptation to complex and variable environments, and such adaptations would likely have favored widespread contacts between peoples.

Economy and Technology at the Beginning of the First Millennium

The starting point of our survey is roughly the mid-point of an arid episode lasting from about 300 b.c. to a.d. 300, which was succeeded by a considerably wetter and more stable environmental regime between a.d. 300 and a.d. 1100 (Maley 1981; Nicholson 1976:73–97). This seems to have been associated with increases in site size and number, and so presumably population, through much of West Africa. Climatic variability and demands of time and labor have encouraged the development of African farming systems based upon the exploitation of a variety of domesti-

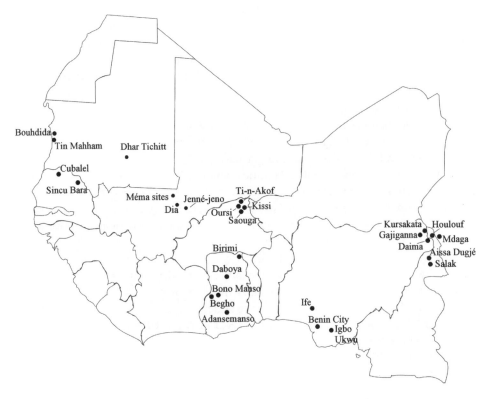

Figure 18.1. West African archaeological sites of the first millennium a.d.

cated, semi-domesticated, and wild plant resources, specialization in certain food-production activities by certain groups, and detailed knowledge of a range of famine foods to be used when crops fail (Harlan 1993; Harlan et al. 1976; Chapter 10). R. McIntosh (1998) describes the appearance of such agricultural systems in the IND (Figure 18.1) based upon cattle, fish, and African rice (*Oryza glaberrima*), but with evidence for use of wild plants and animals as well during the late first millennium B.C.

Other West African sites show similar broad-based adaptations. Bouhdida and Tin Mahham occupations on the Atlantic coast of Mauritania between 600 b.c. and a.d. 400 (Vernet 1993:343–378; 2000) depended upon cattle-herding, hunting, fishing, and shellfish-collecting, with populations at some points occupying substantial seasonal settlements. At Gajiganna and Kursakata in northeastern Nigeria, people cultivated pearl millet (*Pennisetum glaucum*), kept domesticated cattle and small stock, hunted and fished, and made extensive use of wild grasses as a source of cereals (Breunig et al. 1996; Neumann 1999). In similar environments at Ti-n-Akof and Oursi in northern Burkina Faso, there is as yet no evidence for domesticated animals, but otherwise the same food sources were used (Vogelsang et al. 1999).

In savanna areas of northern Ghana, Kintampo populations of the second millennium b.c. farmed pearl millet and gathered other wild grasses and plants, while
related groups living in the forests to the south made more extensive use of wild
plants, including oil palm, kept sheep/goats, and hunted wild game (Chapter 9).
Use of these wild species was common in West African forest subsistence systems
through the first millennium a.d., perhaps accompanied by the cultivation of indigenous tubers. Stone-tool-using hunter-gatherer populations may have persisted in
the West African forests until the end of the first millennium a.d. (Chapter 9), before
being absorbed into neighboring farming groups. If so, they would probably have
been able to furnish forest products to their farmer neighbors in exchange for cultivated goods, as Pygmy populations have in Central Africa in the recent past.

Architecturally, the first millennium b.c. witnessed a significant change in West
African site formation. Before this, savanna and forest sites were for the most part
small and ephemeral, with slow rates of deposition of cultural material. By the
middle of the first millennium b.c., the large mounds and mound clusters that are
one of the most recognizable archaeological features of the West African savanna
began to appear, although in many areas mound formation seems to have accelerated after A.D. 300 (Bourges et al. 1999; Connah 1981; Holl 1987; Lamotte and
Marliac 1989; S. McIntosh, ed., 1995; Togola 1996; Vogelsang et al. 1999). These
changes were probably associated with greater degrees of sedentism and the adoption of more permanent structures, built using clay architecture rather than organic
materials. In the forest zones of Ghana, Stahl (1993:271) suggests that there may
have been a shift from Kintampo rockshelters to open sites on alluvium in the first
millennium b.c., a shift that made these later sites more difficult to find and identify. Remarkably few forest sites dating from between the end of the Kintampo
period and a.d. 1000 have been located.

By the beginning of the first millennium a.d., pottery forms one of the basic
indications of human habitation on West African sites. The early first millennium
a.d. saw changes in ceramic assemblages in some areas (Connah 1976:342;
MacEachern 1996; S. McIntosh, ed., 1995), including increased quantities and a
change from finer, thinner-walled vessels to thicker-walled pottery that would better
withstand prolonged exposure to fire. This may be traced to changes in cooking
techniques, from an emphasis on grilling and roasting to the boiled cereals, stews,
and sauces characteristic of much of modern West African cuisine (S. McIntosh,
ed., 1995:160–161), and possibly to an increase in sedentism. Such changes were
of more than culinary importance; sharing of food and beer remains an important
means of coordinating communal labor today.

Evidence for ironworking first appears on sites in Nigeria, Cameroon, and Niger
by at least 500 b.c. (Woodhouse 1998). The beginning of iron production is often
seen as the most fundamental technological change during this period, so much so
that archaeologists talk about the start of the Iron Age. However, such a division
of West African history implies that the replacement of some kinds of stone or
wooden tools (for example, axes, hoes, or different kinds of weapons) by iron is a
transformative process, more important than other social or cultural processes going
on at the same time. It also implies that the transition from Neolithic to Iron Age

was a singular event of relatively short duration (Holl 1993:330–332; Sinclair et al. 1993:3–9; Chapter 11).

The date of first appearance of iron on savanna sites varies between 500 b.c. and a.d. 500, and there are cases where iron appears centuries earlier or later in neighboring areas (MacEachern 1996; Marliac and Langlois 1996; Vernet, 1993: 353–363). Varying numbers of stone tools (which are usually assumed to have been replaced by iron) continue to be found on sites where there is evidence of iron being used. There is no evidence for use of iron in the tropical forest of West Africa until after a.d. 500, in contrast to the situation in nearby areas of Central Africa, where evidence of ironworking from sites is a thousand years older (de Barros 1986:158–159; Woodhouse 1998:168–170). It is possible that the early use of iron in Central Africa is associated with banana cultivation by about 500 b.c. (Mbida et al. 2001); the two innovations together would probably have facilitated more intensive use of the forest.

All of this implies a more gradual and piecemeal adoption of iron technologies than is often assumed (Chapter 11). If iron were as transformative a technology as has traditionally been thought, we might expect to see a cascade of economic and social changes quickly result from its use. Yet the correlation between adoption of iron and other such changes – in ceramic styles and architecture, or in settlement patterning – varies considerably from one part of West Africa to another, and is often weak. Iron was no doubt an important factor for the communities that adopted it, one that eventually transformed Africans societies and landscapes, but it did not do so all at once.

Our picture of technological and economic patterning in West Africa in the centuries around A.D. 1 is thus extremely complex. Instead of simple and simultaneous adoptions of new technologies, we see a complex mosaic of adaptations to different and variable environments. Communities combined the use of ancient and well-understood technical systems with new approaches, involving various combinations of innovative material technologies, new agricultural elements, and new rhythms of site formation and occupation.

Communities and Societies in the First Millennium A.D.

Archaeologists have often assumed (below) that West African societies of two millennia ago were small in scale, without significant social hierarchies and with only local political affiliations and interests, and that more complex social and political structures were introduced from outside the subcontinent. As outlined in Chapter 13, work in the Middle Niger area throws this model into doubt. Between A.D. 400 and A.D. 900 the size and complexity of some of these sites indicate the existence of truly urban modes of life (S. McIntosh and R. McIntosh 1993a). These sites are too early to plausibly be ascribed to foreign influences. References in Islamic sources to the lands south of the Sahara date only to the eighth century A.D. onward (Levtzion and Hopkins 1981:19ff), although these initial contacts probably took place along trade routes that had already been in operation for some centuries.

More importantly, these innovations are rooted in West African cultural developments, not North African ones. Islamic travelers in West Africa frequently expressed
surprise and shock at the foreign characteristics of the communities they visited.

The features of early trans-Saharan trade are indicated by discoveries at the Kissi
3 site in northeastern Burkina Faso (Magnavita et al. 2002), where graves of high-
status individuals date to the period a.d. 400–700. These graves yielded brass and
other copper alloy anklets, cowrie shells, glass and carnelian beads, and weapons
that had probably been brought into the region from the southern Sahara, and ultimately from North Africa and beyond. Again, the remains from Kissi 3 and related
sites in the area are firmly placed within regional cultural traditions stretching back
into the first millennium b.c., with mixed agricultural systems very similar to those
found on contemporary West African savanna sites (Magnavita et al. 2002:38–48).
The exotic goods found at Kissi 3 may well have provided new and very effective
ways of signaling elite status, but there is no evidence that new social and political
arrangements were introduced with trade across the desert to the north.

The Méma sites west of the Middle Niger link that region with the Dhar Tichitt
area of Mauritania, where over 90 habitation sites of varying sizes existed in a four-
level settlement hierarchy between about 1500 and 500 b.c. (Holl 1993). Such hierarchies, along with the internal characteristics of regional centers, indicate some
degree of political centralization at a very early period and in communities under
some environmental stress. The extent to which a Dhar Tichitt polity may have
served as a point of articulation between pastoralist and equestrian elites in a desiccating southern Sahara and later political organizations of the West Africa savanna
zone (cf. MacDonald 1998b) remains to be investigated.

The period between a.d. 300 and a.d. 1100 followed six centuries of very arid
conditions, and saw significant changes in many areas of the West African savanna
and forest. The sites clustered around Jenné-jeno reached their greatest size during
this time, while other middle Niger mound sites also displayed impressive levels of
internal complexity. In the Middle Senegal River valley, the appearance of mound
(Cubalel) and flat (Sincu Bara) sites in the first millennium A.D. attests to a diversity of settlement patterns; extensive and episodic occupations at the latter site, a
more settled life, and increasing populations at the former (S. McIntosh 1999c; S.
McIntosh and Bocoum 2000). During the last half of the millennium, an extraordinary period of funerary mound and megalith construction began between the
Niger and southern Senegambia, spreading to northern Senegal early in the second
millennium A.D. (S. McIntosh and R. McIntosh 1993b; Raimbault and Sanogo,
eds., 1991). To this point relatively little has been published on the occupation sites
that presumably accompany these funeral monuments in Senegambia (cf. Lawson
2001). Between the Senegal River and Nouakchott to the north, "medieval"
Mauritanian populations of the late first millennium a.d. abandoned the mixed
pastoral/marine orientations of their Bouhdida and Tin Mahham predecessors to
follow a more specialized pastoral way of life (Vernet 1993:365–376).

A substantial episode of mound formation began in northern Burkina Faso early
in the first millennium a.d. The Oursi and Saouga sites show evidence for millet
cultivation, and for the cultivation of pulses (*Voandzeia* groundnuts and cowpeas

[*Vigna unguiculata*]) and exploitation of a variety of tree species, including jujube, *karité*, and acacia (Neumann and Vogelsang 1996; Vogelsang et al. 1999). These plants and their various products are still essential to West African agricultural systems. At the same time, rates of sediment accumulation and artifact deposition increase on sites in the southern Lake Chad basin, including Daima, Houlouf, Kursakata, Aissa Dugjé, and Mege, and architectural features like potsherd pavements and external walls appear (Bourges et al. 1999; Connah, 1981:165; Gronenborn 1998; Holl 1988). It is likely that occupation of many of the "Sao" mound sites of northern Cameroon and Chad excavated by Jean-Paul and Annie Lebeuf and their collaborators (A. Lebeuf et al. 1980; J.-P. Lebeuf 1969) began during this period as well. Settlement intensity in the Diamaré region of northern Cameroon, at Salak and Mongossi for example, seems to increase significantly during the middle of the first millennium a.d. (Marliac 1991:713–793; Marliac and Langlois 1996).

Mound sites are relatively easy to locate during survey work, and it is probable that many people living in the region during the first millennium a.d. did not live in these communities. There does, however, seem to be a real change in the intensity of occupation in some regions. A variety of factors may have contributed, including the effects of the a.d. 300 climatic amelioration. Data from Mauritania and Mali indicate that agricultural systems were becoming more specialized over this period, with a greater differentiation between farmers and pastoralists. Increased sedentism associated with more specialized farming techniques would have in turn affected the rate of accumulation of sediments on sites. Greater use of iron and the introduction of a new cereal crop, sorghum (*Sorghum bicolor*) may have increased the productivity of agricultural systems, although whether sorghum was in widespread use before the late first millennium a.d. remains debatable (Connah 1981:189; S. McIntosh, ed., 1995:350; Magnavita 2002; Neumann 1999; Rowley-Conwy et al. 1999). Millet continues to dominate in most areas.

Archaeologists know much less about occupation in and around the West African tropical forest in the first millennium a.d., in large part because of problems with survey in forested environments. Sites like Daboya (Shinnie and Kense 1989), Begho/Atwetwebooso (Stahl 1994:80) and Bono Manso (Effah-Gyamfi 1985:79–86, 206) just north of the forest in Ghana, indicate the presence of iron-using populations early in the millennium, but there is little evidence for iron use in the forest or on the coast. If Stahl's (1993) hypothesis that post-Kintampo farmers in this area were living on open sites in alluvium is correct, it may be that forest-dwelling populations were too small or mobile, or sedimentation rates too high, for sites of the period to easily be found. Excavations at Adansemanso, near Kumasi in central Ghana, indicate that this situation had changed by the end of the first millennium a.d. (Vivian 1996). The linear mounds found on the Adansemanso site are not like the contemporary, generally circular, mounds found to the north, but they display evidence for substantial architectural features, including clay-lined pits and floors.

The intensity and complexity of settlement in southern Nigeria by the time of European contact from the 15th century A.D. imply a significant period of *in situ* development in that area. Again, however, details of such occupations are scarce.

Settlement at the urban center of Ife probably began late in the first millennium a.d. (Shaw 1980:377), although we know little about the processes through which such occupation took place. Darling (1984, 1998) placed the early construction phases of the remarkable earthwork complexes of the Benin/Ishan region – over 16,000 linear kilometers of earthworks in a 4,000 km^2 area – in the same period. These processes of forest colonization and land partitioning may parallel the cultural trajectories that resulted in sites like Adansemanso in Ghana (above), albeit with different material results. In both Nigeria and Ghana, evidence for human activity in the forest is more abundant after the beginning of the second millennium a.d. (e.g., Ogundiran 2002).

The extraordinary site of Igbo-Ukwu (Shaw 1970) in southeastern Nigeria, with its burial chamber and storage areas, its beautiful cast bronzes and vast numbers of beads, similarly dates to the late first millennium a.d. and lacks local precedents. The Igbo-Ukwu glass beads are exotic to the region, although their ultimate point of origin – Venice, the Near East, and India have all been suggested – and the routes by which they arrived in Nigeria, whether across the Sahara or westward from the Nile Valley, are not definitively known (Insoll and Shaw 1997; Sutton 2001). This implies that the forest zone of southern Nigeria was by this time tied into continental trading networks that spanned a significant part of the Old World, but there is little other proof of such contacts.

Even more perplexing than the external relations of Igbo-Ukwu is the matter of its local meaning. The contents of the site suggest burial of a very important person indeed, someone whom archaeologists would in other contexts identify as a member of a local elite group, perhaps a king. The Igbo peoples who inhabit the area today are, however, relatively egalitarian, without the sort of centralized political hierarchy that would concentrate so much wealth in the burial of a ruler. The ritual contexts of the burial are similar to that of a holder of the title *eze nri*, an important social and ritual status in modern Igbo society (Ray 1987; Shaw 1970:268–270), although there are also significant differences between Igbo-Ukwu and recent Ibo practice.

These complexities in interpreting Igbo-Ukwu should serve as a cautionary tale for researchers: we are often too willing to impose modern assumptions about power and prestige on ancient cases that may have worked according to very different logics. Such assumptions implicitly deny the historicity and dynamism of West African societies through time. They also ignore the effects of cultural disruptions during the slave trade and colonial periods, and more recently. As we will see below, David and Sterner (1999), R. McIntosh (1999), and S. McIntosh (1999a) argue that social and political systems in the Mandara Mountains and along the Middle Niger could in fact diverge considerably from recently attested examples, with changes in those characteristics sometimes happening quite quickly. Guyer and Belinga (1995), using data from Equatorial Africa, present a model of social action and knowledge not well reflected in dominant reconstructions of "traditional" African societies. Such investigations, sensitive to changes in meaning and organization through space and time, could profitably be extended to other areas of West Africa as well.

Political Structures: Hierarchy and Heterarchy, States and Non-States

How do we think about political structures in West Africa during the late first and early second millennium A.D.? Early research assumed that these would look like their presumed antecedents north of the Sahara, particularly in their political and religious characteristics. Under the influence of social evolutionary thought, it was further assumed that simple, egalitarian societies developed into complex and hierarchical ones through a succession of stages (cf. Chapters 1, 13, 16).

In a parallel process rooted in British social anthropology, African political systems were dichotomized into "stateless" (or "tribal") and "state" forms (Fortes and Evans-Pritchard 1940; Horton 1976), with the former occupying subordinate and peripheral statuses, although capable in some cases of evolving into states. These models serve a valuable purpose when they are used to look for common features in cultural systems and processes of social and political change, but become much less useful when they obscure the particularities of specific historical sequences. Over the last decade, critiques of such models have multiplied, in both African and non-African contexts (S. McIntosh 1999b; Possehl 1998; Sharpe 1986; Stahl 1999; Yoffee 1991).

Igbo-Ukwu has provided more material for reconstructions of ancient systems of authority than has almost any contemporary site in West Africa, and those materials are profoundly ambiguous. On the one hand, the material symbolism can be interpreted in modern terms, associated with an important ritual leader in a society without centralized political power. On the other hand, the richness of the remains may indicate that such power was more concentrated in a single person or status in the past. In that case, are we looking at a case of political "devolution" (S. McIntosh 1999b) from more to less centralized political hierarchy, a direction of development opposite to that assumed by the evolutionary models mentioned above? Use of the term "devolution" suggests some decrease in complexity, perhaps even a loss of vitality; however, neither image agrees well with the vibrancy of communities in southern Nigeria as Europeans encountered them from the 16th century onward (Hodgkins 1975; Pacheco Pereira 1937).

The evidence for first-millennium political hierarchies and state development in other areas of West Africa is equally ambiguous. As outlined in Chapter 13, Susan and Roderick McIntosh (R. McIntosh 1993; S. McIntosh 1999a; S. McIntosh and R. McIntosh, 1993a) argue that models of centralized, hierarchical power do not fully explain features of the site clusters at Jenné-jeno and elsewhere in the IND, nor cultural dynamics in the Méma and the Middle Senegal Valley. Heterarchical models, which emphasize complex relationships between unranked or variably ranked elements in a system (Ehrenreich et al., eds., 1995), may prove useful in analyzing these communities.

There is, however, other evidence for hierarchy in social and political relations in this part of West Africa. Jenné-jeno seems to have declined in importance early in the second millennium A.D., after evidence for defensive wall construction and contacts with North Africa appears, and was abandoned by about A.D. 1400. The funeral mounds found between the Niger River and Senegambia are frequently accompanied by rich burial goods, and on at least one occasion (at Koï Gourrey) by what seem to be human sacrifices (Connah 2001:125–130; R. McIntosh 1998:219–233). These sites appear to provide substantial evidence for concentrations of wealth and power in the hands of local elites. However, we should remember the example of Igbo-Ukwu when evaluating such sites. Roderick McIntosh (1998:227–229) raises the possibility that at least some of them are associated with small-scale political units interacting across the region, but still displaying relatively low levels of inter-community conflict and intra-community stratification. (It appears unlikely that such explanations can comfortably accommodate the dead at Koï Gourrey.) This provides an alternative to explanations that use Arabic historical sources (Levtzion and Hopkins 1981:77–110) to emphasize processes of state formation and elite conversion to Islam between the Niger and Senegal rivers at the end of the first millennium A.D.

There is clustering of mound sites in northern Burkina Faso (Vogelsang et al. 1999:53, 59) and around the Mandara Mountains in Cameroon and Nigeria, where both inselberg edges and river margins served as foci for human settlement (Bourges et al. 1999; Langlois 1995; Marliac et al. 2000:71–73). Modern villages in the latter region are often made up of clusters of spatially (and sometimes ethnically) segregated neighborhoods, which may correspond in function to such site clusters (MacEachern 2002). In the *firki* clay plains south of Lake Chad, a more dispersed pattern of solitary mound sites in the first and early second millennium a.d. (Connah 1981:46; J.-P. Lebeuf 1969) may relate to differential distribution of resources. There is no indication of major disparities in wealth or political power at sites like Daima (Connah 1981:99–196), Aissa Dugjé (Bourges et al. 1999), Mdaga (A. Lebeuf et al. 1980), or Salak (Marliac 1991). The horses found at Aissa Dugjé (MacEachern et al. 2001) from the middle of the first millennium A.D. onward do not themselves indicate an increase in social hierarchy, although horses later supplied vital military and symbolic support to emergent elites in the second millennium A.D. (Holl 1994).

Historical sources from the second millennium A.D. (Forkl 1995; Lange 1989) indicate that local and weak hierarchical political units south of Lake Chad were incorporated into larger, centralized states. At the same time, archaeological and ethnographic evidence demonstrates the dangers of such simple models of state encroachment. Even powerful states of the late second millennium A.D. did not control all of the lands that they claimed: they were surrounded by smaller-scale and more egalitarian societies, which provided them with vitally needed resources (Reyna 1990), acted as laboratories for the development of new social and political forms (Kopytoff 1987), or both. Until the colonial period, centralized states were always associated with smaller-scale societies in this region, and the relations between these units were often extremely complex. That complexity has often been obscured in historical and ethnographic writing on the area (Sharpe 1986). Closely related communities in the Mandara region are found at a variety of levels of social and political centralization, and their transitions between such levels appear to owe

Figure 18.2. Abandoned stone structures in the Mandara Mountains
Photo by Nicholas David; printed with permission.

as much to particular historical circumstances as to universal laws of cultural evolution (David and Sterner 1999). Those transitions could involve decreases as well as increases in degree of social hierarchy and political centralization, in some cases involving abandonment of quite spectacular architectural constructions (Figure 18.2). As among the Igbo, such "devolution" appears to have taken place in a vital and expansive cultural milieu.

Change and Adaptation in the Second Millennium A.D.

The 12th century saw the end of a period of relatively benign climates that had lasted for about 800 years, and was succeeded by significantly less predictable climates into the modern period (Maley 1981; Nicholson 1976:98–158). This change may be associated with a gradual abandonment of savanna mound sites in many areas through the middle of the second millennium A.D. (J.-P. Lebeuf 1969; R. McIntosh 1998:241–250; Marliac et al. 2000:75; Sanogo 1991; Togola 1996:105; Vogelsang et al. 1999:65). North of the forests, the increasing importance of expansionist states, with elite ideological charters increasingly marked by adherence to Islam, probably played a role in this process as well. The historical narratives of second-millennium West Africa emphasize state formation and imperial grandeur. That grandeur often came, however, at the expense of rich agrarian traditions that had to that point persisted for many centuries.

Those traditions did not, however, disappear after a.d. 1200. West Africans since that time have existed in a world in which states have become steadily more hierarchical and hegemonic, extending their control over larger and larger areas. At the same time, many communities maintained a surprising degree of local integrity well into the 20th century. The abundant evidence for human migration through the last millennium (Brooks 1993; Lentz 2000; McNaughton 1992; Rossi et al. 1991) testifies in part to the desire for individual and community autonomy among African populations. There is also, however, a great deal of evidence for continuity in human culture through these periods, in economies and technology, and even in many elements of ideology and ritual systems (R. McIntosh 1993; McNaughton 1992). I will assume such continuity through my description of events during the second millennium A.D., and concentrate instead on changes through this period. This may yield a more fragmented view of African history over the last eight centuries, but such fragmentation is also characteristic of archaeological research during this period, as investigators struggle to reconcile their data with the historical and ethnographic record.

Historical narratives of empire have significantly affected the way archaeology has been done in West Africa as research focused on locating population centers associated with second-millennium states, and detecting foreign cultural contacts. The reasons for this are straightforward: Arabic written accounts were privileged as historical sources, because West African societies were supposed to have "entered history" (Trevor-Roper 1965) through Arab contact, and those accounts particularly emphasized population centers. Significant fieldwork has taken place at a number of large settlement sites in West Africa (Figure 18.3): (1) Jenné-jeno (abandoned ca. A.D. 1400); (2) Kumbi Saleh (occupied through the first half of the millennium – Berthier 1997); (3) Tegdaoust (between the eighth and 12th centuries – Devisse 1983; Polet 1985; Robert et al., eds., 1970; Robert-Chaleix 1989); (4) Gao (from the seventh to the 19th centuries – Insoll 1996); (5) Hamdallahi (occupied for a short period in the 19th century – Mayor et al. 1990); (6) Begho (ca. a.d. 1100–1800 – Crossland and Posnansky 1978); (7) Old Oyo (most of the second millennium A.D. – Soper and Darling 1980): (8) Ife (late in the first millennium a.d. until the present – Shaw 1980); and (9) Benin City (from the 13th to the 19th centuries a.d. – Connah 1972). A number of other important sites occupied during this period, including Timbuktu, Kano, and other Hausa urban sites in northern Nigeria and Kong in Côte d'Ivoire, have not been systematically examined.

Archaeologists now know a substantial amount about chronologies of occupation on these sites, although there is as always more to be done. Excavations have generated data on exchange systems and cultural contacts within and beyond West Africa, and especially with the Arab world. Indeed, in many of these cases we know more about such long-distance connections than about relations between the people occupying these sites and their neighbors living in smaller-scale communities only a few kilometers away (see Chapter 13). This "city-centric" view of cultural processes is often accompanied by a corresponding lack of attention to regional settlement systems (S. McIntosh and R. McIntosh 1984:76–84). With few exceptions (i.e., Jenné-jeno and Benin City), little is known about these sites in regional contexts.

Figure 18.3. West African archaeological sites of the second millennium a.d.

These large settlements are quite variable in their characteristics. Sahelian and savanna communities (including Jenné-jeno, Kumbi Saleh, Tegdaoust, and Gao) flourished in the early second millennium A.D., but many declined in population and importance at mid-millennium, a decline probably associated with climate change and increased levels of state conflict. Large settlement sites at the edge of and within the forests appear to persist longer, to varying degrees supported and ultimately destabilized by European trade and contacts. Size – in hectares and in human numbers – and layout of these large sites varied widely, affected on the one hand by limits on population densities and governability, and on the other hand by necessities of defense (Fletcher 1998). The ramifying earthwork complexes around and beyond Benin City (Darling 1984) indicate that a simple rural/urban dichotomy may not reflect the complexity of African settlement systems.

Historical and archaeological data indicate the sophistication of the communities that occupied these sites. The artistic traditions of southwestern Nigeria (Willett and Eyo 1980), with figures depicted in bronze/brass, ceramics, and stone, offer a striking testament to an extraordinarily accomplished group of artisans. The imported goods found throughout West Africa, from the marble gravestones near

Gao on the Niger River to the scattered trade beads found on sites across the sub-continent (Connah 2001:139; Insoll 1996:17–24, 58), show the reach (although certainly not the magnitude) of external trade systems. The remarkable cache of hippopotamus ivory found in Gao (Insoll 1995) provides rare archaeological evidence of the African goods (especially gold, slaves, and ivory) that would have been exported in return (also Stahl and Stahl 2004). For the most part, however, these investigations have not really challenged pre-existing historical assumptions about the development of these settlements, or of the political units of which they were a part. They are still all too often treated as isolated occurrences, lacking social and cultural context.

Even less is known about the villages, hamlets, and homesteads where the vast majority of West Africans lived through the second millennium A.D. Few research projects integrate prehistoric data with historical and ethnographic information on recent communities. In northern Cameroon, investigation by French researchers in the Diamaré region has resulted in such a sequence (Marliac and Langlois 1996; Marliac et al. 2000), based primarily on ceramic variation and changes in site occupation that track regional cultural traditions into the historic period. The authors note that such research should not be thought of as a form of "palaeo-ethnohistory," devoted to establishing the origins of modern ethnic groups, themselves dynamic and changeable entities. Rather, historical and archaeological research most fruitfully meshes in regional analyses of cultural process and interaction. In this area, the disruptions of the early second millennium A.D. were followed by changes in indigenous material culture, but also by an increasing level of regional population migrations, as Sudanic states (Kanem, Borno, Wandala, and so on) exerted control at longer distances from their centers. In the Chad basin to the north, indigenous populations were politically, and eventually ethnically, incorporated into those same states (Connah 1981; Gronenborn 2001; Holl 1994), a fascinating comparative example of the effects of state formation and expansion on a regional level.

In the IND, Swiss researchers have taken the opposite approach, combining ethnoarchaeological research on modern ceramic traditions with archaeological research designed to place those traditions in historical context (Gallay 1994; Gallay et al. 1995; Huysecom and Mayor 1995). This has resulted in a very useful analysis of the development of material culture distributions among Fulbe, Songhai, and other ethnic groups, but such a direct historical approach does not easily lend itself to the examination of very great time depths. On the other hand, examination of the history of Dogon groups has generated a great deal of data on population movements and recombinations in this part of southern Mali (Bedaux and Lange 1983; Gallay et al. 1995).

Work in Bassar territories in modern Togo (de Barros 2001) has focused on significant scales of iron production and export, and provides an effective counterexample to the assumption that cultural change in West Africa during the mid-second millennium A.D. was invariably linked to European influence (below). Intensification of iron production in this region began around A.D. 1300, for local use and export, and was associated with indigenous technological and political developments (de Barros 2001:64–75). Use of both locally made and imported pottery seems to have increased with the greater populations and prosperity that this iron industry made possible. This area was somewhat sheltered from direct European influence until late in the 18th century, when an increase in slave-raiding led to some changes in settlement patterning but does not seem to have disrupted iron production. It was only a century later, just before the arrival of German colonialists in the 1890s, that ironworking declined in the region. It has often been assumed that West African ironworking traditions were destroyed by competition from European imports by the end of the 18th century, but Goucher (1981) suggests that African iron stock remained quite competitive and that abandonment of these ironworking industries was in large part due to environmental change, particularly deforestation.

In southwestern Nigeria, Nigerian archaeologists have undertaken very fruitful investigations of interactions between the well-known major polities of the region, Ile-Ife, Benin, and Old Oyo, and the impacts of those centers upon their hinterlands through the second millennium A.D. (Ogundiran 2002; Usman 2001). One goal of this research has been the examination of the ways in which regions peripheral to those centers participated in the economic, cultural, and political processes that led to state formation in this area in the period before European contact. Core–periphery and frontier models have been used extensively in this analysis, offering a theoretical understanding of these processes that goes well beyond traditional concerns with chronology and large urban sites.

Research on cultural change in Senegambia over the period A.D. 1500–1900 (Guèye 2002; McIntosh and Thiaw 2001) has examined the impact of the trans-Atlantic slave trade, and more generally changes in lifeways through a turbulent period. Ceramic data lend some support to the idea that social systems were disturbed (possibly by slave-raiding, warfare, and/or environmental reverses) in the Middle Senegal Valley, but other areas seem to have gained population, and there is evidence for broad continuity in social systems and elite burial ritual through the area. Such syntheses are valuable, because they provide an alternative to historical schema that assume such periods to be dominated by a rupture between "pre-[European] contact" and "post-contact" social circumstances.

The Vectors of European Contact

The most ambitious attempt to transcend such a dichotomized view of West African history is Stahl's (2001) work in the Banda area of central Ghana. Stahl used data from the archaeological sites of Kuulo Kataa and Makala Kataa, occupied over the period A.D. 1350–1900, as well as African and European historical sources, to examine second-millennium cultural processes in this region. This project has been directed toward two broad goals: analysis of the ways in which Banda social systems were embedded within wider political economies, at regional to intercontinental scales; and examination of the production of Banda history by local people and by outsiders. As in the contemporary societies of Bassar territory to the east, evidence of subsistence activity, craft production, and trade in Banda indicates a complex history of relations with neighboring communities, including the town of Begho.

The picture that emerges is of small-scale communities responsive to external influences, whether from the savanna trading states to the north, the expansive Asante kingdom of the late 18th century, the forces of Samori in the 19th century, or European contact. At the same time, such exotic elements were being reformulated and incorporated into indigenous cultural structures. Historical accounts have conventionally treated this period as one where African communities opened up to a wider world, but Stahl's data are more complex, indicating both expansions and contractions of trade and regional linkages over the last half of the second millennium A.D. This study provides a fascinating glimpse of community life on an internal frontier (Kopytoff 1987) through a tumultuous time.

Direct European contact with West Africa began in the middle of the 15th century A.D. Over the next 150 years, European powers gradually extended their trading and military networks eastward along the Atlantic coast, from Mauritania to Cameroon, and the contexts of European contact are generally held to have involved trade, raids, diplomacy, and eventually governance and conversion. However, this view ignores some of the most important forms of contact, which were never systematically documented. For example, New World food crops – especially maize, sweet potatoes, peanuts, and tobacco – spread far beyond sites where contact was taking place, becoming staple crops in some areas (Alpern 1991; Philips 1983) and drastically changing African agricultural systems. Tobacco pipes and evidence of maize use (grains themselves, or the use of cobs as roulettes) are occasionally found on West African archaeological sites (e.g., Connah 1981:165; Effah-Gyamfi 1985; Jones 2001:57; Stahl 2001:134, 140–143; Wesler 1998:11–14), and indicate that these domesticates spread very quickly indeed away from the shores of the Atlantic. This introduction of New World domesticates was just one element in the continuing development of West African farming practices, which had seen the increasing use of indigenous sorghum by the early second millennium A.D., and probably agricultural and culinary influences from the Mediterranean basin and Asia in the same period.

Most archaeological research on the last five centuries in West Africa has involved investigation of the encounter between Europeans and Africans. Much has taken place at coastal trading sites, including Elmina in Ghana (DeCorse 2001a), and Savi and Ouidah in Bénin (Kelly 1997, 2001). A primary goal of these projects has been examination of the lifeways of inhabitants of these settlements, using interpretive models in which the agency and activity of Africans are explicitly recognized. Researchers emphasize the degree to which Europeans and European practices and technologies were incorporated into cultural systems that remain distinctively African, and the strategies employed by African elites to manage the opportunities and dangers presented by the newcomers. This approach parallels recent historical writing on the area (Brooks 1993). At the same time, the histories of these sites – Elmina and Ouidah developing as appendages to European outposts, Savi destroyed in a struggle for control over the slave trade – remind us that these African initiatives developed in a context of increasing European domination along the coasts of West Africa, and ultimately inland as well.

Some archaeological preservation work has been undertaken at other contact-period sites along the Atlantic coast, including Cape Coast Castle and Fort St. Jago in Ghana and Gorée in Senegal (DeCorse 2001b:8–9; Samb 1997). These sites figure prominently in national and international initiatives designed to open West Africa up to cultural tourism (Bruner 1996). Many of them were directly associated with the trans-Atlantic slave trade, and it is ironic that such tourism focuses upon the experiences of Africans only as they enter slavery and the European world, rather than upon their lives before that. Archaeological research has provided valuable data on the varying cultural encounters between Europeans and Africans that accompanied the trans-Atlantic trade (e.g., articles in DeCorse, ed. 2001). However, DeCorse (2001b) points out that virtually all of this work has been done on European structures and precincts, with far less attention paid to African settlement areas. Relatively little work has been undertaken on the material features and processes of the slave trade itself, beyond these investigations of its architecture and some research on the social transformations that accompanied that trade in different parts of West Africa (Holl 2001; MacEachern 2001).

There has been very little archaeological research undertaken at contact sites away from the West African coast, but work has been done at Fort Senudébu on the Faleme River in Senegal (McIntosh and Thiaw 2001), Fort Ruychaver in southern Ghana (Posnansky and van Dantzig 1976, in Wesler 1998:16–17) and the early 20th-century British colonial settlement at Zungeru in northern Nigeria (Ogedengbe 1998). There is obviously a great deal of potential in the further study of cultural interactions away from the Atlantic coast, for periods of initial contact and for the slave trade and colonial periods.

Conclusion

West African history over the last 2,000 years cannot usefully be encompassed within a set of progressive transitions between contrasted and idealized cultural forms: Neolithic to Iron Age, statelessness to states, pre- and post-European contact. Neither can it be described as a steady progression toward any sort of evolutionary goal. Despite the claims of an earlier generation of researchers, the continent certainly has had a history, but that history has not been directed toward any final end: reality – like archaeology – is messier, and more interesting, than that. The data indicate a situation well known to archaeologists working in other areas of the world, where a great diversity of local cultural elements and historical sequences coexists with broad commonalities at a regional and even subcontinental level. There is evidence in different areas for population increase and decline, for variable degrees of political centralization, and for the productive interaction of very different economic and social systems. In these interactions, zones of environmental transition played a vital role, acting not as barriers to human movement but as privileged locations allowing access to diverse resources.

There is a great deal that archaeologists do not know about West African history during the last two millennia. Many of these gaps in our knowledge are the result of environmental and political conditions that restrict the ability of researchers to work in certain areas (Chapter 17). We are even today faced with the necessity of building basic archaeological chronologies and culture histories for many areas of West Africa, and with the need for far more detailed understandings of cultural processes almost everywhere. We especially need to learn more about such processes throughout the forest zones for this period, and far more – indeed, almost everything – about the prehistory of the countries between Ghana and Senegal. Other gaps reflect the size of the subcontinent, and the small number of people who have worked there. Still others can be traced back to the preoccupations of different archaeologists, the problems that are seen as most important, and the deference sometimes accorded to historical sources.

Archaeologists working in West Africa have tended to use systems of interpretation developed for other areas of the world, formulated with other goals in mind, and inappropriate to West African cases. There is, however, no real reason why such paradigms need to be used, and researchers working in this part of Africa are increasingly developing interpretations that try to avoid resort to the dismissive assumptions that plagued earlier systems. From this point of view, the fact that West African archaeology is still at a relatively early stage of development may be something of an advantage, if we can construct models of cultural process that are faithful to the data and to the needs of communities in West Africa today. It is, I hope, obvious from this survey that the last two decades have been an extremely productive period in West African archaeology, and we may hope to learn a great deal more about the history of the region in years to come.

REFERENCES

Alpern, Stanley, 1991 The European Introduction of Crops into West Africa in Precolonial Times. History in Africa 19:13–43.

Bedaux, Rogier, and A. G. Lange, 1983 Tellem, Reconnaissance archéologique d'une culture de l'ouest africaine au Moyen Age: La Poterie. Journal de la Société des Africanistes 53:5–59.

Berthier, Sophie, 1997 Recherches archéologiques sur la capitale de l'empire de Ghana: Étude d'un secteur d'habitat à Koumbi Saleh, Mauritanie. Campagnes II-III-IV-V (1975–1976)–(1980–1981). Oxford: Archaeopress.

Bourges, Claire, Scott MacEachern, and Maureen Reeves, 1999 Excavations at Aissa Hardé, 1995 and 1996. Nyame Akuma 51:6–13.

Breunig, Peter, Katharina Neumann, and Wim van Neer, 1996 New Research on the Holocene Settlement and Environment of the Chad Basin of Nigeria. African Archaeological Review 13:111–143.

Brooks, George, 1993 Landlords and Strangers: Ecology, Society, and Trade in Western Africa, 1000–1630. Boulder, CO: Westview Press.

Bruner, Edward, 1996 Tourism in Ghana: The Representation of Slavery and the Return of the Black Diaspora. American Anthropologist 98:290–304.

Connah, Graham, 1972 Archaeology in Benin. Journal of African History 13:25–38.

——1976 The Daima Sequence and the Prehistoric Chronology of the Lake Chad Region of Nigeria. Journal of African History 17:321–352.

——1981 Three Thousand Years in Africa: Man and his Environment in the Lake Chad Region of Nigeria. Cambridge: Cambridge University Press.

——2001 African Civilizations: An Archaeological Perspective. 2nd edition. Cambridge: Cambridge University Press.

Conte, Edouard, 1991 Herders, Hunters and Smiths: Mobile Populations in the History of Kanem. In Herders, Warriors and Traders: Pastoralism in Africa. J. Galaty and P. Bonte, eds. pp. 221–247. Boulder, CO: Westview Press.

Crossland, Leonard, and Merrick Posnansky, 1978 Pottery, People and Trade at Begho, Ghana. In Spatial Organisation of Culture. I. Hodder, ed. pp. 77–89. London: Duckworth.

Cruciani, F., P. Santolamazza, P. Shen, V. Macaulay, P. Moral, A. Olckers, D. Modiano, S. Holmes, G. Destro-Bisol, V. Coia, D. Wallace, P. Oefner, A. Torroni, L. L. Cavalli-Sforza, R. Scozzari, and P. Underhill, 2002 A Back Migration from Asia to Sub-Saharan Africa Is Supported by High-Resolution Analysis of Human Y-Chromosome Haplotypes. American Journal of Human Genetics 70:1197–1214.

Darling, Patrick, 1984 Archaeology and History in Southern Nigeria: The Ancient Linear Earthworks of Benin and Ishan. 2 vols. BAR International Series, 215. Cambridge: British Archaeological Reports.

——1998 A Legacy in Earth – Ancient Benin and Ishan, Southern Nigeria. In Historical Archaeology in Nigeria. K. Wesler, ed. pp. 143–197. Trenton, NJ: Africa World Press.

David, Nicholas, and Judith Sterner, 1999 Wonderful Society: The Burgess Shale Creatures, Mandara Polities and the Nature of Prehistory. In Beyond Chiefdoms: Pathways to Complexity in Africa. Susan K. McIntosh, ed. pp. 96–109. Cambridge: Cambridge University Press.

Davies, Oliver, 1980 The Ntereso Culture in Ghana. In West African Culture Dynamics. B. K. Swartz and R. E. Dumett, eds. pp. 205–226. The Hague: Mouton.

de Barros, Philip, 1986 Bassar: A Quantified, Chronologically Controlled, Regional Approach to a Traditional Iron Production Centre in West Africa. Africa 56(2):148–174.

——2001 The Effects of the Slave Trade Upon the Bassar Ironworking Society. In West Africa During the Atlantic Slave Trade: Archaeological Perspectives. Christopher DeCorse, ed. pp. 59–80. London: Leicester University Press.

DeCorse, Christopher, 2001a An Archaeology of Elmina: Africans and Europeans on the Gold Coast, 1400–1900. Washington, DC: Smithsonian Institution Press.

——2001b Introduction. In West Africa During the Atlantic Slave Trade: Archaeological Perspectives. Christopher DeCorse, ed. pp. 1–13. London: Leicester University Press.

DeCorse, Christopher, ed. 2001 West Africa During the Atlantic Slave Trade: Archaeological Perspectives. London: Leicester University Press.

Devisse, Jean, ed. 1983 Tegdaoust III. Recherches sur Aoudaghost. Campagnes 1960–1965, enquêtes générales. Paris: ADPF.

Effah-Gyamfi, Kwaku, 1985 Bono Manso: An Archaeological Investigation into Early Akan Urbanism. Calgary: University of Calgary Press.

Ehrenreich, Robert, Carol Crumley, and Janet Levy, eds., 1995 Heterarchy and the Analysis of Complex Societies. Archaeological Papers of the American Anthropological Association, 6. Arlington: American Anthropological Association.

Fleming, Harold, 1983 Chadic External Relations. In Studies in Chadic and Afroasiatic Linguistics. E. Wolff and H. Meyer-Bahlburg, eds. pp. 17–31. Hamburg: Buske.

Fletcher, Roland, 1998 African Urbanism: Scale, Mobility and Transformations. *In* Transformations in Africa: Essays on Africa's Later Past. Graham Connah, ed. pp. 104–138. London: Leicester University Press.

Forkl, Hermann, 1995 Politik zwischen den Zeilen. Arabische Handschriften der Wandalá in Nordkamerun. Berlin: Klaus Schwarz Verlag.

Fortes, Meyer, and E. E. Evans-Pritchard, 1940 Introduction. *In* African Political Systems. Meyer Fortes and E. E. Evans-Pritchard, eds. pp. 1–23. London: Oxford University Press.

Gallay, Alain, 1994 Sociétés englobées et traditions céramiques: Le Cas du pays Dogon (Mali) depuis le 13ème siècle. *In* Terre cuite et société: La Céramique, document technique, économique, culturel, Juan les-Pins, 1994, pp. 435–457. Éditions APDCA (Association pour la Promotion et la Diffusion des Connaissances Archéologiques.).

Gallay, Alain, Eric Huysecom, and Anne Mayor, 1995 Archéologie, histoire et traditions orales: Trois clés pour découvrir le passé Dogon. *In* Die Kunst der Dogon: Museum Rietberg, Zurich. L. Homberger, ed. pp. 19–43, 132–135. Zurich: Museum Rietberg.

Goucher, Candice L., 1981 Iron Is Iron 'Til It Is Rust: Trade and Ecology in the Decline of West African Iron-Smelting. Journal of African History 22:179–189.

Gronenborn, Detlef, 1998 Archaeological and Ethnohistorical Investigations along the Southern Fringes of Lake Chad, 1993–1996. African Archaeological Review 14:225–259.

———2001 Kanem-Borno – a Brief Summary of the History and Archaeology of an Empire in the Central Bilad-El-Sudan. *In* West Africa During the Atlantic Slave Trade: Archaeological Perspectives. Christopher DeCorse, ed. pp. 101–130. London: Leicester University Press.

Guèye, Ndeye Sokhna, 2002 Ethnoarchéologie, ethnohistoire et interprétation de la distribution des poteries de la moyenne Vallée du Fleuve Sénégal du XVe au XXe siècle. Nyame Akuma 57:21–33.

Guyer, Jane, and Samuel Belinga, 1995 Wealth in People as Wealth in Knowledge: Accumulation and Composition in Equatorial Africa. Journal of African History 36:91–120.

Harlan, Jack R., 1993 The Tropical African Cereals. *In* The Archaeology of Africa: Food Metal and Towns. Thurstan Shaw, Paul Sinclair, Bassey Andah, and Alex Okpoko, eds. pp. 53–60. New York: Routledge.

Harlan, Jack R., Jan M. J. de Wet, and Ann B. L. Stemler, 1976 Plant Domestication and Indigenous African Agriculture. *In* Origins of African Plant Domestication. Jack R. Harlan, Jan M. J. de Wet, and Ann B. L. Stemler, eds. pp. 3–22. The Hague: Mouton.

Hodgkins, T., 1975 Nigerian Perspectives: An Historical Anthology. London: Oxford University Press.

Holl, Augustin, 1987 Mound Formation Processes and Societal Transformations: A Case Study from the Perichadian Plain. Journal of Anthropological Archaeology 6:122–158.

———1988 Houlouf I: Archéologie des sociétés protohistoriques du Nord-Cameroun. BAR International Series, 456. Oxford: British Archaeological Reports.

———1993 Late Neolithic Cultural Landscape in Southeastern Mauritania: An Essay in Spatiometrics. *In* Spatial Boundaries and Social Dynamics: Case Studies from Food-Producing Societies. Augustin Holl and Thomas E. Levy, eds. pp. 95–133. Ethnoarchaeological Series 2. Ann Arbor: International Monographs in Prehistory.

———1994 The Cemetery of Houlouf in Northern Cameroon (AD 1500–1600): Fragments of a Past Social System. The African Archaeological Review 12:133–170.

———2001 Five Hundred Years in the Cameroons: Making Sense of the Archaeological Record. *In* West Africa During the Atlantic Slave Trade: Archaeological Perspectives. Christopher DeCorse, ed. pp. 152–178. London: Leicester University Press.

Horton, Robin, 1976 Stateless Societies in the History of West Africa. *In* History of West Africa, vol. 1. J. F. A. Ajayi and M. Crowder, eds. pp. 72–113. New York: Columbia University Press.

Huysecom, Eric, and Anne Mayor, 1995 Les Traditions céramiques du delta intérieur du Niger: Présent et passé. *In* Vallées du Niger: Catalogue d'exposition. pp. 297–313. Paris: Éditions de la Réunion des Musées Nationaux.

Insoll, Timothy, 1995 A Cache of Hippopotamus Ivory at Gao, Mali; and a Hypothesis of its Use. Antiquity 69:327–336.

—— 1996 Islam, Archaeology and History: Gao Region (Mali) *Ca* Ad 900–1250. Oxford: Tempus Reparatum.

Insoll, Timothy, and Thurstan Shaw, 1997 Gao and Igbo-Ukwu: Beads, Interregional Trade and Beyond. African Archaeological Review 14:9–24.

Jones, Kimberley, 2001 The Archaeology of Doulo, Cameroon. Unpublished MA thesis, Department of Archaeology, University of Calgary.

Kelly, Kenneth, 1997 The Archaeology of African–European Interaction: Investigating the Social Roles of Trade, Traders and the Use of Space in the Seventeenth and Eighteenth Century Huéda Kingdom, Republic of Bénin. World Archaeology 28(3):351–369.

—— 2001 Change and Continuity in Coastal Bénin. *In* West Africa During the Atlantic Slave Trade: Archaeological Perspectives. Christopher DeCorse, ed. pp. 80–100. London: Leicester University Press.

Kopytoff, Igor, 1987 The Internal African Frontier: The Making of African Political Culture. *In* The African Frontier: The Reproduction of Traditional African Societies. Igor Kopytoff, ed. pp. 3–84. Bloomington: Indiana University Press.

Lamotte, M., and A. Marliac, 1989 Des structures complexes résultant de processus naturels et anthropiques: Exemple du Tertre de Mongossi au Nord-Cameroun. Bulletin de la Société Préhistorique Française 10/12:420–428.

Lange, Dierk, 1989 Préliminaires pour une histoire des Sao. Journal of African History 30:189–210.

Langlois, O., 1995 Histoire du peuplement post-néolithique du Diamaré. Doctoral dissertation, Université de Paris I – Panthéon Sorbonne.

Law, Robin, 1983 Trade and Politics Behind the Slave Coast: The Lagoon Traffic and the Rise of Lagos, 1500–1800. Journal of African History 24:321–348.

Lawson, Amy, 2001 Recent Archaeological Research on Gambian Iron Age Habitation. Nyame Akuma 55:32–35.

Lebeuf, A. M. D., J.-P. Lebeuf, F. Treinen-Claustre, and J. Courtin, 1980 Le Gisement Sao de Mdaga (Tchad): Fouilles 1960–1968. Paris: Société d'Ethnographie.

Lebeuf, Jean-Paul, 1969 Carte archéologique des abords du Lac Tchad (Cameroun, Nigeria, Tchad). Paris: Éditions du CNRS.

Lentz, Carola, 2000 Der Jäger, die Ziegen und der Erdschrein. Politik mit oralen Traditionen zur Siedlungsgeschichte in Nordghana. Zeitschrift für Ethnologie 125(2):281–304.

Levtzion, Nehemiah, and J. H. Hopkins, 1981 Corpus of Early Arabic Sources for West African History. Cambridge: Cambridge University Press.

MacDonald, Kevin C., 1998a Archaeology, Language and the Peopling of West Africa: A Consideration of the Evidence. *In* Archaeology and Language II: Archaeological Data and Linguistic Hypotheses. R. Blench and M. Spriggs, eds. pp. 33–66. One World Archaeology 29. London: Routledge.

—— 1998b Before the Empire of Ghana: Pastoralism and the Origins of Cultural Complexity in the Sahel. *In* Transformations in Africa: Essays on Africa's Later Past. Graham Connah, ed. pp. 71–103. London: Leicester University Press.

MacEachern, Scott, 1996 Iron Age Beginnings North of the Mandara Mountains, Cameroon and Nigeria. *In* Aspects of African Archaeology: Proceedings of the 10th Pan-African Congress. Gilbert Pwiti and Robert Soper, eds. pp. 489–495. Harare: University of Zimbabwe Press.

——2001 State Formation and Enslavement in the Southern Lake Chad Basin. *In* West Africa During the Atlantic Slave Trade: Archaeological Perspectives. Christopher DeCorse, ed. pp. 130–151. London: Leicester University Press.

——2002 Beyond the Belly of the House: Space and Power in the Mandara Mountains. Journal of Social Archaeology 2(2):179–219.

MacEachern, Scott, Claire Bourges, and Maureen Reeves, 2001 Early Horse Remains from Northern Cameroon. Antiquity 75:62–67.

McIntosh, Roderick J., 1993 The Pulse Model: Genesis and Accommodation of Specialization in the Middle Niger. Journal of African History 34:181–220.

——1998 The Peoples of the Middle Niger: The Island of Gold. Oxford: Blackwell.

——1999 Clustered Cities and Alternative Courses to Authority in Prehistory. Journal of East Asian Archaeology 13(1):63–86.

——2000 Social Memory in Mande. *In* The Way the Wind Blows: Climate, History and Human Action. Roderick J. McIntosh, J. Tainter, and Susan K. McIntosh, eds. pp. 141–180. New York: Columbia University Press.

McIntosh, Susan Keech, 1999a Modelling Political Organization in Large-Scale Settlement Clusters: A Case Study from the Inland Niger Delta. *In* Beyond Chiefdoms: Pathways to Complexity in Africa. Susan Keech McIntosh, ed. pp. 66–79. New Directions in Archaeology. Cambridge: Cambridge University Press.

——1999b Pathways to Complexity: An African Perspective. *In* Beyond Chiefdoms: Pathways to Complexity in Africa. Susan Keech McIntosh, ed. pp. 1–30. Cambridge: Cambridge University Press.

——1999c A Tale of Two Floodplains: Comparative Perspectives on the Emergence of Complex Societies and Urbanism in the Middle Niger and Senegal Valleys. *In* East African Urban Origins in World Perspective: Proceedings of the Second WAC Intercongress. Paul J. J. Sinclair, ed. Electronic book, <http://www.arkeologi.uu.se/afr/projects/BOOK/Mcintosh/mcintosh.pdf>.

McIntosh, Susan Keech, ed., 1995 Excavations at Jenné-jeno, Hambarketolo and Kaniana (Inland Niger Delta, Mali), the 1981 Season. Berkeley: University of California Press.

McIntosh, Susan Keech, and Hamady Bocoum, 2000 New Perspectives on Sincu Bara, a First Millennium Site in the Senegal Valley. African Archaeological Review 17:1–43.

McIntosh, Susan Keech, and Roderick J. McIntosh, 1980 Prehistoric Investigations at Jenné, Mali. 2 vols. Cambridge Monographs in African Archaeology, 2. Oxford: British Archaeological Reports.

———1984 The Early City in West Africa: Towards an Understanding. The African Archaeological Review 2:73–98.

———1993a Cities without Citadels: Understanding Urban Origins along the Middle Niger. *In* Archaeology of Africa: Food, Metals and Towns. Thurstan Shaw, Paul J. J. Sinclair, Bassey Andah, and Alex I. Okpoko, eds. pp. 622–641. London: Routledge.

———1993b Field Survey in the Tumulus Zone of Senegal. The African Archaeological Review 11:73–108.

McIntosh, Susan Keech, and Ibrahima Thiaw, 2001 Tools for Understanding Transformation and Continuity in Senegambian Society: 1500–1900. *In* West Africa During the Atlantic Slave Trade: Archaeological Perspectives. Christopher DeCorse, ed. pp. 14–37. London: Leicester University Press.

464 SCOTT MACEACHERN

McNaughton, Patrick, 1992 From Mande Komo to Jukun Akuma: Approaching the Difficult Problem of History. African Arts 25(2):76–85, 99–100.

Magnavita, Carlos, 2002 Recent Archaeological Finds of Domesticated *Sorghum Bicolor* in the Lake Chad Region. Nyame Akuma 57:14–20.

Magnavita, Sonja, Maya Hallier, Christoph Pelzer, Stefanie Kahlheber, and Veerle Linseele, 2002 Nobles, guerriers, paysans: Une nécropole de l'Age du Fer et son emplacement dans l'oudalan pré- et protohistorique. Beiträge zur Allgemeinen und Vergleichenden Archäologie 22:21–64.

Maley, Jean, 1981 Études palynologiques dans le Bassin du Tchad et paléoclimatologie de l'afrique nord-tropicale de 30,000 ans à l'époque actuelle. Paris: Éditions de l'ORSTOM.

—— 1989 Late Quaternary Climatic Changes in the African Rain Forest: Forest Refugia and the Major Role of Sea Surface Temperature Variations. *In* Paleoclimatology and Paleometeorology: Modern and Past Patterns of Global Atmospheric Transport. M. Leinen and M. Sarnthein, eds. pp. 585–616. NATO ASI Series, Series C. Dordrecht: Kluwer Academic Publishers.

Marliac, A., 1991 De la préhistoire à l'histoire au Cameroun septentrionale. 2 vols. Paris: ORSTOM.

Marliac, A., and O. Langlois, 1996 Les Civilisations de l'Age du Fer au Diamaré (Cameroun Septentrionale): Des cultures aux ethnies. L'Anthropologie 100(2/3):420–456.

Marliac, Alain, Olivier Langlois, and Michèle Delneuf, 2000 Archéologie de la région Mandara-Diamaré. *In* Atlas de la province extrême-nord, Cameroun. C. Seignobos and O. Iyebi-Mandjek, eds. pp. 71–76. Paris: Éditions de l'IRD.

Mayor, Anne, Eric Huysecom, Matthieu Honegger, and Alain Gallay, 1990 Hamdallahi, capitale de l'empire Peul du Massina, Mali. Première Fouille Archéologique, Études Historiques et Ethnoarchéologiques. Stuttgart: Franz Steiner Verlag.

Mbida, Christophe, Hugues Doutrelepont, Luc Vrydaghs, Rony Swennen, Rudy Swennen, Hans Beeckman, Edmond De Langhe, and Pierre de Maret, 2001 First Archaeological Evidence of Banana Cultivation in Central Africa during the Third Millennium Before Present. Vegetation History and Archaeobotany 10:1–6.

Neumann, Katharina, 1999 Early Plant Food Production in the West African Sahel. *In* The Exploitation of Plant Resources in Ancient Africa. M. van der Veen, ed. pp. 73–80. New York: Kluwer Academic/Plenum Publishers.

Neumann, Katharina, and Ralf Vogelsang, 1996 Paléoenvironnement et préhistoire au sahel du Burkina Faso. Berichte des Sonderforschungsbereichs 268 7:177–186.

Nicholson, Sharon, 1976 A Climatic Chronology for Africa: Synthesis of Geological, Historical, and Meteorological Information and Data. Ph.D. dissertation, Department of Meteorology, University of Wisconsin.

Ogedengbe, A. Yinka, 1998 A Historical Archaeology of Zungeru Colonial Settlement: A Case Study. *In* Historical Archaeology in Nigeria. Kit Wesler, ed. pp. 273–310. Trenton, NJ: Africa World Press.

Ogundiran, Akinwumi, 2002 Filling a Gap in the Ife-Benin Interaction Field (Thirteenth–Sixteenth Centuries AD): Excavations in Iloyi Settlement, Ijesaland. African Archaeological Review 19(1):27–60.

Pacheco Pereira, D., 1937 Esmeraldo De Situ Orbis. G. H. T. Kimble, trans. London: Hakluyt Society.

Philips, John Edward, 1983 African Smoking and Pipes. Journal of African History 24:303–319.

Polet, Jean, 1985 Tegdaoust IV. Fouille d'un quartier de Tegdaoust (Mauritanie Orientale). Urbanisation, Architecture, Utilisation de l'Espace Construit. Paris: ADPF.

Posnansky, Merrick, and Albert van Dantzig, 1976 Fort Ruychaver Rediscovered. Sankofa 2:7–18.

Possehl, Gregory, 1998 Sociocultural Complexity without the State: The Indus Civilization. In Archaic States. Gary Feinman and Joyce Marcus, eds. pp. 260–291. Santa Fe, NM: School of American Research Press.

Raimbault, Michel, and Klèna Sanogo, eds., 1991 Recherches archéologiques au Mali: Les Sites protohistoriques de la Zone Lacustre. Paris: Karthala.

Ray, Keith, 1987 Material Metaphor, Social Interactions and Historical Reconstructions: Exploring Patterns of Association and Symbolism in the Igbo-Ukwu Corpus. In The Archaeology of Contextual Meanings. Ian Hodder, ed. pp. 66–77. Cambridge: Cambridge University Press.

Reyna, S. P., 1990 Wars without End: The Political Economy of a Precolonial African State. Hanover: University Press of New England.

Robert, Denise, Serge Robert, and Jean Devisse, eds., 1970 Tegdaoust: Recherches sur Aoudaghost, vol. 1. Paris: Arts et Métiers Graphiques.

Robert-Chaleix, Denise, 1989 Tegdaoust V. Recherches sur Aoudaghost. Une concession médiévale à Tegdaoust: Implantation, évolution d'une unité d'habitation. Paris: ADPF.

Rossi, P. F., C. Battaggia, B. Sansonetti, G. Destro-Bisol, E. Capucci, M. L. Aebischer, L. Kaptué, and G. Spedini, 1991 Les Foulbe du Nord-Cameroun: Origine, migrations, peuplement et variabilité génétique. Revista de Antropologia 59:49–72.

Rowley-Conwy, Peter, William Deakin, and Charles Shaw, 1999 Ancient DNA from Sorghum: The Evidence from Qasr Ibrim, Egyptian Nubia. In The Exploitation of Plant Resources in Ancient Africa. M. van der Veen, ed. pp. 55–61. New York: Kluwer Academic/Plenum Publishers.

Samb, Djibril, 1997 Gorée et l'esclavage. Actes du Séminaire sur "Gorée dans la Traite Atlantique: Mythes et Réalités." Dakar: IFAN.

Sanogo, Klèna, 1991 Conclusions. In Recherches archéologiques au Mali: Les Lites protohistoriques de la Zone Lacustre. M. Raimbault and K. Sanogo, eds. pp. 510–517. Paris: Karthala.

Sharpe, Barrie, 1986 Ethnography and a Regional System: Mental Maps and the Myth of States and Tribes in North-Central Nigeria. Critique of Anthropology 6(3):33–65.

Shaw, Thurstan, 1970 Igbo-Ukwu: An Account of Archaeological Discoveries in Eastern Nigeria. 2 vols. Evanston, IL: Northwestern University Press.

—— 1980 New Data on the Pre-European Civilizations of Southern Nigeria. In Proceedings of the 8th Pan-African Congress of Prehistory and Quaternary Studies. Richard Leakey and B. Ogot, eds. pp. 376–378. Nairobi: The International Louis Leakey Memorial Institute for African Prehistory.

Shinnie, Peter, and François J. Kense, 1989 Archaeology of Gonja, Ghana: Excavations at Daboya. Calgary: University of Calgary Press.

Sinclair, Paul J. J., Thurstan Shaw, and Bassey Andah, 1993 Introduction. In Archaeology of Africa: Food, Metals and Towns. Thurstan Shaw, Paul Sinclair, Bassey Andah, and Alex I. Okpoko, eds. pp. 1–31. London: Routledge.

Smith, Andrew B., 1992 Pastoralism in Africa: Origins and Development Ecology. London: Hurst.

Soper, Robert, and Patrick Darling, 1980 The Walls of Old Oyo. West African Journal of Archaeology 10:61–81.

Sowunmi, M. A., 1981 Late Quaternary Environmental Changes in Nigeria. Pollen et Spores 23(1):125–148.

Stahl, Ann B., 1985 Reinvestigation of Kintampo 6 Rock Shelter, Ghana: Implications for the Nature of Culture Change. The African Archaeological Review 3:117–150.

—— 1993 Intensification in the West African Late Stone Age: A View from Central Ghana. In Archaeology of Africa: Food, Metals and Towns. Thurstan Shaw, Paul Sinclair, Bassey Andah, and Alex I. Okpoko, eds. pp. 261–273. London: Routledge.

—— 1994 Innovation, Diffusion, and Culture Contact: The Holocene Archaeology of Ghana. Journal of World Prehistory 8(1):51–112.

—— 1999 Perceiving Variability in Time and Space: The Evolutionary Mapping of African Societies. In Beyond Chiefdoms: Pathways to Complexity in Africa. Susan Keech McIntosh, ed. pp. 39–55. Cambridge: Cambridge University Press.

—— 2001 Making History in Banda: Anthropological Visions of Africa's Past. Cambridge: Cambridge University Press.

Stahl, Ann B., and Peter W. Stahl, 2004 Early Second Millennium AD Ivory Production and Consumption in Ghana: Implications for Modeling West African Trade. Antiquity.

Stenning, D. J., 1957 Transhumance, Migratory Drift, Migration: Patterns of Pastoral Fulani Nomadism. Journal of the Royal Anthropological Institute 87:57–73.

Sutton, John E. G., 2001 Igbo-Ukwu and the Nile. African Archaeological Review 18:49–62.

Togola, Téréba, 1996 Iron Age Occupation in the Méma Region, Mali. African Archaeological Review 13:91–110.

Trevor-Roper, Hugh, 1965 The Rise of Christian Europe. London: Thames & Hudson.

Usman, Aribidesi, 2001 State-Periphery Relations and Sociopolitical Development in Igbominaland, North-Central Yoruba, Nigeria. Oral-Ethnohistorical and Archaeological Perspectives. BAR International Series, 993. Oxford: British Archaeological Reports.

Vernet, Robert, 1993 Préhistoire de la Mauritanie. Nouakchott: Centre Culturel Français A. de Saint Exupéry-SEPIA.

—— 2000 Un habitat de l'Age du Cuivre (2500 B.P.) de la région du Nouakchott (Mauritanie Occidentale): Imbich-Est. Sahara 12:83–90.

Vivian, Brian C., 1996 Recent Excavations at Adansemanso. Nyame Akuma 46:37–40.

Vogelsang, Ralf, Klaus-Dieter Albert, and Stefanie Kahlheber, 1999 Le Sable savant: Les Cordons dunaires sahéliens au Burkina Faso comme archive archéologique et paléoécologique du Holocène. Sahara 11:51–68.

Wesler, Kit, 1998 Historical Archaeology in West Africa. In Historical Archaeology in Nigeria. Kit Wesler, ed. pp. 1–39. Trenton, NJ: Africa World Press.

Willett, Frank, and Ekpo Eyo, 1980 Treasures of Ancient Nigeria. New York: Knopf.

Woodhouse, James, 1998 Iron in Africa: Metal from Nowhere. In Transformations in Africa: Essays on Africa's Later Past. Graham Connah, ed. pp. 160–185. London: Leicester University Press.

Yoffee, Norman, 1991 Too Many Chiefs? (or, Safe Texts for the 90s). In Archaeological Theory: Who Sets the Agenda? Norman Yoffee and Andrew Sherratt, eds. pp. 60–78. Cambridge: Cambridge University Press.

Zeltner, J. C, 1979 Les Arabes dans la région du Lac Tchad: Problèmes d'origine et de chronologie. Sahr: Centre d'Études Linguistiques.

Index

Bold numbers refer to tables; *italic* numbers refer to illustrations.

289, 294; interdisciplinary approaches 276, 277, 282; mining 276, 280, 282–3, 287, 289, 291, 338, 379, 383, 386, 434; origins 11, 12, 276–81, 424–5, 436; pyrotechnical expertise 278–81; smelting 276, 278–86, 288, 291, 293, 294; and trade 289–90

microliths 150, 156, 162, 166, 174, 175, 225, 229–33, 235; geometric 111, 121, 139, 140, 230

microwear 68, 162, 165, 230

Middle Awash 56, **58**, 71

Middle Paleolithic 7, 8, 97, 103, 106, 108, 113, 115, 117, 119, 144–5

Middle Range Theory 35, 73

Middle Stone Age 8, 93–123, 130–45; antiquity 103, 107–10, 112, 113, 134–6; Central Africa 106; climate change 107–9, 130, 141; distribution 120; East Africa 106, 109, 110; exchange 114, 120, 122; hearths 141–3; hominid fossils 98, 100, 136–9; modern behavior 104, 112–16, 120, 122, 132, 138, 141, 144; North Africa 106–9; regional variation 104, 111, 121; southern Africa 106, 107, 111–13; subsistence 108, 110–13, 116, 117, 119, 120, 122, 130, 131, 141–4; technology 104, *105*, 110, 111, 113–15, 120–2, 140; West Africa 107, 232

Middleton, J. 341

migration 8, 10, 152, 175, 182, 184, 226, 232, 234, 236, 238, 240, 252, 258, 379, 392, 400, 404, 429, 453, 455; archaeological signatures 182, 312; Bantu 281, 309, 312, 314–17, 322, 393, 428; Fulbe 182, 443; seasonal 182, 199, 260

military 281, 290, 315, 341, 367, 435, 451, 457

milk 191, 194, 197, 239, 400

mining 6, 276, 282, 283, 287, 291, 379; copper 280, 338, 434; gold 283, 289, 338, 383, 386

Mirabib 210

missionaries 362, 404, 425, 426, 431

mobility: decreased 229, 235, 238; Middle Stone Age 122; pastoralism 188, 189, 197, 206, 212, 214; seasonal 151, 157–9

modeling 96, 152, 154, 184, 345; language relationships 305, 312–14, 317–18

modern humans 93, 136, 138, 152; behavior 97, 98, 113, 131, 144; fossil evidence 98–100, 150; origins 8, 93, 94, 96–8, 113–20, 144, 145

Mombasa 340, *380*

Mongossi 448

Monomatapa 386

Montague Cave 99, 102, 112

Moojane 365

Morgan, L. H. 328, 359

Morocco 100, 107, 181, 280

Mortelmans, G. 106, 428, 429

mosaics 3, 15, 371, 393, *394*, 400, 403; approaches to the study of 393, 395–7; Central African 423, 424; Central Rift Valley 207, 397–402; Great Lakes region 402, 403; Taita-Tsavo 404–6, 410–12; West Africa 226, 228, 446, 451, 458

mosques 339, 340, 342

Mossel Bay Industry 140

Mosu 365

Moula-Guercy 138

mounds 259, 335, 403, 445, 447, 448, 451, 452

Mousterian 107–9, 114

Mozambique 339, 379, *380*, 381, 382

MSA I 133, 135, 140

MSA II 133, 140

MSA III 133, 135, 140

MSA IV 133, 140

Mulongo ware 431, 432

Multiregional Continuity model 96–7

Mumba Rockshelter 99, 110

Mumute *233*, 237

Munsa 403

Munson, P. 259

Murdock, G. P. 10, 14, 254, 303, 307, 312

museums 167, 359, 368, 425, 428, 429

Mutapa 32, 336, 339, 386

Mwenezi *380*, 382

Nabta Playa 194, 198, **200**, *201*, 203, 206, *252*, 256

Naivasha Lake basin 397

Naivasha Railway Rockshelter 399

Nakuru Lake basin 397

Namibia 28, 152, 166, 167, 210, 211, 353, 355, *356*, 364, 368, 369, 379